Contemporary Ireland

Other titles published by UCD Press

Health Policy and Practice in Ireland
edited by DESMOND MCCLUSKEY

Sport and the Irish
edited by ALAN BAIRNER

Mapping Irish Media: Critical Explorations
edited by JOHN HORGAN, BARBARA O'CONNOR
and HELENA SHEEHAN

*Moral Monopoly: The Rise and Fall of the
Catholic Church in Modern Ireland*
TOM INGLIS

*Becoming Conspicuous: Irish Travellers,
Society and the State 1922–70*
AOIFE BHREATNACH

*Truth, Power and Lies: Irish Society and
the Case of the Kerry Babies*
TOM INGLIS

*Timeless Wisdom: What Irish Proverbs
Tell Us About Ourselves*
AIDAN MORAN and MICHAEL O'CONNELL

Contemporary Ireland
A Sociological map

edited by
Sara O'Sullivan

University College Dublin Press

Preas Choláiste Ollscoile
Bhaile Átha Cliath

First published 2007
by University College Dublin Press
Newman House
86 St Stephen's Green
Dublin 2
Ireland
www.ucdpress.ie

© the editors and contributors 2007

Artwork © individual artists/organisations, 2007
Figure 8.2 UCD Sport; Figure 8.3 Croke Park
Figure 11.1 Public Communications Company
Figure 12.1 Martyn Turner
Figure 16.1 J. & L. Grubb Ltd
Figure 16.2 James Scanlon
Figures 21.1, 21.2 and 23.2 Pacemaker Press International

ISBN 978-1-904558-87-3

Cataloguing in Publication data
available from the British Library

Typeset in Ireland in
Adobe Garamond and Trade Gothic
by Elaine Burberry, Bantry, Co. Cork
Index by Jane Rogers
Text design by Lyn Davies
Printed in England on acid-free
paper by Athenæum Press, Gateshead

Contents

Acknowledgements

Although only one name appears on the cover of this book, this has been a collective effort. I am particularly indebted to Kieran Allen who, as Head of UCD School of Sociology, initiated the project. I was also fortunate to have the ongoing support of an excellent School editorial committee, consisting of Tom Inglis, Kieran Allen and Ronnie Moore. Their contributions were substantial, involving, amongst other things, valuable advice at the different stages of the project, and detailed feedback and commentary on each of the chapters. I very much appreciate the spirit of collegiality and generosity which characterised their involvement. I would also like to thank all the contributors to the book for their commitment to the project. I wish to thank those individuals and organisations that gave permission for images to be used in the book. Finally I would like to thank Aogán Mulcahy, James Scanlon, Stephen Mennell, and also Barbara Mennell at UCD Press.

SARA O'SULLIVAN
UCD School of Sociology, Dublin
July 2007

Contributors to this volume

KIERAN ALLEN is a Senior Lecturer in the UCD School of Sociology. He was a member of the School editorial committee that provided support to the editor of this collection.

PAT CLANCY is an Associate Professor of Sociology at UCD.

COLIN COULTER is a Senior Lecturer in Sociology at NUI Maynooth.

TONY FAHEY is Professor of Social Policy at UCD.

MARK HAUGAARD is a Lecturer in the Department of Political Science and Sociology, NUI Galway.

BETTY HILLIARD is a Lecturer in the UCD School of Sociology.

GORETTI HORGAN is a Research Fellow in the School of Policy Studies, University of Ulster at Magee and Chair of the Northern Ireland Anti-Poverty Network.

TOM INGLIS is an Associate Professor of Sociology at UCD. He was a member of the School editorial committee that provided support to the editor of this collection.

MARY KELLY is a Senior Lecturer in the UCD School of Sociology.

KATIE LISTON is a Senior Lecturer in the Department of Sport and Exercise Sciences, and Chester Centre for Research into Sport and Society, University of Chester.

STEVEN LOYAL is a Senior Lecturer in the UCD School of Sociology.

PATRICIA LUNDY is a Lecturer in Sociology at the University of Ulster, Jordanstown.

MARK MCGOVERN is Reader and Research Co-ordinator, Department of Social and Psychological Sciences, Edge Hill University, Ormskirk.

ROBBIE MCVEIGH is a researcher and writer and has published extensively on racism and sectarianism.

RONNIE MOORE is a Lecturer in Medical Anthropology and Sociology at UCD. He was a member of the School editorial committee that provided support to the editor of this collection.

AOGÁN MULCAHY is a Senior Lecturer in the UCD School of Sociology.

RONALDO MUNCK is Professor of Sociology and Theme Leader for Internationalisation, Interculturalism and Social Development at Dublin City University.

PETER MURRAY is a Lecturer in Sociology at NUI Maynooth.

SEÁN Ó RIAIN is Professor of Sociology at NUI Maynooth.

SARA O'SULLIVAN is a Lecturer in the UCD School of Sociology.

MICHAEL PUNCH is a Lecturer in the UCD School of Sociology.

KEVIN RYAN is a Lecturer in the Department of Political Science and Sociology, NUI Galway.

PETER SHIRLOW is a Senior Lecturer in Law at the Queen's University Belfast.

HILARY TOVEY is a Senior Lecturer in Sociology at Trinity College Dublin, and a Fellow of TCD.

IARFHLAITH WATSON is a Lecturer in the UCD School of Sociology.

JAMES WICKHAM is the Director of the Employment Research Centre and Jean Monnet Professor of European Labour Market Studies in the Department of Sociology at Trinity College Dublin.

Abbreviations

ABC	Acceptable Behaviour Contract
ACP	Ardoyne Commemoration Project
ASBO	Anti-Social Behaviour Order
CAB	Criminal Assets Bureau
CAT	Committee on the Administration of Justice
CCPR	Central Council for Physical Recreation (UK)
CCTV	Closed Circuit Television
CEO	Chief Executive Officer
CLAR	Committee on Irish Language Attitudes Research
CPI	Consumer Price Index
CRC	Community Relations Commission
CRE	Commission for Racial Equality (UK)
CSO	Central Statistics Office
CTO	Chief Technical Officer
DART	Dublin Area Rapid Transport
DES	Department of Education and Science
DUP	Democratic Unionist Party
DUP	Direct Unproductive Profit-seeking
ECNI	Equality Commission for Northern Ireland
EEA	European Economic Area
EEC	European Economic Community
EPO	European Patent Office
EQUA	Equality Impact Assessment
ESRI	Economic and Social Research Institute
EU	European Union
EVS	European Values Study
FÁS	Foras Áiseanna Saothar (Training and Employment Authority)
FIFA	Fédération Internationale de Football Association
FMD	Foot and Mouth Disease
GCSB	Garda Síochána Complaints Board
GDA	Greater Dublin Area
GDP	Gross Domestic Product
GFA	Good Friday Agreement
GNP	Gross National Project
HBAI	Households Below Average Income
HEA	Higher Education Authority
ICT	Information and Communication Technologies
IDA	Industrial Development Authority

IMF	International Monetary Fund
INCORE	Centre for International Conflict Research (United Nations University and the University of Ulster)
IOM	International Organisation for Migration
IPA	Institute of Public Administration
IRA	Irish Republican Army
ISSP	International Social Survey Programme
IT	Information Technology
ITÉ	Institiúid Teangeolaíochta na hÉireann (Linguistics Association of Ireland)
JPC	Joint Policing Committee
LCA	Leaving Certificate Applied
MLA	Member of the Legislative Assembly (Northern Ireland)
NCCRI	National Consultative Committee on Racism and Interculturalism
NDA	National Disability Authority
NESC	National Economc and Social Council
NGO	Non-Governmental Organisation
NI	Northern Ireland
NIC	Newly Industrialising Countries
NICS	Northern Ireland Civil Service
NILT	Northern Ireland Life and Times Survey
NIO	Northern Ireland Office
NISRA	Northern Ireland Statistics and Research Agency
NUI	National University of Ireland
OECD	Organisation for Economic Co-operation and Development
OFMDFM	Office of the First Minister and Deputy First Minister
PE	Physical Education
PRSA	Personal Retirement Savings Account
PSNI	Police Service of Northern Ireland
PULSE	Police Using Leading Systems Effectively
REPS	Rural Environmental Protection Scheme
RIC	Royal Irish Constabulary
RICS	Royal Institute of Chartered Surveyors
RIR	Royal Irish Regiment
RUC	Royal Ulster Constabulary
SDLP	Social Democratic and Labour Party
SES	Socio-Economic Status
SME	Small and Medium Enterprises
SWA	Supplementary Welfare Assistance
TASC	Think Tank for Action on Social Change
TCD	Trinity College Dublin

TD	Teachta Dála
TFR	Total Fertility Rate
TNC	Transnational Corporation
UCD	University College Dublin
UN	United Nations
UNDP	United Nations Development Programme
UNESCO	United Nations Educational, Scientific and Cultural Organisation
UUP	Ulster Unionist Party

Introduction

Ireland 1995–2005

Sara O'Sullivan

Ireland has been through a period of significant change: the old social order has given way. What was a slow, traditional society has become one of the fastest growing economies in the world. What was fifty years ago a predominantly rural society revolving around small farms has become a cosmopolitan, urban society oriented towards a global economy. A generation ago, people were still flooding out of Ireland to find jobs, now people are flocking into the country. Ireland is rapidly becoming a multi-ethnic, multi-cultural society. The pace of change has been quite dramatic; very few societies have undergone such rapid social, economic and cultural change in such a short time. 'Poor old Ireland' has become one of the richest societies in the world. The aim of this book is to provide a broad, general description and analysis of these transformations.

The book concentrates on changes that occurred during the decade 1995–2005. This was the period that saw the birth of the Celtic Tiger economy in the South and the gradual ending of 'the troubles' in the North. During this period Ireland became open to the world. It became more Europeanised and globalised: Ireland is increasingly governed as much by Brussels as it is by Dublin. The success of the Irish economy has been dependent on foreign direct investment through mostly American-based transnational corporations. Despite becoming very rich very quickly, inequalities based on class, gender and ethnicity persist and the gap between rich and poor in Irish society has increased. Despite the rhetoric of social inclusion underpinning social partnership and the Good Friday Agreement, new inequalities based on race have emerged. Somewhat paradoxically, minority rights have also been highlighted and formalised through a range of equality legislation enacted by the state.

Increased affluence created changes at both the micro and macro levels. There was growing consumption in the many out-of-town retail parks and shopping centres that mushroomed over the period. Spending on consumer goods and services increased from €8,140 per capita in 1995, to €17,884 per capita in 2005 (Central Bank 2005: 3). Personal indebtedness also increased from €37,257 million in 1995 to €258,810 million in 2005 (Central Bank 2005: 4). This was the decade when air travel doubled from 13 million passengers passing through Dublin, Cork, Shannon and Belfast airports in 1995, to 26.7 million in 2004 (CSO 2005a; Civil Aviation Authority 2005, 1998). Many Irish people acquired a second home, either to travel to during their leisure time, or as an investment. In the new Ireland consumption is seen as both the solution to the stresses of modern life, and the route to self-fulfilment. We are repeatedly told we both need and deserve multiple trips abroad each year, the latest electronic gadgets, and the most exclusive designer clothes, shoes and handbags.

Concerns about these changes, and about the real beneficiaries of the boom, have been articulated by social commentators, politicians and ordinary citizens. These include concerns about the state of the health service, traffic gridlock, poor public transport provision, immigration, the cost of housing, levels of crime, gangland activity, childcare provision and environmental degradation. Many of these concerns are addressed in this volume, either directly or indirectly.

The single most important political event in the period 1995–2005 was the 1998 Good Friday Agreement, which led to the transformation of political institutions in Northern Ireland. The decade was also characterised by tribunals of inquiry in the South. Issues of accountability, legitimacy and trust were highlighted by the tribunals' public sittings and findings. A perception of Irish society as corrupt, although not new, gained hold. The tribunals are not addressed directly in this volume, but their contribution to a growing lack of trust in public institutions, a phenomenon alluded to in several contributions, should be noted.

Neo-liberalism became increasingly identifiable as the dominant ideology across Irish political, business and economic thought. The logic of the free market predominated and the new mantra was competition. Essential services became increasingly commodified. League tables for schools and hospital cleanliness audits were published, positioning parents, students and patients as consumers rather than citizens. At the same time, educational and health inequalities persisted (Balanda and Wilde 2001), although these were largely obscured by the language of the market. In 2000, the then Tánaiste argued that '[g]eographically we [Ireland] are closer to Berlin than Boston. Spiritually we are probably a lot closer to Boston than Berlin' (Harney 2000). Many similarities with American society are noted across the chapters and – in terms of dominant ideologies and the economy – the analyses confirm that Ireland is indeed closer to Boston.

The context for these changes was, and is, broader processes of social change occurring throughout western societies, such as globalisation, individualisation, credentialisation, secularisation, materialism, consumerism, and declining trust in institutions. These processes can be seen as common threads that run throughout the book.

The book is a response to a need for an empirically based sociological account of Irish society in a period of rapid economic and social change. The collection brings together work on a broad range of topics relevant to Irish society. Each of the contributors is expert in their field. The majority of the chapters focus on the South. An overarching theme is the changing distribution of resources, power and status in Irish society. Many of the authors take a critical and sometimes sceptical approach to increased globalisation and economic growth.

The chapters concentrate on a specific aspect of changing Ireland over this period. There is a similar format adopted in most chapters. The main changes that have occurred in the area are summarised. The reader is then introduced to some of the key sociological theories and concepts that help to explain these changes. Towards the end of the chapter, the authors try to envision the future of Irish society in this field in the coming decade. The discussion focuses, in the main, on macro-level phenomena. One of the strengths of the collection is the range and quality of the empirical evidence utilised by the authors. Another is the range of different sociological perspectives employed, showcasing many different ways of doing sociology. The classical theories of Durkheim, Weber and Marx, the dominant perspective of the twentieth century, functionalism, and contemporary theorists, most notably Bourdieu, all feature prominently.

The contributors use Ireland as a case study. Although we live in an increasingly globalised world, the nation state remains an important unit of analysis. However, Ireland is not presented as an exceptional society, and links both to other national and global contexts and issues are made throughout the book. Some of the changes analysed in this volume are best understood in a comparative context, while in other instances local processes have equal or superior explanatory power.

Contours of a changing Ireland

The book opens with Fahey's overview of demographic trends in the South since the start of the twentieth century. This provides valuable background and context for the remainder of the book. Ireland has seen an increase in population since the 1990s and this has been both the cause of, and the context in which, recent economic growth took place. The interplay between population growth and economic development is of particular interest to sociologists. The demographic situation in the South is currently advantageous, with a growing population, inward migration, low levels of age dependency, rising birth rate and decreasing mortality rate. Overall Irish population trends are different from the rest of Europe, and more similar to those found in the USA. It is important to study such trends so that current and future employment, public health, education and housing needs can be determined.

It should be noted here that the population of Northern Ireland is also increasing, much of which can be accounted for by natural increases, although inward migration is also a factor (see NISRA 2005: table 2.2). However, the overall demographic picture is not as favourable as that found in the South. Birth and marriage rates are lower, and the death rate is higher than in the South (NISRA 2005: table 1.9). The proportion of the population aged 65 and over is also higher (NISRA 2005: table 2.1).

Immigration is one of the changes to Irish society that is evident in our everyday lives. In a typical day we now come in contact with people from other countries in our work, communities and as we shop and access various services. In chapter 2, Loyal examines immigration, unpacking the processes that come under this generic term, a distinction rarely made. Migrants come to Ireland for numerous different reasons. Once here their treatment, and the rights granted to them, are related to the basis on which they entered the country – on work permits, as students, entrepreneurs or asylum seekers. Policy and legislation governing immigration into Ireland and Irish citizenship are critically analysed. The response of Irish people to migrants is also identified as an area of concern, with racist attitudes pervasive. Racism is presented as one response to the uncertainty associated with broader social and economic changes in train. As one of the major social changes that characterise the period, the topic of immigration is one that the majority of the remaining chapters also touch on.

In chapter 3, Wickham argues that those in professional occupations are the most mobile group in Irish society. Experiences of migration, concentrated in the period before marriage and children, mean that they are the occupational group least likely to have lived in Ireland all their lives. He proposes a sociology of mobility which incorporates the nature and experience of different forms of physical travel, including those associated with migration. His analysis of Dublin's traffic gridlock will be of interest to anyone who commutes to college or work, or who has sat in gridlock on the M50. His argument is that the everyday traffic chaos characteristic of Irish cities is not an inevitable consequence of economic progress, but a result of socio-economic decisions related to planning, combined with the dismantling of public transport system from the 1950s onwards. In this context, car dependency leads to immobility rather than individual freedom. A final change discussed is how air travel has now become a routine part of Irish working life and leisure time, often involving travel to second homes overseas.

Institutions

Institutions often appear as fixed and unchanging, but are products of the society and culture in which they are located and so as the society changes so do they. This is evident when we look at how the institution of the Irish family has changed, a process that has accelerated recently (chapter 5). Hilliard shows a diversity of family types evident and argues that the term family has many different meanings. One change to note is the increase in cohabitation and non-marital births, a trend also evident in Northern Ireland (see chapter 18). The passing of the 1996 Divorce Act was another significant change; however it is noted that the numbers applying for divorce since then have been relatively small in comparison to numbers elsewhere.

Another institution that has seen considerable change is education. As has happened in other western capitalist societies, Ireland has seen an expansion and diversification of the education system in recent decades, and massive expansion of the third-level sector in the past decade. Changes in the education system in the South are presented in chapter 6 by Clancy. In the past only a minority continued their education past Second Level. Now the majority of those in the Republic of Ireland aged between 18 and 22 are enrolled in higher education and numbers of undergraduate students have also increased in Northern Ireland. Increasingly specialised educational qualifications are essential for those wishing to compete in the Irish labour market. Government policy is to increase the numbers studying at postgraduate level and undergraduate students in the South are more likely to continue to postgraduate study than their counterparts in the North (47 per cent as compared to 27 per cent of undergraduates in 2000–1, NISRA 2003: 43). Clancy's discussion shows that class remains central to educational outcomes and this is of concern, given the relationship between educational attainment and life chances.

The Catholic Church in Ireland has lost much of the institutional power it once held over individuals, although it retains considerable power in the education system, where religious congregations own and control the majority of primary and secondary schools (chapter 6). However, in spite of this, Inglis argues that religion remains central to the way we understand ourselves. Many of those who do not consider themselves religious rely on the Church when they wish to celebrate events such as baptism or marriage. In an otherwise individualistic society Catholicism has become an unique inherited and collective social identity, to which people feel they 'belong' although they may or may not accept its central tenets (chapter 4).

Over the past decade, crime has become a major topic of debate and discussion. Ireland is now perceived as a society where crime is a major social problem, a perception highlighted and reaffirmed by the daily news headlines.

However, as Mulcahy details in chapter 7, the crime rate remains low by international standards, and in fact has declined since 1995, although there has been an increase in the number of homicides recorded. Crime can be seen as another vehicle through which more general anxieties about a changing Ireland are both expressed and manipulated by politicians and the media. The fear of crime generated as a result of this misrepresentation of social reality limits people's lives.

The mass media are the key institution for creating and circulating information about our society, some of which is accurate, and some of which is not – as the example of crime rates, above, illustrates. Central issues raised by McCullagh in chapter 8 relate to the perceived power of the media, and the interests various media serve, be they political, economic, ideological or social. The issue of declining trust in institutions is also raised; this may lead to the audience not believing what they read, hear or see on television, a development which would change the power currently attributed to the media. This chapter returns to the issue of immigration, specifically the role played by the media in the creation of racist attitudes. Although much coverage has presented immigration and immigrants in a negative manner, there has also been coverage critical of government policy and racist attitudes. While the media may have a role to play in the creation and circulation of racist discourses, it also may provide a resource for those involved in resisting or challenging racism.

Participation in sport is assumed to have positive outcomes for individuals – for example, improved fitness and health – and for society – for example, social integration and social inclusion. As a result, sport is an institution that is seen as a social good and is viewed positively. In chapter 9, Liston critically examines such taken-for-granted notions and argues that this argument both ignores the social context in which participation in sport takes place, and is not supported by the available empirical evidence. She also raises the question of whose interests are served by this rhetoric about sport. Once again the role of the sociologist as someone who questions background assumptions about our society is highlighted.

Governance

The 1998 Good Friday Agreement led to changes in the political field in Northern Ireland. Particularly contentious were those sections of the Agreement that dealt with prisoners and decommissioning. Coulter and Shirlow discuss the responses to attempts to implement these sections in chapter 10. Their analysis of the peace process highlights the social and political context, in order to understand how and why the peace process has taken the course that it has. This approach is in marked contrast to much media discussion of its ups and downs, which are often presented as irrational, arbitrary or the result of deliberate mischief making. Changes in Northern Irish society after the troubles, in particular the changing fortunes of Catholics and Protestants, are outlined (see also chapter 18). Increasing poverty and disadvantage in working-class loyalist communities are identified as threats to the entire peace process.

Haugaard and Ryan examine how power and governance operate in Irish society. The drafting of the 1996 Partnership Agreement involved the participation of many minority groups, and seemed to indicate a move towards a more inclusive society. In this analysis, the Agreement is part of an emerging form of governance, which involves citizens being conferred with rights (which they had demanded), but simultaneously being curtailed by responsibilities, which involve techniques of self-discipline. They use the example of Travellers' rights, and the 2002 Housing Act, to highlight how empowerment is conditional and partnership can have unintended negative consequences – in this case the reinstatement of an assimilationist policy leading to exclusion, rather than the inclusion promised.

One of the negative features of recent economic growth has been the accompanying environmental problems. Kelly argues that environmental concerns are increasing in Ireland, although these are not accompanied by a desire to curtail economic growth. Instead, there is confidence amongst the public that the state can use scientific expertise to solve environmental problems as and when they arise. The high level of support for state regulation in this area is contrasted with government's reluctance to implement EU policy directives over the period. Critical environmental voices have been marginalised and stigmatised, and their challenge to the mantra of growth suppressed. Where they have been successful is in mobilising local opposition to development, seen as something imposed by outside elites without consultation with the community, a no-no in the Partnership era.

Economy, development and the Celtic Tiger

From 1995 to 2005, there was an increase in the numbers of people in the Irish labour force and this is the subject of the fourth section of the book. The theme of inequalities is central to much of the discussion, and inequalities based on class, ethnicity and gender affecting workers are considered. Social inequalities are argued by Allen in chapter 13 to have increased during the boom, although they were often obscured by rhetoric about social inclusion, equality and partnership. The period also saw the emergence of a segmented labour market, polarised by very different pay and conditions for those in elite sectors of the economy, in comparison to those in the secondary labour market, according to Murray and Ó Riain (chapter 14). Women are disproportionately located in the latter sector. Other inequalities facing women in the workforce are considered by O'Sullivan (chapter 15) and Horgan (chapter 18). Both in the South and in the North, women's increased labour force participation has not led to the disappearance of gender inequalities in the workforce and many difficulties remain for Irish women, including low pay, unequal pay, horizontal segregation, vertical segregation and discrimination on the grounds of gender.

A second theme is the changing structure of the Irish labour market. New areas of employment have emerged during the boom period, and the economy has seen a change away from 'export-based, internationally competitive manufacturing and services to an economy fuelled by domestic consumption and, particularly, construction' (chapter 14). These changes lead to questions being asked about the sustainability of the Celtic Tiger economy.

Changes in the agricultural sector are central to Tovey's discussion of the production of food in Ireland, part of both a changing rural society and agricultural sector. In an increasingly global food market, food is both detached from place of production, and its distribution and supply are dominated by transnational corporations and international chains. Ireland is part of this global food system, although food exports decreased over the period under study. The discussion focuses on competing notions of local food, through which issues of sustainable development are raised. On the one hand, branded local food is an 'authentic' luxury product attracting a premium price nationally and internationally. On the other hand, smaller scale initiatives, such as farmers' markets, seek to supply the local consumer with quality, unprocessed food, often directly from the producer. The latter explicitly draws on ideas of rural sustainable development, whereas the former is more in line with the dominant neo-liberal orthodoxies found elsewhere in the economy, albeit with more attention to environmental impacts than might be found in other sectors.

Class, equality and inequality

The concept of class retains considerable explanatory power when examining Irish society, North and South. Munck argues that the Celtic Tiger economy has not created a society of equals (chapter 17). Rather, the gap between rich and poor has increased, income differentials have become more polarised and consumption cleavages have emerged, most significantly in relation to housing. Similar trends are also evident in education provision and educational outcomes, as evident from Clancy's analysis of the Irish education system (chapter 6).

Although inequalities in the South are high in comparison to the rest of the EU, those found in the North are higher still. Despite this, class based inequalities are often overlooked and ethno-religious divisions are considered to be more important. However, as Horgan illustrates in chapter 18, these divisions intersect with class divisions. When considering issues such as life expectancy or educational attainment, class has considerable explanatory power. Changes in the class structure in Northern Ireland are also evident, with increasing numbers of rich Catholics and poor Protestants, although Catholics remain overrepresented amongst the poor and the unemployed.

Punch's discussion of housing trends draws attention to one dimension of deepening social inequalities in the South. Housing boom and housing crisis exist simultaneously in contemporary Ireland. The decade of 1995–2005 was characterised by high levels of housing output, spiralling house prices and levels of personal indebtedness on the one hand, and increased levels of housing need, including homelessness, on the other. In an increasingly com-modified housing market, policy changes have benefited developers and investors to a greater extent than they have those on low incomes or otherwise marginalised. This is food for thought in a society where indi-vidualistic concerns about property prices – will I, or my children, ever be able to afford a house in my preferred town or neighbourhood? – often obscure the wider picture.

Identity, diversity and culture

Issues of identity are highlighted at times of rapid social change and are the focus of the final section of the book. The demographic, social, economic and political changes discussed in the previous sections are the context for many of the issues arising in relation to Irish identity.

In chapter 20, Watson examines the ever-changing relationship between language, nationality and identity. Nationality is an important aspect of Irish social identity and the Irish language continues to be a symbol of national identity, even if English remains the language used by the majority. Despite a sharp increase in the numbers of children attending all-Irish schools over the past decade, the numbers speaking Irish continue to decline. The Irish language is now positioned as a minority language, and Irish speakers are a minority group with linguistic rights.

The remainder of this section focuses on Northern Irish society. Identity is the focus of chapters 21 and 22, which examine Catholic and Protestant habitus in the period following the Good Friday Agreement. The discussion complements and further develops Coulter and Shirlow's discussion of the peace process (chapter 10), and Horgan's analysis of class in Northern Ireland (chapter 18). In both chapters heterogeneity is emphasised, and the notion of a single Catholic or Protestant habitus problematised.

Lundy and McGovern focus on post-conflict transition in the Ardoyne, a working-class Catholic community in north Belfast, bordered on three sides by Protestant working-class areas. Their interest is intra-community relationships. The people of the Ardoyne suffered disproportionately during the conflict – economically, socially, and in terms of fatalities and injuries. A tightly knit community emerged, based on the two central social institutions that played a central role in everyday life in the area, the IRA and the Catholic Church. The discussion examines how contentious events from the past have been addressed as a part of the process of post-conflict transition. The resources that enabled this community to deal with such difficult issues point to both changes and continuities in habitus.

Moore focuses on inter-community relationships in his discussion of Protestant habitus, examining how Protestant and Catholic values and lifestyles are perceived as different. He argues that, in comparison to the cohesive Catholic community described by Lundy and McGovern, Protestantism is individualistic, fragmented and so does not facilitate a collective identity. This is evident if the competing ideologies of unionism (associated with the middle classes) and loyalism (associated with the working classes) are considered.

In the final chapter, McVeigh critically investigates the idea that racism has become more of a problem than sectarianism in the period following the 1998 Good Friday Agreement. He argues that this notion is not supported by the available empirical evidence, but is related to the state's continuing reluctance to address sectarianism directly as well as problems with its equality mechanisms. This is not to say that racism is not a problem in Northern Ireland: as in the South, racism and racist violence are significant problems (see chapter 2). It is the relationship posited between sectarianism and racism that is challenged.

Overall the chapters combine to provide a cohesive and comprehensive description and analysis of recent transformations in Irish society. In examining the main changes that have occurred over the past decade through a sociological lens, the book provides an alternative to the economic perspective that dominates so much of our society. Sociology allows the questioning of many of the taken-for-granted norms dominant in Irish society. A sociological perspective allows changing societal priorities to be critically investigated, asking whose interests these changes serve.

Section I   Contours of a
changing
Ireland

Chapter 1

Population

Tony Fahey

Introduction

A half-century ago Ireland seemed stricken by an inability to keep up, much less increase, its population numbers. Crippling waves of emigration and an extraordinary reluctance among Irish people to marry and form families had given Ireland's population trends a pathological quality, the only country in modern times to have sustained more than a hundred years of population decline. As a balance sheet of national performance, the Census of population in 1961 was a dismal document. It reported the smallest population in the country at any time since records began and showed that Ireland's demographic malaise had deepened rather than eased in what for the rest of the developed world were the golden years of the 1950s (for accounts of the historical background to this malaise, see Guinnane 1997; Kennedy 1973).

The demographic recovery that began in the 1960s was notable for bringing the previous long history of population contraction to an end. But in international terms it did no more than put Ireland on the same kind of population growth path that was normal everywhere else. That normalisation of Irish population trends was disrupted in one direction for a short time in the late 1980s, when there was a brief recurrence of high emigration and population decline. That proved a temporary blip, however, and as the 1990s advanced population growth returned. Ireland thus became a demographic exception in a novel direction, namely, as one of the few countries in the rich world that continued to experience steady population expansion as the twentieth century came to a close. Ireland's population upswing over the past decade and a half has coincided with an incipient sluggishness in the demography of most other western countries, as reflected both in stalled growth in numbers and rapid population ageing, neither of which is characteristic of Ireland at present. It thereby accentuates the gloss on the social and economic performance of the Celtic Tiger era.

The purpose of this chapter is to provide a brief overview of recent population trends in Ireland, viewed in the context of both Ireland's previous demographic performance and contemporary developments in other countries, especially in Europe. It looks first at population size and age structure and then examines at the main components of population change, namely, fertility, mortality and migration. Brief mention is also made of trends in couple formation indicated by marriage rates and the rising incidence of cohabitation.

Population size and age structure

Figure 1.1 shows the trend in population size by major age group since 1926 and a forecast up to 2036. Population size stagnated from the 1920s to the 1940s and then dipped during the depressed 1950s, falling to a low of 2.82 million in 1961. The decline of the 1950s arose mainly from a contraction of population in the active age ranges as a result of heavy emigration among young adults. The demographic recovery in the 1970s turned that pattern around, in that the active-age ranges showed the greatest growth, fuelled in part by the return of almost 50,000 migrants between 1971 and 1981. Those returning migrants brought some 50,000 children with them and that, combined with a marriage surge and a consequent fertility surge (on which more below), raised the population of children from 877,000 in 1961 to above the million mark from the mid-1970s to the mid-1980s. Population had risen to 3.54 million by 1986. Following a slight dip in total population in the late 1980s, which was caused by economic stagnation and a period of high emigration, strong upward movement returned in the 1990s. Total population, which stood at 3.53 million in 1991, rose to 3.92 million by Census 2002 and then jumped to 4.23 million in Census 2006. The latter represented an 8.1 per cent increase in four years, which, at 2 per cent growth per year, was the highest population growth rate on record for Ireland. Projections for the coming decades suggest that population will continue to grow and, for the next two decades at least, that rising numbers of active-age adults will continue to be the main component of growth. The latter feature in particular is distinctive among present-day western countries, where relative (if not absolute) decline in the size of the active age group is the norm.

A related feature of the trends presented in figure 1.1 is the long-term stability of the share of the population accounted for by the elderly. From the 1920s to the 1960s, the share of the population aged 65 and over rose slightly, from just over 9 per cent to just over 11 per cent (figure 1.2), and that was exceptionally high by international standards at the time. Between 1961 and 2002, the *absolute* number of older people increased from 315,000 to 436,000, but their share of the total population remained almost unchanged at around 11 per cent throughout the period. Population ageing was by then rapidly advancing in other countries, thus making Ireland's elderly population share

Figure 1.1 **Size and age-composition of population of Ireland, 1926–2036**

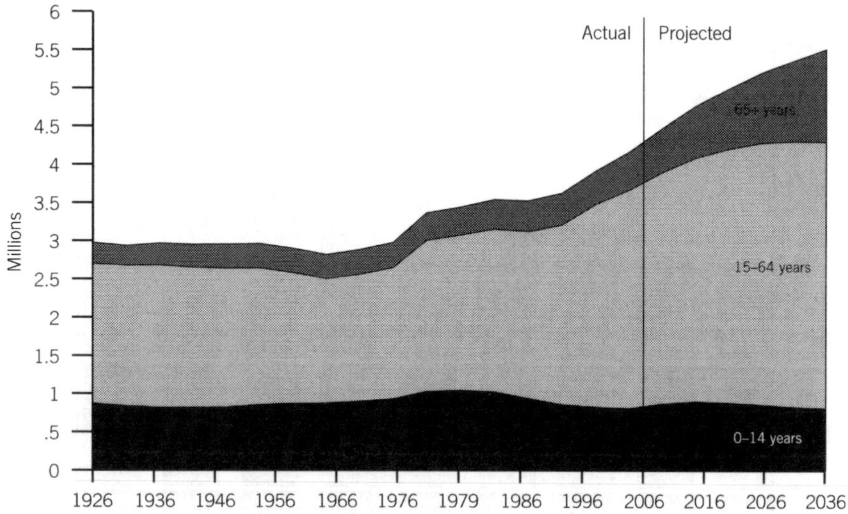

Source: Censuses of Population 1926–2002; CSO Population and Migration Estimates April 2005; CSO Population and Labour Force Projections 2006–2036 (M1F3 assumptions).

in this period seem in relative terms both small and static. In the EU15,[1] for example, the percentage of the population aged 65 or over rose from 12.2 per cent in 1970 to 17 per cent in 2004. A number of features of demographic development in Ireland account for the recent non-ageing of its population. One is the relatively high birth rates by rich country standards found in Ireland, even up to today, which keeps the youth population at a relatively large size. The other is high emigration of young adults in the 1950s, which meant that the cohorts entering old age in the 1990s and early part of this decade were smaller than they otherwise would have been. A third reason is the slow rate of improvement in older-age longevity in Ireland in the second half of the twentieth century, especially among men, a topic we will return to in considering mortality trends below.

These population trends translate into favourable movement in 'age dependency ratios', which refer to the relative balance between those in the 'active' age ranges, who produce most of the country's economic output, and those in younger and older age groups, who depend on others for their economic support. These ratios are important since if the numbers of dependants become large relative to the numbers of the economically active, social and economic strains can arise as a result. For simplicity, the young in this sense are usually defined as those aged 0–15 years, the old as those aged 65 years or over, and the active ages as those in between.[2]

Figure 1.2 **Older people (aged 65+) in Ireland, 1961–2002: number and percentage of population**

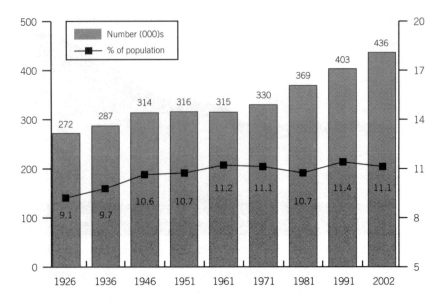

Source: Censuses of Population 1926–2002; CSO Population and Migration Estimates April 2005; CSO Population and Labour Force Projections 2006–2036 (M1F3 assumptions).

Figure 1.3 shows trends in age-dependency ratios, that is, the numbers of young, of old and of young and old combined per 100 persons in the active ages. As a result of the heavy emigration losses among those in the active age ranges in the 1950s and early 1960s, age dependency rose in the 1960s to levels that were exceptionally high both by Irish standards of earlier decades and by comparison with contemporary patterns in other developed countries. At the peak of age dependency in the 1960s, there were 73 young and old combined for every 100 persons aged 15–64. Despite growth in the child population, these levels began to decline slowly in the 1970s because of simultaneous recovery in the size of the active population. After 1986, continued growth in the active population, coupled with decline in the child population and an elderly population that grew only slowly, set age-dependency trends on a more sharply downward slope. At present, historically low levels of age dependency have been reached: there are now 46 young and old people combined for every 100 persons aged 15–64, a dependency ratio that is less two thirds of that of the 1960s. Over the coming decades, age dependency is projected to increase steadily, driven upwards by growth in the numbers of older people. However, the slowness in the increase in age dependency after 2006, coupled with the low base from which it is starting out, mean

Figure 1.3 **Age dependency ratios, 1926–2036**

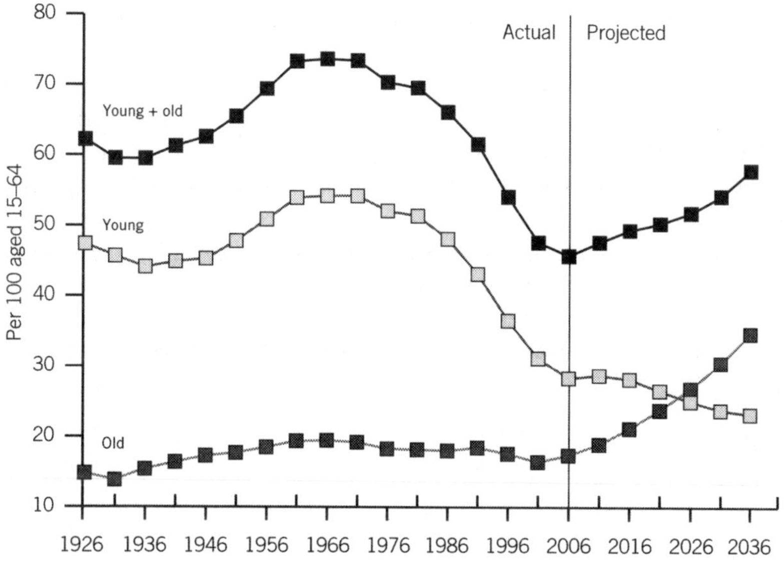

Source: Censuses of Population 1926–2002; CSO Population and Migration Estimates April 2005; CSO Population and Labour Force Projections 2006–2036 (M1F3 assumptions)

that in 2036 age dependency will still be well below the peaks which were reached in the 1960s.

Components of population change

Population growth is the outcome of the interaction between natural increase in the population, which itself is the balance between births and deaths, and net migration, which is the balance between inward and outward migration. Figure 1.4 shows the annual averages of natural increase, net migration and the resulting population change for the period 1926 to 2006. In the 1920s, 1930s and 1940s, natural increase was cancelled out by net outward migration, leading to more or less zero population growth. Net migration became more heavily negative in the 1950s, with a total net outflow of population over the decade of approximately 400,000, or about one eighth of the population. In the 1960s, the turnaround began: net migration remained negative but less so than previously, while natural increase was strong enough to produce a net positive effect on population change. Economic boom in the late 1960s and early 1970s gave rise to a period of net *inward* migration and combined it with strong natural increase. This gave a boost to population growth, the first time this had occurred since the 1840s. In the 1980s, the positive trend came unstuck as net migration turned negative again, particularly in the latter part of the decade, and natural increase declined on account of falling birth rates. Population growth fizzled out and turned into slight decline in the period 1986–91. However, a further turnaround came in 1990s, though slowly at first. In the first half of the 1990s, net migration on average was zero and a modest level of natural increase caused small population growth. Since then, the pace of population growth has intensified. Natural increase has risen as high as ever before, as births have risen and deaths declined (see further below). Inward migration has soared to the point where it now considerably exceeds natural increase as a source of population growth.

Figure 1.4 **Annual average natural increase, net migration and population change, 1926–2006**

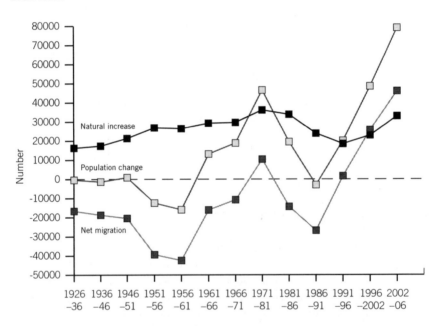

Sources: Censuses of Population 1926–2002, CSO Population and Migration Estimates April 2005.

The unusual level and nature of Ireland's current population growth in European terms is suggested in figure 1.5, which shows the components of population change in 2002 in a number of European countries, including Turkey. Only Spain and Turkey had a population growth rate in that year similar to that of Ireland. In Ireland, however, migration and natural increase contributed equally to growth, while in Spain inward migration accounted for nearly all growth and in Turkey natural increase did so. In all other

Figure 1.5 **Population change (per cent) in European countries, 2002**

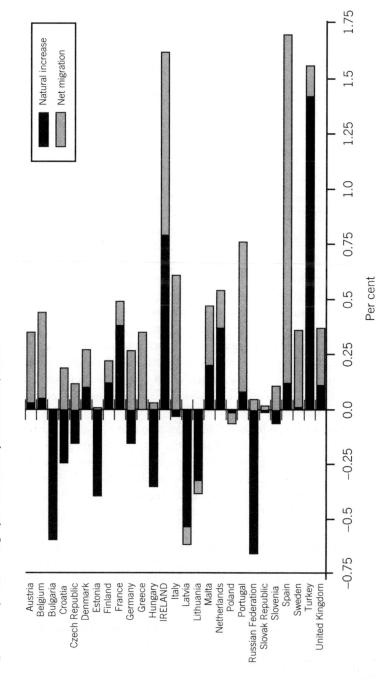

Per cent

Source: Derived from Council of Europe population database

countries, growth was either small or completely absent, if not negative, and only in France and the Netherlands was there any significant degree of natural increase. In Italy, Germany and many countries of eastern Europe natural increase was negative, and the degree to which population growth occurred or not was dependent entirely on migration. Thus Ireland is now exceptional both in having a substantial rate of population growth and in drawing both on natural increase and migration for that growth.

Fertility

Reflecting on the weak demographic performance in Europe just referred to, the European Commission's Green Paper on demographic change expressed the view that the EU no longer has a 'demographic motor' (European Commission 2005a). The key problem is the very low birth rates now found in Europe (figure 1.6). For the past 15 years, the total fertility rate (TFR)[3] in the EU15 has been at less than three-quarters the level needed to replace the population. The TFR for the EU15 in 2004 was 1.52, while the replacement TFR is conventionally defined as 2.1.[4] The ten new member states have an even weaker reproductive performance, with a TFR in 2004 of 1.27.[5] In the United States, by contrast, the fertility record of recent decades has been considerably stronger. Having fallen to a historical low in the 1970s, the TFR in the USA has recovered somewhat since then and for the past 15 years has hovered around 2, a fertility rate, which when coupled with modest inward migration, is sufficient to ensure that total US population will continue to grow for the foreseeable future.

The level of fertility in Ireland is now closer to that of the USA than of the rest of Europe, and this was also true in the 1950s and early 1960s (see also Fahey 2001). The Irish TFR remained at a high level until 1970, at which point it commenced a rapid decline that persisted for two decades. The decline bottomed out in the 1990s and then recovered slightly. By 2004 it was somewhat higher (at 1.98) than it had been in 1995 (when it was 1.84).

A surge in the formation of new families, rather than a return to larger family sizes, has been the main cause of the recovery in fertility in the Ireland since the early 1990s. First births rose by 45 per cent between 1994 and 2005 (figure 1.7). The boom in first births was such that their numbers in the early years of the present decade have been the highest ever recorded in Ireland, even though total births are now well below the previous peak. If we take the birth of a first child as a marker of new family formation, we can thus say that since the mid-1990s, Ireland has experienced an unprecedented level of creation of new families. The large increase in first births between 1994 and 2005 carried forward into a slightly lesser increase in second births, which rose

Figure 1.6 **Total fertility rates in Ireland, the EU15 and the USA, 1960–2004**

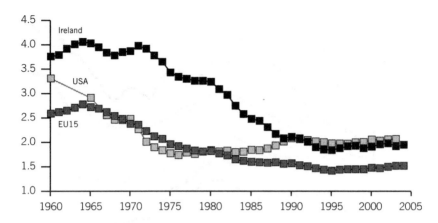

Source: CSO, Eurostat.

by 36 per cent over the same period. The number of second births in 2002 and 2003 have also been the highest on record. Third births showed a much smaller increase, but in the context of the trend towards very small families found elsewhere in Europe it is significant that there was any increase at all. At the other extreme of family size, fifth and higher order births continued their long-term decline. In the 1960s, higher order births were exceptionally common in Ireland. In 1960, for example, for every 100 firstborn children, over 150 children were fifth-born or higher. By 2003, for every 100 firstborn children, only 10 children were fifth-born or higher. Thus, the very large family, which little more than a generation ago was very common, has now become rare.

Women in Ireland have traditionally had children at a late age (Kennedy 1973), and this tradition persists. In 1960, the average age of women giving birth was 31.6 years. Over the following two decades, that age shifted slightly downwards and was 28.8 years in 1980. Thereafter it edged slowly upwards again, and by 2003 had reached 30.6 years. These rather small movements in the average age of childbearing have been accompanied by larger movements in the age-spread of childbearing around the mean, especially since the 1970s: childbearing has declined among women aged in their 20s and 40s and has become increasingly concentrated among women aged in their 30s (figure 1.8). In 1971, the age group 25–29 had the highest number of births, but over the past ten years the age group 30–34 has taken over as the dominant age for childbearing among women. Teenage birth rates are low, account for less than 6 per cent of births, and have fallen slightly since the early 1980s. At the other end of the maternal age range, the birth rate among women aged 40–44 is now less than a third of what it was in the early 1970s, while

Figure 1.7 **Number of births by birth order in Ireland, 1960–2005**

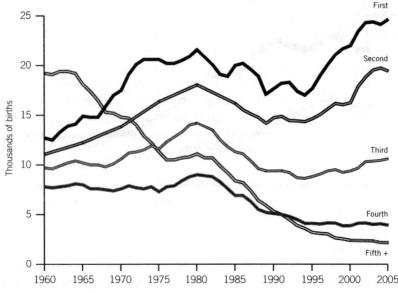

Source: CSO Vital Statistics

births among those aged 45 or over, while always unusual, have also declined since the 1970s. The latter trends are significant since they indicate that while the average age of childbearing among women has risen in recent years, this has not meant that more mothers are having children in the higher-risk older ages.

Analysis of fertility trends in developed countries since the 1980s has gone some way to identifying the factors that might account for the recent recovery and relatively high level of fertility in Ireland (D'Addio and Mira d'Ercole 2005; Sleebos 2003; Ahn and Mira 2002). On the one hand, cross-country differences in fertility seem to be affected only to a limited degree by variations in the generosity or lack of it in state support for families with children. Those countries with the highest fertility rates (such as the United States, Ireland and New Zealand) tend to have relatively low levels of state support for families and children: state provision of pre-school childcare is typically slight, maternity leave is short, and tax-benefit supports for either two-parent or lone-parent families are ungenerous. The key to strong performance in this area seems to lie instead in general economic buoyancy, particularly where that gives rise to high levels of demand for female labour. A recent OECD analysis of fertility rates in developed countries in the period 1980–99 identified factors such as the female employment rate and the availability of part-time jobs for women as the main positive influences on

Figure 1.8 **Age-specific fertility rates, 1961–2005**

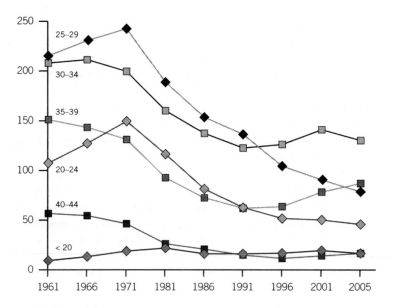

Source: CSO Vital Statistics

fertility rates, while the female unemployment rate was a strong negative influence (D'Addio and Mira d'Ercole 2005). The Irish experience is broadly consistent with these patterns, as the recovery in birth rates since 1995 coincided with the boom in the economy that got under way at the same time and the rapid growth of employment, especially of married women's employment. In the high-job scenario that emerged in Ireland, disincentives to childbearing that are concentrated in early childhood (such as high direct costs of childcare and high costs of housing in the early stages of house purchase), coupled with weak state supports for families with children, may have had some deterrent effect on family formation and birth rates, but they seem to have been counter-balanced by positive economic conditions, perhaps as these gave women confidence in their longer-term employment prospects.

Couple formation

For much of the first half of the twentieth century, Irish people were exceptionally slow to marry: they either married late or never married at all. This pattern reached an extreme in the 1930s, at which point over half of 30–34 years in Ireland were single and 27 per cent of 50–54 year-olds were single. No other population in human history had by then recorded as high an incidence of non-marriage as this (Guinnane 1997). From the low point of the 1930s, the incidence of marriage increased steadily, with a particularly sharp rise as economic conditions improved in the 1960s and early 1970s. The annual number of marriages reached a twentieth-century peak in 1974, with 22,800 marriages in that year. This was followed by two decades of decline, coupled with a rise in the age at which people married. By the early 1990s, the annual number of marriages was hovering around 16,000, a level that was only 70 per cent of the peak of 1974, and the average age of marriage had risen by two years for both men and women. As with births, however, the 1990s brought the period of decline to an end and turned it into recovery. In 2004, there were 20,600 marriages, less than the peak of 1974 but 32 per cent more than in 1995. Some of this increase was simply a function of the growing size of the relevant age cohorts, but there was also some rise in the propensity of people to marry. The marriage rate among those aged 16–49 rose from 17.7 per 1,000 persons in 1996 to 19.7 in 2002 in the case of males and from 17.8 to 20.2 in the case of females. At the same time, the average age of marriage rose sharply, in contrast to the growing youthfulness of marriage that occurred in the marriage boom of the 1960s and 1970s. Having risen by two years in the 1980s, average age at marriage jumped by a further four years between 1990 and 2002, rising to 32.5 years for men and 30 years for women – high ages of marriage not seen since the 1940s. These age patterns suggest that the marriage surge of recent years is probably best interpreted in part as a consequence of catch-up among those who deferred marriage during the depressed 1980s and early 1990s and then crowded into marriage from the mid-1990s onwards. The introduction of divorce in 1997 also contributed to both the higher incidence and older age of marriage, as it enabled those whose marriages had broken down to remarry. However, it is not possible to say what share of the upward trend was due to this factor.

Partnership outside marriage is a growing aspect of family life in Ireland and partly accounts for the rising age of marriage, as young adults cohabit before marrying. The Census of Population in 1996 for the first time included a count of the number of cohabiting couples and their children and the same issue was also examined in the Census 2002, though there were small changes in the format of relevant question between the two censuses. The 1996 Census counted 31,300 cohabiting couples, of whom 40.5 per cent (12,700) had children aged less than 15 years. They amounted to 3.9 per cent of all family units. By 2006, the incidence of cohabitation had increased fourfold. The number had risen to 121,800, and the proportion of all family units accounted for by cohabiters had increased to 11.6 per cent, though the proportion of cohabiting couples who had children had fallen to 36 per cent. Cohabiting couples with children aged under 15 accounted for 8.7 per cent of all families with children of that age in 2006, and 6.7 per cent of children in that age were living in cohabiting couple families. Partners of the same sex account for a small proportion of all cohabiting couples but that proportion rose more than fourfold between 1996 and 2006. In 1996, 0.4 per cent of cohabiting couples were same-sex partnerships, but by 2006 that had risen to 1.7 per cent (the absolute increase was from 150 couples in 1996 to 2,090 in 2006).

Halpin and O'Donoghue (2004) examined patterns of cohabitation in more detail using panel data for Ireland from the European Community Household Panel Survey. They found that for all the increase in cohabitation, it does not appear to be developing as a major alternative to marriage. Rather, in their view, it is most often a temporary arrangement found mainly among young urban adults that either dissolves after a relatively short period or leads on to marriage. They characterised cohabitation as a stage on the road to marriage and concluded that 'in the near future . . . new marriages will be more likely than not to be preceded by cohabitation' (2004: 10).

Mortality

Stronger population growth is in part the consequence of improvements in population health and the resulting falling mortality. The number of deaths per 1,000 of the population has halved over the past 80 years, falling from an annual average of 14.45 deaths in the 1920s to 7.31 in 2003. Some 43,000 people died each year in the 1920s, out of a population of some 2.9 million. Today, less than 30,000 people die per year out of a population of over 4 million.

As a result of these improvements, life expectancy at birth has risen from 57.9 years for both sexes in 1926 to 80.3 years for women and 75.1 years for men in 2002 (figure 1.9). Thus women on average have gained an extra 22 years of life since the 1920s, while men have gained an extra 17 years. From the 1930s to the 1950s, the main cause of improved life expectancy was a sharp fall in death rates among infants and young adults. Mortality rates among older people were slower to improve. This was especially so among older men: in 1986, life expectancy among men at age 60 (15.9 years) was virtually the same as it had been in 1926 (15.8 years). Since the late 1980s, however, older men's longevity has improved, with life expectancy at age 60 for men rising to 19.2 years by 2002, a 21 per cent increase since 1986. Older women's life expectancy has risen more steadily over time, particularly since the 1950s.

In the early part of the twentieth century, the main contributor to the decline in mortality was a fall in deaths due to infectious and parasitic diseases, such as bronchial and digestive infections among children and tuberculosis among adults. With the conquest of infectious diseases, degenerative diseases – those arising from the decay of organs and cells in the body – have

Figure 1.9 **Life expectancy at ages 0 and 60, 1926–2002**

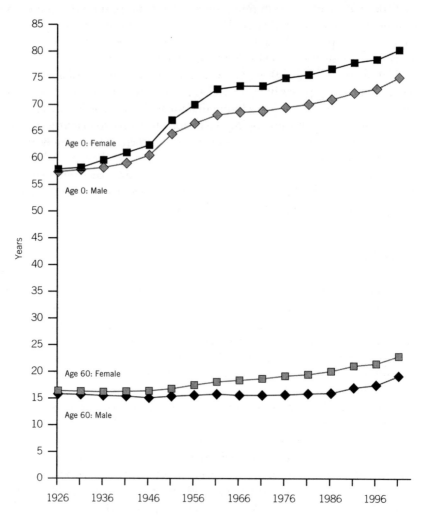

Source: CSO Irish Life Tables

taken over as the primary killers. In recent years also, most these causes of death have shown declines. In particular, deaths from diseases of the circulatory system, such as heart disease and strokes, have fallen sharply (figure 1.10). In the 1970s, there were in the region of 600 deaths per 100,000 population from diseases of the circulatory system. By 2002, this had fallen to less than 300 deaths per 100,000 population. However, deaths from cancer have shown no similar decline, and cancer has already taken over from heart disease as a cause of death in Ireland.

Figure 1.10 **Age-standardised death rates by major cause, per 100,000 population, 1970–2002**

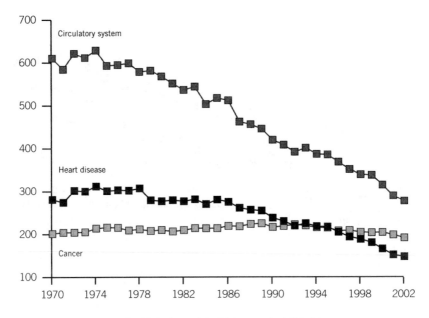

Source: WHO European Health For All database – http://data.euro.who.int/hfadb/

Migration

The long-term trend in net migration has already been outlined on pp. 17–18. Here we focus on the new migration regime that has emerged since the 1980s, when Ireland has become a country of destination rather than of origin for migration flows. Figure 1.11 shows the trend in inward and outward migration and the net balance between the two for each year from 1987 to 2005. As has been outlined earlier, the late 1980s witnessed a return of high emigration. In 1989, the worst year for emigration in this period, 70,000 people left the country while 26,000 came in, yielding a net outflow of 44,000. The gross outflows dropped below 40,000 in the early 1990s and the gross inflows rose to similar levels, so that the net movement hovered around zero up to 1995. Since then the inflows have risen steadily, apart from dips in 2003 and 2004, while outflows have declined slightly, leading to large increases in the net inflow. In the year to April 2006, a record 87,000 immigrants entered the country, while only 17,000 emigrants left, yielding a net inward flow of 70,000 (note that data on inward migration may underestimate the true level of inward flow since some immigrants may be missed by the counting exercises on which these estimates are based).

Figure 1.11 **Immigration, emigration and net migration, 1987–2005**

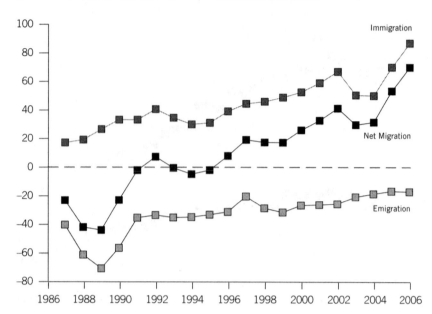

Source: CSO Population and Migration Estimates, September 2006

The first phase of increase in migration flows to Ireland was driven in large part by returning Irish migrants: in 1998, as figure 1.12 shows, over half of the inward migrants were Irish, while the next largest category were from the UK (19 per cent). As inward migration continued, returning Irish migrants became less important, as did migrants from the UK, while non-traditional sources of migration grew in significance. By 2006, migrants from the new member states of the EU (the east European countries that joined in 2004) had taken over as the dominant source of immigrants, accounting for 43 per cent of the total. Returning Irish had reduced by well over half in relative terms (to 23 per cent) and migrants from the UK had reduced to 9 per cent. Thus inward migration has become ethnically more diverse in composition over time and has brought a new degree of multiculturalism to Ireland. However, the cultural diversity of migrant flows into Ireland in recent years is still limited. Even in 2006, seven out of every eight immigrants were from within the European Union and thus were white and from countries with a Christian cultural background. Ireland still has very few non-whites or non-Christians in its population, in contrast to the more multi-racial and multi-religious situation found in most other rich western countries.

Figure 1.12 **Immigrants classified by nationality, 1998 and 2006 (per cent)**

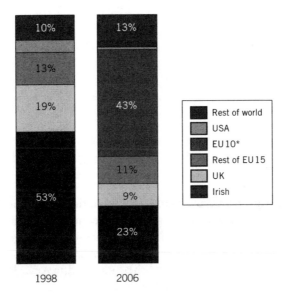

* 10 new member states from May 2004. In the data for 1998, the EU10 are included in Rest of World.
Source: CSO Population and Migration Estimates 2003, 2005

Conclusion

By the standards of both its own past and the present situation in much of the rich world, Ireland is now in a favourable phase of population development. Total population numbers are rising, where they are static or falling in Europe as a whole, and the population has not yet entered the era of rapid population ageing that is found elsewhere. Birth rates rose slightly in the 1990s and have now stabilised at a level that suits Ireland's current circumstances – much lower than in the past and technically below population replacement level, but when combined with even modest inward migration high enough to keep total population growing. Since deaths have declined at the same time, we now have a healthy level of natural increase in the population. The turnaround in migration patterns is the most dramatic of Ireland's recent population changes: people now want to enter rather than leave the country and this is a powerful indicator of the degree to which Ireland's overall social and economic fortunes are in a stronger position than ever before.

Chapter 2

Immigration

Steven Loyal

Introduction

Ireland has historically been a country of emigration. From the Great Famine of the 1840s to the 1950s, Ireland's population continued to decline. Although other demographic factors including birth rate and marriage rate were also important in explaining this decline, emigration played the central role. High rates of emigration continued until the 1960s and 1970s, when, as the economy strengthened, they started to fall. However, the 1980s again saw the emigration figures rise. Many emigrants went to the UK, the USA, Canada, Australia, and some even travelled to Argentina, creating a vast Irish diaspora estimated (in its most capacious interpretation) to be somewhere between 70 million and 80 million people. Given the continued migration of generations of people for almost a century and a half, Irish emigration became an accepted feature of the social landscape. In a slow stagnant economy, characterised by poor growth rates and low employment prospects, itself underlain by a rural insular ideology, emigration not only appealed to the needs of Irish people looking to better themselves materially or to escape a repressive social and cultural climate, but also served the needs of the state by operating as a safety valve for discontented or frustrated citizens unable to find work.

The 1990s, however, witnessed a dramatic reversal in migration flows. From having a net emigration of 70,000 people as recently as between 1988 and 1999, Ireland had a net immigration of 70,000 in 2005 (see figure 2.1).

Given the size of the population, the immigration rate in Ireland is very high by European standards, with only Luxembourg having a higher rate (Mac Éinrí 2003: 17). The reasons for the shift from emigration to immigration are multifold and include a variety of social, political, ideological, and especially economic factors. The opening of the economy to foreign direct investment and low corporation taxes formed the basis of a knowledge economy and an economic policy aimed at attracting computing and pharmaceutical industries (O'Hearn 1998). In addition, membership of the European Union had significant economic benefits. However, the social and economic implications of the

Figure 2.1 **Migration 1987–2006**

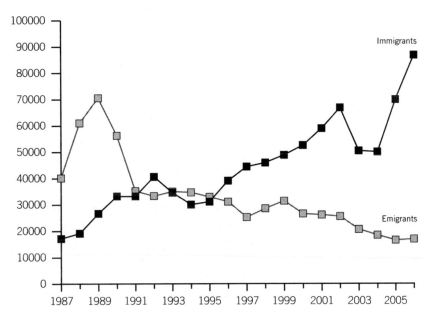

Source: CSO 2006a: 9

rise in immigration, particularly within a protracted period, have been enormous. Immigration has brought increasing diversity to Irish society and has implications for constructions of Irish national identity, the operation of the labour market, Irish culture, and how the state regulates political and civic rights.

Theorising migration

Migration as a process has long formed a central feature of the global social, political and economic landscape and has increasingly come to the fore in Ireland following the dramatic changes wrought by the Celtic Tiger economy. The concept of migration is a generic concept covering a wide variety of complex, multilayered processes and phenomena. Similarly, the term migrant homogenises a very disparate group from a variety of nationalities, class backgrounds, ethnicities and religions. Although processes of migration are considered the exception within the context of a global modern nation-state system, they were for a long time the rule. William McNeil (1979) has argued that when our ancestors first became fully human they were already migratory. Having left what is considered humanity's cradleland – tropical Africa – and moving first to the Near East and eventually to Oceania, it is believed that the great migration was completed by 8,000 BC. Moreover, much early agriculture was itself migratory – slash and burn – and included the development of pastoral nomadry from about 3,000. The emergence of civilisations such as Sumerian cities after about 4,000 BC was also important in shaping societies and population development.

In Western Europe from the sixteenth century onwards migration played a central role in modernisation and industrialisation. From the end of the Middle Ages, the development of European states and their colonisation of the rest of the world, which coincided with the development of capitalism, gave a new impetus to international migrations of many different kinds. European states colonised significant areas of Africa, Asia, Oceania and the Americas. Capitalism made use of both free and unfree workers in every phase of its development (Castles and Miller 1998: 49). The enslavement and deportation of conquered people was a frequent early form of labour migration and colonisation is itself a different form of migration. The development of slavery, the coolie system, and indentured workers generated huge population movements (Potts 1991). A second period of extensive migration followed rapid industrial expansion in the mid nineteenth century, and saw more than 45 million people leave Europe between 1800 and 1925. Much of this emigration was concentrated in five main destinations: Argentina, Australia, Canada, New Zealand and the USA (Massey 2000: 34). Other significant periods of migration followed the First and Second World Wars. Moreover, migration has become an increasingly global and pervasive force since the 1960s with the number of migrants from Asia, Africa and Latin America overshadowing those emigrating from Europe.

How we theorise migration has often followed the existing dominant patterns of migration. A variety of theoretical models have been proposed to explain why people migrate, with each perspective employing different conceptual and analytical frameworks. Moreover, in explaining migration these theories have often proceeded through various unhelpful sociological dichotomies, many of which have reproduced and reconfigured the debate concerning micro–macro approaches, the relationship between agency and structure, or individual versus society. The earliest approach to explaining migration was arguably E. G. Ravenstein's classic *The Laws of Migration* (1885). Drawing on census data, Ravenstein outlined 11 major laws of migration including that migrants preferred to travel short distances; those travelling long distances usually moved to centres of commerce or industry; the natives of towns were less migratory than those of rural areas; women migrated more within their country of birth, and men outside their country of birth; migration increased in volume as industries and commerce developed and transport improved; and that the major causes of migration were economic. In terms of the latter, Ravenstein noted, that there were many reasons for migration: '[b]ad or oppressive laws, heavy taxation, an unattractive climate, uncongenial social surroundings, and even compulsion (slave trade, transportation)', but he added, 'none of these currents can compare in volume with that which arises from the desire inherent in most men [*sic*] to "better" themselves in material respects' (Ravenstein 1976: 286).

Ravenstein's arguments have been highly influential in the field of migration (Lee 1969; Zolberg, 1989), particularly his hypothesis that migration was essentially caused by economic factors. This axiom also constitutes the central platform from which rational-choice theories of migration proceed. Central to the rational-choice approach is an independent individual, who rationally weighs the costs and benefits of leaving one area for another in order to maximise his or her utility. The choice of whether to migrate or not is often based on factors which include whether the immigrant will get higher returns on their skill levels, and the costs of travelling, of language difficulties, and of leaving one's family and friends behind. Such a decision-making model has been modified in the work of the 'new economics of migration' which focuses on the family as a decision-making entity rather than the individual agent and which incorporates the idea of risk rather than simply aggregate income as a crucial factor in the decision to migrate.

Such models are often associated with a push–pull framework whereby the causes of migration are seen as a combination of push factors impelling people to leave their areas of origin, and of pull factors, attracting them to other countries. Push factors in the country of origin may include excessive demographic growth, low living standards, lack of economic opportunities, and political repression, while pull factors in the destination country include demand for labour, availability of land, good economic opportunities and presence of greater political freedoms (Castles and Miller 1998).

By contrast, structural approaches have tended to emphasise more macro causes for migration. These approaches also look to push and pull factors. They link immigration to the structural requirements of modern industrial economies: the pull factors include economic, demographic and social developments whilst the push factors comprise unemployment, poverty and underdevelopment (Piore 1979). As Castles and Kosack argue, 'the motivations of the movement [of immigrants] have been primarily economic' (1973: 3) so that the movement of migrants has 'developed in accordance with the economic needs of the industry on the one hand and of the migrants on the other' (1973: 26). Nevertheless, despite acknowledging the economic needs of migrants, the causes of migration are essentially structural – the macro needs of the capitalist system for labour power (Harris 1995). Migration is analysed as 'a movement of workers propelled by the dynamics of the transnational capitalist economy, which simultaneously determines both the "push" and the "pull"' (Zolberg 1989: 407). Structuralist approaches are not all cut from one cloth. Marxist interpretations of migration which emphasise the needs of capital and the costs of reproduction of labour power have often been supplemented with world system theory approaches which emphasise the unequal distribution of geopolitical power across the nations. Capitalism, they argue, not only perpetuates inequalities, but – following the penetration of capitalist economic relations into what are essentially non-capitalist traditional economies – engenders emigration from less developed economies to more developed countries. Since the cost of educating the migrant worker has been met by the developing nation, this also constitutes a further source of exploitation as well as often resulting in 'brain drain'.

A third approach, which partly arose in order to remedy the deficiencies of the aforementioned standpoints by synthesising their insights, focuses on social networks rather than singularly on economic factors (Massey et al. 1987; 1993; 1994). Here migration is conceived as a cumulative process whose operation is governed by six principles which the authors outline: that migration originates historically in transformations of social and economic structures in sending and receiving societies; that once begun, migrant networks form to support migration on a mass basis; that as international migration becomes widely accessible, families make it part of their survival strategies and use it during phases of life-cycle when dependence is greatest; that individual motivations, household strategies, and community structures are altered by migration in ways that make further migration more likely; that even among temporary migrants, there is an inevitable process of settlement abroad; and that among settlers, there is a process of return migration (Massey et al. 1987: 6–7).

Theoretical approaches to migration in the social sciences have often been characterised by 'methodological nationalism' in which the nation state is taken as constitutive of what we mean by society and used as the framework through which to interpret migration. Thus, rather than looking at humanity as a whole, or looking at a global interstate system as the framework for interpreting migration, the focus of sociologists has generally been on one nation which is seen as co-extensive with the idea of what a society is. Such a correlation has long been questioned in sociological analysis generally (Elias 1978a; Mann 1986), but it remains a dominant feature of much migration research (Wimmer and Glick Schiller 2002). This has a number of implications which have been rightly criticised by Abdelmalek Sayad (2004). Sayad has argued that it is impossible to write an adequate sociology of immigration without simultaneously outlining a sociology of emigration: the two components form 'indissociable aspects of a single reality' (2004: 1). An understanding the country of origin of the migrant as well as his or her country of reception not only avoids a residual ethnocentrism in which it is implied that an immigrant's life begins when he enters the host nation, but facilitates an account of migration which avoids yielding to a problematic in which the adaptation of the migrant to the host society is prioritised.

Moreover, Sayad argues that it is imperative to understand processes of migration in terms of power relationships, not only between the emigrant and the receiving state, but, importantly, as inter-state relations that bear the imprint of past relations of colonialism – as for example an Irish cleaner and her English employer working in the UK.

Irish immigration

The first major piece of legislation that regulated immigration into Ireland was the Irish Aliens Act of 1935 which drew heavily on the British Aliens Restriction Act of 1914 and the Restriction Amendment Act of 1919. This act gave enormous powers of discretion to the Minister for Justice in relation to state security and allowed the minister to determine whether an immigrant would be allowed entry into Ireland, where he or she could live, or if he or she should be deported. The act also curtailed rights of residency and work amongst prospective immigrants. Together with the Irish Nationality and Citizenship Act of 1935 this legislation defines the access, rights and entitlements of individuals as citizens and non-citizens. Until the citizenship referendum of 2004, citizenship was flexibly conferred both upon persons who were born on the island of Ireland (*ius soli*), and to the children of Irish nationals (*ius sanguinis*).

More recently, the Irish state has introduced various pieces of legislation to regulate migration. These include the Refugee Act of 1996, the Illegal Immigrants Trafficking Act 2000, the Immigration Bill 2004, the Employment Permits Act of 2003 and 2006, and the Immigration and Residence Bill 2007. Despite increasing migration, and increasing migration laws, the Irish state, in comparison to most other developed countries, still lacks a coherent official immigration policy. By and large, immigration policy and legislation has developed in a pragmatic and *ad hoc* way. This is partly reflected in the Irish state's failure to designate overall responsibility for overseeing immigration. Instead this is distributed across various state departments. The Department of Justice, Equality and Law Reform is responsible for entry and residence in the state, the Department of Enterprise, Trade and Employment for issuing work permits and work visas/authorisations, and the Department of Foreign Affairs for issuing work visas/authorisations abroad.[1]

Immigration into Ireland cannot be understood independently of an international and European context. Events within Europe, but especially within the United Kingdom because of the Common Travel Area, have a significant impact on migration issues within Ireland. The disputed territory

in Northern Ireland has meant that immigration policies which are introduced in the UK are often mirrored in Ireland. Since individuals who are EU
nationals can freely travel to Ireland there are four major ways in which third
area nationals can enter: through a work permit/visa/authorisation system,
through setting up a business, as students, or as asylum seekers.[2]

Despite this unusually broad citizenship policy, the Irish state has from its
foundation been consistently restrictive concerning the entry of 'aliens' into
its national space. It would be mistaken to believe that contemporary asylum
seekers and economic migrants are disrupting the contours of an otherwise
unitary and homogenous Irish society. Such notions of homogeneity invariably
form a central part of nationalistic state discourses (Calhoun 1997). The
presence of Travellers, Protestants and Black-Irish bears witness to the fact
that Irish society, though relatively homogeneous in terms of whiteness and
Catholicism, was always more diverse than it claimed to be. Moreover, limited
but culturally significant Jewish immigration at the turn of the century, and
the arrival of a number of programme refugees including Hungarians,
Chileans, Vietnamese and Bosnians after the 1950s meant that the experience
and impact of asylum seekers and work permit holders was not unprecedented.[3] Nevertheless, compared to other European countries Ireland was for
various historical reasons remarkably homogeneous.

Although issues concerning migration have become centre stage, little
is known about the exact ethnic and national composition of the country.
Statistical information from the major government departments which collect
data on various aspects of immigration – the Department of Justice, Law, and
Equality, the Department of Social Welfare, the Central Statistics Office
Quarterly Household National Survey, and the Census – is not standardised.
The most extensive database is the 2006 Irish Census. This registered an
overall population of just over 4.2 million people, 419,773 of whom (about 10
per cent) were non-Irish nationals, an 88 per cent increase on the 2002 census
figure. The majority of non-Irish nationals were from the EU (275,775),
followed by Asia (46,952), Africa (35,326), and North and South America
(21,124). The UK continued to account for the largest number of non-Irish
nationals living in Ireland (112,548), followed by citizens from Poland
(63,276), Lithuania (24,638), Nigeria (16,300), Latvia (13,319) and China
(11,161). It is noteworthy that 95 per cent of the total population in Ireland in
the 2006 Census identified themselves as white, and only 1.3 per cent of the
population identified themselves as Asian and 1 per cent as Black. However,
those working with foreign national groups believe that these official statistics
significantly underestimate the actual number of foreign workers and non-
Irish nationals living in Ireland since they fail to include undocumented or
irregular workers, and family reunification. Although the percentage of
foreign born individuals living and working in Ireland is relatively high and

comparable to the UK, what makes the Irish situation *vis-à-vis* migration and increasing diversity even more remarkable is the condensed ten-year timeframe within which this shift towards diversity through immigration has occurred.

Asylum seekers in Ireland

The Department of Justice, Equality and Law Reform has responsibility for asylum policy and dealing with asylum claims. The asylum system contains three major components: the Office of the Refugee Applications Commissioner (ORAC), Refugee Appeals Tribunal (RAT), and the Reception and Integration Agency (RIA). Though each state has significant latitude in interpreting and implementing policy towards asylum seekers and refugees they have to operate according to the 1951 UN Convention which Ireland signed up to in 1957. According to the 1951 Convention, it is the right of any person from any country in the world to invoke the asylum procedure and for individuals to seek recognition as a refugee. The Refugee Act (1996), not fully passed until November 2000, is the act of law which the Irish government uses to guide its asylum procedure and to interpret the 1951 Convention. The Refugee Act (1996) has an unusually progressive definition of an asylum seeker as:

> A person who, owing to a well-founded fear of being persecuted for reasons of race, religion, nationality, membership of a particular social group or political opinion, is outside the country of his or her nationality or, owing to such fear, is unwilling to avail himself or herself of the protection of that country.

In contrast to the majority of Europe where labour migration preceded the arrival of asylum seekers, early debates on migration in Ireland focused on asylum seekers or refugees. In 1992, Ireland received only 39 applications for asylum. By 1996, this figure had risen to 1,179, then to 10,325 in 2001, and peaking at 11,634 in 2002. By 2003 it began to fall, reaching 7,900 at the end of that year and falling further to 4,323 by the end of 2005. This last figure represented a 63 per cent fall in applications from the 2002 figure. The majority of asylum seekers in 2005 were from Nigeria, Romania, Somalia, Sudan and Iran (Irish Refugee Council 2006).

In absolute terms, Ireland in 2004 received only 1.6 per cent of the total number of asylum applications within the EU25 (France received 21.18 per cent and the UK 17.82 per cent). According to the European Council on Refugees and Exiles, compared to the UK which received 393,830, between 2000 and 2004 Ireland only received 45,730 applications for asylum (ECRE 2005: 3). However, in relative terms in relation to per capita of the population, Ireland was fifth out of 25 countries in Europe.

Asylum seekers in Ireland are not permitted to leave the state nor to seek or enter into employment nor to carry on any business or to trade prior to the final determination of their case. Those asylum seekers who entered Ireland before April 2000 are usually in receipt of full Supplementary Welfare Assistance (SWA) payments and rent supplement if they secure private rented accommodation. However, in marked contrast, asylum seekers who arrived in the state after April 2000 are provided for through a system of dispersal and direct provision. Under this system asylum seekers are involuntarily housed around the country in hostels, prefabricated buildings and mobile homes. In contrast to earlier asylum seekers, they receive €19.05 per adult and €9.52 per child per week in addition to the provision of fixed meals and basic accommodation. At present there are approximately 4,858 asylum seekers dispersed in 67 centres around Ireland. Those asylum seekers on direct provision therefore represent the poorest of the poor. With an income below 20 per cent of the average income (Fanning and Veale 2001), they live in cramped conditions, sometimes with three or four individuals or a family sharing one room, and those living in remote areas in Ireland often have little social and cultural support. Moreover, in 2004 child benefit was withdrawn from asylum seekers cutting an already low family income by about 40 per cent. However, a large majority of dispersed asylum seekers have disappeared from the asylum system; many are believed to have returned to Dublin to work illegally in the black economy.

When asylum seekers initially arrived in Ireland, a liberal agenda was dominant. However, this did not persist. With growing inequality characterising the Celtic Tiger, media and political campaigns began defining asylum seekers as 'spongers' responsible for crime, the housing crisis and a general social malaise affecting the country. The result of these political and media discourses – groups with significant power to define the social world – was an increase in the restrictions against asylum seekers, and a rise in racism. Both the government and media made much of the putative difference between 'genuine' refugees of whom there are few, and 'bogus' refugees, of whom there are too many. This discourse of entitlement echoed older distinctions between the 'deserving' and 'undeserving' poor. Government and media statements frequently referred to the way that the Irish welfare regime was attracting 'economic migrants'. The implication was that an overly generous and prosperous Ireland, the land of a hundred thousand welcomes, was being systematically abused by unscrupulous asylum seekers who were taking Irish jobs and draining the country's resources. Equally, banner tabloid newspaper headlines portrayed asylum seekers as 'spongers', here to milk the system, or responsible for rising crime rates, housing shortages, and general social problems. Such a discourse formed the basis of the Minister of Justice's (Michael McDowell) support for a referendum to reduce citizenship from *ius soli* to *ius sanguine.* According to McDowell Irish hospitals were being overrun by pregnant asylum seeking women here to gain citizenship by giving birth to children in Ireland. The referendum was passed with almost 80 per cent of the population's support.

Moreover, mirroring the restrictive practices which developed in Europe in the mid-1990s, the number of asylum seekers granted refugee status relative to the number of applications in Ireland, like other European states, remained consistently low. From a total number of about 48,000 asylum applications between 2000 to the end of March 2005, only 6,087 were recognised as refugees (Irish Refugee Council 2006). Of these, just under 40 per cent (2,431) were at first instance and just over 60 per cent (3,656) were at appeals. In both absolute and comparative terms, such a recognition rate remains very low. The restrictive operation of the asylum system was further evidenced in the introduction of a 'manifestly unfounded' procedure whereby certain categories of claimant could be processed using accelerated determination procedures where a claim was one that was 'clearly fraudulent'. Since 1999 this procedure has been increasingly used to deal with asylum claims. With a high number of refusals, deportation has also become a major factor in asylum policy. In common with the rest of the European Union, greater use was made of 'safe country' and 'safe third countries' in assessing applications. Since 1999, a total of 2,268 deportations have been carried out (Irish Refugee Council 2006).

Despite the media, political and popular outcry about asylum seekers, immigration into Ireland refers to the arrival not only of people from Africa and Asia, who are predominantly 'people of colour', but also of people from Romania and Poland, as well as from Australia, Canada and the United States. The semantic correlation of non-Irish immigrants with black asylum seekers or refugees was an ideological effect of social relations of domination, specifically those of state and media discourses. Thus between 1995 and 2000, asylum seekers constituted less than ten per cent of all immigrants who entered Ireland (Mac Éinrí 2003) with returning Irish and those on work permits constituting the majority. Notwithstanding the social and juridical division between those arriving before and after dispersal and direct provision, asylum seekers overall have the least access and entitlements to social and material resources of all the groups who live in Irish society. They are the most disempowered group in Irish society since they lack certain fundamental civil, political and economic rights – including the right to work.

Economic migration

The second major mode of entry for immigrants into Ireland has been through the work permits/visa/authorisation system. The economic boom in Ireland during the 1990s, often referred to as the Celtic Tiger, has had enormous impact on the size and content of the Irish population. According to CSO figures, just over 1.1 million were employed in the economy in 1988 by the end of 2005 the figure stood at over 2 million. Equally, unemployment in Ireland has remained low at 4.2 per cent, one of the lowest levels amongst all 25 EU member states.

With economic growth as the central plank in government policy, and given the rate of labour market expansion, the government estimated that some 200,000 new workers would be needed by 2006 as part of its National Development Plan. It was envisaged that about half these workers would be returning Irish migrants, one-quarter would be from the European Economic Area (EEA)[4] and the remainder would be non-EU workers. Similarly the Enterprise Strategy Group estimated that Ireland would need over 400,000 new workers by 2010 with the majority of this labour force recruited from outside Ireland (Labour Relations Commission 2005: 5). A large source of labour demand during the 1990s up to now has come from unskilled sectors, such as hotels and catering, and other low-grade services, with a number of employers claiming that they could not recruit, primarily as a result of the low rates of pay on offer. A failure to address the labour shortage could undermine the Irish Republic's economic growth, since wage rates and the availability of skilled workers remained central concerns for multinational companies in relation to investment decisions. As a result, temporary work permits, renewable on a yearly basis, were issued to meet labour demands. However, such permits were non-transferable and tied to specific jobs. Employers had to demonstrate that it had not been possible to fill the vacancy with indigenous labour or with EEA workers. Employers had to pay €500 for the permit, charges which could not be passed to the employee. The holders of work permits have no automatic right to family reunification. Unlike the asylum system which is largely overseen by the Department of Justice, Equality and Law Reform, the work permit system fell largely within the purview of the Department of Enterprise, Trade and Employment.

In 1993, 1,103 work permits were issued. By the end of 2001 this figure stood at 36,431, peaking at 47, 551 by 2003. Between 1999 and 2003, the number of work permits issued increased by 700 per cent (Ruhs 2005: 15). However, following the admittance of ten Accession states into the EU in May 2004 (including Poland, Latvia and Lithuania), which allowed their nationals to freely live and work in Ireland, the figure had fallen to 34,067. At the end of 2005 the number of permits issued stood at 27,136. Up to 2003 the majority of the permits issued were given to individuals from Latvia, Lithuania, Poland, the Philippines, (9.8 per cent of work permits went to Latvia; 9.6 per cent Lithuania; 8 per cent Philippines; 7.8 per cent Poland; 6.1 per cent Romania; 5.6 per cent South Africa; 5.2 per cent Brazil; 3 per cent China; 2.1 per cent India). And although permits were issued to individuals from over 150 countries, the top five countries accounted for 41.3 per cent of work permits in 2002 (Ruhs 2005: 15). However, after the Baltic States the highest numbers of permits in 2005 went to the Philippines (4,192), followed by the Ukraine, South Africa and India.

As a result of continuing labour shortages, business organisations and government bodies such as the National Competitiveness Council and FÁS called for the creation of a fast-track work authorisation/visa system. These fast-track visas/authorisations were introduced specifically to facilitate the recruitment of workers in specialist categories: professionals in information technology and construction, as well as nurses. Work visas are more flexible than work permits in that they allow the recipient to move jobs within a specified sector. Unlike work permits, visas are renewable on a two-year basis and workers with these visas are allowed to apply for family reunion after three months. Since their introduction in 2000 about 10,000 work permits have been issued (3,749 in 2001; 2,610 in 2002; 1,158 in 2003; and 1,003 in 2004). In 2004 the majority of work visas went to Indian and Filipino nurses and 314 work authorisations to South Africans and Australians. Since February 2004, spouses of workers under this scheme have an automatic right to work.

The result, then, of the state's strategy is the construction of an elaborate set of social categories which crudely construct human beings according to their relative use for the needs of Irish capitalism. A multi-tiered migrant work regime has been created with differential rights for highly skilled visa immigrants, on the one hand, and lower-skilled work permit immigrants.

The result of this policy is the formation of a dual labour market and a two-tiered work regime (Piore 1979). Specifically, the expansion of highly skilled, well paid computer and information technology work can be contrasted with the expansion in the unskilled services sector. The marked increase in need for office cleaners, dishwashers and fast-food operatives, agricultural workers, factory workers, nurses, builders and waiters and waitresses has meant an increase in vacancies in these areas. The latter has generally been characterised by difficult, unpleasant and low-paid work. About 75 per cent of all of these work permits were allocated to relatively low skilled occupations. In 2005, the majority of work permits went to individuals working in the services and industry sector followed by the hotel and catering sector. Such unskilled positions generally lack a career path and are characterised by wages that fall well below the national average. Whereas in the past women and young people had filled these positions, a shortage of workers, together with the rising aspirations of indigenous workers, meant that immigrants now did so, with some also taking up work in the black economy or illegally.

According to Quinn and Hughes (2004), work permit holders are earning up to 14 per cent less than indigenous workers, despite the fact that they are on the whole better qualified with over 54 per cent having third-level qualifications as compared to just 27 per cent of the native population. Many are therefore not employed at a level that reflects their educational status (Expert Group on Future Skills Needs 2005). Given the precarious, non-unionised and often illegal status of those employed in the unskilled sector, again reflecting a wider European pattern, exploitation in these areas has been rife. The work permit system is modelled on the idea of the guest-worker system that was devised by the big industrial powers after the Second World War. It is a highly flexible system designed to suit the needs of employers, while denying workers a number of social and political rights. Workers are tied to a particular employer and have to leave the country before applying for new jobs. As they were dependent on their employers, they were unlikely to complain about lower wages, sexual harassment, or join a trade union. Immigrant workers constitute cheap, flexible labour and, because they lack some important social and political rights, also in many cases lack certain economic rights. The number of cases that the Labour Relations Commission Rights Commissioner Service has processed involving foreign workers has continually increased. In 2002, of the 5,692 cases processed only 2 per cent of involved migrant workers; by 2003 the proportion of cases had risen to 3.5 per cent of 4,737 processed and in the first eight months of 2004, migrant workers brought 8 per cent of all cases processed (Labour Relations Commission 2005: 12). In 2002 over 80 per cent of these claims were settled in favour of the claimants. There has also been a steady increase in the number of cases dealt with by the Equality Tribunal on employment equality grounds, from two in 2000 to 71 in 2004. In 2003 85 cases related solely to racial discrimination with an unspecified number also falling within the 76 undertaken on multiple grounds. Similarly, in that year, 43 cases relating to racial discrimination took place under the equal status criterion in relation to access to goods and services, with again an unspecified number within the 202 that took place under multiple grounds. These investigations into employment violations included a variety of offences: the employment of migrant workers with unequal pay and conditions in comparison with other Irish or EEA staff; failure by employers to pay workers pre-arranged wage rates; paying workers below the minimum wage; workers being subject to excessive working hours; illegal pay deductions, with recruitment costs to be borne by the prospective employee; and the non-payment of overtime or holiday pay. Recorded abuses of workers' rights tended to be prevalent in most employment sectors. In 2002 the hotel and catering industry accounted for 31 per cent of all migrant worker claims to the Rights

Commissioner Service and for 26 per cent of such claims in 2003 (Labour Relations Commission 2005: 13). Other sectors of employment included the retail sector, farming, contract cleaning, construction and security, industry, transport, recycling, nursing homes and crèches. Though it has been argued by some that the highest levels of exploitation were occurring in horticulture, the meat industry and construction industry (Labour Relations Commission 2005: 13), for others it is in the domestic service sector (Migrant Rights Centre 2004). The lowest weekly wages given to work-permit holders in 2003 was to those (largely women) working in private homes in Ireland who were paid €253 per week: a figure equivalent to the minimum wage (Ruhs 2005).

Although a complex issue, there are at least four major analytically distinct though interlocking processes that account for the treatment and level of exploitation of migrant workers. Firstly, the limited nature of migrant worker social, political and economic rights. Although we tend to see the social world as composed of humans or individuals, in modern nation states individuals are positioned in terms of specific social roles and forms of classification and categorisation. Thus states categorise and classify individuals and confer different levels of civic and political rights upon them. This is largely through the institution of citizenship. Those on work permits and visas as well as those from Europe are accorded different rights to Irish citizens. This restricts their access to a number of social and economic resources – from the ability to move from employer to employer to their ability to gain social welfare. It also means that many migrant workers are afraid that they would be deported or those on work permits and visas that their work permits would not be renewed, if they spoke out against abuse and exploitation. Secondly, the government's regulation of various employment sectors in terms of maintaining labour standards, fining employers who exploit their workers, and employing labour inspectors is crucial in determining levels of exploitation of migrant workers. There are currently only 90 labour inspectors covering a working population of almost 2 million. Thirdly, the level of trade union activity in specific employment sectors, as well as the levels of migrant recruitment and migrant community organisation, also affects the exploitation of migrant workers. Finally, levels of racism and discrimination of migrant workers, including sexism, will influence the modes and intensity of ethno-racial domination of migrant workers.

Integration and racism

The increase in the number of work permits being granted also saw the growth of racism in the workplace both with the employer and, as Conroy and Brennan (2003) have shown, with fellow workers. However, this narrow economic concern has always been mediated by a restricted notion of Irish nationhood of whiteness and Catholicism. Consequently, the Irish government expects non-EEA workers to return (voluntarily or otherwise) to their country of origin once their labour is no longer needed: they are seen as temporary workers. Such a standpoint echoes the restrictive policy of other European nation states and effectively denies the reality of long-term trends in immigration. Most European states have recognised that the integration of migrant workers is necessary for social cohesion and economic efficiency. However, Ireland has no holistic or long-term integration policy. Much of the work of integration is currently carried out by NGOs, community and voluntary organisations That is, Ireland's immigration policy is market driven and seeks to attract temporary workers to fill skills and labour shortages. Despite the differences between those given work permits – described as 'bonded labour' – and those holding visas, both lack social and political rights, including access to free education, medical care and social welfare entitlements. Neither group benefits from any holistic integration strategy or even from access to language classes. As a result, asylum seekers and some economic migrants have a great deal in common. They are generally at the bottom end of the socio-economic ladder, share similar racialised disadvantages in terms of housing and educational opportunities, experience low standards of living, poverty and social exclusion, and are equally targets of informal and institutional racism, discrimination and hostility.

Racism can be broadly defined as any belief or practice which attributes negative characteristics to any group or persons either intentionally or unintentionally on the basis of their supposed 'race' or ethnicity within the context of differential relations of power. The term is highly contested, however, and because of its elasticity some have argued that we should no longer use it (Wacquant 1997). Despite Ireland's image as a welcoming, hospitable nation and its unparalleled economic boom, many members of black and ethnic minority groups have experienced racism since arriving in Ireland. The culmination of this growing racism was the murder of a Chinese student in Dublin, Zhao Liu Toa in February 2002. In an Amnesty survey in 2001 (O' Mahony et al. 2000), 79 per cent of individuals from black or ethnic minority groups living in Ireland claimed they had experienced some form of racism or discrimination. Moreover, many of these racist attacks were not one-off or incidental occurrences. Hence, when asked how often they had received insulting comments 36.2 per cent stated that this had occurred 'frequently', and 32.3 per cent said that it had occurred 'occasionally'. As a survey of 1,200 people for Know Racism by Millward Brown (2004) shows, although 41 per cent of people believe that ethnic groups living in this country make Ireland a more interesting place, the same amount also believed that immigrants came because of economic reasons due to poor conditions in their own country, but do not intend to work. In fact 51 per cent believed that ethnic groups were taking jobs from the Irish and 48 per cent that one can only be Irish if one was born in Ireland of Irish parentage. Moreover, 48 per cent considered that Irish society was racist or very racist. These figures are borne out by the National Consultative Committee on Racism and Interculturalism's (NCCRI) figures for racist incidents which has recorded at least 40 incidents every six months since it began in 2001.

Although all societies are characterised by conflictual relations between established and outsiders (Elias and Scotson 1994), these processes take on specific characteristics depending on the historical and social context. In Ireland media and political discourses defining immigrants as problematic have been hugely influential. However, their influence can only have effect or these ideas can only be taken up in specific material contexts. It is important therefore to recognise, instead of the liberal view of a society as composed of sovereign individuals, a more radical view which emphasises the importance of racialisation within broader cultural and economic differences in power and social domination.

The recent development of contemporary Irish society is inherently para-doxical. At the same time as producing unprecedented wealth it has created poverty and social exclusion. It is largely, though not exclusively, by reference to this paradox that we can understand the growth of racism in Ireland. The current debate about immigrants concerns displacement. Following the Irish government's decision to allow workers from the ten accession states joining the EU to work in Ireland, a debate ensued concerning their impact. Here two interrelated questions dominate. Firstly, whether non-Irish nationals are displacing Irish workers; secondly, whether migrant workers are reducing wage rates and the level of working conditions in specific sectors of employment.

Although racism may take the form of a relatively coherent theory, it can also appear in the form of a less coherent assembly of stereotypes, images, attributions, and as an explanation that is constructed and employed by individuals to negotiate their everyday lives. As Miles (1989) notes, racism can be characterised as practically adequate in the sense that it refracts in thought certain observed regularities in the social world and constructs a causal inter-pretation which is presented as consistent with those regularities. Such images and stereotypes rarely emerge spontaneously and often arise from state and media discourses with their monopoly over the powers of governance, diffusion and representation. Thus asylum seekers and refugees in Ireland are often represented as being responsible for a number of social and economic problems (which usually existed well before their arrival), such as housing shortages, unemployment and the general lack of adequate statutory provisions, and immigrants for displacing indigenous workers or lowering their wages through displacement. For many disempowered sections of the population racist discourses often constitute a description of, and explanation for, the world experienced on a day-to-day basis. It is an ideological account of the social world that recognises and offers an explanation for the housing crisis, for the lack of jobs available, for the continuance of poverty, for redundancy – experiences which many marginalised groups face. As a correlate of racialisation, racism therefore serves to link observed, real material differences in Irish society, with signified phenotypical and cultural differences of black and ethnic minorities in a causal explanation. It helps to make sense of the economic and social changes accompanying poverty, urban decline and social exclusion as they are experienced by sections of the working class within the context of a booming Celtic Tiger economy. Such problems may grow worse if the economy experiences a recession.

Conclusion

Rapid economic growth has created a structural tension between the logic of capital accumulation and that of political nationalism. The 'imagined community' which emerged during the early years of the Republic embodied a highly restricted notion of citizenship and ethnicity which, despite undergoing significant modification during the economic boom, has remained essentially exclusionary. Since the foundation of the state, Irishness and citizenship have been correlated with whiteness and Catholicism which implicitly acted as the measure against which difference was constructed. However, this restricted, hegemonic, view of 'Irishness' is now coming into conflict with the labour market imperatives of the increasingly globalised Tiger economy. Hence, there is a need for immigrant labour, *yet also* a hierarchical racialisation of that labour. The free movement of people has not matched the free and accelerating movement of goods and capital across national borders. Despite the acute labour needs of the Irish economy, the Irish government has remained cautious with regard to the entry of non-nationals. The Irish state is currently imposing a new restrictive binary framework involving EU and non-EU migrants. Government policy, especially as evidenced with the recent Employment Permits Act 2006, currently involves filling unskilled jobs with Eastern European nationals who have recently joined the expanded EU, and filling the remainder with non-EU nationals on work permits. Occupational shortages in skilled sectors which cannot be filled by Irish or European workers are to be filled through a 'green card' system. However, application for the green card is restricted to certain occupations with a requisite salary level. Firstly, those earning over €60,000 or more in all occupations are eligible to apply. Secondly, those earning between €30,000 and €59,999 in certain delimited occupations are also allowed to apply for a green card. By contrast, work permits will be issued to certain occupations with a salary of over €30,000 and only 'in very limited circumstances' to occupations with a salary of below €30,000. Such a policy will have dramatic and restrictive consequences for the entry of non-EU nationals into Ireland, with many in the future having to enter through family reunification.

Migration and debates concerning immigration into Ireland will continue to be central concerns in Irish society. It has been estimated by the CSO that the number of foreign-born individuals could reach 1 million by 2030 (CSO 2006a). This will have significant implications for diversity and pluralism in Irish society. Although many immigrants will continue to arrive as migrant workers, issues such as family reunification will almost certainly also become prominent.

Chapter 3

Irish mobilities

James Wickham

Introduction

Like many people in the world today, Irish people spend a lot of time *moving* from place to place. The different sites where people live their lives are increasingly separated by physical distance and linked by means of transport. For most people home and work are joined by the daily commute, but for an increasing number the home is joined to a second holiday home by cheap air travel. 'Ireland' itself becomes less obviously the unit of people's lives, when many people who are employed on the island consider their home to be Poland and travel frequently between the two.

Such phenomena fuel the 'mobility turn' in sociology which is outlined in the first part of the chapter. Sociological theorising is now coming to terms with the importance of physical mobility. I suggest that the discussion of 'fluidity' opens up new empirical questions: how mobilities are created and also constrained and what usages actors make of their new opportunities. I then exemplify some of these issues through four aspects of contemporary Irish mobilities: car usage in Dublin; migration to and from Ireland in particular by professional workers; the expansion of business air travel; the growth of Irish-owned domestic property abroad.

The mobility turn

Until very recently sociology studied migration, but paid little attention to other forms of physical travel. Although social commentary and social history have long studied tourism, it only entered sociology with Urry's discussion of 'the tourist gaze' (Urry 1990). The sociology of transport as a specific theme hardly existed. For example, a study of the decline of urban transit in the USA and Europe (Yago 1984) remained almost the only work in the field for nearly twenty years.

Sociology's increasing awareness of all forms of physical movement has followed its awareness of the importance of electronic communication or of what could be called virtual travel. This has led to the 'mobility turn' in sociology. The most explicit representative is John Urry who has argued that sociology can no longer be the study of societies (2000). Whereas this appeared to call for a radical reformulation of the entire discipline, his more recent call for a new 'mobility paradigm' (Sheller and Urry 2006) seems to set out a new area of research *within sociology*.

Even within Urry's own writings, the mobility turn thus comes in a 'strong' and a 'weak' version. The weak version suggests that *mobility* is a valid general topic of research for sociology, just like gender, ethnicity, deviance or whatever. The study of mobility involves not just the study of physical movement, but also the study of location: how particular activities are located in particular physical places to which or from which people then have to *move*. This leads us to consider barriers to mobility (for example, national boundaries) and also the technologies that enable people to move – the technologies of transport. From this perspective the commuter's daily journey to work and the movement of migrants from one country to another both form part of the study of mobility. This 'weak' version of the mobility turn highlights how mobility is an important, and hitherto largely neglected, aspect of social life.

Alternatively, a strong version claims that that the very nature of social life has changed. Society is seen as involving 'flows' and has become 'liquid' (for example, Bauman, 2005). Thus the strong version challenges the assumption – embedded in the title of this collection – that sociology studies 'societies', whereby a 'society' is a delimited social structure within a territorial space bounded by the borders of a specific nation state. The equivalence of 'society' with the nation state was a defining characteristic of twentieth-century sociology – as in all those undergraduate courses in 'Irish society'. Intriguingly, there is some evidence that across Europe as a whole sociologists are more 'national' than some other social scientists: an ongoing study of the careers of Socrates students (Teichler 2006) notes that sociology graduates are *particularly unlikely* to use their experience of foreign study to develop careers outside their country of origin. One probable reason is that empirical sociology has long been interwoven with social policy and hence with the specific institutions of each nation state. 'Practical' sociologists have needed to develop a national knowledge in a way that is now less true for those working in either conventional business or in the new culture industries.

Social historians and political philosophers have long argued that nation states are *constructed*, that whereas national ideologies always appeal to pre-existing nations, actually it was the national ideology and the institutions of the state that created – or at least constituted – the nation. The literature here is extensive and the titles suggestive: from *Peasants into Frenchmen* (Weber 1979) to *Britons* (Colley 1992); as early as the late nineteenth century Renan remarked that nations are not eternal and that the creation of the nation is a lesson in forgetting (Schnapper 2003). Furthermore, such studies also suggest that new forms of mobility were part of the *creation* of nation states. In Europe from the nineteenth century people became national citizens who could freely move around within a delimited national territory. Such citizens crossed national boundaries with national passports: the creation of freedom of movement for national citizens *within* the national territory at the same time involved control by the state of the *boundaries* of the same national territory (Noiriel 2001).

Given this long intellectual tradition, it is not particularly novel to problematise the nation state analytically. The importance of the mobility theorists is rather their claim that the nation state no longer provides the main institutional framework for people's lives. The empirical sections of the chapter will show how many people are moving *through* the nation state of Ireland rather than simply living *in* Ireland, how people who work in Ireland spend time working outside Ireland, and how many people whose home is in Ireland also have homes outside Ireland. At the same time, however, the policies that shape mobility are partly (though only partly) decided at national level. The nation state has not disappeared, and so nor have national societies.

Studying mobility necessarily involves grappling with transport technologies. For nineteenth-century social commentators it was self-evident that theirs was a society based on speed and the railway, epitomised by J. M. W. Turner's famous painting *Rain, Steam and Speed – The Great Western Railway* (1844). Equally, in the late twentieth-century information technology became seen as constituting contemporary 'information societies' and sociologists such as Castells (1996) contributed to this view. By contrast, sociology has never really developed any extensive analysis of car transport technologies. Even more striking, while political journalists have noticed how cheap air travel is changing Europeans' self-understandings (Reid 2004), the sociology of air transport technology remains a complete blank. Here the mobility turn is drawing our attention to issues to which sociology has long been blind.

A focus on transport technology also brings into focus the material consequences of flows of mobility. Transport technologies, in particular the private car and the airplane, have major environmental impacts. Understanding the form of mobility thus contributes to our understanding of how social actions impact on the environment.

The sociology of mobility has to deal with social structures. Just because people *move* they do not enter a world without constraints. On the one hand different people have different resources, while on the other hand the available transportation technologies facilitate some forms of movement and hamper others. As the empirical sections of this chapter will show, there are significant variations in the extent to which people are now 'mobile'. While individuals' mobility depends on the choices they make, based on their personal values and ideologies, their opportunities for mobility are also shaped by political structures and public policies – not least transport policies themselves.

The concept of mobility highlights certain aspects of contemporary life that are often not discussed within sociology; it also puts some issues in a new light. The purpose of the rest of this chapter is not to construct a grandiloquent overarching theory of 'mobility'. Indeed, as Kaufmann (2002) points out, one of the striking features of sociological theories of mobility is that they seem to have no relationship to empirical research. Instead, this chapter works the other way round. It selects four aspects of mobility in contemporary Ireland. Each is seen as interesting in its own right, but also used to evaluate *some* of the more general arguments found in the mobility literature.

Auto-mobility: the car system in Dublin

For most people in Ireland, the continued expansion of travel by car is the defining feature of mobility over the last few decades. Meanwhile the transport crisis in the capital city is now a major topic of public debate. This section of the chapter documents how the growing *car dependency* of Dublin is in part the result of socio-political choices. Dublin's traffic jams are thus a long way away from the 'liquid society' of the mobility gurus. However, recent changes in mobility within Dublin do lend *some* support to the notion that greater physical mobility is part of a growing individualisation of contemporary society.

The expanding car system
In Ireland as a whole car ownership has been rising faster than population, even though Irish car ownership figures are still below the average for the EU15. Car usage has also been increasing. In 1981 45 per cent of all those at work reached travelled to work by private car; by 2002 this had reached 59 per cent. Equally, whereas in 1981 20 per cent of children travelled to school by private car, by 2002 this had reached fully 50 per cent (Wickham 2006: 67). All of this has immediate physical consequences: more space dedicated to cars, and a growing physical impact on the environment through CO_2 emissions (figure 3.1). The expansion of car-based mobility in Ireland is thus a major component of the increasingly negative impact of Irish 'society' on the environment (EPA 2006).

One response to this is that expanding car usage is somehow a 'natural' consequence of economic growth. However, even accepting conventional

Figure 3.1 **Growth, greenhouse gases and energy usage: transport in Ireland 1990–2003**

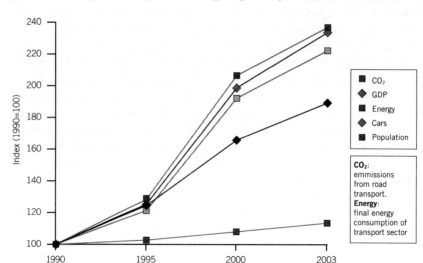

Source: CSO, Environment and Principal Statistics; CSO 2004 National Income and Expenditure

economic measures of economic growth, some societies are more successful than others at 'uncoupling' economic growth and, for example, energy usage or CO_2 emissions. For instance, Americans not only drive more than other people, they use more energy than anybody else for every kilometre travelled (Olsthoorn 2003). In these terms Ireland really is closer to Boston (or Los Angeles) than Berlin: the country's recent economic growth has been remarkable for the extent to which energy usage and CO_2 emissions have simply risen in parallel with GDP.

If rising car usage was the inevitable result of economic growth, it would be difficult to explain why cities of similar wealth vary in the extent to which people use private cars (Newman et al. 1995). At its simplest, where population density is higher, people are less likely to buy a car *and* less likely to use one when they have one. A further issue is land-use planning. Some European cities such as Copenhagen or Helsinki have as low a population density as Dublin, but most development is clustered around public transport nodes. Consequently, people can move relatively easily across much of the urban space by public transport. Such cities also invested continually in public transport in the second half of the twentieth century, so ensuring that they have relatively integrated public transport systems. By contrast, suburbanised Dublin has ineffective land-use planning and notoriously poor public transport. Thus in 1990, before the 'Celtic Tiger' economic boom, Dublin already had one of the highest levels of travel to work by private car in Europe, but still had a low level of car ownership. Indeed, 1990 data from 15 European cities suggests that sometimes the extent of driving to work and the extent of car ownership are negatively related. In cities such as Helsinki or – especially – Bologna, car *ownership* was far higher than in Dublin, but people were significantly less likely to drive to work (Wickham 2006: 21).

Whereas public discussion often sees Dublin's traffic problems as an unpleasant by-product of recent economic success, the evidence shows that they are far more deep-rooted. From the 1950s onwards public transport in the city was destroyed, ensuring that compared to many other European cities there was only a limited *legacy system* of tram and rail that could later be recycled and renovated. Equally, unlike some other European cities, there was little attempt in the 1970s to restrain car usage in the city centre and, apart from the railway electrification programme that produced the DART in the 1980s, little investment in public transport. Accordingly, Dublin's transport history is close to that of American cities whose motorisation was described by Yago (1984). And just as even a simple comparison between sprawling American cities and the less dispersed Canadian ones challenges some abstract geographical determinism (Goldberg and Mercer 1992), comparisons within Europe show that Dublin's precocious car usage highlights the role of socio-political choice.

Car usage and individualisation

Part of the attraction of the car as a form of mobility has long been its promise of freedom. The car driver can travel where he or she wants to go, at a time of his or her choice. More analytically, the expansion of car usage can be seen as a technology of greater individualisation, the process whereby individuals are more and more 'freed' from the constraints of specific institutions.

The move from a situation where the car is owned by a household or family to one where the car is owned by the individual would parallel changes in other domestic technologies, such as the shift from the family's house phone to the individual's mobile phone or even the move from the family to the individual television set. The car can be used to connect spaces and activities. In a society in which activities have become increasingly fragmented, occurring in different places and with their own distinct timetables, individuals can use the car, like the mobile phone, as a connecting technology with which to manage and *integrate* disparate parts of their lives (Shove 1998).

A more political economy approach might refer to a shift from 'fordist' mobility to post-fordist mobility, from mass consumption based on the domestic family unit to more individualised consumption. Thus previously car journeys were made, usually by the male 'head of household', between the home and the workplace for regular work ('nine to five'); work occurred in the city centre and home was located in the suburbs; recreation, which might also involve the car, was carried out by the family. By contrast, post-fordist journeys are made by individuals across an urban space in which home and work are randomly located; both women and men work but their working hours vary so that travel times have become much more diverse.

We can assess the extent to which such changes have actually occurred by studying mobility within the Dublin city-region. The Greater Dublin Area (GDA) comprises seven local authorities: Dublin City Council, here referred to as the city centre; South Dublin, Fingal, and Dun Laoghaire/Rathdown, the 'inner suburbs'; Kildare, Meath and Wicklow, the 'outer suburbs'. Mobility patterns within the GDA can be explored using the micro-data from the 2002 Census, which for the first time collected information from individuals about their place of residence, their place of work and their travel to work.[1]

Census data clearly show the rise of *individual* car ownership and *individual* car usage. According to the 2002 Census, within the GDA 53 per cent of all households have access to at least two cars; within 'couple' households (with or without children) the proportion rises to 62 per cent. Here as in so many other areas, liberal society undermines gender differences, so that gendered access to private transport has become an issue only for the poorer income groups and for older people. Research in a low income suburb (Jobstown in Tallaght) showed that women were significantly less likely to be able to drive than men; where there was a motor vehicle owned by the household it was usually used by men (Wickham 2006: 120). However, such gender differences are disappearing in the general population. Within the GDA, older men (55 to 59) are more likely to drive to work than women of the same age, but in some of the younger age groups women are *more* likely to drive to work than men (table 3.1).

Table 3.1 **Driving to work by gender: selected age groups (Greater Dublin Area)**

Age group	Percentage in each category driving to work		
	Men	*Women*	*All*
25–29	46.6	48.3	47.5
35–39	60.5	65.2	62.4
45–49	63.9	60.4	62.4
55–59	64.8	53.2	60.6
All age groups	54.6	52.5	53.7

Source: Place of Work Sample of Anonymised Records (POWSAR)

The travel to work data can also be used to see if car-drivers have a more 'individualistic' or at least a more post-fordist mobility pattern. Not surprisingly, the further away from the city centre people live, the less likely they are to work there. Thus of those who live in Dublin City 75 per cent also work there, as opposed to 40 per cent of those who live in South Dublin (as an example of the inner suburbs) and only 23 per cent of those who live in Kildare (as an example of the 'outer suburbs'). In the suburbs, those who do not work in the city centre tend to work within their own county.

However, comparing those who travel to work by car with all those who travel by other means shows how car drivers are distinctive (table 3.2). Of all those who live in the GDA, car drivers are much less likely to work in Dublin City than non-car drivers (60 per cent as opposed to 41 per cent). Car drivers are also less likely to work in their own area than those who do not travel by car. Thus 63 per cent of those who live in Dublin City and who travel to work by car actually have workplaces in the city centre, as opposed to 83 per cent of non-car drivers. More than a third of these Dublin City car drivers therefore commute *outwards* to the counties around the city, and traffic counts on the M50 around the city show a small peak of outward bound journeys in the morning as well as the much larger peak in the early evening (Dublin Transportation Office 2005: 15). Equally in the inner and outer suburbs car drivers are more likely to travel to other suburbs than those who do not travel by car. In other words, whereas non-car drivers work locally *or* in the city centre, car drivers' workplaces are more dispersed across the entire city region.

Table 3.2 **Place of residence and place of work, car-drivers and non-car-drivers, Greater Dublin Area 2002**

	Dublin City		South Dublin		Kildare		All GDA	
	car	non-car	car	non-car	car	non-car	car	non-car
Workplace	(%)	(%)	(%)	(%)	(%)	(%)	(%)	(%)
Dublin City	63.1	83.3	42.3	48.1	19.5	28.8	40.8	59.9
South Dublin	11.5	5.0	38.4	42.9	17.8	8.1	15.1	9.9
Other inner suburbs	14.4	10.5	13.3	6.6	7.6	3.2	24.0	17.0
Kildare	1.3	.3	4.0	1.3	48.0	55.7	8.1	5.1
Other outer suburbs	1.2	.4	1.3	.5	3.1	2.1	9.6	7.2
Outside GDA	.7	.4	.7.8	.4	3.9	2.1	2.5	1.0
Total	100.0	100.0	100.0	100.0	100.0	100.0	100.0	100.0

Source: Place of Work Sample of Anonymised Records (POWSAR)

These changes mean *some* movement away from 'modern' forms of mobility. Travelling from the suburb to the city centre in the morning and back in the evening remains the most common journey to work. However, this is decreasingly the case as workplaces, and also working times, become

more varied. And journeys to work probably amount to a declining proportion of all travel time within Ireland, in particular where the car is concerned.
The result is that traffic problems and above all traffic jams can occur anytime
and in almost any place: the postmodern traffic jam has arrived.

Such forms of mobility appear unstructured compared to the regular
journeys to limited destinations of the previous period. Yet this argument
ignores both the variety of individual values *and* the variety of social contexts,
both of which challenge a simple one-to-one relationship between individualisation and universal car ownership. At the individual level it is quite clear that
some people actively choose forms of life and mobility which reduce their use
of the private car. Thus a study of Bologna reported that older people preferred to use public transport because they found it more sociable (Wickham
2006: 144). Similarly, a study of mobility usage in Swiss and French cities
identified minorities, mostly of young men and women, who preferred to use
public transport 'out of respect for the environment' (Kaufmann 2002: 71).
The process of individualisation is not necessarily incompatible with an
'individual' choice not to use a car.

However, for individuals effectively not to use the private car, alternatives
to the car have to exist through which people can satisfy their mobility needs.
In Kaufmann's study for example, the groups who actively chose public transport were larger in those cities with more effective public transport. In Dublin
such minorities are probably very small. For most people, the interlocking
policy failures of low density, suburbanisation and poor public transport
provision ensure there is no realistic alternative to the car.

At the same time, the relationship between the car and individual freedom
is itself deceptive. The new mobility produces its own constraints on mobility.
More roads encourage more cars, and the result is more congestion and even
gridlock. The expansion of the car system is an example of the 'network effect'
(Dupuy 1999) whereby people have to use a specific technology if they are
to participate in the society. As the city becomes built around the car, the
expansion of the car system drives out other forms of mobility, from walking and cycling to public transport. Such 'car dependency' is hardly a new age
of freedom.

Migration and mobility: the temporary Irish workforce?

Car-based mobility in Ireland and particularly in Dublin, is, as we have seen,
shaped by public policy. Another aspect of the increased mobility of contemporary Ireland is the extent to which people move into Ireland from outside
the country. Both the expansion of car-based mobility and the increase in
immigration are sometimes presented as natural or inevitable consequences of

economic growth and even of 'globalisation', but in the case of immigration the overall importance of public policy is more obvious. At its very simplest, government policy determines or at least influences who is allowed to enter the country and on what basis.[2] However, it is useful to consider immigration as a form of migration and hence as another form of mobility (Salt 2001: 95). In particular, understanding migration as mobility avoids the common-sense assumption that 'integration' (or even 'assimilation') is the key issue both for policy and for research; as this section will show, it facilitates questions about the extent of this mobility and the motivations of the mobile.

In Ireland today over ten per cent of the population were born abroad, but it is also well known that, particularly during the 1990s, many 'immigrants' had themselves been born in Ireland and were therefore returning *emigrants*. Rather than categorising the population into 'natives' and 'immigrants', it can be conceptualised as comprising more or less mobile elements: at one extreme those born in Ireland and living here all their life, and at the other extreme those arriving here recently for the first time. Between these extremes lie different forms of mobility, from those born in Ireland but who have lived abroad for some time, to those born abroad who have lived here for some time.

Table 3.3 presents one such possible classification, again using the 2002 Census micro-data.[3] The bottom row shows the share of the groups in the overall population. The mobile can be defined as all those who have lived outside Ireland: those born in Ireland and lived abroad, those born abroad and long-term resident in Ireland, those born abroad and recently arrived. In 2002 the mobile as a whole comprised just over a fifth of the total population. Comparing the top row ('Professional workers') with the bottom row shows the extent to which professional workers are more mobile than other groups: nearly a third of all professionals were in some sense 'mobile'. At the other extreme the 'non-manual' group were least mobile: here 83 per cent had never lived abroad.

Mobility experience is also related to education. Table 3.4 shows that the higher the level of education, the more likely people are to have lived outside of Ireland. Thus of those who had achieved only primary education, 84 per cent had lived in Ireland all their lives. At the other extreme, of those with at least a third-level degree only 57 per cent were 'immobile' and had never lived outside Ireland. In Ireland today, to be educated is to be mobile.

Within the mobile category, however, there is an interesting difference in the use of educational qualifications. On the one hand returning emigrants who have third-level qualifications do better occupationally than those than those graduates who have stayed in Ireland. Further analysis of the data shows that of those who had a degree and who were working full time, 79 per cent of the 'immobile' held a managerial or professional job, but this rose to 82 per cent of all those who were born in Ireland but had lived abroad. This

Table 3.3 **Mobility and social class**

	Born and lived in Ireland	Born in Ireland lived abroad	Born abroad long-term resident	Born abroad arrived 1996–2002	Total
Professional workers (%)	69.1	14.1	6.7	10.1	100.0
Managerial and technical (%)	77.2	11.5	3.9	7.4	100.0
Non-manual (%)	83.8	7.8	2.5	5.8	100.0
Skilled manual (%)	81.4	8.7	3.0	6.9	100.0
Semi-skilled (%)	81.6	8.1	3.0	7.3	100.0
Unskilled (%)	82.3	9.7	2.2	5.9	100.0
All others gainfully occupied and unknown (%)	77.3	7.7	3.9	11.0	100.0
All (%)	79.3	9.4	3.5	7.8	100.0

Source: Census of Population Sample of Anonymised Records (COPSAR).

demonstrates again the 'emigration premium' for Irish-born graduates (Gash and O'Connell 2000). By contrast, amongst graduates who were born abroad, only 71 per cent of long-term residents and 72 per cent of the recent arrivals had reached managerial or professional jobs. At the same time it is important to keep this in proportion. Most of those born abroad are in a job which is broadly consistent with their educational qualification and many are able to use their qualifications more effectively than they would have been able to at 'home'.

Table 3.4 **Mobility and educational level**

	Born and lived in Ireland	Born in Ireland lived abroad	Born abroad long-term resident	Born abroad arrived 1996–2002	Total
Primary (including no formal education) (%)	83.6	11.7	.7	4.0	100.0
Lower secondary (%)	82.3	8.1	2.2	7.5	100.0
Upper secondary (%)	78.1	10.1	3.2	8.6	100.0
Third level – non-degree (%)	71.1	15.3	4.4	9.1	100.0
Third level – degree or higher (%)	56.6	19.7	8.8	14.9	100.0
All (%)	79.3	9.4	3.5	7.8	100.0

Source: Census of Population Sample of Anonymised Records (COPSAR)

The focus on 'mobility' rather than 'immigration' therefore alerts us to the extent to which the population *of* Ireland is actually flowing *through* or *across* Ireland. Furthermore, this focus on the different mobility experiences within the population alerts us to the importance of mobility over the life cycle. Rather than just considering those people currently in Ireland, we need to focus on mobile *careers*. Although immigrants' current intentions are a notoriously bad guide to their future actions, it is clear that many of those currently resident in Ireland do not intend to stay here. For example, according to the Polish Labour Force Survey, most of those who have left Poland recently define themselves as 'temporary' emigrants (Kaczmarczyk 2006).

According to some theorists, much professional work now occurs within increasingly trans-national labour markets: for 'symbolic analysts' (Reich 1991) or members of the 'creative class' (Florida 2004) traditional ties of place have little meaning. An ongoing study (Bruff and Wickham 2005) of migration within the Irish software sector shows both the reality and the limits of such arguments. For many across the globe with some experience and/or qualifications in software, Ireland is now just one of several 'hot spots' where they could work:

> I was just looking at the Net, and I found some articles which said that after the US Ireland is the second biggest exporter of software. I hadn't thought about it until then . . . I found these Irish job sites. *Just for the heck of it I sent off my CVs* (Javed, 32, Indian, has worked in the Irish software industry for a few years; emphasis added).

From this perspective, the initial decision to end up in Ireland has an almost arbitrary quality. At the same time, for some the decision to stay in Ireland rather than move to the USA, allegedly the ultimate destination for many professionals, is sometimes based on a conscious rejection of US values:

> I was the in the States eight, nine years ago . . . I didn't like the lifestyle there: it's so different. Ireland was different, but in a positive way . . . We have a lot of conference calls with the Americans, and they start at seven or earlier [in the morning], and sometimes they are still [working] when I arrive back at the office in the morning, and they have much fewer holidays [as well]. (Tibor, 34, Hungarian, has worked in the Irish software industry for several years).

This interviewee's deliberate rejection of possible mobility exemplifies the argument that it is important to distinguish between mobility potential ('motility') and the actual use of that potential (Kaufmann 2002). Equally the decision to stay in Ireland is shaped by family considerations and position in the life cycle. Marriage and children make mobility more problematic:

My plan was to stay here for only two years and then go . . . wherever the opportunities were going to be. Unfortunately, or fortunately . . . I met my [Irish] wife, so I didn't continue with the plan that I had. (Richard, 30, Venezuelan, has worked in Ireland for various software firms over several years)

Sometimes, however, children are a spur to returning to the real 'home':

We are planning to move back even if the economy is doing well. I really would like our daughter to start her schooling in India, because after that it would be difficult to move back . . . So we are hoping that we can go back in two years (Murali, 36, Indian, has worked in the Irish software industry for several years).

Software workers such as these interviewees face a new international labour market for their specialised qualifications. However, their ability – and their desire – to take advantage of it is shaped by their personal ideologies, their values and, often omitted in the literature, their stage in the life cycle. In these terms at least, the new mobility opportunities have not removed some rather traditional constraints.

Business travel: working on the move

Travelling to work and travelling from one country to another are in one sense 'traditional' mobilities: the journey itself is a means to an end (to reach work, to move home). Business travel often involves working *while travelling*, so that travel time is no longer 'time out', but another form of working time (Felstead et al. 2005). On such journeys the physical location of the traveller becomes in one sense irrelevant, in that s/he remains in contact with colleagues, customers and clients. As one interviewee in an ongoing study of business travel in the Irish software industry (Wickham and Vecchi 2006b) remarks:

I travel with my laptop and often it doesn't matter if I'm in the office, working from home, or away on business, but there are many reasons why I need to be with a customer or an analyst or a manager. (CEO (Chief Executive Officer) of a company producing software for the telecommunications sector.)

Figure 3.2 shows the travel pattern of a senior marketing communications manager for a Dublin software company. For her, travel is clearly part of the job. Such mobility across national borders means that at any one time many Irish professionals are away on business, even if, as we have already seen, they also remain connected to their organisation. Our research suggests that the software industry is in fact particularly travel-intensive, with managers

Figure 3.2 **EK's business travel pattern**

January	Two periods in the UK
February	Major trade show in France (1 week)
March	Press talks in the US (2 weeks)
April	No travel
May	Two trade shows (1 in Europe, 1 in Sri Lanka)
June	Two weeks in Singapore
July	Little travel
August	One foreign trip
September	Three foreign trips (2 in the UK, 1 in the USA)
October	Some foreign travel
November	Little travel
December	Little travel

and professionals continually on the move. At first sight this is paradoxical, since precisely in this industry competence with ICT (Information and Communication Technologies) is most extensive and so managers should be able to replace physical travel with electronic communication. In fact, most research shows that, just as the telegraph and the steam railway were complementary in the nineteenth century, so too at the end of the twentieth century are electronic communication and air travel.

Such mobility is necessary to create temporary *physical proximity*. Business interaction requires 'handshakes' to build up trust and exchange complex information in ways that cannot be achieved purely by phone calls, e-mail or other forms of electronic communication (Leamer and Storper 2001). However, as we shall now see, such mobility is clearly patterned (Wickham and Vecchi 2006a). Consider for example the case of a small Irish software company producing videogames. Here the CEO, the CTO (Chief Technical Officer) and the sales director travel frequently, not least to the USA which is its main market. The CTO goes to Los Angeles every five to six weeks and he stays there for ten days. The sales director travels extensively all around the USA to meet up with potential publishers and he on average gives a presentation every three weeks. The entire team goes to two main tradeshows: one, the Game Developers Conference in March, which is very technical therefore the entire team needs to attend 'to keep eveyone in the loop'; the other one is held in May in Los Angeles and is open to the public.

Indeed, keeping up with technical developments thus requires frequent electronic communication *and intermittent physical proximity*. The case also highlights another paradox. Precisely in this 'weightless' industry, certain physical locations become clusters of activity. Dublin itself is now a software cluster, just as Los Angeles is for the videogame industry. Such clusters around the globe are linked by 'pipelines' (Bathelt et al. 2004) transferring news and ideas, and here physical travel is as unavoidable as electronic communication. The two trade fairs which are so important for the company are temporary clusters – here industry members from around the globe meet in physical proximity for a few days, and although the actual location of the trade show may be incidental to its purpose, it is essential that it occurs in *some* physical location. Finally, the rather different travel pattern of the sales director with its wider range of destinations is produced by the need to liaise with actual and potential customers, and once again, there is no substitute for temporary physical proximity – and hence for extensive short-term mobility.

Foreign property: travelling to the second home

Another development creating more physical mobility is that many Irish people now own assets outside the country. Ireland has one of the highest levels of home-ownership within the EU (Fahey 2003), yet today Irish residents seem more likely than almost all other Europeans to own second homes – and to be private landlords – outside the country.

There are no reliable figures for the numbers of Irish residents who own second homes abroad, partly because the boundary between a second home and an investment property is hard to draw. In 2004 'around 60,000 Irish residents' were reported to have bought properties in Europe during the previous five years (*Irish Independent,* 17 June 2004); Irish 'investors' are now reported to own 100,000 properties in Spain (*Irish Times,* 10 July 2006). Individual Irish investors are particularly adventurous in Central and Eastern markets, buying property in Berlin (*Financial Times,* 10–11 June 2006), and Croatia; newspaper property pages advertise apartments in Dubai and even exhibitions of Bulgarian property. *Irish Property Buyer* magazine has two pages in Polish about buying property in Ireland – and nearly thirty editorial pages on property abroad (*Irish Property Buyer,* September 2006).

In Europe in absolute terms the British own more second homes abroad than residents of any other country. Over a quarter of a million UK households were estimated to own residential property outside the UK in 2003–4 (Aspden 2005); the growing numbers of British retiring to their second homes probably explains the 60 per cent leap in British immigration to France between 1999 and 2004 (Borrel 2006; *Financial Times,* 24 August 2006). However, in relative terms Irish households would now appear to be at least twice as likely to own property abroad than households in the UK. By contrast, it is now

Continental Europeans who are home-bound: a recent survey in the leading Milan newspaper carefully listed second-home prices per square metre in a range of Italian resorts, but did not even mention opportunities outside Italy (*Corriere della Sera*, 15 May 2006).

Affluent Irish families can now partly live outside Ireland because of cheap air travel, especially to smaller regional airports. For example Ryanair's flights to Carcassonne in South-West France have led to the emergence of an Irish colony which is beginning to rival the British 'Dordogneshire' further North. Further afield, direct flights to Cape Town and more recently Dubai are making even these destinations possible second homes.

This precocious level of second-home ownership has little to do with the features of 'liquid society' in general and a lot to do with the specific national political economy. Two issues are important here. Firstly, the Irish-based carrier Ryanair has been central to the European low fares revolution (Creaton 2005). Ryanair is a political lobbyist, skilled at creating new coalitions of interest (for example with small regional airports) which in turn promote further deregulation. Secondly, along with the UK, Ireland now has one of the highest levels of personal debt in Europe. The two countries have extensive *retail* financial services which, compared to most other European countries, enable consumers to have easy access to retail credit and in particular mortgage finance (RICS Research 2006; Donnelly et al. 2005). In the context of economic boom this ensured that many people in Ireland have been able to turn housing from an immobile and illiquid asset into a financial asset which can be leveraged to access *further* property. In turn, rising house prices in Ireland create financial opportunities for arbitrage between Irish and foreign property prices. Such foreign property ownership generates a novel form of mobility and weakens the boundaries between *home* and *abroad*. The mobility occurs as *some* individuals seize the opportunities provided by a very specific national financial system combined with changes in the organisation of air travel.

Conclusion

The study of mobilities in Ireland is just beginning. This chapter has indicated how increased mobility is changing Irish life, but understanding this mobility has involved rather conventional sociological concerns. The 'strong' version of the mobility turn thus appears an exaggeration of little relevance to empirical sociology.

By contrast, the 'weak' version of the mobility turn suggests many new areas of research. One issue suggested by the different case studies is the regulation or *governance* of mobility. Although mobility is partly about the crossing of national boundaries, the national state remains surprisingly important.

While this is obvious in the case of the most local of our four mobilities, Dublin's precocious car-based mobility, the equally precocious extent of Irish foreign home ownership is also largely shaped by national level financial structures and policies. Mobility is at very least shaped by the broader political context. How the politics and social processes of mobility interact is thus one important area for future study.

Section II   # Institutions

Chapter 4

Individualisation and secularisation in Catholic Ireland

Tom Inglis

Introduction

Catholic Ireland is not what it used to be. The Church was once the backbone of strong, cohesive family networks and community structures that created a sense of identity and belonging. It provided meaning, comfort and consolation in times of trouble. The Church was a spiritual and moral colossus. It stretched out over the country like a giant sacred canopy. Its teachings permeated the hearts and minds of every Catholic man, woman and child. It was central to the way in which they understood themselves and the world in which they lived. Irish Catholics were a deeply spiritual, pious, humble people devoted to their Church. They embodied their beliefs. The simple faith was not just in their minds and on their lips: it was in their bowed heads and their awkward, shy, embarrassed bodies. Their piety and humility were reflected in their demeanour, in the practice of self-denial and self-deprecation. It was a land in which priests, nuns and brothers reigned with great dignity and respect. They epitomised a life of spirituality and frugal comfort. They were paragons of virtue.

The Church was also a major institutional player. In many important social fields such as family, education, health and social welfare, it rivalled the state. It may not have been so powerful a player in business, politics and the media, but because it had a monopoly over the socialisation of each new generation, it was able to ensure that the individuals who played powerful roles in these institutions, thought and acted from a Catholic moral viewpoint.

The question at the heart of this chapter is what happened to the power and influence of the Church. How did it lose control of the hearts and minds of Irish Catholics? How did it cease to be the moral guardian of the state and Irish civil society – what Ryan (1979) termed the social conscience of society. Obviously, the scandals in the 1990s concerning bishops, priests and brothers, particularly in relation to child sexual abuse, were central to the Church finally falling from its pedestal (Fuller 2002: 250–68; Garvin 2004: 275; Inglis 1998: 216–19; Kenny 1997: 369–77). But the reality is that scandals were just the final act in a long play of structural transformations that began in the 1960s and which slowly but surely ate away at the base of the Church's power and influence that had been established in the nineteenth century during the first phase of Irish modernisation.[1]

Having gained a monopoly position within civil society and culture, the Church was able to ensure that a Catholic habitus permeated all social classes. Once the Catholic elite came to power with the foundation of the new Irish state in 1922, it was able to set about creating a Catholic civil society that would mark out Ireland as unique in the West (L'Estrange 2005). The vision of this society, was outlined by the then Taoiseach, Eamon de Valera in his famous radio speech on St Patrick's Day 1943 when he referred to people 'being satisfied with frugal comfort and devoted their leisure to things of the spirit' (see Garvin 2004: 44–9). At that time it seemed as if the happy marriage between Church and state might last forever (Inglis 1985). However, during the second half of the twentieth century, the state began to abandon its Catholic vision of Irish society and to push through a new phase of modernisation based on economic growth. The expansion of the media and the market ushered in a new habitus that was based on liberal-individualism, materialism and consumerism, the very things against which the Church had preached so vehemently for generations.

The Catholic Church is still the largest interest group in Irish society. It has a membership of close to 90 per cent of the population. If those members ever acted in unison they could bring down any government and radically alter the way people live their lives. The reality is that although the Church is the largest interest group, it plays third fiddle to the market and the media who, with their messages of self-fulfilment, narcissism and hedonism have come to dominate the hearts and minds of Irish Catholics. Many older people were shocked by the sex scandals, but for many young people they were irrelevant, because the Church itself had already become irrelevant to their lives. It no longer instils the same awe and respect. It was no longer an authority that had to be obeyed. Young Irish Catholics are not afraid of the men in black. They have moved from a Catholic habitus of fear, self-deprecation and self-denial to a new individualism (Elliot and Lemert 2006; Inglis 2006a).

Although most Irish Catholics still see and understand themselves as Catholics, and still go to Mass on Sundays, they have become emotionally detached from the institutional Church. It no longer fills their everyday lives. They have become more inner-worldly, rational and materialistic and less oriented to the supernatural, transcendental and magical. Moreover, like the younger generation, older Catholics are no longer afraid of what priests and bishops might do to them. They are no longer afraid of eternal damnation:

belief in hell is declining rapidly. The teachings of the Church have less influence in their everyday lives. It is not just that many Catholics are choosing the teachings to which they will adhere, but an increasing number appear to be bypassing the Church, developing their own relationship with God and Jesus, and ultimately devising their own path to salvation. It is not that Catholics are leaving the Church to join other Christian churches and sects. It is more that in becoming detached from the institutional Church, in developing their own relationship with God, and in deciding more for themselves what is right and wrong, they are, in terms of their religiosity, becoming more like Protestants (Hervieu-Léger 2003). This is what I mean by the individualisation of Catholic Ireland.

At the same time, the influence of the Church in Irish society has declined significantly. It no longer has the same influence over politicians, the state, the market, the media and public opinion. It used to be that the Catholic Church heavily influenced what happened in other social fields in Ireland. Ireland may never have come close to being a theocratic state, but the Church's influence over education, health and social welfare meant that it came very close to being a theocratic society. In such a society being a good Catholic was central to maintaining and developing social position and influence. This is no longer the case. Today, it is not necessary to be religious, let alone a good Catholic, to be seen as a good person, attain position and status, gain access to educational, health and social welfare services, attract customers, get elected and so forth (Inglis 2003a). This, in turn, has resulted in a detachment from the institutional Church which has left it starved of money and human resources. This is the secularisation of Catholic Ireland.

Conceptualising religious change

Before examining individualisation and secularisation in more detail, I want to draw a broader theoretical picture of how religious change takes place. Bourdieu (1986; 1990; 1991; 1998) has provided a framework in which we can think of social life taking place within numerous different social fields – economic, family, sport, media – one of which is the religious field. The dominant institutions and organisations within each field, in this case churches, through their discourses structure the conceptions people have of being religious. In Ireland, the Catholic Church developed a monopoly position in the religious field and was able to exert a dominant influence over the way people were moral and spiritual (Inglis 1998; 2003a). This gave rise to a predisposed, second-nature, generally unquestioned, almost automatic way of being Catholic, which following Bourdieu (1990: 50–65) we can call a Catholic habitus. This habitus structured what Catholics did and said. What they did and said, how they embodied the beliefs and practices of the Church were important to attaining what, again following Bourdieu (1986), we can call religious capital. In Ireland, religious capital was not only important in obtaining a good position in the religious field, it was also important in attaining other forms of capital: economic (wealth), political (power), social (connections) and symbolic (honour) as well as positions in other social fields.

What has happened in Ireland over the past fifty years is that the religious field is no longer as significant as it used to be. In particular, the Catholic Church is no longer a major institutional player in the field of politics, particularly influence over the state, the media, health, social welfare and, to a lesser extent, education. Secondly, the Catholic Church has suffered significant intrusions from the market promoting a secular, liberal-individualist, hedonistic lifestyle, the state regulating and controlling its activities and the media making it accountable for its actions. These institutional intrusions have led to a new Catholic habitus which is less structured by and more detached from institutional Church teaching – religious individualisation. Finally, these changes have led to a decline in the importance of religious capital in attaining other forms of capital.

Individualisation of Irish Catholicism

If we consider all the different religions, churches and sects as belonging to a religious field, we can notice that one of the characteristics of the religious field in the Irish Republic is the dominance of the Catholic Church (Inglis 2005: 63–8). In the Census of Population 2002, 89 per cent identified themselves as Roman Catholics. This is a decline of only five per cent since 1971 and has less to do with disaffiliation and more because, since the mid-1990s, there has been a significant immigration of Protestants, Muslims, Hindus and Buddhists (Inglis 2006b). And yet, excluding entries for the Roman Catholic Church and Church of Ireland, there are over 40 different churches listed in the Dublin Phone Directory. This suggests a very diverse religious field. The reality, however, is that the membership of these churches is very low. There is little evidence of any significant numbers of Roman Catholics switching religion.

But while identification with the Catholic Church has remained steady, there have been dramatic changes in the nature of being Catholic. Being Catholic was so ingrained in everyday social life, so taken for granted, that it was like a fish swimming in water (Bourdieu and Wacquant 1992: 122). It penetrated into the heart and soul of family and community. Each new generation was socialised not just into the teachings and practices of the Church, but into a Catholic way of seeing and understanding oneself and the world in which one lived. There was a time in Catholic Ireland when the majority of Irish Catholics fully accepted orthodox Catholic beliefs and went to church regularly, not just for Sunday Mass but for devotions, novenas and missions. They accepted the Church's teachings on a variety of moral issues, felt guilty and ashamed when they transgressed these teachings, and regularly told their sins to a priest in Confession. Being Catholic was a public matter. It was not compartmentalised into religious occasions. The year was divided into holy days of obligation, feast and pattern days, Lent, May and October devotions, Advent and Christmas. Catholic prayers and rituals were ingrained into the calendar of their lives and the spaces in which they lived. Catholic homes were like miniature shrines filled with crucifixes, pictures, statues, lamps and holy-water fonts.

In 1973–4, the most detailed study of Irish religiosity was undertaken with a sample of 2,499 Catholics (see Nic Ghiolla Phádraig 1976). The findings revealed that the majority of Irish Catholics were very pious and devoted to the Catholic Church and its rituals, beliefs, teachings and practices. The survey results reveal a deeply devout, highly orthodox, Catholic people. What was remarkable was the extent to which Catholics fully accepted the fundamental beliefs of their religion. Even though they were offered the choice of 'accept with difficulty' and 'partly accept/partly reject' for most of the beliefs a clear majority said they fully accepted the belief in question. An indication of the level of loyalty and commitment to the Church was that more than eight in ten respondents said they fully accepted institutional teachings, that the Catholic Church was the one true Church, that sins were forgiven in Confession, and the Immaculate Conception and Assumption of Our Lady.

What is equally significant is the high levels of religious practice, particularly daily prayer, weekly Mass and monthly Confession. Thirty years ago, nine in ten Irish Catholics went to Mass at least once a week and eight in ten prayed every day. Practising their religion was central to who they were and how they understood themselves. Nearly two thirds of those Catholics surveyed saw their religious principles influencing their occupational, social and family life and, if there was a clash with other interests, most would stand by these religious principles. The permeation of religion into everyday social life is also seen in the regularity with which priests visited people in their homes. Half of the respondents said that they had been visited in their home in the previous six months. This represents a very strong level of pastoral care and attachment to the institutional Church. It also provided a means for the clergy to monitor and supervise the laity (Inglis 1998: 44–5).

Even then there were signs of changes to come. The level of belief in the Devil and Hell were significantly lower than that for other orthodox beliefs, a sign that the institutionalised culture of fear of eternal damnation was beginning to wane and, with it, control over the hearts and minds of the laity. The level of acceptance of papal infallibility was also low, perhaps a sign that

Table 4.1 **Elements of Irish Catholic religiosity, 1973–4**

Religious belief	%
Accept fully belief in:	
God	96
Resurrection of Christ	93
People can sin	94
Sins are forgiven in Confession	87
Transubstantiation	89
Assumption of Our Lady	88
Immaculate Conception	87
Catholic Church is one true church	83
Papal Infallibility	69
Devil	50
Hell	51
Religious practice:	
Mass at least once a week	91
Communion at least once a month	66
Confession at least once a month	47
Pray daily	80
Religious principles always influence:	
Spare time activities	63
Occupation	64
Family life	73
In clash would always choose religion over:	
Spare time activities	77
Occupation	70
Family	53
Always wrong:	
A man and woman having sexual relations before marriage	71
Not marrying in Church	73
Having an abortion	74
Using contraceptives	50
Parish visitation:	
Visit by priest to home in previous six months	34

Source: Research and Development Commission, *Survey of Religious Practice, Attitudes and Beliefs in Republic of Ireland 1973–74*, vols 1–4. Dublin: 1975–6. See Nic Ghiolla Phádraig (1976) for details of the survey.

four years after *Humanae Vitae* many Catholics were having difficulty with the Church's teaching on sexual morality. This was echoed in the findings on religious moral values. Over a quarter of respondents felt that there were occasions when it was permissible for a man and woman to have sexual relations before marriage, for having an abortion, and for not marrying in Church. Most significant of all, two thirds of Catholics felt that there were instances where it was right or permissible to use contraceptives.

Another indication of a change in the nature of being Catholic was the impact of education. Analysis of the survey findings showed that the higher the level of education, the lower the level of orthodox religious belief, acceptance of Church teaching, and attendance at Confession (Nic Ghiolla Phádraig 1976: 144). The impact of education was confirmed through the findings of a survey of university students in 1976 (Inglis 1980). These showed that the proportion of students who fully accepted many of the orthodox teachings in table 4.1 were often 20 points lower than that of the general population of Catholics three years previously. The proportion of students who fully accepted Papal Infallibility was only 22 per cent. There were also tell-tale signs of the Church no longer being able to obtain adherence to its teachings on sexual morality. Six in ten of the students said that it was right to use contraceptives and one third that it was right for a man and woman to have sexual intercourse before marriage.

There were major changes in the nature of Irish Catholic religiosity in the next 30 years. By the end of the century, religious practice had declined significantly. Results from the 1998 International Social Survey Programme (ISSP) indicated that attendance at Church services (which invariably can be taken to be Mass) had declined by almost 30 points to 62 per cent – at which level it seems, as revealed by European Social Survey results, to have stayed until 2004. The 1999 European Values Study (EVS) showed that the level of daily prayer had fallen to 49 per cent. This study also showed that the number of people who believed it was wrong for a man and woman to have sexual relations outside marriage had fallen from 71 per cent in 1973 to 26 per cent. More important perhaps is that there seemed to have been a significant change in the understanding of salvation and the Church's role in helping people to attain it. In the ISSP survey in 1998, just over a quarter of Catholics (26 per cent) definitely believed in Hell.

The decline in attendance at Confession was even more dramatic. The level of attendance at monthly confession had declined from 47 per cent in 1974 to 14 per cent in 1995 (Inglis 1998: 209). This would suggest that there has been a significant change in people's beliefs about salvation. It may be that it is not just a question of people deciding for themselves the best way to get into heaven and avoid going to hell. It may be that salvation itself is no longer a major issue or concern for many Catholics. But there is also evidence to suggest that an increasing number of Catholics no longer see the Church as providing a good guide to leading a moral life.

An opinion poll in 2005 suggested that when it came to sexual morality the rupture between what the laity accepted and what the Church taught had become significant (*Sunday Tribune*, 24 April 2005). The majority of those interviewed found the following acceptable: living with partner before marriage (79 per cent), sex before marriage (77 per cent), having a child outside marriage (73 per cent). An earlier 1990 EVS survey showed that by 1990 only 42 per cent of Irish Catholics considered that the Church gave adequate answers to moral problems and needs of the individual (Hornsby-Smith and Whelan 1994: 41) Sexual morality has always been central not just to Catholic Church teaching but to all salvationary ethical religions. If the majority of Irish Catholics disregard the Church's teaching on sexual morality, does this mean they no longer regard (a) Church teaching on sexual morality as specifically relevant to attaining salvation? (b) Church teaching in general as a guide to salvation? or (c) salvation itself as relevant?

It is difficult to decipher the role of Church teaching for Irish Catholics in their struggle to attain salvation. A earlier 1990 European Values survey found that 89 per cent believed in heaven and that 88 per cent believed in sin. But the connection between these and Church teaching is not clear. Is it that an increasing number of Irish Catholics believe in heaven and that sinning will prevent them getting into heaven, but that the Church is no longer the sole, or indeed, the main guide to what is sinful? If this is so, what does it mean to be a Catholic? Is it that they believe in God, Christ and salvation, but that the Church is no longer the means to these salvationary ends and therefore there is no longer any need to be so attached to the Church – what Davie (1994) refers to as 'believing without belonging'? But Davie (2000) sees 'believing without belonging' as characteristic of European Protestantism. This suggests that Irish Catholics, like other European Catholics, may be slowly beginning to act and think like Protestants against whom they have identified and defined themselves for centuries.[2]

There is another possible interpretation. If people believe in orthodox Christian teachings and that eternal salvation and entry into heaven are dependent on what one does in this life, then one would expect that the level of engagement in religious life would be higher. One would expect that, as in 1973–4, more Catholics would practise what they believed. What we may then be witnessing is not so much 'believing without belonging' as 'belonging without really believing'. In other words, it may well be that for an increasing number of people, being Catholic in Ireland may have more to do with belonging to an inherited social identity. Participating in rituals may reaffirm that collective consciousness but have less to do with any rigorous pursuit of salvation. Insofar as they actively pursue salvation, more Catholics may increasingly be bypassing the Church and its teachings, rules and regulations and developing a more direct, personal relationship with Jesus and God and, within that relationship, deciding more for themselves what is right and wrong.

Secularisation

The debate about secularisation continues to dominate the sociology of religion (Bruce 2002b; Davie 1994; Dobbelaere 1981; Stark and Bainbridge 1987; Wilson 2000). There are those who argue that eventually reason, rationality and science will slowly erase belief in and dependence on magic, gods and supernatural explanations for the meaning of life and death. Although there are important exceptions such as the United States, it is argued that the process of secularisation has been spreading progressively throughout Europe (Bruce 2002a). Secularisation involves three interrelated processes which revolve around the decline in the significance of religion in society. At the first level, the religion, particularly the churches, sects and religious organisations within the religious field, have less influence on social life. In Ireland, the Catholic Church's influence over the state, the media, the family, interest groups, civil society and politics began to decline during the second half of the twentieth century. Concomitantly, at the second level, other social institutions, particularly the state, the market and the media, had increasing influence over churches and religious behaviour. Finally, at the third level, the value of religious capital begins to decline

Decline in influence of Church

The level of influence of the Catholic Church over the Irish state during the twentieth century has been the subject of considerable debate (Whyte 1980; Keogh 1995; Ferriter 2004; Fuller 2002; Garvin 2004; Inglis 1998). Whyte (1980: 366) concluded his comprehensive analysis of Church-state relations by arguing that while the Republic of Ireland was not a theocratic state, the influence of the Catholic Church was such that it was like no other interest group. The failure of Whyte to capture fully the influence of the Church lay in his theoretical model. For the first forty years of the state, there was little need for the Church to lobby the state on most of the fundamental issues about social and economic policies. When it came to understanding what was good for Ireland they both engaged in the same discourse: metaphorically they sang from the same hymn sheet. Priests and politicians imagined Ireland as a deeply devout Catholic country in which people preferred to be spiritual rather than seeking material reward. Although there was a gradual separation of the Church and state's view during the 1960s, there were still many who took the view, represented by Bishop Newman,[3] of Ireland being based on an predominantly agricultural economy, that was built on strong Catholic farming communities that were excellent spawning grounds for vocations (Garvin 2004: 46). What is important to emphasise is that toeing the Catholic line was not just some empty rhetoric that was embodied passively and hypocritically. Of course, the vast majority of Catholics were deeply committed to the Church. But this did not mean that the Church did not have power. It did and it was able to reach down to every community, family and individual. While the state was able to influence the behaviour of people through the laws it passed, the Church was able to control people's souls, the way they thought, what they did and said. People were devout, but they were also afraid to resist and challenge the Church. On the other hand, those who were good prac-tising Catholics were often well rewarded. The Irish Catholic community which formed the basis of Irish civil society was, in this sense, a live and active community rather than an imagined one (Anderson 1983). The Catholic Church symbolically dominated the state and Irish society. Catholic discourse became, in Bourdieu's terms, not just the dominant orthodoxy, but *doxa*, something that was unquestionable (1977: 168). This *doxa* made it impossible to talk about the Church as an organisation interested in creating and main-taining its power (Inglis 2002). Such was the level of control over knowledge and ideas – the level of *doxa* – that it was not seen or recognised. It was, for example as Garvin (2004: 216) has argued 'impossible to suggest in public that one of the central reasons for Irish under-development and poverty was the Catholic practice, imposed by the clergy on women in the absence of contraception, of having large families regardless of the prospects of rearing children in any kind of real prosperity'.

The question then is what caused the demise of Catholic Ireland. The simple answer is that the rising tide of materialism and consumerism, and with them the individualisation and secularisation of social life, eventually broke through the sandcastle walls which the Church had built to keep Ireland holy and Catholic (Whyte 1981: 116; Garvin 2004: 285). But this is not the full answer. The reality is that during the twentieth century, a new urban Catholic bourgeoisie began to emerge, who had a different vision of Irish society. When they seized political control, they opened the castle doors and let the tide of materialism, consumerism and individualism sweep into the country. In doing so, it lifted the standard of living and welfare of most Irish boats, but torpedoed the Catholic battleship.

The main damage to the Church was caused by the rapid increase in the availability of transistor radios and televisions, combined with a relaxation of the law on censorship and a willingness of producers and editors to take greater risks in the content of programmes. The gradual rise in the standard of living through the 1960s together with the emergence of credit and hire-purchase meant that people could gain regular access to the media. The arrival of the television into the heart of Irish homes was the death knell of Catholic Irish society. Quietly, but quickly and effectively, the messages within British and American programmes, as well as advertising, began to shake the foundations of the Church's power. It was not just that people spent more time watching television than practising religion, but the content of the message meant that adults and children were being swamped with secular messages and role-models which led to new forms of personal identity and alternative conceptions of what was right and wrong. In particular, listeners and viewers were stimulated to discover and pursue their pleasures and desires.

In this climate of rapid social and cultural change, Pope Paul VI's Encyclical *Humanae Vitae* in 1968 was to act like a final straw that broke the back of devotion to the Church. The long-term effect was to turn women, particularly mothers, away from an orthodox adherence to the Church and its teachings. Instead of being exemplary Catholic prophets who told their children, particularly their daughters, to do as they had done, mothers now began to reflect critically about their lives and see how they had been burdened by uncontrolled fertility. With the emergence of the women's movement in the 1970s and increasing availability of contraceptives, young women began to disregard Church teaching not just on sexual morality but on women generally. Most important of all, there is evidence that mothers began to support their daughters (Hilliard 2003). Once women, and in particular mothers, began to turn away from the Church as their primary source of status and power, once they no longer saw Our Lady and the virgin martyrs as their role models, one of the mainstays of Church's power and monopoly over morality was removed.

Mothers were the lynchpin of the Church. Once they became alienated they no longer passed on 'the faith' in the same way to their children; they no longer helped to create the vocations on which the Church depended. In 1966, there were 1,409 vocations to all forms of the religious life – priests, nuns and brothers. By 1998, the number of vocations had declined to 92 (Inglis 1998: 212). The effect of the cut off in human resources has meant that the average age and, consequently, the mortality rate among religious in Ireland increased dramatically. Soon the Church no longer had the priests, nuns and brothers necessary to run the myriad of churches, hospitals, schools and welfare homes on which its institutional power had been founded.

What may have been a more rapid process of secularisation has been averted through the Church's continuing dominant position in the field of Irish education. Although it has very few teachers and provides little of the capital or current costs, the Church continues to maintain ownership and managerial control of the vast majority of the 3,300 primary schools in the country. And while there is more variety at second level, almost half of all secondary students attend a Catholic school. Again, most of the capital and current costs are paid for by the state. The maintenance of managerial control is central to maintaining a Catholic ethos not just in the schools, but in families. Parents who may have become more individualist in their approach to religion will often be encouraged to engage in Catholic rhetoric and practice to gain entry and acceptance within the local school.

One of the problems the Church has in maintaining a Catholic ethos in their primary schools is the rapid decline in the number of religious chairpersons which is directly linked to the decline in vocations. The number of lay chairpersons of primary school management boards increased from 395 in 1997 to 892 in 2003 (*Irish Times*, 7 March 2005). Another problem is the dramatic increase in immigration in recent years. This has meant that an increasing number of Catholic schools are being forced to take in children from different ethnic and religious backgrounds. In 2005, one school in West Dublin was reported to have 40 nationalities while in another primary school in the same area, non-Irish nationals accounted for 40 per cent of enrolments (*Irish Times*, 12 April 2005).

Intrusions into the Church

The sacredness of society can be identified by the extent to which the religious field and the institutions, organisations and groups within it are able to limit and control what is said and done in other social fields, particularly the state, the economy and the media. Correspondingly, the secularity of society is evident from the demise of religious domination of political, economic and social life. In Ireland, over the last half of the twentieth century, the state, the market and the media have slowly eroded the influence of the Catholic Church. This has mainly occurred through these institutions propagating discourses and practices that were antithetical to Catholic Church teaching. The state legalised contraception in 1979 and homosexuality in 1993. The market made available a whole range of goods and services that led Catholics away from a life of frugal comfort, spirituality and piety. The media told stories and propagated images that made a mockery of chastity, humility, self-denial and self-deprecation.

Other more direct challenges to the authority of the Church occurred. There have always been troublesome priests in Catholic Ireland who have appeared before state courts, mostly in relation to republican political issues and civil misdemeanours. But the pursuit and prosecution of sexually deviant priests and brothers by the state was a revolt against Church power. It was the inability of the Church to deal with child sexual abuse involving Catholic priests in the Diocese of Ferns that lead to the state carrying out an Inquiry that began in 2003 and reported two years later (*Ferns Report* 2005). This was the first time that the state had formally investigated the Church and, effectively, made the bishops and priests confess to it.

It was the media who first entered the religious field and through investigative reporting and documentaries forced the Catholic Church to give an account of itself and the activities of its priests, nuns and brothers. Until the 1990s the Church managed not just to remain aloof from the media, but to prevent it telling stories that were contrary to its interests. There was a cultural ring of steel that protected the Church from being investigated by the media. When the *Irish Times* was approached in 1992 with a story about Bishop Eamon Casey having an affair with an American divorcée Annie Murphy and fathering a son with her, the editor Conor Brady was reluctant to break it. The stakes were very high. If the story were true it would contribute to the increasing detachment by Catholics from the institutional Church. And, as one senior clergyman told Brady, 'if you're wrong or if you can't prove it, the church will destroy *The Irish Times*' (8 October 2005). The newspaper was right and while the story did not destroy the Church, it severely damaged it.

Over the last fifty years, the marketplace has directly challenged the Church and its teachings against materialism and consumerism through a subversion of the traditional value of keeping Sundays holy and not engaging in servile work. Irish Catholics, particularly those living in urban areas, have developed a peaceful co-existence between Church and market and to render unto the Church the time at the weekend that belongs to it and to Mammon and his cathedrals and churches of consumption any time that is left.

Decline in the value of being a good Catholic

Pure religious behaviour revolves around being spiritual and moral which, in turn, in most world religions is linked to attaining salvation. However, as Weber pointed out, being religious is never divorced from fulfilling other interests. Catholics in Ireland still go to Mass to be spiritually and morally inspired. But they also go, as they always have, for other reasons such as attaining the respect of their neighbours and friends, maintaining their social and occupational position, keeping up social contacts and perhaps even being romantically and erotically inspired by members of the opposite sex. There was a time in Catholic Ireland when being a good Catholic led to the attainment of religious capital which could then be exchanged for other forms of capital in other social fields. Orthodox Catholics, who complied with Church teachings, regularly engaged in Church practices and generally embodied a Catholic ethos in their everyday lives, were more easily able to attain resources and compliance with their demands (political capital), obtain positions, promotions and do business (economic capital), grant and receive favours within social networks (social capital), and obtain the honour and respect of others (symbolic capital).

The decline in the exchange value of religious capital in other social fields is central to the secularisation of Catholic Ireland. It may still have value in fields such as education, health and social welfare in which the Church is still a major institutional player. It is still often difficult for a primary school-teacher to gain employment in a rural school under the patronage of the local parish priest without holding Catholic religious capital. However, as most social fields move out from under the umbrella of the Catholic Church, as institutions and organisations become more rational and bureaucratic, the value of religious capital has declined. It is no longer necessary for politicians, business people and civil servants to be good Catholics. More significantly, it is no longer necessary for women to be good Catholics to be regarded as virtuous women. Most significant of all, it is becoming less necessary for children to be good Catholics to attain and maintain the love of their mothers and fathers. It is the decline in the value of religious capital that links the decline of the institutional Church to the micro-world of everyday life and the secularisation of Irish society.

Institutional identity

The secularisation of Catholic Ireland has been linked to transformations in Catholic patterns of religiosity. An increasing number of Catholics have become emotionally detached from the Church. We can use a continuum of involvement and detachment from the institutional Church to differentiate four different types of Catholics. The first type has a high level of identifi-cation with the institutional Church. These are the *orthodox* Catholics who adhere strongly to its teachings, beliefs and values, and engage regularly in Church rituals and practices. Orthodox Catholics have been the backbone of Catholic Ireland. They have funded the Church and provided it with the vocations that were central to its institutional success in developing a Catholic society. Despite the scandals, and despite teachings which they find difficult to accept, they are emotionally attached, deeply loyal and committed to the institution.

An increasing number of Catholics in Ireland reach out to other religions and, more recently to New Age Religions, for alternative forms of spirituality, transcendental experience and ways of caring for their bodies and souls. These Catholics no longer confine themselves to the Catholic menu so to speak as to how to be spiritual, but look at other religious and spiritual menus and mix and match these beliefs and practices with traditional Catholic ones. They still see themselves as Catholics but they incorporate ways of being religious that may have origins in Buddhism, Taoism, Paganism, and New Age Religion. They may practise yoga and believe in the healing power of crystals, but they also go to Mass regularly. We can refer to these as *creative* Catholics. This type also includes those Catholics who engage critically with Church theology, debate and discuss theological issues, and are willing to follow their own moral conscience.

Cultural Catholics identify less with the institutional Church but strongly with their Catholic heritage and tradition. They may go to Mass, receive the sacraments, send their children to Catholic schools, but they do not see the Church as a spiritual or moral force in their lives. They have strong links to the Catholic chain of collective memory (Hervieu-Léger 2000). Being Catholic is an indelible part of their social identity and they are committed to maintaining and developing religious capital. Finally, an increasing number of *individualist* Catholics see themselves as Catholics, but have little or no identity not just with the institutional Church but other Catholics. They may have spiritual and transcendental experiences, but they do not seek them out in any deliberate or organised way and, if they do have such experiences, are not anxious to debate and discuss them with others. They have no interest in accumulating religious capital.

Conclusion

Catholic Ireland is a good example of the debate about secularisation within sociology. From one perspective, Catholic Ireland is becoming increasing individualist and secular (Bruce 2002a; 2002b; Voas and Crockett 2005). An increasing number of Irish Catholics are becoming more detached from the institutional Church, are selective about the teachings, rules and regulations which they follow, are devising their own paths to salvation and are finding alternative ways of being spiritual. At the same time, the institutional church has decreasing influence in other social fields, particularly economic, political, media, health, social welfare and education. These changes have resulted in a decline in the value of religious capital generally and, specifically, the value of being a good Catholic in order to attain other forms of capital, particularly honour and respect. From this perspective, Irish Catholicism is moving away not just from an other-worldly to an inner-worldly orientation, that is from less involvement and concern with God, Christ and the supernatural generally in their daily lives, but perhaps even from a concern with salvation. It would appear that the decline of the power of the Church has led to a decline in the fear of going to hell and perhaps an increasing optimism of going to heaven. It could also be that because of this optimism, salvation or getting into heaven is no longer a major issue for many Catholics.

From another perspective it is not so much that Ireland is becoming secular but that there has been a move away from institutional forms of religious belief and experience to more individual, alternative forms (Hervieu-Léger 2000; Davie 1994, 2002). From this perspective, being religious is about searching for meaning and transcendental spiritual experiences that bring people to a higher level of consciousness beyond their materialist, animal self and create a feeling of connectedness and belonging to a wider realm of being. In other words, being religious is central to being human, but the searching for meaning and transcendental experience has varied throughout history along a continuum from being more or less institutionalised. What is happening, then, in Ireland at present is that religion is becoming less institutional but this does not mean that Irish Catholics are becoming less religious, but rather that they are developing alternative, more personal, paths to meaning and transcendental experience. This perspective is linked to a soft rather than a hard definition of religion. In other words, some sociologists see being religious as not necessarily involving a belief in God or the supernatural, but rather see religion revolving around transcendental experiences that generate a sense of collective consciousness. This can be generated through participation in effervescent rituals such as community and family gatherings, musical concerts, sports events, national mourning which, when repeated regularly, can become sacred. From this perspective, the interest in religion among Irish Catholics, as among the rest of human beings, remains constant, but the ideas, beliefs and practices by which this interest is fulfilled vary across culture and history. From this perspective, what is happening in Ireland is that Catholic ideas about what it is to be religious are changing rapidly, resulting in their religious interest being shifted down a different track from that provided by the institutional Church.

Chapter 5

Family

Betty Hilliard

Conceptualising 'family'

Most of us are born into a family, and all of us probably think we have some idea of what 'family' means. In practice, however, if asked to provide a concise and comprehensive definition of the term, few of us would find it an easy task. This is particularly so in recent times, when we have become more aware of extensive diversity in family forms. Such diversity is not necessarily a new phenomenon; there have always been families where a parent has been absent, owing to death, imprisonment, desertion, war or an occupation necessitating periods away from home. There have always been childless unions. Couples have not always formalised their relationship by contract or church witness. Same-sex couples are not an entirely new phenomenon. Adult siblings sharing a household surely count as 'family'. While mating and family formation seem to be very central human activities, we can see from the above that the specific form a family takes can vary considerably. This makes us question what exactly we mean by 'the' family.

In Ireland, family has been a very central feature of life. In their account of research carried out in Clare in the 1930s, the anthropologists Arensberg and Kimball (1940) described a society characterised by familism. By this they meant a society where other major dimensions of the society such as economy, community, leisure and religion are basically focused on or structured around the family. In short, the family was the major structuring principle in the society. They identified a family type which is often thought of as the typical 'traditional' family. They described this as consisting of several generations living under one roof, and functioning to keep the family small farm intact by passing it on to only one successor, typically the eldest son. The other children were then dispersed, leaving the elderly couple, the inheriting son and his wife, and their children, in possession of the family home. This type of family was strongly embedded in the community, was uncompromisingly patriarchal, and was characterised by coolness in emotional relations between members. The issue of bequeathing assets to only one heir and the nature of gender roles were portrayed as consensual.

Although for many years the model of the 'traditional' family utilised in English-language sociology was that put forward by Arensberg and Kimball (1940), its typicality is vigorously contested by other writers, for example Gibbon (1973). Other studies of 'traditional' communities, for example on the Aran Islands (Messenger 1969), Tory Island (Fox 1967, 1978) and elsewhere suggest variability in family forms, inheritance patterns, and in levels of consensus about family roles. On the Aran Islands Messenger reported much sibling rivalry especially among brothers about inheritance, and considerable resentment and dissatisfaction among women regarding the gendered division of labour. On Tory, Fox found a high tolerance of illegitimacy, nato-local marriage, and the practice of partible inheritance (where assets may be bequeathed to more than one heir). The model also differs from the type of rural Irish family identified by Brody (1973) in the 1960s, which was not multi-generational and was characterised by much greater autonomy on the part of adult children. Indeed, Brody summed up the putative demise of the 'traditional' family by claiming that 'with the son selling cattle at the fair and a daughter out drinking in the bar, traditional family life is overthrown' (Brody 1973: 128). The work of Hannan and Katsiaounai (1977) showed that by the 1970s Irish families even in rural areas had changed very considerably from Arensberg and Kimball's model in terms of expressive relations and gender roles, with the existence of a number of different family types not conforming to either a classical traditional or a modern urban nuclear model. As we will see below, recent censuses indicate that there are many different types of groupings recognised as family units in Ireland today.

Despite the wide diversity in family forms, both within cultures and across different cultures, a certain model of a 'normal' family has operated in sociology, and in the popular imagination as reflected in the media, for many years. This 'normal' family is often referred to as the 'nuclear' family: it consisted of a married heterosexual couple with two or more children, in which the breadwinner for the family was the adult male and the adult female serviced the family in the home and did not participate in paid employment. Conflict was scarcely considered as an aspect of this grouping. Portrayal of the nuclear family as 'the' family in sociology was due in part to the powerful position of structural-functionalism in the discipline in the English-speaking West in much of the twentieth century. This conceptualisation of family is associated in particular with the writings of the American sociologist Talcott Parsons, who exercised enormous influence over English-language sociology in the twentieth century, and was described by an eminent writer in the field as '*the* modern theorist on the family' (Morgan 1975: 25). This 'nuclear' family type is thought of by many people as the 'natural' family unit. It can be seen, however, that it is but one of a range of family forms. Talcott Parsons (1943) suggested that this smaller form of the family emerged in America as a response to changes in the economic and occupational system; he argued that people needed to be mobile in order to pursue employment opportunities, and smaller family groupings were easier to move around than larger kin groupings. Other writers (for example, Millward 1998) have argued that the extended family continued to be of importance in modern societies. In recent times in Ireland there has been a significant increase in families which are neither extended nor nuclear, for example single-parent families and families consisting of cohabiting adults with or without children (see table 5.1, p. 88).

The definition of the family which operated in sociology for many years was that of the functionalist George Murdock, who defined the family as 'a social group characterised by a common residence, economic co-operation and reproduction, [containing] adults of both sexes, at least two of whom maintain a socially approved sexual relationship, and one or more children, own or adopted, of the sexually cohabiting adults' (Murdock 1949: 1). Such a definition of the family was adopted extensively in texts on the family in the mid twentieth century. Gradually, however, this hegemonic conception of family came to be questioned, and today many textbooks and dictionaries of sociology avoid defining the family at all. In an influential article in the 1980s Bernardes (1985) asked 'Do we really know what the family is?' In this he argues that our inadequate conceptualisation of family has indeed stemmed from the conservative bias of functionalism, which served to obscure the existence of other family forms, or to portray them as 'deviant' or even 'dysfunctional'.

Other theoretical perspectives on the family did of course exist, with quite different ways of conceptualising 'family'. In the symbolic interactionist tradition, Burgess (1926) emphasised the fluid and dynamic nature of family relationships when he defined family as 'a unity of interacting personalities', arguing that 'the actual unity of family life has its existence not in any legal conception, nor in any formal contract, but in the interaction of its members . . . The family lives as long as interaction is taking place and only dies when it ceases.' (Burgess 1926: 5) Another writer in this tradition, W. I. Thomas, argued that conflict was a very normal part of family life (Thomas and Znaniecki 1918). This was in contrast to the functionalist position which tended to see such conflict as a form of social disorganisation and a threat to family life.

Many writers drew attention to the fact that family groupings varied over the life course, pointing out that a family which consisted of a young couple with one infant was quite different to a family where the adult children have left – again, alerting us to the fact that when we talk of family it can mean very different things at different times.

In sociology, the undermining of popular misconceptions about 'the' family owes much to the influence of feminism, which combines a focus on the internal workings of families with an analysis of structural factors which serve to mould and constrain them (as for example in the work of Delphy and Leonard 1992). Feminist theory was perhaps the most significant contributor to thinking on the family in the late twentieth century. Although feminist interest in family life goes back very much further, in sociology the 1970s were marked by the emergence of feminist writers who made visible aspects of family life hitherto neglected, if not indeed denied. Examples are the work of Oakley (1974) exposing the reality of the 'homemaker' role and the nature of housework, and that of Bernard (1973) who spoke of the 'wife's marriage' and 'the husband's marriage', identifying the very different experience that people in a family may have of their relationship. Hartmann (1981) identified the potential for conflict that arises from the fact that the family is not so much a unit as a group within which individuals have differential access to resources. Around this time, too, family violence began to emerge as a major theme in family sociology. In our own time, a greater sensitivity towards other cultures further contributes to a realisation that the old certainties regarding 'the' family can no longer be relied upon.

Almost parallel to the feminist focus on the variable experience and position of individuals within the family, a focus on individual agency developed in sociology in general, as distinct from the structural. This is associated with the work of Giddens, Bauman and others; the suggestion is that the myriad of choices that confront us in modern society lead to the self becoming a 'reflexive product' (Giddens 1991: 32), with individuals choosing and planning their lifestyles and biographies. In this perspective the individual becomes responsible for the creation of the 'self'. In contrast to this, Lash (1994: 120) insists on the need to be conscious of how structures may constrain the choices available to individuals, while Anthias (1999) highlights the significance of social or structural divisions, such as class, race and gender.

A recognition of the trend towards individualisation can be discerned in the work of Parsons, both in his early writings and in his recognition that the differentiation and pluralism of modern society would 'positively . . . favour individuality' (Parsons 1977: 198). The concern with individualisation emerged more forcefully in family sociology in the work of Jones et al. (1990), Beck and Beck-Gernsheim (2002) and Beck-Gernsheim (2002). Individualisation is not necessarily seen as having a negative impact on family: it is argued that it generates not just a claim for a life of one's own, but also 'a longing for ties, closeness and community' (Beck-Gernsheim 2002: 8).

While individualisation suggests a high degree of personal choice, people still live out their lives dependent on institutions; an over-emphasis on choice underestimates the extent to which most of us live our lives within very real constraints. In family sociology this lopsided emphasis on choice is especially evident in Hakim's so-called 'preference theory'. Hakim claims that in our individualised society, agency becomes 'more important than the social structure as a determinant of behaviour' (Hakim 2000: 12). This allows Hakim to underplay the structural constraints which colour the contexts within which women make decisions in relation to family and employment. She represents these as predominantly lifestyle choices, and asserts that the occupational inequalities experienced by women are of their own choosing. However, as McRae (2003) points out, structural constraints limit the choices which are realistically available.

It is clear then that thinking about family from a sociological perspective has passed through many prisms, making problematic a reliance on earlier understandings and definitions of the family as adequately comprehensive. This section has addressed many of the ways of thinking about family which have characterised the sociological quest for an understanding of the term, and emphasised an awareness of diversity and change. Bearing in mind the reciprocal relationship between the theoretical and the empirical in sociology, it is appropriate to look next at the evidence for this diversity and change; in this, the emphasis will be on data for Ireland.

Trends: demographic and statistical

The model of the 'traditional' family utilised in English-language sociology for many years was, as explained above, that put forward by Arensberg and Kimball (1940). This was the 'stem' family, 'a three-generational structure which functioned to retain its original location [land and or house] by means of dispersing most younger members, while preserving the main family stem by a principle of single inheritance' (Gibbon and Curtin 1978: 429). In contrast to this, the 'modern' family was identified as characterised by role segregation being minimised or absent, power gradients minimised, much jointness in decision making, and mutually supportive behaviour, as well as openness in interpersonal relationships (Hannan and Katsiaounai 1977: 15). Hannan and Katsiaounai's (1977: 150) analysis led them to question the appropriateness of the essentially functionalist conceptualisation of family change as evolutionary along a continuum ranging from 'traditional' to 'modern'. Certainly, many of the family units of today cannot be adequately described by either model. In the Census data for Ireland, for example, six types of family units are identified, none of which approximates to the stem family.

It is clear from this census data that the nuclear family of married spouses with children is still overwhelmingly the modal type of unit in Ireland, and hence in a statistical sense the norm. Nonetheless, it is equally clear that significant change is taking place in family formation, and that the rate of change is accelerating. Changes in Irish family formation in recent times are addressed in detail by Fahey and Russell (2001). In this regard, it is

Table 5.1 **Types of family unit 1996–2006**

Family unit types	1996		2006	
	N	%	N	%
Married couple with children	491,567	61.0	516,413	49.0
Married couple without children	154,854	19.2	225,805	21.4
Lone mother with children	108,282	13.4	162,496	15.4
Lone father with children	20,834	2.6	26,717	2.5
Cohabiting couple without children	18,640	2.4	77,782	7.4
Cohabiting couple with children	12,658	1.6	43,977	4.2
Total family units:	806,835		1,053,190	

worth considering the data on family units emerging from the 1996 and 2002 censuses.

Perhaps the most striking aspect of this table is the increase in cohabiting couples, both with and without children (+247 per cent and +317 per cent respectively). Also striking is the increase in reported same-sex cohabitation. In 1996 only 150 same sex cohabiting couples were recorded; this rose to 1,300 couples in 2002 and 2,090 in 2006. Two thirds of these were male couples. In addition to diversity in types of family units, other indicators of demographic change which impact on the family need to be considered. One such indicator is change in fertility, which impacts on completed family size. Despite the short-lived 'baby boom' in some countries after the Second World War, a drop in fertility has been evident in developed countries for almost half a century. In Ireland, fertility began to drop in the 1980s, the birth rate reaching a low of 13.4 in 1994. Marriage rates also showed a decline in recent decades, as table 5.2 indicates, while later average age of brides and grooms (see chapter 1) clearly indicates the postponement of marriage. With increased economic prosperity – for some at least – in the 1990s, some reversal of these trends occurred, excluding age at marriage. It is worth remembering, however, that in a European context Ireland was traditionally characterised by a late age at marriage. The more recent trends are shown in table 5.2 below.

A trend not evidenced in table 5.2 is the increase in non-marital births. From the introduction of compulsory registration of births in 1864, the percentage of non-marital births remained at three per cent for 100 years. In 1977 it increased to four per cent, a decade later it had trebled to 12 per cent (1988). From there the rate increased sharply, exceeding the EU average of 23 per cent in 1996 by two per cent. In 1999 it was 30.9 per cent and in 2005 it reached 31.4 per cent. It is notable that rates for non-marital births vary significantly by region: the rate in Leinster in 2005 was 34.1 per cent, compared to 21.9 per cent for Connaught.

Table 5.2 **Marriage and birth rates; trends for divorce**

Year	Marriage rate (per 1,000 of population)	Live birth rate (per 1,000 of population)	Number of divorces granted
1950–1960	5.4	21.4	
1970	7.1	21.9	
1980	6.4	21.8	
1990	5.1	15.1	
1996	4.5	13.9	
1997	4.3	14.3	95
1998	4.5	14.5	1,421
1999	5.0	14.3	2,333
2000	5.1	14.3	2,740
2001	5.0	15.0	2,838
2002	5.2	15.5	2,591
2003	5.1	15.5	2,970
2004	5.1	15.3	3,347
2005	5.0	14.8	3,433

Divorce in Ireland was banned under the 1939 Constitution: following new legislation, the first new divorces granted here were in 1997. Prior to its reinstatement the nature and extent of marital breakdown in Ireland was examined by Fahey and Lyons (1995) in the context of family law provision here; there were thousands of separations in Ireland in the 1980s. It was popularly feared that there would be a deluge of divorce applications once divorce became available. However, divorce in Ireland can only be applied for under certain conditions: these include the stipulation that the couple should have been living apart for four out of the five years previous to applying for divorce, that there is no reasonable prospect of reconciliation, and that arrangements are made for the maintenance and welfare of the spouse and dependent children.

Table 5.2 clearly shows the upward trend since 1997. Forecasts about the future are usually based on current trends; speaking of countries in which divorce has been legal for a relatively long time, Jones et al. claim that 'In North America and most countries of western Europe, the best forecasts are that 40 per cent to 50 per cent of first marriages in the 1990s will end in divorce' (Jones et al. 1995: 84). Numbers in Ireland, however, are still relatively small and appeared to plateau in recent years. A report in the *Irish Times* in 1996 claimed that over 60,000 people were eligible for divorce because they had been separated for more than four years (*Irish Times*, 28 November 1996). However, the anticipated floodgates to divorce did not materialise. Burley and Regan (2002) identify a complex set of factors which they argue are responsible for the relatively low number of people seeking divorce in Ireland, at least in the first five years. Whether this continues to be the norm remains to be seen.

Two other statistically identifiable trends are important to mention here. One is the highly significant increase in women, especially mothers, in paid employment, and the other is the increased reporting of domestic violence in our society.

Although the proportion of all women in the Irish labour force remained fairly stable for sixty years, being 32 per cent in 1926 and 31 per cent in 1986, the proportion of *married* women, and more specifically mothers, changed significantly from the 1970s on. In 1971 only eight per cent of married women were in the labour force; in 1981 this had more than doubled to 17 per cent, and by 1991 it was 27 per cent. By 1996, 36.6 per cent of married women were in the labour force. Ten years later the most recent figures available at the time of writing show clearly the acceleration of this trend. The labour force participation rate for females of 15 and over stood at 52.2 per cent in the first quarter of 2006; for married women, the rate was 52.4 per cent. Rates for married women in the main childbearing years of 25 to 44, though lower than for single women and widows, were higher than the average: 71.7 per cent of married women aged 25–34 and 64 per cent of those aged 35–44 were in the labour force.

When married women began to participate in the labour force in large numbers in Britain and the USA, the focus in sociology was on the supposedly negative impact of this on the family, and children in particular. This was one of the major themes in the 1970s. As this participation became more and more the norm, attention turned to issues of childcare and work–family balance, and more recently to considerations of work orientations of men and women. In this regard the findings of McCabe (2007) are of interest, recording high levels of commitment to work among women. Ireland still has one of the worst records in Europe for the facilitation of working parents in terms of availability of childcare facilities, and provision for parental leave. This has been the subject of repeated submissions to government by the National Women's Council of Ireland, who identify the lack of affordable or subsidised childcare provision as a fundamental factor in determining the extent of women's access to the labour force. It also has implications for extended family, particularly ageing parents, who are often called on to assume a demanding childcare role.

The other important body of data mentioned above as of relevance to our knowledge of family life is that pertaining to violence in the family. As many commentators have pointed out, domestic violence is by no means a new phenomenon. In many cultures violence against women and children was explicitly allowed. The relative normalcy of such violence in Judaeo-Christian societies is widely attributed to their patriarchal nature, which indeed is shared by many other religious cultures.

The phenomenon emerged as a theme in family sociology in the 1970s and rates of reported incidents of this nature have escalated alarmingly since then. The difficulty of establishing meaningful statistics in this area is notorious. For example, studies of violence against wives in Canada were found to vary significantly depending on the source of the data. Police statistics recorded 46,800 such assaults in 1993, the General Social Survey recorded over double this (107,500) for the same year, and a Violence Against Women Survey of 1993 recorded 201,000. In Ireland, the number of reported incidents of domestic violence ranged from 3,951 in 1994 to 10,877 in 2,000, dropping again to 8,452 in 2003 (Annual Reports of An Gárda Siochána). Conviction rates tend to be small: in 2003 there were 650 convictions recorded. A study by Kelleher et al. (1995) clearly indicates that police statistics for Ireland record only a tiny proportion of domestic violence experienced. It is generally accepted that about one in four families experiences domestic violence.

It is considered likely by workers in the field that the increase in reported levels of family violence does not reflect *actual* increased levels of the phenomenon, but is a feature of greater openness in society, a hope on the part of victims that something will be done about it, and the fact that such violence is now recognised as a crime. One of the difficulties in establishing reliable knowledge in this area is that of conceptualising violence for purposes of measurement. A commonly used method of recording data on violence, the Conflict Tactics Scale, has been criticised as not distinguishing adequately between levels of severity. Feminists argue that the use of such a scale may record behaviour but does not set it in context: for example, a violent act may be an extreme strategy of control or may be a defensive reaction to a violent attack. This issue has been usefully addressed by Johnson and Ferraro (2000), who identify four different levels of violence and point out that couple violence is not peculiar to heterosexuals. In this section trends in family life as evidenced in official statistics have been examined. In the next section trends of a more cultural nature, in the sense of changing attitudes and values, will be addressed.

Trends: social and cultural

Since the 1960s there has been a popular belief in the growth of egalitarianism, combined with increased individualism and secularisation as features of modernisation in the western world. Such trends can be discerned in sociological writing on the family and in research on attitudes to marriage, gender roles and to the domestic division of labour. In the next section the extent to which such attitudes carry over into *behaviour* will be discussed; firstly these beliefs and attitudes are examined.

A number of large-scale studies demonstrate a move away from an acceptance of rigid family role stereotypes towards more 'liberal' attitudes in relation to intimate partnerships, commitment, gender roles, and parenting. Particularly valuable is the data on these issues from the International Social Survey Programme (ISSP), which records attitudes to such topics in up to 40 countries at a number of points in time. Looking at the data for Ireland, it is possible to discern very significant change in attitudes as the twentieth century blended into the twenty-first. In 1988, 1994 and 2002 this survey contained an extensive range of statements about family and gender. Table 5.3 shows how attitudes changed towards a number of pertinent issues over this period. It is clear that traditional views on cohabitation, marriage and divorce underwent considerable change between 1994 and 2002. As divorce was not available in Ireland until 1997, it is not surprising that the question on divorce did not appear in 1988. The fact that the question on cohabitation was not asked then either surely indicates how marginal such practice was perceived to be at the time.

Table 5.3 **Attitudes to cohabitation, marriage and divorce**

Statement	% agreeing 1988	% agreeing 1994	% agreeing 2002
It is all right for a couple to live together without intending to get married.	Not asked	51	60
People who want children ought to get married.	83	72	53
Married people are generally happier than unmarried.	47	33	31
Divorce is usually the best solution when a couple can't seem to work out their marriage problems	Not asked	51	58

Clearly cohabitation and divorce gained considerable acceptability in the four years between 1994 and 2002. A further indication of secularisation is to be found in the increasing number of marriages that take place in a non-church setting. In 1990 there were 656 civil marriage ceremonies conducted in the state; in 1996 the figure was 928, and in 2002 it had jumped almost fourfold to 3,683.

Tolerance of unmarried people raising children also rose very significantly. The idea that married people are generally happier than unmarried lost support, especially among the young, among women, among the married, and not surprisingly among the divorced. This is probably reflected in the increasing popularity of cohabitation, as shown in table 5.1; it does not necessarily imply a rejection of marriage at some stage, and a high proportion of cohabitations end in marriage. Table 5.2 indicated that the marriage rate is remaining relatively stable, although the age at marriage is later. In a recent informal survey of second-year university students which I conducted, over 90 per cent of unmarried respondents said they would like to marry at some stage in their lives. This is clearly an area that would warrant further study. Whatever people's feelings about cohabitation, marriage and divorce, family still plays a major role in people's lives, as Scott (1997) has shown. In Ireland, positive attitudes to family are clear in the European Values Studies of 1990 and 1999–2000 (Whelan 1994, Fahey et al. 2005).

As regards gender roles in families, a popular theme in sociology since the 1960s was the so-called 'equality hypothesis'. Previous research had in the 1950s identified rigid gender role segregation and the dominance of males in marriage (Young and Willmott 1957). In the 1960s, however, a popular belief grew up that spousal roles had become equal and that relationships between spouses were those of 'partners' (Humphreys 1966). In 1973 Young and Willmott claimed that there had been a dramatic transformation in the status of wife in the period since their earlier research. This was a view widely shared and reflected in many influential texts of the period (for example, Fletcher 1966). Writing in 1980 on the methodology of the research on which the equality hypothesis was founded, Edgell pointed out the shortcomings of such claims and data since then have undermined the idea that much has changed in practice in gender roles in the family, especially with the advent of children. In the next section data in relation to the *enactment* of roles will be examined. What is clear is that *attitudes* to roles have changed very significantly. Table 5.4 indicates the extent of change in Ireland. While the decline in support for the first two statements indicates a liberalising of attitudes in relation to gender roles, it is harder to interpret the drop in support for the third statement. It may indicate an awareness of the difficulty in reality of combining paid employment with childrearing, especially for women. This is further suggested by the drop in support for the idea that one parent can bring

Table 5.4 **Attitudes to statements regarding gender roles in families, 1988–2002**

Statement	% agreeing 1988	% agreeing 1994	% agreeing 2002
A man's job is to earn money: a woman's job is to look after home and family	41	35	18
Women should stay at home when a child is under school age	Not asked	49	34
Both partners should contribute to household income	65	77	69

up a child as well as two parents together; in 1994 47 per cent agreed with this position, but agreement dropped to 44 per cent in 2002.

While it is well established that children in the past may have been an economic asset, especially in farming communities and prior to the introduction of pension entitlements, today they are clearly a liability in economic terms. Attitudes to parenthood continued to be overwhelmingly positive, however; 81 per cent in 2002 agreed that watching children grow up was life's greatest joy. Nonetheless, life without children was viewed less negatively over the course of the ISSP studies; in 1988 50 per cent of respondents agreed that 'People who have never had children lead empty lives', but this dropped very significantly to 22 per cent in 1994 and to 15 per cent in 2002.

From all of the above one can see that a high value is placed on family, while attitudes to and beliefs about marriage, cohabitation, gender roles and having children are increasingly liberal, with an emphasis on equality and choice. The extent to which such attitudes are reflected in reality is addressed in the next section.

Behaviour versus belief

One of the beliefs widespread in Western society is that our choice of partner is individual and free. This is seen as in contrast to the past, when economic issues were to the forefront in the negotiation of marriages, as documented, for example, in the account of Arensberg and Kimball (1940). However, a process of negotiation still operates in the establishment of long-term relationships, albeit implicit. The difference today is that such negotiation involves attributes beyond the economic, although these continue to operate to some extent. An example of this is to be found in the work of Jagger, who shows that although the chips may have changed, a process of bargaining is still very much alive in the search for a mate (Jagger 1998). Where substantial fortunes are concerned, as in the case of media personalities, pre-nuptial agreements regarding assets are common. Choice is still structurally limited: homogamy in terms of age, education, race and employment status is still very much a feature of contemporary Irish marriage. Interestingly, homogamy in cohabiting couples is not as marked (see Halpin and Chan 2003; Halpin and O'Donoghue 2004).

The popular belief that partners in intimate relationships in the developed West are somehow 'equal' is reflected in more liberal interpretations of gender roles in family relationships. In practice, despite popular belief to the contrary, actual gender roles within marriage have changed very little. Gelles (1995) pointed out that as a relationship progresses from courtship to cohabitation to marriage to parenting, gender roles in the home become increasingly traditional. Change in women's roles *outside* the family has clearly been enormous, as the figures for labour force participation have shown. Within the family, however, there is not a corresponding change in gender behaviour. Hochschild (1989: 11) refers to this as 'the stalled revolution', which effectively means that despite liberal beliefs about equality, women continue to perform the majority of 'family work'. She estimated that American women work 15 hours more than their husbands each week in all types of work – that is, both paid and unpaid, amounting to a full month in a year.

The identification of domestic labour as 'work' is associated in sociology in particular with the research of Oakley (1974). She argued that male ideologies dominated sociological thinking, resulting in a distorted portrayal of women and the trivialisation of their contribution to the economy through housework. Similarly, Fahey (1992) highlights the significance of household work for Irish GNP. He points out that housework can be seen as the service sector of the household economy, as do Delphy and Leonard (1992). Shelton and John's overview of work on the division of household labour and its consequences addresses the issue of measurement and the comparability of findings. Arguing that relative resources, time constraints, and ideology affect the division of domestic labour, they nonetheless conclude that 'gender remains a more important determinant of housework time than any other factor' (Shelton and John 1996: 317). This is a view shared by Davis and Greenstein (2004) and Kroska (2004). Coltrane (2000), in his overview of over 200 scholarly articles and books published between 1989 and 1999, suggests that housework as a topic worthy of academic study 'only came of age in the 1990s' (Coltrane 2000: 1208), although this downplays the important contributions of some earlier writers. It emerges from Coltrane's overview that women have slightly reduced the numbers of hours they spend in housework, while men have slightly increased their contribution. Sullivan (2000) also identifies a trend towards greater participation of men in domestic work. However, Coltrane concluded that on average women do three times as much housework as men. He points out that women do more housework when they marry and become mothers, while men do less when they marry and become fathers, with 'married men creating about as much demand for household labour as they perform' (Coltrane 2000: 1226.) Coltrane also draws attention to issues of measurement, and to the symbolic dimension of housework, an area which is of particular relevance to gender studies. In Ireland, data from the International Social Survey Programme for 1994 and 2002 (table 5.5) show just how slow the rate of change is here in terms of the performance of household tasks. There is a small increase in the proportion of Irish men in relationships who 'always or usually' care for a sick family member, from one per cent in 1994 to three per cent in 2002. This is also the task in which there is most sharing by partners; 37 per cent of people in relationships reported that this aspect of family life is carried out 'jointly always or usually'.

Table 5.5 **Performance of family tasks by sex, 1994–2002**

Task	Women always or usually		Men always or usually	
	1994	*2002*	*1994*	*2002*
	%	%	%	%
Laundry	88	86	0	3
Preparing meals	Not asked	71	Not asked	6
Cleaning	Not asked	68	Not asked	3
Shopping for groceries	67	63	5	8
Care for sick family member	52	54	1	3
Small repairs	8	13	71	69

Source: Hilliard 2006: 40. Asked of individuals in partnerships. Jointness in tasks not included here.

Of course, family work is not confined to domestic labour, which is often distinguished from childcare, 'solidary labour' and 'love labour' (see Lynch 1995; Lynch and McLaughlin 1995). The main increase in men's contribution to family work tends to be in the area of childcare; this raises the question of men as fathers, a topic which has received increased attention in family sociology in recent times. Traditionally in sociology fathers were portrayed as playing a task-oriented, instrumental role, a conceptualisation that owes much to the functionalist orientation of the work of Zelditch (1956), Bales and Slater (1956), and Parsons and Bales (1956). Fathers in more recent times have been portrayed as playing a more nurturing role, although La Rossa (1995) argues that this 'new' father is more imagined than real. McKeown and Ferguson (1998) suggest that the role of father was traditionally defined by 'investment', understood as the provider role, while that of mother was characterised by 'involvement'. They claim that 'investment without involvement no longer carries the esteem that it once did' (McKeown and Ferguson 1998: 28), and that various other societal changes such as women in paid employment, male unemployment in Ireland in the 1980s, and the growth of one parent families (in which the parent is mother in the vast majority of cases), have resulted in confusion about the role of fathers. This is potentially problematic in terms of ambivalence and disappointed expectations leading to conflict. O'Connor (1998), reflecting on the trend in voluntarily one-parent female-headed families, identifies a possible marginalisation of men within the family.

Increased involvement by fathers in childcare has been widely identified; however, it would seem that this involvement frequently takes the form of play rather than the more labour-intensive services such as washing and feeding. In a 1996 study in which children were the informants, the single most common activity in which children spent time with their fathers was trips/outings; they also reported spending more time in play with their fathers (32 per cent) than with their mothers (27 per cent). However, the majority of everyday interaction with a parent was with the mother, as table 5.6 shows:

Table 5.6 **Children's reporting of activities with parents**

Activities with parents in past week	Mothers %	Fathers %
Shopping	77	19
Things around the house	72	47
Had a good chat	64	42
Trip/outing	57	57
Went to park/walks	46	31
Homework/reading together	36	19
Played together	27	32
Visited him/her at work	8	11

Source: Devine et al. (2004) citing *Children on Childhood*: ISPCC 1996

Of course, the reality is that many fathers work long hours, and women are more likely to be in part-time employment than men. It is argued that fathers spend more time in working outside the home than mothers or non-fathers, which makes them less available in terms of time with children. The relationship between work and family is an increasingly salient topic in family sociology, and it is to this that we now turn.

Work and family

There has been a reluctance in sociology to discuss family relationships in terms of economics, despite the identification of housework as productive economic activity in the work of Oakley (1974), Fahey (1992) and Delphy and Leonard (1992). This is understandable in a system such as that in contemporary Western society where there is a belief in the free choice of partners for long-term relationships and a high value is placed on romance and personal choice. In recent times the dimension of economics, in terms of earned income by partners, is recognised as a central feature of most long-term intimate relationships. Also, the economic value of home-making is recognised, to some extent, by provision in law for contribution to the home on the part of stay-at-home partners in the event of marital breakdown.

The domain of 'work and family' emerged as a distinct area of research in the 1960s and 1970s. The issue of women working outside the home – more specifically, mothers working – became a major focus for debate with the rise in married women in the paid workforce in the 1970s. For many years the focus was on the implications of mothers' paid employment for children's well-being. More recently this has broadened somewhat to a wider interest in consequences of both male and female work for the quality of family life and the development of family members in both the short term and the long term. A new debate in this domain emerged about ten years ago in British sociology when Hakim (1995) made the claim that women have less commitment to work than men. Her arguments were robustly countered by established writers in the field on several grounds. Apart from a selective use of data, one of the main shortcomings of her argument has been the spurious emphasis on 'lifestyle choice' and the simplistic neglect of structural factors.

In day-to-day life, the impact of the engagement of both partners in the labour force is increasingly of concern to the social sciences, not least because of its implications for family life and social policy. Amongst the implications are the need for childcare, the availability of time for partners to spend with each other or with their children, children's use of time, and working parents as role models. The quality of childcare is a major concern for parents; satisfaction with the arrangement in respect of the emotional well-being of the child has been found to be at least as important as economic considerations (Wheelock and Jones 2002). Devine et al. (2004) report that Irish day-care arrangements are becoming increasingly formalised. ISSP data indicates that while working parents rarely go to work too tired to function well because of household tasks, a significant majority came home from work 'too tired to do chores', with women more likely than men to report this tiredness (Hilliard 2006: 38).

Perhaps one of the most significant aspects of the interface between family and work is the fact that the values and rationalities of each are diametrically opposed. While not overlooking issues of power and differentiated access to resources in domestic settings, family is ideally characterised by nurturing, kindness, communication, trust and altruism. The world of work operates on quite different priorities. Jones et al. (1995: 110) argue that 'The assumption underlying all highly paid careers is that work will take priority over every-thing else'. The push for productivity at almost any cost is clearly at odds with the affective priorities of family life.

Commitment in the workplace is often judged by the number of hours employees are available to work, and sometimes by the availability of workers for out-of-work socialising. Looking at the realities of limited time, it is difficult to see how family and career commitments *cannot* come into conflict, especially for women, who continue to carry the major responsibility for family func-tioning. Some of the strategies which couples employ to bridge the work–family dilemma are non-standard/shift work, working from home, and flexible working. All of these strategies have their drawbacks. Couples who work hours which mean that one of them can be home while the other is in paid employment obviously cannot see very much of each other; 'working from home' underplays the concentration necessitated for many forms of work, which is quite incompatible with being available to children. Flexible working, including job-sharing, may sound family friendly, but in practice organisational culture may not be supportive to such arrangements, so that women may be reluctant to take them up (Thompson et al. 1999). Availing themselves of such arrangements may in fact work against women's prospects of career advancement (Fynes et al. 1996). A change in workplace culture is clearly needed, as Humphreys et al. (2000) have argued. Such change necessitates a recognition of men's responsibility for family well-being beyond the economic; it is notable that research on childcare tends to attribute concern with this issue to the mother, rather than to the father or to both parents.

Conclusion

In the latter decades of the twentieth century English language sociology went from a body of theory heavily influenced by structural analyses of society to a growing interest in the role of agency on the part of the social actor. This movement was echoed in the changing theoretical perspectives in family sociology, as outlined in the first part of this chapter. The emphasis on individual agency raises important issues which, though not unique to family sociology, are central to it. In many respects modern society is of course characterised by greater choice and opportunities for agency on the part of many people than were earlier times. However, an excessive belief in individual autonomy can have at least two dangerous consequences. One is that individuals whose biographies are seen to be out of line with the priorities of 'success' in their society (for example remaining poor in a rich world) will be blamed not only for their individual 'failure', but for woes afflicting the wider society, as single mothers were in Britain in the last few decades of the twentieth century. The structural problems of a society can then be explained as the shortcomings of individuals or groups, perhaps immigrants, ethnic groups, or the unemployed. Secondly, and extremely pertinent for family sociology, the reality of intimate relationships is that entering into them successfully entails time, negotiation, trust, vulnerability, altruism and the relinquishment of a degree of individual freedom. This clearly suggests a certain tension between an individual's autonomy, their commitment to others in a family grouping, and the demands of work. It is likely that familial relations in Ireland will be characterised by such tensions for some time to come. As long as love and intimacy remain human aspirations – and there is no indication to the contrary – the implications of those opposing realities need to be confronted, not only for families, but for individuals, for social policy, and for society as a whole. This would involve real debate about our societal priorities; in the current social, political and economic climate the prospects for this are gloomy.

Chapter 6

Education

Patrick Clancy

Introduction

The massive and continuing expansion of education in recent decades, in almost all societies, points to the centrality of education in the project of modernity. Between 1970 and 2000, globally, average enrolments in secondary education increased by 180 per cent, while over the same period enrolments in tertiary education have nearly quadrupled (Gradstein and Nikitin 2004). By the start of this century, a child aged five could expect to be enrolled in school for 11 years on average. This school life expectancy ranges from eight years for Africa and ten years for Asia to 14 years in North America and 16 years in Europe (UNESCO 2005). In more and more countries public policy targets have evolved from that of achieving universal completion of primary education, to achieving universal completion of secondary education, towards achieving mass enrolment in higher education. An analysis of this expansion has attracted the attention of several analysts. In a recent review of the worldwide expansion of higher education Schofer and Meyer (2005: 916–17) argue that this expansion reflects global institutional changes linked to the rise of a new model of society: increasing democratisation and human rights, scientisation and the advent of development planning. In a review of the consequences of global educational expansion, Hannum and Buchmann (2003) have identified six related assumptions which underpin this process. These include a belief that education leads to the following: economic development of societies and enhanced earnings for individuals; improved health and slower population growth; a reduction in social inequalities and enhanced democracy. And while not all of these assumptions are supported by empirical research findings, a widespread belief in these and related propositions has underpinned educational expansion.

The Irish experience fits well into this global picture. From 1973 to 2003 secondary-level enrolments increased by 47 per cent while third-level enrolments increased fivefold. By international standards Irish second-level enrolments were already relatively high in the 1970s, thus the percentage increase at this level was smaller; the increase in enrolments at third level was, however, higher than the global figure. Currently the second-level completion rate in Ireland is about 81 per cent (or 85 per cent if second chance and other equivalent further education programmes are included); while this is below that achieved in some, especially Scandinavian countries, it is above average for all EU25 countries (Department of Education and Science 2005a). Country comparisons of third-level enrolments and graduations are more complex because of variations in types of higher education and in the age range of third-level students. Full-time Irish higher education students tend to be somewhat younger and relatively high percentages follow short-cycle pro-grammes (mainly in the institutes of technology), while in many other conti-nental countries students enter higher education later and enrol on programmes of longer duration. In respect of the percentage of labour force participants (aged 25–64) with third-level qualifications, Ireland is among the top third of EU countries (OECD 2005). In contrast, if we look at gross enrolments (total number of third-level students, regardless of age, expressed as a percentage of the theoretical age group for this level, typically aged 18–22) the Irish rate is the bottom third of EU countries (UNESCO 2005).[1]

Following this brief introduction the chapter is divided into three main sections. The first section describes the main sociological approaches to understanding education. In the second section I describe how the structure of the educational system has evolved to cater for the enrolment expansion while in the third section the problem of inequality in education is the focus, the topic that has attracted the most sustained interest by sociologists.

Sociological approaches to education

How do sociologists come to understand this key social process? Since there are a variety of sociological perspectives it is no surprise to find a range of different approaches. Most of the sociological research and analysis within the field of education has been carried out within a structuralist perspective, and this emphasis is reflected in this chapter. Traditionally, sociologists have taken the total society as their unit of analysis and have sought to understand the contribution of the educational system to the maintenance and development of that society. This macro approach tended to leave the social processes and internal dynamics of the school unexamined. Increasingly, sociologists, using interpretative approaches, have turned their attention to the functioning of the school organisation and have examined the pattern of interaction within the classroom, and the nature of the curriculum through which the explicit goals of schooling are realised (see, for example, Jordan 2003; Woods 1983).

An assertion that most sociological analysis of education can be located within a structuralist perspective should not be taken to imply that all sociologists using this approach share a common view on the role of education in society. In reality, two groups of scholars, functionalists and Marxists, hold antithetical views about the functions of education in contemporary society. However, in spite of fundamentally contrary views, their approaches towards an understanding of education reveal a remarkable similarity.

Talcott Parsons, the leading exponent of structural functionalist sociology, set the agenda for many sociologists of education when he identified the 'dual problem' with which schools have to contend. Schools are simultaneously agencies of socialisation and selection. As a socialisation agency, the school is responsible for the development in individuals of the commitments and capacities which are prerequisites for their future role performance. This socialisation has both a technical and a moral component. At a technical level, schools teach the capacities and skills required for adult role performance. In an age of increasing technological sophistication society is becoming more dependent on the educational system to equip people with the range of skills necessary for the occupational world. For Parsons, the role of the school as an agency of moral socialisation was even more crucial. As a normative functionalist he insisted that value consensus was essential for society to operate effectively. Hence the significance of schooling where young people are socialised into the basic values of society (Parsons 1959).

A key value which schools teach and which is of strategic importance to society is that of achievement. Within the family the child's status is ascribed; it is fixed by birth. However, status in adult life is largely achieved; for example, an individual achieves his or her occupational role. At school, students are encouraged to strive for high levels of academic attainment and by rewarding those who do strive, the school fosters the value of achievement. The functionalist analysis suggests that the school's commitment to meritocratic principles (i.e. rewarding ability and effort) becomes the essential mechanism by which our society accepts the principle of differential rewards. Both the winners (the high achievers), and the losers (the low achievers) will see the system as equitable since status is achieved in a situation where all seem to have an equal chance.

This discussion of the way in which the norm of achievement is internalised leads us to an analysis of the school's selection function, the second element of Parsons's dual problem. The school functions as a crucial mechanism for the selection of individuals for their future occupational role in society. An important dimension of schooling is the ongoing process of evaluation. Schools differentiate between pupils on the basis of their achievement. The differentiation which teachers make between students within the school prepares students for differential allocation in the labour market.

On the face of it, the strident critique of schooling which is contained in the neo-Marxist approach to education would seem to have little in common with the functionalist approach. While functionalists consider education to be an equalising force in society, Marxist-oriented scholars argue that education merely serves the interest of the capitalist class. The meritocratic hypothesis, with its assumption that schools are efficient ways of selecting talented people, is emphatically rejected. Instead it is argued that schools work to convince people that selection is meritocratic. It is essential for the legitimacy of the capitalist order that the population be convinced that people in high status positions deserve their positions, that they are more talented and work harder than others. Schools are an essential prop of this legitimacy. The essentially optimistic functionalist view that education is intrinsically good, that it leads to individual emancipation and self-realisation, is countered by the neo-Marxists who stress its repressive features. They view the educational system as an instrument of cultural domination; its real function is best understood in terms of the need for social control in an unequal and rapidly changing social order. However, in spite of these antithetical views, and in spite of the use of very different terminology, both approaches to the analysis of education are strikingly similar. This similarity in approach is evident from an examination of the work of the American neo-Marxists, Bowles and Gintis (1976).

Bowles and Gintis's analysis of the educational system begins with an assessment of the labour force requirement of capitalism. Education functions as an agency to supply appropriately educated labour power to the economy. Two modes of appropriateness are identified: firstly, the release of young men and women from the educational system at different ages and with different technical capacities and qualifications, and secondly, the production of personalities, attitudes and orientations which facilitate integration into the wage labour system with its attendant hierarchical division of labour. This latter objective is achieved through the operation of the 'correspondence principle'. Bowles and Gintis argue that major aspects of educational organisation replicate the relationships of dominance and subordinacy in the economic sphere. Thus, the social relations of schooling reproduce the social relations of production.

The dominance of structural approaches, whether functionalist or neo-Marxist, has been challenged in recent years by a range of alternatives. For example, in their book *Schools and Society in Ireland* Drudy and Lynch (1993) identify three further perspectives which have been influential: symbolic interactionism, feminist theory and the neo-Weberian perspective. The first of these is unique in that it offers no general perspective on the role schools play in society. Instead it aspires to describe in detail what goes on in particular instances in schools and classrooms and offers an interpretation of the way people think and act in schools. While there is a wide range of feminist perspectives within the sociology of education (Arnot et al. 1999), all of them seek to place women and their lives and gender roles at the centre of any attempt to understand social relations. A continuing important theoretical tradition within the sociology of education is that inspired by the work of Max Weber who attempted to bridge the gap between micro and macro social processes. Weberian sociology seeks to 'interpret' the behaviour of human beings to understand the subjective meaning of their actions, but it also attempts to locate individual behaviour in its social context, accepting that all action takes place within a social and economic structure which, to some extent, limits what the individual can do. From this perspective Collins (1979) has examined the ways in which education is used by individuals and groups in the struggle for economic advantage, status and domination. Education, he argues, can be seen as a 'positional' good in the sense that it is a screening device for selecting and allocating individuals to the labour market. However, he points out that it is not because of the technical skills they certify that credentials are used increasingly for occupational selection. Rather he suggests that the lengthy course of study required by business and professional schools exist in good part to raise the status of the profession and to form the barrier of socialisation between practitioners and the lay public.

I now turn to examine some of the structural features of the changing educational system. My account is deliberately neutral in that it lends itself to different interpretations. Those who seek to apply a functionalist interpretation will read it as an account of how the socialisation experience is being structured and how the educational system is adapting to the changing labour market. Those who wish to apply a neo-Marxist perspective will see this as an account of how schools are involved in the production of consciousness and in the reproduction of the class structure. An adjudication on the latter issues should await an assessment of the final section of the chapter which deals with inequality.

The Irish educational system: continuities and change

It is evident from the introduction that coping with expansion has constituted the major challenge for the Irish education system. This is most obvious at the post-compulsory level with rising retention rates at second level and massive expansion at third level. Enrolment expansion at these levels has been accompanied by significant diversification of provision, which will be examined below. It is not possible within the scope of this chapter to deal with two other evolving features of the Irish educational system, the trend to extend the educational system back to include formal provision for pre-school and to the development of a Further Education and Adult Education sector. Both developments which relate to what have frequently been described as 'Cinderella sectors' have been the subject of government White Papers (Department of Education and Science 1999; 2000). Before examining the expansion and diversification of the educational system it is appropriate to refer to some features of the administrative/governance structure of primary and post-primary education, which have been the focus of debate and some policy development.

Perhaps the most distinctive feature of the Irish education system is the level of Church involvement and control at primary and secondary level. This Church control of education is rooted in the ownership and management of schools and dates back to the emergence of the national school system in the second quarter of the nineteenth century (see Clancy 2005). Currently almost 99 per cent of children of primary-schoolgoing age (4–12) attend state-supported national schools, although the term 'national' is somewhat misleading since, while the state may be the paymaster, the schools are not owned by the state. The vast majority of these are denominational, with 93 per cent under the patronage of the Catholic Church. This leaves the churches in a privileged position with respect to the socialisation process, in control of the 'moral curriculum', and free to maintain the religious ethos of the school.

In response to demands by parents and teachers for more democratic participation in the management of schools and in an attempt to redefine the appropriate role of the state and of denominational authorities in the control of education, some changes have been effected in the governance of national schools. Traditionally the patron (usually the bishop of the diocese, or the head of the religious congregation) appointed the manager who administered the school in accordance with the regulations laid down by the Department of Education. Initially, in 1975, the single manager was replaced by a board of management in which the patron's nominees formed the majority, and more recently, following extensive debate at the National Education Convention, boards have equal representation of patrons nominees, teachers and parents. The patron retains the prerogative to select one of these members to serve as chairperson of the board (Clancy 2005: 86–90).

There is evidence that this resolution will not last indefinitely. With declining levels of religious practice, growing pluralism and multiculturalism more and more parents are unhappy with the denominational structure. While some of this has been catered for by the creation of multi-denominational schools and by a greater variety of denominational schools (such as the addition of a Muslim school), it will be difficult to continue to provide a greater variety of school types (including Gaelscoileanna) to cater for a relatively small population, especially in areas of low density outside the larger cities. In this context it is of interest to note the call made by the leader of the Labour

Party, Pat Rabbitte, who proposed the removal of the religious from the management of primary schools. He called for a system whereby all religious groups were accommodated together and where the churches would move out of management of schools and focus on the formation and education of children in their faith (*Irish Independent,* 3 February 2006).

The Church involvement in secondary schools, which enrol about 56 per cent of all second-level students, broadly parallels that of the situation at primary level. While the state is the paymaster and determines the secular curriculum, the great majority of these schools are owned and controlled by Catholic religious communities. The churches are also involved, in partnership with vocational education committees, in the management and control of comprehensive and community schools which educate about 15 per cent of students in this sector.

Returning to the theme of expansion and diversification it is of interest to look at developments at second level. The most visible change has been the increase in retention rates exceeding eighty per cent by 2002 (see above, p. 102). One measure of change is to compare the percentage of the population in full-time education in the years after compulsory schooling, which now ends at age 16. In the school year 2002–3, 83 per cent of 17 year olds and more than 64 per cent of 18 year olds were in full-time education. This compares with 25 per cent of 17 year olds and 14 per cent of 18 year olds in 1963–4. This expansion has been accompanied by a diversification of provision. Until the mid-1960s the second-level system was a binary one with the majority of pupils in secondary schools and a minority in vocational schools. The curricular pattern of secondary schools was firmly fixed within the humanist grammar school tradition where language and literary studies predominated. In contrast, the vocational schools emphasised practical training in preparation for skilled and semi-skilled manual occupations for boys, and commercial courses and domestic economy for girls.

By the 1960s there was a growing realisation that the structure of the post-primary system in the Republic was unsatisfactory. The new policy adopted was designed to erode the academic/technical distinction, to raise the status of the vocational school and to encourage the provision of a more comprehensive-type curriculum in both secondary and vocational schools. In addition, a new form of post-primary school, initially comprehensive (1963), and subsequently community (1970), was to be established. These schools were to be co-educational, open to all classes and levels of ability, and offering a wide curriculum to match the full range of pupil aptitudes and aspirations. Considerations of efficiency would appear to be the principal rationale for the establishment of these new school types although some consideration was given to educational arguments which pointed to the intrinsic superiority of a common comprehensive school. What was noticeably absent from the debate, however, was any detailed exploration of egalitarian principles, which questioned the invidious status distinctions between the education offered for mainly middle-class children in secondary schools and mainly working-class children in vocational schools. This absence is in sharp contrast to the intense ideological debates that accompanied the transition from binary to comprehensive schools in Britain and Sweden and some other European countries (O'Sullivan 1989: 240–3). This was indeed an Irish solution to an Irish problem. In Sweden and in the UK (although less emphatically) the introduction of comprehensive schools implied a complete dismantling of the binary systems and their replacement by comprehensive schools. In Ireland we retained the existing secondary and vocational schools (with their accompanying class divisions) and we added two additional types of school, comprehensive and community,[2] which catered for a more balanced enrolment of all social groups.

The proliferation of different types of second-level schools was augmented by a further differentiation of the secondary school sector when, on the introduction of free secondary education in 1967, a substantial number of secondary school decided not to opt into the free education scheme and continued to charge tuition fees. These fee-paying secondary schools would appear to have the best of both worlds. On the one hand the teachers' salaries are paid by the state and increasingly, at the discretion of the Minister for Education, these schools receive some support for capital development, yet they charge tuition fees which greatly exceed the state capitation grant that is paid to secondary schools which opted to join the free education scheme. In most other countries private schools are fully financed by the fees paid by clients while in Ireland what have become private schools use tuition fees to supplement the state's contribution. It is in effect a state-subsidised private system.

The differentiation of types of secondary schools is matched by a growing differentiation of study programmes. The trend here has not been uniform. Initially the pressure was to reduce differentiation in the study programmes. Traditionally the vocational schools prepared students for a separate and terminal Group Certificate taken after two years of 'continuing education' in a strongly vocational programme in contrast to the Intermediate Certificate and Leaving Certificate programmes, which secondary school students took after three and five (or six) years of study of a more academic programme. Following decisions taken in the 1960s, vocational schools were permitted to offer both the Intermediate and Leaving Certificate programmes. The Group Certificate curriculum was integrated with that of the Intermediate Certificate curriculum, being designed to constitute two thirds of the latter programme. More recently, in 1989, the two separate programmes were replaced by an integrated and more broadly based Junior Certificate programme.

Since the mid-1990s policy has moved in the opposite direction towards a further differentiation of the curriculum, this time at the senior cycle. In pursuit of higher retention levels, with a target of achieving 90 per cent completion, the suitability of the traditional Leaving Certificate programme has been questioned. One strand of criticism, that there is not enough emphasis in Irish second-level education on technical and vocational training, emerged from some business leaders and was best captured by the Culliton Report (1992: 53). (For a contrary view see Lynch 1992). Support for a stronger technical/vocational element at second level had previously been voiced in the OECD (1991) report which commented on the enormous weight of the classical humanist tradition in Irish education. These criticisms were supported by research by Hannan and Shortall (1991) suggesting that the academic curriculum was not suited to a significant proportion of the age cohort.

A major restructuring of the senior cycle involving four main elements has been effected. This involves the availability of the transition-year programme for all second-level schools; the revision of syllabuses for the established Leaving Certificate programme; the development of the Leaving Certificate Vocational programme; and the introduction of a new Leaving Certificate Applied programme. The transition year programme is interdisciplinary and student-centred, emphasising interpersonal and experiential learning and practical skills which are difficult to accommodate in the pressurised Leaving Certificate cycle. The introduction of the Leaving Certificate Applied (LCA) represents the most radical restructuring at senior-cycle level. This programme is built around three main strands: vocational preparation, which includes work experience; vocational education in selected occupational areas; and general education. The LCA is designed as a separate and distinct form of Leaving Certificate, a vocationally oriented stream which will provide for the needs of those students for whom the traditional Leaving Certificate was deemed inappropriate.

A second and less radical alternative to the traditional Leaving Certificate, the Leaving Certificate Vocational programme, has been available in schools since 1989. It was originally devised as a subset of the Leaving Certificate course with an emphasis on a limited number of technical subjects. In its present form it involves five subjects from the existing Leaving Certificate programme, including two subjects chosen from a set of vocational subjects, a recognised course in a modern European language and three mandatory link modules (enterprise education, preparation for work, and work experience). In 2000–1, of the total 53,025 students in the final year of the senior cycle, six per cent were taking the Leaving Certificate Applied while a further 29 per cent were taking the Leaving Certificate Vocational Programme.

It is at third level that we see the most profound changes in Irish education. In the introduction to this chapter, reference was made to the fivefold increase in third-level enrolment over the past 30 years. Currently about 55 per cent of the age cohort now enrol in full-time courses in higher education in the Republic of Ireland and if account is taken of those from the Republic going to Northern Ireland and Britain the admission rate is about 60 per cent (O'Connell et al. 2006). The expansion in enrolment has been matched by a diversification of the system (Clancy 1989). The major growth area has been the technological sector. Traditionally third-level education was synonymous with university education; as recently as 1968–69, 78 per cent of total enrolments in higher education were in the university sector. However, by 1992–3 only 51 per cent of new entrants enrolled in the university sector. Almost all of the new third-level institutions which have been developed are in the technological sector. The establishment of 13 Regional Technical Colleges, which were subsequently renamed Institutes of Technology, and two National Institutes of Higher Education (which subsequently became the University of Limerick and Dublin City University), were all designed to bolster the provision of technologically oriented education in the fields of applied science, engineering and business studies. One interpretation of this diversification is that it marks the vocationalisation of higher education (Clancy 2003) and signals the triumph of the 'human capital' paradigm over the more traditional 'personal development' paradigm which prevailed until the 1960s (O'Sullivan 1989). This predominantly utilitarian conception of higher education is vigorously endorsed by government, and enthusiastically supported by the OECD, which recently reviewed the Irish higher education system (OECD 2004).

Inequality in education

Perhaps the most enduring focus of interest by sociologists with an interest in education has been with the notion of equality of opportunity. This concern is linked to the central role which education plays in the status attainment process and in the reward structure of society. This development is in turn related to rapid changes in the occupational structure, with a growth in employment opportunities for those with technical and professional qualifications and the demise of employment opportunities for those who lack advanced education and training. The decline in the percentage of the workforce employed in agriculture gives one indicator to these changes. In 1926, 53 per cent of the workforce were employed in agriculture; by 2004 this percentage had dropped to six per cent. By the last quarter of the twentieth century the basic structuring principle of the stratification system had changed. The importance of inheritance as a determinant of future status has declined with a sharp reduction in the number of young people who enter family employment with the prospect of inheritance. Increasingly, educational qualifications have become *the* currency for employment. Moreover, it is not simply the case that educational qualifications serve as a screening device, which allocates people to their respective position in a hierarchical labour market, but the absence of valued educational credentials leads to a very high risk of unemployment.

The apparent triumph of 'achievement' over 'ascription' held out the prospect for the realisation of equality of opportunity. In the changing opportunity structure many people had hoped that meritocracy would prevail: ability and effort would determine who succeeded to the most prestigious and highest rewarded jobs. Research in Ireland and in other countries over recent decades has revealed that these expectations were very naïve. Middle-class families have utilised, or some would argue monopolised, the educational system to maintain their advantaged position. Social reproduction has continued. While the mediating mechanism may have changed, achievement in education may have replaced inheritance, but the outcomes are very similar: the class structure is reproduced.

The middle-class domination of the education system starts with pre-school education and reaches its climax in higher education. With the exception of the modest range of DES funded targeted initiatives focusing on particular children at risk, pre-school education in Ireland is privately funded and hence confined to those families who can afford to pay. Thus at the point of entry to primary education (at age four or five) those children who come with the advantages of pre-school already have a head-start over their less affluent peers. In any event, quite apart from whatever initial advantages are associated with pre-school education, clear differentials by social group emerge in the levels of achievement through the primary school years. The most recent evidence on this comes from the 2004 national assessment of English reading (Eivers et al. 2005). Lower pupil achievement was linked to a number of characteristics of children's families: unemployment of parents, low socio-economic status, and low parental educational attainment. These differences were evident as early as first class and continued through the fifth class sample. Broadly similar socio-economic differences were also found in an earlier study of achievement in mathematics in primary school (Shiel and Kelly 2001).

Social class differences in educational achievement become most pronounced at second and third level. This process of progressive selectivity by social background is best understood as a series of 'transitions' (Clancy 1999; 2001). Increasingly success in education is defined in terms of securing entry to higher education. To achieve entry to higher education it is necessary to negotiate three vital transitions. First, one must remain in school long enough to take the Leaving Certificate examination. Second, one must achieve a level of performance in this examination to meet the college entry requirements and thirdly, one must apply for and ultimately take up a place in higher education. The most recent evidence on these transitions shows clear social class differentials in these transitions, especially in respect of the first two (O'Connell et al. 2006). Combining the results from the school leavers' surveys of 2002 and 2004 it can be noted that 81 per cent completed the Leaving Certificate. This ranges from 90 per cent for the Higher Professional Class to 77 per cent from the Semi-skilled and Unskilled Manual Class. Of those who sat the Leaving Certificate the levels of attainment vary by social background; 42 per cent of students from the Higher Professional Class achieved 'honours' in five of more subjects by comparison with just 15 per cent of the Semi-skilled and Unskilled Manual Class. Finally, in respect of the third transition, of those who achieved at least five passes in the Leaving Certificate enrolment rates in higher education also vary by social class: these range from more than 66 per cent of the professional classes to 41 per cent for the Semi-skilled and Unskilled Manual Class (O'Connell et al. 2006: 56–9).

These differences in retention, examination performance and transition to third level are underscored by persistent differentials in tests of achievement such as those carried out on a sample of 15 year olds for the Programme for International Student Assessment (PISA) (OECD 2004). While overall Irish scores compare satisfactorily with other countries that have participated in the PISA study,[3] clear differences in performance by socio-economic group and parental educational attainment are evident. Students with high socio-economic status (SES), and high parental education significantly outperform students with medium or low scores on these variables in tests of Reading, Mathematics and Science (Cosgrove et al. 2005: 104–6).

It is at the point of entry to third level that we can measure the cumulative impact of class differentials in educational achievement. These inequalities were first identified in the *Investment in Education* (1965) report and have been documented by the author in four successive studies over a period of almost two decades (Clancy 2001) and more recently by O'Connell et al. (2006). Because these studies cover a 40-year period and because of the changes in occupational structure and the changes in how these occupational groups are combined to form socio-economic and social class groups it is not possible to combine these findings in an single integrated table. Instead I have shown some results from these studies in three separate panels in table 6.1. In panel 1, I compare the findings from Investment in Education, which relate only to university entrance, with the findings for university entrants from the author's first national survey of 1980 entrants. In the second panel, I report in summary form changes in the social background of all higher education entrants between 1980 and 1998 while in the third panel, the findings from 1998 and 2004 are compared.

It can be noted from the first panel in table 6.1 that in 1963 some four per cent of the college-going age cohort entered university and that this admission rate had doubled by 1980. What is of interest here is the socio-economic group inequalities: in 1963 these admission rates ranged from less than half of one per cent for the semi-skilled and unskilled manual group to almost 13 per

Table 6.1 **Changing inequalities in access to higher education in Ireland, 1963–2004: selected findings**

1 Estimated percentage of the age cohort entering full-time university education in 1963 and 1980		
Fathers' socio-economic group	*1963*	*1980*
Farmers	3.2	7.6
Professional/intermediate non-manual	12.8	19.3
Other non-manual	1.2	3.0
Skilled manual	1.6	2.3
Semi-skilled/unskilled manual	0.3	1.8
Total	4.0	8.0
2 Estimated percentage of the age cohort entering full-time higher education in 1980 and 1998		
Fathers' socio-economic groups	*1980*	*1998*
Six higher socio-economic groups	35.0	59.0
Five lower socio-economic groups	8.0	29.0
Total	20.0	44.0
3 Estimated percentage of the age cohort entering full-time higher education in 1998 and 2004		
Fathers' social class	*1998*	*2004*
Professional workers	89.0	117.0
Managerial and technical	56.0	64.0
Other non-manual	38.0	36.0
Skilled manual	41.0	58.0
Semi-skilled and unskilled manual	27.0	38.0
Total	44.0	55.0

Source: Panel 1, reproduced from Clancy (1996), calculated from Investment in Education (1965) and Clancy (1982); Panel 2 calculated from Clancy (1982) and Clancy (2001); Panel 3 reproduced from O'Connell et al. (2006); 2004 figures are based on analysis using adjusted Census data, the figure for Professional workers is an overestimate.

cent for the professional, managerial and intermediate non-manual group. By 1980 these admission rates had changed to two per cent and 19 per cent, respectively, for these two socio-economic groups.

In the second panel admission rates to all of higher education are examined. The eleven socio-economic groups used in the Census of Population are collapsed into two. The six higher socio-economic groups (Higher professionals, Lower professionals, Employers and managers, Salaried employees, and Intermediate non-manual and Farmers) are those which were 'over-represented' in higher education relative to their proportionate representation in the population. The five lower socio-economic groups (Skilled, Semi-skilled and Unskilled Manual, Other Non-Manual and Other Agricultural Occupations) were 'underrepresented' in higher education. These findings do not lend themselves to easy interpretation. Optimists will point to the more than threefold increase of the lower socio-economic groups from eight to 29 per cent while pessimists will note that the percentage differences between the two aggregate groups have increased over the 18-year period, from 27 per cent (35 per cent – 8 per cent) to 30 per cent (59 per cent – 29 per cent). It is suggested that the best way to measure changing inequalities is to calculate odds ratios (Clancy 2001: 178–9). These calculations suggest that there has been a reduction in socio-economic group inequalities of about 39 per cent over the 18-year period.

The third panel, using social-class grouping, compares the findings from 1998 with those from 2004. With one exception (Other Non-Manual) all groups have increased their representation. While the figure for Professional workers is clearly an overestimate it does suggest that this group has now reached saturation level in higher education. The significant increase in the manual groups, especially the semi-skilled and unskilled group is noteworthy suggesting a reduction in class inequalities. However, the social-class differentials are still highly significant with the probability of the Other Non-Manual and the Semi- and Unskilled manual groups entering higher education being about a third of that of the Professional workers' group.

Notwithstanding some reduction in the scale of inequalities, Irish research findings conform to the main thrust of international findings which is one of 'persisting inequalities' (Shavit and Blossfeld 1993). Arising out of their analysis of the relationship between equality and expanded educational provision in Ireland over the period 1921–75, Raftery and Hout (1993) advance the hypothesis of Maximally Maintained Inequality (MMI). The essence of the MMI hypothesis is that while expansion allows a greater absolute number of persons to pass through the educational system, relative inequalities between classes are likely to change only when demand for advanced schooling from the privileged classes is saturated. This happened in the 1960s with respect to the transition to second-level education and there is evidence that this is now happening with respect to the transition to higher education. In the report of the fourth national survey it was suggested that demand for places in higher education from the Higher Professional group had reached saturation level,[4] thus providing scope for a reduction in equality given continuing increased provision and a decline in the college entry age cohort (Clancy, 2001). The results from the most recent survey seem to confirm this prediction (O'Connell et al. 2006).

A key assumption of the MMI hypothesis is that expanded provision is the key to reducing inequalities since where access to a scarce resource is governed by competition this will always favour those who bring superior resources with them to this competition. In this context it is important to note a consistent feature of the finding from the surveys of access to higher education that the social selectivity of higher education as a whole is complemented by further selectivity by sector and field of study. Expanded higher education systems, as noted above, tend to be diversified. This diversification can be by type of institution and by field of study within a single institution. Thus, as Collins (1979) would have predicted, middle-class groups are more strongly represented in the universities than in the ITs and within the universities they are especially strongly represented in the most prestigious professional faculties such as Medicine and Law. Not surprisingly those segments of the higher education system that exhibit most social selectivity are those which have the highest earning potential for graduates.

Because of the persistence of the close relationship between social class and educational achievement and because of the implications of this differential achievement for labour market placement, income and lifestyle, much research has been devoted to finding an explanation for this relationship. Most attention has focused on the differences in home background of students. Initially the focus was on differences in material circumstances of the home, such as employment status, income, family size and housing conditions. Subsequently much of the search for correlates of differential educational achievement shifted towards an analysis of cultural features of the family which were found to have greater explanatory power. Parental attitudes towards education and differences in more fundamental value orientations were found to be important. For example, a Dublin study highlighted the importance of future-orientation (especially mothers) as a determinant of the propensity of adolescents to stay in school beyond the minimum school leaving age (Craft 1974). Bernstein's research on the existence of two linguistic codes (restricted and elaborated) has also been invoked as providing a possible explanation for differential educational attainment. Bernstein suggested that in contrast to the middle class who have access to both codes many working class families will be limited to the restricted code and thus will be at a serious disadvantage in the school where the elaborated code is in use. While the applicability of Bernstein's work has been challenged especially in so far as the restricted code is deemed to be inferior (Labov 1973), it is of interest to note how the theory of linguistic codes parallels in some ways the work of the French sociologist, Pierre Bourdieu, whose work is now especially influential within the sociology of education.

For Bourdieu the study of education becomes the study of cultural transmission. By using the concept of 'cultural capital' he seeks to show how general cultural background, knowledge, dispositions and skills, initially acquired in the home, are analogous to economic capital, which is produced and consumed by individuals and groups. Each social group possesses its own 'habitus' that is a system of schemes of thought, perception, appreciation and action. Schooling involves the imposition of a 'cultural arbitrary' whereby the socially acquired capacities of one group (the middle class) are transformed into intrinsic virtues. The culture of the school reflects middle-class culture, thus for middle-class children the transition to school is one of continuity; in contrast the working class bring to school a culture which is out of kilter with that of the school and hence experience a sense of discontinuity. The school 'demands of everyone alike that they have what it does not give' (Bourdieu and Passeron 1977: 494). An important feature of Bourdieu's work is the attempt to link objective structure with subjective dispositions and structured action. His analytic model seeks to show how objective structure (such as family circumstances) leads to the development of subjective dispositions, which in turn produce structured actions. In turn these actions (for example, decisions about remaining in education beyond the compulsory stage) lead to differential outcomes that serve to reproduce the existing class structure.

In recognition of the enduring impact of differences in the material and economic circumstances of families in determining educational outcomes, governments have to varying degrees engaged in affirmative action to assist families from disadvantaged backgrounds to make better use of educational opportunities. In one review the Department of Education and Science listed a total of more than 60 initiatives, which it funds. While the plethora of schemes suggests that this is a matter of some priority in public policy, it may also point to some overlap and lack of systematic focus, a matter that was raised by the Educational Disadvantage Committee (2003). More recently the Department of Education and Science has published what it considers to be a more integrated plan, *Delivering Equality of Opportunity in Schools* (Department of Education and Science 2005b). The new School Support Programme proposes to integrate over a five-year period all of the existing schemes including: Early Start (pre-school programme); the various primary Disadvantaged Areas schemes; the Home/School/Community Liaison scheme; the School Completion Scheme; and the Disadvantaged Areas Scheme for second-level schools (Department of Education and Science 2005b: 10). Estimated government expenditure on 'social inclusion' measures for all levels of education in 2006 is €636 million and represented about eight per cent of the total Department of Education and Science budget. Lynch's (1989: 126–8) analysis of the role of interest groups, including that of 'state managers' in determining education policy, helps to put in perspective the scale of this intervention. She argues that state managers, which include politicians and civil servants, face a dual problem: they must ensure that the knowledge and skills required for capital accumulation are transmitted in schools but they must also ensure that the educational system is seen to treat pupils fairly – a failure to eliminate gross inequalities would destabilise the political system. However, the extent of state intervention is subject to two restrictions. At one level, monies devoted to tackling disadvantage would leave fewer resources for the development of a technical elite. At another level state intervention to improve the consumption capacity[5] of working- class students would threaten the 'inheritance' interests of middle-class groups who rely on cultural capital to transmit privilege to their children. It is, in the final analysis, for each citizen to make her/his own judgment as to whether the balance achieved in the case of Ireland is reasonable or equitable. In making this judgment it is also necessary to take into account the role of the school.

A second strand of research concerning class differentials in educational attainment arises from an analysis of the role of the school in producing these different outcomes. This shift of focus suggests that instead of analysing the class characteristics of those who succeed and those who fail it may be more appropriate to examine the class characteristics of the educational experience at which they succeed or fail. Some researchers have approached this question using ethnographic approaches. In these studies the researcher typically uses observation and qualitative interviews with pupils and teachers to identify the social processes which are at work inside the school and classroom. A second distinctive body of research, which has come to be know as the school effectiveness literature, adopts a more quantitative approach. This literature has addressed a number of questions. First, what are the relative impacts of home background versus school on student learning? Second, if schools do matter what are the characteristics of the effective school?

Starting with the famous Coleman Report (Coleman et al. 1966) a succession of large-scale empirical studies concluded that schools had very little independent effect on attainment (Jencks et al. 1972). By implication it did not seem to matter what type of school a child attended since educational outcomes were almost entirely determined by individual and family back-ground characteristics. While more recent research has suggested that schools do matter and that some schools are clearly more effective than others (see, for example, Rutter et al. 1979; Mortimore et al. 1988), it has proved difficult to identify the essential characteristics of the effective school. More significantly, notwithstanding the burgeoning 'school improvement' industry in many countries, the design and implementation of successful change strategies remain problematic.

An important theoretical and substantive finding to emerge from the literature on school effectiveness is that differences in the socio-economic composition, academic balance and value climate of the student body represent important contextual variables which influence individual outcomes. This is especially relevant in the Republic of Ireland at the post-primary level. As described in the previous section, the present system of post-primary education is a highly differentiated one where variations in social selectivity, prestige and academic emphasis range from those found in fee-paying secondary schools through non-fee paying secondary, comprehensive, community schools, community colleges and vocational schools. These different school types have different retention rates and different transfer rates to higher education (Clancy 2001). While it is clear that the differential performance of the various types of schools reflects differences in individual pupil characteristics at intake, it would also appear that the social-class composition of the schools has a significant effect on student aspirations and achievement, independent of the social-class background of any individual student. The institutional-isation, within a system of publicly funded education, of invidious status hierarchies between different post-primary schools serves to reproduce existing status hierarchies. The willing co-operation by the state with those religious communities which operate fee-paying secondary schools demonstrates a distinct lack of commitment to meritocratic principles.

This issue has come to renewed prominence with the current preoccupation with league tables which have become something of a spectator sport fostered by the daily newspapers. Every year we now have listings of the number of students from each second-level school gaining access to university and other forms of higher education. Not surprisingly, private grind schools, which specialise in offering repeat Leaving Certificate programmes, and elite fee-paying secondary schools feature prominently towards the top of this list. Ambitious and affluent parents assume that these schools offer a superior education and seek to have their children enrolled in these schools. There is clear evidence that these schools are experiencing buoyant demand while simultaneously many non-fee-paying secondary schools are faced with declining enrolments. Taking account of the international evidence on school effectiveness, it is likely that to the extent that fee-paying schools may offer a superior educational environment this is directly a function of the class characteristics of the student clientele. Thus state and church support for maintaining an elite sector is directly creating unequal opportunities. Paradoxically this results in offering a more privileged environment for those who are already rich in economic, social and cultural capital.

Conclusion

This analysis of the role of education has necessarily been selective. The concentration on socio-economic issues has been to the neglect of other critical identities, such as gender,[6] disability and ethnicity, which mediate the impact of the educational system. While asserting the centrality of education in a rapidly changing society, I have sought to demonstrate how sociologists differ in their interpretation and evaluation of the education process. Some offer a benign interpretation and stress the contribution to economic development and the potential offered for personal emancipation and development, and the achievement of a more inclusive society. It is this latter assertion, which attracts the most critical response. Education does not operate in a vacuum: wider socio-economic forces set the parameters of its operation and mediate its impact. Since education is a public service there is a heavy responsibility on policy makers to ensure that it serves the common good rather than any sectional interest. Thus, while there is a solid record of achievement over recent decades, the persistence of serious inequality presents a major challenge for public policy.

Chapter 7

Crime, policing and social control

Aogán Mulcahy

Introduction

In the late 1950s, newspaper headlines of 'crime waves' made their first sustained appearance in Ireland (Allen 1999: 152–3). Crime figures for 1958 indicate that 16,587 indictable offences were recorded by the police, including eight murders. Despite the concern these figures generated, by contemporary standards such crime levels for a country with a then population of nearly three million people would be extraordinarily low. In 2005, for instance, the police recorded 101,659 crimes, including 54 murders. What do such comparisons suggest about the changing nature of Irish society? And how may we also account for the fact that, despite these dramatic increases, crime levels in Ireland remain low by international measures?

Researchers working in criminology and related fields seek to answer such questions by focusing on three main aspects of crime and crime control. First, they consider the 'criminalisation' process through which particular actions are designated crimes. For behaviour to be criminalised, it generally involves identifying it as so socially harmful that it requires a legally imposed sanction. However, this process is very uneven. Why, for instance, is it illegal to consume some drugs, but legal to consume others (including tobacco which is sold with the label 'smoking kills', and which results in thousands of deaths in Ireland each year)? Why are burglars and robbers sentenced far more severely than tax evaders, even though the value of property stolen in burglaries and robberies is far less than the amount of money stolen from the state through tax evasion? The scale of this differential is staggering. In 2005, the value of property stolen in burglaries, robberies and thefts was €78 million, while the amount of money retrieved to date by the state through various tax evasion investigations has reached nearly €2 billion from over 27,000 cases (O'Riordan 2006: 18). This suggests that much of our concern about crime is not necessarily based on an objective assessment of the facts, but instead reflects more dubious factors such as journalistic practices and how politicians use crime in election campaigns.

The second main dimension of criminology concerns crime itself, and involves analysing levels and forms of crime, as well as explaining criminal behaviour generally. While some patterns of crime tend to hold across most societies – that males commit more crime than females, that most crime is property-related rather than violent in nature, and that young people tend to commit more crime than older people – levels of crime vary considerably from era to era and from society to society, suggesting that particular forms of social organisation give rise to more crime than others. Explanations of crime have also highlighted the social dimension of criminal activity. While some early explanations of crime focused on the individual traits of convicted criminals (including their physique and the shape of their skull), later theories focused on the relationship between crime and the wider social environment, and examined the impact of such factors as levels of unemployment, gender equality, the extent of welfare provision, and processes of individualisation and consumerism.

Third, criminology examines how societies respond to crime and deviance, particularly through the different elements of the criminal justice system (including the police, the judicial system, and prisons). When we compare how societies respond to crime, we find considerable and often dramatic differences in the structure and powers of police forces, the sentencing practices used by the courts, and rates of imprisonment from society to society. Moreover, there does not appear to be a convincing relationship between levels of crime and how severely a society responds to crime.

What these three aspects of criminology demonstrate is that societies differ in terms of the problems each believes requires a legal sanction, and the specific form that sanction will take. There is no uniformity in terms of levels of crime, and social responses to crime. In other words, to understand patterns of crime and social control, we must situate these issues within their broad social context.

This chapter applies a criminological perspective to the development of crime and crime control in the Irish Republic in light of the profound social changes that have unfolded over recent decades, and since the mid-1990s in particular. While the scale and pace of these changes prompted much debate generally, their impact was particularly evident within the sphere of crime and criminal justice. Against a historical backdrop of low crime rates and relative stability within the criminal justice system, during the 1990s there was an unprecedented level of public debate on these issues. Part of this was prompted by a newfound politicisation of 'law and order', while a number of policy initiatives emerged in response to various policing scandals.

The nature of these developments, and their similarity with experiences elsewhere, raises the question of whether a global pattern of social control is emerging, characterised by policies that on the one hand focus on 'partnership' approaches to crime prevention, and on the other are more punitive in nature (Garland 2001). In the remainder of this chapter I consider recent Irish developments in light of these various themes. The discussion examines in turn: crime levels and trends; the politicisation of crime control; recent developments in relation to policing; and a number of significant emerging issues. I begin by outlining the historical context of crime and criminology in Ireland.

Crime and criminology in Ireland: the historical context

Debate on crime and criminal justice in Ireland has, historically, been hampered by the lack of sustained scrutiny applied to these issues. Irish criminology was slow to develop and historically few academics and researchers worked in the area. The criminological writing that did emerge was largely limited to overviews based on secondary analysis of official figures, and critical commentary on various aspects of the criminal justice system (for example, McCullagh 1996). Little original research was undertaken that could provide a counterpoint to official data and its limitations, and many aspects of crime and justice were characterised by an abundance of ignorance rather than information.

This ignorance, however, was not just the product of criminology's state of development. It also reflected the low salience of these issues within the sphere of government. Many state agencies whose activities directly concerned crime and justice often paid – at best – only minimal attention to data collection, leading to 'massive data deficits' (O'Donnell 2005a: 100) even in relation to baseline information. As a consequence, policy making has largely been driven by political pressures and public concerns, rather than by sustained analysis and research. Although the number of people working in these areas increased during the 1990s, huge gaps remain in our knowledge of these issues in Ireland (for valuable overviews, see Kilcommins et al. 2004; O'Donnell 2005a; and O'Mahony 2002).

Crime levels and trends

Any discussion of crime levels must immediately confront the grave limitations of the available data. While all forms of data are problematic, official data on crime – generally the statistics gathered by the police – are particularly so, and are compromised by a number of factors. Legal changes often make long-term analysis of crime levels difficult, and changes in organisational structures (such as the redrawing of a police force's boundaries, or changes in its recording practices) undermine the validity of the data that is gathered. Cultural values also shape our knowledge of and responses to crime. Members of the public may not be aware that specific forms of behaviour are criminal, they may be tolerant of specific forms of crime (perhaps drink-driving), or they may not report a crime because they believe the police will be unable to do anything about it. The dominant values within the occupational culture of rank-and-file officers also shape police responsiveness to various issues (such as political corruption, domestic violence or racially motivated attacks), and officers' willingness even to record such behaviour as crime. Victimisation surveys offer one way of overcoming some of these difficulties by asking respondents about their experiences of crime. These surveys have their own limitations and few have been conducted in Ireland, but they confirm that a significant proportion of crime is not reported to the police (see, for example, Watson 2000). The full scale of under-reporting is unknown, but the 2005–6 British Crime Survey (a well-established victimisation survey) recorded twice as much crime as the police did: 10.9 million versus 5.6 million offences (Walker et al. 2006). Overall, though, and despite their obvious failings, the sheer scale of police statistics far exceeds any other data source and so they continue to feature in most analyses of crime levels.

Traditionally, crimes were divided into two main categories. Indictable crimes comprised the more serious offences that could be tried before a judge and jury, and were divided into four categories: offences against the person, offences against property, larcenies, and other matters. Non-indictable crimes generally were offences of a less serious nature that could be dealt with summarily by a judge. From 1947, when national crime statistics were first published, through to 1999, crime data were presented using these two main categories of offence. In 2000, however, crime figures were reclassified into the two categories of headline and non-headline offences. This occurred due to the introduction of a major police computer system (PULSE – Police Using Leading Systems Effectively) whose purpose was the enhancement and improvement of police data systems, but it has hampered long-term analysis of crime levels as the categories of indictable/headline offences do not fully correspond. Also, in the first years of its operation, further (albeit relatively minor) changes occurred in the presentation of these data.

Historically, Ireland was characterised as a 'low-crime' society, one that stood almost as an exception to the 'high' crime levels expected in Western industrialised societies (Kilcommins et al. 2004). From the mid-1960s onwards, however, recorded crime began to increase quite dramatically. The level of crime almost doubled between 1964 and 1970, and increased sixfold in the 20-year period 1964–83, when for the first time in Irish history the number of indictable crimes recorded exceeded 100,000 offences. After 1983 crime levels dropped considerably until 1987 (by 17 per cent), and then began to rise again, reaching a new peak of 102,484 offences in 1995. Between 1995 and 2000 recorded crime dropped by 29 per cent, although the plausibility of this significant drop is called into question given that it coincided with the re-categorisation of crimes from indictable to headline offences. For instance,

Kilcommins et al. (2004: 114) note that the disappearance of the offence category of 'malicious injury to property' 'explains almost all of the supposed fall in crime between 1999 and 2000'. While 2000 marked the lowest point in recent years in terms of crime levels (the last time recorded offences dropped below that figure was in the late 1970s), in subsequent years crime levels increased again, to an all-time high of 106,415 headline offences in 2002, dropping to just under 101,659 headline offences in 2005 (with an additional 316,389 non-headline offences recorded that same year). Examining the trend in crimes per 100,000 population provides a means of taking into account changes in Ireland's population, and this also indicates a peak in 2002 and relative stability in crime levels in recent years. Overall, levels for most crimes in Ireland remain low by international standards and when compared with mean figures for the European Union (for detailed discussion of these issues, see Kilcommins et al. 2004: 90–132).

Table 7.1 **Indictable/headline offences in Ireland, 1995–2005**

	Recorded offences	*Rate per 100,000 population*
1995	102,484	2,846
1996	100,785	2,779
1997	90,875	2,480
1998	85,627	2,337
1999	81,274	2,195
2000	73,276	1,958
2001	86,633	2,252
2002	106,415	2,717
2003	103,366	2,596
2004	98,964	2,447
2005	101,659	2,457

Source: An Garda Síochána Annual Reports, and CSO Population Estimates.

While the vast bulk of crime is property related – crimes of arson, theft, burglary and fraud comprised 87 per cent of recorded crime in 2005 – violent crime has increased as a proportion of overall crime. Violence associated with public disorder – often alcohol-related – was a prominent dimension of this (Institute of Criminology 2003), but one of the most striking changes to emerge was in relation to homicides (murder and manslaughter offences). The annual homicide rate itself increased quite considerably, from about four per million population in the 1960s to about 14 per million population by the turn of the century (O'Donnell 2005b). Whereas the bulk of homicides in previous decades tended to arise within domestic relationships, or minor disputes that escalated into fatal confrontations, from the 1990s onwards an increasing proportion of homicides arose from disputes between individuals involved in criminal – often drug-related – enterprises, and in which firearms were used.

The politics of crime control

From the mid-1990s onwards, 'law and order' became politicised to an extent that was previously unknown in the Irish context (O'Donnell and O'Sullivan 2001). Although these issues had become prominent features of the political landscape in many jurisdictions – a process that was especially evident in the USA and the UK (Garland 2001) – this had never been the case in Ireland. Political and public concern had, of course, been routinely expressed at various points in time, but crime and the criminal justice usually featured low down the political agenda. Moreover, despite the rapid rise in crime from the mid-1960s onwards and the fact that in some marginalised communities it exercised a huge impact on quality of life, public concern about crime remained strikingly low, leading Adler (1983) to characterise Ireland as a society 'not obsessed by crime'. As Kilcommins *et al.* (2004: 132–41) demonstrate, successive public opinion surveys from 1981 onwards found that, in terms of electoral priorities, respondents generally placed the issue of crime/crime control at the bottom of their list of priorities. Concern over issues related to the economy and public services dwarfed whatever concern was expressed about crime.

From the mid-1990s onwards, a number of key factors propelled crime-related issues up the political and public agenda, and O'Donnell (2005a) identifies 1996 as a 'tipping point' in the political field of crime control. Historically Fine Gael had occupied the role of 'law and order' party, although the strength of this association paled in comparison with the links forged in other contexts, such as the links evident in Britain in the 1970s and 1980s between the Conservative Party and the police. By the mid-1990s, however, Fianna Fáil began a prominent campaign that centred on issues of crime control, and John O'Donoghue (the party's justice spokesperson), became a vocal advocate of 'zero tolerance' policing and other 'tough-on-crime' punitive measures.

Zero tolerance was associated with the 'broken windows' thesis advanced by US academics James Q. Wilson and George Kelling (1982). They suggested that the nature and level of crime and disorder in an area tended to escalate (reflected in an increase in the number of 'broken windows') if it became apparent that minor infringements were not being addressed by the police or other relevant bodies. Zero tolerance policing, therefore, involved a crackdown

on minor infringements of the criminal law (what many would have characterised as 'disorder' and 'anti-social behaviour' rather than crime). The New
York Police Department became closely associated with this policy, and during
the 1990s the city experienced a dramatic reduction in crime, especially
murders. Although it is likely that this reduction was largely due to factors
other than the introduction of this policing model – other cities that did not
introduce this policy also witnessed large reductions in crime (Bowling 1999)
– the apparent success of this policy and its uncompromising 'tough-on-
crime' rhetoric ensured considerable publicity for zero tolerance policing, and
it was enthusiastically embraced in many societies, Ireland included.

Some commentators suggest that the transfer of these policies reflects the
formation of a 'culture of control', whereby societies worldwide appear
increasingly preoccupied with crime and its control, and have become
increasingly fearful and reactionary in responding to these issues (Garland
2001). Wacquant (1999) argues that the diffusion of these measures reflects
the cultural dominance of 'neo-liberal' ideology in contemporary society in
which the pressures of economic insecurity are manifested in governmental
efforts to exercise greater control over those on the margins of society.
Whatever their precise origins, their impact on the landscape of social control
in Ireland was immense. Zero tolerance became a major plank of Fianna Fáil's
crime policy, which was elaborated into proposals to expand police numbers
considerably and embark on an extensive prison building programme, and to
introduce new measures to target crime and disorder, including lengthy
sentences for drug offenders, a police crackdown on public 'disorder', and a
constitutional amendment to limit access to bail.

A number of violent crimes generated unprecedented levels of debate on
the effectiveness of the criminal justice system generally. In January 1996,
three murders in rural areas caused enormous disquiet, particularly in light of
the traditional characterisation of rural Ireland as a bastion of tranquillity
(McCullagh 1999). These were followed later that year by two particularly
prominent murders: those of Garda Jerry McCabe and journalist Veronica
Guerin. McCabe was shot dead in the village of Adare in Co. Limerick during
an armed robbery by republican paramilitaries. While Garda McCabe's killing
generated enormous outrage and sparked a further crisis within the volatile
Northern Ireland peace process, the murder of Guerin – a prominent crime
reporter who had written extensively on organised crime – questioned the
ability of the criminal justice system to cope with the challenges posed by
violent criminals, and it became a touchstone event in the emergence of this
new law and order agenda. As a consequence of the measures introduced in the
wake of these events, the average daily prison population increased from 2,141 in
1994 to 3,199 by 2004, while police numbers increased from 10,816 in 1995 to
12,445 by March 2006 (with the goal of reaching 14,000 officers and trainees by
the end of 2006).

Policing and the police

When An Garda Síochána, Ireland's national police service, was established following independence, it was immediately faced with the task of providing safety and security, while also seeking to secure its legitimacy. In doing so, it sought to distinguish itself from its predecessor, the Royal Irish Constabulary (RIC), which had been widely recognised as efficient, but whose role as enforcer for the United Kingdom parliament ensured that it was always faced with a degree of political opposition. Even though An Garda Síochána closely resembled the RIC in its structure and organisation, its self-proclaimed ethos – reflected in its name, 'guardians of the peace' – was intended to reflect a different relationship with the public from that enjoyed by the RIC: the force was routinely unarmed, and officers were strongly encouraged to develop close links with the communities in which they were based. As the first Garda Commissioner proclaimed: 'The Civic Guard will succeed not by force, or numbers, but on their moral authority as servants of the people' (Allen 1999).

In seeking to achieve this goal the force enjoyed considerable success. Once the political turmoil surrounding the formation of the state subsided, the legitimacy of An Garda Síochána was largely established. Low crime levels, a socio-political environment characterised by stasis if not stagnation, and a persistent climate of economic austerity, ensured that few demands for changes in policing were made. Policing did come into dispute on occasion – due to various factors including the dramatic rise in crime levels from the mid-1960s onwards, the strains associated with the Northern Ireland conflict (Mulcahy 2005) and wider social processes of secularisation and urbanisation (Inglis 2003b). Nevertheless, the basic structures of policing established in the 1920s (which themselves were based on structures developed in the 1800s) remained intact. By the mid-1990s, however, Irish policing stood at somewhat of a crossroads as the force came under a level of scrutiny never before experienced.

Police–community relations

Historically, the few analyses of policing that were undertaken in Ireland supported the view that the Garda Síochána had secured the confidence of the wider public, and that the force was, as McNiffe (1997: 175) put it, 'one of the striking successes of the new state'. On the basis of a large public-opinion study exploring dimensions of prejudice in Irish society, Mac Gréil (1996) found that members of the public were generally more willing to accept police officers as potential neighbours and as part of their kinship network (through intermarriage), than individuals from other spheres or backgrounds. He noted that members of An Garda Síochána were one of Ireland's 'in-groups' (p. 68), and that 'It would be difficult to find a police force in any other country with such a high national standing' (p. 271). Allen (1999: 136) also stated that 'their place in the social life of the community could not reasonably have been higher'.

Surveys examining police–community relations repeatedly found high levels of public confidence in the police. Table 7.2 indicates that with the exception of one occasion (discussed further below), satisfaction ratings ranged from a low of 81 per cent to a high of 89 per cent.

Table 7.2 **Public satisfaction ratings of the police, 1986–2005**

Year of Survey	Overall Satisfaction Rating – %
1986	86
1994	89
1996	86
1999	89
2002	87
2003	81
2004	85
2004a	57
2005	83

Sources: T. O'Donnell (2004), *Irish Times*, 10 February 2004, and O'Dwyer et al. (2005).

Such findings, however, offer at best only a partial glimpse into police–community relations. Perhaps the biggest criticism to be made of such surveys is simply that the majority of respondents who express an opinion probably do so on the basis of little or no actual contact – confrontational or otherwise – with the police. In such circumstances, the 'confidence' they express is likely to reflect a pre-established ideological position, or one formed in ignorance, rather than an empirically based assessment of police actions. It is striking that the only significant departure from the broad pattern outlined in Table 7.2 is the figure of 57 per cent confidence in the police obtained in a survey conducted in February 2004. This survey was conducted shortly after a *Prime Time* television programme was broadcast that featured several serious allegations of police misconduct, and while several tribunals of inquiry were under way into police actions. People's views of the police also appear to be nuanced in important respects. For instance, while Bohan and Yorke's (1987) survey found that 85 per cent of respondents expressed confidence in the police, the study also found that 57 per cent of respondents agreed with the statement that gardaí sometimes abuse suspects physically and mentally, and 40 per cent agreed that 'in court, some gardaí would rather cover up the facts than lose face'. This indicates that 'confidence' in the police does not always equate with belief in their professionalism or propriety, and can in fact readily co-exist with bleaker assessments of police behaviour.

Furthermore, reporting the results of such surveys in terms of a single 'confidence' or 'satisfaction' rating masks the significant variations between the views held by various groups. While surveys found that confidence levels were generally high for all age groups, the lowest levels of confidence were consistently found among young males from working-class backgrounds. The scale of distrust in some quarters was such that conflict between police and public was a persistent feature of life in many marginalised areas (Association of Garda Sergeants and Inspectors 1982; Interdepartmental Group on Urban Crime and Disorder 1992; McAuliffe and Fahy 1999; Mulcahy and O'Mahony 2005). A recent study found that the policing style in 'Parkway', a Dublin suburb with an 'established, negative history' in the eyes of gardaí, was noticeably 'more confrontational' than that evident in other research sites (Institute of Criminology 2003: 67–8). Gardaí tended to view 'Parkway' negatively, and routinely used belligerent language to resolve public order situations, such as 'fuck off home, now' (2003: 68). As the researchers noted, gardaí there 'simply asserted their authority and appeared unconcerned about the nature of the reaction that might be elicited as a consequence' (2003: 69).

Significant measures to address police–community relations are contained in the Garda Síochána Act 2005. Although accountability structures formed one of its main themes (discussed further below), the Act broke new ground in police–community relations and the field of community safety more generally. For the first time in Irish history, the Act placed a legal requirement on the Garda Commissioner to obtain the public's views on policing. More significantly, it provided for greater public involvement in policing structures. Although the proposal to establish a Garda Reserve – a body of volunteers who would work in support of attested members of the force – generated most publicity, not least through the opposition of Garda representative bodies, the Act's provisions in relation to the crime prevention responsibilities of local authorities are arguably of far greater significance. In this respect, the Act significantly extended the mandate of local authorities, specifying that these should 'have regard to the importance of taking steps to prevent crime, disorder and anti-social behaviour within its area of responsibility' (37.1). It also required each local authority – in conjunction with the Garda Commissioner – to establish a 'joint policing committee' (JPC) whose function is 'to serve as a forum for consultation, discussions and recommendations on matters affecting the policing of the local authority's administrative area' (Section 36.2).

Although various types of community policing schemes had been in operation for a several years, these had largely developed in an *ad hoc* fashion, with little direction, co-ordination or evaluation of their impact (Bowden and Higgins 2000). The most pervasive scheme was a nationwide system of Neighbourhood Watch committees rolled out in the 1980s, but these suffered from the familiar problem of being easiest to establish where they were least needed, and hardest to establish where crime levels were high and police–community relations were poor. Moreover, their impact on crime was never systematically examined, and their role was confined to that of 'talking shops' – they appeared largely devoid of a focus or work programme. As one evaluation of Neighbourhood Watch schemes noted, some 'barely have enough to do to keep them active' (McKeown and Brosnan 2001: 118). Other community policing schemes emerged on a pilot basis in parts of Dublin in the late 1990s with the goal of improving police–community relations, although their impact was uneven (Bissett 1999; Connolly, J. 2002; Mulcahy and O'Mahony 2005).

While the network of JPCs currently being established serves as a structured means of police-public consultation, the Act left most of the details on their structure, operation and activities to be outlined in Ministerial guidelines that were published in 2006. However, as these indicate, the focus of JPCs remains firmly on consultation: there is no requirement that the relevant authorities act on the recommendations of the JPC, nor is there any provision for a research budget to facilitate JPCs establishing their own initiatives. The guidelines' recommendation that procedures should be as informal as possible (a point made four times in the guidelines), and that two meetings per annum should generally prove adequate, also suggests a rather minimalist understanding of police–public involvement in which JPCs merely serve as public conduits for communicating with the police, rather than real partners in the production of public safety and security.

Accountability structures

Despite high satisfaction ratings for the police, at the turn of the century the issue of police accountability was what generated most public debate. From the inception of An Garda Síochána, complaints against police officers were recorded and investigated by other members of the force. With the establishment in 1987 of the Garda Síochána Complaints Board (GCSB) an independent element was introduced into this process, whereby police continued to conduct the actual complaint investigations but these were overseen by the GCSB. However, unusually for organisations, the GCSB itself in its annual reports repeatedly highlighted the inadequacies of the powers and resources available to it. It noted that over most of its existence it had 'complained of the absence of resources' and highlighted 'the grave shortcomings of the legislation' under which it operated (GSCB 2002: 12).

Public disquiet about police accountability came to a head in relation to a number of high-profile incidents. First, John Carthy was shot dead by members of the elite Garda Emergency Response Unit in the village of Abbeylara in Co. Longford (Barr Tribunal 2006). Carthy, who had a history of mental disturbance, was shot after he walked out of the house in which he had barricaded himself. Despite the numbers of officers present, there appeared to have been little planning for him exiting the house, and further concerns were raised about the manner in which the police had negotiated with him during the siege. The shooting also raised concerns that even with the high level of risk associated with Carthy's behaviour – he had fired his shotgun numerous times within the house over the course of the siege – a consensually based approach to policing had given way to a more militarised response.

Second, in May 2002 a 'reclaim the streets' protest in Dublin city centre was the subject of further controversy. Although protesters had engaged in some disruptive behaviour – including releasing a smoke bomb inside a parked car – this was relatively minor in nature. As the protest reached College Green, one of Dublin's busiest streets, a number of gardaí engaged in what appeared to be blatant and unprovoked assaults on some of those present. This included repeatedly striking some protesters about the head and neck with garda batons. Public alarm over these events was compounded by difficulties experienced by the GCSB when it conducted an investigation into these events. The GSCB criticised the widespread lack of co-operation it received, and noted the 'particularly disturbing' fact that not a single garda proved able or willing to identify any other garda in pictures and video footage of these events (*Irish Times*, 19 November 2002).

Third, the most far-reaching scandal concerned events in Donegal that became the subject of the ongoing Morris Tribunal (Nolan 2005). These included allegations that garda officers manufactured and buried explosives, and then 'discovered' them in a bid to advance their careers; and engaged in systematic harassment and other illegal conduct towards members of the McBrearty family in relation to the police investigation into the death of Richie Barron. Frank Shortt, who had been imprisoned for drug-related offences, received a miscarriage of justice certificate after it emerged that gardaí implicated in corrupt activities had been accused of fabricating evidence against him. He successfully sued the state and in 2005 was awarded €1.93 million damages and full legal costs.

As a consequence of these and other concerns, The Garda Síochána Act 2005 constituted perhaps the most significant review of policing undertaken since the force was first established. In relation to internal management, the Act provided for the introduction of performance measures, and the establishment of a 'professional standards unit' within the force. It also introduced the requirement that members of the force would henceforth have to account for their actions when ordered to do so by a senior officer. The Act further provided for the establishment of a Garda Inspectorate, the function of which would be to ensure that the police maintained 'the highest levels of efficiency and effectiveness in its operation and administration' (117.1).

The Act also provided for the establishment of a Garda Síochána Ombudsman Commission (GSOC), constituting the first fully independent police complaints system established in Ireland. The Commission was given the power to make reports to the Minister for Justice on matters concerning grave or exceptional circumstances (80.5), and to 'examine' a 'practice, policy or procedure' of An Garda Síochána with a view to preventing or reducing the incidence of complaints associated with them (106.1), although this latter power was undermined by the fact that it required an invitation from the Minister for Justice to do so.

Emerging issues in the landscape of social control

In addition to the concerns outlined above, a number of further issues have significant implications for the criminal justice system: the ethnic diversification of Irish society; corruption and organised crime; and cross-border and international developments.

Ethnic diversity and the criminal justice system

Historically, Irishness was in most quarters synonymous with whiteness. Despite the longstanding presence of ethnic minority groups in Irish society, these tended to be small in number and had a low political profile. By 2006, however, census figures indicated that ten per cent of the population were foreign nationals. The scale of this recent ethnic diversification, in turn, poses a number of challenges for the criminal justice system.

The issue of racially motivated crime gained prominence (the police recorded 81 such incidents in 2003, 84 in 2004, and 94 in 2005, although these figures are likely to significantly underestimate its scale), as did crimes committed by members of ethnic groups. For instance, in 2004 over 20 per cent of the persons committed to prison were foreign nationals drawn from a total of more than 115 different States (Irish Prison Service 2004), many of whom were detained pending deportation.

The Garda Síochána established the Garda Racial and Intercultural Unit in 2001 as a means of developing and monitoring organisational responses to ethnic and cultural diversity. Ethnic Liaison Officers were also appointed in each sub-divisional area (approximately 145 officers in total). In 2005, and in light of the ongoing recruitment campaigns to increase the size of the force, the Minister for Justice announced a major public relations drive to increase the representation of ethnic minorities within the force. Previous recruitment criteria did not specify that that applicants had to be Irish citizens, but the requirement that applicants speak both English and Irish effectively amounted to a nationality test. This language requirement was amended so that new applicants now had to be proficient either in English or Irish (even though the possibility of applications being received from individuals who were proficient in Irish but not in English must be considered remote). Soon afterwards, the October 2005 round of recruitment attracted approximately 800 applications from ethnic minorities, including 588 from Chinese applicants. In other respects, though, the profile of applicants merely confirmed the marginal status of some groups: only eight Travellers applied, despite (or perhaps because of) the historical and contemporary difficulties in their relationship with the police. Moreover, garda involvement in immigration proved controversial. Although the role of ethnic liaison officers was ostensibly to cultivate good relations between the police and ethnic minority groups, their impact was considerably undermined by the fact that they also participated in garda operations to round up suspected illegal immigrants for deportation.

Corruption, white-collar crime and organised crime

The economic expansion heralded by the Celtic Tiger had further significant consequences. As the price of housing and land zoned for development purposes increased exponentially in the 1990s, so too did the potential gains to be made from corruption within the planning process. Transparency International's (2005) compilation of perceptions of corruption across various countries found that Ireland's position dropped from joint 11th in 1995 to 23rd by 2002. As McCarthy (2003: 6) noted, 'No other EU country experienced a drop in score or in rank close to the Irish decline.' Much of this occurred through the revelations of several tribunals established to investigate allegations surrounding the links between politicians and the business sector, including the Moriarty Tribunal into payments to politicians, and the Flood/Mahon Tribunal into planning corruption in Dublin. These allegations reached the highest political levels. The McCracken Tribunal, for instance, documented payments totalling several million euro to the former Taoiseach, Charles Haughey, while a former Justice minister, Ray Burke, was among those deemed corrupt by the Flood/Mahon Tribunal.

One of the most significant measures established to deal with organised crime was the establishment in 1996 of the Criminal Assets Bureau (CAB). Emerging from a context of increased concern over organised crime, especially in light of Veronica Guerin's murder, the CAB was a novel development in two important respects. First, its focus was on the financial gains obtained from criminal behaviour, rather than crime itself. Second, its approach circumvented a pivotal element of the criminal justice process. Instead of pursing alleged criminals through the criminal courts in which the standard of proof required to secure a conviction was that of 'beyond a reasonable doubt', the CAB pursued individuals through civil means involving a lower standard of proof. In effect, those who were the subject of CAB actions had to prove that the assets involved had been obtained in lawful ways (irrespective of whether those involved had been convicted of related crimes or not).

Cross-border and international dimensions

Into the future, it is also likely that social control in Ireland will increasingly reflect various international patterns. Part of this stems from the greater emphasis on international co-ordination arising from the attacks of 11 September 2001, but it also reflects the implications of the Northern Ireland peace process for cross-border initiatives generally. Given the historical difficulties surrounding policing and security in Northern Ireland, police reform was a core dimension of the peace process. The Patten Commission's 1999 report recommended a series of innovative measures to address issues of accountability, composition, ethos, operational effectiveness, and links with the community. The widespread recognition of the Commission's Report as an expression of international 'best practice' in terms of policing (Mulcahy 2006) has given considerable momentum to the development of cross-border initiatives and protocols. An Garda Síochána and the Police Service of Northern Ireland are currently involved in establishing a joint anti-racism training programme. The Garda Síochána Act 2005 formally provided for personnel secondment and exchange, while efforts to improve co-ordination in dealing with organised crime and disaster planning have also been considered (see, for example, An Garda Síochána/PSNI 2004). However, it is clear that certain recommendations of the Patten Report were considered inappropriate for the Irish Republic. For instance, the establishment of an oversight body akin to the Policing Board of Northern Ireland was rejected on the grounds that it would undermine the Dáil's role in monitoring the police. Despite considerable evidence that the Dáil had been singularly ineffective in monitoring the police, the Minister for Justice maintained that: 'What is good for Northern Ireland is not necessarily good for a sovereign state' (Joint Committee on Justice, Equality, Defence and Women's Rights 2005: 28). In this respect, while some aspects of policing are likely to be more closely aligned on a cross-border basis, the differing political environments in Northern Ireland and the Irish Republic may inhibit wholesale transfer of policies between jurisdictions.

Conclusion

Recent criminological writing suggests that the landscape of crime and social control is being drastically reconfigured, as significant crime rises in recent decades have been accompanied by new and potentially far-reaching policies of crime control – policies that on the one hand are punitive and exclusive, politically driven and emotionally charged; and on the other are preventive and inclusive, and underpinned by the elements of crime prevention partnership, risk assessment and the like (Garland 2001). At first glance events in Ireland do appear to correspond with this suggested pattern. Crime levels did undergo a remarkable rise from the 1960s; 'law and order' has become considerably more politicised; and a number of policies have been introduced to forge new 'partnership' approaches to crime control, most noticeably in a number of measures contained in the Garda Síochána Act 2005.

While some of these measures are clearly international in origin, this does not in itself demonstrate that Irish social control policies now correspond to an emerging global pattern. As Kilcommins et al. (2004) have convincingly argued, the experience of the USA and the UK – on which Garland (2001) bases his thesis that a 'culture of control' is now sweeping the world – is in many ways atypical of what has occurred in many Western countries. Some of the most significant developments to occur in Ireland are firmly rooted in local rather than global processes. For instance, the Fianna Fáil/Progressive Democrat 'law and order' programme emerged in the context of political opportunism and a series of high-profile murders. Moreover, one of the potentially greatest impacts that the social changes associated with the Celtic Tiger exerted on crime and justice in modern Ireland was that the Irish government finally had the economic capacity to undertake many of the initiatives that had been considered over the years (albeit with different levels of commitment), but set aside on the grounds of expense. As the government's coffers swelled through increased tax revenues, the costs associated with the expansion of An Garda Síochána and an extensive prison-building programme could finally be absorbed. In this respect, political responses to local conditions and events coincided with the economic expansion arising from Ireland's strategic position within the global economy. Given the scale of the developments outlined here, and the fact that their full implementation and impact has yet to be seen, teasing out the detailed and complex interaction between such local and global factors remains one of the key challenges facing researchers working in this area.

Chapter 8

Modern Ireland, modern media, same old story?

Ciarán McCullagh

Introduction

The last ten years have seen the Irish media develop many of the character-istics that have been noted of the media in other modern societies. These include the increasing concentration of media ownership, the rise of a tabloid press, the relentless promotion of a celebrity culture, an increasingly compe-titive media environment, and a fragmentation of the media audience. These changes in media organisation at a global level have been reflected in the theoretical and empirical concerns of the sociology of the mass media. They have led to the unfreezing of the old binary that had come to mark media sociology. This could be characterised, and to some degree caricatured, as the distinction between the view that the media are all powerful and the view that the audience has considerable capacity to resist their influence.

This binary has been transformed in a number of ways, though the main focus of this chapter will be on how it has altered our understanding of the issues of ownership and control. There is increasing concern in media sociology with combating the idea that the media are servants of the powerful and there is a growing interest in suggesting that the relationship between the media and social power is considerably more intricate than this. It is no longer appropriate, if it ever was, to see media content as reflecting the interests of the powerful. It is now more fruitful to see it as having a complex relationship with the economy, the surrounding culture, the power structure and the experiences of its users.

These changes in how we understand issues of ownership and control will be outlined and then some of the tools of analysis developed below will be applied to the media coverage of immigration in Ireland and the extent to which the media create, reflect or challenge a growing culture of racism.

Media as propaganda for the powerful

One of the central working assumptions of media sociology is that, as John Corner (2003: 370) puts it, the media are 'economically and socially constrained agencies'. But this is, as Corner goes on to argue, not necessarily a 'challenging new insight'. The key issue is whose interests these constraints reflect and what their impact is on media content and media influence.

One particularly important view of the nature of the constraints on the media comes from Edward Herman and Noam Chomsky (2002). They identify five filters through which information must go before it is refined and deemed suitable for entry into the public domain. The first is ownership. The media are basically profit-seeking entities owned by a relatively small number of wealthy people, generally men. Though they compete aggressively for market share they have a certain level of solidarity with each other and with government elites and this generally produces a common view of the world. Thus the material that gets into the media is that which is compatible with this worldview.

The issue of limited ownership is an increasing pertinent one in Ireland. National readership surveys, for example, suggest that over 90 per cent of the adult population reads a newspaper and this level of readership appears to be spread across the population. This looks at first sight like an encouraging figure. But the problem, as the Democracy Commission (Harris 2005) points out, is that almost 80 per cent of newspapers sold in Ireland are published by companies fully or partially owned by Independent Newspapers PLC. This makes it the dominant force in the Irish newspaper industry and one that is increasingly becoming a player on the world media market with significant media interests in Britain, South Africa, Australia, New Zealand, Portugal and Mexico. It also owns the two largest cable television operations in the Republic and has an increasing presence on the internet (Shaw 2005: 61). This has led a number of commentators, including John Horgan (2001: 171), to wonder whether this could be a constraining factor in the diversity of views available in the media. It has also been argued that this kind of concentration of ownership has given management at Independent Newspapers and particularly its owner, Tony O'Reilly, a level of access to and influence over politicians that is not available to the ordinary citizen.

Groups like Indymedia (see www.indymedia.ie) argue that this kind of media concentration allows Independent Newspapers to use its newspapers to attack its commercial and ideological competitors. Two incidents can be used to illustrate these concerns. One is the general election in 1997. In a departure from established practice the *Irish Independent* published its editorial on the front page of the newspaper. It was headed 'Payback Time' and encouraged a vote against the then coalition government. Some critics say that this occurred at a time when the owner of the newspaper group was in conflict with the government over their unwillingness to act against illegal television deflectors, a factor of considerable concern to cable television owners (see Horgan 2001: 170). The other is the dropping of a column in 2005 by a senior *Independent* journalist, Justine McCarthy, on corporate greed. This was written against the background of a dispute in Irish Ferries over the replacement of Irish workers by cheaper foreign labour (Murphy 2005), a move that some saw as a concrete expression of such greed in action. It also coincided with the replacement of their industrial relations correspondent allegedly because of complaints from Irish Ferries over a story he had written – and wished to stand by – about the willingness of the company to use tear gas against its employees. This version of events is, not surprisingly, contested both by Irish Ferries and by Independent Newspapers.

Concern over the effects of the concentration of ownership has been compounded by the current situation of the national broadcaster, RTÉ. It has lost its monopoly position as the only national broadcaster and it now operates in a highly competitive environment. Apart from the competition that it has faced from the ready availability of stations from Britain, it now has to deal with competition from two new national television stations. TV3 is currently owned mainly by international conglomerates – CanWest Global and Granada Television. It has a limited level of news and current affairs and its main menu is the simultaneous broadcast of soap opera and reality television programmes from ITV (Horgan 2001: 183). It has since been joined by Channel 6 owned by Irish business people and with no obligation to broadcast either news or sports. It is aimed at the 15–35 age group and largely shows films and imported drama and comedy from the United States.

The combined effect of the ready availability of competing national and UK commercial stations has placed pressures on RTÉ to 'dumb down' the schedule in an effort to maintain its share of the audience. According to Kinsella (quoted in Harris 2005: 14), 'private interests are re-defining its [RTÉ's] role towards a certain type of programming at the expense of its public service role.' This can be seen in the pressure to 'lighten' the amount of investigative newsgathering and to broaden and dilute what passes as factual programming. Some critics have suggested that reality television and format shows, already a central part of the global media menu, are now 'the name of the game' (Shaw 2005: 63) in Irish television.

The combination of the high level of concentration of ownership in newspapers and the growing power of private corporations to set the environment in which the national broadcaster is forced to operate – and to which it is forced to respond – raises the question of power. Do these changed patterns of ownership give to powerful interests a control over the media agenda and through that a capacity to shape the content of public consciousness? In the view of writers like Herman and Chomsky (2002), the answer is quite clearly in the affirmative.

The second filter is advertising. This makes a major contribution to the profits of the media and it is essential to commercial success that audiences are attracted by the media so that they can in turn be sold to advertisers. But in return for this revenue, advertisers want their products displayed in what Herman (1998: 192) calls a 'supportive selling environment'. This means that the media must walk a careful tightrope between attracting an audience but not entertaining or distracting them to such a degree that they do not pay attention to the advertising breaks that dictate the tempo of the television schedules. In effect, according to this model advertising agencies have effective if not direct control over what gets into the media.

Herman and Chomsky's third filter is the role of sourcing. Journalists and media personnel do not generally witness the events they report on but they depend on 'reliable sources' to provide them with accounts and interpretations of what is going on in the world. This means that the sources that can provide the media with reliable copy will get more prominent coverage. This suits dominant elites. Government spokespeople, for example, are presumed to be credible and when that is tied in with their capacity to provide timely press releases, advance copies of speeches, appropriately staged photo opportunities and controlled access to the powerful, it means they obtain favoured treatment by the media. This allows them to influence which events are seen as important and allows them to dictate how these events will be presented in the media.

One of the areas where the power of sources is evident in Ireland is in the media coverage of crime, much of which is influenced and shaped by the use of unnamed gardaí as sources. They have been able to shape our understanding of many incidents by their capacity to provide the media with information without being identified and without there necessarily being any means available to those named or to their relatives to challenge this. A representative case in point is that of two young Dublin people found dead in a hotel in late August 2006. On 1 September the *Irish Times* reported that the priest at the funeral said '[W]e can't and don't understand what has happened.' But the report went on to say that while the gardaí were not releasing information 'a source said that cocaine was found at the scene', a release of information that implicitly offers an explanation for their deaths. Similarly the way in which unnamed gardaí can, in the wake of murder, tell the media that the victim was 'known to the gardaí' somehow neutralises the impact of the killing. Whether intended to or not the phrase carries with it the notion that when people who are 'known to the gardaí' are killed then they are the kind of people who have a certain familiarity with violence and so are in some way partly responsible for their own deaths and consequently less deserving of our sympathy (see McCullagh 2003).

Finally, for information and interpretation to get into the media it must also be consistent with the fifth and final filter, that of the dominant ideology. In the 1980s this, according to Herman and Chomsky, was anti-communism. It has since been replaced by the frame of the 'inevitability' and 'progressiveness' of globalisation. This has forced non-market or state-directed economic options off the media agenda. Market ideology has now been joined, post 9/11, by the ideology of the war on terror. This has, in its turn, squeezed any informed discussion of radical oppositional politics out of the mainstream media.

These filters have clear similarities to the term *doxa*, used by Pierre Bourdieu (1998b). This refers to the presuppositions that are regarded as self-evident and so outside the field of discussion. They could be regarded as setting clear limits to the terms within which arguments can be conducted and between which the media feel the obligation to be objective and balanced. In the Irish context one of the most prominent of such filters is the 'peace process'. The Minister for Justice proposed in 2004 that it be made an offence for journalists to publish stories that would 'undermine the peace process' (Williams 2004: xvi). The degree to which the creation of such an offence might be necessary is hard to evaluate but even without this legislation it often seems that the media in the Republic are more prominent in protecting the peace process than in commenting objectively on it (see Spencer 2004 for a discussion of the pressures from the media for politicians to conclude the Good Friday Agreement in 1998).

The argument of Herman and Chomsky is that these filters interact with and reinforce each other and this interaction sets limits to the media agenda. They are the means through which the powerful frame news and limit the terms of public debate and discussion. As Klaehn (2002: 152) puts it 'news content is framed so as to (re)produce "privileged" interpretations of the news which are ideologically serviceable to corporate and monied interests'. In effect, according to this model, the media are a propaganda system, with the ability to 'to mobilise an elite consensus, to give the appearance of democratic consent, and to create enough confusion, misunderstanding and apathy in the general population to allow elite programs to go forward' (Herman 1998: 194).

Responding to the propaganda model: manufacturing dissent

While the propaganda model synthesises much of the thinking on the media by critical thinkers in the United States over the last 25 years, it has, according to John Corner (2003: 367) 'very little by way of new theoretical insight . . . to bring to European media research'. He criticises the model on two main grounds. One is the way in which it presents media professionals. They are seen as 'comfortably if numbly functional' (2003: 372), tricked by the socialisation and reward systems in media organisations into being servants of power. Yet this is a view of their role and function with which many journalists have little patience.

They argue that if they are the servants of power then their masters do not particularly appreciate them. Most politicians see journalists if not as the enemy then most appropriately supped with in the much the same way as the devil, with a very long spoon. The relationship between the powerful and the media is not experienced by either group as cosy and mutually supportive but as suspicious and conflictual. In addition it is hard to square the model's view of the relationship with the amounts of money that politicians and powerful groups feel they have to expend on media relations or spin doctoring to control and manage the kind of press coverage that they get.

Arguments like Herman and Chomsky's fail to take into account what Hallin (1987) has called 'the maturing of journalist professionalism'. This is where the commitment to professional values gives journalists autonomy from powerful interests and provides an ideology through which their demands can be resisted. It may be a limited form of resistance but the journalistic imperative to get the other side of the story, even if interpreted in a narrow sense of the term by confining that to other powerful interests, still ensures some space for alternative views.

The only empirical study of journalists in the major newspapers and television stations in Ireland would tend to support the notion that their main value commitment is to the profession. Mary Corcoran (2004) found that in general journalists are somewhat more liberal in political terms than the organisations for which they work and the audiences for whom they write. But this does not encourage or permit them to use their professional work as a channel for the expression of their personal values. 'Once they enter the profession', she argues, 'their partisan beliefs become secondary to their professional orientation' (Corcoran 2004: 40).

The propaganda model is also weak on the role of the audience. Herman and Chomsky are more concerned with the controlled nature of media output than with its effects on audiences. Audiences are simply assumed to be 'brainwashed' by the media (Corner 2003: 373). The problem here is that it is now routinely accepted in media sociology that audiences are not cultural dopes but have complex and nuanced reactions to the media. Sometimes they believe what the media say, sometimes they do not, but the balance between these two responses must be considered against the background of a declining appetite for political news and an increasing loss of confidence and trust in the media (Davis 2003). A lot of the time audiences simply do not care.

While there is in effect a considerable area of agreement in media sociology – most scholars agree that factors like ownership, sourcing, advertising and journalistic professionalism are important factors shaping media output – there is also significant disagreement over the degree to which these control media output and over the degree to which the media are open and accessible to those outside the dominant consensus.

The problem for media sociology may be that its almost obsessive interest in the issue of control has led to a comparative neglect of other features of the news media. Three of these are worthy of mention here. These are the role of tabloids in setting the media agenda, the decline of journalistic deference to the powerful, and the rise of celebrity journalism.

The role of the tabloids

The tabloids are the most neglected area in media sociology. The empirical focus in studies of newspaper coverage tends to be on what used to be termed the broadsheets or the quality press. This is partly because of a mistaken and class-based view that, because of their content and their audience, the tabloids are of limited social and political importance. This assumption is hard to square with the evidence that they may be significant in setting the public agenda on issues like crime and public disorder (see O'Connell 2002). It is hardly consistent with their clear lead in sales figures over the more 'serious' papers. It is also difficult to reconcile with the influence that their style of reporting has had on news broadcasting with the rise of what has been termed 'tabloid TV' – short, snappy and highly visual presentations of news items.

Herman and Chomsky's work epitomises this underestimation of the power of tabloids. They argue for a trickle down version of media power. They see the elite media – in the case of the United States, the *New York Times* and the *Washington Post* – as determining 'what topics, issues and events are to be considered "newsworthy" by the lower-tier media' (Klaehn 2002: 157). But this is questionable as arguably the influence equally goes the other way. Thus the quality press may in many cases follow the agenda of the tabloids in terms of the increasing attention given to celebrities and the amount of space that is absorbed by their follow-ups to tabloid led concerns such as paedophilia and violent crime. Also the tabloids have set a particular premium on the 'exclusive'. What they would regard as an exclusive might not be immediately obvious from or reconcilable with the ostensible politics of their owners. Indeed the tabloids are arguably in the vanguard of what some would see as the key change in media coverage and media orientation, that is, the constant search for the populist angle to issues and controversies, a process that makes them unreliable allies for political elites.

The decline of deference

The decline of deference in the relationship between the media and politicians and power holders has been considered by Clayman (2002). This is most evident in what he terms the rise of 'aggressive journalism'. In a research project with John Heritage (Clayman and Heritage 2002) he shows how there has been an increase in the level of antagonistic questioning of American Presidents from Eisenhower in the 1950s through to Ronald Reagan in the 1980s. The underlying theme of the accountability has become more marked. Increasingly politicians are being asked to explain particular policies and actions, but the assumption behind the questions and behind the way they are asked is that politicians are either trying to hide something or that they have done something wrong.

Journalists now use a number of strategies to get around the norm of interactional politeness and deference to powerful people and to get around the risk of being accused of being biased by asking adversarial questions. The main one they use 'to neutralise and legitimate their aggressive conduct' is 'to align themselves with the public' (Clayman 2002: 216). In asking aggressive questions or questions that might in other circumstances be interpreted as rude they claim to be acting on behalf of the people. They use what is in effect the 'Tribune of the People' stance, presenting themselves as 'relaying the concerns of the populace rather than pursuing a personal agenda' (2002: 210). When questions are posed and justified in these terms it is difficult for interviewees to ignore them. The risk for them is that evading the question can in itself become a news item. This means that political interviews are now 'a formidable instrument of political accountability' (Clayman and Heritage 2002). It has also created the situation in which journalists are effectively 'uncontrollable' (Palmer 2002: 349) and where, from the point of view of journalists, nothing is unsayable.

Some journalists may be uncontrollable but Bourdieu (1998b: 6) says that these are probably limited in number. He argues that the current structure of the journalistic field is one in which there is a small core group of star reporters and columnists – the so-called opinion makers – and 'a vast journalistic sub-proletariat'. These are in the majority. They work in short-term contract positions and are never in sufficiently secure employment to be able to exercise their right to either watchdog or attack journalism. The reality of their economic position means they do not have a basis from which they can adopt an adversarial stance against the powerful.

The rise of celebrity journalism

There has also been another significant development in journalism and that is the rise of celebrity journalism. This is a situation in which a small group of journalists or correspondents becomes better known than the people about whom they are reporting. News analysts have noted the way in which over the passage of time there has been a decline in the amount of time and space given in the media to the ideas, policies and speeches of politicians. They have been replaced by a focus on opinion polls and what has been called 'horse-race journalism', a concern with the impact that policies and behaviour of politicians have on their standing in the polls. This has resulted in a change in the frame through which stories are told and in terms of which candidates' behaviour is interpreted. Increasingly political behaviour is presented through a games schema in which their activities are seen as calculated, manipulative and strategic. Political positions are interpreted as being adopted out of a desire to impress public opinion and increase standing in the polls rather than from intrinsic or ideological conviction.

There was some evidence of this in Clancy and Brannick's analysis of the Irish media coverage of the elections to the European parliament in 2004 (Clancy and Brannick 2004). They found that little coverage was given to policy issues. The main focus of the coverage was on the political strategies of the parties and this was part of a growing trend in the media of an increase in coverage of the 'games' aspect (they suggest 'battle' might be a more appropriate term) of the election to the detriment of policy issues. Only eleven per cent of newspaper articles dealt with a policy issue, most of the remainder focused on conflicts between candidates and these conflicts were framed in terms of personal or strategic differences and never in political or policy terms.

This change has been accompanied by a decline in the presence of politicians in the news. Thomas Patterson (1994) writing about the United States has noted how in 1968 the average soundbite from a politician was 42 seconds. By 1988 it had fallen to ten seconds. So if politicians are going out of the news, by whom are they being replaced? Patterson argues that '[T]he voiceless candidate had become the norm: for every minute that the candidate spoke on the evening news in 1988 and 1992, the journalists who were covering them talked for 6 minutes' (Patterson 1994: 75). In this mode of presentation journalists become more important and are more highlighted in the media than the people on whom they are reporting. They end up being better known than politicians and become celebrities in their own right.

The most obvious Irish example is Charlie Bird, the chief news correspondent on RTÉ. Because of his status he has the journalistic authority to investigate aggressively difficult areas like the defrauding of customers by major banks in Ireland (see Lee and Bird 1998). But he has also appeared on the *Ryan*

Tubridy Show on RTÉ television to discuss his personal life and has had his picture used on the front of the *RTÉ Guide*. This almost inevitably attracted the attention of the tabloid press. He claimed that he was followed around Dublin by photographers hoping to obtain pictures of him luring women into what the *Evening Herald* called 'his love-nest'. In the process he has become more famous and more recognisable than the issues and the people on whom he reports (see McCullagh 2005).

Killing kings?

All of these are factors that need to be considered in any model of media power. The problem here is that their interrelationship is in some flux and this makes it difficult to make definitive statements about the relationship between media and political and social power. There are tendencies and pressures in the media such as concentration of ownership and the growing importance of advertising that would lead to a conservative and controlled media agenda. But equally there are tendencies that would lead in the opposite direction. These include the rise of aggressive journalism, the replacement of deference by suspicion in the relationship to politicians and public figures, and the rising influence of the tabloid press. For some, such as Sabato (1991: 3), this has produced a media that is 'more bent on killing kings rather than on making them'. The important question for future work in media sociology is to investigate the circumstances in which the media manufacture consent and those under which they manufacture dissent.

Two factors will be important in this. One is the role of sources. Herman and Chomsky have argued that the way in which media source stories gives an advantage to those in powerful positions. Journalists working in the political world are considered, in Davis's phrase, as having been 'captured by those they report on' (Davis 2003: 683). But this does not automatically mean the suppression of dissent. It has been argued that dissent does get into the media even if it is only in specific circumstances. These are when the powerful do not speak with a single voice. Hence journalists receive conflicting information from their sources and this results in more open and critical accounts being present in the media. Daniel Hallin (1987) had made this clear in relation to the war in Vietnam and it is a point that could be extended to current wars such as that in Iraq. The media acted as cheerleaders in the early part of the war in Vietnam when there was elite unity over its purpose and its chances of success. But when dissent emerged among the elite over the possibility of victory and over the legitimacy of the justifications for the war then that dissent was reflected in the press. It became possible for the media to legitimate this dissent and to avoid the criticism of being unpatriotic by referring to the status of the dissenting voices.

So it is possible to see the use of sources in a more radical fashion than Herman and Chomsky. Paul Williams (2004), for example, has argued that the use of unnamed garda sources has been essential to the revelations about the extent and depth of organised crime in Ireland. It is an area that the government would prefer to see kept under wraps but the willingness of gardaí to act as anonymous sources for journalist like Williams has made this difficult to achieve. The government's response has been to propose legislation that would make it illegal for gardaí to reveal certain kinds of information and for journalists to accept it (see Williams 2004: xvi–xvii).

The second issue is more complex. We are used to speaking of the media as a mass phenomenon but it may now be more appropriate to differentiate between large circulation media and more niche-oriented ones. Arguably a different dynamic applies to the way in which they both work. Large-scale media like large circulation newspapers are in constant search of the space on which they can connect with the concerns of their audiences and become the means through which the emotions of their audiences can be engaged and expressed. This makes them alert to other media, such as radio talk shows, and to the concerns expressed there, which often provide the major stories for such papers. They are trying to identify and reproduce the concerns of their audience rather than those of powerful elites, and that makes them unreliable defenders of the status quo.

In an age when there has been a decline in support for mainstream parties it no longer makes economic sense for the media to be overly concerned with the sensibilities of political parties. Thus the concern about paedophilia has been carried largely by the popular press in Ireland, it has been framed in a particular way through what might be considered a melodramatic and simplified morality of good and evil, and it has become a force in shaping political responses to the issue. It is a force that politicians may be unhappy with but one that they feel they need to acknowledge.

On the other hand there are niche media such as the so-called quality press and high profile television news programmes. Their function has been characterised by Davis (2003: 673), as 'a communications channel for the regular negotiations and decision-making that take place between different elite groups to the exclusion of the mass of citizens'. It is his argument that a significant amount of media discussion is produced by and aimed as what he terms 'decision-making and power-broking elites'. This niche press is the arena within which they promote their political and economic agendas and, effectively speaking, negotiate with each other. It is this function that explains the continued importance of a newspaper like the *Irish Times* whose numerical circulation is not sufficient to justify its sense of self-importance. It is a question of the limited but affluent social groups among whom it circulates. Purchasing and carrying a copy of the *Irish Times* is as much a statement of social capital as a matter of personal or intellectual taste.

If the media have become fragmented in this way then arguably their audience has too. This makes it difficult to study the impact of the media on them. It is generally accepted that we cannot predict media responses from media content and it is now accepted that the impact of media material is filtered through a range of social factors not least the amount of personal experience individuals have of the issue under media attention (see McCullagh 2002). There are also growing indications of significant differentiation in the media audiences in terms of the level of social literacy encouraged by and acquired from television in particular. There are clear gaps in the degree to which factual information promoted and highlighted in the media – such as the names and function of politicians and the geographical location of conflict zones – is actually 'learned' by audiences. Moreover these gaps tend to follow class, age, gender and educational lines. Those who engage with niche media tend to have the most detailed factual knowledge of political and economic issues; those who engage with mainstream media tend to have least (see McCullagh 2002: 174–5).

Manufacturing racism

The issue of immigration is a useful one through which we can explore some of the issues raised here. Ireland only became a country of net immigration in 1996 (see chapter 2 for further discussion). As Boucher (2004) points out, this is much later than for most other European countries. Yet while we are moving, whether willingly or not, towards a multi-racial and multicultural society concern has grown that this has been accompanied by a rise on racist attitudes and increasing levels of violence against people perceived as migrants. As a number of surveys show, social contact between migrants and 'natives' tends to be limited, with many Irish people saying they do not know any migrants personally (see, for example, Millward Brown 2004), so the issue of the source of racist attitudes immediately raises suspicion about the role of the media in the creation of these attitudes.

Guerin (2002: 92) for example argues that 'the media in Ireland has been complicit . . . in creating a context within which racism can flourish and where an anti-immigrant agenda is enabled'. He supports this by reference to a number of studies of Irish newspapers and to the ways in which the papers draw on the 'flood' metaphor to describe the arrival of immigrants in Ireland, the way they focus on the criminal behaviour of some of these immigrants, the emphasis they place on the claim that most asylum seekers are 'bogus' and the creation of a perception that such people are 'spongers' and 'scroungers'. These frames, Guerin argues, set the context within which issues of migration policy are presented and discussed. They set what he calls the 'legitimate parameters of debate on racism'.

This is an analysis which fits very much within the perspective outlined by Herman and Chomsky. The media set the limits for debate in society and these limits are in turn set by the discourse of political parties and other official agencies. Thus media reporting on immigration reproduced in a largely unquestioning manner the pronouncements of politicians and the 'uncorroborated statements by Gardaí and Department of Justice spokespeople' (Guerin 2002: 91). Michael Breen and his colleagues (Breen et al. 2006) make much the same point in their analysis of the media coverage of the constitutional referendum on citizenship held in 2004. They point to the prevalence in media coverage of terms such as 'loophole', 'abuse', 'exploitation' and 'asylum'. These were the predominant frames within which media coverage was organised. This framing was supported by the direct and unexamined use of quotations from statements of politicians in the Dáil. The media seldom pointed out that the information and the assumptions in many of these statements were wrong. The issue of so-called 'maternity tourism' is a case in point. The notion that Irish maternity hospitals were being 'overrun' by pregnant immigrant women was promoted by the Minister for Justice as a reason for the referendum but the claim itself was, according to some, exaggerated and to others it was simply wrong. Yet newspaper reports which recorded the Minister's statements seldom indicated that these had been challenged. 'Politicians', Breen and his colleagues tell us (2006: 67), 'are privileged sources with direct access to the mass media by the simple mechanism of speaking in the Dáil'. This gives them a central role in setting media interpretations and through that in shaping public perceptions of and attitudes to immigrants.

All black and white?

This is not to suggest that the media are overwhelmingly negative in their coverage. There are many examples of articles in the media questioning government policy and criticising the spread of racist attitudes and ideologies. Even newspapers in the Independent Group, often accused of stirring up racial discontent, have carried articles that were more measured and impartial in their consideration of these issues. Similarly Breen et al. (2006) found that both the *Irish Times* and the *Sunday Tribune* were fair and balanced in their editorials on the citizenship referendum. But this is not seen as sufficient to outweigh the negative frames within which the issue was reported. As Watt (quoted in Guerin 2002: 95) put it, 'the cumulative effect of many headlines can serve to neutralise the balanced and objective reporting that can sometimes appear in the same articles elsewhere in the same newspaper'.

This work thus makes an important argument for the role of the media in shaping public perceptions about race and migration. But there are a number of important limitations in this analysis, similar to those that critics claim to find in the work of Herman and Chomsky (2002). These include the assumptions that are made about audiences, the neglect of television representations particularly those in television drama, and the extent of the space that there is in the media to challenge racist framings. No research work is currently available in Ireland which examines the impact of this kind of coverage on audiences and on their attitudes. It is simply assumed that media coverage must be a powerful force in shaping these. Yet while this kind of analysis may be useful in explaining the attitudes that are uncovered in large-scale surveys, it does not seem adequate to explain situations where communities have organised to prevent particular deportations of migrants. And while we do not know the impact of the predominant framings on audiences we similarly do not know the impact of the terms within which the opposition to racism is couched. The major motif here has been the demand that we consider our own experiences of emigration and discrimination and apply some of the lessons to our current situation. This is a way of framing the opposition to racism that may have considerable cultural resonance in a society in which many families have first-hand knowledge of the realities of forced emigration.

Another factor with significant cultural resonance and one that can produce somewhat contradictory media coverage is our concept of the ideal victim or of the victim that we see as deserving compassion. In theory in a world that is increasingly without borders there should be no limits, either social or geographic, on who qualifies as a victim worthy of our sympathy and help. In practice there is. Some victims, as Hoijer (2004: 517) puts it, 'are perceived to deserve our empathy better than others'. These are generally children, women and elderly people. They are 'seen as helpless in a violent situation and therefore they are more suitable than males in their prime' (Hoijer 2004: 517). Men by contrast are neither innocent nor helpless enough to be deserving of our sympathy.

This notion has been applied to media coverage of natural disasters such as famine, flooding and earthquakes but never to the migrants to developed countries. Yet these may well be the kind of immigrants who end up with more positive coverage from the media. So while women were caricatured by the media 'maternity tourists' it is also significant that a number of the campaigns that have been organised in local communities and aided by local and national media with positive coverage have all involved women or children threatened with deportation. There have been no comparable successful campaigns on behalf of men.

The final shortcoming in this work is the emphasis on the print media and the comparative neglect of television and its coverage of the issue. This is partly explained by the lack of ready access to television archives compared to newspaper ones but the cost is a series of studies that use a limited medium –

newspapers – as the major source for large-scale statements about racism. There is a further issue here and that is the neglect of the impact of the representations of race and racism in popular television dramas and most notably in soap operas such as *Fair City*. This has introduced a more diverse range of characters to reflect the growing diversity of the society in which its viewers live and it has used story lines about racism, racial attacks and inter-racial relationships that could be considered to be broadly liberal in orientation. While we cannot be sure about their influence on audiences they must be taken into account in any comprehensive study of the media impact on racism, if only because such programmes reach an audience that is a lot more representative of the wider society than that reached by the print media and especially by the self-styled quality broadsheets.

Conclusion

This chapter has examined a number of questions of contemporary concern in the sociology of the mass media and it has looked at how these issues are pertinent to the media coverage of immigration in Ireland. The underlying assumption in this work, and indeed the reason why the media is of interest to sociologists, is the belief that it is the most important social institution for the creation and circulation of reliable and accurate social and political knowledge in society. Yet, ironically of all the statements in this chapter, it is possible to argue that this is the least securely based. As the media diversify in content but become more restricted in ownership, as their relationship to power becomes more contested and as celebrity journalism continues its apparently inexorable rise, there has also been a slow, steady but significant decline in the level of public trust in media output.

The effects of changes in the social and political landscape appear to be a decline in belief in governments and in politicians but also and significantly a decline in trust in the media that report on them. This is an issue that is not being sufficiently addressed in discussions of the media. Increasingly the focus is on technological developments that will, or so the industry claims, fun-damentally alter our experiences of the mass media and in particular of television. These developments come in many shapes and sizes but can refer, for example, to whether we will be accessing television through satellite, computer or mobile phones or whether we are receiving a digital picture on a plasma screen or not.

Quite what effects these changes will have remain unclear. It could be argued that many of these developments are technologies of individualism and so will encourage and facilitate social isolation by the nature of the media reception that they encourage. Watching television on a mobile phone does not, despite advertising to the contrary, necessarily open opportunities for collective social interaction. Moreover this perspective tends to emphasise the nature of the technology at the expense of a consideration of the content that the technology will be carrying. You may now be watching the news on your mobile phone, but the material has been generated through the same processes as the version that you can see on a conventional television screen.

Thus what is perhaps the most pressing question about the media is being ignored in many contemporary debates. The concern is overwhelmingly with the mode through which we receive information and less with what the media tell us and with whether we believe it or not. In the era of declining trust in public institutions the media have become one of its most significant victims. The reason the powerful may no longer have to worry about the media is the strain of cynicism and indifference that has become the defining characteristic of the modern media audience.

Chapter 9

A question of sport

Katie Liston

Introduction

A decade ago, a Department of Education report on sport in the Republic of Ireland noted that 'Irish people love their sport and either play or follow a wide range of sporting activities'. According to the authors, 'the value of participation in sport and active leisure pursuits in the physical, psychological and social development of individuals [was] *well documented* and *accepted*' (Department of Education 1997: iii, emphases added). In that same year, Taoiseach Bertie Ahern reinforced the perceived social value of sport in his speech announcing the creation of the Department of Tourism, Sport and Recreation (now the Department of Arts, Sport and Tourism):

> I feel strongly that sport has the same importance for national well-being as, for example, arts and culture. Along with the issues we raised in the broader area of sport and recreation, they have the related advantage of helping the disadvantaged and less well off in our society achieve personal betterment, about which I feel strongly.

It is surprising then, given sport's position of importance in public policy, the popularity of individual and team sports as well as the related (if not exalted) public profile of some elite Irish sportspeople, that the sociological study of sport on the island of Ireland is in its infancy. In comparison with other sub-disciplines of sociology, sociologists in Ireland have yet to cast a concerted critical eye towards sports and their social significance. Of the limited sociological research that has been published in this area in the past decade, much is dominated by a focus on sport and the complex relationship between sport and expressions of nationalism in Northern Ireland (see, for example, Bairner 2002, 2003; Fulton 2005; Hassan 2005; Magee 2005). Apart from this Northern Irish focus, other sociologists (Liston 2005a, 2005b, 2006a, 2006b; Liston and Rush 2006; Maguire and Tuck 2005; Kelly and Waddington 2007) have examined the relationship between sport and gender, rugby union and national identity from a predominantly national perspective, and managerial control in professional soccer from an inter-national perspective.

The absence of a concerted sociological commentary on sport in Ireland is notable when we consider some of the wider developments that have occurred in the organisation of sports in the Republic of Ireland in the past ten years including: changes in the statutory provision for sports; the establishment of the Irish Sports Council; the increasing participation of females in formerly male-dominated sports; the shift towards participation in an increasing variety of lifestyle activities; the establishment of the new Irish Institute for Sport; the de-amateurisation of some sports; the influx of ethnically diverse immigrants who play or follow sports not hitherto associated with Ireland; and the increasing commercialisation of others. The statutory changes in the field of sport (such as the organisational power of the Irish Sports Council and the introduction of a national anti-doping framework in sport) have gone along with the publication, by the government and the ESRI, of some descriptive social research on sport at the national level. There have been surveys of sports participation and lifestyles, investigations of the economic and social value of sport in Ireland and commentaries on the relationship between sport and health. There have also been some examinations of children's participation in PE, extra-curricular activities and club- and community-based sports.

Given this current state of knowledge, in this chapter I shall seek to question the ways in which sport is usually approached and understood by bringing to light some dimensions that are often hidden – or ignored by – moral, philosophical or ideological approaches to sport. It is suggested that much of the existing knowledge on sport in Ireland is driven by the unques-tioned and fantasy-laden idea that sport is intrinsically, invariably, unequivo-cally, always and inevitably – for everyone, for individuals and for society – a beneficial thing. I shall, for short, refer to this uncritically accepted idea as the 'sport is good' assumption. In attempting to reflect more deeply on the ways in which we approach sport in Ireland, I explore some of the international theoretical developments in the sub-discipline of sociology that have come to be known as the sociology of sport, and secondly, I examine how some of these developments relate to sport in Ireland and how it is understood.[1] I shall endeavour to adopt the role of the sociologist as the 'destroyer of myths' (Elias 1978a) and, more specifically, to reflect upon the idea that sport is unequivo-cally 'good'. This chapter can be viewed, then, as an attempt to contribute to the nascent sociology of sport in Ireland. It is also predicated on the assump-tion that the full significance of sport lies, not in its prevalence or its economic value (both of which views represent reductionist models of sociological enquiry), but in the manner in which key meanings about identity, ways of living and social norms are imparted through the field of sport.

The sociological study of 'sport in society'

The sub-discipline of sociology known as the sociology of sport emerged in the 1960s and, according to Coakley and Dunning (2000: xxi), 'among the sub-disciplines concerned with the study of sport as a social phenomenon, the sociology of sport was the first to emerge in an institutionalised form'. Research in the sociology of sport has expanded considerably since the 1960s and the sociological lens has been focused in a systematic way on a widening range of social issues in the field of sport including: pain and injury in sport (see, for example, Loland et al. 2006); the sociogenesis of modern sports and, related to this, processes of state-formation and civilisation (see, for example, Dunning 1999; Dunning and Sheard 2004); sport and gender (see, for example, Scraton and Flintoff 2002); national identity (Allison 2000); sport and globalisation (Maguire 1999); sport and health (Waddington 2000); sport and disability (Nixon II 2000), sport and the media (see, for example, Whannel 2000) and sporting bodies (see, for example, Cole 2000).

This widening of the sociological field of vision internationally has not been matched in Ireland, where the sociology of sport as a scientific discipline in the broadest sense is in its infancy. Indeed, Irish sociologists have argued that the discipline of sociology in Ireland has been largely characterised by the absence or underdevelopment of a democratic objective that sets out 'to inform public consciousness' (Calhoun 1996: 429, in Tovey and Share 2003: 41), and others have pointed to the limits of positivistic and problem-solving approaches adopted by sociologists. It is not possible here to examine in detail the reasons for this absence of sociological research on sport and leisure in Ireland. However, we can address this absence indirectly by examining some of the international theoretical developments in the sociology of sport and the ways in which these developments have been shaped, in part, by changing approaches to sport. Two significant features of the theoretical developments in the sociology of sport have been: (i) the desire to demonstrate that sport is a serious topic worthy of social inquiry which requires, in Dunning's (1999: 12) words, 'an analysis of how sport is organically embedded in social life'; and (ii) the need to develop a more adequate sociological approach to sport that moves beyond the assumption that sport is necessarily good.

According to Coakley and Dunning (2000), there are seven major theoretical perspectives in the sociology of sport: functionalism, including structural- and neo-functionalism; Marxist and neo-Marxist theories; cultural studies; feminist theories; interpretative approaches; figurational sociology; and post-structuralist and postmodernist perspectives. A brief sketch follows, contrasting the main themes emanating from functionalism and figurational sociology, which help to reveal the changing approaches to sport by sociologists, and the ways in which these approaches offer us the opportunity to reflect more deeply upon how we think about sport in Ireland. Functionalism was internationally the dominant theoretical school in sociology at large during the two decades following the Second World War, and although it has long since been discredited as an *explicit* theoretical orientation in sociology in general, I shall argue that *implicitly* functionalist assumptions have provided the normative basis of much of the empirical research in sport in Ireland over the past decade or so – and indeed they underlie much factual survey research on many other topics and in many other countries. Of the several schools that could provide a contrast with this implicit functionalism, I choose to focus on 'figurational sociology' – the name often applied to the work of sociologists influenced by Norbert Elias (1897–1900) – because of the pioneering work specifically on the sociology of sport which Elias and his colleague Eric Dunning carried out from the 1960s onwards (Elias and Dunning, 1986; Dunning, 1999). Figurational sociologists have striven to achieve a less normative and more reality-based approach to sport.

This brief theoretical sketch will then be used as the basis for a brief overview of the field of sport in Ireland, and to show some of the ways in which, using sociological ideas, we can raise what are often hidden issues relating to sport for consideration by the public in general.

Theoretical developments in the sociology of sport

Prior to the 1980s, international research in the sociology of sport was dominated by what we might call an empiricist and structural-functionalist model. Functionalists such as Loy and Booth (2000) argued that the key feature of society was the order and relative stability of society as a unified system. Functionalists therefore point to the need to consider sport as one part of this social system and to examine the relationships between sport and other social institutions, such as politics. The functions of modern sport identified by them include integration, socialisation, socio-emotional stability and social mobility. Functionalists have also examined the particular dynamics of sports groups such as sports teams and clubs. Leadership behaviour and the role of task leaders and socio-emotional leaders in sport teams are important themes in their work.

Although this approach contributed to the generation of sports-related data that were previously unavailable, it has also been heavily criticised because it was 'influenced by the notion that societies are most accurately conceptualised as "social systems", possessing "needs" and "goals" and delimited by clear-cut, impermeably and easily determinable boundaries' (Coakley and Dunning 2000: xxviii). Moreover, because of the focus upon social consensus, many of the functionalist sociological approaches to sport have been highly normative; an example is the idea that sport is unequivocally 'good for society' because it fulfils various positive functions, including the development of moral character at the individual and national levels, providing a safe release of aggression and social conflict, and promoting local, regional and international harmony. Since the 1980s, functionalist and neo-functionalist approaches have also been heavily criticised in academic circles for their 'process-reducing assumptions' (Coakley and Dunning 2000: xxix), that is, for reducing complex social processes to more or less determined outcomes, and for being either non-scientific or too scientific. By this, it is meant that functionalist-informed empirical work on a variety of issues – see, for example, Loy et al.'s (1978) work on sports teams as social systems or Karnilowicz's (1982) analysis of the integrative effects of ceremonial occasions like the Super Bowl – is characterised by teleological and tautological conclusions which are often ideologically driven.[2] Functionalist work is also criticised for its overriding concern with problems of consensus.

In response to these criticisms and other exogenous factors, a widening variety of theoretical approaches in the sociology of sport have emerged. Coakley and Dunning (2000: xxviii) suggest that, at the beginning of the twenty-first century, sports sociologists are more likely to acknowledge that the balance and tension between continuity and change in social life, and therefore in sport, have been shifting in favour of the latter so that more recent sociological theories have approached sport as a more dynamic social phenomenon. As a result, more sophisticated and critical theoretical models have emerged which have at their core the desire to understand how modern sports are situated at the centre of social changes and the ways in which modern sports play a key role in social change. For example, we might say that the extension of the range of Olympic sports to include softball, aquatics (including synchronised swimming) and baseball reflects, in part, the pace and dynamics of change in modern societies. At the same time, however, modern sports also reflect, and play a role in promoting, the increasing ossification of some social norms and social patterns. For instance, the continuing class-specific participation in some sports such as polo, golf and rugby union demonstrate that involvement in sport can exacerbate rather than dissolve social class boundaries. This also challenges the functionalist claim that sport fulfils an unambiguously integrative role for socially excluded groups or that sport has an integrative potential in and of itself. For this reason – the desire to capture more adequately the balance between continuity and change in society and in sport – since the 1980s, sociologists of sport have sought to develop more sophisticated theoretical models that utilise a more reality-congruent approach to understanding sport. In other words, sociologists have sought to reduce the impact of ideology on our understanding of sport. They have sought to separate the notion that there is, or has to be, any necessary correspondence between our own wishes and hopes for sport from empirical observations about what sport is in reality.

The emergence of a critical tradition in the sociology of sport

As a result of the desire to understand the tension balance between social change and continuity in sports participation throughout the world, there is a high level of theoretical diversity in the discipline of the sociology of sport today. Currently, many of the discussions in this field are dominated by a debate between what we might call *social* theorists (including the theoretical perspectives of Marxists, feminists, cultural studies writers and post-structuralists) and *sociological* theorists (including figurational or process sociologists for example). In a nutshell, the former advocate the need for action in sociological research because they believe that, given particular interventions, sport can (and should) 'provide some resources of hope' (Jarvie 2006: 385). *Social* theorists seek particular interventions through their research with a view to bringing about an improvement in people's social conditions. *Sociological* theorists, in contrast, argue that, the desirability of social objectives notwithstanding, the normative commitments of sociologists and their related desire for social intervention do not necessarily advance our understanding of sport. In some cases, these commitments can impact negatively upon the adequacy of our understanding of social issues, and the interventions that follow can sometimes have an adverse effect because of this.

One figurational sociologist, Ivan Waddington (2000), has sought to demonstrate this point in his work on approaches to doping in sport. He argues that the issue of doping in sport can be exacerbated further when the desire for an immediate intervention in doping and drug use (such as that reflected in the implementation of a national drug testing programme) can override a more adequate understanding of the historical roots of the 'problem'. Evidence points to the use by athletes of substances to improve sporting performance since ancient Greek times; in other words, drug use is not just a modern 'problem'. Moreover, athletes (particularly at the elite levels) have long sought to improve their performances in various ways because of the increasing competitiveness of sport. In other words, drug use is not an individual 'problem' *per se*. Rather, the actions of athletes can best be understood when we view their behaviour in the context amongst other things of the increasing social expectations placed upon them to succeed. According to Waddington, short-term solutions like the imposition of testing for prohibited substances often unintentionally obfuscates the issue further, because the use of performance-enhancing substances by elite (and increasingly, some non-elite) athletes has been displaced 'behind the scenes' by the very imposition of prohibited lists and various drug-testing measures designed to alleviate the 'problem'.

Another example of the often contentious debate about the role of ideology in understanding sport can be seen in the ways in which some people have argued that the establishment of 'sport in the community' schemes is a panacea for the social ills in society. In other words, sport is, and can be, a prescriptive treatment for the problems associated with crime, deviance and youth delinquency (see, for example, the [British] Central Council of Physical Recreation [CCPR], 2002). However, much of the more adequate empirical research on this type of scheme (in countries other than Ireland) indicates a more complex picture. First, many of the schemes relating to the use of football programmes, street cricket programmes or even initiatives to involve more women in sport preach to the converted, in the sense that participants are either self-selected or predisposed to becoming involved, thereby often excluding those socially segregated populations for whom the schemes were actually intended. Secondly, because evaluations of schemes – such as those that target youth disaffection, for example – are generally conducted over a short period of time, there is little or no evidence to suggest that participation in them contributes to a meaningful and longer-lasting change in the delinquent lifestyles of youths, their levels of self-esteem and their social conscience. Furthermore, delinquent activities may be displaced during participation in these schemes, but we know little about the lives of participants outside this time.

There are also other examples of the problems arising from the assumption that sport has curative properties. In the American context concerns have been raised about the adequacy of Title IX legislation which was introduced in the 1970s as a positive discriminatory mechanism to increase the funding for, and numbers of, female participants in high school and college sports. Whilst there has been a quantitative increase in female participation since then, at the same time we have also seen the unintended disproportionate creation of opportunities for males to be employed as coaches and managers of female athletes by virtue of the organisational requirements for supporting these increasing numbers of female athletes. Here we can see that the ideological desire to address gender differences in high school and college sports in the USA has led, unintentionally, to the exaggeration of this discrimination in other ways.

This debate – the balance between involvement in social life and detachment from it for the purposes of generating a greater understanding of the problem at hand (Elias 2007) – provides the backdrop for the remainder of this discussion, in which I focus attention on the relationship between sport and health in Ireland as defined in two senses. In its broadest sense, the sport–health relationship includes the perceived role of sport in the 'health of the nation'. In its narrowest sense it focuses on the role of sport in levels of physiological well being such as heart rate, weight and maximal oxygen capacities.

The debate outlined above also sets the stage for our examination of some of the more recent changes that have occurred in sport in Ireland, most notably a suggested increase in the participation of people in sports and physical activities. It enables us to examine the ways in which participation in sport in Ireland is usually understood, uncritically and rhetorically, as having positive benefits for sports participants and the nation as a whole. These benefits might include at the individual level the positive outcomes of sports participation for individual self-esteem and improved physiological and mental health. The benefits of sports participation for the wider society might include assisting with problems of obesity, 'couch potatoes' and social exclusion.

First, I outline the current state of knowledge about participation in sports and physical activities in Ireland; secondly, I seek to challenge the ways in which this participation is usually approached; and, thirdly, arising from this, I bring to the surface some hidden dimensions of sport which are not always immediately obvious to us. These dimensions are generally hidden from view because of the levels of emotional attachment to sport in Ireland and to the idea that sport is unreservedly a good thing.

Participation in sports and physical activities in Ireland

Despite the relative dearth of longitudinal research on participation in sport and physical activities in Ireland, most commentators suggest that participation is increasing. Evidence for this claim tends to be drawn from national participation surveys of adults and children conducted over the past ten years or so. For example, in 1996 research by the Department of Education and the Health Promotion Unit found that 77 per cent of men and 71 per cent of women participated in sports and physical activities.[3] As expected, the overall activity rate decreased as the age of participants increased. Just over half (51 per cent) of 55–75 year olds participated in some form of physical activity (though not necessarily 'sport'). While only a slight sex difference was evident in overall rates of participation, there were more apparent differences in the motivations for participation and the popularity of activities by sex. Thirty-eight per cent of the 1996 sample of 2,000 females cited walking as their most popular activity, followed by swimming and aerobics. In contrast, a sample of males cited soccer as their most popular activity, followed by walking and golf. While walking and swimming were equally popular at that time with both males and females, there were also relatively clear differences in the popularity of activities such as dancing for females and snooker and Gaelic football for males. Indeed, more recent national surveys (some of which are outlined next) seem to indicate that these inter-sex differences in the popularity of activities have remained relatively constant, despite some changes within the sex groups in their participation in sports and activities.[4]

Figure 9.1 **Gaelic football**

The National Health and Lifestyles Survey (Department of Health and Children and Health Promotion Unit 1999) examined patterns of physical activity and found that 42 per cent of a national sample of adults engaged in some form of physical activity on average three times per week. Twenty-four per cent reported doing mild forms of physical activity up to four times a week, while 31 per cent did moderate forms of activity up to three times per week. Only nine per cent reported doing strenuous exercise three times weekly. As in the findings of the previous national survey, it was apparent that activity levels decreased with increasing age. The 1999 study also examined children's activity levels and found that 53 per cent of a sample of children exercised four or more times each week, while six per cent exercised less than weekly. In addition to health concerns about lower levels of activity by Irish adults and children relative to European standards, the 1999 report also identified significant sex differences in children's activity levels. Sixty-two per cent of boys exercised four or more times weekly while only 45 per cent of a sample of girls participated in similar levels of exercise. Significantly, only 26 per cent of 15–17 year old girls exercised four or more times each week. In addition, 13 per cent of this age group did not participate in any form of physical activity.

The latest national surveys in 2003 and 2004, entitled the *National Health and Lifestyles Survey* and *Sports Participation and Health among Adults in Ireland* respectively, show little substantial change in levels of physical activity among Irish men and women. In the 2003 report, just over half of a sample of adults (51 per cent) reported some form of activity. Marked differences remained in levels, types and rates of participation in sports and physical activity by sex, and men were much more likely to be strenuously active than women.[5] According to this survey, the numbers of people reporting no physical activity at all had increased among both males (from 21 to 30 per cent) and females (from 20 to 25 per cent). This concern with rising levels of inactivity for adults and children was echoed most recently in the 2004 survey in which it was found that 'about 22 per cent of adults in Ireland are completely inactive in sport or recreational walking' (ESRI 2004: ii). The effects of particular social dynamics such as social class were also identified here as were the enduring popularity of golf, soccer, Gaelic games and swimming for men. By way of contrast, swimming and aerobics remain the most popular physical activities for adult women.

From this research on participation levels in sports and physical activities in Ireland, social commentators have drawn a number of general conclusions about the social desirability and popularity of sports participation, most of which resonate with the fantasy-laden assumption that participation in sport is always and necessarily good in itself. Thus, for example, in 2004 the ESRI argued that 'those who participate in sports are healthier on average, even within age groups, than those who don't' (2004: iv). In the case of children's health, the fact that one in five second-level children were either obese or overweight (ESRI 2005b) was also a cause for concern; and the relatively inconsistent delivery of 'quality' PE to children, in lessons and extra-curricular PE, is another issue which seemingly compounds this problem. Here we can see that, certainly, sport was perceived simply as 'good'.

Besides the concerns raised here about physiological health and the suggested poorer rates of physical activity in Ireland, we might also identify some broader patterns in these surveys which are even more important to us in sociological terms.

Figure 9.2 **Women doing aerobics**

Whilst participation in competitive team sports seems to have remained relatively constant over the past decade (with the exception, perhaps, of the increase in participation in ladies' Gaelic football over the past five years or so), there seems to be an increasing diversity in the kinds of activities in which people participate. For example, we know from these surveys that people are becoming increasingly involved in recreational walking, including hill walking, and a national survey has been commissioned to examine this in greater detail. We also know that the shift towards 'lifestyle' activities for adults is matched, to a greater or lesser degree, by the increasing diversity in young people's participation in sports and leisure activities. Indeed, the provision of choice for some young people in curricular and extra-curricular PE is one extension of this. We might say, therefore, that there seems to be some evidence to

suggest a shift towards, but not in favour of, young people's and adults' participation in 'lifestyle' activities and not just sports *per se*. However, at the same
time there is a body of evidence which suggests that the popularity of competitive team games in Ireland has persisted over time. Part of this dominance is
reflected, for example, in the ways in which some team sports are regarded as
more or less appropriate for the sexes. The continued provision of significant
amounts of government funding for team games is also a reflection of the solid-
ification of the dominance of competitive team games in the national psyche.

Figure 9.3 **Croke Park**

The role of sociology, then, is to consider this evidence and approach it
from a less fantasy-laden position. As part of this approach, we might consider
the ways in which we might dissolve some of the myths associated with sport
and health. Given the evidence outlined here, can we say for example that
sport is, in the words of some commentators, a 'level playing field' – that is,
that it offers equal opportunities to all, or that it has a levelling effect on social
inequalities? And can we argue, prescriptively, that sport is indeed good for the
nation and good for individual people? In seeking to advance our knowledge
in this area, it is necessary to adopt a less involved and more detached approach
to the issues at hand. In other words, it is necessary to consider the ways in
which the uncritical approach to sport and physical activities has imposed
some limits to our understanding of the often complex and unintended
outcomes of sports participation.

'Sport is good' – Or is it?

The idea that 'sport is good' is a leitmotif in our approach to sport in Ireland as elsewhere. While this theme has longer-term origins that I cannot address here, of particular relevance are a number of the contemporary dimensions of this, the first being the assumption that sport can, and does, promote personal development and well being at the individual level and social integration at the national level. In other words, there are contemporary manifestations of the sport–health relationship in its broader and narrower senses. I have dealt with personal development for individuals to some extent earlier in the context of 'sport in the community schemes'. In this section, I focus on social integration as one desirable consequence, and function, of sports participation for the nation's health, in its broader sense. The Taoiseach's statement in 1997 is one example of this assumption, as is the following excerpt from a 2004 report on sport, which arose, according to its authors,

> against the background of considerable international interest in *the social role of sport*, particularly in regard to the generation of 'social capital', that is, the practices and conventions that promote social contact between people, enhance interpersonal trust, and support the shared acceptance of norms and values in society (ESRI 2004: i; emphasis added).[6]

The normative approach taken in these excerpts to the social value of volunteering in sport and to the forms of positive socialisation connected with participation in sport raise a number of sociological dilemmas. Not least of these is the contradiction between what are empirically verified observations about the tendency to generalise (for emotional and scientific reasons) from the 'positive' few to the whole, and research which demonstrates the co-existence and reproduction of social integration *and* disintegration through sport. One example of the tendency to focus wilfully only on the 'positive' effects of sport is seen in research which indicates that, today, 'approximately 400,000 adults, 15 per cent of the adult population, volunteer for sport in some way during the course of the sporting year in Ireland' (ESRI 2005a: ii), while 'amongst men 60 per cent and amongst women, 51 per cent [of the research sample] considered that making new friends and acquaintances was an important benefit they obtained from sport' (ESRI 2005a: iii).

It is not sociologically surprising that sport is assumed to promote the social acceptance of shared values and social integration through activities such as volunteering, precisely because it is widely believed that sport has some intrinsic worth. Nevertheless, while we have a greater understanding – in quantitative terms at least – of the numbers of people involved in sports as volunteers, participants, members of sports clubs and so on, this cannot be taken to mean that these activities *promote* social integration and low-level relationship building *per se* (assuming, of course, that there are clearly identifiable levels of relationship building that can be measured in some way). In taking a more detached approach to this, we might consider some other possibilities:

1   whether other social factors (for example, improvements in infrastructure or urbanisation being only two other factors) may have contributed, either intentionally or unintentionally, to relationship-building between people. In other words, the tendency to identify sport as the sole causal factor in relationship-building ignores the complex interconnections between sport and society and the ways in which social change in sport (as in society) is not captured adequately by a cause–effect model; and,

2   the ways in which relationships between people involved in sport might actually have integrating and disintegrating effects at one and the same time. Indeed, these co-occurring developments might be regarded as being two sides of the same coin.

An obvious example of the co-existence of relationship-building and disintegration is the generation and persistence of sporting rivalries for participants and spectators alike, and the ways in which sporting rivalries at the local, regional and national levels have long persisted over time, some of which have been characterised by social conflict. Other cases of longer lasting social disintegration (or social exclusion at the very least) include the perpetuation of class differences in participation in sport. This has particular implications for the supposed integrative potential of sport and its perceived role in national well being in its broadest sense. Thus, a more adequate statement might be to say that involvement in sport can extend social networks in various directions, not all of which are 'positive' or integrative *per se*. Sociologists might also ask whether, in seeking to understand *if, why* and *how* participation in sport does indeed foster and constrain relationship-building in some way, a focus on what happens in sport alone is but 'the tip of the sociological iceberg'. Thus, we also need to consider the ways in which human beings are always and inevitably intertwined in complex networks 'beyond' sport; and this has obvious implications for the assumed potential of sport as a causal mechanism for integration, and the ways in which we might actually assess this.

If we were to take Coakley and Dunning's (2000: xxviii) advice literally, then a more adequate sociological approach might try to take account of these networks in which sports people are enmeshed. Given that sportspeople's experiences are but one aspect of these networks, the boundaries of sociological enquiry would focus on the ways in which the choices of sportspeople are not just a function of rational choice or free will, but are also the unplanned product 'of the interaction over time of pluralities of conscious, interdependent, differentially powerful, emotional as well as rational "embodied" human beings who make choices'. Thus, in an Irish context we might consider the possibility that volunteering in sport also has unintended and unforeseen consequences for individual people and groups of people such as: constraints on other social activities, social networks and dimensions of their lives which they themselves might not recognise; the reinforcement of a competitive ethos in sport which can have negative consequences for some people's self-images; the reproduction of some gender inequalities in sport, particularly those sports that are televised; increasing contact between adults and young people in sport which, in some contexts, has led to cases of physical, emotional, psychological and sexual abuse of varying degrees;[7] and the reinforcement of the exclusive class patterns of participation in various sports. In short, the involvement of people as sports volunteers could have a number of unforeseen consequences, whose impact can only be brought to the surface when viewed from a more detached and less ideological perspective.

A second dimension of the 'sport is good' rhetoric is the reproduction of the ideology of 'healthism' (in the physiological sense) in sport and in the wider Irish society. Though sport and leisure have been the subject and focus of regular social commentary in Ireland, few proponents of sport or sociologists of sport in the country have to any great degree questioned the idea that 'sport is good for you'. For example, government departments (see, Department of Education and the Health Promotion Unit 1996; Department of Health and Children and the Health Promotion Unit 1999, 2003) and the ESRI (2004) have suggested, in differing ways but along similar ideological lines, that an increase in adults' and young people's participation in sports and physical activities is 'good for the nation's health' because 'those who participate in sport are healthier on average, even within age groups, than those who do not. This is true for both physical and mental health' (ESRI 2004: 54). The ideology of healthism is also evident, for example, in bio-medical research and social commentaries on the supposed effects of sports participation as a cure for obesity, assuming that obesity can be understood (using the causation model) as the result of over-eating particular foods and low levels of inactivity (see *Irish Times*, 19 April 2006; 27 June 2006; 7 July 2006). Interestingly, the ESRI report also identifies 'that the lifestyle effects of sports [such as smoking and drinking] are not entirely positive' (2004: 54) – that is, that they seem to generate some undesirable side effects.[8] However, the origins of these effects – that is, their roots in wider social patterns – are not examined to any great degree. Nor are their consequences for sports participants or spectators examined in any detail.[9] Put more simply, smoking and drinking seem to be regarded as a *necessary* by-product of participation in sport, thereby reaffirming the notion that sport is 'good' even as its by-products are 'bad'.

International research does not suggest that sports *per se* are beneficial for health, but rather that particular forms, amounts and intensities are so;[10] and the tendency in Ireland as elsewhere to conflate the differential activities that are sports, leisure, exercise, play and games into one universal social phenomenon – sport – also obfuscates our understanding of the sport–health relationship further. In particular, it generates problems for evaluating the effectiveness of policies designed to bring about improvements in health in, and through, sport, as well as compounding further the interchangeable use of the term 'sport' in a number of differing senses.[11]

Sociologists point to the ways in which the use of the term 'sport' has changed over time and varies between and across cultures, and thus to the need for a more adequate classification and demarcation of the social phenomenon under study. Contrast the ancient gladiators with the modern Olympic sport of synchronised swimming. Modern definitions of sport differ from their pre-modern predecessors and terms such as 'sportsmanship' can have different meanings for different cultures. Furthermore, ideologically based descriptions of sport often lack reality-congruence: contrast the adequacy of the 'sport for all' and 'sport as a level playing field' rhetoric with the largely class-exclusive and highly competitive cultures associated with elite-level sports such as rugby union, cricket and golf. In short, while the descriptive and positivistic approaches to sport in Ireland have made possible the generation of hitherto unavailable quantitative data on the prevalence of sport in Ireland, the fantasy-laden approaches to sport have undoubtedly hindered the adequacy of the interpretation of the data generated. Sport may not be as adequate a means of combating social exclusion, problems relating to attendance, behaviour and attainment in education, and social disintegration as some have suggested.[12] Moreover, the increased competitiveness of modern sports, and the ways in which this ethos is permeating through to amateur and recreational sports, have contributed to increasing social pressure upon athletes to act in ways that we, the ideologically motivated audience, might regard as 'unsporting'. Sociologically speaking then, we might point out that the perception of 'sport's ills' partly has its origins, not just in the deviant behaviour of individual athletes such as drug users, but rather in the illusionary approach to modern sport.

One example of this illusion is the reinforcement and reproduction of the fair play ethos in modern sports and the subsequent labelling of athletes as 'cheats' if they appear to flout the ethics of fair play. In the case of doping, the identification of substances designed to have performance-enhancing capacities is one mechanism for differentiating 'cheats'. The use of these substances and the motivations of the athletes involved are, however, rarely understood. A number of sociologists (Waddington 2000, for example) have argued that the increasing pressure upon elite athletes to succeed in sport has contributed, in part, to their increasing desire to win and to train, play and compete when in pain, and injured. Indeed, many injuries are managed by athletes through the use of various substances, supplements and scientific support, all of which have performance-enhancing capabilities but are not necessarily included in the designated prohibited list. These include recovery in oxygen tents which has a similar boosting effect on red blood cells as the use of EPO and the use of some vitamin and natural supplements whose effects mirror some of the prohibited substances. The point to be made here is that the expectations placed upon athletes (and these expectations are increasingly permeating to the non-elite levels) reflect the highly emotional and fantasy-laden approach towards modern sports, a central feature of which is the tendency wilfully to view sports in romantic terms – that is, as a social site that is, and should be, free of all 'ills'. In effect, sport in Ireland is, in ideal terms, uncontaminated and untainted. Hence, we tend to ignore or underestimate sports-related 'ills' like the economic costs associated with the treatment of sports- and exercise-related injuries (such as physiotherapy, hospital visits, GP consultations, insurance costs, enforced sick leave, degenerative effects in later life).[13] If we consider these effects for a moment, then the often illusory claims about the economic and health benefits of sport can be seen to be inadequate. So, putting the desirability of the ideal or 'pure' sporting expression aside, it is at least equally important to understand 'the surface connections that are not always made in a field of enquiry that is often awash with ideological pre-conceptions about what [sports] people do' (Smith and Green 2005: 250).

Conclusion

This discussion has sought to focus our attention on the levels of emotional attachment to sport in Ireland and the ways in which this attachment has particular implications for how we approach, and seek to understand, sport as a social phenomenon. The leitmotif in our approach to sport – the role of ideology and its sub-variants, the level of emotional attachment and engagement with our subject matter, sport – has particular resonance for the study of sport in Ireland for a number of reasons. These include: the widespread and uncritical acceptance of the intrinsic value of sport by academics, physical educationalists, sports advocates and the wider public; the related tendency to talk of sport (often in a proselytising manner) as having an identifiable, valuable and universal essence at its heart; the dominance of sports advocates in the field of sport generally, whether as physical educationalists, current (or former) government ministers, officials of governmental and non-statutory sports organisations and so forth; and the 'infant' status of the sociology of sport within sociology. One of the problems that besets social research in Ireland is the difficulty in maintaining an appropriate balance between the desire for action and understanding. In Ireland, this is evident in the dominance of problem-solving and ideologically driven approaches to sports research and in the problems that can arise from this. In the words of Coakley and Dunning:

> When scholars in our field [and here they mean the sociology of sport] place the need for action above the need for understanding, there is the possibility that 'truth claims' will come to rest primarily on normative commitments rather than theory-guided empirical research. (2000: xxxii)

In seeking to raise awareness of the hidden (rather than the presumed or imagined) connections in sport, we can infer some of the ways in which the application of the sociological perspective can enable us better to understand not just why it is that Irish people 'love their sport' (if indeed they do), but also 'what is' in the field of sport and 'how it has come to be'. Key to this is the critical examination of the commonsense and fantasy-laden assumptions about the integrative potential of sport in Ireland which often have statutory and government support precisely because they tend to reflect and reinforce the interests of powerful groups.

At the outset of this chapter, it was suggested that the discussion was to be viewed as an attempt to contribute, in an incremental way, to the nascent sociology of sport in Ireland. Compounding this is the fact that sociological research is, by its very nature, incomplete, given that its subject matter – the systematic study of people and the unplanned outcomes of their complex interactions over time and in space – is characterised by continuity alongside change. The changes associated with immigration in Ireland over the last decade or so are prominent cases in point for sociologists. This chapter was also predicated on the sociological premise that the full significance of sport lies in the manner in which key social meanings about individual and group identities and ways of living are imparted in the field of sport. Much of this significance can remain hidden in the complex webs of interaction between people, and hidden also because of the fantasy-laden approach to sport which I have identified here. If sociological research has a 'public agenda' as part of its remit, then it can be used to bring to the surface these hidden connections; and that can, in turn, inform the ways in which we might intervene in, or try to bring about a desired transformation in the ways in which sports are organised. In short, our understanding of the sporting reality – 'what is' – can inform our attempts to bring about meaningful change – what we think 'ought to be' – in the field of sport rather than *vice versa*. For, as Coakley (2001) puts it: the meaning, purpose and organisation of sport; who participates in sport and the conditions of that participation; and why and how sport is justified and supported, are all examples of the ways in which sports are 'contested activities'. They develop around particular ideas about human potential, human abilities, and what is regarded as important and unimportant to people in Ireland – thereby rendering sport a key topic for sociological enquiry.

Section III   Governance

Chapter 10

The peace process in Northern Ireland

Colin Coulter

Peter Shirlow

Introduction

At midday on 31 August 1994 the Provisional IRA declared that from midnight it would embark upon a 'complete cessation of military operations'. Within six weeks, this seemingly historic move would be echoed in a ceasefire called by the principal paramilitary organisations on the loyalist side. The biggest selling local newspaper sought to capture the sense of relief and perhaps even euphoria that many – though not, of course, all – felt with the banner headline of the *Belfast Telegraph* declaring simply and boldly: 'It's Over!'.

It was always entirely predictable of course that the rhetorical optimism that greeted the first republican ceasefire – in some quarters, at least – would transpire to be rather premature. The era of the troubles had produced several false dawns and hard experience had counselled that there would be many twists in the plot before the conflict could genuinely be said to be over. It was widely anticipated, therefore, that the path to political reconciliation would be a long and arduous one. There were few, however, who could have predicted that the peace process would prove to be as difficult as it has actually been (Cox et al. 2006: 2).

In this chapter, we will seek to explain how and why the 'long war' in Northern Ireland has become the 'long peace'. It is not our intention to document every turn that the political life of the region has taken over the decade that has passed since the ceasefires, but rather to tease out those broad political processes and practices that have marked the era of the peace process with a view to explaining why the cautious optimism of the mid-1990s has given way to the current disillusionment.

The specific developments that have marked the recent political history of Northern Ireland have not of course occurred in a vacuum but rather reflect the ways in which the social life of the region has changed over recent generations. If we are to understand fully the course that the peace process has taken, we need to acknowledge the very particular social context in which it has unfolded. It is, therefore, to the transformations that have occurred within Northern Irish society over recent times that we turn our attention first.

Northern Irish society after the troubles

During the half century that followed partition, the social life of Northern Ireland was defined by the polarisation of power and wealth along ethnoreligious lines. The control of the institutions of state enabled the unionist leadership to engage in practices that were routinely discriminatory and oppressive. In addition, the fact that the principal manufacturing enterprises were in the hands of the Protestant bourgeoisie ensured that the more lucrative and prestigious forms of manual labour were essentially the preserve of working-class unionist men. While most unionists came to identify strongly with the ethos and institutions of the state, the nationalist experience of the Stormont era was one that inevitably engendered widespread disaffection. The exclusion of Catholics from public employment served to ensure that the nationalist middle class remained comparatively small. Furthermore, the discrimination that was endemic throughout the regional economy meant that working- class nationalist communities were forced to endure high levels of unemployment and poverty.

The experience of political and economic dispossession nurtured among Northern Irish nationalists a sense of alienation that would in time fatally undermine the regime at Stormont. The emergence of the civil rights movement in the mid-1960s signalled that the partition settlement had begun to unravel and unleashed forces that would see the region descend into three decades of conflict. The social formation that has emerged from the troubles would appear radically different from that which existed before. Perhaps the most remarkable change has been the emergence of a substantially enlarged Catholic middle class (Smyth and Cebulla forthcoming). Over the period of the troubles, the public sector came to assume an increasingly important role within the local economy and at present one out of every three Northern Irish people who are in work are employed directly by the state (*Sunday Times*, 8 January 2006). The expansion of public employment created opportunities for younger nationalists denied to their predecessors.

The gradual enlargement of a new Catholic middle class in time found expression in patterns of spatial mobility. In Belfast, those affluent neighbourhoods that were once the preserve of the unionist middle classes are increasingly home to upwardly mobile nationalists. The burgeoning wealth of the new Catholic middle classes has found reflection not merely in predictably conspicuous modes of consumption but also a new-found cultural and political self-confidence. It would seem that among younger, more affluent nationalists a strong belief exists in their ability to secure a good life for themselves within the existing constitutional arrangements (Mitchell 2003).

The comfortable lives of the new Catholic middle classes stand in stark contrast to those of others within the nationalist community who have been denied the opportunity of social mobility. The seismic changes that have occurred over the last couple of generations have evidently been insufficient to alter the status of working-class nationalist communities as the most disadvantaged within Northern Ireland. It remains the case that working-class nationalists experience higher rates of unemployment, poverty and reliance upon state benefits than their unionist counterparts. The material disadvantage that working-class Catholics continue to experience does not, however, appear to have inhibited their cultural and political development. Since the outbreak of the troubles, a strong network of relations and institutions has emerged that have nurtured a vibrant civil society within working-class nationalist districts. The existence of such social capital is inevitably most apparent within the urban heartland of republicanism in Northern Ireland. Over the years, the nationalist community in west Belfast has managed to initiate and sustain a major cultural festival, a mass circulation community newspaper, an international film festival and, most recently, a team capable of playing in the top flight of local soccer. The considerable political and cultural self confidence that animates working-class nationalists is often further evident in the fluent delivery of many of the younger people who have joined the ranks of Sinn Féin in recent times.

The changing position and experience of the nationalist community adverts to an important shift in the balance of forces within contemporary Northern Irish society. While the fortunes of nationalists have in the main been in the ascendant, those of unionists have been largely on the wane. The expansion of public expenditure and employment that has created the new Catholic middle classes has also of course been beneficial to many from the other principal ethnopolitical tradition. A considerable swathe of the unionist community enjoys a comfortable lifestyle that centres upon rising house prices, conspicuous consumption and sending their children to some of the best schools in the United Kingdom free of charge (Shirlow and Murtagh 2006). While the affluence of the more privileged elements of unionism has been underwritten, their once enormous political influence has all but evaporated. The operation of direct rule from Westminster over the last 35 years has nurtured a growing political indifference and inactivity among middle-class Protestants.

The processes of social change at work within Northern Ireland have impacted rather less kindly upon the less privileged sections of the unionist community. The reconfiguration of the global economy that coincided with the onset of the troubles eliminated those manufacturing jobs that had for generations been the principal source of both material and symbolic reward within working-class Protestant neighbourhoods (Coulter 1999: 63–95). The advent and persistence of the conflict ensured the creation of a large number of lucrative positions within the security forces that for a time partially filled the void left by deindustrialisation. In the era of the peace process, however, many of these opportunities have begun to evaporate as Northern Ireland moves towards a smaller police force that will draw a growing proportion of its officers from outside the unionist community (Smyth and Cebulla forthcoming).

The paucity of attractive employment available to working-class unionists reflects not only political change but also economic stagnation. In stark contrast to the seeming economic miracle unfolding south of the border, Northern Ireland remains profoundly underdeveloped and reliant upon an annual subvention from the British exchequer (*Sunday Times*, 8 January 2006). In the main, the region has proved unable to generate in sufficient numbers those highly paid and highly skilled jobs that are typically regarded as the hallmark and engine of economic growth. And even if such enviable positions were to begin to flourish in Northern Ireland, most would remain beyond the grasp of working-class unionist communities that typically have the worst records of educational attainment in the six counties. In the near future, therefore, the choice that working-class unionists will continue to encounter will be that between poorly paid and poorly regarded employment and no employment at all (Smyth and Cebulla forthcoming).

The substantial and possibly growing poverty that afflicts working-class unionists finds an echo in their apparent political and cultural underdevelopment. Over the last three decades, poorer Protestant neighbourhoods have been beset by a host of problems in the guise of political upheaval, economic decline and often disastrous urban planning. In contrast to their nationalist equivalents, working class unionists have never quite been able to establish those forms of expression and organisation that might enable them to negotiate an increasingly challenging social environment. The apparent inability of poorer unionist communities to find a progressive way of talking that might enable them to speak both to their own grievances and beyond their own boundaries assumed perhaps its most baleful expression in the blockade of the Holy Cross Catholic Girls' School in the autumn of 2001. The harrowing spectacle of grown men and women barracking nationalist children on their way to class inevitably drew the horrified interest of a global audience and served only to compound the mutual hostility with which loyalists and the outside world would appear to regard one another.

In sum, therefore, the version of Northern Irish society that emerged from three decades of the troubles is one that differs radically from that which existed when the conflict initially erupted. While the social transformations outlined above constitute the context of the peace process, they do so in ways that are both complex and contradictory. The emergence of a confident and largely contented nationalist middle class open to the possibility of a deal that would leave partition intact created an important precondition of a political settlement in Northern Ireland. Moreover, the pervasive sense within the unionist community that the tide of history had turned against them nurtured a willingness to reach a compromise in the present for fear of having to accept a less attractive deal in the future. On the other hand, the economic margin-alisation of working-class unionists has given rise to a widespread disaffection that could serve only to undermine the quest for peace. The complex processes of social change at work have, therefore, acted both to nurture and retard the prospects of political progress in the region. It should scarcely come as a surprise then that the course of the peace process should have taken the form of multiple apparent breakthroughs quickly followed by countless actual reversals. It is to this particular sorry tale that we turn our attention next.

Old habits and New Labour

While the announcement of the ceasefires had inevitably raised hopes that a genuine political breakthrough might be imminent, these would be swiftly dashed by the vagaries of Westminster parliamentary arithmetic. In the mid-1990s the Conservative administration had become reliant upon the votes of Ulster Unionist Party (UUP) MPs to remain in office. In order to retain the favour of the UUP, the Major administration adopted an aggressive stance when dealing with the republican movement. Their insistence that real political negotiations could only commence once the IRA had 'decommissioned' inevitably and quickly served to alienate republicans who evidently presumed that their ceasefire would yield rather more substantial and immediate gains. The growing frustration within republican ranks would soon give rise to a military response in the form of the Canary Wharf bomb. The IRA ceasefire that had sparked such hopes of a lasting peace in Northern Ireland had in fact lasted a mere 18 months.

It would soon become apparent, however, that the Canary Wharf bomb would not signal a return to the dark days of the troubles. Since the late 1980s, the leadership of the republican movement had moved towards the view that the IRA campaign had become a hindrance and that their interests would be best pursued through exclusively political means. The 'political turn' within republicanism ensured that while there would be further 'spectaculars' – most significantly in the centre of Manchester in June 1996 – there would, however, be no return to full-scale hostilities. The resumption of the IRA ceasefire was, therefore, a fairly inevitable development but one that would require a change in the balance of power at Westminster.

On 1 May 1997, New Labour registered a conclusive electoral victory that transformed the political landscape in Northern Ireland. Armed with an enormous majority of 179 seats, the Blair government enjoyed altogether greater freedom than its predecessor to chart a rather bolder course in relation to Northern Ireland. While the initial days of the administration were dogged by the decision to force an Orange Order parade through the nationalist Garvaghy Road district of Portadown, even this would prove insufficient to permanently sour relations between London and the republican movement. On 20 July 1997, the IRA declared that it was reinstating its ceasefire and this second cessation has, after a fashion, remained in place to the present day.

With republicans having committed themselves to pursuing their goals through solely peaceful means, the path was now clear for their inclusion in the political negotiations reconvened in the autumn of 1997. On Good Friday, 10 April 1998, the various parties to the talks announced that they had finally come to an agreement on the political future of Northern Ireland. Not for the first time and not for the last, it appeared for a while that the political fortunes of the region might just have taken a turn for the better.

The Good Friday Agreement

The document that emerged from the multiparty negotiations at Stormont inevitably was detailed, multifaceted and wide-ranging. The terms of the Belfast Agreement sought to address and resolve three different sets of relationships understood to be at the heart of the 'Northern Ireland problem'. In more specific terms, the political deal struck at Stormont set out to nurture and heal relations between the 'two communities' in Northern Ireland, between people living either side of the Irish border and between the various peoples who live either side of the Irish Sea. The first of these relationships is of course the most substantial concern of any solution to the Northern Irish conflict and it is, therefore, the one with which we will concern ourselves.

In large measure, the Belfast Agreement represented an attempt to reach an honourable compromise between the ambitions and identities that often appear to divide the 'two communities' in Northern Ireland. The text of the document sought to allay the enduring fears of the unionist community that they might be forced or duped into a united Ireland. It stated quite categorically that 'Northern Ireland in its entirety remains part of the United Kingdom' (Annex A Part 1 (1)). Furthermore, the text affirmed that any change to the constitutional status of the region could only happen with the concurrent electoral consent of people living in both jurisdictions on the island. While the agreement clearly sought to accord with unionists' ambition to remain citizens of the United Kingdom, it also set out to accommodate nationalists' aspiration that they might in the future become citizens of a united Ireland. The text clearly acknowledged as legitimate both the political objectives and the cultural practices that are associated with the tradition of Irish nationalism. In addition, it was stated that if in the future a majority of people living either side of the border gave their simultaneous support to the unification of Ireland, it would be a 'binding obligation' upon both the British and Irish governments to ensure that this came to pass.

While the Belfast Agreement clearly envisaged that nationalists will remain *de facto* British citizens for some time to come, it also sought to ensure that they would do so on rather more favourable terms than had often been the case in the past. The text agreed in the multiparty talks marked an attempt to resolve historical grievances through the implementation of a sweeping programme of political and institutional reform. The 108 seat Assembly devised under the deal is obliged to operate in a manner that empowers both communities more or less equally. Those matters that come before the legislature that are deemed to be 'key' can only be endorsed on a cross-community basis. Furthermore, the two most senior positions in the proposed Executive – the First and Deputy First Ministers – have to attract the support of both nationalist and unionist Members of the Legislative Assembly (MLAs). The remainder of those holding ministerial posts were to be assigned on the basis of party strengths and according to the d'Hondt system which in effect means that the positions of executive power are in the hands of equal numbers of nationalist and unionist politicians.

The consociational mode of government envisaged by those who framed the Belfast Agreement proved to be emblematic of a broader concern to build an equitable and inclusive social order in Northern Ireland. In effect, the agreement reached at Stormont represented a new deal for nationalists living in the region. One of the most alienating aspects of the nationalist experience in Northern Ireland was dealing with a police force that was drawn almost exclusively from the unionist community and that often conducted itself in a draconian and discriminatory way. The Belfast Agreement sought to redress the grievances of nationalists by promising a 'new beginning to policing' in the region. The text of the deal provided for the creation of an independent commission charged with beginning the arduous task of creating a police force that both reflected the composition and enjoyed the trust of Northern Irish society as a whole. The commitment to a programme of reform was expressed further in the provisions for a review of the criminal justice system and for the establishment of a Human Rights Commission as well as an Equality Commission. Finally, the terms of the agreement sought to underline the need for greater respect for cultural and linguistic diversity. While Ulster-Scots is mentioned in passing, it is of some significance perhaps that it is the Irish language that is discussed at some length as a cultural practice that deserves attention and funding.

New times?

Originally it seemed that the Belfast Agreement might just be that hither-to elusive settlement that could mark a new and more progressive phase in the political life of Northern Ireland. The accord enjoyed the backing of the British, Irish and US administrations as well as all of the mainstream local parties, with the ominous exception of the DUP. More importantly perhaps, the agreement had gained favour among the ranks of those paramilitary groupings on both sides of the divide. While the deal negotiated at Stormont had the blessing of most of the political classes, its broader popular appeal would be tested in the dual referenda scheduled for 22 May 1998. In the Irish Republic, the Belfast Agreement had evidently struck a chord, with 95 per cent of the votes cast being in favour. On the other side of the border, predictably, the outcome of the ballot was rather less clear-cut. In the Northern Irish poll, some 71 per cent of the electorate that exercised their right to vote said 'yes' to the Belfast Agreement. In most electoral circum-stances, such a proportion would be considered a ringing endorsement. A closer examination of voting patterns, however, revealed a marked and potentially dangerous trend. While the overwhelming majority of the nationalist community had cast their votes in favour of the proposed deal, only a very slim majority of unionists had also voted 'yes' (Aughey 2006: 92). What were the reasons for the very different responses that the agreement elicited within the 'two communities'?

In a sense, it was always fairly inevitable that most nationalists would find the Belfast Agreement to their liking. The influence of certain nationalist thinkers was, after all, clearly apparent in the terms of the deal (Aughey 2005: 30; McCall 2006: 303; Tonge 2006b: 79). The notion of the three strands of relationships, the emphasis upon power-sharing and the conviction that the problems of Northern Ireland could only be resolved through political arrangements that both acknowledge and, more importantly, transcend that particular territorial space, all bear the hallmark of the SDLP. The popularity of the Belfast Agreement among constitutional nationalists was always, there-fore, more or less guaranteed. In principle, however, the response of republicans to the deal should perhaps have been rather different.

Over the preceding three decades, the republican movement had waged a brutal military campaign designed to take Northern Ireland out of the Union. The Belfast Agreement, however, quite clearly recognises and guarantees the constitutional status of the region as part of the United Kingdom. While a minority expressed their opposition to the deal, the republican movement *en masse* chose to endorse it. In so doing, republicans would seem to have violated the most central and cherished ideal of their political tradition (Tonge 2006a:

6, 23, 27, 37). Quite conscious perhaps of the betrayal signalled by accepting the Belfast Agreement, the upper echelons of Sinn Féin have sought to shift attention away from the constitutional provisions of the accord and focus upon the benefits that will arise from the programme of reform sketched out in the deal (Aughey 2005: 126). The Sinn Féin leadership attempted to underline those elements of the deal that appear to promise nationalists fairness and equality within Northern Ireland (Tonge 2005: 6; 2006a: 8, 27). While this strategic shift of focus from the 'national question' to the 'democratic question' begs questions of the legitimacy and utility of the IRA campaign over the previous three decades, the emphasis that republicans have placed upon a reform agenda that seems to offer genuine cultural and material parity would appear to have struck a chord within an increasingly pragmatic but confident nationalist community (Aughey 2005: 13, 140; Mitchell 2003).

In principle, there were elements of the Belfast Agreement that had the potential to appeal greatly to most of the unionist community (Tonge 2005: 4). After all, the signatories to the accord had agreed that the constitutional status of Northern Ireland was to be respected and could not change without the voluntary consent of the majority of people living there. In effect, therefore, the deal hammered out at Stormont explicitly endorsed the principal ideal and ambition of the unionist tradition. While the constitutional guarantees enshrined within the Belfast Agreement were attractive to a great many unionists, their appeal was somewhat diminished by two further considerations. Firstly, the fairly generalised sense of mistrust that defines and deforms their political imagination ensured that unionists were unwilling to take at their word a whole range of other political actors and in particular the British state (Aughey 2006: 92, 97; Tonge 2006a: 158). Quite simply, the unionist community was from the outset never entirely convinced that the constitutional guarantees within the Belfast Agreement were in fact worth the paper they were written on. Secondly, those aspects of the deal that were attractive to unionists were from the beginning finely balanced against other elements that they found deeply troubling. While the unionist community hoped that the Belfast Agreement might be a final settlement, they also feared that it would in fact prove to be a process that would undermine their interests and perhaps ultimately sweep them into a united Ireland (Aughey 2005: 34, 51).

Hence, when unionists went to the polls in May 1998, they were torn between an ambition to strike a deal that would finally signal an end to the troubles and an anxiety to avoid being duped into arrangements that would ultimately undermine their position. While more unionists voted for the Belfast Agreement than against, this was the product more of rational calculation than principled or emotional attachment to the deal itself (Aughey 2006: 93). There were clearly many within the unionist community who had severe misgivings about the agreement but who took a leap of faith in the hope that a 'yes' vote might finally bring peace and stability to the region. The precise balance of forces within unionism in the future would hinge largely upon how this particular group of pragmatists who supported the deal in principle would respond to the specific manner in which it was implemented in practice – whether they felt that it was fair, whether they considered that promises had been honoured, whether measures that might have appeared just about tolerable in prospect turned out to be entirely intolerable in reality and so forth (Guelke et al. 2006: 444). A consideration of the specific dynamic between the introduction of the structures and practises envisaged within the Belfast Agreement and the response of the unionist community to it constitutes one of the principal threads of the discussion that follows.

The prisoners issue

The Belfast Agreement would draw radically different responses from the two principal ethnopolitical traditions in Northern Ireland. These differences may in part be traced to the divergent ways in which unionists and nationalists have experienced, practised and perceived politically motivated violence. From the outset of the troubles, considerable support had existed within the nationalist community for the campaign mounted by the IRA against a state often considered to be illegitimate and oppressive. While unequivocal support for the republican movement was principally to be found within those working-class districts that had borne the full force of the repressive aspects of British state policy, it often appeared that there was considerable sympathy for its ideals if not necessarily its practices among middle-class Catholics.

The widespread support that Sinn Féin has come to enjoy finds no parallel, however, on the other side of the communal divide. While many loyalists have of course engaged in acts of political violence, they have never managed to garner widespread support within the wider unionist community. In the main, unionists have turned their backs on the unofficial violence of the loyalist paramilitaries and preferred instead the role of supporters and agents of the official violence of the British state. The poor esteem with which paramilitarism is regarded within the unionist community finds its most crucial expression in electoral trends. In the initial elections to the Northern Ireland Assembly in June 1998, for instance, the two parties associated with armed loyalist groups could only muster fewer than 30,000 votes and secure two seats between them – and that in spite of being the beneficiaries of some suspiciously favourable coverage by the media on both sides of the Irish border. Since that poll, the already meagre fortunes of both have been on the wane.

One of the assumptions that seemed to inform the Belfast Agreement was that there existed something approaching a balance between the experience and interests of the rival ethnopolitical communities whose consent it required. The success of the deal would hinge in part upon a sequence of presumed commonalities – that neither side wished to return to war, that the settlement would offer both more or less comparable benefits and that they would be prepared to implement its terms in a fairly synchronised manner. In reality, however, there was, with the crucial exception of the common desire to avoid the resumption of the conflict, no meaningful symmetry in how the Belfast Agreement was received. This would become all too apparent in relation to the initial controversy that dogged the early days of the deal.

While in many respects a skilfully crafted document, the Belfast Agreement was also largely a fairly predictable one. The agreed text did, however, contain one passage in particular that took many people by surprise. In section 10, provision was made for the release within two years of all prisoners belonging to paramilitary groups successfully maintaining ceasefires. This critical aspect of the political settlement created particular revulsion within the unionist community.

The different responses to the issue of prisoners reflected the divergent ways in which unionists and nationalist have experienced and enacted political violence – and in particular *unofficial* political violence – that we outlined earlier. The terms of the Belfast Agreement entailed of course the early release of loyalist paramilitaries who had inflicted enormous suffering, especially upon working-class Catholic districts. While the sight of loyalist killers walking out of prison to the acclaim of their fellow travellers was inevitably deeply troubling for the nationalist community, it was to some extent offset by the fact that the amnesty also signalled the early release of republican prisoners for whom many nationalists have considerable personal and ideological respect. As a consequence, although the response of most people within the nationalist community to the issue of prisoners was in all likelihood one of pragmatic if grudging acceptance that it was a necessary ingredient of the new political settlement, there was at least a substantial minority of nationalists who regarded the early releases as, on balance, a positive measure.

Within the unionist community, in contrast, the response was rather closer to universal revulsion. The amnesty afforded by the Belfast Agreement meant the premature release of hundreds of IRA members who had been responsible for the murder and maiming of Protestant civilians and members of the security forces. Moreover, that the deal applied equally to paramilitaries drawn from their own community provided scant compensation for the overwhelming majority of unionists. In the main, unionists have come to regard and reject loyalist paramilitary organisations as self-serving thugs and parasites. The early release of loyalist prisoners merely served, therefore, to compound the already acute sense within the unionist community that the peace process was an unprincipled programme that sought to placate and reward 'gangsters' and 'terrorists' (von Tangen Page 2006: 200, 209).

Given the enormous controversy that it generated – especially within unionist ranks – it is perhaps ironic that the prisoner release scheme arguably represents the provision of the Belfast Agreement that might be considered to have been most successful, in its own terms at least (von Tangen Page 2006: 202, 209). To date, some 447 prisoners in total have been released under the programme – 241 republicans, 194 loyalists and 12 non-aligned individuals (Shirlow et al. 2005). In the months after the Belfast Agreement was signed, the issue of early releases was arguably the one that did most to erode the support of those unionists who had made the pragmatic decision to vote 'yes'. While much of the hurt and anger caused by the freeing of paramilitaries remains to this day, the principal focus of unionist ire would soon shift from the prisons to the proposed assembly. The institutions of government that were conceived within the Belfast Agreement rested on the assumption that we have encountered before that there exists a certain balance of experience and intention between the two principal ethnopolitical traditions in the region. In more specific terms, the anticipation that executive authority could be shared presupposed that such an arrangement made equal demands of unionists and nationalists who would be able and willing to leave behind their historical differences in order to move forward together in the interests of all. As we have argued already, however, in reality there is no such ready political symmetry between unionism and nationalism. The prospect and practice of sharing power would, therefore, draw rather different responses from unionists and nationalists.

Guns and government

While the process of making peace necessarily made onerous demands on all sides, these would transpire to be rather more unpalatable for some than for others. The formation of an executive required that politicians agree to co-operate with others whose views and actions in many cases they regarded as odious. The practice of power sharing demanded that nationalists accept that they will in part be subject to the decisions of unionist political figures, some of whom they considered to be indelibly sectarian. With the unedifying image of his victory jig along the lower stretches of the Garvaghy Road fresh in the mind, the prospect of having David Trimble as First Minister cannot have been one that appealed greatly to the nationalist community. Crucially perhaps, the devolution of power to Northern Ireland did not actually require nationalists to enter government with individuals who had been directly involved in politically motivated violence against them. The parties associated with the loyalist paramilitaries have, as we have noted already, only a miniscule presence in the assembly and stand no chance whatsoever of securing ministerial positions.

The same cannot be said of those unionists who were selected for ministerial positions. Over the period of the peace process, the republican movement has made considerable ground at successive elections. Their growing electoral strength meant that when the first power-sharing executive was formed at Stormont, Sinn Féin secured the two key Ministries of Health and Education, thereby placing the party in charge of half of the devolved governmental budget. The composition of the new cabinet inevitably alienated a great many unionists who were appalled at the prospect of crucial decisions concerning their lives being taken by individuals who had orchestrated and rationalised the campaign of violence they considered the IRA to have waged against their community. The outrage that many unionists felt at the advent of republicans being in government was embodied in the figure appointed to the position of Minister of Education. That Martin McGuinness – widely regarded at the time as a long-standing Chief of Staff of the IRA – would now be in charge of their children's schooling struck many within an already sceptical unionist community as emblematic of the insidious and intolerable nature of the entire peace process.

In the referendum, a majority – albeit a slim one – of unionists had of course voted to endorse a deal that they knew would inevitably lead to republicans holding positions of government. The decision of unionists to lend their support to the settlement was, however, a largely pragmatic one that assumed that the unpalatable inclusion of Sinn Féin within the executive would be paired with the disarming and disbanding of the IRA. This issue of the 'decommissioning' of paramilitary weapons represented of course the principal stumbling block that the peace process has faced from the very beginning. The enduring disputes surrounding the fate of the IRA's arsenal and that of other groupings owed their origins to a particular trait of the Belfast Agreement that might be considered both its greatest strength and its principal weakness.

The potential success of any political settlement in Northern Ireland would hinge upon its ability to appear to be able to square the circle of what are in some cases the mutually exclusive demands of the two communities. Those who framed the Belfast Agreement sought to create such an impression through a 'constructive ambiguity' designed to create the impression that the deal signalled a 'loserless' conclusion to the troubles (Aughey 2005: 3, 44–5, 55, 87). Some of the provisions of the text are worded in a manner that both enables and encourages unionists and nationalists to interpret them differently. This characteristic is particularly apparent in section seven which deals with the issue of decommissioning (Shirlow and Murtagh 2006: 47; Tonge 2006a: 191–3). The relevant section of the Belfast Agreement states that all the participants in the talks:

> reaffirm their commitment to the total disarmament of all paramilitary organisations. They also confirm their intention to continue to work constructively and in good faith with the Independent Commission [the official body established to oversee the decommissioning process], and to use any influence they may have, to achieve the decommissioning of all paramilitary arms within two years . . .

While the text that faced them was of course exactly the same, unionists and nationalists almost inevitably chose to read it in ideologically convenient and, therefore, starkly different ways. In the eyes of the unionist community, the Belfast Agreement simply signalled that the IRA and other paramilitary organisations would disarm and disband during the two-year period in which their prisoners would be released. The reading to which the republican movement chose to adhere was predictably rather different. The view consistently offered by the Sinn Féin leadership was that decommissioning would be a long and arduous process that could work only within a context of the wider demilitarisation of Northern Irish society. While republicans acknowledged that the Belfast Agreement required them to use their influence to bring about disarmament, they did not appear to regard the deal as necessarily obliging them to actually bring about this particular outcome.

These different expectations about decommissioning repeatedly thwarted the development of the peace process in Northern Ireland (Darby 2006: 221). The various attempts to break the deadlock over decommissioning have typically assumed an increasingly predictable form (Guelke et al. 2006: 444–9). In the hope of making progress, the then Ulster Unionist Party (UUP) leader David Trimble would take a leap of faith and agree to go into government on the proviso that republicans would disarm during a specified period of time (Aughey 2005: 129–30; 2006: 99–101). During this window of opportunity, the IRA would then either fail to dismantle its armoury or to do so in a manner that unionists found acceptable (Shirlow and Murtagh 2006: 43). The resultant crisis in confidence would see the institutions of government suspended and the whole cycle would begin anew. The latest version of this process came to a conclusion in October 2002 when allegations concerning continuing activity on the part of the IRA – and in particular that republicans were gathering illicit information on their supposed partners in government – led to the executive collapsing for a fourth time (Tonge 2006a: 200). In total, the power-sharing government has operated for a mere 19 months and at the time of writing – the autumn of 2006 – it remains in cold storage.

The stalemate over decommissioning has also unleashed forces that threaten further the prospect of genuine political progress in the region. The dispute over 'guns and government' has inexorably served to polarise political opinion in Northern Ireland (Tonge 2006a: 173–81; 2006b: 70). In the minds of many nationalists, the refusal of unionist politicians to engage in sustained co-operation with Sinn Féin represents a violation of their rights and articulates an abiding sectarian aversion to actually sharing power with the nationalist community. This reading has engendered an alienation that has seen a growing body of nationalists switch their allegiances to Sinn Féin whom they regard as the party more willing and able to face unionists down and assert their interests. In the 2001 Westminster elections, Sinn Féin overtook the SDLP for the first time and the polls held since have amplified the status of the party as the principal voice of contemporary Northern Irish nationalism.

The hardening of nationalist opinion sparked largely by the issue of decommissioning has inevitably found its double within the unionist community. The seeming refusal of republicans to fulfil their presumed obligation to disarm inevitably alienated many within the unionist community. In the summer of 2005, the IRA would complete an independently verified process of decommissioning that signalled their apparent demise as an organisation. But by then, unfortunately, the damage to unionist confidence had already been done. The nagging conviction that republicans were not to be trusted and that their decision to disarm was merely a pragmatic move designed to enable the pursuit of their goals through other means hardened the outlook of the unionist community. This would find electoral expression in the emergence of the DUP as the strongest voice within unionism. In the Westminster elections of 2005, the party secured twice as many votes as the erstwhile pre-eminent UUP which suffered the humiliation of being able to retain only a single seat, in affluent North Down.

This polarisation of political opinion represents a substantial threat to the peace process in Northern Ireland and perhaps signals the end of the particular version of it codified within the Belfast Agreement. While collaboration between the UUP and SDLP proved unworkable, the prospect of co-operation between the two largest parties currently – the DUP and Sinn Féin – is *almost* inconceivable. Sinn Féin continue to demand that the institutions of devolved government be restored to the region. We are faced then with the irony of a republican movement that once sought to 'smash' Stormont being the principal voice demanding its revival. While the DUP have accepted the possibility of sharing power with Sinn Féin in principle, they continue to refuse to do so in practice (Aughey 2005: 157–8; Tonge 2006b: 78). The demands of the party that the Belfast Agreement must be renegotiated have proven popular among a unionist electorate that increasingly regards the peace process as weighted against them (Aughey 2005: 71; McCall 2006: 311).

The most recent instalment of the seemingly endless rounds of talks designed to get the peace process back on track took place in October 2006 in St Andrews. After three days of negotiations, it appeared that perhaps some progress had finally been made. With the now customary fanfare, the British and Irish governments unveiled a series of measures that they agreed would enable the political logjam to be resolved. The provisions of the 'St Andrews Agreement' make demands upon all the principal players in the peace process. Sinn Féin are required to recognise the legitimacy of the police, the DUP are expected to enter into government with republicans and it is anticipated that the British state will introduce measures to advance equality and human rights.

While the St Andrews Agreement was heralded in many quarters as a potentially historic breakthrough, there remain of course considerable grounds for scepticism about the potential for genuine political progress in Northern Ireland (Millar and Moriarty 2006). The refusal of Ian Paisley to meet Gerry Adams a mere four days after the supposed accord suggested that once again efforts to introduce power sharing government to the region might well be stillborn. Indeed, it is questionable how many ordinary people living in the region would actually really care if devolved powers were not in fact to be returned to Stormont in the near future. The recurrent crises of the peace process, coupled with the fact that MLAs continue to draw their substantial salaries even though the assembly has been suspended for the last four years, have conspired to make the general public in Northern Ireland increasingly cynical and indifferent (Aughey 2005: 179). It all feels a very long way from the optimism and excitement of 1994.

New dawn fades

Over the last couple of decades, Northern Irish society has been transformed in ways that have simultaneously enabled and retarded the prospect of political progress. The particular course that the political life of the region has taken has inevitably reflected the opportunities and restraints that have been generated by these complex processes of social change. The era of the peace process has, as we have seen, been punctuated by a sequence of apparent breakthroughs that have with numbing regularity failed to materialise. The dispiriting narrative that forms the recent political history of Northern Ireland has of course posed a major difficulty for those various actors who have a vested interest in at least the semblance of political progress.

From the outset, official discourse has sought to depict the peace process as heralding that the people of the region have finally decided to overcome their historical differences in order to advance towards a brighter future of stability and prosperity. This optimistic narrative has proved increasingly difficult to sustain in view of the recurrent crises that have beset Northern Irish political life since the initial ceasefires were declared. Faced with successive crises, the response of the British and Irish states has been to cross their fingers, close their eyes and remain stoutly on message. The speeches of Tony Blair and Bertie Ahern continue to be littered with references to 'new dawns' and 'historic opportunities'. The Northern Ireland Tourist Board (2006: 4) seeks to entice visitors to the region with the reassurance that '[m]uch has happened in the past few years and old perceptions of the North have had to be rewritten'. And infomercials in the southern Irish press strive to depict the regional capital Belfast as a 'thriving' city in which 'new investments are helping to sustain growth at levels unimaginable a decade ago' (*Irish Times*, 24 April 2006).

The official narrative that seeks to recount the peace process as an era marked overwhelmingly by progress contains, it must be said, a substantial kernel of truth (Aughey 2005: 161–6). In the dozen years since the first IRA ceasefire, many things have changed for the better in Northern Ireland and these should not be dismissed lightly. In particular, the number of fatalities arising from politically motivated violence has fallen considerably. While there were 857 deaths arising out of the conflict in the eleven years that preceded the initial cessations, in the same period afterwards there were 225 (Shirlow and Murtagh 2006: 53). The advent of the peace process has, therefore, ensured that there are several hundred people in Northern Ireland – most of them young working-class men – who are currently alive and well who might otherwise be prematurely in their graves.

Furthermore, over the period of the peace process, there has arguably been rather greater progress has arguably been made on the issue of policing than would once have been considered possible. The independent commission conceived under the Belfast Agreement and chaired by Chris Patten made a series of broadly progressive recommendations that laid the ground for the dissolution of the Royal Ulster Constabulary (RUC) and its replacement in November 2001 by the Police Service of Northern Ireland (PSNI). The latter has a new badge which more fully reflects the range of cultural identities within the region, a revised oath that commits officers to the respect of human rights and a provision that half of all new recruits to the force should be from Catholic backgrounds (Dickson 2006: 173–5). Moreover, unlike its predecessor, the PSNI is subject to greater scrutiny and accountability in the guise principally of the Policing Board and the Office of the Police Ombudsman. The latter, in particular, displayed a willingness to ruffle feathers with its damning report that highlighted the incompetence of the RUC investigation of the bombing of Omagh that claimed 29 lives in August 1998 (O'Rawe forthcoming). While most unionists roundly condemned the dissolution of the RUC as the betrayal of an honourable force that had held the line against 'terrorism' and most nationalists have criticised the pace and extent of change (Dickson 2006: 171), it would seem nonetheless that we may well be entering into a new era of policing in Northern Ireland. The seeming inevitability that Sinn Féin will join the Policing Board in the near future raises the prospect that the PSNI might in time become a body broadly acceptable within the nationalist community (McCall 2006: 305; Tonge 2006a: 196).

While the official narrative of progress accords with some of the ways Northern Irish society has changed in recent times, a couple of deeply disturbing social trends are also evident. The first of these casts serious doubts upon the political course that Northern Ireland has taken over the period of the peace process. When it was signed, the Belfast Agreement was heralded as an historic compromise that would enable and encourage the 'two communities' in the region to transcend their differences and enter a new era of mutual appreciation and cooperation. It has become increasingly apparent, however, that the effect of the deal might have been to have nurtured rather less progressive political dispositions. In the main, the Belfast Agreement presumes and prescribes those very ethnopolitical interests and inclinations that it ostensibly seeks to overcome. The institutions and processes initiated under the deal presuppose that people in Northern Ireland can only mobilise politically as unionists and nationalists respectively and insist that they compete for resources accordingly. The effect of the Belfast Agreement has, therefore, been to reproduce and legitimate many of those forms of ethno-political feeling and competition that sparked the Northern Irish conflict in the first place.

Such ethnoreligious prejudice finds rather starker expression in the everyday life of Northern Ireland. While the peace process has often been depicted as facilitating an era of enhanced intercommunal relations, it has become apparent that sectarian feeling has not only failed to dissipate but may even have hardened in some districts. In recent years, research has indicated that reactionary ethnopolitical stereotypes are part of the outlook even of infants (Connolly et al. 2002) and central to the mindset of many teenagers in the region. In the particular context of Belfast, these sectarian prejudices both articulate and are articulated through the organisation of physical space. The growing spatial segregation of Belfast offers a further dramatic reminder that the peace process has failed to stem the tide of communal polarisation in Northern Ireland (Leonard 2006). Since the advent of the Belfast Agreement, six new 'peacelines' have been constructed and eleven existing ones heightened and/or extended (Tonge 2006a: 212).

The second disturbing social trend that needs to be acknowledged here is intimately associated with the first. One of the assumptions that has often informed official discourse is that the resolution of the Northern Irish conflict would usher in an era of greater prosperity that would serve the interests of all.

It has become increasingly evident, however, that insofar as there can actually be said to have been a peace dividend its benefits have not been evenly distributed. The middle classes in the region continue to enjoy an affluence that, for the time being at least, remains underwritten by the British taxpayer (*Sunday Times*, 8 January 2006). While there are clear cultural and political differences between the unionist and nationalist middle classes respectively, these are typically overwritten by a shared interest in the status quo. As time passes, the concern of middle-class unionists and nationalists alike increasingly drifts from shifting electoral trends towards that most potent of all contemporary bourgeois totems, spiralling house prices (Shirlow and Murtagh 2006: 101–23).

The manner in which the poorer sections of Northern Irish society have experienced the peace process has been rather less beneficial. In reality, there has been little discernible peace dividend for working-class people living in the region. The ongoing underdevelopment of the local economy has ensured that the less advantaged within Northern Ireland still have relatively few opportunities for material advancement. While unemployment has admittedly declined, working-class communities in the six counties continue to endure high levels of impoverishment. The multiple social problems that are rife within many working-class neighbourhoods have predictably provided a fertile breeding ground for the production and reproduction of ethnopolitical hatred. It is in the marginalised districts of north and west Belfast rather than the leafy avenues that grace the south of the city that the most virulent forms of sectarian enmity continue to fester (Shirlow and Murtagh 2006). The intimate association between poverty and prejudice suggests that the cause of progress in Northern Ireland demands not merely the creation of sustainable political arrangements but also the radical redistribution of wealth and opportunity. If there is to be a genuine and lasting peace in the region, those marginalised communities that invariably give voice to the most vehement forms of sectarianism will require the material and cultural resources that are necessary to persuade them that they are valued members of the society in which they live.

During the period of the troubles, the gnawing disaffection of working-class nationalists was evidently the most palpable source and emblem of the political instability prevalent within Northern Irish society. The alienation that defines the outlook and experience of republican communities has been mirrored during the peace process in the growing disenchantment increasingly apparent within poorer unionist districts. In the period since the ceasefires were called, it has become painfully apparent that working-class unionists have derived little benefit from the supposedly historic political developments unfolding around them. While rates of poverty in nationalist areas appear to be slowly declining, those in loyalist neighbourhoods are in fact on the rise (see chapter 18).

Such disadvantage has inevitably served to alienate many working-class unionists from a peace process which they consider to have conferred benefit upon others but not upon them. The disenchantment rife within loyalist communities has given rise both to stern opposition to the Belfast Agreement and to various troubling forms of political violence. The widespread rioting that ignited in north and west Belfast in September 2005 and in which members of the PSNI came under sustained assault represents possibly the most troubling manifestation to date of the political alienation common among the less advantaged sections of unionism. It might perhaps be suggested that the mood of sullen disaffection that has descended upon working-class unionist districts constitutes the single most significant threat to the entire peace process. If there is to be meaningful political progress in Northern Ireland then the poorer sections of unionism will have to be able to see that there are benefits that accrue from the compromises that any durable settlement will inevitably demand. In the dozen years since the ceasefires were called, however, there has been no tangible peace dividend that might encourage working-class unionists to feel that they are among the beneficiaries of the substantial political changes afoot in the six counties. Until such time that they do so, Northern Ireland will continue to represent a society that while no longer at war, is not yet quite truly at peace with itself.

Postscript: Never say 'Never, never, never, never' again

And then it transpired that the almost inconceivable was in fact not quite so inconceivable after all. On 8 May 2007, Ian Paisley and Martin McGuinness were inaugurated as the First and Deputy First Ministers in a power sharing government that challenged all logic and defied more than a few predictions. As the previously implacable foes shared smiles and wisecracks before an audience of the global media, it was hard to resist the temptation to wonder what precisely those four decades of murder and mayhem had been all about after all. But then again, those feelings of incredulity were rarely far away at any stage over the last 40, miserable, utterly pointless years. It is, of course, rather too early to judge how this improbable new venture in power sharing between Sinn Féin and the DUP will work out. But it is probably reasonable to suggest that Northern Irish history has displayed a perennial compulsion towards complex narrative and it is, therefore, entirely likely that there will be a few more twists in the strange tale of the peace process yet to come.

Chapter 11

Power and powerlessness

Mark Haugaard
Kevin Ryan

Introduction

When the National Agreement entitled *Partnership 2000 for Inclusion, Employment and Competitiveness* was published in 1996, it was heralded by many as a turning point in the social and political history of modern Ireland. Some 14 organisations representing, among others, the unemployed, women, gays and lesbians, lone parents, Travellers and the disabled participated in drafting the agreement, and it seemed that the pattern of past injuries relating to questions of inequality and discrimination was going to be definitively addressed. If these groups had been excluded in the past, they were now to be recognised as citizens and empowered through a combination of rights and inclusion into the decision-making process known as 'social partnership'.

Partnership 2000 was, in fact, but one sign of what the media called a 'new dawn'. Two reports relating to disability were published the same year (*Towards and Independent Future* and the *Report of the Commission on the Status of People with Disabilities*), and in 1997 a new National Disability Authority (NDA) was established to oversee policy and services to disabled people, with the Minister for Justice, Equality and Law Reform announcing that this would 'enable people with disabilities to achieve and exercise their economic, social, cultural, political, and civil rights' (Pollak 1997; *Irish Independent*, 19 November 1997).

In the case of Travellers, the *Partnership 2000* framework followed the *Report of the Task Force on the Travelling Community* (Task Force 1995), which led to the 1998 Housing (Traveller Accommodation) Act and a national Traveller Accommodation Strategy (Galway Travellers Support Group 1999). Further to this, and in response to recommendations by the Task Force to promote intercultural dialogue between Travellers and the 'settled' community, a Traveller Communication Committee was established in 1999 with financial support from the Department of Justice, Equality and Law Reform.

Putting these markers of change together, it is possible to suggest that we have witnessed an innovation in the arts of government which has transformed democracy in Ireland. All citizens, including the marginalised and the disadvantaged, are incorporated into the democratic process through mechanisms of consultation, participation and negotiation. The word 'government', which is generally understood as a centralised executive power, is now routinely supplemented in political discourse with references to 'governance'. Governance is a process which has the potential to empower citizens. However, governance is also a specific mode of discipline, which becomes apparent only if power is examined as a relation rather then something possessed by the powerful and exercised over the powerless. In fact, if we are really to understand the new inclusive model of democracy, then what is required is not a single analytical tool called 'power' but rather the conceptual equivalent of a toolbox. Consequently, the first part of this chapter is concerned with assembling this toolbox, while the second uses it to conduct a critical analysis of how inclusion both empowers and disciplines, focusing specifically on the case of Travellers.

Power and powerlessness, some theoretical considerations

Power is not one single entity with a specific essence, whereby one can say 'this is power and that is not', in the same way as one can confidently assert that 'this is an orange and that is an apple'. In social life, power has many manifestations and the use of the concept is frequently determined by the kind of theoretical context in which one is arguing. The concept is what the philosopher Wittgenstein (1967) termed a 'family resemblance' concept. Imagine a large family in which each member resembles the other but there is no core essence tying them together – Mary has the chin of her mother and long legs of her father, while John has his mother's hair and so on. In practice this means that it is better to speak of different types of power, rather than just power in general.

In the debates on power there is a fundamental opposition between those who view power consensually and those who consider it a conflictual phenomenon. The former emphasise 'power to' while the latter think of power purely as 'power over'.

The consensual theorists consider power as an essentially desirable phenomenon. It is our capacity 'to do' things. It is what enables us to be 'agents' with a capacity for action. A 'powerful' car is powerful by virtue of its capacity for action – to drive fast. Similarly, powerful people are powerful by virtue of their capacity for action or ability to make things happen (Barnes 1988). There are two sources of such power: the physical world and membership of a society. The former includes machines such as cars, while the latter is derived from our ability to act in collaboration with others. The latter we will term 'power to' and it corresponds (to paraphrase the words of Hannah Arendt) to the human ability to act in concert with others (Arendt 1970: 44).

'Power to' is what people have in mind when they think of 'empowerment'. A person is empowered if they are given a capacity for action by virtue of their membership of a collective. This can be seen most clearly in the example of simple organisations which are established for the purposes of realising a specific goal – a golf club for example, or a society for the preservation of a dying language or endangered species. You join the organisation and by virtue of that membership you are empowered to accomplish a shared goal.

It is a neo-liberal orthodoxy that political systems and societies are different from organisations in that they do not have an ultimate end (Hayek 1960). The central idea is that political systems are simply there as a neutral 'watchman' to ensure 'fair play'. As a strong claim this view is theoretically unsupportable, as any liberal capitalist democracy presupposes members with, for instance, basic literacy and good health. Although it remains a political decision as to the quality and scope of the services provided, the state is a collective organisation that empowers its members through the provision of public goods and social services such as schools and hospitals. Thus we would say that the state 'empowers' people by giving them 'power to' accomplish certain tasks. This capacity for action, or social power, is one that they would not have at their disposal if they were not members of society.

While the idea of empowerment is a positive one it also has its converse side. The state does not necessarily empower equally. For democrats who believe in political equality, this may raise normative issues concerning how society should be constituted. When a specific group finds itself cut off from the 'power to' of society we speak of 'social exclusion'. This need not mean that the group is excluded as some kind of pariah group, simply that it is excluded from the 'power to' which society delivers to the majority of its members.

We have already argued that education gives a capacity for action. So, for instance, if we find that one group is systematically excluded from participating in the educational system, then this is of normative concern. This is especially the case if we find, which is usually the case, that those who are excluded from educationally based power resources are the very same group who are excluded from 'power to' in other aspects of their lives. Furthermore, we may find that those who already have a great deal of 'power over' others are the same as those who are benefiting most from collective power. For instance, it is usually the case that the children of the well-off tend to benefit more from state education than those from disadvantaged backgrounds, who frequently find it difficult to access educational resources (see chapter 6 for further discussion).

So far we have focused primarily on 'power to', or power as empowerment. We have begun with this aspect of power because it is frequently
overshadowed by the characterisation of power as something which is
exercised by some people over others (generally referred to as 'power over').
While clearly related to questions of domination and resistance, there are
also many instances where the exercise of 'power over' is deemed legitimate.
Legitimacy can of course be defined in purely legal terms, but this is not
entirely correct, for legitimacy is also linked to the reactions of those over
whom power is exercised. If they willingly consent, it is legitimate. On the
other hand, if they consciously resist, then it may be because it is illegitimate
in their eyes. In this case, the exercise of power is illegitimate despite its
legal formality.

While we shall return to this in more detail later on, here we can note that
the attempt to 'settle' the travelling people in Ireland is a case in point.
Sponsored by the state and organised by voluntary settlement committees,
the settlement policy established during the 1960s was implicated in what is
now called cultural genocide. And yet, within the context of nation building,
the policy was perceived by those who supported it as a benevolent gesture,
bestowing the benefits of full citizenship upon Travellers. This was not a
viewpoint shared by Travellers, however, and they began to organise to resist
what they experienced as the illegitimate exercise of power.

This is an example of how, in practice, what we call authority is not
necessarily based upon legitimacy all the way down. There will always be
some who resist an exercise of power over them. Consequently, those in
authority also have access to coercive power, which is the kind of power Max
Weber had in mind when he wrote of power in terms of getting people to do
things despite their resistance: 'Power is the probability that one actor within
a social relationship will be in a position to carry out his will despite resistance,
regardless of the basis on which this probability rests' (1978: 53). Though
frequently quoted as a definition of power itself, Weber actually intended it as
a definition of *Macht* (as distinct from *Herrschaft*), which translates more
accurately as coercive power. Coercive power is based upon the threat of
deprivation or punishment, so that individuals comply because they are
threatened with either material deprivation (fines and so on) or physical
punishment (violence or prison).

The phenomenon of coercive power raises a number of conceptual issues
which are central to democratic theory. Essentially it throws up the question,
when is it legitimate to coerce people? Liberal democracies are based upon the
idea that government is founded upon on the consent of 'the people'. While
the latter is a slightly vague term, the manifest withdrawal of consent by a
large number of people undermines perceptions of legitimacy. The effectiveness of public demonstrations is based upon this tacit ideal. Consequently,

coercing large sections of the population is considered illegitimate. Authority based upon legitimacy is the most effective source of power, while the use of coercive power is the manifestation of illegitimacy.

In liberal democracies the use of coercion against 'free-riders' is considered legitimate. Free-riders are individuals who are seen to benefit from a system without making their due contribution. These people take 'power to' from the system without giving back the compliance that gives those with authority 'power over'. The tax defaulter is a case in point. In much of liberal political theory this relates to the notion of the social contract, which is a metaphor for the idea that accepting 'power to' from society entails consequent obligations, or compliance with authoritative 'power over'.

In ideal circumstances, the 'power over' which people in authority have should be there to maximise the 'power to' of all members of society. The need to organise entails that some are given authoritative power over others, but if the less powerful gain 'power to' from this relationship it is entirely logical that they consent to the power of the powerful. However, if they do not find themselves empowered by society then it is only natural that they will resist. Consequently, they will continually have to be coerced into compliance, with the result that these excluded groups will be overrepresented in the various penitentiary institutions of the state. If a group is genuinely excluded from 'power to', then it cannot be argued that this is the case of a free-rider breaking some kind of tacit social contract. It is not the case that they gain 'power to' from society but rather that they are unwilling to give back compliance to 'power over'. This raises fundamental normative issues concerning how society might be better organised in order to be more 'inclusive'. After all, it is unjust to expect certain individuals and groups to consent to power that is exercised over them without their deriving any 'power to' from society.

Inclusion in a social order is not necessarily a simple exchange whereby, for example, certain social agents who have been excluded from 'power to' are given access to power resources in exchange for compliance to 'power over'. Every social order presupposes a certain kind of social agent. As observed by Gellner (1983), the early modern period of capitalism was premised upon a labour force which had internalised certain social norms which were fundamentally different from the norms required for traditional agrarian societies. It is for this reason that the development of capitalism was accompanied by the emergence of state education. The latter is essentially a process whereby socialisation is removed from the home and taken over by the state, thus creating a relatively homogenised population of social agents whose behavioural patterns are compatible with the emerging modes of mass production. At the same time, within sovereign states a given dialect and culture became the 'national' culture, while local dialects, languages and customs were wiped out. In some instances, local social practices proved to be particularly resilient to the norm, with the result that minority movements emerged. Again Irish Travellers provide a good example. As Travellers organised against the settlement policy, they demanded a differentiated understanding of citizenship which would recognise their 'right to retain their own identity and tradition' (Gmelch, 1987: 306). However, this type of resistance often takes time to emerge, if it emerges at all. And in some cases, as with Travellers, it emerged against the strain of assimilation programmes (see Fanning 2002).

It is in this context of nation building that education can be conceptualised as a social technology, the aim of which is to create predictable patterns of behaviour on the part of the individual and the population. As observed by Foucault (1977), the school is a disciplinary organisation and an artificial order that the social agent internalises. If successful, then the predispositions which are learnt through this mode of training become part of the 'natural order of things'. Modelled on the Panopticon,[1] the school is both a building and a mode of inspection through which the behaviour of the individual and the group is shaped through principles of observation, examination and ranking. Education then is a judgemental regime that looks for and acts upon a whole series of 'illegalities' or departures from the norm: crimes of 'time (lateness, absence, interruptions of tasks), of activity (inattention, negligence, lack of zeal), of behaviour (impoliteness, disobedience), of speech' (Foucault 1977: 178). Within the school there is, of course, coercion, but the aim of this is still socialisation, so that once recalcitrant individuals have internalised the correct social norms, then coercion is no longer required. If socialisation fails in the school then a whole series of corrective institutions wait in the wings as a sort of 'carceral net', such as reformatories and prisons, all of which mirror the school in terms of strategic objective: to create a specific kind of social subject who has internalised the norms appropriate to a specific system of authority. Returning to the case of Travellers, the policy of settlement was an attempt to subject Travellers to educational programmes so that they would learn to relinquish their 'itinerant habits' (Commission on Itinerancy 1963: 110–11). It was hoped that education, delivered within the confines of camps managed by local settlement committees, would gradually 'absorb' the travelling people so that they would be indistinct from the majority 'settled' population.

We began by observing that in the case of authority, 'power over' is based upon the consent of those over whom it is exercised. The most straightforward source of consent is in terms of benefits: a person gives consent to 'power over' because they hope to gain 'power to' through their membership of society. This is the kind of consent upon which liberal democracy is premised. However, as noted above, consent emerges from specific forms of social agency which are created within the state through its disciplinary institutions. Consequently, the consent to legitimate systems of power is created through organised socialisation on a mass scale which, it could be argued, is ultimately coercive. However, to the upholders of the status quo, because they have internalised these norms, this order does not appear artificial and coerced but rather part of the natural order of things. From the perspective of those who uphold the social order, deviation from the norms of a particular society is seen to reflect the innate character or disposition of people who are either inadequate or 'anti-social', and so it is legitimate to 'protect' or, if necessary, to coerce them. In the same way, because we tend to overlook the fact that our perceptions of social life are largely constructed through conventions which are particular to our society and culture, so those defined as defective or deviant are frequently essentialised. An essentialist claim is one to the effect that specific types of persons have certain essences which define them, and these essences can have positive or negative connotations in terms of power. It may be that a specific group is thought to be endowed with an essence that renders them fit to rule. The aristocracy used to make this kind of claim in an explicit way, employing rituals of pomp and ceremony to communicate their superiority to the lower ranks. In contemporary society members of the middle classes often make similar claims, although in more implicit and subtle ways than the elites of traditional societies.

In modern democracies inequalities in power frequently come about through negative essentialist claims rather than positively essentialist ones. A certain group is identified with essentialist meanings which has the effect of naturalising their relative powerlessness. Travellers, for example, were long thought to be 'primitive', with the relation between power and knowledge naturalising negative meanings relating to dirt and a lack of respect for private property. Even as the travelling people were impoverished by an order which constrained their nomadic culture, so it was their poverty – manifest in inadequate shelter, poor health, and lack of access to water and sanitation for example – which became the proof of the primitive 'itinerant' or 'tinker' disposition, and this in turn made the policy of settlement appear both necessary and inevitable.

When we think of authority we tend to think of it in terms of high politics – politicians and so on. In reality, however, all social agents have some authority. If you are a parent, you have authority with regard to your children. That authority is not a generalised thing but is tied to specific meanings. When we say that a parent should not do such and such with regard to a child in their care we are claiming that the meaning of what it is to be a parent is inconsistent with a specific exercise of power; in other words, they are going beyond what is considered to be their legitimate authority. Membership of a group may also result in a loss of authority with regard to the rest of society. The baseline for authority within democratic politics – one that cuts through differences of class and status and defines the relationship between individual and state – is 'citizenship'. Citizenship is clearly not equivalent to unconstrained freedom, for the citizen is expected to play according to the rules of the game which constitute the dominant norms of a society. These are the norms which are necessary for authority, thus effective 'power to' and 'power over'. The attempt to claim rights without accepting responsibilities, for example, brings us back to the issue of free-riderism, which can be legitimately coerced. In cases where transgression crosses the threshold of law, then punishment may entail suspending the rights and freedoms that come with citizenship, and yet the status of citizenship cannot be suspended or revoked by anyone. It requires legitimate authority. It is the claim to citizenship which has, in part, enabled groups such as Travellers to challenge the way in which they have been essentialised in the past and excluded from the benefits of social power. As we shall see, this claim to citizenship can be granted on a provisional basis, and it can be used to leverage compliance to social and legal norms.

Between inclusion and exclusion: the case of Travellers

Among the larger Traveller organisations in Ireland are Pavee Point and the Irish Traveller Movement, both of which define Travellers as the nomads of Ireland and an indigenous minority, ethnically distinct from the Roma and Sinti of continental Europe, and distinguished from the sedentary ('settled') majority population of Ireland by a shared history, value system and language. This claim to ethnic specificity is both a claim to historical fact,[2] and a way of challenging the idea that the difference between Travellers and the majority society reflects a failure of socialisation. In other words, the claim to ethnic identity refuses the long-standing tendency – noted above – to define Travellers as indigenous primitives, a label which has been used to legitimise programmes to 'absorb' (assimilate), 'rehabilitate' (educate), and 'settle' (modernise) them as a group.

When we consider the treatment of Travellers in the past it is important to note that what is at issue is more than illegitimate coercive state power being exercised over a marginalised group. The programmes to which Travellers were subjected emerged in large part through efforts to create a stable society appropriate to modern systems of authority. Some suggestions on how to resolve the 'tinker menace' were ruthless, such as the idea that the children of 'itinerants' be removed from their parents and placed in 'nursery homes', where they would be trained in the habits and values of 'decent citizens' (Pro Bono Publico 1931; also Helleiner 2000: 68–72). The dominant strategy, however, and one that had widespread support, was the policy of 'settlement', which deployed the model of the camp (Commission on Itinerancy 1963). Part prison, part school and part factory, the camp was a way of concentrating the travelling people so that they could be subjected, both as individuals and as a group, to a combination of surveillance and training. The Irish state certainly played an important role in instituting the settlement policy, but so did the many settlement committees that emerged organically in civil society. Similarly, the policy was challenged not only by Travellers as they became politically organised, but also by the many tenant and resident associations who campaigned against housing Travellers in their neighbourhoods, that is, beyond what was considered a fair 'quota'.

Struggle and conflict thus played a significant role both in creating and contesting the settlement policy. There were individuals and organisations who spoke for or on behalf of 'itinerants' and wanted to help them (a type of intervention that often entailed infantilising the travelling people), while others demanded explicitly punitive forms of intervention. This disempowering complex of meanings was built on a body of expertise that made the 'itinerant problem' possible in the first place, from the gypsiologists of the nineteenth century to the folklorists of the twentieth century. For those who subscribed to a theory of social change which opposed the 'modern' to the 'traditional', the travelling form of life was destined to wither and die, and this axiom lent legitimacy to the idea that the inevitable should be brought about sooner rather than later (see Helleiner 2000; Delaney 2001, 2003).

Modern social order necessitates the inclusion and exclusion of specific conducts, dispositions, relations and desires on the part of its subjects. Those who did not, would not, or were unable to conform to dominant norms were classified in the negative, often incarcerated, and usually subjected to programmes of education and training. Examples from twentieth-century Ireland would include the categories of 'juvenile delinquent', 'mental defective', 'unmarried mother', and 'itinerant', all of which brought together a complex of authorities pertaining to scientific knowledge, philanthropy, social work, religion, and public administration. In the closing decades of the twentieth century this paradigm was challenged both politically and through structural transformations, opening out the possibility for a new type of order.

In the introduction to this chapter, we sketched a number of landmark changes which were seen to herald a new dawn for those people long excluded from the benefits of social membership, tangible signs that the new inclusive mode of governance was delivering not only greater prosperity (the Celtic Tiger economy) but also greater equality. Among these was the Citizen Traveller campaign. Established in 1999, Citizen Traveller was to facilitate inter-cultural dialogue between Travellers and the 'settled' community while also providing a means to re-present the meaning of 'Traveller'. No longer indigenous primitives to be 'rehabilitated' or 'absorbed', Travellers presented themselves as citizens: the universal subject of the Irish Republic.[3]

Organised initially through a Traveller Communication Committee, the Citizen Traveller project was managed jointly by the Irish Traveller Movement, the Parish of the Travelling People, Pavee Point and the National Traveller Women's Forum. With financial support from the Department of Justice, Equality and Law Reform, the Committee was charged with developing a communications programme to 'promote the visibility and participation of Travellers within Irish society, to nurture the development of Traveller pride and self confidence, and to give Travellers a sense of community identity that could be expressed internally and externally' (Irish Traveller Movement 1999). As part of the programme, a series of posters was produced depicting the faces of individual Travellers – one of a woman, another of a man, and a third of a young girl – overlaid with words such as 'mother', 'singer', 'daughter', 'storyteller', 'best friend', 'husband'. Common to all of the posters were two words: 'Traveller' and 'Citizen', and the message: 'It's time to value Travellers as people with their own culture, needs and contribution' (Irish Traveller Movement 1999). The posters might be considered the cultural equivalent of T. H. Marshall's famous essay on *Citizenship and Social Class* ([1950]1992): though cultural differences exist in Irish society (Marshall would have said class differences), all share the status of citizenship. The mode of representation both diffuses and de-essentialises difference, for though Travellers embody and value certain things and meanings which are culturally specific, any individual Traveller also has much in common with non-Travellers (as a 'mother', 'best friend', 'singer', and so on). Rejecting both essentialist meanings and the type of authority that ties essence to exclusion, the declaration of 'citizenship' is a claim to a specific type of equality: one derived from the idea of social contract.

Figure 11.1 **Advertisement from Citizen Traveller campaign 1999**

Research on the effectiveness of the Citizen Traveller campaign was generally positive (Department of Justice, Equality and Law Reform 2002: 10), yet the programme ran into difficulty before the end of its three-year funding cycle. When representatives of the Communications Committee met with the Taoiseach to discuss funding in 2002, they were questioned about anti-social behaviour on the part of Travellers, a concern raised again in a subsequent meeting with the Department of Justice (Department of Justice, Equality and Law Reform 2002: 15–18). This was almost certainly a reference to Traveller encampments along the banks of the Dodder River in Dublin the previous summer, something the media seized on in a series of reports focusing not only on the usual suspects of dirt and nuisance, but also something new: extortion. On the one hand, Travellers were reported to be using dirt and nuisance to extract cash from landowners, and on the other to be abusing equality legislation by blackmailing publicans (*Sunday World*, 2 December 2001; Hennessy 2001a; *Irish Times*, 15 May 2001; *Irish Times*, 11 March 2001; *Irish Times*, 31 December 2001; Farragher 2001; Department of Justice, Equality and Law Reform 2002: 13). The charge of anti-social behaviour – and the terminology is important – seems to have been instrumental in the passage of the Housing (Miscellaneous Provisions) Act 2002 through the Dáil, which empowers the Gardai to arrest trespassers without a warrant and to confiscate property, including caravans, while those charged under the act face a fine and possibly a prison term (see Haughey 2002; Hennessy 2001a, 2001b). It should be noted that even as the new legislation came into existence, the targets set by the National Traveller Accommodation Strategy had failed to materialise beyond a token 129 units (Community Workers Cooperative 2002; Delaney 2003).

Travellers responded to the 2002 Act through the resources of the Citizen Traveller campaign, creating a billboard poster to disseminate the following message (endorsed by Amnesty International, see Love 2002): 'Suddenly, in caring Ireland, to be a Traveller is a terrible crime. The racist and unworkable law on trespass criminalises 1200 unaccommodated Traveller families.' The message claimed that the legislation did not simply target 'anti-social' behaviour but instead essentialised Travellers as a group, outlawed Traveller culture, and further excluded Travellers from society. On the one hand, the Citizen Traveller strategy had given substance to the otherwise vague notion of social inclusion, but, on the other, it had become apparent that the meaning of both inclusion and citizenship were being shaped by political struggle. As explained above, the concept of citizenship is not without constraints. In Ireland and Britain in recent years, the concept has been hugely influenced by communitarian discourse, with 'rights' (freedoms) set against responsibilities (constraints). The work of Etzioni (1993) and Putnam (2000) for example, which has clearly influenced Blair and Third Way thinking more generally, has also transferred to Irish policy.

For Travellers, what was at stake in the Citizen Traveller campaign was recognition and entitlement to specific goods, such as culturally appropriate accommodation, which had failed to materialise. For the state – and it should be noted that this was consistent with the thrust of public debate at this time – recognition was twinned with a contractual conception of citizenship, emphasising responsibilities or obligations so that failure to live up to these obligations was interpreted as free-riderism, thus a legitimate target for coercion. Travellers had deployed a conception of citizenship which made room for vigorous dissent, which of course reflected their long struggle against exclusion, while the state was sponsoring a more compliant and consensual notion of the citizen. The Citizen Traveller strategy had brought Travellers and the state into partnership, yet from the perspective of Travellers the Housing Act had rendered citizenship tentative and revocable. In fact what had happened was that the boundaries of the law had shifted, and what in the past had been governed as a departure from social norms (Traveller encampments) had now become a strictly legal transgression. Thus, the basis of excluding Travellers has been redefined. Noting our earlier definition of legitimacy as entailing social recognition, the issue here is whether the new mode of exclusion can be considered legitimate.

The state responded to the final dissenting gesture of Citizen Traveller by commissioning an independent (and thus apparently impartial) agency – Talbot Associates – to conduct a 'value for money' audit of the Citizen Traveller project in 2002 (Department of Justice, Equality and Law Reform 2002). Following the publication of the Talbot report the Minister for Justice announced that the strategy had 'represented the Traveller perspective exclusively and did not address the concerns of the settled community', and that 'Government objectives for Citizen Traveller were unlikely to be met in the future'. As the funding was withdrawn it became apparent that, irrespective of how Travellers conducted themselves as individuals, the strategy of intercultural dialogue had failed sufficiently to modify their conduct as a *group*. Not only does this reveal how 'inclusion' and 'partnership' can reinstate the old policy of assimilation, it also reveals what may be a weakness in a struggle for inclusion organised on the basis of a collective identity, or more specifically, a fixed-primordial ethnic identity. Travellers as a group are held responsible not only for the (alleged) wrongdoings of 'anti-social' individuals who happen to be Travellers, but also for 'anti-social' behaviours *associated* with Traveller culture as an abstract entity, which does not necessarily bear a direct relationship to any specific Travellers. What seems to be happening here, as an unintended effect rather than an insidious design, is that the collective identity of 'Traveller' has become entangled in a discursive web which deploys the theme of 'anti-social' conduct to symbolise the difference between those who should be included into society and those who should be excluded.

From the Citizen Traveller strategy we can see that inclusion can both empower and discipline, and to understand the mechanics of this we need to examine the relation between the 2002 Housing Act and the emergent discourse of anti-social behaviour in more detail, which is arguably most developed in the UK. The recent Anti-Social Behaviour Act of 2003, for example, covers aggravated trespass in the UK and can, in practice, be applied to anyone occupying private property. It has been suggested that the trespass dimension of the legislation is directed specifically at Travellers, ravers and political activists, which is to say those who represent cultural alterity and/or political dissent (see Padfield 2004: 723–4). In Ireland the current Minister for Justice is in the process of drawing up legislation to introduce British-style Anti-Social Behaviour Orders. From the case of Travellers it could be argued that legislation directed at anti-social behaviour has already been enacted, and while it might seem like an unlikely place to look, we shall be arguing that the new child-care legislation in Ireland is part of the same discursive web.

Anti-social behaviour

The Anti-Social Behaviour Order (ASBO) came into existence in the UK through the Crime and Disorder Act of 1998, and has been met with a number of criticisms. Foremost among these is the problem of defining 'anti-social behaviour'. The 1998 Act defines it as acting in a manner which has caused or is 'likely' to cause 'harassment, alarm or distress to one or more persons', while the more recent Act of 2003 defines it as conduct 'capable of causing nuisance or annoyance to any person' (Home Office 2002; Ramsay 2004; Padfield 2004). Behaviour associated with annoyance and nuisance may well reflect the perspective of those who make the allegation, and when coupled to behaviour 'likely to cause' such things as harassment and annoyance, then there is the danger that the rule of law moves beyond things which have happened to the judgement of *possible* misdeeds. Critics of the ASBO are thus concerned with a discretionary power which is insufficiently constrained by due process and may encroach on individual rights and liberties.

Legal opinion is also worried about the hybrid nature of the ASBO. While an ASBO is basically a civil injunction, breaching it is a criminal offence which may lead to a custodial sentence (Jones and Sagar 2001; Irish Youth Justice Alliance 2005). Yet another concern is the way it augments the shift away from social supports to punitive methods of control. In some instances, local authorities have distributed flyers identifying young people who have been issued with an ASBO, the objective both to 'name and shame' while also recruiting local residents into the task of surveillance (Squires and Stephen 2005; also Jones and Sagar 2001).

The ASBO is thus perceived by its critics as a slippery slope to an authoritarian state, yet there is in fact much more to this than the ASBO itself, and it involves more than one modality of power. In the UK the ASBO is supplemented by Acceptable Behaviour Contracts (ABCs), which are voluntary agreements that organise the anti-social individual into partnership with local authorities, such as the police, housing and school authorities. Likewise, local authorities have a duty to develop a crime reduction strategy by facilitating a synergistic relationship between probation committees, health authorities, voluntary sector agencies, and representatives from the business sector, all co-operating as a 'crime prevention partnership'. When examined together, the ASBO and the ABC insert the 'problem' individual into a form of community governance or 'parochial control' (Crawford 2003), flanked on one side by a voluntary contract and on the other by a compulsory order. While it clearly has its punitive moment as it passes from civil injunction to crime, this apparatus could also be described as a technology of citizenship (Cruikshank 1999). Here the otherwise tacit social contract is made manifest. The individual is granted agency, thus 'power to', and in exchange they undertake to uphold certain social norms. If they fail to do so then they will meet with sanctions – not sanctions predicated on essentialist constructions, but sanctions to enforce a relation of reciprocal obligations, between citizens and the state.

In Ireland all the major political parties are currently striving to instil a sense of responsibility into 'anti-social' individuals and communities, and this is also recoding the relation between Travellers and the settled community. While acknowledging the link between anti-social behaviour and socio-economic disadvantage, the Irish Labour Party (now an overtly Third Way party) has published a position document titled *Taking Back the Neighbourhood*, which emphasises responsibility and endorses the introduction of ASBOs (Labour Party 2005). Fine Gael stands over a similar message, arguing through its *Safe Streets* strategy that 'it's the perpetrator, not the law-abiding citizen and community who must pay the price' of anti-social behaviour (Fine Gael, 2005). And foregrounding all of this is the Minister for Justice in the current coalition government, who is preparing legislation for the introduction of ASBOs.

Child welfare agencies and experts in Ireland argue that if the ASBO is introduced it will undermine the Children Act of 2001. Designed to bring the juvenile justice system into alignment with the UN Convention on the Rights of the Child, the legislation emphasises prevention, diversion, supervision and counselling within the community so that detention will be used only as a measure of last resort (Dooley and Corbett 2002). While the legal framework is different in Ireland and England, the same apparatus is nonetheless apparent in both cases. In Ireland – if the new childcare legislation if fully implemented – young people who accept responsibility for criminal behaviour will be admitted to diversion programmes, while young offenders will be managed within the community through a technique called the 'conference'. Here a facilitator is to be charged with formulating an action plan with and for the offender, in partnership with his or her parents/ guardians, in consultation with the victim (restorative justice), and with the assistance of police, health services, probation and welfare services, and school authorities (Children Act 2001).

If we examine this bundle of innovations as a whole – noting that all are techniques of prevention and control which are modelled on the contract (Crawford, 2003) – then the Citizen Traveller programme might be interpreted as a pilot project which is about to be mainstreamed.

Those who support the new childcare legislation see it as an opportunity finally and decisively to break with the old punitive model of treatment, whether in the industrial school, the reformatory school, or the borstal (and to this list we would add the camp). The penitentiary waits in the wings to punish those who break the law or breach an ASBO (that is, if and when the ASBO is introduced to Ireland), and this is where we find coercive power. Yet this is merely the outer limit of something more encompassing, and it is this we need to focus on if we are to explain how it is that the inclusion of Travellers (granting them 'power to') involves both empowerment and discipline. For between inclusion and exclusion are technologies of citizenship that recruit the subject (Travellers, the disabled, the unemployed, lone parents) into the work of governing their 'self'. We would argue that the discourse of anti-social behaviour circumscribes an administrative apparatus which can be unpacked as follows:

Dimensions of discourse of anti-social behaviour

- *Responsibility*: at once individual and social, rights come with responsibilities, which is an axiom of contemporary communitarian views of citizenship connecting freedom to (self-) discipline.
- *Authority*: has its central points in coerceive power (the police, the law, the prison) but is also dispersed through forms of partnership and contractual relationships, which organise a variety of authorities into the task of securing order at the local level.
- *Order*: the discourse of 'anti-social' aims to secure order by creating a wholly negative representation of undesirable conducts, dispositions and relations. The 'anti' signifies pure negation, reaching beyond the concern with certain individuals and groups to the government of social conduct and social relations more generally.
- *Contract*: the sometimes implicit, sometimes explicit, idea that empowerment entails obligations, and so the exercise of freedom must be constrained, and if necessary controlled.

Whether targeting 'anti-social' youths or Travellers, it seems that power increasingly operates through forms of partnership, with empowerment coupled to pedagogic techniques which aim to inculcate self-discipline. Those coded as anti-social, whether an individual or a community, are to be tutored through a mode of authority that brings a variety of agencies together in the same discursive space, and here we find power – as a relation – both empowering and disciplining. In other words 'power over' and 'power to' form a mutually constitutive relation: responsibility is being devolved to individuals and communities in response to demands on the part of individuals and communities to be empowered through inclusion into the political and policy-making processes. Empowerment is conditional and inclusion comes with a contract, and though often only tacitly acknowledged, the disciplinary force of the contract is made visible in the discourse of anti-social behaviour.

Reflections

In recent decades we have witnessed a transformation which, though not of the same magnitude as the revolution envisaged by socialism, looks a little like the Marxist prophecy, minus the utopian end-state. While the economy has not been democratised and the state has not withered away, the old distinctions are becoming less clearly defined as the public folds into the private, work dissolves into leisure, the separation between culture and nature is increasingly difficult to define, and 'government' is no longer thought of as something external to its subject. The new inclusive model of democracy, or governing through 'governance', attempts to address the forms of exclusion engendered by the 'power to' of modern social formation. As a mode of social organisation, social partnership operates through mechanisms of consultation and negotiation, and this confers legitimacy on the authority structures of society by making each and all party to the social contract. Certain dispositions and conducts are still excluded (those coded as 'anti-social') but it is claimed that these are not attributed to specific groups, such as Travellers. Of course things may turn out differently in reality, but nonetheless it is here that we can locate the legitimacy of this apparatus. For even as groups such as Travellers are charged with failing to actualise the ideals of citizenship, and even as this is resisted, so it seems that the ideals themselves are not radically contested. Travellers have clearly not (yet) acquired the kind of justice they demand, yet Traveller organisations and representatives continue to struggle for inclusion and for recognition as citizens. In principle, if not necessarily in practice, citizenship no longer excludes on the basis of negatively essentialised identities.

Both 'power to' and authoritatively based 'power over' constitute a field of relations within which we are positioned as individuals and through which we act in concert. While we have not suggested that power is conferred equally among all individuals and groups, what we have examined is the way in which social agency inevitably comes with a cost to freedom: the forms of discipline enforced through both legal and social sanctions and engendered through programmes to educate and train us in the arts of self-government. Furthermore, we are suggesting that between the Citizen Traveller campaign and the various strategies emerging through the discourse of anti-social behaviour is an outline of the subject of inclusive governance: a constellation of norms which, though ill-defined, nonetheless circumscribes a more or less definite field of possibilities and constraints. As the socially excluded become the subject of inclusion, so they are tutored in the arts of self-government. Defined against states of dependency, passivity and unemployability, the subject of inclusive governance is (to be) self-actualising, flexible, reflexive, independent and entrepreneurial. Both individualised while also dependent on social networks ('communities') as the basis of support, this is the citizen as defined within the discourses of communitarianism, neo-liberalism and the Third Way. Whether all members of society are equipped or prepared to play this role, however, remains to be seen.

Chapter 12

The environment and civil society

Mary Kelly

Introduction

Has recognition of the scale of the waste mountain, of the contribution of car dependency to global warming, of the danger of overuse of fertilisers for water pollution influenced the policies and practices of the state, of economic interest groups or of citizens and consumers in Ireland? To what extent has local environmental mobilisation against incineration and road building, and against toxic, oil and mining industries been successful, and what can sociology contribute to our understanding of these protests? Research shows that public concern to protect the environment is increasing in Ireland. This concern is nonetheless challenged by a perhaps even stronger interest in maintaining economic growth. Can these two interests be reconciled? What can sociological perspectives and research contribute to exploring and understanding these potentially conflicting concerns which lie at the heart of contemporary society?

Four sociological perspectives prevalent within the sociology of the environment and relevant to this question will be examined in this chapter. It will outline the debate between risk society, green socialist, civil society and ecological modernist theorists regarding the nature and level of current environmental risks and the socio-economic characteristics of the society that has produced them. Also examined will be their different perspectives on what can and should be done.

The elaboration of each of these theories will be followed by an exploration of how they help to raise relevant sociological questions regarding the relationship between society and the environment in Ireland and help us to understand changes that have occurred in the last few decades. Regarding a risk society perspective, research on changing perceptions of risk and of science among the general public and among mobilised environmental groups will be examined. Regarding a green socialist perspective, research evidence indicative of the priority given to economic growth over environmental protection will be reviewed, as will attempts to align political and economic interest in the development of such environmental policies as waste management. With reference to a civil society model, research on environmental protest movements and their articulation of a discourse on democracy and rights will be discussed. Finally, within an ecological modernist perspective, the development of a state environmental regulatory regime and the influence of the EU in this, as well as responses at a local level, will be analysed.

Risk society

Ulrich Beck's *Risk Society* (1992) and *World Risk Society* (1999) offer a theory of contemporary industrial society which places the origins and consequences of environmental degradation at its centre. Two of the pertinent questions for Beck are: What are the characteristics of a society which is seriously undermining the very bio-physical world on which all human life depends? Secondly, can we identify the social and cultural resources within that society which can question and change the kind of destructive industrial society we have created?

He argues that modern industrial societies are characterised by a level of humanly created environmental risks unknown in previous societies. He particularly focuses on such environmental risks as nuclear explosions, genetic engineering and chemical pollution. These he argues present new forms of environmental risks in that they cannot be immediately seen or smelt or felt, and cannot be limited in terms of time or place. As Beck notes, the injured of Chernobyl are today, years after the catastrophe, all not even born yet. Beck argues that, in the early stages of industrialisation, the overwhelming emphasis on economic progress led to an almost total blindness regarding the consequences of this 'progress' for the natural environment. It was exploited indiscriminately as both a production resource and as a sink in which to dump extensive industrial and other waste. There was little public debate regarding environmental issues. However, as we move into the later stages of modernity, recognition of these risks leads to an increased questioning of the kind of society we have created. Adding to these societal concerns is the perception that existing state and economic institutions appear unable to deal adequately with them or ensure the safety of the public, leading to increased questioning of these major institutions. Thus risk society is a self-critical society, characterised by 'reflexive modernisation', or 'self-confrontation with the consequences of risk society which cannot (adequately) be addressed and overcome in the system of industrial society' (Beck 1999: 73).

The role of science and technology in relation to environmental risk is of particular interest to Beck. He notes the role of scientists in contributing to the creation of environmental risks as well as their role in analysing and attempting to lessen these risks. As the state, economic institutions and the public attempt to grapple with environmental issues, scientists play a central but increasingly ambivalent role, being unable to provide the definitive 'right answer' regarding, for example, culturally acceptable levels of risk. As Beck (1999: 42) comments, 'There are no expert solutions in risk discourse, because experts can only supply factual information and are never able to assess which solutions are culturally acceptable.' Thus, for example, the scientific information of the chance of industrial pollution or a nuclear explosion occurring, may be interpreted very differently by state officials pursuing economic growth, by industrials seeking to make profits, or by the local community living beside the potentially polluting facility. Furthermore, different applied scientists and engineers may themselves offer different advice regarding what are 'acceptable' levels of risk. This lack of clear answers further increases the sense of risk, insecurity and fear in society, and a sense that major institutions in society cannot protect its members thus leading to further societal questioning. Within risk society, some scientists also play other roles, contributing to the production of greener technologies or, as they become more reflexive themselves, contributing their expertise to oppositional environmental groups.

Beck identifies three potential future paths for risk society. One is to continue the industrial practices of the past, ignoring the environmental consequences. The second is for major institutions in society, especially the state, to put in place environmental regulations to limit environmental destruction. This is frequently entitled ecological modernisation and will be discussed later in the chapter. A third option, and that favoured by Beck, is the promotion of ecological democracy, where the decisions of the two most powerful societal institutions – the state and the economy – would be more open to critical public debate, challenge and change, and particularly open to debate with critical environmental groups.

Beck's characterisation of contemporary society as 'risk society' has been criticised for its over-emphasis on the importance of ecological issues especially within the political sphere. It is argued that the mainstream electorate is still primarily concerned with economic growth, increasing prosperity and jobs, and it is in these terms that political parties continue to appeal to them. And while class issues may have decreased in importance, 'it is not clear that risk issues have come to outweigh production and consumption issues' (Goldblatt 1996: 178).

Risk society and Irish research

To what extent does empirical research indicate that Ireland might be characterised as a risk society or has entered what Beck has called 'reflexive modernity'? Certainly survey research undertaken in 2002 indicates that Irish respondents feel that environmental issues are of concern to them, 95 per cent stating that they perceived nuclear power stations as dangerous to the environment (45 per cent stating that they were extremely dangerous), while almost 90 per cent or more judged a range of environmental issues, including the pollution of rivers and lakes, air pollution by industry and by cars, and pesticides in farming, as dangerous, with between 15 and 22 per cent judging them to be extremely dangerous. With regard to the rise in the world's temperature, 86 per cent felt this to be dangerous (18 per cent extremely dangerous) and 76 per cent thought genetic modification of crops to be dangerous, 15 per cent extremely dangerous (Motherway et al. 2003: 37).

However, the percentages assessing these environmental problems as *extremely* dangerous had declined since similar research questions were asked in 1993, although the overall totals of concerns remained the same (Motherway et al. 2003: 35). It would thus appear that the Irish public have become more moderate in their environmental concerns. This pattern of moderation is also a feature of Northern European countries including the Netherlands, Denmark, and the Scandinavian countries (Kelly et al. 2004: 3–4) most frequently characterised by ecological modernist (or eco-modernist) policies. A sense that something can and is being done by state and industry appears to contribute to lowering the levels of extreme anxiety regarding environmental issues, although this is less the case in Germany, Austria and Switzerland.

A characteristic of ecological modernisation is a belief that science and state environmental regulation can help to resolve at least some environmental problems. Survey research in Ireland shows a somewhat increased belief in the efficacy of science over the last decade (Motherway et al. 2003: 18), and a continuing strong belief that the state is responsible for ensuring the environment is protected (Motherway et al. 2003: 40). However, while emphasis is placed on the role of the state, there is little evidence that the public feels that environmental issues, despite their concerns, should be top of the political agenda. Health, crime, education and the economy were found to be given greater priority than the environment by all 12 groups included in research on environmental discourses. This research used a qualitative focus group methodology, drawing groups from the general public living in Dublin, the midlands and the west of Ireland (Kelly 2007).[1]

Evidence of a belief that science can solve environmental problems is also offered by Tovey (2002b) in her analysis of the response to the foot and mouth (FMD) outbreak in Ireland (and indeed across Europe) in 2001. The response to this risk (in the event, only one sheep in the Republic was confirmed with FDM) by state bureaucracies, the agric-food industry, veterinarian scientists and the general public was that scientific advice should be immediately sought and strictly followed. The state rapidly mobilised what Tovey (2002b: 28) characterises as a modernist, 'military style application of technical bodies of knowledge to solve a technocratic problem', justifying this in terms of the national interest. Farms were turned into fortresses, 55,000 sheep, cattle and pigs slaughtered, and the public agreed to forgo travel and leisure time in the countryside while sports events, and even St Patrick's Day celebrations, were cancelled. Driving this policy, she argues, was protection of the meat industry and its exports. What did not happen in response to this potential risk was a reflexive questioning of the dominant role of the food industry in shaping contemporary attitudes to nature, in particular the strongly anthropocentric 'cultural interpretation of food animals as technological artefacts placed at human disposal' (Tovey 2002b: 37). Thus, Tovey concludes, 'the food industry remains in its treatment of animals a relentless production machine which is the epitome of modern dominating rationality' (Tovey 2002b: 37).

The above empirical findings would indicate that Irish society and polity show more of the characteristics of one form of eco-modernisation than of risk society. The empirical evidence of the widespread development of that reflexivity which is characteristic of risk society, that is, a self-questioning among members regarding the kind of society they have created, in particular criticism of a society which produces a self-destructive level of environmental risk, is somewhat weak. On the contrary, a predominant interest in further economic growth is evident as will be apparent from the discussion under a green socialist perspective below. Nonetheless, there is evidence of considerable environmental mobilisation at the local level, protesting against perceived local environmental threats and drawing on discourses of rights and democracy and of risk, safety and threats to health to do so (see for example *The Great Corrib Gas Controversy*, Centre for Public Inquiry 2005).

However, there is also considerable research evidence of how such critical environmental discourses are marginalised by an alliance of state and industrial interests, and the scientists they employ. Studies have been undertaken of two public hearings held by An Bord Pleanála and the Environmental Protection Agency. The first was to hear public protests against the siting of a chemical factory in East Cork in 1988 (see Peace 1993), the second against a proposed toxic waste incinerator by a pharmaceutical company in Clare in 1996 (see Keohane 1998). In both these cases the voices of the protesting local rural population and environmental groups and their scientific advisers were marginalised by the dominant bureaucratic and technocratic language of the hearing, the well-resourced scientific voices of the multi-national companies privileged by the hearings, as well as the latter's arguments regarding what was economically feasible.

Nevertheless, environmental mobilisation at the local level, often networking with other environmental groups and experts at local, national and international levels, indicates the perhaps increasing demand from below for that greater reflexivity which characterises risk society, and certainly a demand for greater involvement in decision making regarding proposed developments in one's own locality. Thus in the mosaic of conflicting Irish cultural values and social groups addressing environmental issues, some elements characteristic of risk society are visible, if only to be strongly challenged and marginalised by others, especially by economic and political elites.

Green socialist perspectives

This perspective proposes that central to the capitalist system is its continuous demand for economic growth and the accumulation of profits and that it is these forces which are the most important drivers of environmental depletion and destruction. Some theorists within this perspective would argue that the demand for economic growth can be described in terms of the 'treadmill of production' and the 'treadmill of consumption' (see Schnaiberg and Gould 1994; Bell 1998). The former describes the central role of competition within capitalism, continuously driving increased overall production levels. The consequent increased supply of products drives prices down so that profits decline, driving the need for further production to maintain profit levels. Thus the treadmill of production is continuously fed by competition and profit making, diverting attention from the environmental and human costs of this exploitative production process.

Interrelated with the treadmill of production is the treadmill of consumption. The increased supply of products must continuously be bought and consumed. These high levels of consumption (at least among the rich and in rich nations) are supported and encouraged by a culture in which status and success are demonstrated through increased and conspicuous consumption, aided and abetted by the advertising industry. Green socialists argue that together these treadmills of production and consumption have contributed to unsustainable levels of resource depletion and environmental pollution, as well as increasing levels of inequality, both within states and globally between the developed and the developing majority worlds. Indeed it points to capitalism's severe destruction of the very natural resources on which both it, and indeed all human life, depends.

Ted Benton (2002) argues for a green socialist perspective noting that, while green socialism emphasises the causal importance of capitalist accumulation in generating environmental destruction, it also examines those political, legal and cultural factors that are interrelated with capitalist accumulation and which may have a specific influence on environmental issues. He discusses Beck's argument regarding the role of reflexive modernisation in contributing to increased environmental consciousness and to eco-modernist policies to protect the environment, concluding that this theory is incomplete without an analysis of the economics of capitalism. Regarding scientific and techno-logical innovation and the extent to which they can contribute to limiting environment deterioration, he suggests the importance of examining how such 'knowledge communities' may be aligned with particular elite interests and policy groups, and the need to explore the extent to which scientific exploration may be subordinated to the competitive priorities of private capital, and indeed the role of the state in this. A green socialist perspective advocates, as does Beck, the opening up of contentious scientific and technological decision making to public debate, thus promoting greater democratic involvement in decision making about the development and deployment of new technologies.

A further criticism Benton (as well as others, see Goldblatt 1996) would make of Beck's risk society thesis is its claim that the role of social class within politics has been greatly diminished. This postulate of 'the death of class' is, they would argue, premature. While accepting that its role has been weakened with the increasing importance of, for example, identity politics as well as environmental politics, they note that class patterns can still be observed in voting, that there is still considerable support for the politics of redistribution, and that class issues continue to be of importance at the level of the shop floor and indeed in the environmental justice movement. The latter describes the mobilisation of working class and marginalised groups to protect their envi-ronmental and social interests, for example by mobilising to protest the locating of dirty industries in their areas of residence while also pointing out the inequity in such siting decisions. Green socialists are particularly interested in studying those environmental justice movements in which environmental movements join with class-based social forces, focusing not only on environ-mental issues but those of social justice and accountability (see Szatz 1994; 1997; Agyeman et al. 2003).

This perspective concludes that ecological sustainability is improbable unless there are fundamental challenges to the power of capital. It recognises the difficulties this entails, especially owing to the way in which state institutions align themselves, and facilitate and support capitalist interests. Indeed it would note that state support has increased since the 1970s as the power of transnational corporations (TNCs) has grown relative to that of the state. This increase in power of TNCs is particularly related to their ability to move elsewhere if the policies of a particular state do not facilitate them. It is to research on the role of the Irish state in relation to economic growth and its environmental consequences to which we now turn.

How relevant is a green socialist perspective to understanding environmental issues in Ireland?

Rapid economic growth in Ireland based on foreign direct investment, with some related indigenous developments, along with an explosion in the services sector and in construction, have significantly contributed to Ireland's environmental problems. Two aspects of this economic growth will be discussed below. One is the role of the state in promoting and legitimating economic growth, in particular looking at how the state has attempted to deal with one of the major downsides of this growth – the ever-increasing waste mountain; the second is evidence of the extent to which the public is critical of the type of economic growth which has been achieved and the consequences of this growth for the environment.

Mark Boyle (2002) has looked at the relationship between the type of economy in Ireland and the government's response to the EU's demand that the waste issue be tackled. Drawing on Ó Riain's (2000) research, he argues that Ireland has the characteristics of a 'flexible developmental state' within which economic growth is the key governmental goal. Thus priority is given to government policies and practices that attract and keep foreign transnationals and that support the globalising (and hence competitive) strategies of key types of indigenous companies. Boyle argues that the way the government has attempted to deal with the waste problem since the mid-1990s has been fundamentally influenced by its concern not to interfere with this primary goal of economic growth and the means it has chosen to achieve it. Rather than disrupt the treadmills of production and consumption by a policy of radically reducing waste production (through for example strongly supporting and facilitating recycling, although some such recycling services aimed at the consumer have been belatedly increased), the waste policies introduced emphasised the disposal of the existing (and annually increasing) waste mountain through incineration and super-dumps. Furthermore, the policy ultimately removed responsibility for making controversial decisions regarding incineration and super-dumps from democratically elected local authorities to unelected local authority managers.

The government's waste policies thus attempted to marginalise both local concerns and local democracy. Consequently the state's plans have run into serious difficulties, especially in the face of local opposition to the siting of major waste facilities. Some of these highly vocal protests are articulated around the public's concern that having a thermal treatment plant located in one's locality will lower the amenity value of the neighbourhood, despite the authorities stating otherwise; that waste is a toxic substance possessing serious health implications; that science and modern technologies cannot easily resolve these difficulties; and, drawing on an environmental justice discourse (see further below), that communities have a right to be consulted.

Strong commitment to a continuous high level of economic growth – indeed it would appear its idolisation – is evident among all the main political parties, and the government's mantra regarding the need to maintain competitiveness rings true to the treadmill of production thesis. Trade unions also express strong allegiance to the ideology of growth, and especially for the jobs and wage rates it is expected to deliver.

Figure 12.1 **Carbon credits: The purchase of carbon credits, rather than the reduction of carbon emissions, is the current method of meeting Ireland's Kyoto targets. Cartoon: Martyn Turner,** *Irish Times*, **15 December 2006.**

Focus group research among the general population indicates that they also recognise the major benefits to Ireland offered by economic growth (Kelly 2007). However there is also evidence from both qualitative and quantitative research of an increasing emphasis on the need to balance economic growth with environmental concerns. While a quarter of survey respondents in 2002 agreed when asked if they felt the economy should be prioritised over the environment, this had declined from over a half in 1993. Furthermore over a half agreed that 'economic progress in Ireland will slow down unless we look after the environment better' (Motherway et al. 2003: 19).

Focus group respondents also readily acknowledge that the Irish economy is a highly dependent part of a global economic system, a system over which they perceive the Irish government and people have little control. There is recognition that this globalised economic system deals a radically unfair hand to the developing majority world. However, the public response to this inequality tends to be a sense of passivity and futility in attempting to challenge or change it. Typically, the response is, 'What can we do?' Acknowledgement of being on the receiving end of the rewards of this economic system and its consumer gravy train is widespread – the treadmill of consumption appears alive and very well in Ireland (Kelly 2007).

Research has also indicated the successful marginalisation of critical voices, including environmental voices. The processes of marginalisation include the repeated valorisation of economic growth stories in the media, even when reporting on ostensibly environmental events (Skillington 1997, 1998); the characterisation of voices of protest as unreasonable and emotional at, for example, An Bord Pleanála public hearings, as well as the narrow terms of reference given to such public consultation processes (Peace 1993); and the stigmatising of radical environmentalists and their forms of protest – some of the most frequent, if least offensive, labels being 'tree huggers', or 'woolly hats' (Kelly 2007).

On the other hand, there is also recognition among a significant minority of the important environmental and democratic role played by protest groups (see further below). There is also within Irish political culture an expressed commitment to the value of greater equity and redistribution in society (see Coakley 1999: 60–1). Research has also indicated that those who hold the strongest pro-environmental values tend to also be committed to equity issues and to an active political culture (Kelly et al. 2003; Taylor and Flynn 2003).

Civil society approaches, including constructionist, cultural and social movement perspectives

Increased awareness of environmental issues and concerns regarding environmental protection are evident in both national and international survey research. A number of interrelated sociological approaches are relevant to exploring the processes whereby issues come to be defined as problematic and placed on the public agenda. One is a social constructionist approach asking how environmental issues, for example climate change, come to be defined in a particular way; a second is a more broadly based cultural approach which asks what cultural values, including ethical and religious perspectives, exist within a society regarding the interrelationship and interdependence between humans, society and the environment, how these values are institutionalised and practised within that society, and how they are drawn upon by citizens mobilising to protect the environment; while a third approach asks, how and why environmental social movements mobilise, organise and gain – or lose – influence.

A constructionist perspective examines how environmental claims and environmental problems are defined, legitimated, contested and acted upon by different social actors with various, and indeed frequently conflicting, interests. It analyses how claims are articulated in terms of the rhetoric used, the evidence mobilised and the justification given for action (see Hannigan 1995). It studies who the claims-makers are. In the context of environmental policy making it may thus examine the different and contested claims of industrialists, farmers, various government departments and officials, scientists and professional groups, as well as environmental and locally based community groups. Finally it also explores the claims-making process, asking what are the social, political and cultural processes, as well as the institutional settings, in which various claims-makers articulate their positions? How do they seek to publicise their claims, for example through the media, and attempt to influence decisions? It places the social actor at the centre of its analysis, recognising the importance of understanding how actors define issues, and how they mobilise appropriate cultural and knowledge resources to advance their case.

A cultural perspective, while related to a constructionst approach, asks which cultural values and discourses (that is, ways of representing aspects of the world from a particular perspective (see Fairclough 2003)) exist within society regarding the appropriate relationship between humans, society and non-human nature. Thus, for example, are humans seen as but one species dwelling within nature and not necessarily superior to other species as claimed within eco-centric or deep-green perspectives and by some animal rights activists? Or, are humans defined as superior to non-human nature, legitimating their right to exploit, or indeed over-exploit, it as some forms of anthropocentrism claim? A cultural perspective would ask how, historically, such values arise. To what extent and by whom are they articulated in contemporary society? How are these discourses argued for and by whom, and how are discourse coalitions formed (see Hajer 1995; Kelly, 2007).

To understand the latter questions, cultural researchers are particularly interested in identifying the forms of knowledge and narratives or storylines articulated by and used strategically by different groups. Thus, for example, regarding environmental discourses, this approach may be particularly interested in the discourses articulated by scientists and ecologists, in how these discourses are used by powerful groups and how they may differ from the discourses and storylines embedded in the 'lay knowledge' of local community members. A further discourse frequently articulated by locally based environmental movements is that of environmental justice, emphasising the rights of citizens and local communities to be consulted about developments in their own areas, their right to be given accurate information, and a timely, respectful and unbiased hearing (Capek 1993).

Examining the mobilisation of environmental protest groups, whether internationally, nationally or locally based, may draw on further, if related, perspectives. Within civil society at least four different types of environmental and other social movements can be identified, and the research questions related to each may differ. One form is the very locally based group which may originally form to contest a particular environmental issue in the neighbourhood. Typically over time such groups network with other groups outside the community with similar problems to gain and share knowledge, to seek advice regarding appropriate strategies and to get support. They may indeed become more environmentally and socially radical in the process, linking their analysis of the environmental issue with issues of power or inequality. A second form of social movement may be constituted by a relatively loose network of individuals and groups who share a strong concern with environmental destruction locally, nationally or internationally, and with the cultural values that underpin this destruction. This may characterise the stage before a formal environmental organisation is formed, contributing to the shared development of a collective sense of identity, of critical forms of consciousness, and of everyday forms of action which put these critical perspectives into practice. A third form is the more centralised social movement organisation, such as Greenpeace, which campaigns for change. One particular research perspective drawn upon to explore the latter, entitled resource mobilisation theory, examines how such organisations insert themselves into the political process to bring about change, how they organise, attract and hold members, and the cultural resources they draw upon to strategise and campaign (see McAdam et al. 1996)

Environmental social movements in Ireland

One way of examining some of the cultural values and practices in civil society in relation to the environment is to examine them through the lens of environmental movements. Membership of environmental movements in Ireland is not high. Nationally based survey research indicates that four per cent of the population claim membership of environmental groups, while five per cent state that they had taken part in a protest or demonstration about the environment over the last five years (Motherway et al. 2003: 46 and 84). These percentages have remained constant over the last decade. However, higher percentages state that they supported environmental groups by giving them money (20 per cent) or signing environmental petitions (25 per cent) over the last five years. Thus there would appear to be a small core of active members which can mobilise more general public support when necessary. This pattern has been confirmed by qualitative research which shows that as well as a few centralised environmental groups, there exist relatively extensive locally based groups. In these the core membership may be small, but they network with other similar groups based elsewhere when necessary, and are sufficiently in touch with local interests that when an environmental issue, especially with implications for the locality, arises, they can provide leadership, information and organisational capabilities (see Tovey 2007).

An important discourse frequently drawn upon by environmental groups operating at the local level is that of democracy, especially the democratic right to be consulted regarding developments in one's own area, and the related storyline of the felt lack of respect involved in marginalising local knowledge by what are seen as economic and political elites from outside the area. This discourse can be immediately articulated against decisions taken by what are seen as unrepresentative elites, including industrialists and what are perceived as their aligned scientist-advisers and politicians (see Kelly 2007). On the contrary, locally mobilised groups claim the right to be involved in local decisions and legitimate this not only in terms of their democratic right, but in terms of their local knowledge, their attachment to the local area, as well as local livelihood and residential interests. They frequently bolster their claim by drawing on alternative scientific knowledge of the environmental issue involved or on an alternative interpretation of scientific data. The use of new communications technologies including the web and email greatly facilitate this quest.

While the above describes the cultural resources and actions of environmental groups acting to defend what they perceive as their existing local environmental interests, environmental groups may also act in more culturally creative manner by working and living a lifestyle that in itself offers an alternative to that of the majority, and which offers a critique of the cultural mainstream. Some involved in the organic farming movement offer such a critique both in their production and consumption practices. They offer a critique of mainstream intensive and high-fertiliser input agricultural practices by their alternative of extensive farming with low fertiliser use and less intensive rearing of farm animals and fowl. They also provide a critique of contemporary globalised food production and transportation by their emphasis on direct selling to and communication with customers in, for example, local farmers' markets as well as a critique of increased consumption of processed foods by their emphasis on wholefoods, locally grown and fresh (see Tovey 1997 and 2002a).

Ecological modernisation

A fourth perspective is that of ecological modernisation. This is a perspective which is particularly useful in raising questions about the role of the state in environmental policy making, especially in relation to economic growth and the role of industry and agriculture. It offers a way of characterising and analysing the reformist socio-democratic political processes which are characteristic of some states where political and economic institutions are modernised in order to protect the environment. Here the eco-modernist state takes responsibility for ensuring the curtailment of environmental degradation, encourages industry to invest in green production and in green markets in which waste in particular is reduced and thus efficiency as well as environmental protection promoted. Furthermore the citizen/consumer is mobilised (through for example green carbon taxes or waste charges or support for eco-friendly consumption) to consume and behave in a more environmentally sensitive manner. Two of the most well-known theorists in this area are the Dutch sociologists Arthur Mol and Gert Spaargaren (see for example, Spaargaren et al. 2000). The environmental policies of the EU are frequently seen as eco-modernist, and through the EU influence Irish environmental policy.

It is argued that, with eco-modernisation policies in place, economic growth can continue while the environment is also protected. Thus through further progressive modernisation or rationalisation of both state and economic institutions environmental risks can be limited. This is popularised through such slogans as 'pollution prevention pays', the 'polluter pays principle', or 'reduce, reuse, recycle'. Indeed protecting the environment can offer further possibilities for economic expansion into eco-industries. Beck notes of eco-modernist economic practices that the group most likely to benefit may be big business who can afford to transform themselves into green businesses. Thus a pattern of secondary industrialisation, including expanding markets and green consumerism, occurs. To Beck (1992: 175) this expansion simply permits 'the transformation of mistakes and problems [of the past] into market booms.'

Strongly contributing to this process of further rationalisation are applied science and economics. Applied science and technology are looked to for solutions to environmental problems, especially in terms of reducing pollution and efficiency in resource usage, while applied economics is called upon in, for example, advising on the introduction of environmental taxes and charges. Thus policy makers turn to 'experts' in developing 'ecological rationality', to encourage (though fiscal policies and penalties as well as technological changes) the taking into account of environmental concerns in production, in pricing, in creating markets and in green consumption.

This is a perspective which, in its stronger and more democratic form, although it does not argue for radical economic or social change, recognises the importance of reflexivity if both political and economic institutions are to be modernised. Furthermore it seeks to encourage not only elite mobilisation but that of consumers and citizens. This mobilisation in the interests of the environment is best brought about, according to an eco-modernist perspective, not by hierarchical command and control mechanisms but by encouraging a partnership approach which includes negotiation with not only major economic interests but with mobilised citizens in, for example environmental and community groups, regarding environmental decision making. To ensure compliance, the ideal policy style is the use of legal mechanisms and civil liability law as well as the use of environmental taxes and environmental policy incentives. Ecological modernisation as a policy initiative can range from a weak form in which technocratic and managerialist perspectives are emphasised, to a much stronger form in which ecological democracy is more firmly embedded. In the latter, the ideal is the establishment of deliberative, integrative and participative (often called DIPs) forums where citizens' opinions can be heard and have some influence in the formulation and implementation of environmental policies along with the views of other stakeholders.

One of the more important criticisms of eco-modernisation is that it is applicable to only a limited number of countries where a strong socio-democratic state is already in existence and in which a relatively high level of environmental mobilisation among citizens already exists (see Leroy and van Tatenhove 2000). At the present time, these are characteristics of Northern European countries and the Netherlands, as well as Germany, Austria and Switzerland. Furthermore, major inconsistencies may occur even in these states' environmental policies, including the fact that, while some eco-modernisation policies are pursued, the state may at the same time be promoting, for example, nuclear industries and major infrastructural projects such as roads, as well as the privatisation of public utilities, all of which may have major negative environmental consequences. A third criticism is that offered by green socialism which would argue that eco-modernisation neither adequately analyses nor tackles the root cause of environmental destruction which lies in the way the capitalist system works.

Is Ireland an ecological modernist state?

From the previous discussion it would appear that Ireland has at least some of the characteristics of an eco-modernist state. Fundamental to this perspective is the assumption that economic growth can accommodate environmental protection and that it is important to facilitate both. Survey research, as noted above, indicates that the Irish public increasing think this is the case, and hold an increasingly positive attitude to the role of science in environmental protection. They also state a slightly increased willingness to pay higher taxes in order to protect the environment, although the willingness to pay higher prices is greater (Motherway et al. 2003: 26). Levels of recycling have increased, albeit from a low base. Indeed focus group research with groups from the general public indicated that, in 2003, there was extensive criticism of the government for its lethargy in providing sufficient convenient and accessible facilities to encourage increased recycling. Overall, there is a continuing high level of support among the public for state regulation of environmental issues.

One of the major eco-modernisation policy drivers is the EU. Its environmental policy directives regarding for example waste disposal, habitat protection and water quality, require the Irish state to ensure that institutional structures and regulations are in place to limit pollution and to protect fragile ecosystems and threatened species of birds and fish. The Irish state has, however, been relatively slow to transpose these directives into Irish law or to significantly increase the institutional capacity of the state to deliver on environmental protection at either the central or local authority levels. The special interests of particular groups including industry, business and construction firms, farmers and fishermen, and their alliances with political parties would appear to contribute to this hesitancy, as does the overriding commitment of political parties to economic growth. Also contributing would appear to be fear of alienating an electorate lulled by low taxation policies and hence perhaps loath to accept, for example, a carbon tax that may contribute to limiting car pollution. However, the question may be raised as to whether the results of the survey research quoted above indicate that the attitudes of the electorate may have in fact moved at a faster rate in a pro-environmental direction that those of the political establishment.

If the state is slowly moving in an eco-modernist direction, prodded by the EU, it is towards a weaker form of this policy emphasising its managerialist and technocratic orientation rather than its more democratic potential. This can be clearly seen in its approach to waste management and especially its support for incineration favoured in the regional waste plans as already noted. Specialist engineering consultancy firms drafted these regional plans. Davies (2005: 382) notes the importance of these engineering consultancy firms in setting the waste agenda, 'The consultants have been key decision-influencers in the waste-management debate, being pivotal in defining the initial strategic vision for waste in Ireland', a vision that included incineration and super-dumps along with increased recycling. The government characterised the resulting public protest to incineration plans as 'alarmist' and without scientific evidence, and 'attempted to reassure publics that science, engineering and technology would resolve remaining technical difficulties' (Davies 2005: 388). When protesting groups were not mollified and local authorities, sensitive to these protests, began to reject regional waste plans, the government strengthened its managerialist arm by removing responsibility for the adoption of waste management plans from local councillors to the county or city manager, who is appointed by central government.

In relation to the government's attempt to institutionalise a relatively strong technocratic and managerialist form of ecological modernisation, it is relevant to take note of the survey research evidence of the public's lack of trust in the environmental information provided to them by both government and industry. When asked, 'How much trust do you have in each of the following groups to give you correct information about the causes of pollution?' only seven per cent stated they had a great deal or quite a lot of trust in the pollution information provided by business and industry, while 25 per cent stated the same in relation to information from government departments. However, much larger percentages (61 per cent and 70 per cent respectively) trusted the pollution information coming from environmental groups and university research centres (Motherway et al. 2003: 42). Low levels of trust were also evident in the focus group research already noted. Here high levels of distrust were expressed regarding what was seen as an elite alliance of business and political interests who did not take seriously what was seen as the democratic right of local communities to be involved and consulted in matters regarding their own interests and their own communities. The mobilisation of citizens and consumers, if eco-modernisation policies are to be successfully institutionalised, may well be inhibited by these low levels of trust.

Conclusion

The mosaic of conflicting attitudes to the environment among Irish people has been attested to in the above discussion, whatever theoretical perspective is drawn upon. Environmental issues have become contentious at this time of rapid change. This conflict often appears to be used symbolically to flag a strong sense of anger at what is perceived as a lack of respect by political and economic elites for the views of ordinary citizens and is fuelled by a lack of trust between them. On the other hand, there is also popular recognition and assent to what are seen as the benefits of economic growth and little evidence of a sustained challenge to the globalised economic system on which that growth is based. Furthermore, while particular local issues may be highly significant at the local level, and on occasions reach the national level, environmental problems are not, at least as yet, top of the political agenda for most groups.

Research findings indicate that in Ireland only a few of the characteristics of Beck's risk society can be observed. Environmental problems and concerns, while they certainly exist, are not, for most, at the centre of the Irish polity, culture or society. Indeed the environmental movement has to battle its corner in the face of marginalisation by political and economic elites. There is little evidence that the majority of the population seriously questions the kind of society Ireland has become, or questions the forces of globalisation that are recognised as shaping it and indeed much of the world, as might be expected if Ireland had moved to 'reflexive modernity'. Nor can the Irish state be characterised as strongly ecomodernist; delivery of eco-modernist policies on the ground in Ireland is slow, despite EU prompting, as governments prioritise economic interests and marginalise what are seen as troublesome environmental issues and groups.

Nonetheless, environmental activism is alive and well in Ireland. While the core membership of environmental groups in Ireland is small (four per cent of the population), this core can call on more broadly based support, indeed a fifth of the population reported having supported an environmental group in the last five years. A particular pattern of environmental mobilisation in Ireland is that of the small core group organised locally, networking with other similar groups and with the ability to mobilise more general support in the light of significant local environmental issues. Informing these groups is a strong sense of what has become known as an environmental justice discourse, emphasising their democratic right to organise and question those with economic and political power, a sense of their right to be involved in decision making regarding their world and their own efficacy, as well as a detailed knowledge of their own area, an appreciation of its natural environment and its vulnerability, and a strong impetus to protect it. Such localism does not negate global concerns but may feed into activism regarding the protection of humanity's fragile natural environment from such global threats as climate change, biodiversity loss and possibly increasing nuclear energy facilities to combat fossil fuel depletion. Indeed the future of the biophysical world of which humanity is part and without which it cannot survive depends on such mobilisation.

Section IV

Economy, development and the Celtic Tiger

Chapter 13

Globalisation, the state and Ireland's miracle economy

Kieran Allen

Introduction

The Celtic Tiger refers to the spectacular growth that has taken place in the Irish economy since the early nineties. The name was invented by an economist working with the Morgan Stanley Bank, who compared it with the more commonly known Asian Tigers of the time – Hong Kong, Singapore, South Korea and Taiwan. The Celtic and Asian tigers were viewed as Newly Industrialising Countries (NICs) who overcame decades of backwardness through an 'export orientated strategy'. Instead of restricting foreign goods through tariffs, these countries welcomed foreign direct investment and embraced globalisation.

Ireland is supposed to be a showcase for how globalisation works. Despite having only one per cent of the EU population, it has attracted 25 per cent of US investment in the EU over the last decade. In 2003, US investment flow into Ireland was roughly $9.1 billion, two and half times the amount of US investment into China (US Department of State 2005). As a result of this huge surge of inward investment, Ireland became one of the fastest-growing economies in the world.

The Celtic Tiger is therefore held up as model which others are urged to follow. One of the most prominent columnists of the *New York Times* has recommended that France and Germany change their ways and catch up with the 'leapin' leprechaun' (Friedman 2005). From a national point of view, this might appear complimentary but what exactly is the Irish model that is being promoted? What are these economic policies which are supposed to have brought success?

Rather insensitively, Thomas Friedman attributes the growth to an 'Anglo-Saxon' model of flexible labour markets. He suggests that,

> The Germans and French may want to take a few tips from the Celtic Tiger. One of the first reforms Ireland instituted was to make it easier to fire people, without

having to pay years of severance. Sounds brutal, I know. But the easier it is to fire
people, the more willing companies are to hire people (Friedman 2005).

Here the Irish model is being used as evidence for neo-liberal policies. By neo-
liberalism, we mean, a theory that human well-being can best be served by
liberating individual entrepreneurship within an institutional framework
characterised by strong private property rights, free markets and free trade
(Harvey 2005: 2). In other words a form of capitalism that is 'liberated' from
the constraints of the welfare state. Ireland is often used as evidence for the
success of this model by its advocates. The prominent right-wing think tank,
the Cato Institute, has published an article on the Celtic Tiger to prove that
its growth came after it fully embraced 'economic freedom' (Powell 2003).

The South African President Thabo Mbeki has taken a slightly different
approach and pointed to Ireland's social partnership model as the key to its
success. He argued that 'the union's role in the new social pacts is to participate in enhancing the competitiveness of the national economy [and] in
exchange the unions gain access to policy making' (Mbeki 2005). Impressed
by the Irish experience, he has created a Millennium Labour Council where
business and union leaders interact as partners. Yet the South African government is also committed to the agenda of neo-liberalism, often claiming that it
is powerless before the force of globalisation (Bond 2005). It still, however,
maintains links with trade unions and Mbeki's reference to the Irish model
was made in the course of a May Day address. This may explain the different
emphases on what constitutes the success of the Irish model, but the interpretations of Friedman and Mbeki are by no means incompatible. Mbeki is looking
for a mechanism by which society as a whole lends support for 'competitiveness'
while Friedman is more robust in his embrace of the globalisation model.
One is concerned with legitimation while the other is concerned with the
economic content. Both, however, share the same assumptions that neo-liberal
policies offer the best way forward.

How are we to assess these arguments? One approach might be simply to
revel in a certain form of national pride and soak up the praise. The problem,
however, is that a nationalist standpoint leads to an uncritical examination of
the wider social processes that underlie the apparent success story. Nationalist
modes of thought permeate everyday discourse and nowhere more so than in
Ireland. In the past, Irish nationalism was focused on ending partition and
retaking the fourth green field or Ulster. Today, however, this traditional discourse slides over into economic nationalism where we assume that if Ireland
wins the battle for competitiveness it must be a good thing. From the very
moment of birth, we are marked out as citizens of a particular country. Our
birth certificate gives access to a particular passport which in turn confers a
host of rights or privileges. In school, we learn national history which recounts

the heroic struggles of one society. When we listen to the media, we hear an interpretation of the world from an 'Irish' perspective. Despite the fact that Ireland has, for example, ceased to be an agricultural country, EU decisions which cut price supports for food are often presented as bad for 'Ireland'. All of this means that when we approach the study of society, we often start within a national framework – even without realising it.

Has globalisation removed the importance of nationality in our thinking? At the heart of globalisation according to one writer is 'a stretching process in so far as modes of connection between different social contexts or regions become networked across the earth's surface as a whole' (Giddens 1990: 4). The attack on the twin towers on September 11th came as a dramatic shock to people in Leitrim almost as much as Lexington, USA. The food we eat, the books we read, the films we watch are almost identical the world over. These impressionistic observations might lead one to claim that the nation state no longer matters – and indeed some do. According to Kenichi Ohmae (2003: 207), 'nation states have already lost their role as meaningful units of participation in the global economy of today's borderless world'.

A cursory glance at the issue of migration indicates that this is an extremely exaggerated claim. Each year 175 million, or one in every 35 people on the planet, become international migrants. It is one of the most tangible signs of globalisation, with the numbers doubling over the past forty years (International Organisation for Migration 2005: 379). Without their labour power, the economies of most developed countries could not function and these economies will become in future even more reliant on migrant labour owing to their increased age-dependency ratios – the ratio of pensioners to the working population. Yet migration is surrounded by all sort of national restrictions and up to half of the international movement of workers may take place in a clandestine fashion (Harris 2003: 256). Millions are forced to work in the invisible economy without legal protection simply because they have the wrong passport. Ohmae's concept of a 'borderless' world in this context seems absurd. But even if we reject his exaggerated claims, we can still think about migration through national spectacles. We may assume, for example, that having a passport is only natural and that migration poses dangers to 'national cultures'. Starting from these assumptions, we arrive at the conclusion that migration is a 'problem' that has to be managed carefully.

The great value of sociological theory is that it questions these nationalistic perspectives and asks its readers to stand back from their own socialisation process and become critical. It helps to clarify unspoken assumptions behind our arguments by connecting particular experiences to a wider body of concepts and debates. This is relevant when we come to consider the oft-repeated claims about the success story of the Celtic Tiger, because explanations of why development takes place are often connected to visions about how its society and economy *should* be organised. In assessing the Celtic Tiger, we shall therefore leave aside a national vision and examine how that story is used to promote neo-liberal globalisation. In order to do this, we shall first examine the debates about the wider sociological theories of economic development and indicate how some of this literature has been used to interpret the Irish experience. We shall then outline our own alternative view which seeks to analyse the experience of the Celtic Tiger from a class rather than national perspective.

Neo-liberalism and development theory

1   Modernisation theory

One of the earliest texts on development theory was *The Stages of Economic Growth* by W. W. Rostow. Subtitled a Non-Communist Manifesto, it was a product of the Cold War (Rostow 1960). Its author was a security adviser to Presidents Kennedy and Johnson and was an ardent supporter of the Vietnam War until the end of his life. Nevertheless the book raised interesting questions about the relationship between culture and economic development and became the founding statement on what was known as modernisation theory.

Modernisation theorists such as Rostow and Samuel Huntington (1968) drew on the work of the US sociologist Talcott Parsons to emphasise an ideal type distinction between the culture of 'traditional' and 'modern' societies. Parsons had argued that traditional societies were constructed around certain values such as 'ascription' rather than 'achievement'. In these societies one judged individuals on the basis of their ascribed characteristics – such as bloodlines or marriage ties rather than on the basis of what they had achieved in a more socially mobile society. Clearly this blocked innovation, entrepreneurship and development.

Using these assumptions, modernisation theorists suggested that the key factor in underdevelopment was the internal culture that prevailed inside poorer countries. The transition from traditional to modern society had already taken place in the West and it was assumed that the underdeveloped countries could follow on this same path – provided there was internal cultural change. This change would mainly occur through the dissemination of modern values by an elite. The elite might be formed either through a colonial power or through a nationalist movement that resisted that power but simultaneously took on some of its values. Rostow attempted to chart this process through five stages of growth: (1) traditional society; (2) preconditions for take off; (3) take-off; (4) drive to maturity; and (5) the époque of high mass consumption.

Many of these arguments fitted in neatly with the aims of US Foreign Policy because development was equated with private capitalism and culminated in a mass consumer society – rather than the communist model (Gendzier 1985). The focus on a modernising elite dovetailed with the Kennedy administration's aim to promote a middle class in Latin America. Most crucially, modernisation theory closed off questions about the relationship between the underdeveloped society and metropolitan countries like the USA. Instead it tended to take a benign view of America's role in the world.

Modernisation theory's focus on how the internal culture blocked development in Ireland is well represented in the work of Joe Lee and later Tom Garvin. The former attributed Ireland's original underdevelopment to the fact that 'Irish manufacturers were not psychologically prepared for expansion.' (Lee 1969: 57). After independence, a culture emerged which encouraged conformity over risk-taking and so professional employment was preferred to entrepreneurship. Garvin takes up a similar theme in his *Preventing the Future*, arguing that after 1945 Ireland made a series of 'non-decisions' which were disastrous. The causes were partially structural such as 'a curious alliance between the welfare dependent and the politically powerful privileged against the innovative, the energetic and original' (Garvin 2004: 17) and partially cultural, such as a mindset 'that thought in static and rural ways and in ethical rather than scientific terms' (Garvin 2004: 3). Garvin also argued that a local elite, or as he puts it 'the actions of good citizens in key positions', was the key locus of change (2004: 7).

The problem with such analysis is its sheer voluntarism. How this elite were able to perform the Herculean task of changing culture and develop an economy is not fully theorised. Even if we were to assume that rising education and democratic structures led to a more secular culture, it is by no means clear how this alone brought about economic change. And if it did, why did it happen in Ireland rather than, say, Turkey? And, why Ireland in the nineties rather than Ireland in the seventies? There is also little analysis of how different social classes have fared once culture has changed. From a modernist perspective, Ireland is simply a success story that is to be celebrated rather than subjected to critical inquiry.

2 Dependency theory

Modernisation theory was originally attacked principally by a number of Latin American intellectuals. Starting with Raul Prebisch, who led the UN agency, the Economic Commission for Latin America, these emphasised the wider structural relationships into which poorer countries were inserted. They argued that the nations on the periphery were often forced to supply primary produce to metropolitan countries in return for industrial and consumer goods. Far from gaining a comparative advantage by specialising in exporting products where they had natural advantages, peripheral countries had to produce more and more primary goods to obtain the same quantity of manufactured goods. The solution, according to Prebisch, was import substitutionism where tariffs were imposed on goods from industrialised countries so that a space was created for domestic manufacturers to produce simple consumer goods (Roxborough 1979).

Dependency theory soon took on a more radical direction in the hands of Paul Baran (1957) and Andre Günter Frank (1967). For Baran, dependency was characterised by a dual economy comprising a large agriculture sector with extremely low productivity and a small industrial enclave that could not find a domestic market for its goods. Shifting Marx's paradigm, Baran argued that a surplus was extracted from the peasantry and appropriated by land-owners, moneylenders, merchants and a mainly foreign capitalist class. These groupings had little interest in development and often functioned as a 'comprador class', siphoning off the surplus to foreign capital and gaining privileges as a result. The only solution was extensive state intervention to promote national development.

Frank agreed that the cause of underdevelopment was the extraction of a surplus by metropolitan countries. This, however, occurred primarily through trade itself rather than through a dualistic structure of the economy. The trading relationship with the metropolis affected all sectors of society and led to the draining away of resources. There was no original state of under-development from which such countries had to incubate – rather they were underdeveloped through coming into contact with the metropolitan powers. The route to development lay, therefore, in de-linking from the world economy.

The conflict between modernisation and dependency theorists dominated debates in the sociology of development up to the 1980s. Broadly speaking it often appeared as an argument between Left and Right, with the Left appearing to champion state led national development and the Right focusing on the need to modernise the value system. Sometimes the argument shifted when, for example, F. H. Carduso (1972) broke from the orthodoxy of dependency theory and suggested that some development could occur in the periphery. Using the concept of dependent development, he returned to Baran's argument about a dualistic structure within an economy but acknowledged nevertheless that some development was possible.

Dependency theory in Ireland is best represented in the writings of Denis O'Hearn who produces a highly perceptive analysis by locating Ireland within with the Atlantic economy of Britain and the USA. He disputes the sugges-tion that a 'lazy' or psychologically ill-adapted bourgeoisie caused underde-velopment and instead focuses on Ireland's historical relationship with the British Empire. He also argues that the spectacular growth of the Celtic Tiger did not occur simply because the government invited in foreign capital because, 'The orthodoxy that foreign capital would cause prosperity by transferring capital, technology and jobs to the host country was accepted in Ireland by the 1950s' (O'Hearn 2001: 142). What needs explanation is why the growth occurred in the nineties rather than before. For O'Hearn, the main factor has been the surge of US investment which was motivated by a desire to gain access to the EU single market before tariff barriers came down. Ireland was used both as a site to shift US products to Europe and as a tax haven. The Celtic Tiger was thus a case of dependent development where the primary beneficiaries were foreign capitalists.

O'Hearn's realism about Irish dependence on US investment is welcome but some of his arguments are questionable. He claims, for example, that 'the main recipients of the fruits of growth were the foreign capitalist class rather than the domestic one' and that 'this form of dependent development contributed to class inequality . . . because it produced returns primarily for a foreign class' (O'Hearn 2001: 187–8). While foreign capital gained considerably, it hardly did so at the expense of domestic capital. Nor can it be plausibly argued that domestic capital did not benefit from Ireland's status as a tax haven. Why the Irish state might look after foreign capital exclusively or even to the detriment of Irish capital is not explained. The claim that foreign capital contributed more to class inequality looks, therefore, suspiciously like an alibi that might excuse the actions of domestic capital. Implicit in dependency theory is a suggestion that the interests of workers are best served by a nationally controlled economy. However, it is doubtful if this is the case. While Ireland ranks high in the inequality index of the industrialised world, it still manages only to come second to the nearest approximation to a fully developed nationally controlled economy: namely, the USA.

3 Neo-liberalism

By the 1980s, the arguments between these two opposing frameworks of modernisation and dependency theory had run aground. The rise of the NICs meant that it was no longer possible to talk about one undifferentiated Third World. The modernisation of internal values was by no means the key factor in determining whether countries experienced rapid economic development. Taiwan, for example, maintained many traditional elements within its society but its location in an area of high US military spending gave it an extra spurt to growth. The NICs also represented a fundamental challenge to dependency theorists. The argument that all contact with foreign investment brought further underdevelopment was no longer sustainable. More generally, the shared assumption of both schools that development implied an autocentric economy, where each element of the world system was replicated internally within each national economy, was questioned.

Something more fundamental than intellectual debates also occurred. The debt crisis, which affected many developing countries, forced them to go to the International Monetary Fund (IMF) and the World Bank for assistance.

These institutions had, in turn, embraced the new view of the US Treasury about the developing world. Essentially, this demanded an opening up of economies so that foreign capital could move freely in and out; that state assets should be sold off; that a tight financial regime would be maintained through high interest rates; and that countries remove barriers to imports and expand their own exports. Known as the Washington Consensus this was a blueprint for rolling back the state in Latin America and Africa. Loans from the IMF and the World Bank became conditional on the acceptance of stabil-isation and Structural Adjustment Programmes. In effect, this brought about the forcible reintegration of many poorer countries into the global economy. Between 1982 and 1988, for example, 28 of the 32 nations in Latin America and the Caribbean had agreed to an IMF stabilisation plan (Panayiotopoulos and Capps 2001: 49). The era of state-led development of national capitalism appeared to be over.

This was the context in which neo-liberalism rose to a hegemonic position. Neo-liberal ideas were highly marginal until the 1970s and were only sustained by small right-wing think tanks such as the Mont Perelin society, which promoted the ideas of Friedrich von Hayek. Hayek's ideas won a hear-ing among economists in the Chicago School of Economics who argued for a fundamentalist style return to the market. Their moment, however, came with the first major global recession of the post-war era – commonly known as the oil crisis. The ending of the post-war boom and the return of recession threw conventional Keynesian economic ideas into crises and neo-liberalism grew quickly in the Thatcher–Reagan era. It attacked the idea of social solidarity and state regulation and called for new emphasis on individualism, private property and personal gain. As Thatcher put it, 'Economics was the method but the object is to change the soul' (Harvey 2005: 23).

The leading agency for promoting these ideas in the context of develop-ment studies was the World Bank. Its regular World Development Reports argued that government policies led to price distortions which impeded eco-nomic growth. The state was analysed as a set of economic actors who engaged in 'direct unproductive profit-seeking' or DUP behaviour. Its use of licences to regulate trade, for example, created monopolies which were exchanged through political patronage or corruption. The state tended to expand its range of operations because its employees had a direct interest in plunder or 'rent seeking' behaviour. This in turn hindered the free functioning of the market which was the only real source of economic efficiency. The ideal solution was for governments to 'institute a speedy bonfire of all controls and Ulysses-like tie itself to the mast by signing a stabilization and structural adjustment programme with an international organisation' (Lal 1993: 118)

The place of the state could then be occupied by free competition between individuals and companies. While acknowledging that markets might sometimes fail, the neo-liberals argued they were still preferable to government failures. Development, they argued, would not spring from major state-led projects but by getting the pricing structure right and encouraging micro-efficiency. Bauer's study of Malaysia argued that development was the result of 'the individual response of millions of people to emerging or expanding opportunities created largely by external contacts and brought to their notice in a variety of ways, primarily through the operation of the market' (Bauer 1984: 30–1). The main thrust of neo-liberal policy was measures such as privatisation, liberalisation of trade and stringent controls over state spending.

Neo-liberal arguments about the Irish success story abound in conventional economics. Indeed the discipline has adopted a fortress-like attitude to social critiques and has elevated neo-liberal assumptions to the status of an official dogma. The idea that the world should approximate as closely as possible to a pure market is barely questioned. Instead the arguments of neo-liberalism are presented in technical terms as if it were part of the architecture of economics itself, barely requiring any justification. Sometimes, however, the veil of value freedom slips and a straightforward morality tale is recounted. Here, for example, is Professor Dermot McAleese on the Celtic Tiger:

> The economic boom is an exemplar for the good things that follow from adopting new (or Washington) consensus policies built around the twin pillars of macroeconomic stability, globalisation and competition in the market place. (2000: 50).

Even though neo-liberal approaches have become a new orthodoxy, there was little evidence that they led to significant growth in most parts of the globe. In Latin America, only three countries have grown faster during the 1990s than in the 1950–80 period – and one of these was Argentina, whose economy crashed in 2001. Among the former communist countries, real output stood below 1990 levels for a long period in all but four of them. In Sub-Saharan Africa, the situation is far worse than that which obtained prior to the late 1970s. By contrast the success stories of the last two decades, China and South Korea, for example, are characterised by a high level of state activism and, in the case of China, weaker property rights. All of which makes the Irish case one of the few remaining success stories for the thesis that minimal state intervention may be the key to economic success.

4 New institutionalism

Before examining this case, let us look finally at one intellectual reaction against neo-liberalism. Known as the 'new institutionalism' or the 'new political economy', it disputes the emphasis on individual entrepreneurship and asserts that the market needs social institutions. Drawing on the economic sociology of Mark Granovetter (1985) and before him Karl Polanyi (1944), the key concept used is 'embeddedness'. This suggests that economic actions do not follow a simple individual path of profit maximisation but are organised around complex networks. In other words, markets only function smoothly when they are embedded in wider social structures. There needs to be, for example, a trust relationship before any contract can be signed; a culture of impersonal rather than entirely personal relations; a stable state which guarantees adherence to contracts.

One of the key writers to focus on the role of state institutions is Peter Evans. Evans distinguishes between different types of state which can assist or hinder economic development and challenges the neo-liberal view that state activism is always detrimental to economic progress. There are indeed 'predatory states' such as that which prevailed in Zaire, where rent seeking or plunder became endemic. But there are also 'developmental states' where the state interacts with the private sector in a constructive manner (Evans 1995). The key characteristic of these states is that they are embedded in civil society via a dense web of networks but do not become colonised by any one sector of that society. Rather they have a degree of autonomy that allows them to present a wider vision for economic transformation.

The 'new institutionalism' is an advance beyond neo-liberalism but, unfortunately, also subsumes some of its major assumptions. It challenges the idea of a reified market that is not connected to social relations. It undermines the dogmatic assertions about the benefits of a pure market by examining empirical links between states and markets. And it dismisses the idea that individuals are the only efficient economic actors. However, there are also key weaknesses in this mild-mannered critique. First, the market is accepted as the fundamental driver of efficiency. It may have to be embedded in other networks, but it is still the prime mechanism for allocation of resources in an efficient manner. Second, social class is dissolved into a host of social networks or collective actors who navigate the embedded economy. There are no fundamental conflicts of interest between larger class formations but rather a Weberian world of competition between status and economic groups. From this perspective, the question of how the resources are being distributed becomes a secondary question – if it is asked at all. Finally, in practice, the new institutionalism comes up with solutions that merely modify the supposed imperatives of globalisation. Typically it promotes liberalisation but argues the state can still function as an active agent in assisting and sustaining this process (Rodrik 2002). The difference between the post-Washington consensus and the Washington consensus is often about the speed and method of 'reform' – social partnership, for example, versus full flexibility – rather than the central thrust of economic policy.

The new institutionalism is best represented in Ireland by both Sean Ó Riain's *The Politics of High Tech Growth* and Peadar Kirby's *Celtic Tiger in Distress*. Ó Riain argues that Ireland's Developmental Network State was the key to its success. By this he means 'the institutional transformation of the Irish state and the emergence of the new state-society alliances'. This institutional transformation included social partnership which grew alongside a corrupt political system as a 'more efficient and accountable mode of governance' (Ó Riain 2004: 10). Through social partnership the Irish state became more embedded in civil society but simultaneously, through agencies like the Industrial Development Authority (IDA), it retained its autonomy from particular interest groups. Peadar Kirby is more sceptical about the benign functioning of the Irish state and sees it as a 'competition state' because it prioritises international competitiveness over social development.' (Kirby 2002: 143). Both, however, see social partnership as a vehicle by which market–state–civil society relationships can be adjusted to promote better social well being. Ó Riain, in particular, dissolves the question of class into the clash between 'two middles classes of a post industrial world' (technical professional and state employees) who become more distant from low-paid service workers (2004: 140).

This argument about the role of the state comes up against an important point raised by O'Hearn: namely, that the Irish state has not made any essential change in its industrial strategy since the 1970s. For three decades it targeted sectors such as electronics or pharmaceuticals yet only in the 1990s did this bear fruit. Social partnership began with National Wage Agreements in 1970 and developed into National Understandings in the early 1980s. There was already quite a sophisticated exchange between wage restraint and union inputs into state policy by the early 1980s. Yet the spectacular economic growth did not occur until the 1990s.

The notion that the Irish state is both embedded in civil society but still autonomous invites a further question: is it really autonomous from capital itself? The whole thrust of Irish state policy is to reduce taxes and regulation on both foreign and domestic corporations. Ó Riain's own evidence on how the IDA functions as a representative for foreign capital within the state structure surely raises questions about the notion of autonomy. The corruption scandals that have plagued the Celtic Tiger would also appear to indicate a very close relationship between the political and economic elites.

The claim that social partnership is designed to promote solidarity and better social well being also fails to explain how Ireland developed as one of the most neo-liberal societies in the world. It may be that the rhetoric of social partnership agreements makes much play about 'social inclusion' and ending poverty. But it might equally be argued that this rhetoric is aspirational and serves mainly to demobilise opposition to the elite. In any event, as we shall see, Ireland ranks as one of the most unequal societies in the world and robust neo-liberals like Thomas Freedman have little difficulty holding it up as a model for others to follow.

An alternative account

An alternative Marxist account of the Irish model makes class relations rather than national development the primary focus of analysis. One way it does this is to critique the morality tales about the birth of the Celtic Tiger and indicate the special conjunctural factors that caused the boom. Such an approach also questions the teleological assumption that Ireland's growth has now become self-sustaining. If the boom arose from a relatively unique set of circumstances, there is no good reason to suspect that Ireland will uniquely escape the return of a business cycle. Moreover, instead of seeing national development as a benefit in itself, the Marxist approach also examines how that development was shaped according to the interests of particular social classes. Rather than seeing a conflict of interest between foreign and national capital, it focuses on their shared alliance and their combined opposition to the working class. Overall, therefore, the most interesting question may not be about the relatively unique conditions that caused Ireland to develop but rather who benefited from the boom and what impact this had on the wider Irish society.

Just as nations often develop 'myths of origin' to strengthen an imagined community, so too have myths been created about the birth of the Celtic Tiger. Typically they suggest its birth was due to a certain chain of decision making by the political elite. The success story is then taken as evidence for the theoretical reasoning which informed such decision making. So neo-liberals point to deregulation and flexibility, while the institutionalists point to social partnership and state–civil society links. What both ignore is the sheer anarchy and inability of any one state – no matter how large – to exercise a significant level of control within current global system. This is one of the main reasons why supposed prescriptions for economic success turn out to be *post hoc* explanations which cannot be repeated elsewhere.

Looked at from this angle, it is questionable if the 'right policies' or institutions of the Irish state brought about a boom. It is more likely that policies which had *failed* in the past worked because of wider changes in the global economy. Specifically, the emergence of an EU single market forced US corporations to find new manufacturing bases inside its boundaries. Whereas in 1985, the EU share of foreign direct investment had fallen to 31 per cent of the global total, it rose again to 42 per cent by 1990 and remained at 39 per cent in 1995 (Barrell and Pain 1997). US companies were to the fore in this surge of investment, racing to gain advantage over their Japanese rivals in areas like office equipment and computers. Ireland's success lay in attracting a vastly disproportionate share of that investment and so the most interesting question is: why?

Quite clearly there were the host of factors at work, such as pay levels, educational attainment, a stable right-wing political structure and an English-speaking culture. However one issue stands out: the tax regime. The low 12.5 per cent rate of corporation tax on profits is famous but this was only the headline figure. Ireland provides a host of other measures to reduce tax on profits and wealth such as, for example, exempting income from patents and intellectual property from tax. Most crucially, it has no legislation to outlaw the practice of transfer pricing whereby multinational corporations artificially manipulate prices to declare profits in countries they regard as tax havens.

Between 1999 and 2002, profits from US companies in Ireland doubled from $13.4 billion to $26.8 billion. One of the reasons was that a new double taxation agreement was signed between the US and Ireland in 1997 which widened opportunities for avoiding US taxes. The Irish government succeeded in effectively exempting items such as royalties, profits earned from inter-national transport and interest from tax. Similarly, it was agreed to reduce the normal US withholding tax on dividends from 30 per cent to 15 per cent in some cases and 5 per cent in others (Revenue Commissioners 1997).

US tax expert, Martin Sullivan, has argued that a 'seismic shift' occurred in the late 1990s in international taxation. Subsidiaries of US corporations declared 58 per cent of their profits earned abroad to be in tax havens like Ireland or Bermuda. Ireland differs from Bermuda in that real business activity takes place here – as against being a location for front companies. Precisely because of this, however, it is a more respectable destination that allows corporations to slip below the radar screen of public opprobrium. As a result Ireland now tops the list of global tax havens for US companies (Sullivan 2004).

Ireland was able to get away with tax dumping because of its tiny size and its previous underdeveloped status. It benefited from Europe's social model as regional aid flowed to assist it to overcome underdevelopment. But it then undercut that model by introducing the lowest rate of corporation tax. Few EU governments originally objected because it took such a small share of foreign direct investment. Later, of course, there were calls for tax harmon-isation but by then it was too late. Ireland thus boldly embraced a neo-liberal project – even while receiving hand-outs from a social Europe. The very uniqueness of the case provides little evidence for neo-liberalism as a general strategy for development.

The effect, however, on Irish society was to cause a systematic transfer of wealth to the existing owners capital and property. Table 13.1 presents data on the adjusted wage share of the total economy and indicates that the share going to wages has declined faster in Ireland than in the EU in general. More interestingly, the decline occurred as the number of employees increased dramatically. The figures indicate a significant shift in class power within Ireland in this period.

Table 13.1 **Adjusted wage share of total economy: compensation per employees as percentage of GDP at factor cost per person employed**

	EU15	*Ireland*
1960–70	n/a	77.9
1971–80	74.5	75.9
1980–90	71.8	71.2
1991–2000	68.7	62.3
2001–7	67.3	54.0

Source: European Commission Statistical Annex of European Economy, table 32

This huge transfer of the share of the economy away from employees was not the 'inevitable result of globalisation' but the effect of a deliberate state policy. Using a rhetoric about wealth generation and competitiveness, the government systematically de-regulated Irish society. When democratic governments retreat from social regulation, it does not leave behind a vacuum but rather a new space for the power of capital. Table 13.2 indicates how the share of the economy going to large capitalists, the self-employed and landlords, has increased at the expense of wage earners.

Table 13.2 **Share of non-agricultural incomes (percentages)**

	1987	*1997*	*2004*
Profits, rent and self employed earnings	30.7	43.7	48.1
Wages, pensions and social security	69.2	56.3	52.1

Source: CSO, National Income and Expenditure Annual Results for 2004

Another indication of the transfer of wealth is the systematic reduction of the social wage. Ireland has the lowest level of spending on social protection in the EU and, contrary to the general trends, is reducing it further, as table 13.3 indicates. Means-testing rather than universal social insurance is more prevalent, with 29 per cent of total expenditure on benefits being means-tested as against an EU average of 10 per cent (European Commission 2001: 21). Ireland also has one of the lowest levels of spending on pensions, at only

3.7 per cent of GDP as against, at the other extreme, 14.7 per cent in Italy (Eurostat 2005: 138). One result is that Irish workers have longer working lives, with the average exit age of 64.4 as against an average of 61.0 across the EU (European Commission 2005b: 59). In the private sector, pension coverage is abysmal with only 38 per cent of employees being covered for pensions. (Pensions Board 2005: 38). The main reason is that neo-liberalism has brought low social security costs for employers and promoted instead an ethos of 'individual responsibility'.

Table 13.3 **Total expenditure on social protection as percentage of GDP at current prices**

	1991	1994	1997	2000	2002
EU15	26.1	28.0	27.8	27.2	27.9
Ireland	19.6	19.7	16.6	14.3	16.0

Source: Europe in Figures, Eurostat Yearbook 2005

The total tax take in Ireland represents only 29 per cent of GDP compared to an EU average of 40 per cent (Eurostat 2004). This means that there is less money available for public services than elsewhere. Or to put it differently, the population subsidies the corporations by putting up with poorer services. Nowhere is this more evident than in the public health system. Maev-Ann Wren has chronicled the effects of the historic underspending.

> Irish waiting lists compare poorly with those in other states. The UK's NHS, despite its well publicised difficulties, does remarkable better. In September 2002 in England only 6 patients in total had waited longer than 18 months for either inpatient or day treatment. Only 3 patients in every 10,000 had waited over a year. This compared to 21 adult patients in every 10,000 people who had waited for over a year in the Republic. In France, there are, quite simply, no waiting lists. All surgery is planned under a booking system in which a patient is given a date for surgery immediately it is prescribed, although this may involve a few months wait (2003: 146).

No wonder Ireland is sometimes described as a first world economy with third world public services.

All of this developed under the aegis of social partnership that exchanged wage restraint for a union input into state policy. The input was conditioned, however, by an acceptance of 'competitiveness' and an embrace of business unionism. The price of gaining an influence into state policy was that the unions aligned their policies with the dominant neo-liberal consensus. Instead of campaigning for free publicly run crèches, the unions supported tax breaks for parents; instead of arguing that employers had to make increased pension contributions, the unions supported the more individualised Personal Retirement Savings Account (PRSA) option; and in contrast to their British counterparts, the Irish unions supported, rather than criticised, the formation of public–private partnerships.

The logic of social partnership was that costs on corporations should be kept low in order to enhance competitiveness and this in turn produced its own contradictions. Despite having a wider say in state policy, the unions have not been able to show many substantive gains on non-wage issues for their members. Annual leave and public holidays in Ireland are the third lowest among the EU15 with total leave amounting to 29 days in contrast to 37 for Greece or 38 for Austria (Mercer 2003). Casualisation has grown by stealth among the workforce. The Irish state does not keep proper statistics on the use of temporary agency staff but one survey conducted for the European Foundation for the Improvement of Living and Working Conditions found that Ireland had the highest percentage of such staff (5.2 per cent) as against an EU average of 2.2 per cent (Conroy and Pierce 2002: 16). The partnership agreements have also ceded many more areas to managerial prerogatives as performance management, benchmarking and outsourcing of 'non-core' work have become accepted.

With a tighter labour market, one would normally expect the balance of power to swing towards workers during a comparatively long boom. This has not occurred in the Celtic Tiger because this common economic pattern has been superseded by political choices. The state has embraced neo-liberalism while social partnership has induced a voluntary restraint among workers. Given these two conditions, the Celtic Tiger has produced a far greater class polarisation than before.

How long that boom will last is an open question. What is certain, however, is that there is no set pattern of sustained success, as economic miracles tend to be as transitory as they are surprising. In 1987, the Italians celebrated the *sorpasso*, when their GDP overtook Britain's, but in the next 15 years their growth rates were amongst the lowest in Europe. In the 1970s, Chile was celebrated as a miracle economy and proof of the success of neo-liberalism. But then it faced major difficulties until 1983. In the 1980s, Japanese management techniques were all in vogue because Japan's growth rates were so remarkable. Yet in the 1990s it entered one of the severest long-term recessions in the modern world. The Asian Tigers were once hailed as miraculous only to be denounced by some of their former admirers for 'crony capitalism' after their crash in 1997.

There are already warning signs in Ireland. US investment into Ireland has begun to fall, dropping from $21.6 billion in 2003 to $9.1 billion in 2004. Some of this reflects the fact that companies were repaying internal loans but there may also be a pattern of relocation. There has also been a more general decline in manufacturing, with over 30,000 workers losing their jobs from this sector. It may, indeed, be more accurate to speak not so much of one Celtic Tiger economy but rather a Tiger and hare economy.

The Celtic Tiger proper lasted from 1993 to 2001. During this period, US investment increased its flow and manufacturing expanded. After the initial slowdown, the state intensified its neo-liberal policy and encouraged growth in the construction and financial services. The construction sector now accounts for a much higher proportion of the economy than in most other countries. But the building boom in turn is fuelled by high levels of debt and an influx of migrants seeking accommodation. The Irish economy may continue to race ahead for a period but has more the character of a lightweight hare than a strong tiger.

Looked at from a broader historical angle, therefore, there is no certainty that the high level of growth is self-sustaining. The more interesting question may not be what caused Ireland to develop but rather how was the boom squandered to suit a small minority. A critical sociology that is not aligned with state policies on 'national development' is therefore crucial. There are just too many questions to be asked about social class and inequality in modern Ireland.

Chapter 14

Work transformed: two faces of the new Irish workplace

Peter Murray
Seán Ó Riain

Two faces of the brave new workplace

One of the regular features of the *Harvard Business Review* is the HBR Case Study. These 'cases, which are fictional, present common managerial dilemmas and offer concrete solutions from experts'. In November 2005 the journal's readers were presented, under the headline 'Riding the Celtic Tiger', with the case of John Dooley, Dublin-based vice president of strategic research with a global biotechnology corporation (Roche 2005).

John had grown up in Dublin but left an economically depressed Ireland for the USA in the late 1980s, where he added a doctorate to his primary degree and worked for a couple of 'leading-edge' biotechnology firms before taking the job that brought him back to a booming Ireland at the end of the 1990s. John's current dilemma is the offer he has received of a top job at corporate headquarters in California. The opportunity tempts John 'who had always loved the start-up phase of a project – the feeling of endless possibility, the challenge of assembling the right team, the excitement of discovering something entirely new'. But other considerations incline him towards staying in Ireland. He and his wife had returned to Dublin 'wanting their son to grow up knowing his grandparents and other relatives, to learn Irish history, and to play hurling and Gaelic football rather than baseball'. Career-wise, John also has local options: a senior position with a smaller Irish company is being dangled in front of him by a head-hunter. But, he muses, 'how long is Ireland's economy going to keep up like this?'

In the same month the invited experts and readers of the *Harvard Business Review* mulled over the fictional John's dilemma, other Dubliners were also encountering problems at work. On a winter's Saturday night the Skerries lifeboat crew rescued a group of 13 Latvian periwinkle pickers from a small, uninhabited island. Dropped off on the island, they had received a phone call saying that the boat that was supposed to bring them back had engine trouble and that they would not be collected until the following day. But for the lifeboat's arrival they faced a night for which high winds and heavy rain were forecast without food or warm clothing. As nationals of a European Union member state, Latvians are legally entitled to work in Ireland but, once back on shore, the pickers quickly left the scene. The few interviewed by a local garda 'had little or no English. They wouldn't tell me who their boss was' (*Irish Times*, 9 November 2005). The incident attracted media and political attention. In addition to the gardaí, three government departments or statutory agencies carried out investigations. But no official action resulted as 'it has not been possible to establish any detail of an employment relationship and the Latvian interviewees made no complaint' (*Irish Times*, 8 December 2005).

Segmenting work and workers

The fictional John Dooley and the flesh-and-blood periwinkle pickers inhabit the same globalised economy in which a premium is placed upon the flexibility of workers. However, their working experiences within this common environment are poles apart. The co-existence of 'good' and 'bad' jobs in the modern labour market and the patterned allocation of these different types of jobs to different social groups are the basis of labour market segmentation theory (Reich et al. 1973). According to this theory it is inaccurate to talk about *the* labour market. There is in reality no such single entity. Instead the hiring of workers takes place within a series of distinct *segments* that together comprise the overall market for labour. Within this divided labour market the crucial boundary lines run between the *primary* labour market and the *secondary* labour market. What differentiates the two is the degree of stability and security of employment offered within the labour market.

In the primary labour market jobs:

- require, and develop, stable working habits
- provide opportunities for the acquisition of skills
- offer relatively high wages
- form part of job ladders offering promotion prospects

In the secondary labour market jobs:

- do not require, and often discourage, stable working habits
- offer low wages
- are subject to high turnover and do not put their occupants upon any ladder to something better

Segments vary along other lines too. In each segment of the labour market different approaches are taken to the control of labour, and to ensuring that workers gave full levels of commitment to their work. Direct methods of control, relying on close managerial supervision and direction, or technical control, using assembly line technologies, predominated in the secondary labour market (Edwards 1979). However, professional and craft workers proved difficult to control with these methods and firms often turned to strategies of 'responsible autonomy' that involved relying on these workers to monitor their own effort and commitment (Friedman 1977). Goldthorpe (1982) argued that expert workers are part of the 'service class' defined by a relationship to their employers which is very different from that applying to less-skilled employees. While less skilled employees are bound to the firm by their labour contract, managers and experts are bound to the firm by a 'service relationship' where they are promised not only the immediate benefits of salary and so on but also the long-term benefits of a career: 'in place of any attempt at the immediate linking of performance and pay, the employment contract envisages, even if implicitly as much as explicitly, a quite diffuse exchange of service to the organisation in return for compensation in which the prospective element is crucial; and, by the same token, the contract is understood as having a long-term rather than a short-term basis' (Goldthorpe 2000: 220).

Since its formulation in the 1970s, segmentation theory has continued to attract international interest. Some scholars regard its perspective on the patterned inequalities observable in labour markets as being more plausible than that proffered by conventional economic theories that emphasise differences in human capital endowment between individuals – the differences in people's education, skills, experience and know-how. Since the 1970s segmentation theory has been further developed by specifying a number of qualitatively different types of primary location while retaining the fundamental primary/secondary distinction. Schemes allocating different industrial groups and occupations to particular segments have also been devised. This has meant that the validity of propositions derived from segmentation theory can now be more rigorously tested against empirical evidence gathered by surveys than was the case when this theory was first formulated.

Irish survey data have been used to carry out such testing by Hughes and Nolan (1997 and 2000) in relation to earnings and to pension entitlements. Possibly owing to the relatively high level of trade union influence in the Irish economy, the analysis of earnings provides limited support for regarding the Irish labour market as a segmented one but in the case of pension entitlements 'tests of these two theories favour the segmentation model over the competitive model' (Hughes and Nolan 2000: 140). Interestingly their work (see table 14.1) suggests that the distribution of workers across segments in Ireland is very similar to the pattern found in the USA, with in both cases

Table 14.1 **Distribution of employment in four labour market segments in Ireland in 1994 and in the United States in 1987**

Labour Market Segment	Ireland %	United States %
Independent primary professional	29.4	29.3
Independent primary craft	11.4	10.8
Subordinate primary	30.9	33.9
Secondary	28.3	26.0

Source: Hughes and Nolan (2000), table 6.9

almost 30 per cent being located in the secondary labour market. Compared to their counterparts in the primary segments, the Irish secondary labour market workforce is, as table 14.2 shows, more feminised, less unionised and more part-time.

In the early days of labour market segmentation theory there was some debate about whether dualism in the labour market could cut through firms, making it possible for a single employer to contain both primary and secondary labour markets (Barron and Norris 1976: 49). The influential concept of the flexible firm formulated in Britain during the 1980s argued that within a changing 'post-Fordist' economic environment such a co-existence of segments within the firm was becoming the norm (Atkinson and Meager 1986). The flexible firm has a core of multi-skilled workers that it seeks to retain through satisfaction with tasks, seniority within the organisation and monetary rewards. It also has a periphery of workers pulled into or pushed out of the firm according to the needs of the situation. The numerical flexibility through which a firm quickly and easily changes the size of its workforce in response

Table 14.2 **Perecentage female, unionised, part-time, with pension entitlement and average length of job in four labour market segments in Ireland in 1994**

Segment	Female (1987) %	Union members (1987) %	Part-time (18 hours) %	With pension entitlement %	Average job length years
Independent primary professional	40.2	54.0	4.3	70.0	9.95
Independent primary craft	13.3	51.4	0.8	47.4	7.43
Subordinate primary	38.2	61.4	3.5	63.6	7.05
Secondary	55.9	29.1	16.2	18.9	6.16

Source: Hughes and Nolan (2000), Table 6.10

to changes in market demand is obtained by the growing use of what are termed 'atypical' work arrangements such as part-time work, temporary employment, self-employment and contracting out.

As we enter an information economy firms come to value knowledge, skills and control over intellectual property; it is the workers who most directly create, and partly control, this knowledge and who have the most bargaining power in dealing with their employers. While all workers bring their knowledge to bear in the workplace, recent decades have seen a growing international class of knowledge workers who are valued almost entirely for their ability to apply or create new bodies of knowledge. It is these workers who are now the main recipients of the privileges of the primary labour market in the firm's core. However, the contemporary workplace has been stripped of the bureaucratic layers through which a typical primary labour market career once ascended. Even while they may offer greater financial rewards, stocks and other inducements, the employers of workers like John Dooley have rowed back on their previous commitments to long-term employment security, pension guarantees and other features aimed at keeping employees with the firm. In the information technology sectors which are at the heart of these new arrangements, the iconic employment arrangements are now those of job-hopping Silicon Valley rather than the lifetime employment promises of IBM (see Sennett 1998 for a discussion of the social consequences). The weakening of organisational protections for careers and job security raised the stakes for workers. While more workers were working under conditions similar to the secondary labour market, the rewards of success expanded as wage inequality increased rapidly in the USA and Ireland in the 1990s. Workers were renegotiating their working lives in a context where the rewards for success were greater than ever but where the bulk of workers faced insecure and unpredictable working lives.

Structural changes in a polarising world

Even as employment has expanded enormously in Ireland, we have also seen a significant transformation in work and employment itself. Having largely missed the Fordist era of mass production, Irish workers are for the first time participating at home in an advanced industrial economy in which flexible work and employment loom large. Before going on to explore the specific experiences of workers at the top and bottom of the labour market, we shall examine the major changes shaping the shift from Fordist to flexible work.

Techno-economic change: new jobs and occupations

The work taking place within these new kinds of firms and workplaces is increasingly wrapped up in new kinds of jobs – and particularly various forms of service work. Even as manufacturing boomed in Ireland in the 1990s, and our industrial revolution finally arrived, Ireland made an even more rapid shift towards a service economy with the greatest increase in employment in professional and personal service occupations. The term 'services' covers a multitude of different kinds of work, and is at the heart of both employment growth and of polarisation in the labour market. At the top of the services hierarchy are the 'symbolic analysts' like John Dooley, workers who spend their time handling and analysing information and symbols – scientists, managers, marketing executives, financial gurus, and so on (Reich 1991). Less fortunate are those workers providing 'personal services' directly to customers – the cleaners, hairdressers and hotel staff often working for poor pay and conditions. They, along with the workers at the sharp end of agriculture and manufacturing such as the periwinkle pickers, experience a quite different version of the flexible workplace. Work is therefore taking place in a quite different *techno-economic context* – as new technologies such as information and communication technologies help to reshape the profile of work and jobs in the economy. This combines with the dramatic move of many of the tasks previously carried out in the home into the marketplace, as first food production, then production of goods and now caring, cleaning and food provision have historically moved into the world of exchange (Esping-Andersen 1999).

Socio-spatial change: new work spaces

The global economy looms large in the lives of contemporary Irish workers – whether it is John Dooley considering lucrative corporate career options on two continents or the Latvian workers buffeted on the rougher seas of the low end of the European labour market. The dominant image of these workplaces is that of places lifted out of time and space, places where communication and innovation are free from the drag of local cultures and practices and untainted by power relations, and where new information and communication technologies make it possible and even necessary to reorganise firms into 'global webs' and employees into global telecommuters (Reich 1991). For others, this perspective is too benign. The speeding up of the global economy destroys local space – time annihilates space, melting away 'solid' local places into the 'air' of the global economy and the once autonomous local space of the worker is increasingly dominated by global corporations and the ever more rapid pace of economic life under capitalism (Berman 1982; Burawoy 1985; Harvey 1989). Yet the local context still matters – it is the concentration of the Celtic Tiger boom in a single location within the European economy that has made return to his native city viable for John Dooley at the same time that it has drawn the Latvian workers to the latest boomtown in search of survival. Work increasingly takes place in a new *socio-spatial context*, where workers are connected to the global through migration flows, multinational corporations and competition with workers elsewhere, but are also deeply affected by local economic conditions.

Political organisational change: new work organisations

Ultimately then, since its emergence around the beginning of the 1980s as a ubiquitous buzzword in discussions of work, flexibility has had its nasty and its nice versions. The nice version of flexibility paints a picture in which skilled and satisfying work can be, and is being, offered within environments where the most advanced technology is being utilised. People with science doctorates working in the biotechnology sector fit this bill. Its nasty version sees flexibility replacing well-paid and reasonably secure jobs whose occupants were protected by trade union organisation with various forms of 'atypical' work where – for many people – pay, protection and prospects are poor. This is the case with jobs where 'any detail of an employment relationship' eludes enquiring government labour inspectors.

Flexibility came to the fore after the capitalist 'long boom' enjoyed by North America and Western Europe following the Second World War ended in the early 1970s. National economies had been relatively self-contained and within most of them planning by an interventionist state with the support of bureaucratic business corporations and organised labour was the order of the day. But, under US leadership, a liberalised system of international trade was established in this period. Over time this exposed the established industrial economies to external low-cost competition. By investing abroad to take advantage of low costs, business created a new international division of labour while the states of the capitalist world embraced market neo-liberalism and drew back from planning. These changes repudiated the class compromises of the 'long boom' era, put organised labour on the defensive and facilitated radical economic restructuring. Aided by revolutionary new information technology, a process of globalisation gathered pace. This quickened with the collapse of the 'second world' of Communist economies from the end of the 1980s.

Globalisation has meant that work increasingly takes place within a *political-organisational context* where labour regulation and protection are weakened; where large hierarchical firms increasingly operate within complex networks of contracting, outsourcing and strategic alliances; and where promises of lifetime employment and job security are increasingly limited (Osterman 1999; Sennett 1998).

Precarious work at the bottom

Despite the boom times, there are still many in Ireland for whom the work-place is a precarious environment – the kind of worker who, on entering the 'hidden abode of production' is perhaps still, as in Marx's classic image, 'timid and holds back, like someone who has brought his own hide to the market and now has nothing to expect but – a tanning' (Marx 1976: 280). In this section we review Irish research evidence on working at the bottom end of the labour market.

A significant research focus on atypical work forms, and particularly on part-time work, had developed in Ireland by the end of the 1980s (Daly 1985; Drew 1991; Dineen 1992: Blackwell 1995). This was partly a response to statistical trends – against a background of mounting economic difficulty, part-time work 'accounted for all of the modest growth in employment between 1983 and 1993', a period in which the total numbers in full-time employment actually suffered a decline (O'Connell 2000: 77). In addition, the growing number of part-time workers did not enjoy the same rights as the declining number of full-time ones. Protection against unfair dismissal as well as the right to a minimum period of notice, the right to redundancy com-pensation and – particularly important since so many part-time workers are women – the right to maternity leave were all linked to a threshold of 18 hours per week below which workers were not covered.

This was broadly in line in with British arrangements but out of line with European norms which tended to apply on a *pro rata* basis the same rights to part-time as to full-time workers. Prompted in part by social research findings, the Worker Protection (Regular Part-time Employees) Act 1991 began a process of bringing Irish legal treatment of atypical work situations into line with European practice. EU directives subsequently continued this trend. In 2000 both typical and atypical workers benefited from a move away from the historical British model of setting minimum wage rates for a limited number of designated occupations through Joint Labour Committees (Nolan 1993) to a European one of comprehensive protection (Bazen and Benhayoun 1992) with the introduction of a statutory minimum wage. While employer organisations consistently opposed the introduction of this legislation on competitiveness grounds, a survey to gauge the minimum wage's impact found that 'over 80 per cent of firms said that, in the light of trends in the Irish labour market, they would have had to increase wage rates anyway' (Nolan et al. 2002: ii)

After 1993, with Ireland's 'employment miracle' getting under way, the percentage share of part-time working in total employment continued to edge upwards although the majority of the new jobs being created were full-time. This changed context fostered a more positive view of the role part-time work plays in the Irish economy. It was pointed out that, while rising, Irish rates of part-time working remained comparatively low by European standards. The Irish pattern thus seemed to be converging with an established international norm. New legislation had, as noted above, removed the incentive that used to exist for Irish employers to exploit part-time workers. That lack of child care provision and other factors constrain the choices that women with families can make was acknowledged (Russell et al. 2002), although the rapid increase in the numbers of women in the labour force led some to label Ireland the 'Celtic Tigress' (O'Connell, 2000). Yet the falling proportion of part-timers classified by official statistics as being underemployed made part-time work look increasingly like an option voluntarily chosen by the workers engaged in it (O'Connell 2000: 77–9).

However, it remains the case that 'there has been little research to date into part-time work in the Republic, so little is known about the pay and conditions, about how much part-time work is voluntary or otherwise, nor about the stability of such work' (O'Connell 1999: 228). Here two studies, though limited by the age of their data, are noteworthy. Surveys of workplaces conducted in eight EU states during 1989 and 1990 have been drawn upon by Wickham (1997) to explore the respective contributions of employer objectives and employee preferences to the shaping of part-time work patterns. This work qualifies the relatively sanguine view that 'with regard to both part-time working and temporary contracts, Ireland has participated in a common European trend towards increased flexibility' (O'Connell 2000: 81) with its conclusion that:

> In Ireland part-time work is more contested than in any other country in the study. While Irish managers find more advantages in part-time work than their colleagues in any other country, Irish employee representatives can find very few advantages to it indeed. They appear to be hostile to part-time work firstly because they believe many of those they represent are compelled to do it against their will, and secondly, because they consider management exploits part-timers by paying them lower wages and benefits. Within a European context, Ireland emerges as an example of bad practice, of how not to use part-time work (Wickham 1997: 149–50)

Tormey (1999) emphasises the heterogeneity of part-time workers – on which see also Smyth and McCoy (2004) – while presenting a generally negative picture based on two retail sector case studies. These were carried out in first half of the 1990s 'when unemployment was high and the economy was not yet experiencing the Celtic Tigress boom period'. With the boom, he notes, 'employers may make the jobs more attractive to ensure that they are filled' or 'alternatively they may recruit from an even more marginalized workforce, such as immigrants' (Tormey 1999: 85, 95)

Ireland has historically been a country of emigration rather than immigration and into the mid-1990s it continued to be one of the most mono-ethnic societies in Europe. Up to this point in time Irish discussions of inequality and exploitation at work referred almost exclusively to women who were white and Irish-born. Citizens of other EU states were entitled to work in Ireland, but few did so, and a similar entitlement was extended to quite small numbers of 'programme refugees' who have since the mid-1950s been periodically admitted to Ireland following displacement from war-torn countries such as Vietnam in the 1970s or Bosnia-Herzegovina in the 1990s.

Over the past decade this picture has changed dramatically as large numbers of foreign workers have flowed into a booming economy (see chapter 2 for further discussion of migration). An upsurge in an already large inflow followed EU enlargement in 2004 when ten new, mostly former Communist central and eastern European states were admitted. Most EU members restricted the access of citizens of these Accession States to their labour markets. Ireland, however, was one of a small number of states (along with Sweden and the UK) that opted to permit full access. In 2003 just under 5,000 Irish work permits were issued to Polish citizens (Grabowska 2005: table 1): in spring 2006, Personal Public Service Number applications indicated that at least 5,000 Poles per month were arriving in the state, making up over half a total monthly flow of more than 10,000 people from the newest member states (*Irish Times*, 13 March 2006).

The construction industry, where employment has undergone massive growth as a huge rise in property prices has fuelled a boom in apartment and house building, has become a major employer of foreign labour – and a notable source of disturbing stories about its treatment. With a strong tradition of craft and general union organisation, this industry has historically been predominantly associated with primary labour characteristics and retains an important trade union presence. The publicised cases its unions have drawn attention to provide food for thought about what may be happening in the classic secondary market locations where much of the foreign workforce is to be found and (excepting Cunningham et al. 2005; Kropiwiec and King-O'Riain, 2006) little research has been carried out.

Concerns about employment abuses can only be exacerbated by the fact that, while the state has a large volume of protective legislation on its statute book, it has left the enforcement of these laws grossly under-resourced. As the labour force changed and grew in a manner that heightened concerns about worker exploitation, the number of workplace inspections fell from 8,372 to 5,160 between 2002 and 2004. Towards the end of 2005 the Republic of Ireland had only 21 labour inspectors. There were plans to increase this number to 31 – a figure that, as one trade union official noted, was still less than the number of dog wardens in the state (*Irish Times*, 12 November 2005)

Opportunities and uncertainties at the top

As we noted earlier, vulnerable workers with weak bargaining power co-exist with workers who enter the workplace filled with a confidence that stems from their possession of scarce and valued skills. The Silicon Valley software developer is perhaps the iconic figure of these workers today – but there are many others, from financial advisers to marketing managers and from educational consultants to electronic engineers.

Not so long ago employers would typically have sought to secure the commitment of these workers by offering them the prospect of moving up a career ladder. But now organisations are flatter, leaner (and meaner) with the old middle layers up through which such careers used to progress stripped out. This gives rise to a crucial tension in the organisation of work in Silicon Valley and beyond. While work has become more socialised with the rise of teamwork, careers have become more individualised, with growing use of individualised performance pay within firms and job insecurity and job hopping across firms. Teams are assembled from a mobile labour force to put together the right mix of skills. However, there is a deep tension here – the bonds that make for good teamwork are consistently bruised and broken by the arrival and departure of new co-workers (Benner 2002). For Irish software workers this tension has been found to be just as much a reality as for those in Silicon Valley (Ó Riain, 2000). With high turnover, individualised human resource management strategies, and non-union approaches to workers dominating, Irish high tech looked a great deal like Silicon Valley for workers – perhaps not surprisingly given the massive influence of US and Silicon Valley companies such as HP and Intel in the Irish information economy.

We can get some idea of how widespread these patterns are among the new services and informational industries by comparing key features of a variety of sectors, using data from a national survey of employees in 2003. Software stands out as the most extreme example of these new trends with high rates of team working, performance pay, job mobility (2000–3 incorporate periods of boom and bust in IT industries) and very low trade union membership. But these patterns are widespread across these leading sectors of the 'new economy' with team working, performance pay and mobility more widespread than in the rest of the economy, and union membership lower. There are differences – financial services workers often work for commission, while professional services workers are often 'freelancers', with less teamwork and higher mobility. Overall, however, the combination of socialised work and individualised employment is increasingly prevalent, particularly in these new information industries.

If there has been a global shift away from individualised work and collective reward systems towards socialised work and individualised careers, these

Table 14.3 **Prevalence of teams, performance pay, job mobility and trade union membership in selected sectors, 2003**

Sector (N)	Work in a team %	Performance related pay in the workplace %	More than one job in previous 3 years %	Member of trade union %
Software(55)	56	55	52	5
Computer/semiconductor (56)	48	49	25	19
Telecommunications (66)	55	55	19	62
Medical instruments(52)	45	55	31	40
Pharmaceuticals (77)	53	51	30	42
Financial services (262)	44	63	28	41
Professional services (207)	24	35	34	11
Other (4309)	33	18	27	45

Source: National Centre for Partnership and Performance Survey of the Changing Workplace, 2003. Data available from Irish Social Science Data Archive

patterns are compatible with a wide variety of forms of social relations in the workplace. Drawing on a EU wide survey from 2000, Lorenz and Valeyre (2004) identify two new models of production across Europe, in addition to 'traditional' models of craft organisation and managerial control of the direct and technical kind. The 'learning' model is a relatively decentralised model where teams have a great deal of autonomy in controlling their own work and have strong employment security guarantees. The 'lean' model is a more hierarchical model which uses teams extensively but where managers more tightly regulate individual or group work pace, as well as offering fewer employment security guarantees. Team-based production has proven to be compatible with the hierarchical corporate employment relations of leading Japanese firms, with the workplace solidarity and worker autonomy of Swedish workplaces and with the individualised careers of US firms (Cole 1992). How has the team model institutionalised in high tech in Ireland been embedded within the social relations of the workplace?

Even controlling for occupation, sector and establishment size, Ireland shows a clear tendency to adopt the lean model (Lorenz and Valeyre 2004). The employment model that combines socialised work with individualised careers appears to have been imported into Ireland in a way that is most closely tied to the approach that prevails in the USA, with relatively little employee autonomy and close managerial control. This comparative perspective is borne out by the results of a national survey of workplaces in

Ireland in 1997. Roche and Geary (2000) find that high levels of responsibility for work process improvement (90 per cent of workplaces giving teams the lead) and quality (71 per cent) and that half of workplaces give teams the lead role in scheduling work, setting the pace of work and controlling time keeping. A third or more give teams the lead in relational issues such as allocating work and controlling attendance within teams, addressing/resolving problems with other teams and dealing with customers and suppliers. Managers were, however, much more reluctant to cede control of selection of team members and team leaders (Geary 1999: 877).

Similarly management prerogative remains paramount as the approach to tackling crucial strategic issues such as investment and divestment plans, employment levels and promotion systems and criteria in both union and non-union workplaces. Employees, whether directly or through their unions, are more likely to be involved in shaping decisions most closely related to the performance of work itself (work practices, new forms of team-working, working time, employee involvement and identifying strategies for attaining the corporate goals that have been set further up the hierarchy) (Roche and Geary 2000: 19 and 22). These results indicate an emerging Irish pattern of 'lean production'. Here strong employee involvement in work and quality improvement, along with widespread diffusion of team handling of crucial production relationships, co-exists with the retention of high levels of managerial control of key decisions and information.

We know relatively little about how these arrangements play out within Irish workplaces. The only sector where such arrangements have been explored in detailed ethnographic studies is the software industry (Greco 2005; O'Carroll 2005; Ó Riain 2000, 2002, 2006). While software developers may move quite regularly from job to job, they have an intense relationship with each other once in a particular job. The core of the typical software organisation workplace – and perhaps of the knowledge economy itself – is the autonomous project team. In a case study of a US software firm in Ireland, the deadline set the rhythms of the workplace: in the weeks before the team's next major deadline, life in the team cubicle became busier and busier. The team worked longer hours and became more and more isolated from the life of the company around them (Ó Riain 2000, 2006). The combination of the high level of autonomy software workers have at work with severe pressures to get the work done was striking. Decent pay, conditions and autonomy at work are not in and of themselves a protection against pressures to work long hours (Ó Riain 2000, 2006).

Research in the USA shows that individualised pay structures and the pervasive job insecurity of the industry reinforce the pressure to work long hours and a commitment to work above all else (Perlow 1997; Sharone 2004). The system in the USA encourages engineers to do whatever it takes to solve an immediate crisis while ignoring any costs imposed by interruptions or failures of co-ordination and long-term planning. These pressures seemed less extreme in Ireland. Although good data are hard to find, the hours worked appear somewhat fewer than in the US. Research by O'Carroll (2005) shows that in many Irish firms workers were able to impose a set of time norms of their own, which included a more reasonable set of expectations around working to deadlines and restricting longer hours, while it is the absence of an industry-wide set of norms about acceptable working hours that allows excessive working hours to persist in certain firms and at certain times.

Caught in the squeeze: gender, social services and the market

The two faces of the new workplace look each other squarely in the face in the crucial area of the social reproduction of labour. Harried workers at the top (and in the middle) increasingly face problems of child care and turn to the market and extended family in order to keep the household ticking over. But many of these tasks are carried out by unpaid family members or relatively poorly paid personal service workers.

Societies face choices as to how to deal with these central issues of social reproduction that are linked intimately to the gendering of work in the household and paid employment. Esping-Andersen (2003) notes that we see two main models of how societies are dealing with these choices. One model relies heavily on the expansion of public sector services and employment, improving pay and conditions and paid for by taxation, while the second relies primarily on the market, with individuals and households buying in personal services from low-paid workers. With poorly funded social services and expanding personal service employment, Ireland seems to be moving closer to the latter model – or at least towards the extension into new areas of its 'two tier' secondary education and health *status quo* in which public subsidy helps to pay for private advantage.

NESC has warned recently of the delicate balance between income support, activation schemes and social insurance in the Irish welfare state, suggesting that we are approaching a crucial tipping point where many middle-class people will abandon public services for the state-subsidised private sector and the social insurance system (NESC, 2005). It is worth noting here that 'private sector' initiatives are often heavily publicly subsidised – including fee-paying schools which receive extensive public funding, and the planned private hospitals that are likely to rely heavily on the state bankrolled National Treatment Purchase Fund for a market.

The work of social reproduction, typically viewed as 'women's' work', has often been rendered invisible, portrayed as 'natural' and therefore devalued

(Lynch and McLaughlin 1995). This work is increasingly public and work that was once the preserve of the family has entered the realm of state services, through health and education, and the market, through personal services such as cleaning and food preparation. Even as women have entered the workforce, they have often moved into precisely these already feminised areas of work and patterns of occupational segregation have not shifted significantly in Ireland during the Celtic Tiger years (Fahey et al. 2000).

If employers are to have a labour force to employ, a massive system of social investment and emotional and social care must be in place, and the previously invisible issues of care and social reproduction are increasingly on policy agendas as child care, education, health, housing and transport become key political issues and major factors shaping work and employment (see Cronin 2002 and Wickham 2006). Questions of social reproduction and gender have been placed firmly on the political agenda, driven in many respects by pressures generated from the world of work and employment.

Issues and prospects

The pace of recent employment change in Ireland has been truly extraordinary. In the seven years 1994–2000, GNP grew an average of 8.4 per cent per annum and, more significantly, a total of 468,000 additional jobs were created. Where the economy had been stabilised and was improving prior to 1994, these were the years when the Celtic Tiger roared. Employment has boomed further since 2000 but the dynamic of economic growth has shifted firmly from export-based, internationally competitive manufacturing and services to an economy fuelled by domestic consumption and, particularly, construction. When construction slows down, as it must since even with substantial immigration a population base of around four million people can hardly sustain indefinitely a demand for 90,000 new dwellings every year, it will be easier to distinguish the durable from the ephemeral features of Irish workplace change. Reappraisal of the development strategy that provides the context for this change may also be timely.

The irony of the inequalities and polarisation in the Irish workplace is that they have developed within the context of social partnership institutions that are typically associated with increasing wage equality and social solidarity (Hicks and Kenworthy 1998). Social partnership institutions in Ireland attempt to hold together from the centre what is an increasingly diverse set of workplace regimes – ranging from professionalised workplaces in the informational industries with their team work and individualised careers through unionised public sector bureaucracies to the poorly regulated sectors of construction, agriculture, retail and personal services at the 'sharp end' of which a heavily immigrant workforce is exposed to poor pay, conditions and insecurity.

The Celtic Tiger emerged when two social forces mobilised to try to reverse the disastrous situation of the 1980s. State investment in education and pursuit of inward investment had created a burgeoning professional class, many of whom emigrated but enough of whom stayed behind to form a new industrial development coalition with dissident elements from the Industrial Development Authority (IDA) and other, more marginal, state agencies. This coalition became the basis of indigenous industrial upgrading and deepening in the 1990s. A second group of unionised workers were mobilised through the union movement to enter a series of social partnership agreements which sought to restore macroeconomic and fiscal stability by centrally negotiating wages and other distributional issues. These two coalitions between different groups of employees, employers and sections of the state existed in an arms-length but complementary relationship. The modified industrial policy finally created a strong dynamic of growth and development. The union movement's commitment to partnership was sustained, although non-union regimes prevailed throughout the tiger economy's dynamic knowledge sector industries. While the terms of this accord between the state and the social partners ensured that basic levels of protection were guaranteed to those excluded from national economic recovery, the inequality-lessening effects associated with corporatism or neo-corporatism in other countries were less evident (O'Riain 2004).

Now, however, as Ireland's international economic competitiveness and its union density is declining while its property market continues to boom, the two coalitions no longer seem to complement one another so well. Growth has become concentrated in the low productivity construction sector and not among the industries populated by knowledge professionals. The Irish unions already faced a US-style slow strangulation (Freeman and Medoff 1984) in a private sector where union density was falling sharply. Now they also confront unprecedented conditions of open European labour market exposure. As well as cases of employment abuse referred to above, these have produced the emblematic Irish Ferries case where well-paid jobs previously filled by unionised Irish seamen were 'outsourced' through a Cyprus-based management company to Latvian workers who were to be paid much lower wages and to have different conditions of employment. What has been termed 'one of the truly momentous disputes of modern Irish industrial relations' (*IRN* 2006) brought huge numbers out on to the streets in protest but ended on settlement terms whose main positive feature was the doubling of the intended rate of pay of the Latvian seamen to the level of the Irish statutory minimum wage.

Almost fifty years ago a hugely significant shift in strategy identified the creation of a capacity to compete in export markets as being central to Irish economic development. Today, the question is whether something like the alignment of forces that fostered the growth of the Tiger economy up to 2000 can be restored to working order, or whether some new coalition can be assembled to reinvigorate a sustainable form of economic and social development in place of the present boom's unsavoury mix of property speculation and immigrant exploitation. Important as its role as a catalyst for change was in the 1980s, it remains to seen whether the partnership system is now capable of providing a forum in which an answer to this question can be formulated.

Chapter 15

Gender and the workforce

Sara O'Sullivan

Introduction

For years, the majority of Irish women worked in the home, without pay, for most of their lives. There they fulfilled what was considered their most important role, as caring wives, mothers and daughters and, for the most part, their work was not adequately acknowledged or rewarded. Now, the majority participate in the formerly male terrain of the paid labour force, a key factor in the creation of the Celtic Tiger economy in the 1990s (Russell et al. 2002: 1). This points to a major social change – both in Irish women's everyday lives, and in the wider economy and society.

Girls now outperform boys in the Junior and Leaving Certificates (Department of Education and Science 2005c) and are increasingly ambitious and career-focused. They constitute a majority of those entering those bastions of male prestige and power, the legal and medical professions. Given this advantageous position *vis-à-vis* their male counterparts, a key question is whether gender inequalities that have been found to be endemic in the Irish workplace will wither away in the face of this new reality, or persist (O'Connor 1998). Will these girls be unencumbered by the kind of gender discrimination that affected women in the 1980s and 1990s? Or will their successes be short lived?

The current situation is that increases in Irish women's labour force participation do not mean they have achieved equality in the labour market. Although overt discrimination against women is now illegal, many difficulties remain for Irish women in the workforce. Overall, women earn lower wages than men (CSO 2005b) and are not paid at the same rates as their male counterparts (Russell et al. 2005). Promotional opportunities are not equally available to women, a phenomenon known as 'the glass ceiling'. This invisible barrier restricts women's upward mobility in organisations. Discrimination on the grounds of gender remains a problem for Irish women in the work-force (Equality Authority 2006).[1] Women in Irish society still do not have the same access to power, money or status as their male counterparts (see

O'Connor 2000; Baker et al. 2004). The challenge for sociology is to explain these disadvantages.

The discussion will examine the increase in the number of women in the paid workforce, identifying both continuities and changes. Changes in the structure of the labour market in the Republic have created employment opportunities for Irish women. However, despite their changing roles outside the home, Irish women have also retained primary responsibility for caring (Hilliard 2006). This creates difficulties for many women, mothers or not, both at home and in the workplace. These difficulties are often experienced as individual problems and so are not always visible as gender inequalities. However, for sociologists, the patterning of these difficulties leads us away from a focus on the individuals experiencing these difficulties, to search for the broader social processes or 'conditions' in play (Bauman 2001: 7). As O'Connor (2000: 81) reminds us, this way of organising work in the home is reflective of 'the interests of powerful men' and operates for the benefit of most men. A related issue to be considered is the response to this change both in the workplace, at the policy level, and by men as a group.

To understand these continuities and changes it is necessary to examine how work is organised in our society, and how gender plays a central role in this organisation. Historically, men and women's participation in both paid and unpaid work has been quite different. Women have been more likely than men to be involved in unpaid work in the home and men and women tend to do different types of work in the paid labour force. Sociologists call this organisation of work the gendered division of labour. According to Connell (1987) the gendered division of labour is one of the structures supporting the way gender is currently organised, which he terms the gender order. Underpinning this structure are dominant norms and ideals about gender. As individuals we can be both enabled and restricted by our understandings of what is normal, appropriate and desirable for men and women. As Kramer (2000: 5) argues 'experiences, opportunities, and burdens are differentially available to males and to females because of social views about maleness and femaleness'.

What is gender?

Sociologists define gender as 'that complex of social meanings that is attached to biological sex' (Kimmel and Messner 1995: xv). For sociologists the way gender operates throughout society, including the world of work, cannot be understood without paying attention to its symbolic dimensions (Connell 2002). Two different understandings of gender are relevant here, essentialist and social constructionist. From an essentialist perspective biological differences between men and women are argued to create fixed masculine and feminine roles, behaviours and identities. Gender differences are seen as natural. Men and women are presented as different species, with different needs, abilities, interests and personalities. For example Irwing and Lynn (2005) argue that women are less intelligent than men. This understanding creates a tendency to emphasise differences between men and women and ignore or underplay similarities. The most fundamental split here is between the (male) bread-winner and (female) carer roles, seen to reflect men and women's natural talents and abilities. A related issue is the value attached to these roles; the breadwinner role is positioned as more valuable than the role of carer (O'Connor 2000: 97; O'Connor 2005). As Leonard (2004) has argued, such traditional understandings of gender persist in Irish society (see also Goodwin 2002). However, tensions have also been created by the increased participation of Irish women, and particularly of married women, in the paid labour force (Kennedy 2001: 81).

These gender myths may be common in popular culture, but this does not mean they are true. Biology provides some of the parameters for behaviour but explains very little. It cannot explain variations in cultural norms sur-rounding gender, why and how cultural norms vary over time, or the diversity of gender systems that exist globally. Essentialist arguments also overlook the variations that exist between men, and between women, and the similarities and overlaps that can be found across the two categories. Finally, given the decline in the importance of manual labour in western societies, the biological differences that exist between men and women cannot adequately explain the differential value placed on men and women's work or the unequal treatment of men and women (De Beauvoir 1972).

As far back as 1792, Mary Wollstonecraft was making the case that 'gender role characteristics were the result of . . . social learning' and could not be reduced to biological difference (Andersen 1998: 326). This is a social con-structivist approach, which sees gender as socially constructed within society by men and by women. From this perspective, gender norms and gender systems can be accounted for by the different social and cultural contexts in operation in a particular place and at a particular time.

Margaret Mead (1962) reports different norms pertaining to work in the different cultures she studied. In Samoa work is not divided along gender lines and both men and women cook, garden and fish. In Arapesh both men and women do heavy work, childcare, make fires and gather from the nearby bush. Balinese men and women are both reported to work equally hard, although they do different tasks. In contrast the Itmul headhunters of the Middle Sepik River organise work according to gender and in a manner similar to that found in hunter-gatherer societies. The women take care of much of the daily work, for example catching fish, gathering wood for the fire and cooking; 'women work steadily at unexciting tasks' (Mead 1962: 167). The men's work is described as 'episodic' and exciting (Mead 1962: 167). They build the houses, make the canoes and go hunting. The men are described as working 'with a will' as none of these are jobs that must be done regularly (1962: 167). This anthropological evidence leads Mead to argue that the gendered division of labour is arbitrary rather than natural.

Masculinity and femininity are produced by social experience and are not natural phenomena. Current constructions of gender in Ireland reflect dominant norms about men and women and are influenced by broader changes in Irish society. These include the decline in the power of the Catholic Church (Inglis 1998), the increasing ethnic diversity of Irish society, the increasing power of the mass media and the increased prosperity associated particularly with the middle classes in Celtic Tiger Ireland. This is not to suggest that men and women's lives are completely determined by existing structures. Individuals do play a role in the construction of gender and can challenge the norms in operation (Garfinkel 1967). However, gender is always constructed within existing social structures, which limits the scope for manoeuvre (Connell 2002: 54). Sanctions may be applied to people who break gender norms.

The gendered division of labour is understood quite differently from within this perspective. A strong link is identified between understandings of masculinity and femininity and the division of labour in relation to both paid and unpaid work. These are not linked to any biological difference in men's and women's capacity for paid work or for caring. Rather, the roles played by men and women, respectively, in the past, and the expectations we have of men and women in the present, play a central role. This corresponds with the available evidence: we can all think of examples of individuals who do not fit the traditional mould – men who are primary caregivers or women who are breadwinners – and who are clearly well suited to their roles. Because they are social constructions, any definition or understanding of masculinity and femininity is not fixed or absolute. Changing practices challenge traditional understandings. This is especially true in times of change, when contradictions in existing arrangements may become apparent. Over the past decade there has been some focus on the changing role of Irish men and the pressures of being a man in contemporary Irish society (Cleary 2005: 4) – including male suicide and the legal rights of fathers – reflecting a broader change in the sociology of gender away from a focus exclusively on women. As Weeks (2005: 53) argues, 'The question of what men are and what they want has become central to public debates and private concerns'. Connell (2002: 61), writing about Australian society, argues that despite such crisis points, the prevailing norms about men and women's work remain strong; 'the whole economic sphere is culturally defined as men's world (regardless of the presence of women in it), while domestic life is defined as women's world (regardless of the presence of men in it)'. This is an issue that I shall revisit in relation to Irish society; does women's increased labour force participation challenge this norm or does the strong association between women and the domestic sphere nullify this?

Finally, it has already been argued that not all men and women are the same and that these are broad, heterogeneous categories. Feminist writers such as bell hooks (1994), and those writing from the men's studies tradition (Connell 1987) have argued that it makes no sense to speak of 'men' and 'women' ignoring social differences which may advantage or disadvantage them, such as race, class, age, occupation, sexuality, education, disability and so on. Instead, we should recognise that there are both powerful women and powerless men in our society. Nowhere is this more evident than in the world of work.

Gender and work

Work has been the focus of different feminist theorists trying to explain why women and men occupy unequal positions in society. For both liberal and Marxist feminists the inequality of women in society has a material basis, that is women are powerless because they lack economic power. In 1851, John Stuart Mill and Harriet Taylor Mill argued that women should have the same economic opportunities as men. Taylor focuses on the benefits for women; 'in order to be partners rather than servants of their husbands, wives must earn an income outside the home' (Tong 1998: 17). Mills's work emphasises the benefits that would accrue to society if women were afforded the same rights and opportunities as men. However, both agreed that women were responsible for child rearing and there is no suggestion that the division of domestic labour should be altered so that both men and women could participate fully in the world of work.

There is an optimism inherent in this approach; inequality is seen as the legacy of traditional society which can be removed through societal reforms. A range of legislation aiming to tackle such barriers has been enacted in the Republic of Ireland over the past decade. The Equal Status Acts (2000 and 2004) and the Employment Equality Act (1998) prohibit discrimination on the grounds of gender or family status,[2] making it illegal to treat women and those with children less favourably than others in the workforce. The Maternity Protection Act (1994 and 2004) gives a woman the entitlement to a period of maternity leave from her job (currently 22 weeks, with the possibility of 12 weeks additional leave). Employers are obliged to keep the position open for this period, but are not obliged to pay women while they are on leave, although some do. Unpaid parental leave was introduced in 1998, and entitles both parents to 14 weeks leave before their child reaches the age of eight. These legislative changes met a key demand of liberal feminism – the elimination of practices or laws that discriminate against women in an overt manner. The prediction was that once a level playing field was established, the material basis for gender inequality would wither away and a gender-neutral society would emerge.

Contemporary liberal feminists continued in a similar vein to Taylor and Mills. For example, Betty Friedan (1982) was critical of American society in which college-educated women became housewives after marriage, taking up the traditional female role. She saw this as a waste of human potential as well as an ordeal for these women. Her proposed solution was that women should enter the paid workforce and abandon the housewife role entirely. The current situation in Ireland is that, although women have entered the paid workforce, thereby gaining access to economic power, they have done this without complying with the second part of Friedan's solution. This raises the question of why and how this has happened. One sociologist, not a feminist, has explained this by arguing that family, and not work, is the most important thing for women and that this represents their (valid) choice (Hakim 1995). However, others would be more critical. Connell (1987), for example, argues that gender inequality is the product of both economic and cultural power wielded by men. This suggests that the strategy proposed by liberal feminism was never going to solve the problem of gender inequality. It is not just the institution of work that must be reformed and so the optimism of liberal feminism in relation to gender inequality is largely unfounded.

Girls outperform boys at the Leaving Certificate, and more women than men go on to third-level education.[3] This performance is reflected in a new self-confidence. In my gender classes, there is optimism amongst the majority of female students about their life chances; they believe they can 'have it all', they can see their advantageous position in the educational system and are looking forward to combining successful careers, children and marriage. They believe in a fair and meritocratic society – a gender-blind society – where exam results, qualifications and hard work count and gender does not (see also Leonard 2004; Ging 2005). In a study of the legal profession in Ireland, Bacik et al. (2003: 153) termed this widespread optimism in the power of numerical superiority the 'trickle-up' fallacy: 'the powerful misperception that women's progress as lawyers is simply a matter of time, with increasing numbers of women studying the law and entering the profession'. This optimism is inherently conservative as no organisational or structural change is seen to be required and so no such changes are sought by these optimists. The optimism is also misplaced as 'the assumption that change occurs inevitably is not borne out by the empirical data' (Bacik et al. 2003: 316).

Engels (1884) argued that 'Male dominance . . . is simply the result of the class division between the propertied man and the propertyless woman' (cited in Tong, 1998: 103). So, for Marxist feminists, this dominance will remain as long as the capitalist system stays intact. Contemporary Marxist feminists have argued that gender inequality is functional for capitalism. For example, women's unpaid work in the family is necessary to maintain the workforce. The solution is therefore to overthrow capitalism. Socialist feminists are critical of this analysis, arguing that it is false to claim that capitalism caused gender inequalities: 'women's oppression extends beyond the area of economic production' (Andersen 1998: 356) and the end of capitalism will not be enough to end oppression of women. Hartmann (1994: 576) argues that both capitalism and patriarchy 'can be surprisingly flexible and adaptable'. Her historical analysis charts the relationship between these two systems in order 'to explain the ways in which capitalism intersects with patriarchy to oppress women more . . . than men' (Tong 1998: 119). The way capitalism currently works comes under scrutiny. Women's wages do not allow most to live independently. This wage differential is seen by Hartmann as central. It allows women's work to be considered less important than men's and also contributes to women's economic dependence on men. As we shall see, the issue of differential pay remains a key issue for Irish women in the present situation and contributes to their position of relative powerlessness.

Ryan (2003) points to an additional material factor that applies in the current situation. In Ireland, the rise of consumer culture has led to the triumph of the idea that couples 'need' two incomes to service their mortgage and other consumption. In this analysis, the dual income family is economically rational (indeed it has been essential for the Celtic Tiger boom) and this rationality obscures the gender inequalities associated with it. The economy's need for the extra capacity offered by women workers, including mothers, is the macro-level driver behind recent changes rather than any restructuring of gender roles. Women workers have been central to Ireland's recent economic success. However, the labour force remains largely 'unfeminised', despite the changes in its composition. By this I mean that it remains a workforce designed for a worker with no family responsibilities, and good behind-the-scenes support – a male worker in short.

Finally, as we have already seen, the work of Connell draws our attention to additional structures in operation in relation to gender. The organisation of work is central, but it is not the sole or even the primary foundation of the current gender order. He argues that any analysis of how gender operates must also pay attention to the way power is distributed (echoing socialist feminists), the way emotional and sexual relations are organised (the central theme of radical feminism), as well as the symbolic dimensions of gender, including representations of ideal forms of masculinity and femininity. Women's unequal position in the workforce is related to and reinforced by their unequal position in these other domains.

Gender and the workforce in the Irish Republic 1995–2005

The proportion of Irish women in the labour force has been on the increase since the mid-1980s. The past decade has seen particularly rapid increases. In 1995, 41.6 per cent of Irish women were in the labour force, a figure lower than the EU average. By 2005 this figure had risen dramatically to 58 per cent, a figure slightly higher than the EU average (CSO 2005b: 11). Since 1999, the majority of Irish women are in the paid labour force. Those working exclusively in the home are now in a minority (33 per cent) (CSO 2005b: 25). In comparison, in 1996, 41 per cent of women were working exclusively in the home, almost the same as the number of women in the labour force at the time (Kennedy 2001: 70). This represents a major change.

O'Connor (1998) has shown that younger women are much more likely than older ones to participate in the paid workforce. In 1996, 71 per cent of those aged 25–34 participated, compared to 29 per cent of those aged 55–59 and only 17 per cent of those aged 60–64 (O'Connor 1998: 193). The most recent data show an increase in the participation rates for all age groups; the largest change was in the 45–54 age group where the percentage in the labour force increased from 42 to 63 per cent of the cohort. It is interesting to compare men and women's participation across the life cycle. (see figure 15.1).

Figure 15.1 **Ireland: Labour force participation rate by age group, 2005**

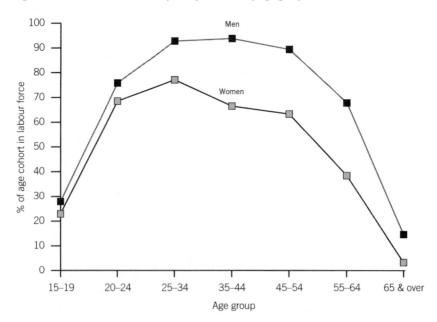

Source: CSO 2005b

The pattern for both in 2005 is broadly similar, an inverted 'U', but the big difference is that men's participation rate is higher than women's at every point across the life cycle. Women's participation peaks in the 25–34 age group, while for men the peak is in the 35–44 age group. There is a drop in overall labour force participation for women during the peak childbearing years. Older women are much less likely than their male counterparts to be in the labour force, only 38 per cent of women aged 55–64 compared to 67.8 per cent of men. Some of these women would have joined the labour force pre-1973 when the marriage bar was in place, meaning that if they worked in the public service they were obliged to leave their jobs when they married, and this discrepancy may therefore be explained by historical factors. So despite the increases in older women's labour force participation overall, age remains an important factor.

The percentage of married women in paid employment has increased, from 45 per cent in 1997, to 51.2 per cent in June/August 2005 (CSO 2006b). The majority of married women are now working outside the home, a big change from the 1970s when these women were forced to give up their jobs if they worked in the public service. Dual income couples are more common as a result. Another trend is that more mothers are now working, whereas in the past it was the norm for them to exit the workforce, for a period or permanently. In 2004 the Quarterly National Household Survey identified 282,700 couples with children under 18 where the woman works and 59,000 working lone parents (Department of Justice Equality and Law Reform 2004: 10). A normative expectation is emerging that to be an adult is to be a worker, irrespective of one's gender or marital status. The legislative changes mentioned earlier have been crucial in facilitating this.

Segmentation or segregation?
A key issue in relation to women in the labour force is the extent to which they are vertically segregated (work mostly with other women in lower status and low paid areas) and, despite their educational credentials, horizontally segregated (concentrated at the bottom of occupational hierarchies). Table 15.1 shows us that vertical segregation remains an important feature of the Irish labour market (see also Galligan 2000), and some gender specific areas have become more rather than less gendered over the past decade; plant and machine operatives and craft workers were more likely to be male in 2005 than in 1997 and clerical, secretarial and sales workers were more likely to be women. Professional work is the only sector with an even gender balance. This is a sector that saw expansion in the period under discussion, increasing from 147,500 employees in 1997 (10 per cent of the total labour force) to 224,700 in 2005 (11.3 per cent of labour force).

Table 15.1 **Persons in employment classified by sex and occupation (percentages)**

Broad occupational group	Men		Women	
	1997	2005	1997	2005
Managers and administrators	76.6	69.5	23.4	30.5
Professional	56.0	51.1	44.0	48.9
Associate professional and technical	45.3	41.8	54.7	58.2
Clerical and secretarial	25.5	24.1	74.5	75.9
Craft and related	91.5	95.9	8.5	4.1
Personal and protective service	44.9	36.3	55.1	63.7
Sales	41.8	38.7	58.2	61.3
Plant and machine operatives	72.0	83.9	28.0	16.1
Other	59.0	63.3	41.0	36.7

Source: CSO 2006b: table 4, figures for September–November 1997 and 2005

Fahey et al. (2000: 266) identify a polarising trend in the labour force 'encompassing growing numbers of highly qualified, professional and managerial level women and a growing band of female sales workers, personal service workers and part-time workers'. As Kennedy (2003) has argued, there is a class dimension to Irish women's experience of the labour market. This may be overlooked owing to the tendency to speak about women as if they are a homogeneous category.

Women occupy a minority of positions of power in Irish society, as figure 15.2 demonstrates. In the 2002–2007 Dáil, only 13 per cent of deputies were women. This compares unfavourably to an average of 22.5 per cent across the 25 countries of the EU.[4] Only Greece, Slovenia, France, Italy, Malta and Hungary elect fewer female representatives than Ireland (CSO 2005b: 21).

Figure 15.2 **Women and men in decision making, 2005**

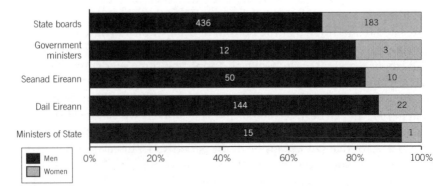

Source: CSO 2005b: 21.

In terms of horizontal segregation the picture remains relatively bleak for Irish women. As evident from table 15.1 women make up less than one third of those classified as managers and administrators, although this figure has increased by seven per cent between 1997 and 2005. If this change continues at a similar pace, women would make up 50 per cent of this group by 2029. However, as O'Connor (1998: 218) argues, it is difficult to identify the precise location of the women in this group, particularly whether they are in high or low status areas of the economy. An article on the Chief Executive Officers (CEOs) of the top thousand companies in the Republic of Ireland indicates that only 4.6 per cent of this elite group are women, including four of the CEOs of companies in the top 50 – Apple Computers, Dunnes Stores, Vodaphone Ireland and O$_2$ Ireland (*Irish Times*, 26 May 2006); only one of the top 50 companies in Northern Ireland listed has a female CEO. So some women are getting the top jobs and the sectors in which they are doing so are interesting to consider: six of these CEOs are in telecommunications and eight are in the banking and financial services sector, neither of which is traditionally considered a 'female' sector.

The data available for the public sector have improved greatly over the past decade and we now have some very useful data on horizontal segregation in education, health and the civil service. In education, the majority of teachers at both 1st (primary) and 2nd level (secondary) are women (CSO 2005b: 42). Primary schoolteaching is a particularly feminised occupation with women making up 86 per cent of primary schoolteachers. The gender breakdown at principal level is quite different. Men constitute only 14.4 per cent of primary schoolteachers but, despite this numerical disadvantage, they make up almost half of those at school principal level. At secondary level women do better, but still only make up 32.3 per cent of school principals despite being in the majority in the sector. As well as seeming inequitable, such obvious horizontal segregation sends out messages to both girls and boys about the association between gender and authority.

In the health service the majority of employees are women, outnumbering their male counterparts by more than four to one (CSO 2005b: 50). Almost 100,000 women work in this sector, making it a major source of female employment. It is also a sector where there is evidence of both vertical and horizontal segregation. Women make up the majority of those in management in the health service (approximately 16 per cent of all women at this level are working in the health service), but the top job in the sector in terms of pay and status is that of consultant and not manager. Women are the majority of those at all grades except consultant and non-consultant doctors and dentists. Women make up 91.5 per cent of nurses and only 29 per cent of consultants (CSO 2005b: 50).

In the civil service, the picture is broadly similar (see table 15.2). Women are the majority of those working in the civil service (64.6 per cent) and are concentrated at the lower levels: 94.1 per cent of Secretary Generals, 88.6 per cent of Deputy and Assistant Secretaries and 79.6 per cent of Principal Officers are men. Women are in the majority at the Clerical Officer (79 per cent) and Staff Officer (80 per cent) grades.

Table 15.2 **Distribution of women across civil service grades, 1995 and 2003**

Grade	Number of women as % of grade		
	1995	*2003*	*% change*
Secretary General	4	6	+ 2
Deputy and Assistant Secretary	6	11	+ 5
Principal Officer	13	20	+ 7
Assistant Principal	23	33	+ 10
Administrative Officer	21	53	+ 32
Higher Executive Officer	37	48	+ 11
Executive Officer	51	65	+ 14
Staff Officer	75	80	+ 5
Clerical Officer	79	79	0

Source: CSO 2005b: 22 rounded down; O'Connor 1998: 221.

Between 1995 and 2003 increases in the numbers of women were recorded at all grades, with the exception of Clerical Officer. The increases are most modest in the top three and the bottom two grades, reflecting underlying horizontal and vertical segregation. The highest increase recorded is at Administrative Officer level and women now make up the majority of those at this grade. So there is evidence here of moves in a positive direction for women in the civil service, albeit at a slow pace at the top levels.

Unequal and low pay
Women earn less than men and are concentrated in the lower income bands. In 2003 64.3 per cent of women had an annual income of less than €20,000; for men, the figure was 46.4 per cent. Men dominate the higher income bands; 18.7 per cent of men and only 7.9 per cent of women had an income of more than €40,000 in 2003 (CSO 2005b: 16). In addition women's average incomes overall were only 65.6 per cent of men's in 2003 (CSO 2005b: 16). For women aged 25–34, incomes are, on average, 80.9 per cent of men of the same age. Factors which explain this discrepancy include women's shorter working hours, vertical segregation of women in areas which are low status and lower paid, and unequal pay which will be discussed in more detail below. In addition, many women returning to work after periods of unpaid work in

the home experience downward mobility (Russell et al. 2002: viii), that is, the jobs they return to are of a lower grade than the ones they previously occupied.

The discrepancy between male and female incomes is particularly acute for women aged 45 and above, whose income is only 55.3 per cent of that of men in the same age group, perhaps reflective of both horizontal segregation (men are more likely to be promoted as they get older) and older women's lower labour force participation rates. Poverty remains a key issue for Irish women; the proportion of women at risk of poverty was almost 23 per cent in Ireland in 2004, while the corresponding figure for men was 18 per cent (CSO 2005b: 10).

The problem of a pay differential persists, and the most recent estimate is that Irish women earn 14 per cent less than their male counterparts (CSO 2005b: 17). In a recent study of graduates three years after graduation, Russell et al. (2005) found an eight per cent pay gap (hourly pay) between men and women graduates working in the private sector, and seven per cent in the public sector (if teachers are excluded) (2005: 19). Men in this study were more likely to receive training, bonuses and other fringe benefits (2005: 24–5). What makes these findings particularly interesting is the cohort studied: those who graduated in 2001 and had entered the labour market the following year. The rationale for this choice is that, at this stage of a career, differences in qualifications or experience are not common. More importantly, perhaps, given that the average age at which women have their first child was 28.3 in 2003 (CSO 2005b: 34), only a small minority of women in the cohort would already have children. Despite progress in terms of women's overall participation in the labour force, and some progress in terms of promotional prospects, women's economic power remains weaker then men's overall and this disadvantage begins early in women's working lives. In a heterosexual couple, this makes it seem logical and economically rational to define a woman's work as less important than a man's. This can, over time, lead to a situation where the woman's primary role is defined as mother and homemaker, and the man's as breadwinner.

Unpaid work

It has already been argued that traditional understandings of men and women's roles remain powerful. This helps to explain the different experiences of men and women in the workforce following parenthood. Recent figures show that Irish women's participation in paid employment varies according to family status and age of children: 84.8 per cent for women with no children in comparison to 55.3 per cent for women whose youngest child was aged three or under (CSO 2005b: 14). In contrast, male participation rates remain relatively constant irrespective of age or numbers of children. This would suggest that the association between women and the role of mother remains strong. The majority of employers do not facilitate work–life balance and, when they do, initiatives are often directed at, or created exclusively for, women. In a gender neutral society, such entitlements would be targeted at parents, rather than exclusively or primarily at the mother.

Hochschild (1989) has identified what she terms a 'stalled revolution' in American society. She is referring to the fact that women's mass entry into the paid labour force – the first part of the revolution in the gendered division of labour – has not been accompanied by a restructuring or a renegotiation of the gendered division of labour in the home. This unfair division of domestic labour can be seen as reflective of a lack of female power (Connell, 1987). In Ireland, a similar phenomenon can be observed and changes in relation to unpaid work have been much more modest than changes in women's labour force participation (Leonard, 2004). McGinty et al.'s (2005) study of time use in Ireland showed clear gender differences in relation to work done in the home (see table 15.3).

Table 15.3 **Average time spent on domestic labour hh:mm**

	Weekdays			Weekends		
	Men	*Women*	*Time difference**	*Men*	*Women*	*Time difference*
Cooking	0:16	1:09	+0:53	0:18	1:00	+0:42
Cleaning	0:12	1.18	+1:06	0:12	1:07	+0:55
DIY/gardening	0:28	0:14	−0:14	0:44	0:15	−0:29
Shopping	0:16	0:42	+0:26	0:27	0:50	+0:23
Childcare: supervision	0:14	1:50	+1:36	0:26	1.49	+1:23
Childcare: playing, reading	0:17	0:40	+0:23	0:25	0:40	+0:15

*a positive figure indicates that women's total for the task is higher than men's.
Source: McGinty et al. 2005: 7.

The survey also found that Irish men spend more time on paid employment and travelling than women. At the weekends, men's time spent on employment and travelling reduces. In contrast, the time women spend on caring and household remains much the same. The result is that women have 90 minutes less leisure time than men, creating a 'leisure gap' (McGinty et al. 2005: 12). Finally, it is interesting to note that the 'trickle-up fallacy' also appears to operate in relation to unpaid work. In Leonard's (2004) study of teenage girls and housework there was a belief that although the situation for their mothers was unfair, their education and skills would protect them from such problems.

Breen and Cooke (2005) ask why the gendered division of labour remains so strong despite increases in women's labour force participation. They cite US research that might help to explain this seeming paradox: 'as wives become the primary breadwinners, they do more of the domestic tasks to reinforce traditional gender ideologies', highlighting the agency individuals possess in relation to gender (Breen and Cooke 2005: 43). They argue that changes in the gendered division of labour are not inevitable even given women's increased participation in the labour force. They identify two changes that are needed for the gendered division of labour in the home to change. Firstly, there must be an increase in the number of women who are economically independent (so issues such as low pay, unequal pay and segregation are all pertinent). Secondly, there must be 'a sufficiently large proportion of men who, if faced with an economically autonomous woman, would rather participate in domestic tasks than endure marital breakdown' (2005: 43). The combination of these two changes would restructure the balance of power in the home.

Childcare

In Irish society, the mother retains primary responsibility for children and their needs, irrespective of whether or not she is working. Childcare is seen as part of the female role. As we have already seen in table 15.3, women spend, on average, almost two hours more than men looking after children on week-days, and one hour and 38 minutes on weekend days. Women's experience as workers is mediated by motherhood, as well as by education and class. There is no universal and generalisable female experience of the workforce. The lack of state support and childcare provision in Ireland (Kennedy 2001: 77–8; Tovey and Share 2003: 250; Murphy-Lawless 2000) has created a situation whereby childcare was been positioned as a private issue for families to resolve themselves. This is what the OECD (1990) has termed a 'maximum private responsibility' model of childcare, also found in the US and the UK, 'in which the joint problems of childcare, family life and labour force participation are entirely private concerns which are left to the individual to solve' (Coveney et al. 1998: 11). In practice, the individual referred to here is usually the mother.

The argument that childcare is a private issue rather than one for the state is supported by available data on providers of childcare in Ireland. In table 15.4 we see that, in 2002, unpaid relatives looked after 31.2 per cent of pre-school and 46.1 per cent of primary schoolchildren. These unpaid relatives are usually women – a grandmother, aunt, cousin or older sibling of the child. In contrast, only 27.1 per cent of preschools and 6.1 per cent of those at primary school are in formally organised group care.

Coveney et al. (1998), in a small qualitative study of working women in Dublin's inner city, point to problems experienced by women using these

Table 15.4 **Location of children in non-parental care in Ireland 2002**

	Preschool	Primary school
Unpaid relative	31.2	46.1
Paid relative	12.0	14.1
Paid carer	29.4	31.9
Group	27.1	6.1
Other	7.4	4.3

Source: Department of Justice Equality and Law Reform 2004: 7.

types of childcare arrangements. Given the high costs of crèches and childminders, family support may be the only option available to women in low-paid work. This often worked well, but in practice it usually involved obligations for respondents which were not always sustainable in the long term (see also Russell and Corcoran 2000). It is unsurprising, therefore, that such childcare arrangements are not considered optimum by Irish respondents, who in a recent survey said they would prefer to use group or after-school care (Department of Justice Equality and Law Reform 2004: 8). The reasons cited by parents for not using their preferred type of childcare were availability and cost.

Paid carers are another important feature of the Irish childcare system. As inward migration becomes more common in Ireland, we see a situation where female migrants are employed as domestic and childcare workers, often working in the informal economy (Migrant Rights Centre Ireland 2004; see chapter 2 above on Migration for further discussion). Hochschild (2000) has drawn attention to this phenomenon, which is more widespread in the USA. The 'globalisation of mothering' often involves women from the minority world leaving their own families in their home countries, whilst they provide domestic and childcare services for western women, thereby enabling their participation in the labour force.

More recently, childcare has made its way on to the political agenda in Ireland. A series of government reports that dealt with this issue either directly or indirectly were published in the late 1990s, including *Strengthening Families for Life* (1998), *The White Paper on Early Childhood Education* (1998) and *The National Childcare Strategy* (1999). In August 2005 the annual Fianna Fáil 'think in' devoted considerable time to the issue. These events framed the topic of childcare as newsworthy and generated some media coverage and analysis. However, much of this debate positioned childcare as women's responsibility, and so a woman's issue, and, in this way, reinforced rather than challenged the traditional role of the mother. What was challenged in some of the discussion was the quality of life experienced by dual-income families. At present, there is little evidence to suggest that the state plans to step in and take statutory responsibility for childcare as happens elsewhere in Europe. At the moment, women's labour force participation continues apace without it (Collins and Wickham 2004). The preferred solution for Ireland's anticipated labour shortages at the policy level is not to continue the revolution currently stalled, but to solve the problem by using migrant workers to meet any such shortages (see chapter 2 above).

Conclusion

From 1995 to 2005, women's participation in the paid labour force in Ireland has continued to rise. The majority of women between the ages of 20 and 55 are working, irrespective of their marital status and whether or not they have small children. However, this increase in women's participation does not mean that women have achieved equality, either in the labour market or in the home. The Irish situation, therefore, can be characterised as a 'stalled revolution' (Hochschild 1989), one which causes difficulties and tensions. These difficulties and tensions are defined as individual problems at both the micro and macro level. Despite legislative changes, many difficulties remain for Irish women in the workforce, including low pay, unequal pay, horizontal segregation, vertical segregation and discrimination on the grounds of gender. The social and cultural implications of changing female labour force participation have not yet been addressed by Irish society or Irish sociology (O'Connor 2005: 28). The economic rationality of the dual income family obscures the gender inequalities associated with it (Ryan 2003). Women in different class positions are more or less able to deal with difficulties associated with women's participation in the labour force and the stalled revolution. Those with the resources have access to a far greater range of support options; for example, they may subcontract some of their domestic responsibilities by using formal childcare or employing a housekeeper, nanny or au pair. Different concerns arise for those excluded from the Celtic Tiger economy, including the disabled, Traveller women and one-parent families (Kelleher and Associates 2001).

As this discussion of women's participation in the workforce shows, legislation alone is insufficient to tackle the many inequalities that persist. Traditional gender roles remain strong and underpin the gendered division of labour. Irish women currently do it all, and still do not have the same access to power, money and prestige as their male counterparts. The difficulties created by the stalled revolution have begun to be articulated by ordinary women and men, particularly in relation to childcare. As women continue to experience difficulties in the workplace and in the home, the crisis tendencies

(Connell, 1987) underpinning the gendered division of labour will continue to make themselves evident. Changing practices will challenge Irish society's understanding of what women and men should be and want. One possibility is that we shall see another readjustment in the mutually beneficial alliance between patriarchy and capitalism in Irish society, creating a situation in which gender inequalities will persist, albeit in a different form (see Hartmann 1994). Another is that the crisis tendencies will lead both men and women to pay more attention to the costs of the current system, for both men and women, and question in whose interests the current system is operating. What is certain is that women cannot change the gendered division of labour on their own. For the stalled revolution to reignite will require the majority of men to enter the domestic world of unpaid work challenging traditional associations in the same way that many women have done in the paid labour force. Whatever the outcome, it is imperative that Irish sociology continues to examine how gender and power operate in our society.

Chapter 16

Food and rural sustainable development

Hilary Tovey

'Rural Ireland': space or society?

This chapter looks at 'rural Ireland' as the location for productive work on nature – specifically in this instance, the production of food. It uses research from South Tipperary on local projects for rural development to discuss the different ways in which local actors think of 'local food' as a vehicle for sustainable development. These case studies are locally specific, but they can give us an insight into some of the transformations taking place in Irish agriculture and rural society more generally.

Many discussions of the rural understand it primarily as a type of space – characterised by a dispersed population and a low ratio of people to geographic area. From the spatial point of view, the key issues that need to be considered in a discussion of 'rural transformations' are changes in the distribution of populations across space: demographic and migration trends, in particular. From the perspective used in this chapter, however, it is rather changes in the nature of rural livelihoods, economy and society which are important. In the scope of one short chapter it is not easy to bring these two interpretations of 'rural' together; and yet each set of changes clearly interacts with and conditions the other. Here, I shall only sketch some significant spatial changes, preferring to give more room to a discussion of transformations in the rural as a socio-economic category and to changing public and policy understandings of how such a category should be 'managed' and 'developed'.

According to the Census of Population, Irish people are 'rural' if they live in settlements of less than 1,500 persons, including the open countryside. Successive censuses suggest that rural Ireland, in this sense, is gradually disappearing as the society urbanises. The proportion of the population classified as 'rural' has fallen from around 46 per cent in 1981 to around 40 per cent in 2002. Of course, this statistic is distorted by the sheer dominance of the Dublin Metropolitan region, which accounts for nearly one third of people living in Ireland and whose commuting belt now stretches as far as Wexford and Dundalk on the east, and Nenagh and Thurles on the west and south. In the mid-1990s, around 60 per cent of the population, excluding the greater Dublin area, lived in rural areas, and around a third of these were living in farm households (Commins 1996). At that time, analyses of change in rural Ireland still focused primarily on the effects of emigration on the rural population (see for example, Jackson and Haase 1996). Constant emigration removed a high proportion of those of working years from rural areas, leaving a population much of which was elderly, often single-person households living in increasing social isolation. Today, in-migration and return migration are becoming as important as out-migration in shaping rural Ireland. In Tipperary South Riding, for example, where today 10 per cent of the population are not Irish-born, the proportion of the population which the census defines as rural increased from 58 per cent to 61 per cent between 1996 and 2002. While there is still a high rate of movement out of the county by young adults, movement in by young middle-aged people, often married and with young children, is also increasingly significant. However, most incomers settle in towns and villages, rather than in the open countryside, and despite the media attention attracted by disputes around 'one-off housing' in the countryside, much new housing is in fact in ribbon development along improved roads near to existing settlements. There is a general shift in rural population settlement away from the remoter hinterlands and into new suburban locations, and if we add to this the outward spread of Dublin and other large cities, we might conclude that the key trend in spatial settlement today, one which incorporates both 'rural' and 'urban' populations, is not 'urbanisation' so much as 'suburbanisation'.

However, for rural sociologists, and for many rural inhabitants themselves, being 'rural' primarily means living in a distinctive social world. It is distinctive partly, of course, because it is small in scale, but also because it has historical roots in a particular kind of economy – one of productive work on nature, where the rhythms of work, the social relations, the landscape and the culture have all been shaped to a greater or lesser extent by human relationships with natural and biological processes. In this perspective, changes in rural society are intimately linked to changes in agriculture and other similarly nature-based work. These changes have been profound over recent decades: agriculture is shrinking within rural economies, and other economic activities have expanded. State policies for industrialisation through attracting in and building on multinational investment have increased employment alternatives, although the earlier interest in encouraging transnational corporations to locate their branch plants in rural localities has moderated in recent times. But the greatest occupational expansion has been in professional, administrative and service work, often bringing rural women into the paid workforce in much greater numbers than before. In Tipperary South Riding, again, over the 20 years between 1981 and 2002 the numbers working in agriculture fell by half (to 8 per cent), and the numbers in professional, commercial and other service work almost doubled, from 17 per cent to almost 30 per cent of the paid workforce. Other types of work – in manufacturing, construction, and 'unskilled' labouring jobs – remained almost unchanged, again at around 30 per cent. If rural settlement patterns are becoming more 'suburban' in style, rural work appears to be becoming more white-collar, more detached from the transformative work on material nature which gave it its distinctiveness.

In relation to agricultural work, however, the statistics are complex and not easily interpreted. They present evidence of contraction and decline, but also of a complicated pattern of restructuring and reorganisation. From the 1970s on, Irish agriculture was reshaped from a dispersed, mainly small-scale production system to one where commodity output is now concentrated on a small subset of farms – that 20 per cent or so of all farms which possessed the financial and human capital to adopt new technologies and production practices which would intensify their output. Agriculture in this sense, of intensive, science-based commodity production, is located mainly on larger farms in the east and south-east, specialised mainly in dairying, tillage, or cattle finishing (Tovey 2000). The shakeout in farming has produced a cohort of agricultural businessmen, younger on average than European farmers generally, 11 per cent being under 35 years of age and only 20 per cent older than 65 years (compared to EU averages of 8 per cent and 29 per cent). The structure of landholding has changed much less: a market in farmland has only recently started developing, farmers who increase their farm sizes often do so by renting additional land from neighbours, and many of the farms which did not intensify remained as family assets but are worked in ways which allow farming to be combined with off-farm jobs or with semi-retirement. We know little about what is happening now to that land. Some of it has been forested, some sold for house-sites, some rented out, some sold to people from Dublin or overseas interested in 'hobby-farming' or in various experiments in sustainability and self-sufficiency, and some is available to family members to use for new food production ventures.

It is no longer possible to make easy identifications between 'farms' (landholdings), 'farmers' (food producers), and 'farm households'. Perhaps such identifications were never very valid, and are better understood as an ideological construct, the result of state and farming organisations' commitment to 'the full-time viable family farm' as the marker of agrarian progress. Ownership of land, usually by inheritance, is still important for most new entrants to farming, but landownership and an agricultural livelihood are becoming more and more disassociated. Just over half (54 per cent) of Irish farmers today (compared to 30 per cent on average across the EU) also have off-farm work, and many more live in households where most of the household income comes from off-farm work done by a spouse, children or other relatives. In 2003, the annual average income from the agricultural activities of the 54 per cent of 'part-time farmers' was around €7,000, while they received an average of €20,200 from their off-farm work (Department of Agriculture and Food 2005a). The more fluid relations between farming and land owner-ship, diversity in life experiences and family situations among those working in agriculture, changes in the wider rural society and perhaps particularly the arrival of new incomers to rural areas, all help to open up new possibilities for those who have access to land and an interest in using it productively. While National Farm Surveys suggest a continuing decline in the number of farms in Ireland, from 159,000 in 1992 to 135,300 in 2003, with the sharpest decline in the holdings under 30 hectares in size, we should be mindful that these figures are socially constructed: they depend on how both those doing the counting, and those being counted, define what is a 'farm' or who is a 'farmer'.

Transformations in agriculture are an outcome not just of changing economic conditions for farming but also of state and EU 'rural development' policies. Up to 1990, both EU and Irish states understood 'rural' essentially as 'agricultural'; increasing and intensifying agricultural output was the way to bring incomes from farming up to a level comparable with those from indus-trial employment. Before our Accession to the then EEC (1971), Irish state policy included most farms in that goal, even smaller farms in remoter areas and on poorer land; but during the 1980s the EU's Common Agricultural Policy encouraged Irish policy to focus selectively on supporting those farms which were seen as having a capacity to become 'viable farms', that is, larger farms, with 'good demography' (a household including younger members, particularly a potential heir), and the educational and capital resources to become modern intensive businesses. This 'agri-modernisation' (Marsden 2003) policy model assumed that 'non-viable' farmers would move out of agriculture and seek a livelihood elsewhere, in decentralised industry, for example, or in tourism; but many such Irish farmers proved reluctant to sell their land, seeing it as family heritage, potential future capital, or a marginal but still important source of family income.

After 1990, however, policy orientations towards the rural changed significantly. What Marsden calls 'post-productivist' understandings of the countryside began to shape policies for rural areas. As the economic power of European farmers contracted, so did their political control over land and natural resources, whose future became opened up to a range of new debates, particularly influenced by environmental concerns. Post-productivist orienta-tions value the countryside less as a terrain for (agricultural) production, and more as a site for (urban) consumption; the countryside is seen as the legitimate object of public interests, in environmental protection, aesthetic appreciation, leisure and recreation, rather than private economic ones. From a post-productivist policy perspective the countryside appeals as empty space, to be enjoyed by tourists seeking to get away from crowded cities, or even as a suitable space for the 'dumping' of urban problems from waste infill sites to prisons and other communities of the disadvantaged. Rural landholders are not to be encouraged to produce food, of which Europe already has a surplus, but rather to manage the scenery, landscape and biodiversity of rural areas as a public good. While they have been influential, however, post-productivist policies have not been unchallenged. Irish state policies for the rural continued to value rural 'community', for example as a resource for tourism, and the agricultural policy network embedded within Irish state institutions is still strong enough to represent farming as the bedrock of rural community, while recognising that it must become more environmentally sensitive and responsive to public good concerns. Through the Rural Environmental Protection Scheme (REPS) and more recently through LEADER programmes, these networks have been strategically using EU agri-environmental and rural development resources to re-situate farming as a core rural practice. At EU level also, changes to the Common Agricultural Policy – the 'de-coupling' of income supports to farmers from the production of agricultural commodities, agri-environmental support for 'extensifying' farm production – express a new recognition that farming is a 'multi-functional activity' in which the function of food production is as important as, and can be compatible with, its other environmental and social functions.

In summary, rural Ireland today (and indeed, rural Europe) is a contested site, in which discourses of the rural as a site for the protection and enjoyment of nature are challenged by discourses of 'rural development', and increasingly, 'sustainable rural development'. What exactly 'sustainable' means, what 'sustainable development' requires from rural inhabitants, and how it can or should be implemented, remain ambiguous. At a national level, Irish development policy has been committed to a sustainable development discourse since the publication of the Department of the Environment's *Sustainable Development: A Strategy for Ireland* in 1997. Farmers have been drawn into environmental regulation through REPS, through regulation of the disposal of animal wastes, and through implementation of EU nitrates and water directives. However, environmental regulation 'from above' forms only a part of broader understandings of 'sustainable development', in which creating economically sustainable livelihoods, and ensuring social sustainability through a more engaged and active civil society which participates in its own governance, are equally emphasised. A policy approach which only seeks to make farmers 'internalise' their environmental impacts might be better described as 'ecological modernisation' (Spaargaren 2000) than as 'sustainable development'. In the case of rural development, strikingly little attention has been paid in the formulation of Irish policy to the sustainable development of food. Food is both an economic output from farming and a significant 'public good', and it potentially links together all the elements of the concept of 'sustainability' – livelihoods, protection of natural resources, social wellbeing, and participatory self-governance; yet national sustainable development policy documents discuss food primarily in terms of environmental impacts from farming, and food hygiene issues. Nevertheless, as I argue below, there is a strong interest in sustainable food emerging today. And it appears to be emanating from rural and farming actors themselves, rather than from national development agencies. One way in which it expresses itself is through notions of 'local' or 'relocalised' food.

Local food in global context

To talk of 'local food' appears odd, given the extent to which food today is a globalised phenomenon. The food we eat today is increasingly globally constructed and globally traded, although Watts and Goodman (1997) argue that it still remains largely locally produced, not yet organised around a transnational division of labour in the way much industrial production is. Food researchers are still debating whether, given its dependence on bio-logical and natural processes (climatic, temporal and seasonal, for example), food can ever become globalised in that sense, or whether new production technologies, driven by transnational food processing and retailing chains, will eventually detach food production from nature and make it globally transportable. This is also a debate about whether rural localities are inserted into global food chains, or whether the dominant trend is to marginalise and bypass the rural as a food production site.

Global trade in food has certainly intensified and accelerated over the past decade. Of course international trade in food is not a new phenomenon: archaeologists have found residues of traded food, and food containers, in sites from pre-Christian times; the Roman Empire organised its food supply economy around imports from Roman settlements in Spain and in Asia, as well as in Italy; the 'discovery' of America introduced tomatoes, potatoes, corn and turkeys into European diets as well as tobacco into their leisure habits, and opened up markets in the New World for European wheat and livestock. During the seventeenth and eighteenth centuries Ireland became a major exporter of beef and butter to British military and colonial adventures in Europe and further afield; Irish landholding and agrarian social structures were reorganised to produce one of the world's first export-oriented colonial agricultural economies. The British working classes in the nineteenth century had a diet based heavily on imported sugar, stimulants (tea, coffee) and cheap grains and starches, low in nutrition values but high in the energy they needed for factory and other manual work (Mintz 1980). However, the contemporary globalisation of food circulation is extraordinary in its intensification and reach. The proportion of the world's food which is traded internationally increased by around one third between 1990 and 2001 (Fold and Pritchard 2005). In some cases it has nearly doubled: nearly half of all vegetable oils produced in the world in 2001 were exported, nearly one third of all sugar, fish and seafoods, one fifth of all animal fats (primarily butter), 97 per cent of all coffee and tea. The main exception is vegetables, export of which remained at around five per cent of production over the decade despite a doubling of world output (Fold and Pritchard 2005: 6). Fold and Pritchard argue that the 'global' trade in food is actually patterned into specific 'trans-continental' exchanges demarcating distinct food regions of the world (for example, the Australia–South Pacific food trade). In these food regions, poorer countries grow food products for richer countries to import and consume, but increasingly the richer countries also export to the poorer countries both processed food products and branches of their own processing and marketing industries.

In Ireland, although agri-food exports constituted only 8.4 per cent of our total exports in 2003 compared to 20 per cent in 1993, we still largely understand ourselves as a food exporting country. In 2003, exports of our agri-food products totalled nearly €7 billion in value (Department of Agriculture and Food 2005a). However, in the same year we imported over €4 billion worth of agri-food products. The pattern of Irish food imports and exports confirms Fold and Pritchard's food regionalisation thesis: 83 per cent of our food imports came from the EU (42 per cent from the UK), and 78 per cent of our exports went to the EU (41 per cent to the UK). Predictably, exports outweigh imports in live animals, meat and meat products, dairy products and eggs; nevertheless, we do also import all these products, despite being more than self-sufficient in them already. The main food imports are vegetables and fruit, vegetable oils and fats, cereals and cereals products. Ireland today is inserted into an 'open' transnational food trade system where food imports no longer simply make up gaps in what we cannot produce ourselves. State policy for agri-food development endorses this position; despite some encouragement to consumers to 'buy Irish', its main emphasis is on gearing up agriculture and, particularly, the processed food industry, to compete in international food markets.

The accelerating globalisation of food supply systems is underpinned by changes in the global organisation of food trade and the emergence of some new dominant actors within it, who share an interest in removing barriers to food imports in markets around the world. A relatively small number of very large TNCs now dominate food processing, transport, distribution and retailing; some of these (e.g. Cargills) grew from an earlier position of strength in grain or livestock transportation, others (e.g. ICI, Monsanto) moved into food trading from a base in the chemical and petrochemicals or biotechnology industries. Power relations within food chains have also been reorganised, with transnational retailing corporations increasingly controlling both food supply sources and the activities of food processors and traders. On the level of global governance, the key actor is the World Trade Organisation (WTO) which was established in 1994 as a permanent regulatory body charged with achieving agreement on the rules of international trade, arbitrating trade disputes, and promoting trade liberalisation. Agriculture and food have become inscribed within a global regulatory framework concerned to promote free trade in food, subject only to considerations of food safety. Cultural differences in preferred diets or in judgements of food quality, national food security concerns, and concerns about the welfare and sustainability of rural regions and locales, are now liable to challenge under WTO procedures as hidden strategies for re-establishing barriers to free trade.

As food supplies circulate more globally, food consumption also becomes more globally homogenised, although not in a straightforward way (Dixon and Jamieson 2005). The global food regime expands what foods people eat, at least in the affluent North, even if what is presented as 'increased choice' is increasingly regulated by what large retail chains perceive as saleable, sanitary and satisfying foods (Marsden et al. 2001). Even in the South, diets are increasingly penetrated by and reshaped around Northern consumption patterns. Food also becomes more anonymous – detached from its place of production, it passes through often intense transformations in the hands of food processors and packagers as it is transported around the world. Kerry Foods, for example, takes milk from Irish cows and processes it into its constituent elements which are then exported globally for use in the confectionery and fish processing industries; most global consumers have no idea where the crumbs which cover their frozen fish portion have come from, how they have been made, or by whom. Anonymity makes consumers fearful about what they are eating (Beardsworth and Keil 1997). Consumers in affluent societies are becoming 'omnivores' (Fischler 1980), whose now unlimited consumption choices are guided only by considerations of convenience, taste, pleasure, cost, and fears about the impact of foods on their health. Divorced from cultural dietary norms and social prescriptions, food becomes regarded as 'fuel'.

Food has become a lot 'cheaper' in Ireland over the past 30 years – while household incomes have grown exponentially, the labour time needed to buy a basket of staple food items more than halved between 1973 and 2005 (Department of Agriculture and Food 2005b) – yet Irish households spend less on buying food than households in any other part of the EU (6.9 per cent of total household expenditure in 2002, compared to between 16 per cent and 12 per cent in Spain, Greece, Italy and France) (Department of Agriculture and Food 2005a). Yet with affluence we are also seeing an increasing interest in food as 'fashion'. Food journalism has expanded enormously; weekend editions of the main newspapers contain sections on food in which the 'quality' and aesthetics of food receive more attention than price or convenience; celebrity status is bestowed on certain chefs, restaurateurs and quality food retailers. Much food journalism is devoted to creating a new 'taste' in food, a form of cultural capital (Bourdieu 1984) which is represented as bringing distinction and status to the person who possesses and understands it. Eating practices are increasingly linked to social class position: the new rich are encouraged to seek out luxury foods of distinctive origin, while the lower classes, lacking such 'taste', are threatened with nutrition experts and rising tides of obesity.

In 'satiety societies' (Miele 2001) such as Ireland today, where access to food is largely a non-issue and the problem is rather how to discipline dietary choices, the aestheticisation of food is one way of resolving the omnivore's dilemma. A second way is to 'moralise' food consumption choices. 'Moral' food consumers make food consumption choices on the basis of how the food has been produced, in terms of its environmental impacts (e.g. organic consumers), the livelihoods of the producers (e.g. Fair Trade consumers), or the treatment of animals in the production process (vegetarians, consumers of animal-welfare-guaranteed products like free range eggs). Aestheticised and moralised consumers both resist the homogenisation of food consumption linked to a globalised food supply system, and often take an interest in the local origins of foods, although usually for different reasons (aesthetic consumers seek out 'traditional' or 'speciality' local foods, moralised consumers are concerned about the miles which food has travelled to reach them). The emergence of 'moralised' food consumption suggests that for a small but growing proportion of food consumers, what they know about production exercises an influence on how they choose to consume: against a globalised food system where each is anonymous to the other, moralised consumption tends to reintegrate food production and food consumption, through codified knowledge, mutually shared knowledge, or face-to-face relations. The moralisation of eating helps to re-politicise a global food supply system which represents itself as based on unquestionable economic rationality.

Local food in Ireland: contested versions

New discourses of rural sustainability, the growth of social movements in rural Ireland around 'alternative' foods and food systems such as the organic movement, and changing trends among consumers, reconnect 'the rural' and 'rural development' to food. If consumers are emerging who value knowing about the local origin of the foods they eat, then farmers may be able to find a livelihood, not by supplying bulk commodities to global food chains, but by selling 'local food' to knowledgeable consumers.

In the sociology of food literature, and among practitioners, however, 'local food' has varied meanings. It can denote practices to conserve crop and animal varieties traditional to specific rural localities, which have been forgotten, disregarded, or judged as uncommercial by mainstream food industries, and/or the conservation of traditional cuisines closely based on such local varieties. In continental Europe this meaning is particularly associated with Mediterranean food sociologists, with the Italian-based Slow Food Movement, and with attempts by biodiversity activists to save 'heritage' seed varieties in the face of EU attempts to standardise and limit what seeds can be commercially sold. It has been used to develop rural tourism in different localities, where the capacity to offer tourists a particular food or wine 'trail' in which they can sample traditional products is recognised as a marketing advantage; and to develop a brand recognition for food certified as coming from a particular locality (a strategy long used by wine producers) in order to increase their price. Brand certification pays the producer not only for the product but also for his or her specific local knowledge and skills which are embodied in the marketed item (Ray 1998). However, Ireland has few locally specific foodstuffs or cuisines, and Irish 'local food' in this sense is most likely to be an example of 'reinvented tradition' (the construction of a history which represents a new social practice or economic innovation as something which has long existed). In Northern Europe, 'local food' is often used rather differently, to refer to 'short chain' food systems, that is, systems which deliver food to consumers with as few intermediaries and over as short distances as possible, facilitating knowledge and personal relationships between grower and eater and avoiding the environmental costs of food transport. Sociologists using this meaning generally focus their attention on sites and forms of exchange between 'local' producers and 'local' consumers.

However, the question is not just how to define 'local food', but why one might be interested in studying it. Some sociologists are interested in the contribution which local food can make to rural development; others study it as an expression of an 'alternative food' movement, wanting to assess how far it represents a challenge to the social organisation of 'conventional' food systems and the relations of power around which these are structured (Goodman 2003). I suggest that in the Irish case, the meaning given to 'local food' and the type of 'development' envisaged for rural areas are in fact related: local food as 'locally typical food' goes together with a form of development which seeks to integrate rural localities into global food chains, while local food as 'short-chain food' envisages a type of development which disconnects rural localities from global systems, seeing those as routes through which rural natural resources, rural skills and knowledges, and rural social relationships have been systematically commodified and exploited to the benefit of others.

As part of the CORASON project,[1] we recently carried out research on 'local food' actors and networks in south County Tipperary. This is a region known for its history of 'strong farming', its good-sized and prosperous farms on rich land, its early activity within the co-operative movement and in representative farming organisations. Farmers here primarily produce milk and beef (although in the more mountainy parts farms are smaller and land is used for running sheep or, increasingly, for afforestation), and their farming practice has been shaped by three key organisations: the dairy co-operatives, the large-scale beef processors, and Teagasc (the Food and Agricultural Authority) which operates extension services for farmers, advises on state agricultural policy, and conducts R&D research for commodity production and marketing. These institutions have worked to integrate Tipperary farmers into a food processing and exporting system which is oriented to world markets and in which farmers themselves have decreasing power, over their own production practices and over the prices they receive. Developing first as an 'agricultural system' in which the area was incorporated as a producer of raw commodities for food, we can see it transforming into an 'agro-industrial system' dominated by corporate actors who are detached from the local site of production and source their raw inputs globally as well as locally (Basile and Cecchi 2001).

This is also an area where food consumption has become globalised; in the towns around the region, traditional fairs and markets have disappeared, corner shops are decreasing, and food supply is dominated by national (Dunnes) and international (Tesco, Lidl) retail chains. Corner shops are also being displaced by the effects of motorisation: people increasingly shop at petrol stations, along motorways or other main routes, these shops also being often part of an international or national retail chain and acting as 'mini-supermarkets' for a dispersed consumer base. On neither the production nor the consumption side does this seem a likely location for the development of 'local food'.

Yet there is clear evidence of an interest in local food among different social actors in south Tipperary – among some producers, some consumers, and leading local and national development agencies operating the area. It seems to have developed first among local networks associated with 'alternative' social movements, in particular the organic movement which has had a presence in the area since the 1980s. In the past two years it has also been taken up by networks associated with rural development, which include both local and national actors – LEADER, An Bord Bia, Teagasc. The two networks are to some degree overlapping and mutually supportive, but our research indicates that they co-operate around a concept of 'local food' which is deeply ambiguous and contested. For the development actors, 'local food' is primarily food which can be given a distinctive local label or certification

Figure 16.1 **Cashel Blue is one of Ireland's premium cheeses and is exported throughout the world**

which enables it to be sold in national and international markets at a premium price. It is food which can be marketed as 'heritage' and 'high quality' produce, and which is essentially intended to supply what Bourdieu (1984) calls a 'taste of luxury' among specific socio-economic groups of consumers.

'Quality' here prioritises the 'exotic' – locally distinctive, unusual and expensive foodstuffs. For movement actors, however, 'local food' is about 're-localising' food chains: integrating producers and consumers through a system in which food is produced locally, consumed locally, and exchanged through as short a supply chain as possible and preferably through face to face relations. This is food which supplies a 'taste of necessity' – the ordinary food staples which people consume on a daily basis. 'Quality' is also emphasised here, but has to do primarily with flavour, lack of processing, and consumer trust.

In researching that version of local food, we traced the networks – producer and consumer – associated with the first farmers' market to be established in Tipperary, set up in a small town west of Clonmel in 2001. The Irish Farmers' Markets movement itself exhibits some of the same contested understandings (Moore 2006) which we identified in our research locality. The more urbanised types which have multiplied in recent years around Dublin and other eastern regions tend to emphasis organic certification of their produce as a key selling point, and what is sold at them is not always 'local' and can include such 'exotics' as imported organic olives and olive oil, wines and pates. In other parts of the country, the rule that what is sold must have been produced 'locally' (within a radius of 30 miles of the market place) is more strictly applied, and whether the food is certified as organic is less important than whether it has been produced using organic or environmentally sustainable production methods. In the case we studied, only some of the traders had organic certification; others preferred to use their face-to-face relations with customers to explain for themselves how they produced the food in a 'naturally embedded' way.

The farmers' market we studied operates every Saturday morning, in a car park attached to a former grain store which is today a craft shop. It is run by a committee of the stallholders, of whom there are currently eleven, selling breads, vegetables, organic certified meats, fish, jams, fruit, and apple juice among other items. Most of the producers come from within a ten-mile radius of the town, while customers come from a wider area, some travelling from as far as the north of the county to buy what they described as 'food which tastes the way I remember it when I was growing up'. Stallholders and customers both enjoy the market as an opportunity for sociability and social interaction. Stallholders use it as a place to educate and widen local tastes in food (one vegetable stallholder explained how he has introduced locals to eating spinach, a previously almost unknown foodstuff locally), and customers, especially incomers to the area, find it a place where they can make friends and integrate into local social life.

Figure 16.2 **A vegetable stall in a farmers' market**

Among the stallholders, a number are newcomers to the area, or have returned to it after diverse educational and career experiences elsewhere (earlier research in West Cork (Tovey 2007) suggests this may be a common characteristic of 'alternative food' movement actors). One of the vegetable stallholders, for example, grew up on a small farm in Ireland, took a degree in agriculture and a diploma in rural sociology, and worked for the European Commission developing aid projects in Africa before retiring to south Tipperary to set up in small-scale vegetable production. An organic meat stallholder worked for a decade in the meat processing industry and with the Department of Agriculture before returning to take over his parents' farm. They also tend to be active in local and community development generally, not just in relation to food. Tipperary stallholders are involved in strong and supportive networks which have a high degree of 'local embeddedness' (Winter 2003), and which extend beyond this particular market to include traders at other markets, local and artisan producers who 'sell direct' through farm shops or through the 'box system' (where households receive regular deliveries of food in a box or bag), local organic networks, and individuals involved in various types of formal or informal local development associations.

National development agencies also operate through intensive networking, but their networks and their goals are different. The LEADER group for this region came to the idea of food as a vehicle for rural development only in 2004, when it set up a Tipperary Micro-Food Strategy Group which brought together 'stakeholders' from national agricultural and food agencies, university-based food scientists, retailing (supermarket and speciality food chains) and local government. Their initial idea was to start 'some kind of branded initiative', for example a designation of origin label which would certify local foods as typical produce of south Tipperary. This has been put on hold for the moment, and their present strategy is to encourage the direct selling of produce by local farmers, as one way of responding to the new options available under the EU de-coupling regime. In this context, they are promoting the spread of farmers' markets to a number of towns in both south and north Tipperary. As a LEADER officer told us, 'we would view the farmers' markets as an ideal kind of test ground or incubation area for a basic product to get out, and how to modify the product . . .' Direct selling to local customers is understood here as a first step in testing a new product, for example a new farmhouse cheese, which if successful would be supported to enter export retail markets, drawing on the expertise of national agencies such as An Bord Bia and of national and international retail chains. Branding food as a local specialty, like its certification as organic, codifies information about the product in a way which allows it to travel to distant consumers and makes unnecessary the uncodified knowledge exchanged by producer and consumer in face-to-face 'relations of regard' (Sage 2003).

Strategies to sell 'local food' internationally, and strategies to 'relocalise' food exchanges, are both strategies for rural development. From an economic point of view, the former has much greater potential; although some forms of direct selling, such as through a farm shop, can yield a good income, most stallholders at the farmer's market we studied can not secure a full livelihood from this activity, and many rely on additional sources of income, such as a pension from previous employment, off-farm work, REPs payments or cattle commodity farming, to survive. In that, of course, they are little different from the majority of Irish farmers. However, relocalising food spreads income more widely among small-scale producers and may retain it more effectively within the local area, issues which the development agencies' interest in 'picking winners' to promote for international markets do not address. The food 're-localisers', on the other hand, are embedded in and help to reproduce local civil society, at a time when geographic mobility, social and economic change are putting pressure on older forms of rural 'community': they develop interpersonal connections, mobilise local networks, diffuse new ideas about food itself and simultaneously about citizenship and local governance.

Conclusion

Both of the types of local producer we encountered in South Tipperary, whether they were trying to develop a local branded product (for example, a new type of cheese specific to the area) for export markets, or were trying to promote a local food distribution system in which 'good food' is made available direct to local consumers, were concerned to emphasise to us the ecological sensitivity of their production processes: both strive to be 'environmentally sustainable'. Both were likely to have introduced into their production systems, for example, measures to manage in environmentally less harmful ways the waste that food production can generate, or new systems for reducing the use of water supplies in their production system. However, here too we can see different understandings of 'sustainability' in action. 'Local speciality food' producers think of sustainable development as the application of scientific and technological advances which enable food production enterprises to operate with reduced environmental costs. They, and their advisers, are still working with a conception of rural development as modernisation, albeit a form of modernisation which now takes into account environmental as well as economic outcomes. We might describe them as 'ecological modernisers' or 'ecomodernisers' of the countryside. The 'food distribution re-localisers' offer a rather different vision of rural sustainable development; they practise a distinctive lifestyle which tries to holistically integrate economic, social, ecological and participatory ideals around the idea of a 'sustainable rural livelihood'.

In the sociological literature on sustainable development (see for example, Irwin 2001, Jacobs 1999), a similar difference in interpretations is widely recognised; it is usually explained as a division between the global North and South, where the North is said to prioritise the (environmental) 'sustainability' dimension of the concept and the South the 'developmental' (economic, social and political) dimension. Studies of the interaction between these competing interpretations at a local level are less often found. Food 're-localisers' in rural Ireland appear to be pioneering practitioners of a post- or anti-modernisationist form of 'sustainable rural development' unknown to the creators of state sustainable development strategies. The danger is that their vision of a local food system may be socially excluded and marginalised by the more powerful agents and institutions who are beginning to endorse 'local food'.

Section V   Class, equality
and inequality

Chapter 17

Social class and inequality

Ronaldo Munck

Introduction

Ireland today is by all accounts a wealthy society so if 'a rising tide lifts all boats' as most economists argue, then all citizens should be benefiting from this new-found prosperity. However, simple observation of the world around us – such as, for example, the cars people drive – will show us that inequality persists. That inequality matters should be simple enough to understand. As Fintan O'Toole puts it, '[T]he reality is clear: wealth and poverty in Ireland are matters of life and death. And the lives of the poor are worth less than those of their betters' (O'Toole 2003: 81). But what if this inequality is just about the luck of the draw, or a competition with winners and losers? Conjuring up images of status distinctions, no longer deemed relevant in a meritocratic society where 'we are all middle class' or so many people believe, might not be seen as relevant. As Kieran Allen puts it 'Irish society has sometimes had difficulties facing up to the reality of social class' (Allen 2000: 3). Classical sociologists, and their present day followers, have advanced different explanations of why social inequalities exist and how to explain them. This chapter will introduce these explanations, focusing on the various approaches to and understandings of social class. My basic argument will be that, regardless of how we define or measure social class, it remains a major explanatory element in the understanding of social inequality and differing life chances in contemporary Ireland.

It is not only today that social class has an anachronistic ring about it. In his history of Ireland in the twentieth century, Diarmaid Ferriter argues that class has been 'a neglected of Irish history writing' even though 'class differences were in fact blatantly enunciated well after independence' (Ferriter 2005: 697). Certainly the prevailing nationalist politics in this era has cut across class boundaries in building its support and has thus been more effective at managing class politics. Thus none other than the late Charles Haughey, who is now credited with laying the basis of the Celtic Tiger, argued that discussion of class and inequality reflected 'an alien gospel of class warfare, envy and strife [and] is also inherently un-Irish' (cited in Ferriter 2005: 697). Be that as it may, Haughey was himself articulating a class project for those social sectors wishing to 'modernise' Ireland and implement its own version of the neo-liberal economic model then sweeping the Western world. While nationalism has been more prevalent in Ireland than 'classism' as an openly class based analysis and point of departure for politics, that does not mean it is irrelevant, or at least that is what I now seek to demonstrate.

Durkheim and functionalism

Emile Durkheim is usually regarded as one of the founders of sociology. He argued that the different elements of society needed to be balanced according to their function in keeping the whole healthy, from which is derived the theory of 'functionalism' in sociology. In terms of the development of a sociological understanding of social class his most relevant work is *The Division of Labour in Society* (Durkheim 1984), which examines how the social order is main-tained in different types of society. Traditional societies were, for Durkheim, characterised by a 'mechanical solidarity' held together by their commonality, whereas modern societies with their highly complex divisions of labour needed an 'organic solidarity' based on interdependency and shared values.

Durkheim was fully conscious of the negative effects of the division of labour in modern society in terms of anomie, poverty and social tensions. But he argued that complex industrial society will develop a division of labour in which society rewards individuals according to a consensus of values on the importance of particular functions. Durkheim assumes an equality of oppor-tunities for the individual and that it is through competition that the more able and talented rise to the top. This point is important for current debates on social class because it articulates a strong moral justification for social and economic inequality. According to this theory, if there is equality of oppor-tunity for all individuals then any resulting inequalities are fair and not due to structural factors.

The functionalist approach to social inequality that Durkheim first deve-loped really came to fruition in the United States after the Second World War. The classic statement of the functionalist approach to social stratification is that of Davis and Moore for whom 'social inequality is an unconsciously evolved device by which societies ensure that the most important positions are conscientiously filled by the most qualified persons' (Davis and Moore 1966: 48). Social stratification is deemed both functional and necessary for the smooth operation of any social system. The functional importance of a position in society – a factory manager versus a factory shop-floor worker for example – determines its ranking in the stratification system. To ensure that the best-qualified person fills these functional important posts the material resources and prestige attached to them must be made attractive. Company directors' 'pay and perks' packages today reflect this widespread belief.

The problem with a truly equal society, according to Davis and Moore, would be the lack of incentives to take on various positions and the lack of rewards for people performing to the best of their abilities. In practice, the Davis–Moore thesis reflected the optimistic mood in the United States in the 1950s which perceived a truly modern meritocratic society emerging there as a universal model. Even fellow functionalist sociologist Peter Saunders admits that 'Davis and Moore were Americans who assumed that the culture of American capitalism is in some way universal' (Saunders 1990: 61). Essentially they believed that there was consensus in society on the hierarchy of occupations and thus stratification was perceived as legitimate. A class system was thus not going to lead to class conflict as the Marxists argued but, rather, it would ensure that the social system was stable and functioned efficiently.

The Davis and Moore position more or less faded from view in the 1960s and 1970s, but it then re-emerged in the 1980s and 1990s as neo-liberalism became established as the dominant economic perspective. The market was seen as the best and most rational way to allocate resources and determine rewards in society. Peter Saunders took up this perspective arguing that, 'the value of egalitarianism is not necessarily unattainable, but it could only be realised at the price of individual liberty' (Saunders 1990: 67). Social inequality and social stratification (leading to social class formation) are preferable, from this point of view, to the tyranny of the planned society and the totalitarianism of Marxism.

Saunders argues that contemporary society is fundamentally meritocratic in the way it operates, and not exploitative or inherently inegalitarian. If everyone has an equal chance to achieve what they want through merit – equality of opportunity – then we can call that society a meritocracy. For him the critique of the class system is misguided because it cannot accept 'that talents are unevenly distributed among people, that the most talented tend to rise towards the higher social positions, and that they tend to pass on some of their genetic advantages to some of their offspring' (Saunders 1990: 82). How this supposedly natural and genetic imbalance translates into an occupational structure is through the educational system where IQs determine who is best equipped to do which job in society.

In Ireland such a view has been argued by Michael McDowell for whom 'a dynamic liberal economy like ours demands flexibility and inequality in some respects to function' (McGarry 2004). More specifically McDowell argues that 'the current rights culture and equality notion would create a feudal society' because it is inequality 'which provides incentives' for a successful economy (McGarry 2004). This is a view in accordance with the dominant neo-liberal doctrine in economics that sees the free play of market forces as essential and that any social or political moves threatening to curb them must be opposed. Inequality is deemed functional and concerns for inequality are seen as misguided because this may lead to a dampening of creativity and dynamism.

A weaker functionalist or neo-Durkheimian position is articulated in Ireland by the Economic and Social Research Institute (ESRI) a state-funded social research body. Their approach to social class can be seen to be influenced by Durkheim in its acceptance of the meritocratic case and its commitment to the equality of opportunities argument. McDowell's praise for inequality is not, of course, inconsistent with a belief in equal opportunities and the merits of a meritocracy. The ESRI approach to social-class analysis also shares with Durkheim a strong commitment to positivism and focuses on empirical, applied and state-oriented research. I will return to the ESRI approach to social class later in the discussion.

Marx and polarisation

Of all the various sociologists of class it is Karl Marx who most clearly foregrounds its role. The first sentence of *The Communist Manifesto* reads 'The history of all hitherto existing societies is the history of class struggle' (Marx and Engels 1985: 79). For Marx social class is at the core of his theory of social change. In any given mode of production such as capitalism there will, according to Marx, be two predominant classes based on those who produce and those who expropriate the economic surplus. This relationship between those dominant and the exploited class is antagonistic and leads to what Marx calls class struggle. It is through that ongoing process that history is shaped, heading towards the abolition of exploitation and the eventual emergence of a classless society or socialism.

Marx famously distinguished between a 'class in itself' as it is determined by the relations of production, and a 'class for itself' where it becomes conscious politically of its objectives. It is in this political sphere that Marx moves beyond his original two-class scheme and accepts the complexity of the political process. But there is still a separation between 'structure' and 'action' that Marxist sociology shares with other sociologies. It was Anthony Giddens (1971) who carried out the definitive critique of both Marxist structuralism and mainstream sociological functionalism. For Giddens class relationships could not be taken for granted but, rather, are actively structured. This happens through a process of structuration where both structure and agency interact, a process that overcomes Marx's dualism in thinking of classes structurally and only afterwards as in action.

The neo-Marxist revival in the 1960s and 1970s led to many debates around social class and its relevance for contemporary society. As Mike Savage puts it, 'during the 1960s and 1970s defining and conceptualising class became the central feature of Marxist debates' (Savage 2000: 10). The underlying objective was to provide a class map of contemporary capitalism to explain the rise of the new white-collar middle class and show the relevance of class struggle to the ongoing political transformations of the era. One particular area of interest was the distinction between productive and unproductive labour and what that meant for the political prospects of the working class (see Poulantzas 1975). Thus there was discussion about where the boundaries of the working class lay, and whether white collar workers could be classified as working class or not. However, by the 1980s and 1990s the transformations of capitalism and the rise of the information society meant that traditional Marxist categories were no longer deemed relevant and this perspective faded.

In contemporary sociology it is Erik Olin Wright who has most systematically sought to update the original Marxist schema of social classes. His project has been 'to generate a concept capable of mapping in a nuanced way, concrete variations in class structure across capitalist societies' (Wright 1985: 274). Wright's project (like that of Goldthorpe discussed in the next section) is to develop an empirically based international class map for contemporary capitalism by allocating specific jobs people do to the broad class categories. He then adds concepts of control and exploitation that shape the social relations of production in society. He also puts forward the concept of 'contradictory class locations'. In Marx's most simple class scheme the bourgeoisie owned the means of production and the proletariat sold their labour power to the former. However, in the era of advanced capitalism how would we categorise the manager, the small- and medium-scale employer (the SME sector) and those fairly autonomous employees who do not own the means of production but do exercise considerable control over their work, such as university lecturers? For Wright what we see here are jobs that are torn between the two basic class locations in capitalist society, hence the term 'contradictory' class locations. Wright went on later (see Wright 1997) to develop a more nuanced class map with 12 rather than six basic classes that took him closer to parallel work by Weberian sociologists.

Within Marxist sociology there is an alternative to the traditional 'structuralist' approach of Wright, which stresses the 'subjective' process of class formation. This can be traced back to the labour historian E. P. Thompson in particular, who directed his fire against the US functionalist sociologists. In his study of the 'making' of the English working class, Thompson argued that class was 'a *historical phenomenon*. I do not see class as a "structure", nor even as a "category" but as something which in fact happens' [italics in original] (Thompson 1968: 9). From this perspective, social class is less about structural positions in the economy and more about the way in which class experience produces class consciousness. While this reading of class can be seen as culturalist (as against the economism of Marxist and functionalist sociologists alike) Marx would probably have agreed with Thompson's view that 'class is a relationship and not a thing' (Thompson 1968: 9).

In the debates around the Celtic Tiger there is a well-articulated Marxist analysis that foregrounds social class. Firstly, if we take social class to be the underlying form of social inequality as Denis O'Hearn does, then we could examine how economic change affects class inequality. At a broad level we can chart the evolution of what are known as 'factor incomes', namely the share of national income going to wages and salaries on the one hand, and profits on the other hand. This can be taken as a rough indicator of Marx's capitalist and working class incomes respectively. Until the mid-1980s the share of wages as a proportion of non-agricultural incomes stood at around 70 per cent, with profits taking the other 30 per cent. By the mid-1990s as rapid growth began, the share of wages has dropped to 60 per cent and mostly the share going to profits had risen to 40 per cent. For O'Hearn 'this shows conclusively that the overwhelming winners from economic growth are capitalists, who have enjoyed a rapid rise in their profit incomes – not just absolutely but also relative to wages' (O'Hearn 1998: 125).

Another issue that has been taken up by Marxist analysts of the class structure in Ireland is that of class polarisation, namely that the gap between the top and the bottom of the social scale in terms of earnings is getting greater. Proinnsias Breathnach reorganises the 1991 and 1996 census data to examine the social polarisation thesis as it applies to Ireland. The basic data on those sectors with above average growth is shown in table 17.1.

We see at first glance that while all occupations have expanded growth has been greatest at the top and at the bottom of the occupational pyramid. Overall we can conclude that when the Celtic Tiger was kicking off there was not a general upgrading of class but rather a polarisation process occurring.

Table 17.1 **Employment growth sectors 1991–2002**

	Percentage change 1991–2002
All occupations	35.6
Professional/technical	68.9
Employers/managers	92.4
Other professional/non-manual	50.1
Unskilled	40.8
Unskilled (excluding sales)	51.5

Source: Breathnach 2004: 6.

Futhermore, as Breathnach argues, 'the tendency towards occupational polarisation identified here is entirely due to the distinctive behaviour of the female
workforce' (Breathnach 2002: 16), with women accounting for the bulk of the
expansion of unskilled employment and the majority of expansion of
professional/managerial categories.

In more general terms we can deploy official census data in Ireland to
show that class inequality has deepened between the mid-1990s and the end
of the century. If we examine the disposable income of Irish households (see
table 17.2), we see clearly how the gap between the high-income and low-
income households has widened.

Table 17.2 **Average weekly disposable income by gross household income deciles,
1994–95 and 1999–2000**

Gross income decile	1994–5 £	1999–2000 £	Change %
1st decile (poorest)	62.75	83.67	+33.3
2nd decile	98.25	137.37	+39.8
3rd decile	133.84	196.44	+46.8
4th decile	173.72	261.24	+50.4
5th decile	215.16	333.14	+54.8
6th decile	264.04	406.17	+53.8
7th decile	321.60	486.41	+51.2
8th decile	384.41	585.51	+52.3
9th decile	469.92	728.91	+55.1
10th decile (richest)	695.31	1,125.22	+61.8
State	**281.92**	**434.40**	**+54.1**

Source: CSO 2006c

We can learn a great deal from this table. Overall the disposable weekly
income of the Irish household rose by 54 per cent between 1995 and 2000 or in
absolute terms from £281 to £434. But, whereas the top ten per cent of households found their incomes increasing by 62 per cent, the bottom ten per cent
increased their incomes by 33 per cent. What is even more striking is that in
2000, when the Celtic Tiger was probably at its peak, the poorest ten per cent
of households had an average weekly disposable income of £84 whereas the
richest ten per cent had a phenomenal £1,125 to dispose of each week. The optimistic view that a rising tide lifts all boats is only true in a very simplistic way.

In conclusion, the Marxist approach to social class in general and in
relation to Irish social development is an influential one (see O'Hearn 1998
and Kirby 2002). While the original simple two-class model clearly does not

apply today (or never did) class inequality is clearly a major issue. Marx's theory of social class directs us towards the continued importance of structured forms of inequality that the Celtic Tiger has not dissolved. While we certainly need to go beyond Marx to consider how social classes are also structured by gender and ethnicity, we cannot ignore the economic facts of social class. Economic growth creates economic profit and its distribution in terms of employment conditions and economic rewards varies hugely between the owners of property and capital and those who work for a living.

Weber and stratification

Max Weber is usually seen as a fierce opponent of Karl Marx but, on the whole, he accepted much of Marx's theory of social class even though he thought it was limited. While Weber went along with the understanding that the main cleavage in society was that between the owners of the means of production and the propertyless, he also pointed to divisions within these broad social classes. Stratification for Weber referred to 'the distribution of power within a community' (Gerth and Mills 1970: 181) in a general way. This power had an economic aspect (class) but also a social dimension (status) and a political dimension (party). In any particular society, for Weber, class, status and party could interact in various crosscutting ways. For Weber, while class might predominate in periods of economic upheaval, status or social prestige might become the main variable in periods of social stability.

Weberian class analysis comes across as more complex and flexible than the original Marxian scheme. Whereas Marx was concerned primarily with the *structural* determinants of social evolution, Weber focused much more on individual *human action*. Thus for Weber, class situation referred to the life chances of the individual as determined by the market. So the main difference between Marx and Weber in relation to social class is that 'for Marx, class relationships are grounded in exploitation and domination within *production* relations, whereas, for Weber, class situations reflected differing "life chances" in the market' [emphasis in original] (Crompton 1998: 35). In today's market-driven society where the individual and consumerism reign supreme it is easy to see how the Weberian approach to social class would have more purchase in explaining real world events compared to Marx's seemingly archaic focus on production, when the service sector is now dominant anyway.

As Harriet Bradley puts it, 'Weberian class theory is currently dominant, as its more complex, pluralistic vision appears to fit better with the late twentieth century context and our perceptions of change and fragmentation' (Bradley, 1996: 58). From a strict Marxist position, mobility between social classes did not matter insofar as structural 'class positions' did not alter. But

Weberians rightly point out that whether social mobility exists or not has a strong influence on an individual's *perception* of the class structure. Thus many might think that the Irish class structure is less rigid than the British one because they sense there is more upward social mobility. That perception will, in itself, impact on how people live or experience the class system at a subjective level. More generally, the Weberian's pluralistic model of social class is better able to adapt to the fragmentation or break up of traditional class structures in the last quarter of the twentieth century.

In contemporary sociology a broadly Weberian understanding of social class prevails and the analysis of class and status in contemporary society usually occurs through the mapping of occupational structures. The investigation of social inequality today, as John Scott puts it, 'involves assessing the relative importance of class, status and command in the life chances that are associated with particular occupations and groups of occupations' (Scott 2000: 26). It is through employment aggregates that most sociologists seek to measure or approximate to what social class means today. John Goldthorpe has developed the Weberian tradition most and, according to many, moved towards a true social class map through his allocation of class situations to seven separate occupational categories. While he does not see it as completely accurate, John Scott has argued that Goldthorpe's basic scheme (with an eighth elite category added) 'does provide an approximation to an accurate mapping of contemporary class boundaries' (Scott 2000: 31).

The Goldthorpe class scheme, although it has taken various permutations, is as follows:

I   Higher-grade professionals, administrators and officials, large company managers, large proprietors

II   Lower-grade professionals, administrators and officials, small company managers, supervisors of non-manual employees

III   Routine non-manual employees: higher grade (a), lower grade (b)

IV   Small proprietors and artisans etc: with employees (a) and without (b)

IVc   Farmers and smallholders and other self-employed workers in primary production.

V   Lower- grade technicians, supervisors of manual workers

VI   Skilled manual workers

VIIa   Semi- and unskilled manual workers (not in agriculture, etc.)

VIIb   Agricultural and other workers in primary production

Source: Marshall 1997: 23

Goldthorpe's arrangement of occupations into classes closely resembles the conventional lifestyle or prestige ladders used by market researchers and many national censuses. There are particular problems one could identify in this scheme, for example the apparent omission of a ruling class and what might appear as an anachronistic class boundary between manual and non-manual workers. Nor does it seem to recognise that social classes exist only in relation to one another and not just in a hierarchical ladder. There is also a problem in Goldthorpe's apparent rejection of a theoretical framework as a necessary basis from which to do class research, preferring to see his class schemes as purely a research instrument. The major flaw in the Goldthorpe class map, however, is its gender blindness that is its failure to recognise the sexual division of labour that is overlaid on the class divisions of society. When it was first published in 1980, Goldthorpe's work on social mobility was severely criticised for sampling only men, with women relegated to the category of wives. Where women were counted in their own right was only in category III, routine non-manual category. Women, from this perspective, would be classified by class only according to the status of the male bread-winner. But as Rosemary Crompton points out 'although Goldthorpe has at times appeared to be very resistant to feminist criticisms . . . nevertheless, his work has incorporated many changes' (Crompton 1998: 65). In particular a household's class is now inferred from that of the dominant breadwinner who may be a man or a woman. Whether that makes it a gendered approach to class remains a moot point.

In Ireland the dominant approach to social-class analysis is the work associated with the ESRI, a research organisation that works mainly for the state. Richard Breen and Christopher Whelan note that 'our analysis of the social mobility process in Ireland draws on Goldthorpe's model of the mobility process' (Breen and Whelan 1996: 19). These ESRI authors follow Goldthorpe to suggest that the pattern of social fluidity (between social classes) is determined by the barriers to movement between classes and the resources individuals may deploy to achieve upward social mobility. Their application of the Goldthorpe model to Ireland does not support the optimistic view of the Celtic Tiger. Contrary to the liberal view that, with industrialisation, inheritance becomes less important than education (the merit selection hypothesis), the ESRI found that as of the year 2000 'no evidence was found of a significant weakening in either the gross or net relationship between class origins and destinations' (Layte and Whelan 2000: 105).

The ESRI researchers are, however, also concerned to rebut what they see as 'the predominant sociological view [in Ireland] that globalisation, as typified in recent Irish economic development, fuels economic inequality' (Whelan and Layte 2004: 4). There are two aspects to this debate, namely whether economic growth has led to greater 'social fluidity' (as against a heightened inequality of opportunity) and, furthermore whether it has led to increased income inequality. On the first point, the ESRI data show that from a very low historical level absolute social mobility increased in the 1990s to approach the European norm. As to whether increased economic growth generates more social inequality or reduces it, both the international and national evidence contradicts the ESRI argument. The dominant view amongst economists is that globalisation in the 1990s increased the levels of income inequality between the richest and the poorest social groups globally (see Sutcliffe 2004). At a national level table 17.2 also shows this pattern to hold true in Ireland.

The ESRI research has focused largely on relative social mobility in Ireland. We can see in figure 17.1 the percentage of people entering the professional/ managerial class from other class locations and how this has changed over time. There is clear case for upward social mobility from the clerical category and to a lesser degree amongst unskilled manual classes although in percentage terms they make only a small contribution to the numbers employed in professional/managerial occupations. There is not much change in the flow upwards from the other categories but an actual decrease in the number of

Figure 17.1 **Percentage entering the professional and managerial class**

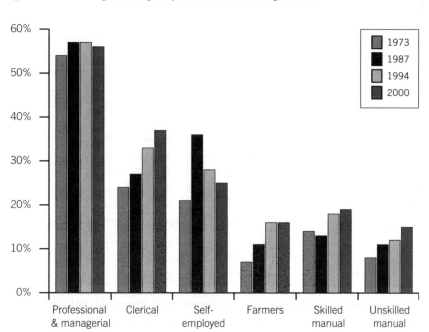

Source: Whelan and Layte 2004: 95.

self-employed making it into the ranks of the professional/managerial class. As to the numbers from the professional and managerial classes who attain professional/managerial posts, this has remained fairly constant.

The ESRI has provided the most systematic database on social class in Ireland that is currently available. The social surveys it carries out for government are an invaluable source of information for the social researcher. From a sociological point of view there are some limitations to this approach. First of all, as with the Goldthorpe tradition from which they borrow their class model, there is a refusal to engage in social theory and a total emphasis on the empirical (positivism). Also, as with Goldthorpe, there is a lack of attention to the gendered nature of class patterns. While there is a chapter on women and class mobility in *Social Mobility and Social Class in Ireland* (Breen and Whelan 1996) the arguments seeking to demonstrate increased social fluidity (as in figure 17.1) are based solely on men. In third place this approach is marked by the limitations of its methodological nationalism insofar as the boundaries of the study are set totally by the nation (26 counties of it in fact) and are geared towards the needs of the state that commissions this research. A more independent and critical analysis starting from the impact of globalisation on Ireland's economy, political system and social structure would throw up a different picture starting from the momentous changes occurring as globalisation restructures the global workforce.

Weber and the neo-Weberian approach to social class have provided huge insight into social stratification and, in particular, the distinction between class and status. Until the 1960s class and status seemed closely associated and we could see a clear upper, middle and working class in most industrial societies. The weaknesses of this approach could be seen in terms of the emergence of a more fragmented class structure since the 1960s (see next section). The Weberian approach also tends to examine only the effects of social class (in terms of the distribution of income) and not its origins. As Rosemary Crompton points out 'neither of the major practitioners of the employment aggregate approach (Goldthorpe and Wright) has incorporated any empirical examination of the *processes* of class formation – for example, the accumulation of wealth, and/or the structuring of employment and labour markets – in the programmes of class analysis' [emphasis in original] (Crompton 1998: 134).

Postmodernism and fragmentation

The founders of sociology (and most of their progeny) belong to the industrial or modern period of capitalism. Since the 1970s, however, various schools of thought within sociology have been advancing a post-industrial and postmodern interpretation of contemporary society. The post-industrial interpretation began to make an impact as far back as the early 1970s with Daniel Bell's, *The Coming of Post-Industrial Society* (Bell 1973). New technology would lead to new forms of work that would, in turn, generate a new type of society. Bell was keen to reject Marxism and class conflict theory generally and posited the emergence of greater material prosperity for all and the end of class conflict. From a more radical position, the postmodernists also began to challenge traditional sociological paradigms. Postmodernism challenged rational development models of social development and the notion that there was an underlying logic in society, be it capitalism or socialism.

The postmodern perspective emphasises the fragmentation and fluidity of our social experience and the complexity of our social identities. Whereas modernism stressed uniformity in the workplace and in the cultural domain, postmodernism stressed difference and diversity. Where modernism often sought a holistic explanation such as class theory, postmodernism focused on local narratives or more small-scale social processes. In terms of research methods this would mean a turn towards cultural rather than economic processes and various qualitative approaches (such as interactionism and ethnomethodology) rather than the large-scale survey that was the favoured instrument of modernist sociology. Where postmodernism took up some of the earlier post-industrial themes was in relation to computerisation, the rise of the information society and the impact they would have on social transformation.

Taken to its logical conclusions the postmodern perspective leads to 'the death of class' (Pakulski and Waters 1996: 3) as the title of one comprehensive deconstruction of class theory puts it. For Pakulski and Waters 'a minimum level of detectable clustering or groupness is essential if we are to say that classes exist' (1996: 3). A sense of difference – of them and us – needs to exist if social class is to be a meaningful category of analysis. What the critics of class analysis argue is that 'if classes are dissolving, a form of analysis that privileges class as an explanatory category has to give way to a more open-ended social analysis' (Pakulski and Waters 1996: 3). From this perspective a class analysis is now historically redundant however much some may lament the fact (see Wood 1986).

We could, however, argue that it is not the death of class we are witnessing but a particular form of 'class essentialism' in which the complexity of contemporary society was reduced to economic determination. According to Gibson-Graham 'what has died or been demobilised is a fiction of the working class and its mission' (Gibson-Graham 1996: 69). The monolithic vision of a usually male manual working class was probably not even true in the 1950s in the industrial heartlands but it is certainly not true today and never was in the majority or 'developing' world. For one thing, there was much more diversity within the working classes that were divided by gender, national and ethnic lines. Furthermore, social groupings were formed for other reasons than sharing a similar role in the economic system. Social groups could bond and form collectivities at a community level, for example, or along political lines.

From a post-structuralist perspective focused on the new globalised condition of social existence we can understand the emergence of new social classes such as the 'cybertariat' (see Huws 2003). In the new 'weightless economy' praised by the postmodernists, a new cybernetic proletariat is emerging. Not only is it a very different working class from the era of Marx and Weber that has emerged but the whole relationship between work and leisure has changed. In Ireland this sector is increasingly important and Seán Ó Riain has studied a small group of Irish software developers from an ethnographic perspective. This group of new economy employees was found to be 'strongly male and Irish' in terms of its workplace culture and owing to the pressures of the new globalised workplace 'work demands came to dominate family life, leaving very little space for workers to find alternative work and family time arrangements' (Ó Riain 2000: 200).

At the other end of the social spectrum the greatly accelerated pace of economic integration known as globalisation and Ireland's own Celtic Tiger has produced a new turbocharged capitalism and capitalist class. At a global level, inequality of income distribution measured through the Gini coefficient (a rather basic measure of economic inequality) has increased in the last quarter of the twentieth century: it is estimated that the richest one per cent in the world today are composed of the richest ten per cent in 13 countries of the affluent North (see Munck 2005).[1] Ireland's Gini coefficient has increased since 2000 and stands at 32 per cent in 2005, high by European standards. Fintan O'Toole provides a graphic journalistic account of this new Ireland, one of the most globalised and most unequal societies in Europe, where the poor, the ill and the migrants meet 'the stern face of State authority' while 'their betters were to get off scot-free' (O'Toole 2003: 53) in terms of tax avoidance and a generally benign view of the free market system.

Another way in which the postmodern perspective has led us to take a new approach to social class divisions is through an emphasis on consumption as the driver of contemporary social development. The postmodern consumer society is seen to stress the individual over social collectives such as class. The typical workplace is no longer the Fordist mass-production labour process but the flexible small-batch production of the new capitalism. The consumer is sovereign, or so we are told, and our identity is shaped by what we consume and our lifestyle, rather than by our occupations. Does the information or knowledge society render production and class irrelevant? For Barry Smart '[C]onsumption is without doubt a vital economic and cultural aspect of the restructuring and reorganisation of capitalist economic life, but it constitutes an "organised extension of the productive forces"' (Baudrillard cited in Smart 2003: 78). In short we can only consume what we produce.

If we examine table 17.3, we can gain some idea of how consumption patterns in Ireland have changed during the Celtic Tiger period. In terms of household appliances, the likes of the washing machine entered virtually all Irish households, whereas the dishwasher increased from 7.6 per cent of households in 1987 to 32 per cent in 2000. The colour TV set and the video player became pretty near universal, whereas the home computer increased its presence from 6.1 per cent of householders in 1987 to 29.3 per cent in 2000. What we see are some products of the consumer society becoming universal but also a consumer divide reflecting the variation in household incomes discussed above. The same applies to household facilities where we see a doubling of the *second* motor car during this period, reflecting the emergence of newly affluent social sectors, and also a great increase in burglar alarms to protect these households from those lacking in the amenities of the consumer society. We could argue that something approximating social class – in the sense of differential power, income and status – can be discerned behind these trends.

Table 17.3 **Household facilities and appliances, 1987, 1994–5 and 1999–2000**

Item description	1987 Households %	1994–5 Households %	1999–2000 Households %
Household appliances			
Vacuum cleaner	79.4	88.0	94.2
Washing machine	77.1	85.6	93.4
Dishwasher	7.6	18.7	32.0
Coloured television set(s)	61.2	88.2	96.2
Video player	16.9	60.9	85.0
Home computer	6.1	16.0	29.3
Household facilities			
Telephone (fixed)	54.3	75.9	89.2
Double glazing	13.0	33.0	53.9
Burglar alarms	3.6	11.7	23.9
Motor car – one only	51.8	51.1	50.1
Motor car – two or more	10.4	14.0	24.2

Source: Household Budget Survey, 1999–2000.

The notion of consumption cleavages was originally focused on by Saunders in his conservative critique of the Weberian/Marxist mainstream in sociology. For Saunders, the privatisation of consumption reached its peak with the privatisation of public housing in Britain during the 1980s (Saunders

1990). It was in relation to housing that we would see the emergence of a new 'underclass' who could not afford to buy their own house. While the notion of a consumption sector replacing occupational categories is debated, the importance of the housing market in contemporary Irish society is undoubted (see chapter 19 for further discussion). Dáithí Downey, on the basis of a survey of access to Irish housing, concludes that 'problems of housing affordability became transformed into a crisis of sustainable access that falls most significantly onto the most unorganised and vulnerable groups in Irish society in a most immediate way' (Downey 2003: 19). Furthermore, we are likely to see conflict between those groups (or classes?) in society in social housing need and those demanding an affordable private dwelling.

The postmodern perspective on social class, if it has done nothing else, has helped us understand class in a more complex and open manner, as a process rather than a structure. It has focused on the fluidity of society in the era of globalisation and the instability and insecurity it creates. We now understand the limits of class analysis, especially if it does not seek actively to integrate the gender and the race/ethnicity dimension. In Ireland this particular perspective is in its infancy but there are signs, especially in terms of recent and new doctoral research topics, that it will gain in importance. One of the problems that need to be addressed is the rather large gap between the mainly ethnographic approach taken here and the dominant large-scale data sets of the quantitative Weberian/ESRI approaches. Not only does this lead to pseudo-debates between incompatible research approaches but also, as Crompton points out, the latter often 'assume that the class concept *is* adequately conceptualised through the applications of sociological . . . class schemes to the occupational order an assumption which is highly problematic' [emphasis in original] (Crompton 1998: 115).

Conclusion

Much of the discussion about social class in Ireland is really about social status. It is not surprising, therefore, that most people would think of themselves as 'middle class': to flaunt an 'upper class' status would be unseemly and who would really want to proclaim an 'under class' status? But we have established in this chapter that social class in the sociological sense is not about ranking in society but, rather, focuses on relations between social groupings based on inequality and exploitation. That is why it is important to question whether equality of opportunity is sufficient to overcome this structural inequality or whether we need to address equality of outcome if we are to establish democratic social relations. Whether we adopt a perspective based on the social-class theories of Durkheim, Marx, Weber or the postmodernists, we need to be clear on these broader parameters and address what is to be done about social class and inequality in contemporary society. In broad comparative terms the inequality of income distribution and at risk of poverty rates in Ireland today are high by comparison with Europe's social economies (see Eurostat 2005: 125–6). What these data do not tell us, however, is anything about the gendered or racialised nature of social inequality and class divisions. There is finally – in the sociologies based in Durkheim, Marx or Weber – an enduring tendency to establish a divide between the public domain of work and the private space of the household, thus ignoring their interrelationship and the way this is structured by gender (see chapter 15).

Chapter 18

The changing working class in Northern Ireland

Goretti Horgan

Introduction

Since the 1998 Belfast Agreement, Northern Ireland[1] has been formally divided into two camps, described as 'communities' – Catholic/nationalist and Protestant/unionist. Such is the extent to which the politics of the North is constructed only around the two communities, that economics' editors of Belfast newspapers find it hard to differentiate between the policies of the four main parties (Cowan 1998). Indeed, the areas on which the parties have been able to agree – socio-economic issues – are the areas that define the division between political parties in other regions. Some commentators have argued that the Agreement has entrenched and perhaps exacerbated sectarian division (Wilson and Wilford 2003). Others have suggested that the Agreement seeks only to 'make the politics of communal rivalry "work" and that only a move towards a politics of class can challenge the communal basis of Northern politics' (McCann 1998: 254). Both of these views remain minority positions, however, since the view that the only identity that matters is community background dominates mainstream discussion of the North.

This chapter is written from a Marxist perspective. It argues that class is the biggest divide in a changing Northern Ireland. Focusing particularly on the experiences of women, it will use facts and figures to show the general trends, and qualitative evidence[2] to demonstrate the lived experience of being working class in Northern Ireland and, in the process, to explore the continuing relevance of class today.

What is class?

When asked: 'Do you ever think of yourself as belonging to any particular class? If yes, which class is that?', 64 per cent of respondents in the 2001 Northern Ireland Life and Times Survey (NILT) said 'yes, working class', compared to 16 per cent who said 'yes, middle class' and 18 per cent who answered no. By contrast, when asked if they thought of themselves as unionist, nationalist or neither, 35 per cent thought of themselves as unionist, 27 per cent as nationalist and 35 per cent as neither. Asked 'if you had to choose, which one best describes the way you think of yourself?' 39 per cent said British, 27 per cent Irish and 22 per cent Northern Irish. This suggests that considerably more people in the North think of themselves as working class than think of themselves as British or Irish, unionist or nationalist.

This class awareness is further supported by other elements in the survey. Just 24 per cent of respondents agreed that 'Ordinary working people get their fair share of the nation's wealth', while only 18 per cent of respondents disagreed with the statement that 'There is one law for the rich and one for the poor'. The views uncovered suggest that the majority of people in the North of Ireland have an understanding of class generally in line with a Marxist approach. In brief, Marxists see the division of society into two main classes as the primary cause of inequality and poverty everywhere. Marxism recognises that in most human societies, the surplus product (the profits on goods or services produced over and above what has to be paid in wages and overheads) is taken and controlled by a tiny elite. This, to Marxists, is the basis of the vast inequalities we see in the world, including Ireland North and South. As Ferguson et al. (2002: 50) note, 'wealth and poverty are linked, they are relational – the poor are poor *because* the rich are rich' [emphasis in original]. This is not to suggest a simplistic two-class model. Marx recognised the complexity of class structure. He argued that 'middle and intermediate strata . . . obliterate lines of demarcation everywhere' (1972: 885). Wright (1997) proposes that these strata occupy 'contradictory class locations', some like line managers close to the working class, others closer or even merging with the dominant class.

Class can only be understood as a relationship formed by the dominant class's ownership and control of the means by which wealth is produced. It takes the bulk of the wealth for itself, giving workers as little as it can get away with paying in wages. Marxists call this 'exploitation'. The historian Geoffrey de Ste Croix, writing about the class nature of ancient Greece, notes:

> Class is the collective social expression of the fact of exploitation, the way in which exploitation is embodied in a social structure . . . A class is a group of persons in a community identified by their position in the whole system of social production, defined above all according to their relationship (primarily in terms of the degree of ownership or control) to the conditions of production . . . and to other classes. (Croix, de Ste 1981: 43)

Thus the Marxist view of class stresses the exploitative nature of social relations between different classes. It is this context that the question 'who is working class?' becomes capable of a clear answer.

Class made a brief official appearance in the Human Rights section of the 1998 Belfast Agreeement. Parties affirmed 'the right to equal opportunity in all social and economic activity, regardless of class, creed, disability, gender or ethnicity'. Typically, however, when it came to legislating to ensure equality, class had disappeared. Section 75 of the Northern Ireland Act 1998 requires public bodies to 'equality proof' policies, publish an Equality Impact Assessment (EQIA) of all decisions, and consult with those likely to be affected by these decisions. The categories covered are: gender, marital status, disability, race, religious belief, political opinion, age, sexual orientation and those with or without dependants. Class has been discarded.

Partly as a result of this legislation, a wide range of information has been made available in relation to each of the Section 75 equality categories. Some of this information includes data on poverty; nonetheless, class is rarely mentioned, even as one among other equally significant variables – despite the fact that class cuts through each of the equality categories. Instead, a whole series of euphemisms is used to mask the reality of class division: 'disadvantaged', 'deprived', 'socially excluded', 'marginalised'. This smokescreen means that the inconvenient issue of class as a social relationship can be sidestepped and, by isolating people living in poverty from wider class relationships, allows them to be demonised, pathologised and subject to regular media moral panics. As Law and Mooney (2006: 529) note in relation to Scotland, to the elite 'the working class tend to feature only as an ever-present source of disappointment'. It could be argued that this is even more the case in Northern Ireland where sectarian clashes and political violence tend to be blamed on unruly 'marginalised communities', without reference to the class dynamics affecting these communities.

The continuing relevance of class

In recent years, it has become fashionable to argue that, 'We are all middle class now', with mass ownership of videos/DVDs, washing machines and cars being cited as evidence. This 'commonsense' attitude reflects what has been willed at the top of society for almost half a century. In the late 1950s and 1960s, for example, rapid socio-economic change led some to argue that we were entering a post-industrial society within which the working class was disappearing and the middle class becoming dominant (Zweig 1961; Bell 1973). This view was echoed by Tony Blair in 1999, when he announced that New Labour wanted to make Britain a 'middle-class society': 'A middle class that will include millions of people who traditionally may see themselves as working class . . . no more ceilings that prevent people from achieving the success they merit' (14 January 1999).

Goldthorpe et al. (1969) examined this 'we are all middle class' idea in their *Affluent Worker* studies of well-paid car assembly workers. Their research found that, despite their high wages, the affluent workers showed working-class attitudes towards family life, unions and politics; most were union members and voted Labour. Their findings emphasised the continuing relevance of class and the continual creation of new types of working class jobs. But the 1990s saw a re-emergence of the idea that class is dead, as neo-liberal ideas of individualism, consumerism and of social division, marked by different lifestyles among a contented majority and persistent failure among the 'underclass', were promoted. In *The Death of Class*, Pakulski and Waters (1996: 4) argued there was a wide redistribution of property, such that 'classes are dissolving and that the most advanced societies are no longer class societies'. More recently, New Labour sociologist Anthony Giddens argued that:

> With the rapid shrinking of the working class and the disappearance of the bipolar world, the salience of class politics, as well as the traditional divisions of left and right, has diminished. (Giddens 1998: 18)

But these advocates for the death of class fail time and again to address the incontrovertible evidence that class does still matter. That is why it is important to return to the classical tradition of Marx and Weber who saw the central divide in society as between the two main classes – capitalist and working class (Callinicos 1983; Allen 2004).

The impact of class

In every society, the impact of class on life and life chances is immense. Being born into a working-class – particularly an unskilled working-class – family brings the risk of a shorter life, physical and mental ill health, lower educational attainment, lower earnings, poorer housing and less control over every aspect of life.

In the North of Ireland, this means that the fifth of the population who are best-off have a life expectancy among the highest in Europe. For the poorest fifth, life expectancy is closer to that of Eastern European countries (General Consumer Council for Northern Ireland 2002). Children living in poverty are 15 times more likely to die as a result of a house fire, five times more likely to die in accidents and four times more likely to die before the age of 20 (Department of Health and Social Services and Public Safety 2000). While considerable publicity is given to the North's very high suicide rate among 15–24 year olds, it is rarely mentioned that young suicides are almost three times higher in the lowest income groups than in the other groups combined (General Consumer Council for Northern Ireland 2002).

From as early as 22 months, children of parents in professional or managerial occupations with high educational qualifications are already 14 percentage points higher up the scale of educational development than children of unskilled or semi-skilled parents with low educational attainment (Child Poverty Action Group 2002: 138).

Educational disadvantage has been further compounded by the North's selective education system. The Eleven Plus has meant that most working-class children were labelled failures at the age of 11. An elite went to grammar schools and this is unlikely to change. Research studies found that schools where there were more working-class children were less likely to achieve A grades in the Eleven Plus (Gallagher and Smith 2000). More than eight out of ten children of professional families went to grammar school, compared to two out of ten children of factory workers and just over one of every ten children with unemployed parents (Daly and Shuttleworth 2000). While the Eleven Plus examination is to be abolished after 2008, the St Andrew's Agreement of October 2006 reversed plans to end academic selection.

Whatever a parent's educational level, not having enough money makes 'free' education expensive. Families living in poverty say they have insufficient money to purchase adequate clothing or books, or to contribute to the activities and items for which 'voluntary contributions' are required. Already, demographic changes mean fewer children competing for places: as a result, 80 per cent of grammar schools accept children with Bs, Cs or even Ds in the Eleven Plus. Increasingly, then, the real criterion for entry to grammar schools is ability to pay. Class dictates what school a child goes to, with all the implications of that for future life chances. As this mother notes:

> it does seem to be the ones that have money do go to these [grammar] schools, which kind of fascinates me, because just because you have money how does that make a child smart? It doesn't, but for some reason all these children's background . . . would be moneyed people. (Mother of three teenagers, Greater Belfast)

Class or creed? Northern Ireland's real divide

There is a growing gap between the rich and the rest in Northern Ireland. Recent UN Development Reports rank the Republic of Ireland among the most unequal developed countries in the world – second only to the USA. Yet the Poverty and Social Exclusion NI survey revealed that inequality in the North is greater – a Gini coefficient of 0.42, compared to 0.36 in the South (Hillyard et al. 2003).[3] Households Below Average Income (HBAI) figures for 2004–5 show more than three quarters of people living below what is the average income (after housing costs) in Britain and more than two out of five individuals living on incomes that are half or less of the British average. But while the majority struggle, the top ten per cent in the North – which includes both Catholics and Protestants – is able to afford second homes and luxury cars. Clear figures for levels of second home and luxury car ownership are hard to establish but indications are that at least 6.5 per cent of Northern Ireland's population own a second home and that the region has the third highest level of luxury car sales in the UK (Hillyard et al. 2003).

As the proportion of Catholics among the rich rises, so does the proportion of Protestants among the poor. Of households living in poverty, 47 per cent are Protestant, 48 per cent Catholic: thus, there being more Protestant households (364,767) than Catholic (247,568), Catholics are overrepresented. Thirty-six per cent of Catholic households are in poverty compared with 25 per cent of Protestant. The difference between Protestants and Catholics is reducing – not because Catholics are becoming more well off, but because Protestants are less well off. A comparison of the 2001 and the 2005 Noble Indices shows Protestant working-class areas making their way up the rank of deprivation in many 'domains'.[4] But while the gap between poor Protestants and poor Catholics is narrowing, the gap between the rich and the poor within each community is widening.

The other big divide in Northern Ireland is between those who have been affected by the conflict and those who have not. What we euphemistically call the Troubles, when viewed proportionately to Northern Ireland's population, could be characterised as a war in scale, intensity and duration. By the end of 2002, 3,352 had died in the conflict. In addition, about 50,000 people were injured. This represents just over three per cent of the population. If we extrapolate these figures to Britain, some 126,000 people would have died – with 1.8 million people injured – representing just under half of all British deaths (265,000) during the Second World War. Extrapolating to the United States, some 608,000 would have died, more than during the Second World War (405,000) and nine times the American death toll in Vietnam (Hayes and McAllister 2005).

A map of the areas where poverty is most concentrated in the North matches very closely the map of areas where the conflict has been most intense. (Fay et al. 1998). In the Poverty and Social Exclusion Northern Ireland survey, half of all household respondents said they knew someone who had been killed in the conflict. (Hillyard et al. 2005) The impact goes far beyond this. The shock of witnessing a violent event, being forced to move house, fear of travelling out of one's own area – these, too, have had a major impact on working-class lives. Yet government responses to poverty generally fail even to mention the conflict, still less address its legacy. Even the 2002 *Investing for Health* strategy, developed under a Sinn Féin Minister for Health, did not address the effects of the conflict on health.

The Households Below Average Income (HBAI) survey for 2004–5 provides information about the percentage of children living in households, broken into quintiles or fifths. Taken before housing cost figures, 43 per cent of Protestant children live in households in the bottom two quintiles of the income distribution which, given the high levels of inequality in the region, puts them below the poverty line. This compares to 59 per cent of Catholic children. This is an unacceptable differential, but small when compared with, for example, the difference between children who live in social as opposed to private housing. More than twice as many children living in Northern Ireland Housing Executive houses live in poverty, compared to 42 per cent of children who live in houses owned with a mortgage. HBAI also provides a deprivation indicator taken as cases where adults responded 'would like to do this but cannot afford'. Eighty-six per cent of poor children were in families that were unable to keep their accommodation warm: no children in the top quintile and just four per cent in the fourth quintile were in this situation. Eighty-eight per cent of poor children had parents who could not afford two pairs of all weather shoes per adult in the household; no children in the top two quintiles had to witness such deprivation. Three quarters of poor children did not get a holiday for one week in the year, compared to one in ten in the fourth quintile and none in the top.

This evidence is further reinforced by reference to levels of social capital in the region. Robert Putnam (1993a, 2000) uses the term to refer to social networks and the neighbourliness, reciprocity and trustworthiness that arise from them. Research has shown that communities with a good 'stock' of social capital are more likely to benefit from lower crime figures, better health, higher educational achievement, and better economic growth.

Several studies of levels of social capital in Northern Ireland have been carried out since the turn of the century, spurred by the widespread view that the Catholic community is better organised and has stronger 'community infrastructure' than Protestant areas. Cairns et al. (2003: 16) found that that the total social capital score 'increased with increasing social class and that this increase was statistically significant' but there was 'no evidence of Catholic/Protestant differences in social capital'. This suggests that the poorer you are, the more isolated you or your community is likely to be – whether you are from a Protestant or a Catholic area. It also confirms Murtagh's findings and supports his view that the evidence 'challenges simplistic notions about the relative strengths of Catholic community infrastructure and capacity for self-organisation compared with Protestants' (Murtagh 2002: 1).

There are, of course, differences between Protestants and Catholics. The unemployment rate for Catholics was 6.9 per cent in 2004, compared to just 2.9 per cent for Protestants. However, a study of labour market dynamics found that while the unemployment rate for both Catholics and Protestants showed a distinct downward trend over the ten years 1994–2004, the rate for Catholics reduced faster than for Protestants, leading to a narrowing of the unemployment gap (Hanvey et al. 2005). There is also an overrepresentation of Catholics among economically 'inactive' people of working age, including those who are 'economically inactive despite wanting to work': this difference is only 2–3 percentage points. Hanvey et al. (2005) also found that the difference between the proportion of workless households that are Catholic and those that are Protestant has halved from six per cent in 1997 to three per cent in 2004. As the Committee on the Administration of Justice (CAJ) points out, this closing of the gap between the two communities is evidence, not of greater prosperity in the Catholic community, but rather of growing impoverishment in the Protestant. The CAJ concludes that 'the recent growth in prosperity has bypassed a significant minority within each community, particularly those living in workless households' (Committee on the Administration of Justice 2006: 65).

The changing working class globally

The composition of the working class changes continually. In the nineteenth century, women and young children worked alongside men in factories in many countries; but with the advent of the 'family wage', women's work was confined to the home and most children were not expected to work (O'Connor et al. 1999). The biggest change over the last half-century has been not a contraction of the working class, but a massive expansion, fuelled by women's entry to the workforce. The entrenchment of industrial capitalism in East and South Asia has seen a huge increase in the size of the global industrial proletariat, both male and female – even before the tens of millions of Chinese workers coming into industry are taken into account.

In *Capital*, Marx showed how the productive process in capitalist society is constantly transformed in the drive for profit. Productive methods have changed in particular branches of industry, and labour has been redistributed among different occupations and industries. New productive technologies have always meant that some workers were no longer useful to the dominant class while other groups became vital to them. The long-term decline of manufacturing and the increase in service industries is an example of this process. Interestingly, some service workers have always been seen as part of the working class. Transport workers, for example, provide a service and not a product, yet they have always been regarded as a 'core' part of the working class. Similarly, workers in the newer service industries like banking, insurance, telecommunications and retail are integral to the capitalist economy: without them huge transnational corporations simply could not operate.

At the same time, we have seen the market encroach on more and more areas of life. The picture painted in the *Communist Manifesto* of a revolutionary mode of production that 'has given a cosmopolitan character to production and consumption' and 'creates a world after its own image' fits the globalised world of today better than that of 1848. Braverman highlighted the dependence of all social life on 'one gigantic marketplace' as capitalist production methods become dominant throughout the world and commodification extends into every part of our lives.

> The social structure built upon the market is such that relations between individuals and social groups do not take place directly as cooperative human encounters but through the market as relations of production and sale. (1974: 277)

Leisure, sport, care of children, older and disabled people, health, education, all become dependent on the market (O'Connor et al. 1999). Labour-saving devices, entertainment, media, improved health care, more widespread education, caring activities and so on are opened to the market and provide new branches of production which employ new groups of workers. The massive rise in the number of women at work is mainly into these jobs – many of them jobs that used to be relatively well paid, high status men's jobs, but which have been de-skilled and demoted in the job hierarchy. Many others are now being paid to do jobs that had traditionally been done without pay by women in the home. Across the world, in services like banking and computers, women have displaced men in positions which are now lower paid and proletarianised – shorthand for a process whereby jobs over which the worker once had a good deal of control are broken down into discrete tasks, with precise instructions given as to how each is to be carried out. Once, for example, different teachers would take different – sometimes innovative, sometimes boring – approaches to educating children and young people. But the education required by global capitalism is not one that opens minds or teaches children to question anything. Rather it is about the production of 'adaptable workers' and 'the development of attitudes necessary for the workplace' (World Bank 1995). To promote these results, strict regulation, as in the National Curriculum in the UK, has been introduced, telling teachers exactly what to teach and how to teach it. Increasingly, the teacher has as little control over how children learn to be useful citizens of the world as the bricklayer does over how a house will be built. Banking used to be a high-status, relatively well-paid job. But over the last 20 years, new technology has allowed banks to recruit young women, who could be paid considerably less than traditional bank workers to carry out simple, repetitive tasks. At the same time, there is a growing number of graduates, almost a quarter in the UK in 2001, in non-graduate jobs, exerting downward pressure on jobs requiring degree-level education (Dolton and Silles 2001). In the North, call centres are known as 'graduate graveyards' for precisely this reason.

The Northern Ireland Civil Service (NICS) illustrates both the continuing importance of class and the problem of occupational classification schemes that lump together different groups who have very different pay and levels of autonomy at work. Almost two thirds of non-manual civil servants work in grades where the pay scales start at between £11,000 and £16,000 per annum and rise to a maximum of £13,000–24,000. By contrast, less than one per cent of civil servants work in grades that start at between £54,000 and £75,000 and rise to a maximum of £159,000. Those at the top earn between three and 12 times those at the bottom. In between, about 16 per cent of civil servants earn between £20,000 and £36,000, while just four per cent earn between £31,000 and £57,000. The interaction of class and gender is clear, too. Women make up 55 per cent of all non-manual civil servants but only 16 per cent of the top grades, rising to 35 per cent of the other well-paid grades. Only when we reach the lowest grades does their composition become half or more female. Those at the bottom do frontline work, dealing with the often frustrated and irate public; much of their work is boring and repetitive. Those at the top have varied, relatively interesting jobs which, according to popular press 'exposés', frequently involve wining and dining in top hotels in various parts of these islands and beyond. Yet many of those who challenge Marxist class analysis place all non-manual civil servants in the same class.

The feminisation of the working class in Northern Ireland

British ministers in the North like to boast about the 30 per cent growth in employee jobs in the period 1990–2005. What they are less likely to explore is the nature of these jobs, overwhelmingly low paid, part-time, in the service sector. Between 1995 and 2003, the number of manufacturing jobs in Northern Ireland fell by 12,084 (12 per cent) while the number of service sector jobs rose by 103,848 (25 per cent). The rise in service jobs was greater than the total rise in employee jobs during the period (Department of Enterprise, Trade and Investment 2005: 50). It is into these service sector jobs that women in the North have poured.

Changes in the participation rates of women in Northern Ireland's workforce have not been as dramatic as in the Republic (see chapter 15), and, of course, participation rates were not so low historically. Nonetheless, there has been a steady increase in the number of women working outside the home since the 1990s. In 1977, the female economic activity rate stood at 42.9 per cent; by 1997 it had risen to 63.8 per cent, and by September 2001, over 65 per cent. By June 2005, over half (51.6 per cent) of all employee jobs in the North were held by women. The low-paid, part-time nature of many of these jobs means that some women are forced to work two or even three jobs in order to achieve a decent income. Women comprised 45 per cent of the workforce in 2005; almost half (48 per cent) of those in paid employment had children.

More than nine out of ten female employees work in the service sector. Of all female full-time employees, 55 per cent are employed in the public administration, education and health service sectors, compared with 27 per cent of males. The other main work area for female full-time employees in the service sector is distribution, hotel and restaurants (15 per cent). For males the figure is 14 per cent. One in ten full-time women employees work in manufacturing compared to one in four men. Twenty-three per cent of women in employment are in administrative and secretarial occupations, compared with six per cent of men. Fourteen per cent of working women are in personal service occupations, such as catering, domestic service and hairdressing; the number of men in this category is too small to be quoted reliably.

This feminisation of the formal workforce has been a contradictory experience for most women (Wichterich 2000; Horgan 2001). On the one hand, becoming economically independent leads to women having more choices about what to do with their lives. On the other, the 'double burden' faced by women because of their role in the family means that their lives are enormously difficult as they try to reconcile work and family life. Working outside the home and being economically independent may mean they do not have to answer to any man, but the 'race to the bottom' on which the expansion of global capital is being built means that, typically, this work entails long hours at low wages and makes caring for children very difficult. This is the case in the North of Ireland, too. Accompanying the growth in participation of women in the labour market has been a marked change in family structures with falling birth rates, increased numbers of children born outside marriage and growth in the number of households headed by women. In 2005, the birth rate was 13.1 per thousand population, down from 17.5 in 1985. The total period fertility rate has dropped correspondingly from 2.45 in 1985 to 1.88. Births outside marriage rose from 11.5 per cent of all births in 1985 to 36.3 per cent of all births in 2005, with over half (56 per cent) of births in Belfast occurring outside marriage. In 2005, of the births outside marriage, three-quarters (76 per cent) were jointly registered by both parents.

Women and class in Northern Ireland

It is sometimes said that Marxism, because of its concentration on relations of production, ignores the oppression of women, failing to address their caring role, or violence against women. But this ignores the theory of alienation.

Ferguson et al. (2002) provide a highly accessible account of how the loss of control over the means of production leads to loss of control by the vast majority of humankind over every aspect of their lives. Marx saw four aspects of alienation, involving the workers' relations to the products of her work; her productive activity; her essential humanity – or what Marx called her 'species being' – and her fellow human beings. Alienation provides an important concept, explaining some of the worst aspects of women's oppression.

Marx also argued for the importance of 'a right to inequality' in order to ensure full equality for all, particularly for those with particular needs and responsibilities.

> one worker is married, another not; one has more children than another, etc. etc. Thus, given an equal amount of work done, and hence an equal share in the social consumption fund, one will in fact receive more than another, one will be richer than another, etc. To avoid all these defects, right will have to be unequal right rather than equal. (1989: 87)

This emphasis on the inequality required for equality has been developed by Sen with his 'capabilities framework'[5] which emphasises the social, economic and environmental barriers to equality (Sen 1980, 1985). Some of those barriers to equality were raised again and again by mothers in the course of the qualitative research, carried out in the most disadvantaged parts of the North in 2003.[6] They spoke of their caring responsibilities for children and for sick or disabled family members. One of the biggest problems was the 'atypical' hours they are expected to work in many of the jobs available to them. Cleaning, caring or home help jobs, even factory work, offer hours that do not fit in with children's school hours; often they are times when it is impossible to get child care – especially for lone parents; and they may be expected to work long hours, often at more than one job in order to bring in enough money. The exhaustion that comes with such long hours, combined with childcare, meant that there is no time for anything but work. Small wonder, then, that few continued this exhausting routine for more than a few years.

> I used to do seven days . . . a lot of hours . . . I was just exhausted. I was literally coming home at 4 o'clock, picking the kids up, making the tea, trying to do washing, trying to do housework, and going to bed at ten o'clock and getting up at five the next morning, trying to get the kids up about 6 to get back out again. [lone mother, Greater Belfast]

One of the main impediments to many of the mothers engaging in paid work was the unsocial hours of many of the jobs available. Some jobs, like cleaning, have traditionally involved early morning or late evening work. This can suit some women. But for lone parents with school-age children, for example, any job that starts before school opens is impracticable. For lone parents with children of different ages, some at primary school, others at secondary and maybe a younger child at nursery, getting to a job with an early start is just not possible.

> My job in the [hospital] now, when [eldest child] was P1, I worked from eight o'clock which meant that I was leaving him with [husband], before I was divorcing him, at before eight o'clock. He was taking him to school; she was still a baby which made it easier. She's up now running about; he's not there. [lone mother, Belfast]

Disability and ill-health were major reasons why both women and men were unable to get paid employment. Most wanted to have a paid job but found that, in spite of the Disability Discrimination Act, employers just do not want to know if someone has any kind of disability. Mothers gave examples of when they or their partner had clear evidence that they were not considered for jobs because of a disability:

> He done his three day trial and at the end of the three day trial they said 'all right we can employ you'. He turned in for work the next morning and they turned round and said 'oh sorry we can't employ you, you have got a back injury'. That's the exact words they said. [married mother, Greater Belfast]

Of those mothers who were not themselves disabled but who cared for a family member with a disability, several said they would love to go out to work 'for a bit of a break' or 'a bit of time to myself'. But few thought this would be possible, because even if a disabled child was at school, hospital and other appointments meant that they always needed to be on call.

These are the reasons why Marx and Sen argue that there is a need to compensate women and others, such as disabled people, for the barriers to equality they face.

Is there an 'underclass'?

The qualitative research confirmed the findings of other studies (Gallie and Vogler 1993; Marshall et al. 1996) that the poorest parts of society do not form an 'underclass'. Rather, they are a core part of the working class, in formal employment as often as possible, living on benefits and working a few hours in the informal economy when possible and necessary. One of main obstacles to formal employment is the general scarcity of jobs, apart from in the Belfast area.

> There were 25 jobs advertised for B&Q and 1,000 people applied for them, it shows you the level of unemployment. [young person, North West]

All participants complained that the only jobs they could get were low paid with poor working conditions and often long or unsocial hours. One of the issues raised by both mothers and young people was the growing lack of security in any job they could get. Despite the traditional view that getting a job in the public sector guarantees 'a job for life', this is clearly no longer the case. As women earn more on average in the public sector than the private (Office for National Statistics 2005), privatisation has a greater impact on female workers than male. Several of the mothers had experience of the jobs they were doing being privatised or contracted out. All who had had such an experience reported that their wages and working conditions had worsened as a result.

> It was the Bru [dole] that employed me first of all. But it was privatised then and I became the supervisor then over the other girls. Because the wages dropped that low, I was getting less for the supervisor's job than what I was as a cleaner . . . While I was in the Bru working then, I heard about a messenger's job going, so I applied for that. It was working direct for the Bru again, so the money went up again. It's weird, like, a messenger getting paid more than a supervisor! [lone mother, North West]

As a result of the difficulties of getting and keeping a job in the formal economy, many of the poorest working-class people have no choice but to move in and out of formal employment and to work in the informal economy – despite very low wages and lack of rights. A 2006 report from the Joseph Rowntree Foundation (Katungi et al. 2006) found that it is economically rational for the poorest sections of society in some areas to engage in the informal rather than formal economy. Further, all the research participants had immediate family members who are part of the formal working class. The participants in the qualitative research are prime candidates for placement in 'the underclass': living in areas of multiple disadvantage where there are families in which second, third, even fourth-generation unemployment is not unusual. Yet they continue to strive to find work, to educate their children and to be part of mainstream society. The work they do may be very low paid, insecure and 'atypical' in its hours and conditions, but the work is very much 'core' to the needs of society. Jobs like cleaning, childcare and elder care cannot be outsourced to India or China. The problem with them is not that they are 'unskilled' or 'semi-skilled' but that the skills involved are under-valued and the wages in line with this undervaluation.

Northern Ireland's equality legislation

The equality provisions in Section 75 of the 1998 Northern Ireland Act have been described as transforming 'how you do equality, and what it might mean to be a citizen' (*The Guardian*, 14 November 2005). But the absence of class (or socio-economic or poverty status) has been the subject of some controversy among those who want to see the strongest possible legislation (McLaughlin and Faris 2004). The importance of strengthening Section 75 by including a class or low-income dimension was raised at every one of 15 workshops during the Northern Ireland Anti Poverty Network's 'Get Heard' consultation. 'Get Heard' gave people living in poverty the opportunity to feed into the UK government's 2006 National Action Plan on Social Inclusion. Participants gave many examples of how, without the inclusion of a class dimension, Section 75 had proved to be too weak to defend the rights of all categories, but especially women, against the neo-liberal onslaught from New Labour. Privatisation proposals to introduce water charges were given as an example of this weakness by many participants. The Impact Assessment in relation to this concluded that because young and old, male and female, disabled and non-disabled etc. will all suffer equally from the introduction of water charges, there were few equality considerations.

Conclusion

Inequalities in Northern Ireland range across religion, race, age and particularly gender. But each of these groups is riven by class, and class intersects with each of the other inequalities to make life most difficult for working class people who are part of one of the 'equality' groups. Thus, while the gender dimension is vital to understanding NI society, when we examine closely the experience of women, the importance of class emerges. This applies also to religion, race, disability and age – while children are more likely to live in poverty than other age groups, the likelihood of them living in poverty depends on the class into which they are born. Although religion is seen as the main divide in the North, the differences between the two communities are small compared to the class divide within each.

Chapter 19

Commodity or home? Critical perspectives on Irish housing

Michael Punch

Introduction

The recent unprecedented era of economic growth in Ireland has coincided with the emergence of one of the most unequal societies in the developed world (O'Hearn 2001; Kirby 2002; UNDP 2005). The problem of uneven development and deepening social inequality is especially evident in housing trends. Simply put, speculators and landowners have made fortunes from a booming housing market, while many others struggle to access suitable, affordable accommodation. Levels of housing need and homelessness have escalated while public housing output has been allowed to dwindle relative to the private sector. For some, the past decade has meant the accumulation of considerable wealth in the shape of capital gains, while others have lived through the harder realities of rising rents, unaffordable prices, long-distance commuting, homelessness and other pressures. In short, a clear contradiction is now starkly evident: a housing boom for some brings a housing crisis for others.

The aim of this chapter is to explore some key changes in Irish housing over the past decade with an emphasis on the links to social change and inequality more broadly. It first examines some of the key theoretical debates about housing, connecting to broader questions about social structure, power and market commodification. These ideas are helpful in interpreting trends in housing in Ireland over the past decade, which are examined in the second part of the chapter. The underlying aim is to shed some critical light on these issues by connecting them to the broader social, economic and political context within which the housing system is located.

Housing and society: theoretical perspectives

At first glance, the housing question has not been well situated theoretically, and this remains an important challenge for the social sciences. The literature both in Ireland and internationally is dominated by policy perspectives, and while this has the advantage of producing a wealth of useful empirical and practical contributions, it has also meant that the field has tended to be somewhat a-theoretical and empiricist in orientation. It will therefore be useful first to draw attention to a number of important conceptual contributions from commentators who have tried to embed the analysis of housing problems in broader considerations of social structure and political economy and to unpack the links between housing systems and broader concerns about power and inequality, commodification and the role of the state and other issues.

One common approach to housing analysis is situated within the confines of neoclassical economics (though these theoretical assumptions are typically not clarified). In this case, housing systems are seen in terms of market relationships between individuals motivated by profit maximisation or utility maximisation. Put simply, the producers and consumers of housing seek to get the best deal possible (variously seeking higher returns on investment or cheaper housing) within housing markets. The key analytical question then has to do with the dynamics of supply and demand, which are seen as the key forces determining the production and distribution of dwelling units. If housing output greatly exceeds demand, the suppliers of housing will find it difficult to sell or let their product and prices will fall. Those seeking homes will benefit from increased choice and falling prices. Conversely, if demand is high and supply does not increase quickly enough in response to these demand signals, prices will rise and those in need of housing will have to pay more to secure it. Equilibrium will occur when supply and demand are 'balanced' at some mystical point where both producers and consumers of housing are reasonably happy with house prices. There are of course many different 'markets' depending on age, architecture, size and location, and the geography of housing markets can get very stretched out – witness the apparently unending expansion of the Dublin housing market to take in many surrounding counties over recent years.

There are many limits to this approach, however. Most importantly, it tends to downplay the role of the state and non-profit sectors, and it fails to situate housing within broader questions about social structure and power. A useful alternative starting point would be to clarify how the market is embedded in social relations, which requires consideration of broader questions about social structure, inequality and housing needs. People have a universal need for housing, regardless of social class, gender, ethnicity, age or income. However, this need cannot be translated into effective demand in a market system unless the household has sufficient economic power to compete for what can be a relatively scarce resource. One can *demand* exactly as much housing as can be paid for, but this may not amount to much (or any) housing if housing income is low or insecure. Accordingly, there is no immediate equation between *demand* and *need* in a market; indeed much need may remain unmet or inadequately met, while a considerable proportion of effective demand may have nothing to do with (basic) need, deriving instead from speculative interest or a desire for second home-ownership. As a result, there may be many under-used dwellings side by side with considerable unmet housing need, including, on the margins, homelessness.

In some respects, there is nothing surprising that housing markets generate considerable problems of inequality and exclusion within a capitalist political economy underpinned by private property social relationships, a structural condition that by definition protects the entitlements of private property owners above the propertyless (Blomley 2006: 3) and emphasises capital accumulation interests over concerns with social development and human needs. In an urban context, this is expressed in the divided city of wealth and squalor, a classical theme in urban sociology (from Engels's Manchester of 1845 to the early twentieth-century Chicago of the urban ecologists) and one which has been re-vivified in recent literature on globalisation and dual cities (Castells 1989; Sassen 1991). In Davis's (1990: 223) colourful field trip through 'post-liberal Los Angeles', for example, the reader is introduced to a landscape 'where the defense of luxury lifestyles is translated into a proliferation of new repressions in space and movement, undergirded by the ubiquitous "armed response"'. In this analysis, the 'hardening of the urban surface' characteristic of the social polarisations of the Reagan era and the 'militarization of city life so grimly visible at the street level' are redolent of 'Hollywood's pop apocalypses and pulp science fiction' (Davis 1990: 226). In deploying such dramatic metaphors, Davis is drawing our attention to the racial and class tensions that underscore the city, and these divisions are most clearly articulated in the residential structuring of the urban form, from the high-class enclaves of Beverly Hills to the ethnic and working-class neighbourhoods of East LA and elsewhere. The general point is that capitalist housing systems are constructed as 'dense landscapes of prohibition, exclusion and security' (Blomley 2006: 3), and people learn quickly to read the codes and hard lines of segregation – gates, CCTV cameras, private security forces, 'no trespassing', 'armed response' signs.

In order to speak to these complex realities, Kemeny (1992) insists we need to consider how housing is embedded in social structure. Following Granovetter (1985), this requires a theoretical approach that is neither 'under-socialised' (viewing housing as non-social and apart from structural factors) or 'oversocialised' (in which housing outcomes are seen to be determined by social relations and therefore of little substantive interest). The challenge is to discern the balance between the two tendencies that achieves the greatest explanatory power. For Kemeny, one way to move towards such a balance is to consider housing as part of the socio-spatial dialectic at various scales, an approach that raises questions about the internal spatial organisation of dwellings and their social use and the spatial organisation of dwellings within the locality or society more generally. This invites us to focus on 'residence', broadly defined to include questions about the relationship between household and dwelling (including aspects of household composition, family cycle, socioeconomic status, tenure, housing quality) and the relationship between household-in-dwelling and the broader society (raising questions about the local town, suburb, village or rural area and the institutions and structural factors that impinge on housing access and mobility). The suggestion is we take seriously the relationship between residence and the dynamics of social change.

The contribution of Harvey (1982, 1985) also explores questions about residence and social structure (among many other related issues), using the toolkit of radical political economy to arrive at a detailed critique of the urban process under capitalism. The key idea here is that capital flows through the built environment in search of profitable returns (rent and capital gains), and in the process an increasing proportion of the housing system can be commodified (for example, turned from a public good to a market commodity) or recommodified (for example, a housing area may be upgraded or demolished, reconstructed and re-branded as high class apartments or lofts). In this dynamic and conflictual process, the housing system is turned to the task of expanding capital and creating new markets. So it is that capital accumulates and circulates through the housing sector, and this has considerable and far-reaching implications for the lives and fortunes of different people and communities. A topical example is the gentrification of city areas involving the replacement of older low-income public housing with intense developments of high-class, high-cost apartments. An example is Sheriff Street in Dublin's docklands, a traditional local authority flats complex which was demolished and replaced by high-class, private apartments built by Chesterbridge Developments in a gated complex renamed 'Custom House Square'. This approach mobilises key concepts from the Marxist tradition in an effort to clarify the fundamental social and economic dynamics of residential space. The work is dense and challenging, and it succeeds in providing quite powerful explanatory tools capable of speaking to the complexity of the production and differentiation of residential space and the contradictions, conflicts and inequalities that inhere to this process.

Housing as a commodity, housing as a home

Analytically, a central problem at issue here relates to 'commodification', an historical process that has had a considerable bearing on the evolution of consumer societies over many decades. The notion of 'commodification' suggests that goods are produced for sale in an anonymous market with the aim of making a profitable return, and the production process generally involves wage labour outside the home. This contrasts with commissioned or planned productive activity to meet certain needs identified by the state (including health, education and housing) or the reciprocal productive activity carried out within households or communities such as domestic work or caring. Indeed, that the commodification of greater areas of everyday life implies both state and household economies reduce in importance as the public sector retreats and people increasingly rely on purchasing goods and services rather than achieving some level of self-reliance through reciprocal productive activity in the household or community.

The commodification of housing implies that it is given both a use-value and an exchange value. The former relates to its real practical purpose, qualitative essence, and material or symbolic worth, such as providing shelter, security or a sense of place. The latter refers to the expected return on investment – the rate of profit it is hoped to extract – and is thus purely quantitative and abstract or phantom-like, lacking any qualitative character. There is an immediate tension, at least in theory, between the economic imperative of maximising the return on investment and the social aim of securing necessary use-values such as shelter. Accordingly, we need to consider carefully the dichotomous role housing is given as both a market commodity for investment and a social good. This also highlights a number of structurally contradictory interests, such as those of landowners, landlords, financiers, investment funds, tenants, those in housing need and the homeless.

In view of the problems linked to commodification and inequality, the state has in fact intervened quite strongly in housing systems over many decades, while various private philanthropic interventions have also been an important feature. In this case, non-market housing provision adopts a different set of priorities and makes use of different processes of production and allocation. Housing is de-commodified, that is, produced in a non-profit manner and directed towards meeting housing needs in the interests of social inclusion, equality and societal development in a broad sense. In practical terms, this has taken many forms, from employer-built housing estates, to co-operative and voluntary housing movements, to the state-driven system of council housing. Of course, no modern housing system is either completely commodified or de-commodified – rather some balance of market and non-market activity will typically exist. Indeed, it is this balance that explains to a large extent the considerable variation between housing systems over time and space. This comparative analytical perspective deserves some brief attention.

Comparative perspectives

Kemeny's (1995) seminal conceptual approach to comparative housing research captures the complexities and dynamics of policy evolution and variation (historically and geographically). A typological distinction is identified between 'dualist' and 'unitary' systems, primarily based on contrasting policies towards rental housing, particularly the role afforded non-profit provision and social renting. In dualist systems, a 'profit-driven market' is kept apart from an effective 'command economy' in social housing. Non-profit provision is suppressed, but maintained as a residual safety net for the casualties of the profit market, which is protected from any competition from non-profit providers. In effect, 'getting into home ownership at all costs' is promoted and heavily supported as the most rational (or 'natural') economic decision, while rental options are downgraded to temporary or secondary roles and therefore become perceived as somewhat unsatisfactory options. A social housing stock is maintained, but only for the most marginalised. Because this sector is now only allowed to house poorer households, the overall rental stream is very limited – something that in turn can leave the sector vulnerable to further attacks from right-wing administrators and politicians since it looks costly from a short-term accounting viewpoint. At the same time, policies and considerable public resources are diverted towards the market sector, supporting and promoting private development and owner occupation. Contrary to the assumptions of neoclassical economics, in this market-dominated approach, competition is discouraged and consumer choice is reduced – getting into home ownership at all costs becomes an imperative and, indeed, given the lack of choice, the only 'sane' option for most households. This imperative is given further impetus through the cultural stigmatisation of the residual public rental tenure, which is often perceived as a less desirable form of housing, even though building quality is often much better in this sector and tenants' rights may be stronger. Kemeny identifies Britain, Australia and New Zealand as typical examples of dualist housing systems.

In a unitary system, by contrast, a *social market* is allowed to evolve, involving both profit- and non-profit provision for general needs. Cost rental models of housing are encouraged, and over the long term these can better meet a range of needs by exploiting the benefits of rent pooling across a mature stock. This approach can go some way to resolving the tensions between exchange-value and use-value interests by opening profit markets up to competition from non-profit providers. It is argued that this can ensure effective tenure choice, de-stigmatise social housing and improve the housing options open to people regardless of income or social status. The economic viability of this kind of system is based essentially on the concept of maturation. While the real cost rent on newly constructed stock may be relatively high, it can be much lower, even negligible, on older stock on which debt has been largely repaid. Thus, as the overall non-profit stock matures, it becomes more economic to offer accommodation at affordable rents to a range of households on different incomes. In essence, the rental income and capital increments associated with a stock of housing held in non-profit ownership over many years cross-subsidise newer construction and the housing of poorer households. A unitary system may be further supported if the cost and availability of land are strategically controlled in the interests of the community through public land banking, a policy that residualises or eliminates speculative activity. Kemeny identifies a number of housing systems that typify unitary systems, namely Sweden, the Netherlands, Germany and Switzerland.

To recap, we find various analytical approaches to housing questions in the literature. Critical social theory and research have brought a diversity of conceptual lenses and practical concerns to the debate, including perspectives on the relationship between housing and social structure, capital accumulation and residential space, commodification and the balance of market and non-market forces and the tendency towards unitary or dualist approaches. How does the Irish housing system measure up in these regards? To what degree is it a 'commodified' system? Does it operate a dualist or a unitary rental system? What does the nature of the housing system reveal about broader questions of power and inequality in Irish society? In order to try to shed some light on these questions, the rest of this chapter explores trends in the Irish housing system over the past decade, a period of considerable transformation and many challenges.

1995–2005: A decade of transformation and challenge

Housing provision, prices and rents

The past ten years have seen high levels of housing output, unprecedented in the history of the state and noteworthy in international terms, with Ireland registering the highest level of new housebuilding in the European Union in 2002, for example (Redmond and Norris 2005). Overall housing output increased from 30,575 in 1995 to 80,957 in 2005. Despite the high levels of private housing output, rapidly escalating house prices in the market for owner occupation have also been a persistent feature since 1995. These long-term trends raise some questions about the neoclassical faith in the mechanics of supply and demand bringing about equilibrium. Average new house prices in the country as a whole increased from €77,994 to €276,221 between 1995 and 2005 (in Dublin prices increased from €86,671 to €350,891). Average second-hand prices increased from €74,313 to €330,399 over the same period (in Dublin prices increased from €88,939 to €438,790). These phenomenal increases have impacted generally around the country – it would be a mistake to assume that this was driven purely by the Dublin housing market. Comparable rates of increase were also recorded in all the major cities and in smaller towns and rural areas. Thus, over the period 1995–2005, new house prices increased by 254 per cent in the country as a whole, 305 per cent in Dublin, 247 per cent in Cork, 213 per cent in Galway, 209 per cent in Limerick, 253 per cent in Waterford, and 254 per cent in other areas outside the main cities. These trends really are quite exceptional, the *Economist* magazine index showing that Ireland had the highest rate of house price inflation in the developed world between 1997 and 2005.

Perhaps the most striking fact about these booming house prices is the divergence from other key relevant indices such as housebuilding costs (labour and materials), average industrial earnings and the consumer price index (CPI). Between 1995 and 2005, while new house prices increased by 254 per cent, average earnings, building costs and the CPI only increased by 58 per cent, 62 per cent and 35 per cent respectively. What accounts for this striking disparity? Most policy attention has focused on problems of supply and demand. This raises concerns about demographic factors, low interest rates, flexible lending practices, rising incomes and speculative activity (buoyed up by the apparently unending cycle of upward price movements and capital gains) fuelling demand, as well as an inadequate supply response (due in part to planning procedures as well as the inevitable time lag involved in construction).

These are undoubtedly important factors, but there are also some other intriguing possibilities. To begin with, a considerable amount of the increase may be linked to rising land costs. Average site prices in Dublin rose by 200 per cent between 1995 and 1998 (a period of considerable house-price escalation as shown above), such that land accounted for 36 per cent of the average house price in 1998 compared to 21 per cent in 1995 (Drudy and Punch 2005). A further possibility is that private-housing suppliers have been able to extract 'super-normal' profits from the whole process, in effect exploiting the developmental importance of shelter and the socially created need for increased levels of housing provision. This suggests the existence of a monopoly-type situation, favouring developers and speculators. Local evidence for this conclusion was available from the non-profit community organisation City Housing Initiative, which in the late 1990s was able to deliver three-bedroom housing units in the highly sought after area of Ringsend in Dublin 4 for no more than €127,000 (City Housing Initiative 1999).

Rental housing takes up a minority position in the contemporary Irish housing system, with 11 per cent of households in private rental accommodation, while just seven per cent are renting from a social landlord (local authority or voluntary housing association). The private rental system also experienced rapid inflation over the past decade. Indeed, by the turn of the century, the rate of rental inflation actually began to outstrip house price increases (Downey 2003), and the highest rates of rental increase in the EU between 1997 and 2001 were recorded in Ireland. Rising demand in the rental system from households priced out of ownership and the resultant rent increases has also meant that poorer households within the system have had greater difficulty finding cheap accommodation. In many ways, the sector is quite polarised between relatively high-income salaried households and others who are either 'working poor' or dependent on social welfare rent supplements, such that this tenure is now reflective of deep social inequalities and disparities in economic power in Irish society more generally (Punch 2005).

The social rental system, meanwhile, offers few options. Access is by definition limited to the most marginalised population, as housing is allocated on a points system (based on various categories of priority need), with rents being geared to income thereafter. New provision in this sector has been limited over the past decade, some efforts to increase output over very recent years, particularly in the voluntary sector, notwithstanding. In 1995, only 13 per cent of new house completions were in the public sector, while in 2005 the performance was even worse with social housing making up only seven per cent of total output, a trend that highlights the low priority afforded social output relative to the private market (Department of the Environment, Heritage and Local Government 2006). The situation is compromised further when one considers the scale of privatisation in the local-authority housing sector due to sales to tenants: allowing for completed sales, the annual addition to the public housing stock was only 2,400 over the period 1995–2005.

Social consequences

These trends in housing and economy have had far-reaching social, geographical and environmental consequences. One immediate concern has to do with housing access – the plight of those unable to get into the market at any level owing to the prohibitive cost of housing and the difficulties associated with taking on a mortgage. The issue was highlighted by recent estimates of the proportion of new households who would not be able to afford to purchase (based on a formula whereby households should not have to spend more than 35 per cent of net income on housing) over the period 2001–6, as calculated by local authorities in their housing strategies. An estimated 33 per cent of all households fell into this category, or 42 per cent in urban areas. The problem of access is also reflected in the diminishing share of new housing purchased by first-time buyers, with investors and households trading up gaining an increasing hold on the market. In 2004, for example, only 34 per cent of house purchases involved first-time buyers.

Even where households have managed to purchase housing, there is the considerable issue of housing indebtedness. Over the past ten years, over €114 billion in housing loans were approved by the relevant agencies. According to one Central Bank economist, if interest rates or unemployment increased, many households would find themselves above any acceptable affordability ratio. Furthermore, the relaxed lending environment is likely to result in a higher rate of mortgage arrears (Kearns 2003).

One strategy adopted by many households to resolve their affordability crisis has been to move considerable distances from the place of work, effectively sacrificing a considerable portion of their lives to commuting in order to purchase a home. In an analysis by Williams et al. (2003), the problem is readily evident from the rapid expansion of towns within Dublin's effective commuter belt, which now stretches at least 80 km from the city. For example, between 1992 and 2002, a number of towns and villages experienced a leap in population, such as Navan (52 per cent), Portlaoise (28 per cent), Rathoath (258 per cent), Enfield (89 per cent) and Dunboyne (74 per cent). The 'stretched-out' residential geography that has emerged in essentially unplanned fashion driven by market forces is a direct reflection of the problem of unaffordability. Put another way, the apparent 'affordability' of home ownership for a large proportion of first-time buyers is premised upon a willingness to accept the social and psychological costs of long-distance commuting for the foreseeable future. These costs include increased use of private transport, fuel consumption, pollution, frustration and reduced quality of life.

Tenants in the private rental sector have also seen considerable price increases, and affordability problems in the private rental system are just as acute, if not worse (Fahey et al. 2004). This has created particular hardships for lower-income households, essentially 'crowded out' by the extra demand pressure from a whole range of households who might traditionally have been expected to purchase (Downey, 1998; Punch, 2005).

The most immediate implication of the relative underdevelopment of the publicly rented sector through much of the last decade or more has been an escalation in official housing need (that is, in the numbers of households assessed as being in need of local authority housing). Between 1996 and 2002, housing need increased by 77 per cent to 48,413 households. Although the most recent assessment of need suggests an apparent reduction to 43,700 households (though some of the major cities have again registered substantial increases), this still represents a considerable failure in the Irish housing system. It should be a matter of urgency given the social plight faced by such households who may currently be paying unaffordable rents, living in overcrowded conditions or unfit accommodation, living homeless in shelters on the streets or on the side of the road, or otherwise facing considerable housing vulnerability. It should also be noted that an unknown number of people in considerable housing need will not be counted in the official figures, including many single people, for example, and there is an ongoing dispute about the real level of housing need.

The most pressing social issue in housing is the experience of various degrees of homelessness. Between 1996 and 2002 homelessness in Ireland increased by 123 per cent to 5,581 people. It is an interesting reflection of power in society that the affordability problems experienced by relatively well-off households have attracted most political and media attention, while the much more urgent concerns of those marginalised by the housing system remain literally and metaphorically on the edge. Arguably, the fact that people who fall into homelessness are faced with considerable and persistent difficulties has to do with the relative powerlessness of the marginalised. The urgent human realities of their situation and their diverse housing needs are easily ignored politically, something that may well have worsened in the years of rising economic growth and hardening inequality. Thus, the lack of accommodation is only the tip of the iceberg in understanding what homelessness means. To be homeless is to feel forgotten, ignored, uncared for, depersonalised, rootless, and without hope. The point is well made by Peter McVerry SJ in an essay on his experiences working with homeless in Dublin's inner city since the 1970s:

> To be homeless is to ask yourself '*why bother to keep going?*' '*What is the point of it all?*' You think that maybe you would be better off dead. Your life has no meaning, no value, no significance. If you were to die, no-one would even notice, you can't think of anyone who would miss you.
>
> To be homeless is to live your life *in the shadows*. In the shadows there is little light, little sun, little warmth. You look out at all those who are busy, rushing here and there, with things to do, people to meet, money to spend; they live in the brightness, where the sun shines and laughter can be heard. But between you and them there is a gulf which prevents you from getting from your side to theirs. And you ask '*Why?*' and no answer is heard [italics in original] (McVerry 2003: 40).

Policy transformation

To fully understand these economic and social issues, it is necessary to consider the evolution of Irish housing policy, which has been considerably restructured over the past decade or more. This is interesting analytically, but it also opens a window on the connection between housing and society, and, in particular, the problems of power and inequality as reflected in the housing experiences of different social groups (highlighted above) and the balance of priorities in policy and the powerful interest groups that tend to influence policy

The underlying aim of housing policy is stated in broad terms by the Department of Environment, Heritage and Local Government with an apparent emphasis on needs, use-values and tenure neutrality: 'to enable every household to have available an affordable dwelling of good quality, suited to its needs, in a good environment and, as far as possible, in the tenure of its choice'. Various strategies are to be deployed to achieve these aims, including the operation of an efficient housing market, the expansion of housing provision, the improvement of housing standards and the facilitation of home ownership. This latter emphasis is interesting insofar as a focus in promoting home ownership as an end in itself carries some ideological undertones regarding an emphasis on private (market) rather than public (non-market) approaches. Although it is popularly asserted that Irish society has a preference for private ownership owing to historical circumstances, it is difficult to verify these cultural assumptions empirically. What is clear is the policy commitment to the aim of promoting a private home-owning society, as reflected in a formidable raft of supports for the owner-occupied tenure. Some of the most important policies of this kind include the abolition of residential rates in 1978, the abolition of residential property tax in 1997, the absence of capital gains tax on sale of the principal residence and the reduction of capital gains tax on other property sales from 40 to 20 per cent in 1997, right-to-buy of local authority houses and a range of shared ownership and affordable housing schemes.

Policy provision for private rental housing has long been considerably less favourable in different ways, so that it has justifiably been labelled the 'forgotten sector' (O'Brien and Dillon 1982) owing to the failure to regulate either standards or rents. A number of important policies have had some effects over recent decades, however. Of particular note is the rent-supplement system provided under the Supplementary Welfare Allowance system. Under this scheme, which cost €350 million in 2004, the private rental system has become a de facto 'alternative' to public housing for a large number of social welfare tenants supported by state subsidies (about 60,000 in 2004). The creation of the Private Residential Tenancies Board under the Residential Tenancies Act of 2004 promises some change in this sector, though the effectiveness of regulation remains to be seen, while it is unlikely to have a significant effect on rental levels since the entire Act is based on the central premise of 'market rents'.

A key policy has involved various tax-incentive schemes to encourage property development in designated areas of inner cities and many towns and villages throughout the country. These schemes (most importantly Section 23 and various urban renewal schemes since 1986) have a number of flaws. They fuel demand for housing and land among investors and they are inherently regressive as they only benefit those with sufficient income to incur tax liability and access to sufficient capital to get involved in property investment. A recent report concluded that such schemes were both costly to the state and regressive (Goodbody Economic Consultants 2005). For example, under the Urban Renewal Scheme of 1998 alone, the cost in tax foregone amounted to

€1,423 million (or €40,917 per residential unit and €498 per square metre of commercial space constructed in the renewal areas). Moreover, most of the benefits were captured by investors, who acquired 90 per cent of the properties built under the scheme. Importantly, a general process of 'incentivised' gentrification seems now to be well established in many urban areas as these schemes attract high-class, high-cost developments in formerly working-class areas such as the Liberties in Dublin (Kelly and MacLaran 2004).

Policy for public rental housing is also weak in some crucial ways. As housing output trends (above) show, the sector is now in a considerable minority position. This is a recent historical departure. From 1932 to 1942, local authorities provided 49,000 units or 60 per cent of total housing output (Drudy and Punch 2005). During the Second World War, public provision represented 65 per cent of total housing and was as high as 70 per cent in 1945–46 (Finnerty 2002). In the early to mid-1950s, public provision always exceeded 50 per cent of housing output. This historic dominance of state investment in housing began to reduce from this time, however, though public housing still represented 33 per cent of total output in 1975. Since then, the system has been dramatically commodified with a turnaround to the current situation where typically less than ten per cent of housing output is in the public sector. This process of commodification has been even more dramatically driven by a long-standing policy of privatisation of public housing through sales to sitting tenants at a significant discount. This 'right-to-buy' arrangement has seen about two thirds of the public housing stock transferred into private ownership. While this has seen a wider band of households accessing home ownership, the difficulty is that at a later stage these formerly public assets are 're-commodified' as they are traded in the market for sums vastly greater than the initial selling price to the tenant. In some cases, local authorities have bought back houses they once owned at much higher prices.

The introduction of Part V of the Planning and Development Act 2000 provided an important central-government impetus for housing policy change with direct implications for social housing. The Act made housing a material consideration of planning, in that it was now a requirement for local authorities to produce a housing strategy as part of their development plans. This included a policy whereby up to 20 per cent of new residential developments could be acquired by the local authority for the purposes of social (for rent from the local authority or housing association) and 'affordable' (for sale at a subsidised price for private ownership) housing, where such a need was identified. This mechanism was also seen as a means of avoiding 'undue' social segregation (in practice, by introducing a policy of tenure mixing). It is striking that this was a market-driven mechanism, depending entirely on the co-operation of private developers to provide housing. This implied reliance on, and vulnerability to, market forces and by implication little public control over location, phasing, design or quality. In any event, the provision came under sustained political attack from special interest groups, particularly in the property construction sector, and it was amended in 2002. Under the original Part V, the local authority could negotiate as a condition of planning permission the transfer of land, sites or completed units. Under the 'new' Part V, the deal could involve these same three transfers within the proposed development or the transfer of land, sites or dwelling units elsewhere, a cash option or a mixture of all of the above. In view of these changes as well as allowable 'exemptions' (developments of less than four units or less than 0.8 hectare), it is perhaps unsurprising that the number of social units returned under Part V agreements has been very limited so far, amounting to a tiny fraction of overall private output as is evident from table 19.1 (below).

Table 19.1 **Social and affordable housing output under Part V**

	Part V Social (local authority)	Part V Social (voluntary)	Part V Affordable	Total	% of total private output
2002	—	—	46	46	0.08
2003	75	—	88	163	0.3
2004	135	82	374	591	0.8
2005	203	206	962	1,371	1.8

Source: Department of the Environment, Heritage and Local Government 2006

Conclusion

This chapter set out a theoretical context for considering housing trends, issues and policies, raising key questions about the limits to a-theoretical, empiricist and neoclassical economic approaches, and exploring important alternative approaches that emphasised the links between housing and social structure and power and inequality in society, capital accumulation, market commodification and the creation of dualist versus unitary housing systems. Arguably, these issues are useful to understanding experiences in Ireland. Over the past decade, key trends include considerably increased levels of housing output (mostly in the private ownership market), rising prices and rents, and a reduced role for publicly rented housing. The social consequences of these trends raise important challenges regarding housing access and need, homelessness, commuting and sustainability, household debt, the reduction and stigmatisation of social housing, and other issues. A key factor in all of this has been the realignment of housing policy, and while there have been many and varied departures and experiments (tax incentive schemes, the

Private Rental Tenancy Board, Part V), some broad overarching tendencies in policy restructuring can be identified. It can be argued that policies have been heavily infused by an emphasis on privatisation and a reliance on market forces. The result is a shift towards an increasingly commodified system constructed in dualist fashion around a dominant private ownership sector with restricted rental options. This is housing for capital accumulation in the first instance, and while the winners in such a system may do very well indeed, the implications for more vulnerable households are stark, including home-lessness at the very edge of the system. Such experiences provide some illuminating insight to the nature of social power and inequality in Irish society. In particular, the restructuring of policy priorities towards the interests of private capital highlights a critical problem and challenge for anyone concerned with the hard everyday realities faced by households disadvantaged both socially and by the operation of the housing system.

Section VI Identity, diversity
and culture

Chapter 20

Identity, language and nationality

Iarfhlaith Watson

Introduction

'*Tá an fear sin ag féachaint orainn.*'[1] With those words the two Irish people abroad reaffirmed their Irish identity. They established themselves as 'us' and the man as the 'other'. Identity tends to work like this – to require an 'other' against which it can be defined. Comparison and contrast are quite fundamental to our ability to comprehend. In language it is difficult to explain a concept without reference to something else. Can you explain mauve[2] without comparing it to other colours? Words come to be linked to some understanding of them that we have in our mind. The opening phrase of this paragraph is meaningless unless we understand what the series of black ink marks represents. Like language, identity also depends on our understanding of a set of meanings and on comparisons which are produced and recreated in social interaction, such as the example of the two Irish people abroad. The similarities between language and identity serve as a useful basis for analogies, but, although I shall make some analogies in this chapter, we shall focus on the specific relationship between the Irish language and Irish national identity. In terms of the example above, we can ask why the two Irish people abroad used the Irish language to establish themselves as Irish. This question will be the central focus for this chapter.

In response to Descartes' claim 'I think therefore I am' (*cogito ergo sum*) one could ask 'who am I?' This is a central human question – a question about identity. Some identities are based on what we regard to be an 'essence' of ourselves, such as sex or race. Other identities, based in social aspects, are regarded as no less essential. The focus of this chapter will be how nationality and the identity which relates to it, despite their appearance as a solid, fixed and lasting essence of ourselves, are in fact subject to processes of change and social construction. Nationality appears to have a history which stretches back into a distant primordial past. Yet, as we shall see below, nations are a modern phenomenon. The reason they appear so fixed and ancient is that they are constructed using the resources of history and essential aspects of human existence, such as language. The objective of this chapter is to take a long-term historical perspective in order to understand sociologically how identity, language and nationality have come together in present-day Ireland.

Identity

Identity is in a continual process of construction, appearing in various social contexts which manifest identity while simultaneously altering it. Stuart Hall (1996: 2) argued that in common-sense language, identity is built on 'a recognition of some common origin or shared characteristics with another person or group, or with an ideal', but he went on to argue that 'in contrast with the "naturalism" of this definition' identity is 'a process never completed – always "in process"'. The changes, which are part of this process, can be gradual, subtle and 'banal' (see Billig 1995) in the overall context of a changing society. At other times changes can be faster and more dramatic. Either way the importance of the Irish language to national identity is the result of a social, not a natural, process.

As two sides of the same coin, identity is both the product of, and can also influence, lived experience. This is a phenomenon that sociologists are well aware of. Society is both the product of individual interaction and that same individual interaction is structured by society. As Norbert Elias (1978b: 221) put it

> one of the peculiarities of the traditional image of man is that people often speak and think of individuals and societies as if these were two phenomena existing separately – of which, moreover, one is often considered 'real' and the other 'unreal' – instead of two different aspects of the same human being.

A simple analogy can be drawn with the spoken language. It exists even if I don't speak, because other people speak. It existed before I was born and will exist after I die and, because other people use it, it has an existence independent of mine. It structures what I can say and some people argue that it even structures our thoughts – see for example the Sapir-Whorf Hypothesis (see Kay and Kempton 1984) or the linguistic theory of Bhartrihari, who lived in India about 1,500 years ago (see Tola and Dragonetti 2003).

In social interaction the reaffirmation of the 'us', who share the sameness of identity, simultaneously reinforces the difference of the 'other'. In this interaction there is the inclusion of the people with the shared identity and the exclusion of others. Identities, according to Hall (1996: 3), 'emerge within the play of specific modalities of power, and thus are more the product of the marking of difference and exclusion, than they are the sign of an identical, naturally constituted unity'. This can be a quite blatant exclusion of individuals from a particular social context, but it can also be manifested in the structural nature of oppression when people who are identified as different are, for example, paid different amounts for the same work or excluded from employment. Identity as a process and as exclusion are contained in Jacques Derrida's (2000) use of the word *différance*. It is a pun in French, in which both of the verbs 'to differ' and 'to defer' (or, more precisely, to postpone) are implied. What this means for us here is that identity is about difference, but that at the same time there is never a fixed and permanent identity – its final meaning is always postponed.

Drawing on the anthropologist Fredrick Barth (1969), one could argue that identity as a process, in which there is inclusion and exclusion, results from the maintenance of a boundary between 'us' and 'them' – not from preservation in social isolation. Furthermore, as Barth (1969: 10) wrote, this boundary is 'maintained despite changing participation and membership'. The boundary which stands between the sameness of those who are included and the difference of those who are excluded is marked symbolically through representational systems. Some examples of more explicit symbolic marking are murals and insignia. This symbolic marking is related to social interaction in which sameness is the product of lived experience. Many approaches to identity tend to celebrate the diversity evident in the symbolic aspect of identity and neglect the structural nature of oppression which is reinforced by the lived experience of sameness and difference.

Language

An extreme example of exclusion and of the explosive potential of opposition between identities is evident in Northern Ireland. In recent years there have been advances made in reducing the violent nature of the clash. A major development of the last decade was the agreement, known as the Good Friday or Belfast Agreement, reached on 10 April 1998. It is of interest in terms of identity, nationality and language. In the agreement the British government undertook to 'promote', 'facilitate' and 'encourage' the use of Irish. There was also the expectation that:

> All participants recognise the importance of respect, understanding and tolerance in relation to linguistic diversity, including in Northern Ireland, the Irish language, Ulster-Scots and the languages of the various ethnic communities, all of which are part of the cultural wealth of the island of Ireland. (Belfast Agreement 1998: 24)

The agreement led to the British-Irish Agreement Act, 1999, in which Foras na Gaeilge was established to deal with the Irish language in both the Republic of Ireland and Northern Ireland. Simultaneously, Tha Boord o Ulstèr-Scotch was established to promote greater awareness and use of Ullans (the Ulster-Scots language). The inclusion of Ullans raises the issue of linguistic diversity in Ireland. It also raises the question of the difference between a language and a dialect.[3]

The difference between language and dialect mirrors the arguments about objective and subjective definitions of the nation which will be mentioned below. A linguist struggles to define objectively the limits of a language and the necessary minimum diversity to qualify as a separate language. This is a difficult task to achieve because languages change constantly. This change is more rapid in a language whose rate of change is not reduced by the relative permanence of the written word. It is also a difficult task to achieve because language is a fundamental element of identity, especially national identity. In this context one can question why it is that Norwegian and Danish are separate languages whereas Alemannic is considered a dialect of German. When criteria of mutual intelligibility (imprecise as they may be) are applied, it is easier for Danish and Norwegian speakers to understand each other than it is for High German and Alemannic speakers. When it comes to language and identity even 'objective' linguistic declarations become part of the political debate. When a group of people believe that they speak a particular language, they will treat it as a language regardless of linguistic definitions to the contrary. If this group is convinced by arguments (whether objective or subjective) that theirs is a dialect, their language, without linguistic changes, can become a dialect. Language is often used as a marker of difference in the political arena of the opposition between national identities. The Irish language has been promoted in Northern Ireland as an element of the identity of Irish nationalists and in that context Ullans became a propitious counterbalance, despite the objective fact that Irish and Ullans have been spoken by people of both 'communities'.

Another language spoken in Ireland is Cant (a language spoken by Irish Travellers and also known as Shelta, Gammon or Sheldru). Ethnologue (www.ethnologue.com – which uses the term Shelta) claims that there are 6,000 speakers of Cant in Ireland and 86,000 worldwide. They also argue that it is a cryptolect or secret language. As the Travellers believe themselves to be an Irish indigenous minority and members of the Irish nation the Cant language is representative of Traveller identity as a component of Irish national identity rather than a separate national identity.

As a result of the recent high rate of immigration into Ireland there are many people now in Ireland speaking many different languages. The most interesting development of this kind is the arrival of people from Poland.

During the period May 2004 to May 2006 alone, it is estimated that over 100,000 people came to Ireland from Poland. The linguistic results are evident in radio advertisements in Polish as well as telecommunications companies offering Polish 'packages' for internet, telephone or cable television. As the Polish people are not racially or religiously distinguishable from the Irish, it will be interesting to see if language becomes a marker of difference in the construction of an Irish-Polish identity, especially as Polish may now be the largest minority language spoken in Ireland (perhaps not ahead of Irish in number of speakers able to hold a basic conversation, but perhaps ahead of Irish in terms of frequency of use and the fluency of its speakers).

The language spoken by most of the people of Ireland most of the time is English. There is no 'natural' reason why the Irish language should have become the important linguistic marker of Irish national identity rather than Hiberno-English. There was enough potential in Hiberno-English for it to have been established as the national language of Ireland associated with Irish national identity. Instead, the language which became the marker of Irish national identity was the largest minority language of Ireland at the time of the Irish nationalist movements a century and more ago. Furthermore, this minority language is in no way mutually intelligible with English. This is the Irish language or Gaeilge.

It is difficult to determine exactly how many Irish speakers there are because of three main elements: attitude, ability and performance. Attitude to the Irish language can influence whether or not people claim to be able to speak Irish. For example attitudes to the Irish language had altered to such an extent in the century and a half between the 1851 and the 2002 censuses that although about 1,500,000[4] people were returned as Irish speakers in both censuses it was most likely underreported in 1851 and most definitely overstated in 2002. Attitudes to the Irish language are so positive today that even people with little ability and little opportunity to speak Irish claim in the census that they are Irish speakers. The more than 1.5 million people who claim to be Irish speakers is 42 per cent of the population (over three years of age). In comparison, the surveys conducted by the Committee on Irish Language Attitudes Research (CLAR) in 1973 and continued by Institiúid Teangeolaíochta na hÉireann (ITÉ, the Linguistics Institute of Ireland) in 1983 and 1993, as well as the International Social Survey Programme (ISSP) modules on national identity in 1995 and 2003, all have found that about 10 to 15 per cent of the whole population of Ireland claim to be able to speak Irish reasonably well. That accounts for about 400,000 people, much fewer than the 1,500,000 in the census. One can also infer from the CLAR/ITÉ surveys that as well as the 400,000 who claim to be able to speak Irish well there are about another 800,000 who can put a few sentences together in Irish. That brings the CLAR/ITÉ figures up to 1,200,000, but still leaves about 300,000 people who claim to be able to speak Irish when most likely they have no more than a few words of Irish. Although the figures here are rough estimates, we can conclude that most of the people who, in the census, claim to be Irish speakers are expressing an attitude rather than ability.

Having briefly examined attitude and ability we can now turn to performance. It appears that, of the 1,500,000 people who claim in the census to be Irish speakers, only 22 per cent speak Irish on a daily basis and a further 10 per cent on a weekly basis. The majority speak Irish either less than weekly (37 per cent) or never (29 per cent). It appears that because Irish is a compulsory subject at school the majority of Irish speakers learn Irish at school (rather than at home) and the longer people stay in school the more likely they are to be able to speak Irish to some extent. Irish speakers are dispersed throughout the country, with only approximately 60,000 Irish speakers living in the Irish-speaking Gaeltacht communities.[5] Many Irish speakers are not part of a community or even a network of Irish speakers. Ó Riagáin, from the ITÉ argued that 'were it not for the fact that the schools continue to produce a small but committed percentage of bilinguals, the maintenance of this small minority of Irish speakers would long since have failed' (Ó Riagáin 1988: 7). The conclusion one could draw from this is that changes in the education system could result in changes in the profile of Irish speakers.

Since the early 1970s some of the compulsory elements associated with the teaching of Irish have been reduced. One result is that Irish speakers are no longer more likely to go on to third-level education than non-Irish speakers. Another development evident in information leaked from unpublished findings of the Department of Education and Science, was that since the mid-1980s the standard of Irish in primary schools has dropped dramatically (*Irish Independent*, 17 February 2006; RTÉ Radio 1 *Five Seven Live*, 17 February 2006 and Enda Kenny, TD statement in the Dáil, 17 February 2006). On the other hand, the percentage of people claiming to be Irish speakers, in the censuses since the early 1970s, has increased gradually from 28 per cent to 42 per cent.[6] This appears to illustrate an increasingly positive attitude to the Irish language because of the less compulsory approach of state policy. Although this may result in a more favourable attitudinal context for the Irish language, it may also result in fewer people with higher levels of ability to communicate effectively in Irish.

Nationality

The compulsory elements of the teaching of Irish can be traced back to independence in 1922. The newly independent Irish state made political use of the education system to attempt to form good citizens, as had the British government previously. Just as there was a new state post-1922, there was also to be a new citizenry. The Irish government decided to use the education system to attempt to revive the Irish language. This then raises the question of why a nationalist objective becomes intertwined with issues of citizenship. The answer to this question lies in the relationship between nation and state.

The first part of this problem can be dealt with by some understanding of what a nation is. Walker Connor (1978: 381) explained that

> The word *nation* comes from the Latin and, when first coined, clearly conveyed the idea of common blood ties. It was derived from the past participle of the verb *nasci* meaning to be born. And hence the Latin noun, *nationem*, connoting *breed* or *race*. . . . At some medieval universities, a student's nation designated the sector of the country from whence he came. But when introduced into the English language in the late thirteenth century, it was with its primary connotation of a blood related group. One etymologist notes, however, that by the early seventeenth century, nation was also being used to describe the inhabitants of a country regardless of that population's ethnonational composition, thereby becoming a substitute for less specific human categories such as *the people* or *the citizenry*.

Perhaps a simpler definition is that a nation is a group of people with shared physical, cultural and other traits (an objective approach to the nation) or a group of people who believe that they share some traits in common (a subjective approach to the nation). This definition then raises confusion between definitions of a nation and of an ethnic group (or nationality and ethnicity). In both cases there is a group of people who share common traits, whether it is objectively imposed or subjectively believed. Both ethnic group and nation are usually based on a belief in things such a shared ancestry, common cultural traits like language and religion, and an 'other' against which to define the group. The Irish during the medieval and early modern eras were recognised by others (such as the English) as a distinct group and they could recognise themselves as a group. We could say then that there was an ethnic group called the Irish. This does not imply some scientifically defined genetic group, but rather a group of people who are believed to have shared certain characteristics; often they are presumed to have a common genealogy or ancestry as well as current cultural similarities. Although the Irish appear to have thought of themselves as a group with shared traits it is hard to find evidence that they thought of themselves as a nation. Today the Irish do think of themselves as a nation and yet, when one examines the traits which are emphasised, it appears no different from an ethnic group. The trait which is most emphasised today is shared ancestry – even more than shared cultural traditions. In an International Social Survey Programme module on national identity which was fielded in 2003, 81 per cent of the respondents agreed that it is important to have Irish ancestry to be Irish. This compares with 52 per cent who agreed that it is impossible for people who do not share Irish customs and traditions to be Irish (up seven per cent from 1995). Perhaps the reason for the emphasis on ancestry is the lack of a distinctively Irish way of life which could distinguish the Irish from the 'other'. On the other hand 91 per cent of the respondents agreed that it is important to have Irish citizenry to be Irish. In nationalist ideology, nationality and citizenship overlap. An examination of the difference between nationality, citizenship and ethnicity should take place in the context of the discussion of the emergence of the modern state.

The origin of the modern state can be traced to the Treaty of Westphalia in the mid seventeenth century, mainly because the treaty resulted in the mutual acknowledgment of each country's sovereignty. There were few nation states in existence at the time, but over the next few centuries more nation states emerged, as well as nationalist movements and the ideology of nationalism. This ideology established the belief that there are groups of people, with shared characteristics, called nations and that they have the right to their own state. Gradually over the centuries the nation state became the ideal.

Within this ideal the Irish nation would have sovereignty. The members of the nation would be Irish citizens. This is where confusion arises between two central aspects of the nation – the civic and the ethnic. Nations tend to contain elements of both, but are classified as primarily belonging to one type or the other. In the ethnic nation the people are members of an ethnic group *qua* nation and the uniqueness of the collective ethnic features of the nation are emphasised. In the civic nation the individual is a citizen with civic rights and responsibilities. Kohn (1944) labelled the Irish nation an ethnic nation in opposition to other Western European nations such as England and France which he labelled civic.

The mixture of features, but with an emphasis on the ethnic, is evident in the actions of the Irish state in the decades following independence. To ensure that members of the Irish nation were 'good' citizens, to ensure that they shared the national traits and to legitimise its own existence the independent Irish state built the nation by imposing on the people of Ireland the 'ethnic' traits which the Irish nationalist intellectuals of the late nineteenth and early twentieth century regarded as essentially Irish. The trait of most relevance here is the Irish language. The state used media such as the national education system and broadcasting for this purpose. The education system has already been mentioned above. Similarly, from 1926, the state used radio to promote the Irish language. It was not until 1972 that there was a dedicated Irish language radio station and 1996 before there was a dedicated Irish language television station. That was, however, after the era of nation building, when these media began to be used to entertain and inform Irish speakers rather than primarily facilitate the mass production of Irish speakers. (See Watson 2003).

If the modern nation state is expected to have been based on a unit called the nation, the question then arises as to when the nation began. It is difficult to determine the origins of individual nations. Nations are, however, phenomena of the modern world. This is most particularly the case from the modernist perspective of authors such as Tom Nairn, Eric Hobsbawm and Ernest Gellner. Nairn argued that the origins of nations are to be found in the wider process of historical development in Europe since the late eighteenth century. This suggests that it is a modern phenomenon. He claimed that '"nationalism" in its most general sense is determined by certain features of the world political economy, in the era between the French and Industrial Revolutions and the present day' (Nairn 1977: 332). Similarly, Hobsbawm (1990) argued that the ideology of nationalism produced nations and not *vice versa*. He argued that the invention of tradition was an important aspect of nations and that the development of primary education was a major element in this. The newly independent Irish state made use of the education system to achieve the nationalist objective of reviving the Irish language, as was mentioned above. Evidence of this nationalist objective can be found decades earlier in 1899 when Fr M. P. O'Hickey, a prominent member of the Gaelic League, had written that 'even though half the subjects in the programme should have to be sacrificed, the language of the country should be taught in all the schools of Ireland' (quoted in Kelly 2002: 6). The state also introduced other subjects into the curriculum to make it more Irish, for example singing, history and geography. In order to reinforce the teaching of Irish these subjects were to be taught through Irish, and elementary science, hygiene, nature studies and domestic studies were to be dropped to make room for the teaching of Irish.

Like Hobsbawm, Gellner (1964: 168) argued that 'nationalism is not the awakening of nations to self-consciousness: it invents nations where they do not exist', and he went on to argue that 'it is the need for growth which generates nationalism, not *vice versa*'. His point here is that with the arrival of industrialisation there was a need for people who could communicate in a manner which could be understood by all others in the country. This meant linguistic homogenisation through the elimination of the diversity of languages and even the standardisation of the favoured language through the elimination of its various dialects. There was also a need for literacy and numeracy as well as technical skills. All of these could be provided through a homogeneous 'national' education system.

For nationalists, on the other hand, the nation is usually a pre-existing unit. Thus, from this perspective, in the Irish case, it is simply a matter of reintroducing the people to their ancient language, traditions, music, folklore, sports, and even history and archaeology. The important point for nationalists is that the nation has existed since time immemorial and remains as an essence with the people of the nation. The role nationalist leaders see for themselves is the revival of that essence. From this perspective a nation is not constructed or invented, it is a pre-existing essence. To a large extent this is the taken-for-granted or common-sense view of the nation. It is accepted that the Irish are a nation with essential features which distinguish them from other nations. Yet the features which distinguish the Irish nation were largely constructed by nineteenth-century nationalists to distinguish the Irish from the English. It is very likely that had the colonisers been French, for example, the features used to distinguish the Irish nation would be quite different. Modernists tend to label this position primordialist. While primordialists claim that nations contain an essence which has existed for a very long time, modernists argue that nations are in fact modern constructions or fabrications. Amongst scholars of nationalism there are no true primordialists. There are scholars, however, whom the modernists have labelled primordialist. These scholars do not accept this label. Recently they have been called ethnosymbolists – a more accurate label. Their position lies between the modernist and primordialist positions.

To illustrate the difference between modernists and ethnosymbolists it is helpful to examine the debate between Smith and Gellner (Gellner and Smith 1996) about the question of whether or not nations have navels. The point is that because the navel results from the existence of the umbilical cord, which had a vital function before birth, it symbolises that the individual was born and not invented or constructed. This is the essential point of the debate – whether nations are modern inventions or born from entities which pre-exist modern times. Gellner (Gellner and Smith 1996) argued that we need not concern ourselves with this issue because (adhering to the analogy) navels are not necessary after birth. He maintained that the modernist perspective gives a sufficient explanation – if it tells half the story that was enough for him.

Smith (Gellner and Smith 1996) argued that it is not enough to tell half the story as modernists do. He argued elsewhere (Smith 1994) that it is also neither correct to regard the nation as an unchanging essence as primordialists do, nor, in a postmodern fashion, to regard history to be like a sweet shop where nationalists pick and mix various features to construct a nation. He argued that although nationalists draw on the resources of history, they do so within certain limits. They rediscover and reinterpret the past according to the demands of the ideology of nationalism, 'scientific evidence, popular resonance and patterning of particular ethnohistories' (Smith 1994: 19). In this way Smith established that his position was neither nationalist or primordialist, nor was it modernist or even postmodernist.

Along with Smith there are authors such as John Armstrong and John Hutchinson residing in the same general theoretical camp (see Armstrong

1982 and Hutchinson 1994). In short, from this perspective, the study of nations should look at *la longue durée* because nations tend to have ethnic origins and are the culmination of a longer process of change. They claim that taking this approach helps us to understand which ethnic groups are likely to develop into nations and it also helps us to understand the importance of traditions, symbols and myths.

Language and nation

In Ireland the Irish language has been promoted since the nineteenth century as a symbol of the Irish nation. It is important therefore to trace the connection between language and nation. In the eighteenth century Johann Gottfried von Herder, in an attempt to defend diversity from what he felt was the uniformity being imposed by the progress and reason of the Enlightenment, argued that language is what makes people human. He claimed that language is thought and, that being the case, each linguistic community has its own mode of thought. Furthermore, he argued that individual governments are the result of an organic historical development as the folk-nation comes into existence on its own (see Breuilly 1982: 336). In other words, if the nation could be protected from outside influences, its own government and culture could develop 'naturally'. Early romantic nationalism was influenced by Herder (amongst others) and, as it developed during the nineteenth century, it influenced Irish nationalists such as Thomas Davis who visited Germany in 1839–40 and adopted the German Romantic idea that the nation is a linguistic and cultural entity. Davis wrote many articles on this topic in his newspaper *The Nation*; he coined the slogan 'educate that you may be free' and brought the two political issues of the Irish language and education together. Particularly from the 1880s onwards, the Irish language movement emphasised the importance of the introduction of Irish into the education system at all levels. As the Irish language movement developed and was closely associated with the political nationalist movement for independence the revival of the Irish language became a nationalist objective and the education system was regarded an important medium for its achievement.

In Ireland the initial decades after independence (particularly after 1932) were dominated by an ideological perspective which was protectionist. This was not only reflected in economic policies, but also in cultural policies such as the compulsory nature of the Irish language in the education system and the inclusion of Irish language programmes on the state-controlled radio station. By the 1960s there was an ideological shift to a less illiberal (perhaps more social democratic) approach (see O'Dowd 1992). In the context of the Irish language this was reflected in the removal of some of the compulsory elements relating to the teaching of Irish and in the establishment of the first Irish language radio station – Raidió na Gaeltachta – in 1972. By the era of the Celtic Tiger in the 1990s there had been another ideological shift to a more (neo-)liberal and individualist perspective. This perspective is based on a rational choice model in which individuals are understood to act 'rationally' to maximise their own advantage.

This has been the approach employed by the state in its language policy only in recent decades. Briefly we can see that initially the Irish language was raised up by Irish intellectuals in the late nineteenth and early twentieth century as a symbol of the Irish nation and that subsequently the Irish state imposed the Irish language on its citizens as a method of producing a distinctively Irish nation. These methods employed by the young state were intended to create a fully Irish-speaking nation and were of little benefit to the existing Irish speakers in the Gaeltacht. In response, during the 1960s, there was a Gaeltacht movement which reflected the civil rights movements in other places such as Northern Ireland and the United States of America. This paralleled or even opposed the national linguistic policy. The restoration policy benefited the urban middle class the most as they had the best access to the employment advantages created by the policy. As a result of this movement the Irish speakers in the Gaeltacht were recognised as a minority and the state became more active in the Gaeltacht. During this era the state, amongst other endeavours, attempted to industrialise the Gaeltacht, founded a Gaeltacht community radio station (Raidió na Gaeltachta) and a Gaeltacht authority (Údarás na Gaeltachta). By the 1990s it was recognised that although there was little which could be called an Irish-speaking community outside the Gaeltacht, there were far more Irish speakers spread throughout the country. Based on the estimated figures discussed above, the Gaeltacht Irish speakers are only ten to 20 per cent of the total population of Irish speakers in the country as a whole.

Although elements of the nation-building era still exist, these days the role of the state appears to be one of providing individuals with the (rational) choice to learn and to speak Irish. Although much is left to individual initiative, the state has been involved in quite a few developments relating to the Irish language in recent years. One already mentioned is the consolidation of Irish language state organisations into Foras na Gaeilge with an all-island remit. Another development which has been mentioned above is the establishment of an Irish language television station at a cost to the state of about IR£12,000,000 per annum initially and about €30,000,000 per annum in recent years. Much of the campaign for Teilifís na Gaeilge (later TG4) was founded on minority rights arguments. By the time the broadcasting began, the minority rights era had already begun to shift to one in which individual rights were paramount. The emergence of TG4 (initially TnaG) represents a point at which there was a shift from minority rights to individual rights and from an emphasis on the Gaeltacht to an emphasis on Irish speakers generally. Pádhraic Ó Ciardha (from TG4) made this clear when he claimed that the *raison d'être* of the channel was to provide a new television service for the Irish public as a whole and that it just happened to be in Irish.[7]

Language and identity

Although the Irish language is still regarded by much of the population as an important symbol of the Irish nation, it has largely remained just that – a symbol. In a recent survey 89 per cent of the respondents agreed that 'promoting the Irish language is important to the country as a whole' (MORI Ireland 2004: 7). This percentage is divided between 57 per cent who also agree that 'promoting the Irish language is important to me personally' and 32 per cent who also agree that 'promoting the Irish language is not important to me personally'. In effect these percentages illustrate the continuing importance of the Irish language as a symbol of the Irish nation – not a commitment to actually speak Irish.

While the Irish language is still a relevant symbol of Irish national identity, it is necessary also to examine the relevance of nationality to social identity in contemporary Ireland. In the International Social Survey Programme module on national identity in 2003 respondents were asked to choose from a list the most important item with which they identify. By far the most important aspect of social identity in Ireland was family or marital status (40 per cent). In an international context of 33, mostly European, countries the percentage is the same or higher in northern European countries as well as Australia, New Zealand, Canada and the United States of America, but lower in southern and eastern European countries. Nationality was the second choice in Ireland (16 per cent), way behind marital status, followed closely by occupation (15.9 per cent) and quite far behind that came gender (8.5 per cent) and religion (eight per cent). In the international context nationality was in fourth place (nine per cent) – much lower than in Ireland.

The importance of nationality is evident in only a few countries other than Ireland. In Europe, Poland (14 per cent), Bulgaria (15 per cent) and France (16 per cent) came close; further afield there was Israel (Jews: 18 per cent and Arabs: 13 per cent), Japan (15 per cent), Uruguay (15 per cent) and Venezuela (16 per cent). These figures are based on the first choice respondents made. The respondents were allowed to choose three items. When the figures are added together, around half of the respondents in Ireland chose nationality as one of the three most important groups with which they identify. This compares with about one third across the 33 countries in the survey. These figures suggest that nationality, although not the most important, is, nonetheless, a very important aspect of social identity in contemporary Ireland.

As long as the Irish nation remains a relevant construct the boundary around the nation will be maintained against the 'other'. Who that other is will influence the relevance of the Irish language to national identity. For many years the state was the most important actor connecting national identity and the Irish language. However, the state has long been withdrawing its policy of producing an Irish-speaking nation and in recent years has focused more on Irish speakers as individuals. One of the clearest examples of this is in the Official Languages Act 2003.

The purpose of the Act is to promote the use of the Irish language for official purposes in the state: in parliament, in the administration of justice, in public bodies, as well as in communicating with or providing services to the public. The Act also established a Coimisinéir Teanga (Language Commissioner) whose principal responsibility is to monitor how public bodies comply with the Act. Essentially this Act makes it possible for Irish speakers as individuals to conduct their business with the state in Irish. In the Coimisinéir Teanga's annual report in 2005, however, there is evidence that there may not be sufficient Irish speakers in the civil service and that they are not being compensated as directed by Government. The Coimisinéir reported that

> in the period since the Government's decision to end compulsory Irish for posts and promotions in the civil service in 1974, four circulars on the matter have been issued by the Department of Finance. These circulars directed that additional marks for competency in both Irish and English be awarded as an alternative to the requirement of compulsory Irish. (Coimisinéir Teanga 2006: 39)

The Coimisinéir went on to argue that although 'it is clear that this system of additional marks was the cornerstone of State policy to ensure that a sufficient number of people competent to provide services in Irish would be available at various levels of the civil service' (Coimisinéir Teanga 2006: 39), half the departments had not been awarding the additional marks. The Coimisinéir also reported that only three per cent of the Department of Education and Science's administrative staff were competent to provide services in Irish. This is a drastic change in a department in which, more than half a century ago, Irish was the working language.

The state has continued to promote the Irish language and appears likely to do so for the foreseeable future. Late in 2006 the government announced that a 20-year plan for the Irish language would be forthcoming within the following two years. Several months later, in early 2007, the Irish language was included in the National Development Plan for 2007–13.

Another interesting recent development has been the acceptance of the Irish language as an official working language of the European Union. This was decided at a meeting of the Foreign Ministers of the EU countries on 13 June 2005 to come into effect on 1 June 2007. It is interesting to consider why the Irish state promoted the Irish language as an official working language of the EU in 2005 and had failed to do so when Ireland joined the European Economic Community (EEC), as it was called, more than three decades ago. The answer can be discovered partly in the relationship between the Irish language and the nation.

In the 1970s, when Ireland joined the EEC there was a de-emphasis of nationalist elements such as the Irish language. Initially there had been a shift away from the earlier policies of building the nation, but later, as a result of the violence in Northern Ireland, nationalism took a new turn and the state began to oppose its own earlier nation building efforts (see Watson 1996). In this context the Irish language was regarded as contrary to the EEC's purposes of uniting European countries which had formerly been divided by nationalist ideologies. By 2005, however, the state had passed through a phase of regarding the Irish language as a minority language and begun to regard it as a language spoken by many individuals. Also, fundamentally, the EU had begun to take notice of the many minority languages within its jurisdiction, especially since the adoption of the European Charter for Regional or Minority Languages in 1992.[8] In this context the Irish state could follow the European trend and regard Irish speakers as having individual rights to speak Irish.

Although the recent inclination has been for the state to treat the Irish language as a language spoken by many individuals, it has continued to regard it as a language of symbolic importance. There is also evidence that a large percentage of people in Ireland continue to regard nationality as an important social identity and the Irish language as an important aspect of it. The fact that the Irish language remains of symbolic importance is not an indication of its usage. The situation appears to be that today, although 89 per cent of the population regard Irish as important for the country as a whole (MORI Ireland 2004), only 39 per cent (down three per cent from 1995) (from ISSP 2003 national identity data) regard speaking Irish as important to being Irish. It appears that the Irish language remains important to national identity, but is primarily of symbolic importance. People are more likely to point to traits they believe they already have as being important to national identity, such as Catholicism (57 per cent) or Irish ancestry (81 per cent) (from ISSP 2003 national identity data), rather than traits they may have to work hard to acquire. This means that the existence of the Irish language is more important than its actual use, except in those few times when individuals want to establish their Irishness in the face of some 'other'.

The future of Irish: the role of schools

The survival of the Irish language as a spoken language appears to remain in a precarious position. Irish as a community language in the Gaeltacht has continued to decline while, over the generations, secondary bilinguals (people who have learnt Irish as a second language) have replaced these Irish speakers. Languages are normally passed on from one generation to the next within the family and wider community. In Ireland the education system appears to have played a crucial role in producing these secondary bilinguals. In the 1950s and 1960s there was a reduction in the number of all-Irish schools. In the following decades there were other changes which made the Irish language a less compulsory subject in the schools, for example in 1973 'the necessity to pass Irish in order to pass the Leaving, Intermediate and Group Certificate examinations was dropped' (Kelly 2002: 38). Such changes, as well as changes in the Irish language curriculum, may have resulted in a more general positive attitude to Irish, but also reduced the state's ability to mass produce Irish speakers.

In recent years Irish speakers more clearly have become a minority. They have their own radio stations, their own television channel, their own schools and the right to use Irish in 'official' business has been reaffirmed. This minority is very fragmented with little community. Following the closure or conversion to English of all-Irish schools in the 1950s and 1960s new all-Irish schools were established from the 1970s onwards. Figure 20.1 presents the founding year of the all-Irish schools which exist today. These all-Irish school were established on the initiative of parents' groups and Irish language organisations. Initiative for establishing all-Irish schools moved from the state to civil society. Although the increase in the number of all-Irish schools appears dramatic in the graph, it represents only schools which exist today and therefore conceals the disappearance of all-Irish schools in the 1950s and 1960s. Furthermore, today only 2.3 per cent of all second level students receive their education partly or completely in Irish (Nic Ghiolla Phádraig and Kilroe 2002). There is still considerable scope for expansion, particularly when considering that about one in five people claimed in an ITÉ survey in the early 1990s that they would send their children to an all-Irish school if there was one nearby (Ó Riagáin and Ó Gliasáin 1994).

The increasingly positive attitude towards Irish and the simultaneous decreasing percentage of the population who regard speaking Irish as necessary for being Irish confirms that many of the elements weaved into national identity are strictly symbolic. That many people would be willing to send their children to all-Irish schools reflects the continuing importance of Irish for national identity, but also people's willingness for others to make the effort. This is no different from how the state's efforts to revive Irish were almost solely focused on the education system.

Figure 20.1 **Increasing number of all-Irish schools in the Republic of Ireland over time**[9]

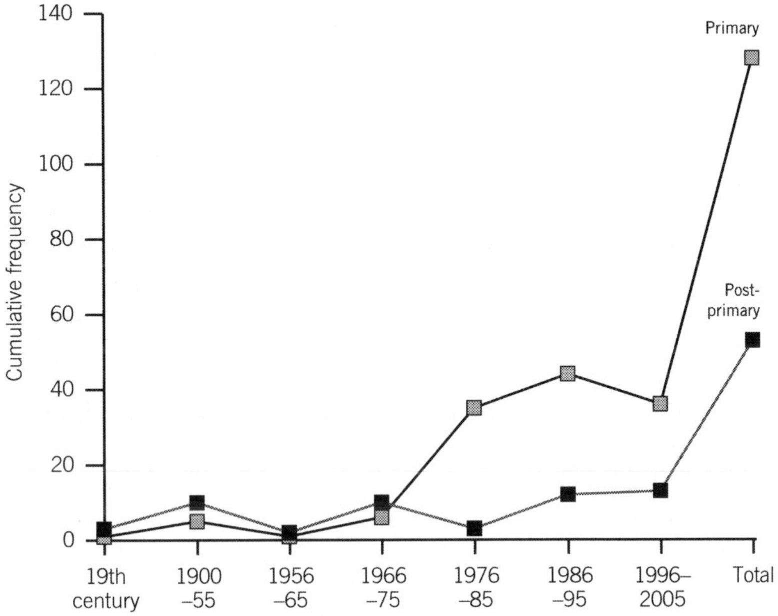

Source: Raw data from www.gaelscoileanna.ie on 13 March 2006.

From the founding of the state the emphasis on the Irish language in the education system and in state employment was primarily of benefit to the middle class who were better equipped to gain access to these positions via the education system. This was to such an extent that in the early 1980s the sociologist Michel Peillon claimed there were two groups of Irish speakers: the peasants in the Gaeltacht and the literati outside the Gaeltacht, mainly in Dublin (Peillon 1982). In Dublin in recent decades the majority of all-Irish schools have been established in middle-class areas. All-Irish primary schools were established in working class areas such as Tallaght and Kilbarrack in the 1980s and these were joined by more in other working-class areas such as Ballymun and Cabra in the 1990s. The production of Irish speakers was more effective in middle-class areas because these students tended to stay in school longer and to aspire to state employment. After the changes of the 1950s–1970s the Irish language was losing ground in working-class areas because the state was no longer providing the same grounding in Irish. With the establishment of all-Irish schools in working-class areas there is a gradual reintroduction of Irish to the working class. For this to be more effective there would be a need for a dramatic increase in the number of all-Irish second-level schools in working-class areas.

After finishing school, according to Murtagh (2003) 'participants from IC3 [immersion schools] were the most likely to continue to speak Irish, to read Irish and to write in Irish. These participants' access to Irish-speaking networks (generally outside of the home) emerged as a factor in facilitating use.' Irish-speaker networks have the potential to become denser in population centres such as Dublin, Cork, Limerick and Galway where there are a number of all-Irish schools. In Dublin there are places where Irish speakers can congregate, such as Club an Chonradh and the more recently established Café Úna and Club Sult. In Irish-speaking networks the chances are increased that Irish speakers will be able to raise their children through Irish both because there is increasing support from fellow Irish speakers and because the partner may also be an Irish speaker. This raises the possibility of the inter-generational transmission of the language within the family and various domains within which Irish can be spoken.

A major development in Irish society mentioned above is the diversity which results from the dramatic increase in the number of immigrants who have arrived in Ireland in the last ten years. Many of these immigrants have come from Eastern Europe and from Africa. This diversity is evident in Irish schools, including all-Irish schools to some extent. Language is a more inclusive element of identity because one can learn a new language, but one cannot create Irish ancestry and one may not wish to convert to Catholicism. It will be interesting to see how Irish national identity will develop in the coming few years. The Irish language could have a role to play.

Conclusion

Although the Irish language became important for national identity a long time ago, it has remained an important symbol of Irishness and appears likely to remain an aspect of national identity, at least in the short term. During the past decade there have been some interesting developments in relation to the Irish language, but despite these developments, the continuing importance of the Irish language to national identity means that the symbolic value of the Irish language overshadows more practical considerations such as Irish-speaking usage or ability. In fact the lived experience of the majority of people in Ireland appears likely to include less usage of Irish over the coming years. On the other hand, with the growth of all-Irish schools, Irish-speaking networks may become denser and the Irish-speaking minority may have more opportunity to use Irish. The ideological shift in state policy, which has resulted in Irish speakers being treated as individuals with linguistic rights, may also offer Irish speakers more opportunity in the longer term to use Irish. The Irish language, not the Irish speaker, is the symbol of Irish national identity. The existence of Irish and not its usage is all that is required for its symbolic use.

Because its boundary requires less regular maintenance, national identity is not of the same consistent importance as other social identities such as gender identity. It has remained, none the less, an important aspect of social identity in contemporary Ireland. As Ireland becomes a more multi-cultural and multi-lingual society it will be interesting to examine how the nation develops as a focus of identity and what role language (and not just the Irish language) will play in the future.

Chapter 21

Habitus, identity, and post-conflict transition in a Catholic working-class community in Northern Ireland

Patricia Lundy
Mark McGovern

Introduction

In 1998 Catholics in Northern Ireland voted overwhelmingly in favour of the Good Friday Agreement (GFA) and have continued to support it ever since. This is largely because the GFA marked a significant moment in the history, social position and attitudes of Northern Catholics. Since its inception in the 1920s Northern Ireland has generally been seen as something of a 'cold place' by (and for) Catholics. The experience of political, economic and social inequality framed the lives and outlook of Northern nationalists and were key causes of the conflict that broke out in 1968 and which over the next 30 years claimed some 3,600 lives (McKittrick et al. 1999). They were also conditions crucial for the development within the Catholic community of internal structures of mutual support and interdependence that often cut across class, locality and other potential lines of cleavage to foster a sense of collective interest and identity (Hepburn 1996; O'Connor 1993). That said, the extent of such cross-class collective solidarity may always have been something of a myth and would be put under real strain with the outbreak of the conflict. Nevertheless, this is what, throughout the history of the Northern state, constituted the organisational and spatial boundaries of the Northern Catholic community as a community.

The question is, has the experience of 30 years of conflict and (perhaps even more significantly) the processes of social and political change emerging as part of post-conflict transition changed that social reality and, as a result, impacted too on that sense of shared identity? Is there still a Northern Catholic community as such and if there is how does it live, experience and view the idea of being a distinct community? Indeed, this raises questions as to how we understand the very concept of 'community' itself. As Gerard Delanty has argued, the term has rarely been more popular in academic and political circles, although there are often very different approaches to understanding what it means (Delanty 2003). The aim of this chapter is therefore to explore the relationship between post-conflict transition, social experience and the formation of collective identity and community amongst Northern Irish Catholics today.

These are big questions, not easily addressed here. To understand community as a matter of *experience* and *practice* (as we will do) raises some difficult issues. Describing and defining everyday social experience – rather than, for example, the formal structure of social organisations – is a notoriously tricky sociological proposition that does not lend itself easily to broad-based methodological approaches. Similarly, the diversity of what we might better refer to as the multiplicity of Catholic identities, experiences and practices is not easily captured. So, rather than address the changing experience and meaning of community amongst Northern Catholics in general terms, the chapter will ultimately cast light on this question by focusing on a particular area and the way its people are facing up to the process of post-conflict transition. The area in question is Ardoyne, an overwhelmingly Catholic, nationalist, and/or republican working-class community of some 7,000 people in north Belfast that was at the forefront of the 30 years of conflict. There are some significant problems in coming to generalised conclusions from the particular experiences of this in some ways untypical community. However, there are also valid insights to be gained by such a focus.

We shall also explore the idea of community and transition by looking at one particular issue within Ardoyne. Ninety-nine people from the area were killed during the conflict, one of the highest rates of fatalities of any community in Northern Ireland (Ardoyne Commemoration Project 2002; Fay et al. 2000). How to deal with the legacy of the past, and the issue of victims in particular, has become an important and often rancorous subject of debate in the last decade. Within Ardoyne a particular problem was presented in the remembrance of all of its victims by divisions that had long existed over certain conflict-related deaths and funerals. Our aim is therefore to explore this issue as a prism through which we might view what can be termed the habitus within Ardoyne. The concept of habitus, particularly as developed in the work of French sociologist Pierre

Figure 21.1 **View of Ardoyne**

Bourdieu, is one that allows us to think about what frames and structures people's everyday experience. Given this focus, questions of habitus and identity will generally be explored in terms of relations *within* this community rather than *between* it and others.

In order to do this the chapter will therefore be divided into four parts. First, we shall briefly outline aspects of social change that are impacting upon Catholics as a whole in Northern Ireland before, in part two, looking at the social situation in Ardoyne. In part three we shall focus on the concept of habitus, particularly as developed in the work of Bourdieu (1990). For Bourdieu the idea of 'habitus' provides us with a means of thinking about the 'socialised subjectivity' through which people perceive and act in their everyday lives. This, it will be argued, provides us with a way to understand how people, at a local and everyday level, react to and cope with issues raised in a situation of conflict and post-conflict transition. Finally, in order to illustrate the workings of habitus, in part four we will concentrate on the example of divisions over conflict-related funerals in Ardoyne and the legacy left as part of post-conflict transition. Funerals are concerned with one of the most fundamental human relationships: the relationship with our dead. Here are crystallised key aspects of the socialised subjectivity of a community. In Ardoyne and other Northern Catholic working-class areas divisions over how certain conflict-related funerals should be conducted and treated profoundly disrupted the taken-for-granted expectation people had for these major life-cycle events. This evidenced a deep disjuncture and tension within the community's identity, polarised by the competition for local leadership between two key social institutions – the Catholic Church and the republican movement. The difficult, at times devastating, way in which these issues played out in Ardoyne (as in many Northern nationalist working-class communities during the conflict) will be explored. The chapter will therefore examine the processes evident today, in the wake of the conflict, for dealing with the legacy of victimhood at the local community level and how this reflects part of the wider story of the habitus of the Catholic community.

Social change and the Catholic community in Northern Ireland

Which social changes have impacted upon Northern Catholics and potentially created a shift in attitudes and sense of identity? What some regard as a growing sense of confidence amongst Northern Catholics may in part be due to demographic change. The proportion of Catholics in the Northern population has certainly grown in recent years. In 1971 they constituted 36.8 per cent of the total, 41.5 per cent by 1991 and 43.8 per cent by 2001, by which time over a quarter of Catholics (27 per cent) were under 16 years old compared to a fifth (20 per cent) of Protestants (Melaugh and McKenna 2002).

Life opportunities may also be changing for at least some Northern Catholics. Economic growth during the last decade has witnessed a significant fall in the overall levels of unemployment and underemployment from the socially devastating heights that marked the 1980s and early 1990s. Sectoral shifts have seen a decline in traditional occupations (for example in manufacturing) and a growth of white collar (particularly middle-class) labour markets where educational credentials are the primary means of accessing employment. Combined with the introduction of more robust measures to enforce equality, employment opportunities have opened up, most obviously in the public sector, for those Catholics in a position to take advantage of such changes (Shuttleworth and Osborne 2004). One result has been the growth of a potentially socially and politically influential Catholic middle class. In addition, Catholics from poorer backgrounds are on average more likely to outperform working-class Protestants in educational achievement; and the decline in manufacturing jobs, where Catholic access to employment had been limited, is also hitting the latter more than the former (Shuttleworth and Osborne 2004). That said, for those members of the Catholic community unable to avail themselves of such life chances, and facing multiple barriers of social exclusion, the story has been somewhat different and Catholics are still more likely to be unemployed than Protestants. One possible long-term consequence may be a tendency to undermine the mutuality of interest and the collective conception of equality that was a foundation of Catholic community identity. It might also mean that those communities facing marginalisation, social exclusion and high levels of social deprivation have to rely, as much if not more than ever, upon the internal resources at their disposal.

In what sense and to what extent are Catholics still Catholic? At the most obvious level, in terms of religious practice, there has been a significant diminution in regular Church attendance. In 1989 86 per cent of Catholics stated that they attended mass at least once a week. By 2001 this had fallen to 66 per cent (Lennon 2004: 3). However, this still represents one of the highest levels of regular religious observance in Europe. In 1999, 48 per cent of people living in Western Europe stated that they rarely if ever go to Church and only in Ireland and Italy do more than a third of the population attend a Church at least once a month (Ferguson 2004: 38). Similarly, while the social power of the Catholic Church has been profoundly undermined by scandals in recent years (such as that over clerical child sex abuse), Church leaders, particularly at a local level, often continue to enjoy an important role in community organisations and leadership. On the other hand, a growing ambivalence to the moral teaching of the Church, particularly in terms of sexual behaviour, is also a marked trend (Lennon 2004: 4) evidencing the limited role many Northern Catholics give to religion and religious teaching in their daily lives.

However, 'Catholic' as an ascription of identity in Northern Ireland goes far beyond the sphere of religiosity. As authors who have sought to define the meaning of the term sectarianism have observed, it has little enough to do with religion as such and much more to do with 'the determination of actions, attitudes and practices by belief about religious difference' (Brewer 1992: 352; see also McVeigh 1998). Such determinations and practices are also embedded in the structural and social realities of segregation and separation, particularly in terms of where people live, work and socialise. A report by Shuttleworth and Osborne (2004) suggests that an increasing number of people work in mixed workplaces although, despite many people's expressed desire to live in mixed areas, residential segregation continues to be a prominent feature of Northern Ireland life. Residential segregation increased significantly between 1971 and 2001 and although some evidence suggests this pattern has stabilised in the last decade (Shuttleworth and Lloyd 2006) there is little sign that it has declined and some have argued that the trend has been upward (Doherty and Poole 1995). It remains the case that at least two thirds of urban dwellers in Northern Ireland live in communities where an overwhelming majority of their neighbours are co-religionists. The pattern of residential segregation continues to be starkest within the working-class communities in the North's major towns and cities. In addition, marital endogamy and other markers of institutional separation (for example, in the education system) remain high.

Catholic social identity has also been closely intertwined with Irish nationalism and/or republicanism. Elections since the Good Friday Agreement have witnessed Sinn Féin replace the Social Democratic and Labour Party (SDLP) as the majority voice of Northern nationalists. In part, this has been dependent on the changing nature of Sinn Fein itself. The party's negotiation of the transition from conflict to post-conflict politics has seen the concept of equality gain an ever-greater prominence and this appears to find a resonance with the outlook and aspirations of most Northern Catholics (McGovern 2004). That said, this also reflects an apparently growing ease that many Catholics feel with self-identifying as Irish and/or nationalists. This is particularly marked amongst the young, with up to 77 per cent of young Catholics identifying themselves as 'Irish' in 2003 and 71 per cent viewing their national identity as either quite or very important (ARK 2003).

These changes in political outlook are undoubtedly closely linked to the end of the conflict and the processes of post-conflict transition which have emerged as a result. Indeed, the greater willingness to self-identify as nationalists may in no small part be due directly, at least for some Catholics, to the cessation of the IRA armed campaign. For others, and particularly those most directly involved in the conflict, that process of transition brought with it a range of different emotions and responses. Most obviously it offered an opportunity to reflect upon the impact and experience of the conflict itself. In a recent survey 18 per cent of Catholics said that they had been a victim of a violent conflict-related incident, 28 per cent stated that a member of their family or a close relative was either injured or killed and as many as 65 per cent said that they knew someone else who had been killed or injured in the conflict (ARK 2004). Whilst these figures apply to all Northern Catholics, conflict-related incidents, injuries and deaths were concentrated in certain areas far more than others (Fay et al. 2000). The places that suffered most were over-whelmingly working-class areas and this differential class experience of the conflict within the Catholic community has undoubtedly had a significant impact. The consequences of such suffering are also therefore likely to have left their mark to a greater extent within those communities where the conflict was primarily fought. This has been manifested not only in the direct social and psychological impact of deaths and injuries, but in a complex of legacies that conflict can leave in its wake.

Community and context in Ardoyne

While a growing 'post-industrial' economy had emerged in Northern Ireland, recent evidence suggests that patterns of social exclusion and poverty remain extensive and deeply entrenched. It has certainly meant little for areas like Ardoyne that are characterised by multiple forms of marginalisation. For example, more than a third of Northern Ireland's children are being brought up in households in poverty (Hillyard et al. 2003: 64). While Catholic children are 50 per cent of the total, they constitute 70 per cent of those living in the 20 per cent 'most deprived wards' in the North, some of which have child poverty rates of anything up to 90 per cent (McLaughlin and Monteith 2006: 100). Ardoyne is amongst those areas with the higher rates of child poverty (McLaughlin and Monteith 2006: 102). Such young people occupy what have been referred to as '"spaces of dispossession", growing up as excluded people in excluded families increasingly characterised by anti-social behaviour, insecurity and threat' (Hillyard et al. 2003: 65). Certainly such conditions frame life in Ardoyne and the problems facing its young people were highlighted in recent years both by the events of the Holy Cross dispute and a much-publicised wave of youth suicides which devastated the area (PIPS Project 2005). Nor is it insignificant that, with over half of the community being under 25 years of age, Ardoyne has one of the highest levels of youth population anywhere in the North. In a recent study of 'multi-deprivation' conducted for Belfast City Council Ardoyne also emerged as one of the ten per cent most severely deprived areas throughout Northern Ireland (Belfast City Council 2005). Any consideration of the processes of identity formation needs to be cognisant of these salient objective structural circumstances.

The material realities of sectarian division are an important part of that story. The segregation of space continues to influence social networks, practices and everyday experience in many parts of the North, but perhaps nowhere more so than in North Belfast. Already a mosaic of sharply drawn 'confessional villages', the fact that more than 20 per cent of all conflict-related deaths took place within a single square mile of North Belfast (including roughly seven out of ten of all explicitly sectarian killings during the conflict) has only served to reinforce spatial division (Fay et al. 2000). Historically this sectarian social geography has done much to define the community life of Ardoyne. While today it is far less isolated than it once was, and the sense of vulnerability that pervaded the area through much of the conflict has to some extent dissipated, Ardoyne remains an enclave Catholic community bordered on three sides by Protestant working-class areas. Indeed recent studies have shown that the peace process has done little to break down the fear, distrust and lack of everyday contact that has long characterised social relations between communities here (Shirlow 1999). Again, this was brought into sharp focus during the Holy Cross dispute and in the tensions that have accompanied the annual 'Tour of the North' Orange parade. The apparent religious homogeneity of the area that is the result has important ramifications for social life in the area, more of which later. So too do the low-level interface tensions that sporadically erupt into larger scale affairs, and that continue to be part and parcel of everyday experience (Jarman 2002a). Again, this has a particular impact on young people. Growing up 'on the interface' represents an additional 'space of dispossession' and compounds their social marginalisation. In addition, and despite a growth of social exclusion and poverty in neighbouring Protestant working-class areas, Catholics in areas like Ardoyne are still significantly more likely to be unemployed than Protestants, evidencing an ongoing issue of Catholic socio-economic disadvantage. Catholic wards are significantly over-represented amongst those with the highest rates of poverty and unemployment and Ardoyne is counted amongst them.

Proportionately, Ardoyne suffered more casualties than most during the conflict. As well as the 99 fatal victims from the area many more were injured and subject to attack. Some events, such as the attacks on the area in August 1969, became ingrained in the collective memory, framing the attitudes and actions not only of those alive at the time but transmitted to future generations. Many people from Ardoyne also became directly involved in the conflict themselves. The Irish Republican Army (IRA) was very active in Ardoyne and many of its residents in various ways participated in it. It is also estimated that roughly a third of all males of adult age spent at least some time in prison for conflict-related reasons. Equally significant was the impact of state counter-insurgency strategies, particularly in terms of the near saturation surveillance. At one time there were over a dozen watch towers situated in and around this relatively small geographical area and this was combined with regular military patrols. Loyalist paramilitaries were responsible for the majority of attacks and deaths of people from the area, but roughly one in four were killed directly by the state amid persistent allegations of collusion between loyalist and state forces (Ardoyne Commemoration Project 2002). The use of informers and psychological operations were also designed to instil a sense of insecurity and vulnerability. These factors combined to create a heightened sense of alienation from the state and distrust of its various agencies, or indeed potentially anyone unknown within the community.

The combination of these factors resulted in an already tight-knit community turning in on itself. Far from being some abstract process, this turning inward was manifested and lived out in everyday practice. For example, socialising took place almost exclusively within the area. In the worst years of the conflict the threat of sectarian attack or being caught up in a bomb blast made travelling to and from the city centre (or merely in and out of the area) for an evening's entertainment a potentially dangerous affair. Many of the local pubs and bars were either destroyed in the initial phase of the conflict or occupied positions that made them vulnerable to attack. As a result, a string of drinking and social clubs sprung up within Ardoyne. Some were identified clearly with the republican movement, others were not. Almost always sited away from the geographical fringes these clubs in turn were invariably windowless and, latterly, surrounded by security doors, fences and cameras. They also formed a key focus for social networks and activities within the community. The Ardoyne Kickham's GAA club is a case in point. Gaelic games can themselves be viewed as the everyday living out of a social, cultural and political identity, and certainly this was reinforced by the circumstances the community was facing. The club also formed an important nexus within the community, an institutional locus for important social bonds. And, of course, almost everyone who took part in the various activities associated with this and the other clubs was from Ardoyne. Social contact with people from outside the community was restricted and limited, particularly at the height of the conflict. The peace process has impacted upon this situation, but it is a slow thaw. While needing to be set against the many positives, the end of the conflict may have also have brought with it a new atmosphere of uncertainty and undermined a sense purpose that adversity can help engender.

Understanding habitus: the work of Pierre Bourdieu

In order to explore the legacies of the conflict in Ardoyne and how they impact upon the lived experience of people in the area we are going to employ the concept of 'habitus'. As developed primarily by Pierre Bourdieu, 'habitus' has gained an important place in contemporary sociology, although it is certainly not without its critics (Calhoun 1993; Jenkins 2002; Lau 2004). For advocates of the term, 'habitus' forms a key element of Bourdieu's wider project to develop ways of thinking about the social world that avoid, or (as he himself suggested) 'transcend', some of the traditional categories evident in much sociological theory. The concept of 'habitus' is particularly designed to circumvent the dualisms of the 'objective' and the 'subjective', of structure and agency, as means of explaining social action. For Bourdieu the problem with 'objectivist' explanations is that they tend to focus too much on the idea that people's actions are determined by social structures. On the other hand, subjectivism over-emphasises the idea that people act intentionally, on the basis of their own conscious choices and decisions. For Bourdieu the way in which people live 'in practice', the way (in other words) they go about their everyday lives, is undoubtedly profoundly affected by social structures, and may involve conscious, intended actions. However, while both are necessary they are not sufficient to explain how people think, act and live. Indeed, what Bourdieu is trying to get away from is this separation of the interior world of mind and body – of consciousness – from the exterior world of an 'objective reality', in our efforts to understand how society works and how people experience how it works. A key way of breaking down that separation is his concept of 'habitus'.

So what does Bourdieu mean by 'habitus'? First it should be said that this raises a number of problems. The way Bourdieu used the term changed over time. It was also often unclear, at different times, precisely what it was meant to mean. Indeed, one major source of criticism for many is that the concept is largely under-theorised. However, in his classic work *The Logic of Practice* (1990) Bourdieu did provide a useful definition of habitus. He described them as 'systems of durable, transposable dispositions' (Bourdieu 1990: 53), to be understood as 'structured structures predisposed to function as structuring structures'. People, Bourdieu suggested, are predisposed to think, act and perceive the world in certain systematic ways that are so much part and parcel of themselves that they become unconscious, literally habitual ways of being. It is in this sense that he thought of such influences on behaviour as becoming 'embodied'. This should not be taken to mean that habitus is little more than a bodily motor skill, rather that such practices are 'non-reflective', derived from experience and become part of the self in a very literal, 'embodied', sense (Lau 2004: 376). In other words these 'dispositions' are internalised, becoming such an intrinsic part of someone's make-up that they do not require a sense of self-awareness to impact on action. As a consequence a person's sense of themselves, and how they act upon that sense of self, is not always a matter of conscious reflection but is rather 'naturalised': understood as the way one simply should act and think given that things are the way things are.

Bourdieu is not, of course, saying such dispositions are actually natural; they are very much a matter of social construction, as 'structured structures'. Two things are primarily involved in shaping these systems of dispositions, in structuring these structures. The first is past experience. Bourdieu places great emphasis upon time as a key frame for understanding how practice happens, and the habitus is very much understood as 'a product of history [that] produces individual and collective practices – more history – in accordance with the schemes generated by history' (Bourdieu 1990: 54). The second, is what Bourdieu terms the 'social field'. By this Bourdieu means a 'structured system of social positions' (Jenkins 2002: 85). The occupants of these positions are also involved in power relations *vis-à-vis* each other on the basis of the extent of limits of their access to 'resource', or different forms of capital. For Bourdieu 'capital' is not solely understood as economic resources (although economic resources are extremely important) but also in cultural, symbolic and social terms.

Ultimately it is therefore the interaction of the habitus and the social field that produces the context within which practice will occur. Yet people still act in this context; there is still a degree to which this context is not all-determining. This is important for Bourdieu in his attempt to get away from what he saw as the straitjacket of determinism, where social action is governed by rules rooted in structure. Structures, he suggests, may shape and frame collective and individual assumptions and actions but they will not lead to a given outcome in each and every case; not always, in other words, in practice. He therefore places great emphasis upon the contingency of experience itself. People encounter issues, problems or events in real time and space. While habitus provides a framework for understanding and acting in this context what people think and do in any given instance is not wholly determined. It will also be dependent on how, both individually and collectively, experience informs strategies to deal with those moments. In this sense habitus should be understood as itself changing through time, both determining and being determined by experience. For Bourdieu, people therefore develop strategies, based on circumstance, framed by the social field, and rooted to some degree or other on the dispositions of their habitus (Jenkins 2002: 82–4). This, then, is the process through which people live out their lives.

The concept of habitus also helps us to focus on the taken-for-granted aspects of social and political identity. Much analysis of political identities tends to look at the nature of competing political ideologies. It is entirely valid

to subject to scrutiny the nature of party political programmes, the machinations of political actors and policy makers or the expressed views and opinions
of different sections of the population. However, this is often describing a
world of interests, rational considerations and political calculation. Habitus,
on the other hand, draws our attention elsewhere, to the way in which
identities can be inscribed and expressed in the day-to-day way people see
themselves and go about their lives. It also points to the importance of the
pre-reflective aspects of identity and how these may be enmeshed and
embedded in the signs, symbols and discourses of social, cultural and political
markers of belonging and difference. This is to understand social and political
identity as interwoven with the very fabric of the everyday lives of social actors
and their commonsensical sense of the world they inhabit.

One of the advantages of Bourdieu's theoretical framework is that it
provides a means to analyse the role of both macro and micro social forces on
the structures, practices and processes of identity formation in a local
community. The multi-faceted nature of social identity is in large part derived
from the complex nature of contemporary society. In order to grasp how
identity is lived and practised it is therefore necessary to keep such complexity
in mind, to avoid the urge to over-simplify, and to identify the diffusion of
influences that shape identity.

It is also necessary to be conscious of the means at the disposal of a
community like Ardoyne to deal with these issues, what Bourdieu has called
its 'social capital'. This concept is important in Bourdieu's work. For Bourdieu
(1986: 248) social capital can be understood as 'the aggregate of the actual or
potential resources which are linked to possession of a durable network of
more or less institutionalised relationships of mutual acquaintance and
recognition – in other words, to membership in a group'. Group membership
produces a specific combination of (stronger or weaker) social and cultural
resources upon which the group member can depend (or not) as a means by
which to negotiate the world around them (Lane 2000). These can be deeply
affected by social and economic conditions and by long-term and deeply
divisive conflict.

Coming to terms with the past: habitus, identity and funerals in Ardoyne

The conflict-related processes impacting upon Ardoyne reinforced the already
existing and extremely strong family and kinship ties which have provided a
key framework for the collective life of the community. Loyalty to place, to a
set of shared social and cultural symbols and to wider political identities are
closely bound up with these affective bonds of community, friendship and

family. These 'durable networks' of 'mutual acquaintance and recognition' similarly flow into and through the social institutions that matter in the area. Two are particularly significant: the Catholic Church and the republican movement. It is therefore important when understanding how these institutions function not to disaggregate them from this embedded character. The way such institutions work at a localised level is often dependent upon the extent to which they can call upon, shape or are seen as an integral part of this less formal nexus of social relations. It is also one of the ways that the ideas and practices of such social institutions can become part and parcel of the taken-for-granted view of the world that people in the area come to hold.

Of course, it needs to be said that the authority of such institutions can also be very much a matter of exerting far less benign forms of power and control. As a counterpoint to Bourdieu we also need to understand that dispositions can be collectively orchestrated and regulated. Indeed, another criticism levelled at Bourdieu's conception of habitus and his theory of practice is that it does not have a comprehensive perspective on the social role and nature of institutions (Jenkins 2002: 90). Understanding how habitus works does also require a complex view of its relationship to conscious action directed explicitly at obedience to rules. Both the republican movement and the Catholic Church are powerful social institutions capable of enforcing, through various means, both formal and informal rules in operation. Republicanism and Catholicism also represent distinct ideological traditions, historically rooted, consciously structured bodies of thought and practice directed toward specific ends. At one level, there is little here of pre-cognitive habitus.

However, it is precisely because the frames for seeing the world constituted through both Irish republicanism and Catholicism are so much part and parcel of an everyday worldview for so many, socialised within a wide range of family and community settings that embed them in the habits of living, that they are such powerful influences on everyday practice. In like manner, the symbiotic relationship between community and organisation evident in processes such as the development of alternative justice systems says a great deal about what happens when expectations for social action are not lived out, or change. This is also highly dependent on context and the onset and long years of the conflict, for all the mutual dependence it instilled also had a deeply disturbing and fracturing effect on social life in Ardoyne. In the midst of such social flux the local Catholic Church and republicans struggled to establish a particular definition of what the ethnographer Frank Burton, in his classic study of 'Anro' (in fact Ardoyne) in the early 1970s called 'Catholic social consciousness': the worldview of people in the community (Burton 1978). In other words, achieving social and political leadership depended upon being able to connect their social outlook with the taken-for-granted understanding of, and practices in, the changed and charged environment within which the community found itself.

Tensions developed around two interlinked issues: the attitude to political violence and community development. Largely masked in the early years of the conflict, arguments between the Church and republicans over whether or not, and in what circumstances, the use of political force could be justified grew fiercer over time (Burton 1978; McElroy 1991). Differences became particularly acute in the wake of the republican hunger strike of 1981, the emergence of Sinn Féin's 'armalite and ballot box' strategy and the consequent rise in the party's electoral support. The ideological ground upon which this struggle for community leadership was fought was the question of political violence. However, the practical terrain was the question of community development and employment. As part of a shift in strategy from the early 1980s, republicans became increasingly involved in community politics. Many such community activists were ex-prisoners. In response the British government introduced a system of political vetting to exclude people they viewed as politically undesirable from such community development work (Political Vetting of Community Work Working Group 1990). It was part of a co-ordinated drive to contain republicanism socially and politically. The Thatcher government also sought alternative avenues through which to channel investment in community development. Church-led organisations became a prime conduit for such funding and this led to a great deal of often bitter division and antagonism. The creation of the Flax Centre in Ardoyne in the early 1980s was a case in point. By the late 1980s relations between these two key local social institutions had reached an all-time low.

It was in this context that disputes over the treatment of funerals, such as that of leading Ardoyne republican Larry Marley, arose. Larry Marley was shot dead in his home by loyalists in June 1987 (Ardoyne Commemoration Project 2002: 418–28). As part of its drive to cut off what it called the 'oxygen of publicity' to republicans, the British government had adopted a policy of mass policing and violent disruption of republican funerals from the early 1980s onwards. Larry Marley's funeral became a focus for these struggles. For three days the cortège was prevented from leaving the family home in the heart of Ardoyne by a huge force of RUC. Eventually, accompanied by a massive crowd, the coffin made its way to the local Holy Cross Chapel for the funeral mass. However, restrictions imposed by the Church limited the nature of the mass and local priests refused to take part in the graveside ceremony if any republican regalia or rituals were involved. Memories of these actions proved to be extremely long-lasting. But why, and what does this reveal?

At its heart the battle over funerals was part of the struggle between the forces of the state (and the RUC in particular) on the one hand and republicanism (and indeed the wider Ardoyne community) on the other.

Figure 21.2 **RUC presence at Larry Marley's funeral**

However, that the local Catholic Church adopted a position and actions that placed it at odds with the latter and seemingly in support of the former is what is of interest here. Funerals were one of the few inevitable points of very public contact between the Church and republicans. In addition, they need to be seen as a complex, ritualised and deeply emotive arena of practice for the display and demonstration of collective solidarity and identity. Embedded in history and culture, the practices that go to make up such funerals are also emblematic of the durable dispositions that constitute the specific habitus of the Northern Catholic working-class experience. Funerals had also largely been seen as, literally, sacrosanct, outside the realm of political division within the community. Some had previously been subject to political dispute and attack (indeed a loyalist bomb had killed two people at a funeral in Ardoyne in 1977) but this was more the exception than the rule. Crucially, such incidents also involved attacks from without and could thus occasion a heightened sense of internal empathy and cohesion. Disputes over funerals such as that of Larry Marley were different. What was revealed now was a fundamental fissure within Ardoyne between the two poles of parish and community. But because it concerned something as fundamental as the collective social practices involved in the burying of the dead it also revealed a crisis in the taken-for-granted view of the world and how one should act in it. Identity of Church, nation, community and family may often be unproblematised, unconscious, taken as read. But the crisis over the funerals meant that people had to consider the divisions revealed in the world around them of things they usually saw as unitary. As a result, they could not ignore a tension revealed in their own sense of themselves and had to adapt as a result. The legacy was the lasting memories that many maintained of these events, whether directly involved in them or not.

Nor were these funerals the only ones that created such tensions within. Quite as troubling, if in a very different way, was the treatment of the funerals and families of informers. A number of people in Ardoyne had been killed by the IRA as alleged informers throughout the years of conflict. However, the issue of informers had always been something of a taboo subject in the area. The social opprobrium accorded to people accused of informing is something again deeply rooted in the culture and history of Northern Catholic working-class communities. This was only heightened during the long years of the conflict and the increasing likelihood that informers, if caught, were killed. Obviously this impacted most upon the families of the dead but there was a wider social impact too. Traditionally, attending wakes and funerals is an extremely important means of evidencing personal and communal recognition and support within the Irish Catholic, working-class culture of Ardoyne. However, the exigencies of war had prevented such a display for certain victims and families and this left its mark not only upon those families but on a far wider circle of people within the community as well. The result was a legacy of pent-up, unarticulated emotions, experiences and memories, a sense of having failed to live up to the demands of decency that were an ingrained, pre-conscious aspect of people's sense of the world. The consequence, again, of a socialised subjectivity and sense of identity thrown into flux by the conflict.

This was the context for the attempts that have emerged in Ardoyne since the signing of the Good Friday Agreement to come to terms with such internal division over the past. Central to this has been the work carried out since 1998 of a community-based 'truth-telling' initiative, the Ardoyne Commemoration Project (ACP), which collated and published 300 testimonies of the relatives and friends of the community's 99 conflict-related victims. The book that was the result, *Ardoyne: the Untold Truth*, was designed to commemorate the lives of those who had died. It soon became clear on the night of its launch, in August 2002 in the Ardoyne GAA club, that this event itself was an act of collective commemoration. Around 500 people were at the launch, almost all were from Ardoyne and the majority were the invited relatives and friends of those who had died. Several speakers had been invited to address the gathering including a local Catholic priest Fr Aidan Troy. Fr Troy had risen to some prominence as a result of his leading role in opposing the loyalist blockade of the nearby Holy Cross Catholic girls' primary school (Cadwallader 2004; Troy 2005). However, no one expected his speech to have the impact that it did.

Fr Troy issued a public apology, on behalf of the local Church, for the way in which the funeral of Larry Marley had been handled. This not only had a massive effect upon those gathered in the hall that night, but became a major talking point throughout the area in the weeks and months to come. It has also been seen as part of a wider process of *rapprochement* between various sections of the community, particularly those associated with the Church and the republican movement working in community development.

After the launch the authors conducted a series of interviews to find out from people who had participated in the work of the book what effect it had upon them (Lundy and McGovern 2005, 2006). Amongst them was a relative of a conflict victim who exemplified the attitude of many when he said:

> Through the whole informer thing the book actually liberated people's thoughts because you were quite happy that they were there and that they were able to cry and do all the things and have all that support. Because it was as if, when it actually happened to them [the death], while people would have sympathised or empathised with them nobody showed it here but secretly they did . . . when someone was killed . . . you know their brothers and their sisters and their ma and da and even most of the time you knew the person who was killed . . . so it [the book] was good because there was a healing process that has to happen in the district.

For this person (a lifelong republican) it had been hugely important that the fate of informers and alleged informers had been raised. Even more significant was that the treatment of their families and funerals had been highlighted. The presence of many of these families at the launch meeting had been regarded as particularly vital in developing a healing process. This again had involved the opening up of a previously excluded subject of dialogue within the community that was seen to have had far wider social consequences.

In both the case of mistreated republican funerals and those of alleged informers the process of post-conflict transition has provided the possibility of revisiting difficult memories and opening up alternative ways to deal with them collectively. A social space had been opened up, at least within the community, to confront the dilemmas people had faced when their taken-for-granted view of the world was profoundly challenged by what was happening around them. The public apology for the Church's role in Larry Marley's funeral, and the collective acknowledgement of the community's shunning of those of alleged informers, were welcomed with a palpable sense of relief that was an echo of a wider reaction to the end of conflict. This centred on a tension that had long existed within the community, and within people themselves, about the rights and wrongs of political violence. For people in an area like Ardoyne this was no distant argument, but part and parcel of their daily experience, of their habitus. That tension was all the greater when the two social institutions central to the structural context of local community living and collective social identity were profoundly at odds with one another. The socialised subjectivity of being, at one and the same time, both Catholic and nationalist/republican could not, in this context, be relegated to the realms of habitus, of a pre-cognitive conception of practice in the world. Choices had to be made, and these involved a social and emotional cost. Such dilemmas were all the more difficult because of the isolation of a community at violent odds both with the state and near neighbours. Social and economic marginalisation, sectarian division and the impact of the conflict made reliance on the durable networks of community a key aspect of collective living. Yet it was precisely these that were challenged by the crisis in intra-community relations exemplified by the tension over the treatment of funerals.

Conclusion

What does this case study of the experiences of contentious conflict-related funerals in Ardoyne reveal about the habitus of Northern Catholics? How to act in relation to the funerals of republicans and alleged informers threw people's taken-for-granted view of the world into crisis. The disputes had such a long-term impact not only because this was a struggle between two key social institutions within the community but because for people in the area how to act in such circumstances had previously been so habitual, 'non-reflective' and 'embodied'. Those actions were also ways of expressing, consciously or not, what it meant to be from Ardoyne and to be a Northern Catholic and/or nationalist. The crisis over the funerals, in this sense, very much happened within people and between them, and could only ultimately be resolved in a similar way, through practice. In doing so, we can see an example of the everyday working through of what a Northern Catholic identity looks and feels like, in practice, in a working-class community like Ardoyne.

The onset of the peace process has created new possibilities. The signing of the Good Friday Agreement and the gradual process of post-conflict transition has had a massive impact on the everyday lives of people in Ardoyne as elsewhere. The combination of high tech surveillance and a regular military presence has largely gone away. Interface tensions, whilst still apparent, have at least partly changed in character and consequences. However, many other problems remain and have been joined by new ones, not least the issues facing the area's young people. Unlike those able increasingly to benefit from new economic growth and the mainstreaming of equality, communities like those in Ardoyne are facing a range of difficulties and dilemmas. The capacity to tackle these relies in no small part upon the durable networks and social capital of which community and grassroots organisations are only the most visible part. Confronting past divisiveness is also therefore a crucial way of providing the community with better means to deal with the issues it now faces. It was a collective strategy, born out of the contingency of the experience of conflict, that could convert that experience into a resource or capacity upon which the community could call in the present. This may be seen as one of the most significant outcomes of the public apology for the Church's treatment of a funeral that happened 15 years before, and the acknowledgement of the loss suffered by the families of alleged informers. Nor were such actions and strategies necessarily the result of conscious and interest-driven decisions. Rather, they were derived from a *sense* of what was needed in the current climate. A sense derived from an often unspoken shared understanding of the socialised subjectivity of (at least significant sections of) a community, emerging from long years of conflict and violence, facing up to new dilemmas for the future. In this sense, in the manner that the habitus of a community constitutes the means through which it handles experiences collectively, the rapprochement over divisive funerals in Ardoyne might be taken as emblematic of the wider and diverse ways in which post-conflict transition is being lived out in the socially excluded working-class Catholic areas of the North.

Chapter 22

Protestants and Protestant habitus in Northern Ireland

Ronnie Moore

But I cannot deny my past to which my self is wed,
The woven figure cannot undo its thread.

Louis MacNeice

Introduction and background

This chapter focuses on Protestants and Protestant identity in Northern Ireland. It draws together key recent themes hitherto undeveloped which are of sociological relevance. This emphasises separate, but interlinked issues. First, it seeks to explore distinctive Protestant and Catholic values and lifestyles which separate each from the other. Secondly, it draws out recent important differences within Protestantism. Thirdly, it suggests that the basis for categorising identities in terms of traditional notions of ethnicity and religion in Northern Ireland is likely to become increasingly problematic.

From a global perspective, Northern Ireland is a very small Province lying at the outer most edge of the European shelf. It has a population of 1,685,000 people (1991 Census).[1] Yet the profile of its history and politics are well known around the world. Even today, it commands a disproportionately high level of attention from of Western world leaders. The reasons for this remarkable focus on the Province are found in a public and academic fascination and interest in Ireland's historical and more recent past. Ireland lies not only within Europe (the Irish Republic is itself an enthusiastic partner of the European Union), but it also links (what has sometimes been described in a somewhat Eurocentric fashion) the 'old world' with the 'new', through various migrations of Scots/Irish, and the later waves of Irish migration, particularly to America. The Irish became particularly dispersed throughout other newly discovered lands such as Canada and Australia and in more recent years they have gone to various parts of the European continent.

Northern and Southern Ireland have undergone rapid and significant changes. Economically, both parts of the island have travelled in different directions. The South of Ireland, within a relatively short timescale, has effectively been transformed from a mainly agrarian based economy into a leading world player in terms of production and output in highly specialised fields (*The Economist* 2004). It has established itself as a major magnet for high tech, high spec (mostly foreign) businesses and peripheral industries. Full membership to the European Economic Community (EEC) connected the Republic of Ireland into a global economy thereby reducing its historical economic dependence on Britain. It is now a major exporter of computers and electrical machinery, with equally major developments in the chemical/ pharmaceutical industries, and it has a telecommunications system which is one of the most sophisticated and advanced in Europe.

Northern Ireland, on the other hand, once a renowned and proud world leader in industry, trade and commerce, has been transformed into an industrial wasteland as traditional industries declined. From the 1920s and 1930s unemployment and later long term or structural unemployment emerged as a major social and political problem in Northern Ireland. As the employment situation steadily worsened much of the academic and public debate focused on the different unemployment rates between Protestants and Catholics. Catholic unemployment in Northern Ireland was recorded as being consistently higher. The social and political consequences of this are discussed elsewhere in various accounts (see for example O'Dowd et al. 1980; McCullough 1986; O'Dowd 1983).

From the 1970s into the 1980s the Province began to experience spectacular job losses, particularly in the greater Belfast region, in construction and manufacturing. As a result Protestant rates of unemployment also began to rise sharply. Some employment had moved into the service economies from the 1950s but particularly from the early 1970s (Howe 1990). This came to replace the varied traditional skill base, which was occupied for the most part by Protestant workers. But jobs in the service sector accounted for a very small portion of total jobs lost.

In recent years the service sector itself has experienced major decline, particularly in the security sectors which had offset unemployment for many Protestants. Unemployment rates between Protestants and Catholics now appear to be converging. Recent figures indicate that across the period 1990 to 2001, 'while the totality of the economically active has increased, the profile for the two communities has differed, with a steady increase in the number of Roman Catholics economically active compared with a much lesser degree of change in the number of Protestants economically active' (NISRA 2001: 6, 8).

Historically, social, political and economic life in Northern Ireland was bound up with Britain via an interconnected social structure. The export industries (linen, shipbuilding and engineering) depended on free access both to internal and external markets for their survival. 'For the Unionists of Ulster, industrial wellbeing, no less than religious liberty or political security, depended upon the maintenance of the British connection' (Lyons 1971: 27).

This connection emerged from the earliest developments of capitalism in the North extending back to Huguenot lace-making and the production of linen in the Lagan valley. [2] Later developments in heavy engineering and shipbuilding and leadership in commerce and industry put Northern Ireland on a world stage. However, Northern Ireland's importance within the British economy has declined severely. The old imperial order has given way to Europeanisation and to global economics and the resulting transformation is showing signs of having profound social, political and economic consequences for Northern Irish Protestants.

Protestants: identity and identities

The issue of identity and group belonging in Northern Ireland has dogged theoretical interpretation of social, political and ethnic conflict. Sport serves to illustrate the problem. While the Northern Ireland football team remains separate from the Republic of Ireland team, the Irish national rugby team has had a long tradition of fielding numerous players from Ulster. The latter code now calls on two anthems before a game. In recognition that the official 'Soldier's Song' may appear militaristic and unwelcoming to the Northern Protestant tradition ('Sons of the Gael! Men of the Pale . . . Out yonder waits the Saxon foe . . .'), a second anthem is now routinely begun in a gesture of solidarity of spirit:

> From the mighty Glens of Antrim
> From the rugged hills of Galway
> From the walls of Limerick
> And Dublin Bay
> From the four proud Provinces of Ireland.
> (excerpt from 'Ireland's Call')

The social and political history of Protestants and Protestantism in Ulster is presented in numerous and voluminous accounts (Falls, 1936; Lyons 1971; Gibbon 1975; Brown, 1991; Barton 1992; Ó Broin, 1995; Canny 2001). Debates focusing specifically on Protestant ideology and Protestant lifestyle have, however, received markedly less attention. Part of the problem is that discussions relating to Protestants have tended to be couched in relation to the Catholic 'other'. Because of this, Protestant ideology, hegemony, motivation and worldview have appeared nebulous and confused. These have therefore been notoriously much more difficult to capture and articulate. This is partly because the position of Protestants has typologically been viewed as problematic. Their identity has often been expressed in terms of their relationship with Britain, and consequently they have been interpreted as either a peripheral element of a British nationalism or as an anomalous population, that, in the age of nationalism, lacked a genuine national identity since it made no claim for an ethnically based state of its own (Miller 1978).[3]

Protestants in Northern Ireland have historically been viewed as colonialist and sectarian. From a Marxist perspective there have been competing interpretations of the position of Ulster Protestants.[4] James Connolly pointed to the paradox of working-class Protestants wanting to remain British within a region which exploited them as workers (Connolly 1913). This was explained as misguided, where Protestants were tricked by a Protestant bourgeois class, and were regarded as having a 'false class consciousness'. The problem with this perspective is its over-reliance on economic determinism at the cost of other important factors such as local culture and religion. It also emphasised a somewhat paternalistic attitude to a Protestant community that seemingly did not know what was good for it. It underestimated the autonomy of a Protestant working class who held a very different value and belief system as well as different cultural, religious and lifestyle preferences.

The point here is that in presenting Protestants as unwitting dupes who did not, or could not, recognise their 'true' cause in a workers' struggle against a bourgeois Protestant class, Marxists signally failed to understand other important dimensions to social and cultural difference in Northern Ireland. A more detailed discussion of class relations in the Protestant community offered by Bew et al. (1979) conceded, for example, the importance of a separate 'Protestant identity' and pointed up the significance of the connection with Britain as an important social, economic and security dimension for Ulster Protestants.

Religion, culture and identity

Historically, Protestants of all shades (and classes) unified in opposition to what they perceived to be the threat of an all-Ireland Catholic church dominated Republic, in which their numbers, their lifestyle and cultural values would quickly erode as evidenced in the declining numbers of Protestants in the Republic of Ireland, and, as they saw it, sanctioned by the *Ne Temere* Catholic Church edict which required that the children of mixed marriages be brought up Catholic (see Ruane and Todd 1996).[5] Bruce underscores Protestant concern. 'The only thing which maintained civil liberties was adherence to the Protestant faith' (Bruce 1989: 91). The significance of this has been articulated in prophecies of doom and predictions by some leading Protestant clergy who remind Protestants of the threat to their culture, religious freedom and way of life. It is a mantra that is embedded in their folklore, tradition and expressed through song and art.

Since the late 1960s, the civil conflict that has characterised Northern Ireland has provided a commanding theme for academic writers, broadcasters, novelists and filmmakers. The very topicality of 'the troubles' has produced what might be described as a 'troubles' industry and this has itself become a problem for academic writers, many of whom are now frustrated with the various machinations, not to mention the breadth and scope of what has been produced.[6] Specific focus on the conflict has been directly dealt with in various introductions and summaries (see for example, Darby 1976; Darby 1986; Whyte 1990; Dunn 1995) and there is now a dedicated website for those who have an interest (see http://cain.ulst.ac.uk/).

For decades, the state of Northern Ireland has been viewed as an awkward outpost to a Britain shedding the final vestiges of colonial rule. In more recent times it has increasingly come to be viewed as an irritant to a buoyant and globally integrated Republic of Ireland economy. The literature has described it variously as 'two sides of the house', 'two Ulsters', 'a place apart', and somehow different from other societies because of overt extreme sectarian social division (Larsen 1982; Kennedy 1986; Murphy 1978). In more recent years, successive leaders, British, Irish and American (along with European influence) have played a significant role in brokering a cessation of political violence by the Provisional IRA. Protestant paramilitary groups, while not standing down, have followed suit. Continued local incidents such as bank robberies, fighting within and between ethnic/religious communities, feuds, and revenge killings, although serious, are routinely downplayed and Northern Ireland is held up triumphantly by Western leaders as an exemplar of how peace can be successfully negotiated.[7]

The historical background to civil unrest in Northern Ireland points to religion and Protestant/Catholic religious affiliation as the bases of physical, social and ethnic divisions. The popular portrayal of Northern Ireland is of two cultures, two religions, and two national identities, British and Irish, and religious affiliation is seen as key to this differentiation. Religion is an important maker for local, regional and national identity (see for example, Geertz 1966). The idea of the nation is an expression of awareness and sentiments of belonging. For Geertz, it is representative of a network of extended kinship or common ancestors. Others, such as Anderson (1983), suggest that even if this is not actually the case, the idea or 'imagination' of what constitutes a community or a nation has important consequences. Anderson's constructionist approach fixes nations and the idea of nationalism (involving notions of family and common ancestry, however fictive) within the context of culture. For Anderson these crucially represent important political communities.

The point is that religion is also an expression of a cultural system, and sense of belonging to a real or 'imagined community'. It thus has conse-quences for social organisation, identity, physical and mental boundaries, as well as a sense of belonging, language and expression, a sense of security, neighbourliness and co-operation, and conflict. A potent representation of religion as culture are the ethnic religious identities of Protestants and Roman Catholics who live in Northern Ireland.

Northern Ireland is highly segregated, in the city and the country. More than 60 per cent of the population live in areas which have more than 80 per cent of one religion (O'Reilly and Stevenson 1998). A University of Ulster study conducted in 1995 indicated that almost 50 per cent of Protestants said they would rather live in an all-Protestant area, and 43 per cent said they would not allow a member of their family to marry a Catholic (Murtagh 1996: 31). This is suggestive of a high degree of exclusivity and homogeneity.

But Northern Ireland is also divided by social class, region and locality. There is strong identification and pride in local community. The effect of political violence has reinforced the idea of group difference and has been influential in shaping identity within groups. It also makes everyday inter-action across the sectarian divide difficult and dangerous even after the Good Friday Agreement – witness the sectarian killing of a young Catholic, Michael McIlveen in Ballymena in early May 2006. In addition, long-term unemploy-ment has meant that whole communities, and not just individuals, experience a more locally centred, encapsulated and ghettoised lifestyle. Ties outside the local community are therefore reduced with consequent effects on stereotyping, worldview, political attitudes and strength of boundaries. The boundaries are strongest in working-class areas, urban and rural. 'Networks that divide are largely based on pragmatic and uniplex relationships . . . Multiplex ties are more likely in the case of the professional classes' (Moore and Sanders 1996: 135).

Historical beliefs and practices tied to ethnic religious differentiation have been and for many remain an important source of division. Yet Catholics and Protestants in Northern Ireland undeniably share a common culture and many of the basic features of modern living in Western society (see Larsen 1982; Moore et al. 1996). The late John Whyte (1990) posed an important question, 'How complete [*sic*] is Northern Ireland divided into two com-munities?' (Whyte 1990: 14). In reviewing the literature he concluded that 'on the whole there is a fair degree of consensus on how distinct the communities are from each other. They are seen as deeply, but not totally divided' (Whyte 1990: 16).

The statement reveals a static concept of division as employed by many sociological and political commentators on Northern Ireland. Such a position, however, has inhibited a deeper discussion of the dynamics of conflict. Apparent contradictions in terms of how and why communities and groups come together and divide via crosscutting ties (fission/fusion) are less foreign to those with an anthropological perspective (see Evans-Pritchard 1940; Harris 1972; Gluckman 1973; Burton 1978).

The historical literature suggests that these communities are separate and yet may integrate. Harris's 'pre troubles' anthropological research in the 1950s in rural Ulster, for example, revealed part of the complexity in social relations in Northern Ireland. The study suggested that Catholic and Protestant farmers maintained courteous relations with each other in spite of stereotypical notions of the other and deeply held suspicions (Harris 1972). There has also been a focus on social processes in the literature on Protestants, especially symbolism and ritual (see Bryan 1995).

The discussion on ethnicity and identity in Northern Ireland, however, is contentious and remains underdeveloped theoretically.[8] Recent alternative political science and sociological theoretical accounts, emphasising the importance of looking at cognitive interactionist and network features and contingency and fluidity in conflict and identity in Northern Ireland, are though now attracting debate (see Brubaker 2001; Brubaker 2002; Ruane and Todd 2003).

There is little doubt, however, that in Ireland, religion and the Christian churches have played a major role in establishing and regulating social, political, cultural, moral and psychological boundaries and social duties. In Northern Ireland religious identity underpins ethnic identity and culture and influences social organisation, competition and co-operation and everyday living in very profound ways. For example, an important ethnographic study of Anro, a Catholic community in Belfast, Burton identifies the 'collective consciousness' and solidarity of Anro as (although by no means homogeneous) typical of the community structure of the Northern Ireland Catholic (Burton 1978).

For Burton, such solidarities are crucial in understanding the conflict in Northern Ireland. The common traits important to local people include kinship and 'friends', class, religion and territory.[9] These cumulatively constructed a sense of identity. Burton suggests that the differences are so profound that, according to local people, an elaborate system of deciphering codes 'telling' signifies and differentiates Protestants from Catholics. For Burton, 'telling' constitutes the syndrome of signs by which Catholics and Protestants arrive at religious ascription in their everyday interactions. It is the method (conscious or otherwise) of working out what religion a person is. But it does rather more than this. It is a demonstrable indication of real social and cultural differences assigned to religious affiliation. The extent and significance of 'telling', as Burton admits, is open to dispute, but that it exists, is important as an indication of real and/or perceived difference (Burton 1978: 37).

Religion and local identity in Northern Ireland prescribe a worldview and concomitant social action. This is sustained by enduring moral and ethical ways of thinking and acting. The French scholar Pierre Bourdieu developed the idea that people's dispositions are shaped by social conventions and practice in society. This imbues a worldview. Bourdieu (1977) refers to this as 'habitus' (see chapter 21 for further discussion of habitus). Habitus is a system of dispositions or cognitive and motivating structures that generate meaningful practices and perceptions. For example, how a person manages their life illustrates their social position. We have differing accents, use of vocabulary, dress code, and even food preferences. Our very person carries social value in demeanour, outlook and action and this makes people distinct from one another.

Habitus means that a person does not necessarily need to be religious *per se* to feel compelled by local obligations, rules and expectations. Therefore, cultural behaviour, ethnic principles and political identity are commonly assigned by virtue of religious affiliation. This directly addresses Connolly's paradox. Inglis, following Bourdieu, offers a more detailed and explicit exposition of the Catholic Church's religious capital and symbolic domination and the religious habitus of Irish Catholics. This explores the link between Irish nationalism and the Catholic collective consciousness in what he describes as the Catholic Church's 'moral monopoly' (Inglis 1998).

Protestant habitus

Protestants in Northern Ireland have an idea of nationhood, of Protestant characteristics and identity. They share key aspects of a common Westernised culture and lifestyle with Catholics from Northern Ireland. They also share some of these with the British (in the same way the Scots and Welsh in Britain and the Basques and Bretons in Spain and France identify with the dominant national culture, but with much that is unique and distinctive).

Protestantism historically emphasised religious freedom and personal piety and stressed autonomy and destiny. Weber saw this as a necessary precondition for the vigour of rational capitalist development (Hamilton 1995). The ethos demanded hard work, thriftiness, self-sufficiency, honesty, individual responsibility and loyalty to family, friend and sovereign. For Ulster Protestants, there was also an emphasis on frontier ancestry, fortitude, determination, discipline, individuality, martial history and prowess (Moore and Sanders 2002; Ruane and Todd 1996). This is an expression of values and tradition, which are embedded culturally and cognitively in Protestants, their social structure, lifestyle and worldview. It emphasised a way or a *modus operandi* for living, a distinctly Protestant habitus. Part of this includes deeply held beliefs not only about the Protestant lifestyle, but also Catholic lifestyles.

In addition, social class has featured more prominently in Protestant communities. The industrial revolution had forged various guilds and skills of tradesmen, managers and employers. The journalist McKay points up some of the perceptions:

> Protestant society is more staid. Catholics are more fun loving. I see that at work too, even in hotels – the ones run by Protestants are different. Protestants are more reserved, shyer. You don't let yourself go. Protestants are worriers too. And they have difficulty asking for help. Catholics will ask for help, but they also give it. The thing about the work ethic is you can lose your soul in all that (Eileen, a Protestant social service worker, in McKay 2000: 234).

Protestants perceived that their religion, values and cultural tradition had forged the industrial economic progress in Northern Ireland and beyond (evidenced, for example, by six former presidents as well as other key figures in the social and economic development of America coming from Ulster descent). The historical evidence in Northern Ireland was proof positive of the industrial might of a tiny Province which produced among other things the largest and most prestigious ships of their time and which boasted, for example, of having the largest rope works in the world. In addition, they had made important sacrifices in defence of the realm. The symbolic representations of this are depicted on gable walls across working-class Protestant Ulster. Add to this new articulations of Ulster culture, such as the current interest in and mainstreaming of the history of the Scots/Irish, its language and distinctive music, as well as the search for 'legitimate' roots (Stewart 1986; Adamson 1986) and attempts by loyalists to reinterpret Irish mythology into loyalist tradition (Moore and Sanders 2002).

Protestants also perceived Catholics and the Catholic way of life in opposition to their cultural values. Catholics are stereotyped as being fickle, lazy, work-shy, disloyal, deliberately living off the state, slavishly obeying the dictates of priests and unable to think for themselves. While Protestants are perceived as stoic, Catholics are seen as being able to work the system (individually and collectively) for personal advantage:

> Protestants were less community spirited than Catholics . . . Catholics look on grants as something they deserve from the system. The Protestant work ethic is very strong. It is very individualistic . . . The converse is that you don't share much. (Eileen, a Protestant social service worker, in McKay 2000: 233).

Similar themes are expressed in various academic writings. Dunn and Morgan (1994), for example, in their small survey of Protestants described how Protestants perceived Catholics to be very good at accessing resources while Protestants were seen to lack the structures of assistance at community level which the Catholic Church provided for Catholics. This perception is pervasive as Beattie further illustrates.

> The RCs are better at claims than us Protestants. That's what they say anyway. They know all the ins and outs of all the forms. It's because they are so good at collecting social security. (Beattie 1992: 11).

The perception is one of betrayal and imbalance, unjust and unfair treatment of those who see themselves as good citizens. McKay's interview with Billy Mitchell a former member of the Ulster Volunteer Force also makes the point. 'They (mainstream Unionists) hate community development. Nationalists had a head start on us on this' (see McKay 2000: 61).

Dunn and Morgan (1994) also reported widespread feeling of unease and uncertainty among Protestants which they described as 'Protestant alienation' and the perception that reverse discrimination and quotas were being used which favoured Catholics. A recurrent theme among working-class Protestants is the idea that they have been betrayed and forgotten (Moore 2004: 141).

A recent ethnographic study of health and related need of two rural communities in Northern Ireland pointed up the connection between habitus and social capital (that is the rules and norms that provide for various coping strategies, networks, family ties, religious ethos, marriage and kinship networks, extra familial support structures and community or religious institutions) and how actual or potential resources effects the health chances of Protestants and Catholics in Northern Ireland in small, but profound ways.[10] This points to a link between habitus, social capital potential and health.

> In Ballymacross [Catholic] and Hunterstown [Protestant], structure, religion and local culture oriented habitus influenced health lifestyles, health chances and health risk. Individuals' health promoting opportunities and decisions, were guided by religious affiliation and local cultural principles. This enabled or inhibited social support networks and information (Moore 2004: 142).

Ethnic/religious identity provided the basis for social capital potential. The communities differed in the degree and scope of social capital potential. The Catholic community was seen as supporting a unified Catholic ethos and identity with the strict involvement of religion and the Church while the Protestant community reflected not only historical denominational divisions, but also more recent fundamental factions in the form of new (inspirational) Protestantism. Protestantism was not supportive of a cohesive collective identity on a day-to-day basis, rather the opposite was true (Moore 2004).

The Protestant principle of subjectivism (*sola fide*) has undermined religious meaning in post-industrial Ulster, has made Protestantism essentially fragmented and has contributed to community division. A unified Protestant doctrine does not exist and is not practised in Northern Ireland. Various members of the Protestant community enforce their own brand of social inclusion/exclusion and social control. Liberalism within Protestantism also promotes secularism. For Protestants there is no one unified church and no overarching moral authority. Rather Protestant formations compete with each other (as well as Catholics) with secularisation, and with the effects of late capitalism and nascent globalisation. This has implications in terms of identity and cohesion. In contemporary society, capitalist moral individualism is a cause of disenchantment, confusion and 'anomie' among Protestants. It is translated into feelings of relative deprivation, powerlessness, fatalistic attitudes and into atomised groups with competing interests. For Catholics, the Church was the single unifying feature in terms of identity. This endured the Reformation, land dispossession, famine, imperialism and civil war. The distinctive symbolic rituals central to Catholicism remain central. The hall-mark is a unified, universal doctrine emphasising social and moral values and religious and political obedience. This contrasts with Protestant habitus which emphasises individualism and is suggestive of Weber's 'inner loneliness' as the consequence of the Calvinist ascetic lifestyle and Protestantism on identity choices (Gerth and Mills 1970).

> Once on its way, the modern economic system was able to support itself without the need of the religious ethic of ascetic Protestantism which in many ways could not help but sow seeds of secularisation in modern society by its own promotion of world activity and consequent expansion of wealth and material well-being. Calvinistic Protestantism was its own gravedigger (Hamilton 1995: 170).

This also had consequences for non-Protestants. For example, Catholics living in Protestant areas were in the most vulnerable position of all, since they experienced a greater degree of physical and social isolation from both their Protestant neighbours and from their Catholic co-religionists (Moore 2004).

Protestants and 'Protestants'

Rapid social change influences cultural transition. The literature suggests that Protestants and Catholics in Northern Ireland display different social, religious and cultural preferences and lifestyles. However, it is inaccurate to talk of a politically homogeneous Protestant population with a common purpose and identity. Protestant unity is expressed at seasonal high times or in opposition to threat from an all-Ireland nationalist Catholic Church-dominated republic.

The social structure of Northern Ireland is complex and requires inspection of multiple (and contingent) forms of identity not only between ethic religious groups but also within these groups. The point here is that within Protestantism there is, and has always been, a very wide spectrum of views. Historically, some of these views have even espoused republican and Irish nationalist identity.

Although some have alluded to important intra religious differences in the past (see for example, Jones 1969) scholars have only relatively recently begun to seriously focus on divisions within sectarian communities. The focus on Protestants and Protestant perspectives, their attitudes, beliefs, motivations and culture is a developing one. Recent debates on Protestant identity have challenged sectarian and popular representations of Protestants as a single coherent homogeneous block (McFarlane 1989; Shirlow and McGovern 1997), 'between sections of Northern Ireland Protestants, there is little sense of commonality or affection, but rather cordial and mutual dislike and disrespect' (Ruane and Todd 2003: 12).

McKay presents narrative illustrating commanding themes exposing such differences. Among these are issues of social class, loyalty and betrayal. McKay's interview with Billy Mitchell a former member of the Ulster Volunteer Force makes the point;

> there is this thing about knowing your place. There is a dichotomy between middle unionism and loyalism. Middle unionism disapproves of loyalists getting above themselves. All this talk about the independence and individuality of Protestants is nonsense. Those of us born into the 'lower orders' felt we were born to follow, and our betters, the people you touched the forelock to, were born to lead. You look at the way mainstream Unionists hate us now. They sneer at our political representatives when they wear suits.' This is a reference to the DUP designation of the fringe loyalists as 'gangsters in suits (McKay 2000: 61).

These are recurrent themes (see also Moore and Sanders 2002; Dunn and Morgan 1994). The peace talks which led to the power-sharing executive at Stormont in 2000 were in fact premised on the recognition that there are more than two internal parties to the conflict, and more than two interpretations of the conflict. Protestant identity exists, but it is given different importance by different individuals and even for those for whom it has a master status, it has varying degrees of importance in different situations. Working-class Protestants have not experienced demonstrable changes in their fortunes following the Good Friday Agreement. The indications are that they are becoming progressively marginalised (Dunn and Morgan 1994; Shirlow and Murtagh 2006).

Protestantism and Protestant ideology is difficult to unravel. Within Protestantism, we see different political attitudes, lifestyles and behaviours and divergent attitudes and interests (Ruane and Todd 1996). While traditional 'unionism' for example, may be viewed as an expression of Protestant middle-class culture, 'loyalism', has come to symbolise working-class Protestant identity.

The famous Northern Protestant republican and founder member of the Irish Republican Brotherhood, Bulmer Hobson, was convinced that the way to unify Ireland was to make an Ireland so prosperous that Ulster cannot afford to stay out of it (Hobson 1968). The extent of the Celtic Tiger's prosperity has made this proposition a reality. Yet far from enticing Protestants into an all Ireland state, Protestants and particularly working-class Protestants appear to have entrenched into more localised notions of culture and identity (Moore and Sanders 2002).

Over the past thirty years Protestants have perceived themselves as unequal in three important ways. First, they saw an erosion of their civil rights. One consequence of this is that the Protestant community has fragmented into separate entities with middle-class Protestantism continually emphasising Britishness and the Union, and working-class Protestants articulating a separate position, a form of nationalism. This is expressed through 'loyalism' and emphasises distinctive and different cultural values. Its primary imagined community is the Northern Irish Protestant population and not the wider British one which emphasises unquestioning loyalty to British values (Moore and Sanders 2002). The emphasis on cultural survival is associated particularly with loyalism. In other words, they appear to be moving from a political folk conception of Northern Ireland to a multicultural, plural society, one in which Protestant culture is seen to be under threat. Their cultural focus has been on Orange institutions and activities such as Orange marches (Cairns 2000) which are seen to be an important expression of cultural identity (Bryan 1995). This may be seen as the benchmark by which cultural erosion is measured.

Secondly, they came to see themselves as colonially exploited people. Exploited by the English who they regard as the 'other' just as much as nationalists/republicans. The English are seen as unprincipled, materialistic and self-serving. Thirdly, they perceive their culture and identity as being ignored by the British and not afforded the same value as Irish or British culture. They see themselves as under attack by Irish nationalism and sold out by the British. In the wake of the Good Friday Agreement the concern is that in an increasing globalising world they would enter into an all-Ireland economic and political entity by default (Aughey 2006; Bew 2006).

They now see themselves as an increasingly vulnerable ethnic group in a rapidly changing world where Europeanisation and gobalisation have brought new identities, languages and cultures to their streets and to their communities. While aspects of the Good Friday Agreement such as the Irish Republic giving up their territorial claim on Northern Ireland are broadly welcomed, Protestants are suspicious about the agreement. There is a general worry among Protestants (and, as they see it, borne out by repeated appeasement of republicans) of betrayal by successive British governments (Moore and Sanders 2002).

Northern Ireland and the people who live there may be viewed at one level as sharing a Westernised common culture. But they may also be viewed as diametrically opposed ethnic/religious entities with distinctive cultural differences and habitus. While ethnic/religious differences have important consequences, the traditional dichotomous explanation has helped to obscure other important factors in contemporary Northern Ireland. It has, for example, clouded the relationship between community conflict and local inequalities, lifestyle preferences, beliefs, and more complex notions of identity. In addition, the myopic ethnocentric focus on two tribes has effectively concealed other important non-Christian ethnic groups, their politics, lifestyles and their problems, such as health concerns (see Hainsworth 1998). These communities, some quite large and very well established, have thrived in the Province and have hitherto not been afforded serious attention until relatively recently.

If we also add to this important recent changes in terms of the makeup of the population of Northern Ireland where European, East European, Filipino and other languages are now becoming more evident, we see a mix of ethnic interest groups which are likely to continue to produce ethnic pluralism or create additional tensions. In the longer term these events and changes present important challenges for academics who are interested in identity, conflict, health and social change in Ireland, North and South.

Chapter 23

Racism and sectarianism in Northern Ireland

Robbie McVeigh

'Racism, like sectarianism, is the product of a destructive and ugly mindset'
Northern Ireland Policing and Security Minister Ian Pearson (*Sunday Life*, 22 August 2004)

'An agreed definition for the promotion of good relations does not currently exist. Therefore, until such times as there may be a more common definition and approach, all people, organisations and institutions will define good relations differently. Organisations will approach this process from their own, unique perspective and with their own particular concerns. For example, words such as sectarianism, racism, equality and diversity can have different and sometimes, loaded meanings as people work through issues from individual and community viewpoints.'
(Community Relations Commission 2004: 6–7)

Introduction

This chapter examines the relationship between sectarianism and racism in Northern Ireland and how these have been understood by sociologists and by the state. In the wake of the 'peace process' and the 1998 Good Friday Agreement (GFA), the notion that racism has 'replaced' sectarianism as the offensive practice of choice in Northern Ireland has gathered momentum. While the commonsense notions that people were not racist during the conflict because they were too busy being sectarian or that there was no racism in the north because there were no black people do not hold up to examination, clearly *something* has changed in terms of racism over the past ten years. Northern Ireland is now dubbed the 'race hate capital of Europe' with Belfast identified as the 'most racist city in the world' (McVeigh 2006a).[1]

What can be characterised as 'replacement theory' – the notion that racism has occupied a space vacated by sectarianism – not only speaks to the escalation in racism but also implies a radical reduction in sectarianism. There is

Figure 23.1 **Headline from Daily Ireland, 27 June 2006. Is Northern Ireland really the** 'race hate capital of Europe'?

The North branded race-hate capital of Europe:
Damning figures reveal rise in racial bigotry as violence continues

---

little evidence of this happening at all. While the war is over, the 'peace' that followed has been characterised by continuing sectarian violence and structural inequality. Sectarian violence – including murder – continues to be commonplace. In fact, in some forms sectarianism – like racism – has *intensified* since the ceasefires and the GFA; for example, many so-called 'peacelines' separating Protestant and Catholic communities have been built or heightened since 1998. While no journalist has made the claim, Northern Ireland might well remain the 'sectarian hate capital of Europe' and Belfast the 'most sectarian city in the world'. It is palpably clear, therefore, that racism has not 'replaced' sectarianism but that both remain defining features of Northern Ireland. The crucial question is why this has been misrecognised both by sociologists and the state. So why has replacement theory taken hold? And what does this suggest about how we understand racism and sectarianism in Northern Ireland?

The growing influence of the replacement thesis has been largely situated in one piece of academic research which made a claim about racist and sectarian attitudes:

> Overall, racial prejudice appears to be around twice as significant than [sic] sectarian prejudice in the initial attitudes of the population in Northern Ireland. Around twice as many respondents in the survey stated that they would be unwilling to accept and/or mix with members of minority ethnic communities than they would members of the other main religious tradition (i.e. Catholic or Protestant) to themselves. Moreover, negative attitudes towards specific minority ethnic groups have become worse over the last few years. (Connolly and Keenan 2000a: 44)

Despite the tentative and problematic nature of this claim, the analysis that racism had 'replaced' sectarianism in Northern Ireland was quickly presented as an academic 'truth'. In turn, this became simply a 'truth'. The influential British anti-racist and anti-fascist magazine *Searchlight* epitomised this approach:

> While there may be fewer gunshots and a lot less manning of the barricades at peace lines throughout the Province of late, it seems that some in the community cannot

survive without meting out a regular dose of intimidation, harassment and violence to those newer arrivals in their community . . . The hatreds remain the same, now it is your colour and your language that make you a target. (Collins 2004)

The media seized on the rise in racism with an unprecedented level of hyperbole – by 2003, for example, the *Belfast Telegraph* was reporting a '900 per cent rise in race hate crimes' (*Belfast Telegraph*, 30 October 2003). There was very little examination of the statistical basis for such claims but they reflected the mood of the moment. Moreover the state in Northern Ireland began to develop policy and practice on 'hate crime' in the context of this new 'reality':

> A research report published last year by the Northern Ireland Statistics and Research Agency, 'Racial Attitudes and Prejudice in Northern Ireland' concluded that racial prejudice appears to be around twice as significant as sectarian prejudice. (Northern Ireland Office 2002: 4)

It bears emphasis that this notion of the 'significance' is rarely explained let alone interrogated in any of these discussions or proposals. Racism had replaced sectarianism in 'significance' and that was all there was to it. This analysis was, however, promulgated at the same time as new 'peace lines' were being built, the Holy Cross school dispute was ongoing and Garvaghy Road remaining 'under siege'. The grim calculus of sectarian murders and assaults also failed to support the 'racism is now worse that sectarianism' thesis (Jarman 2005).

So why did this notion taken hold? The answer has more to do with the Northern Ireland statelet's reluctance to address sectarianism than its commitment to address racism. The state apparatus, of course, presents itself as resolutely opposed to both. Witness Policing and Security Minister Ian Pearson writing in the *Sunday Life* under the banner of 'Race attacks shame us all':

> Racism, like sectarianism, is the product of a destructive and ugly mindset. To abuse and attack vulnerable people, who are making a new life for themselves and their families in a strange country, is shameful and cowardly . . . I wish to make very clear the Government's abhorrence of racist behaviour, and our determination to tackle it. (*Sunday Life*, 22 August 2004)

For all the hand-wringing about racist and sectarian violence, however, the state has not managed to achieve very much in terms of either racist or sectarian violence. Its criminal justice system cannot tell us if it has convicted anyone for racist crimes despite its reputation as the 'race hate capital of Europe'.[2] The Police Service of Northern Ireland (PSNI) only began to record incidents of sectarian violence in 2004 – five years after it had begun

Figure 23.2 **Events surrounding the loyalist picket of Holy Cross – a Catholic girls' primary school in North Belfast – were a reminder of the currency and brutality of sectarian division**

to record incidents of the 'new' phenomenon of racist violence and nearly forty years after the first sectarian murders of the 'troubles'. Despite the problematic nature of these statistics, however, they are likely to remain regarded as the key metre of levels of racism and sectarianism (as well as other 'hate crime') in the future. [3]

This chapter addresses the nexus of racism and sectarianism and state in the emerging post-GFA Northern Ireland. The GFA supposedly guaranteed 'the right to freedom from sectarian harassment', yet sectarian violence and profound sectarian inequality continues alongside the upsurge in racist violence. The British security minister characterises both as the 'product of a destructive and ugly mindset', but the state has shown little commitment or competence in countering either. It has integrated anti-racism and anti-sectarianism within a 'good relations' paradigm without any clear sense of how or why this does anything to address the reality of racism and sectarianism in Northern Ireland, especially hate crime and violence. What do endemic sectarian violence and growing racist violence tell us about the state formation that emerged from the GFA? More specifically what does this focus suggest about the sociology of racism and sectarianism in this context? While academic research has driven the popular construction of the situation, how much has it contributed to understanding – let alone countering – racism and sectarianism?

Table 23.1 **PSNI statistics on crimes and clearance rates with a faith/religion, sectarian, disability, racial or homophobic motivation 2005–6**

	Faith/religion	Sectarian	Disability	Racial	Homophobic
Total number of incidents	70	1,701	70	936	220
Total number of crimes	78	1,470	38	746	148
% clearance rate	17.9	14.4	39.5	20.5	32.4

Source: Police Service of Northern Ireland Statistical Report no. 3.

Making sense of racism and sectarianism in a 'changing Ireland'

Changes in racism and the analysis of racism have been characterised by the growing importance of globalisation alongside theorisation of the 'racial state' (Lentin and McVeigh 2002; 2006a; 2006b). Over the past ten years, 'changing Ireland' has been symbolised by the Celtic Tiger in the south and the peace process in the north. These transformations obviously took place within – and were structured by – wider dynamics. In terms of our focus – racism and sectarianism – there were specific developments which impact directly on the processes of racialisation and sectarianisation. This period saw an intensification of globalisation as well as a reconstitution of US political influence and power across the world. Just how Ireland, North and South, sits in this 'new world order' is central to understanding contemporary racism and sectarianism.

From this perspective, the 'war on terror' and the resonance of its appeals to 'civilisation' and 'post-modern imperialism' (Cooper 2002) invoke new forms of racism. Western political and military intervention around the world – as well as the globalisation process itself – marked a re-emergence of racialised imperialisms. Within the 'new world order', capital, labour, goods and services are distributed and moved in ways that remain inherently racialised. Crucially resources located in places occupied by peoples of colour (the Majority World) are redistributed to places controlled by richer, predominately white people (the USA and EU). This economic dispensation is thus profoundly and unambiguously racially coded. If we want to understand racism and sectarianism, we must engage with a world system in which inequality is palpably encoded by race and ethnicity and nationality. It is also clear, however, that the state continues to play a key role in this 'new world order'. In fact, in the context of globalisation, the role of the state is accentuated rather than diminished (Lentin and McVeigh 2006a: 23–30). Crucially, it is the state which continues to define citizen and non-citizen, national and non-national, legal and illegal. The state remains *the* key mechanism in reproducing and mediating both racism and sectarianism in a globalised world.

In terms of how we understand racism and sectarianism, this paradoxically brings us back to older and more traditional questions. What is the connection between racist and sectarian ideologies and the economic base? Are racism and sectarianism simply to be understood as 'false consciousness'? Do they have some level of 'relative autonomy'? Behind all this theory there is a prosaic reality of the *colour* of the economic system – at a global level, at the level of the nation state and at regional and local level. There is a direct correlation between ethnicity and inequality. There is a continuing specificity to the kind of jobs that are done by Black and minority ethnic people and migrant workers and refugees and asylum seekers and undocumented workers. When we address this reality we begin to unpack the systemic, structural dimensions of racism and sectarianism because at every level we find that race and ethnicity – like gender and class – retain a key explanatory function in sociological analysis. From this perspective, *pace* Ian Pearson, racism and sectarianism are not so much the 'product of evil mindsets' as the product of unequal, globalised social relations.

While this core aspect of understanding racism has not changed all that much over the last ten years, other things undoubtedly have.[4] Perhaps most significant of all has been the developing 'war of/on terror'. In the dynamics of what Agamben terms a 'global civil war' (Agamben 2005: 2–3), Islamophobia became a key tool for understanding the new dynamics of world racism (Allen and Nielsen 2002; Runnymede Trust 1998). While this has had little impact on conceptualisations of sectarianism in Northern Ireland, it further undermines the notion that there is any simple distinction between religion and race. Certainly, if racism in the second half of the twentieth century was defined by the legacy of colonialism and enslavement in apartheid and other forms of racist segregation, the first half of the twenty-first century seems likely to be defined by the racism that emerges from the 'clash of civilisations' engendered by a new, robust and self-confident Western imperialism (Sivanandan 2004).

The British state's Stephen Lawrence Inquiry and the consequent Macpherson Report (1999) also changed the conceptual landscape of racism and anti-racism in Britain and beyond. Its main effects were more practical than theoretical but it had an important democratic function in demystifying the terms racism and institutional racism. Most importantly, perhaps, the Stephen Lawrence Inquiry forced politicians and journalists and ordinary people – as well as academics and activists – to engage with the question of *what racism is*. The Macpherson definitions continue to inform and reconstitute debate and practice around the world:

> *'Racism'* in general terms consists of conduct or words or practices which advantage or disadvantage people because of their colour, culture or ethnic origin. In its more subtle form it is as damaging as in its overt form . . . [and] *'Institutional Racism'* consists of the collective failure of an organisation to provide an appropriate and professional service to people because of their colour, culture or ethnic origin. It can be seen or detected in processes, attitudes and behaviour which amount to discrimination through unwitting prejudice, ignorance, thoughtlessness, and racist stereotyping which disadvantage minority ethnic people. (Macpherson 1999: 6.4, 6.34 [emphases added])

It is important not to exaggerate the consequences of this process – particularly in terms of their practical import. For example, a 2005 inquiry by the Commission for Racial Equality (CRE) characterised the situation in the

British police over five years after MacPherson as one of 'a perma-frost on race issues – thawing on the top, but still frozen solid at the core' (Commission for Racial Equality 2005). The Institute of Race Relations also estimates 'Sixty-eight racist murders [in Britain] since Stephen Lawrence' (Athwal and Kundnani 2006). (This also puts the notion of Northern Ireland as the 'race hate capital of Europe' in brutal context.) Nevertheless, the MacPherson analysis and recommendations had a wide international impact and continue to inform analysis and practice, not least in Ireland, North and South.

Racism and sectarianism: the main sociological changes 1995–2005

Despite and to some extent because of its pervasiveness, sectarianism in Northern Ireland has not been not particularly well researched or analysed. I suggested some 12 years ago that: 'Sectarianism in Ireland is that changing set of ideas and practices, including, crucially, acts of violence, which serves to construct and reproduce the difference between, and unequal status of, Irish Protestants and Catholics' (McVeigh 1995: 643). This approach has been adopted by other academics and researchers and it remains a useful working definition despite the profound sociological and political changes in the intervening period. Although new work is emerging on the persistence of sectarianism after the GFA (McVeigh 2006a; McVeigh and Rolston 2007; Shirlow and Murtagh 2006), there is no definitive text providing an overview of the sociology of contemporary sectarianism.[5] In particular, the relationship between racism and sectarianism remains contested (McVeigh and Rolston 2007). Moreover, some of the more influential analyses are clearly dated, engaging with the sectarianism of a pre-GFA 'war' rather than a post-GFA 'peace' (McVeigh 1995; O'Dowd et al. 1980). In contrast, the subject of racism in Northern Ireland is better served by academic research. Hainsworth's (1998) *Divided Society: Ethnic Minorities and Racism in Northern Ireland* remains the key text although this was produced pre-GFA and before Northern Ireland was recognised as place with any significant problem with racism. Rolston's work on the growth in racist violence (2004) has been supplemented by other more recent work (McVeigh 2006a, 2006b, 2006c; Lentin and McVeigh 2006a, 2006b; McVeigh and Rolston 2007). Gilligan and Lloyd (2006) have also recently usefully analysed social attitudes to race in Northern Ireland in the context of the 'race hate capital of Europe' claim.

Since the GFA, the Northern Ireland state has also begun to generate a volume of work on both racism and sectarianism. The quantitative analyses generated by state equality structures continued in the new Equality Commission for Northern Ireland (ECNI) but the state also began to commission work in academia and the private and community sector. Work on racism by Connolly and Keenan (2000a, 2000b, 2001, 2002; Connolly, P. 2002) and racism and sectarianism by Jarman and others (Jarman 2002b; Jarman and Monaghan 2003a, 2003b; Radford et al. 2006) contributed significantly to the corpus. Something had changed with this, however. A state which had denied the relevance of racism in Northern Ireland right up into the 1990s was now commissioning all this work. In doing so, however, the state was also constructing and defining the situation. Not surprisingly, there was little critical analysis of the role of the Northern Ireland state in all of this. Tellingly, the most direct attempt to address 'institutional racism' in Northern Ireland in the wake of MacPherson – the ECNI commissioned *A Wake Up Call on Race* (Oliver and McGill 2002) – was cursory in its review of policing and hardly addressed the rest of the criminal justice system at all.

Arguably the Northern Ireland state had successfully repositioned itself *vis-à-vis* both racism and sectarianism without any substantive or critical engagement at all with the concepts of institutional racism and sectarianism. More specifically, the concepts of state sectarianism and state racism had disappeared from view. The state continued to actively resist any critical, structural analysis of its responsibility *vis-à-vis* both racism and sectarianism, but now it was situated on the 'right side' – against the 'ugly and destructive mindsets'.

We can and should, however, trace the contours of contemporary racism and sectarianism from a more sociological perspective. First, both the racialised and sectarianised economic base has changed significantly in Northern Ireland over recent years, particularly since the GFA. Second, there is a stark contrast between the economic base of sectarianism and racism. The sectarian economic base was in many ways the core logic for the existence of the Northern Ireland state from partition onwards. The uneven development between the industrialised 'Protestant' north and the rural 'Catholic' south provided the logic for partition and the economic basis for the continued, separate Six County formation – characterised by a very conscious state project to reproduce a sectarian division of labour and protect and co-opt the loyalist working class.

The traditional economic base of the statelet has been further racialised over recent years. While Northern Ireland has lagged well behind the 'economic miracle' model of the Celtic Tiger, it has seen significant economic growth since the GFA. There have been labour shortages in sectors of the economy and these have been met by the arrival of substantial numbers of migrant workers. Some of these come from new accession states of the EU and some from without (Jarman 2006; McVeigh 2006c). Refugees have also arrived for the first time although in relatively small numbers (McVeigh 2002). It bears emphasis, however, that this new racialisation is an *addition to* rather than a *replacement for* traditional sectarian divisions.

We find a whole infrastructure of sectarianism and racism raised upon this economic base. There is no area of social life in Northern Ireland which is not structured in some way by sectarianism. The correlation between political party and 'perceived religion' is as absolute as it ever was. Sectarianism also continues to profoundly structure where people are born, where they go to school, where they live, where they work, where they socialise, what sports teams they support and where they are buried. Moreover, racism in Northern Ireland is itself becoming structured in a similar way – it assumes particular forms precisely because it occurs in a profoundly sectarianised social formation (McVeigh 2006a, 2006b).

There has also been a seismic shift in the dynamics of sectarianism over the last decade. If Northern Ireland remains profoundly sectarianised, it is also undoubtedly sectarianised *in a new way* post GFA. The reduction in armed conflict, the effective disbandment of the Royal Ulster Constabulary and Royal Irish Regiment, and the formation (and suspension) of a cross-sectarian powersharing government all mark significant shifts in the dynamics of sectarianism. Arguably, however, this process has been ill served by academic analysis. Clearly *something* significant has been taking place but there has been no definitive sociology of the peace process. We can, however, suggest that the key to understanding both racism and sectarianism in contemporary Northern Ireland is in the changing nature of the state and its management of both phenomena in the context of the peace process and the GFA.

Arguably the GFA was about a new accommodation in the state management of sectarianism. (The GFA also obviously had a significant – if largely unintended – impact in terms of the dynamics of racism.) This undoubtedly reconfigured the state in Northern Ireland. Certainly it reformed some of the most egregious elements of the sectarian statelet that had characterised Northern Ireland since partition, and the direct rule statelet since 1972. In other words, the structural context for sectarianism was transformed in quite profound ways, however incomplete this transformation. This had a direct impact in terms of institutions. Most obviously the Patten Commission addressed policing directly but the wider criminal justice system was also critiqued (Independent Commission on Policing 1999). Whatever its limitations, the attempt to de-sectarianise policing was undeniably significant. The 50/50 recruitment of Protestants and Catholics was a relatively robust equality model. It bears emphasis that this in no way guaranteed an end to the sectarianisation of policing but it did seem to guarantee that policing would at least be sectarianised in a new way.

New equality legislation was also introduced. The reformist tendency of the Agreement saw anti-sectarian (previously 'fair employment') legislation extended to goods and services to mirror the more recent advances in legislation on racism in the 1997 Race Relations (Northern Ireland) Order (which predated the GFA). The GFA also generated a whole set of new statutory institutions with some responsibility for addressing either sectarianism or racism or both. Most significantly the ECNI emerged from an amalgamation of equality agencies – including the Fair Employment Commission and the Commission for Racial Equality Northern Ireland – so for the first time responsibility for addressing race and sectarian inequality was located in the same body. Equally significantly, however, the Community Relations Commission (CRC) remained in place, despite having played no role in the peace negotiations or the GFA. It emerged strengthened from the GFA with a broader mandate. Despite the fact that it had shown little interest in racism up to this point, it also began to draw anti-racism into its ambit. So the CRC also integrated analyses of racism and sectarianism within a new 'good relations' paradigm. When the CRC launched its *A Good Relations Framework: An Approach to the development of Good Relations* in 2006, 'dealing with' racism had been unambiguously integrated into the community relations/ good relations paradigm:

> Those who have worked on anti-racism and anti-sectarianism approaches in Northern Ireland have acquired decades of experience. The promotion of good relations requires that both these areas of expertise be joined together to provide an approach that will enable racism and sectarianism to be addressed equally and together. (2004: 5)

When the state's 'Good Relations' strategy emerged in the OFMDFM (Office of the First Minister and Deputy First Minister) *A Shared Future* document in 2005 (2005b), the synthesis was complete. Replacement theory was in the ascendant and the blueprint for the 'Good Relations' response to racism and sectarianism was in place.

The rise of 'replacement theory'

Replacement theory became *commonsense* in two distinct ways. first, it was argued that racism replaced sectarianism as the 'evil' of choice. There was a popular notion that in any society there is a predilection to violence and discrimination and, in Northern Ireland post ceasefires, racism replaced sectarianism as the 'ugly mindset' of choice. This thesis assumed that sectarianism was either disappearing or had disappeared. Second, it was argued that racism had become 'more significant' or 'more important' than sectarianism – this, as we have seen, drew directly on the tentative conclusions of the sociological work of Connolly and Keenan (2000a). This thesis also implied that sectarianism was on the wane but it was more focused on the rise in racism than the fall in sectarianism. It failed completely, however, to acknowledge that the 'rise' in racism highlighted by Connolly and Keenan was based on a dubious comparison with earlier, methodologically different social attitudes research.[6] Moreover the most egregious racist attitudes focused upon by Connolly and Keenan were examples of *anti-Traveller racism*.[7] It seems hard to support the thesis that this had 'grown' or 'changed' much at all post GFA since racist and genocidal attitudes towards Travellers had been present in Northern Ireland for decades (McVeigh 1992, 1997). While there is no definitive quantitative research evidence to either support or contradict the thesis, it seems unlikely that anti-Traveller racism was changed *at all* by either the GFA or the rise in racist violence directed at other minority ethnic groups.

Tracing the evolution of the replacement thesis is comparatively easy. As late as 1998, the *Belfast Telegraph* could characterise sectarianism in terms of the *absence* of racism, 'Sectarianism is Ulster's Racism' (*Belfast Telegraph*, 21 July 1998); yet within five years racism was newsworthy enough to become described as 'Ulster's new bigotry' in the same paper (*Belfast Telegraph*, 16 July 2003). By 2003, the BBC News was suggesting that: 'Ethnic minorities in Northern Ireland are more than *twice as likely* to face a racist incident than those in England or Wales, according to a BBC News investigation' (BBC, 13 October 2003, emphasis added). The BBC 'investigation' was little more than a repetition of previous analysis. Moreover, the content of the report completely undermined its own argument: 'Earlier this year, Northern Ireland's Equality Commission noted that racist attacks in Northern Ireland were running at a higher level than in England and Wales. They were running at 16.4 per 1,000 of the minority ethnic population compared to 12.6 in England and Wales, said the commission' (BBC News, 13 October 2003). By now it was accepted uncritically that racist attacks were 'twice as likely' as anything they were compared with, even when the evidence used to support the assertion directly contradicted it.

The replacement argument was replicated by a whole spectrum of commentators from the BBC (BBC News, 14 April 2000) and INCORE[8] (Lewis 2004) to the Irish Labour Party (2005) and the Committee for a Worker's International (2003). At every repetition there was a more permissive interpretation of the thesis. Thus the Committee for a Worker's International reports how: 'A recent report into racial prejudice in Northern Ireland said that racism in the country is now twice as common as sectarianism' (2003); for the Irish Labour Party: 'Connolly and Keenan . . . demonstrated that racism is twice as prevalent as sectarianism' (2005). Despite the fact that it had almost no basis in reality, post ceasefires and post GFA, replacement theory was an idea whose time had come. Most importantly, however, this was taken up by key state actors to shift agendas. As well as the CRC and the ECNI, the Northern Ireland Office (NIO) and various elements in the statutory sector grounded developments in relation to this new 'truth'. People in Northern

Ireland were now 'more likely to be racist that sectarian' because this idea had been so often repeated.

In combination, these ideas about the 'replacement' of sectarianism by racism served to transform the analytic landscape of the Northern Ireland statelet. Thus by 2003, the CRC could, completely erroneously, assert: 'It is a fact that there are more racist attacks in Northern Ireland than in England and Wales and that people in Northern Ireland are more likely to be racist than sectarian. Everyone has a role to play in combating racism.' (Community Relations Commission 2003)

It bears emphasis that this was not a 'fact' in any meaningful sense of the term. There are palpably *not* more racist attacks in Northern Ireland than in England and Wales. (There might conceivably be more racist attacks *per capita* in Northern Ireland but even this assertion is impossible to make given the flimsiness of PSNI recording of racist crime (Jarman 2002b; Jarman and Monaghan 2003a) and the fact that statistics as presently gathered are not directly comparable between the two jurisdictions.) Moreover, as we have seen, the most virulent racist attitudes identified by Connolly and Keenan and used to support the 'people in Northern Ireland are more likely to be racist than sectarian' thesis were the consequence of anti-Traveller racism (2000a: 44). Despite ample opportunity to do so, the CRC (established in 1990) had played almost no role in challenging the anti-Traveller racism that now provided the basis for its call to arms in combating racism.

We therefore find a powerful state-sponsored agency crudely distorting facts to make some kind of political and analytic intervention. Why is replacement theory so dominant in Northern Ireland? And what does this tell us about the relationship of both racism and sectarianism to the Northern Ireland statelet? One piece of sociology was used to hang a whole paradigm shift in how people thought about the north. It is an unusual example of sociology informing state policy alongside wider attitudes in civil society. It is also sociologically interesting, however, because this 'reality' was clearly constructed. The evidence did not support the thesis, yet the thesis was made and continues to dominate thinking and practice on the issue. What was it about replacement theory that made it so appealing to so many people despite the palpable weakness of its evidential basis?

On the one hand, the moral panic spoke to a reality. While it was untrue to suggest that there had been no racism before 1998, there has undoubtedly been much *more* racism since – however that is measured – particularly more racist violence (McVeigh 2006b). In other words, the assertion that there has been a disturbing rise in racism – alongside other 'hate crime' – is fairly uncontestable (House of Commons 2004). But the thesis becomes much more problematic at the point at which it is tied to the notion that sectarianism has diminished and that there is some causal connection between these two developments. The notion that racism has become *more significant* than racism just does not hold – even in the loosest sense of the term significance. For example, people in Northern Ireland continue to vote for parties that are clearly 'sectarian', at least in terms of their association with sections of the population. While the correlation between 'perceived religion' and voting tendency is not absolute, it is much stronger than either class or gender. We might continue in this vein with further examples of how the significance of sectarianism has hardly diminished since the GFA in almost any area of social life (Shirlow and Murtagh 2006). The point is fundamentally fairly simple – there is nothing to suggest that *more racism* in Northern Ireland has led to *less sectarianism*. There is nothing to suggest any inverse correlation between the two phenomena. Any interrogation of notions about 'attitudes' leaves little support for the thesis that racist attitudes are 'more significant' than sectarian ones (Gilligan and Lloyd 2006).

There has been widespread 'ethnic cleansing' of minority ethnic people from loyalist working-class areas (McVeigh 2006b). But this only compares with the continued sectarian segregation of working-class housing in particular. It is simply false to assume or imply that Catholics are moving into loyalist working-class communities as minority ethnic people are being 'put out'. The loyalist working-class communities that have been most associated with expelling minority ethnic groups over recent years – the Village, Donegal Pass, Sandy Row – remain 'no-go' areas for Catholics. There is no sense in which these areas have opened up to Catholics since the GFA. There is more racist segregation post-GFA, but there is not any less sectarian segregation. In this sense, the notion that the 'significance' of sectarianism has declined or abated is not simply inaccurate but also an ideological intervention. Moreover, in terms of race, the only absolute segregation that parallels loyalist and nationalist working-class segregation – demarcated physically and absolutely by 'peace lines' – is between Travellers sites and the settled community. These 'ethnic boundaries' existed long before 'replacement theory' came along. Travellers were living in segregated accommodation in the 'good old days' when there was 'no racism because there were no Black people' in Northern Ireland and sectarianism was 'Ulster's racism'. So when we find academic research being used to support a thesis that is commissioned by and heavily endorsed by the state, we must ask what is going on? Why is the state so keen to promote an idea so plainly contradicted by evidence?

The answer is that the state-defined good relations agenda has trumped both human rights and equality agendas. This shift is absolutely central to understanding racism and sectarianism in Northern Ireland. The core state project was reworked from its focus on persuasion that it was capable of reform, to persuasion that it has been reformed. The target of intervention has shifted from structural inequalities that can be measured – unemployment differentials, relative poverty between communities, incidence of hate crime, even the length and height of 'peacelines' – towards the unquantifiable straw man of 'destructive and ugly mindsets'. Phenomena that can reasonably read as indicators of racism and sectarianism are effectively ignored. This new, post-GFA formation eschews discussion of inequality with its focus on 'relations'.

It bears emphasis that this new construction does a profound disservice to the task of understanding and addressing both sectarianism and racism. Increasingly, state intervention moves away from both subjects. For example, the ECNI Corporate Plan 2003–6 (Equality Commission 2003) mentions both racism and sectarianism *once* and good relations four times. The Race Equality Strategy mentions 'good relations' 32 times and anti-racism twice (Office of the First Minister and Deputy First Minister 2005a); the Shared Future strategy (Office of the First Minister and Deputy First Minister 2005b) mentions good relations 120 times, racism (15) more times than sectarianism (12), and neither anti-racism nor anti-sectarianism at all. This is the post-GFA, post-reformist 'good relations' statelet in action. It is a state formation that repudiates racism and sectarianism as destructive and ugly mindsets. Equally, however, it is questionable whether any state institutions in Northern Ireland would pass the Macpherson test on either institutionalised racism or sectarianism – the 'collective failure of an organisation to provide an appropriate and professional service to people because of their colour, culture or ethnic origin'. This formula was generated by the British state and the New Labour government at its most reformist but it does not have application in the post-GFA Northern Ireland statelet. The Northern Ireland statelet is increasingly incapable of engaging with – let alone dismantling – racism and sectarianism in their structural and systemic forms.

Conclusion

What does this analysis tell us about the nature of racism and sectarianism in the post-GFA state? The GFA was a reformist project. It was an historic compromise that saw republican political violence ended in response to the promise of an end to sectarian inequality. It was assumed that the human rights and equality agendas of the GFA would deliver tangible, if incremental, benefits to Catholics sufficient to legitimise the state – at least to the extent that political violence was no longer supported or justified. In this sense, the GFA was essentially about sectarianism: it promised to 'desectarianise' the state sufficiently to copperfasten peace. The state – like the PSNI – would have a 'new beginning' above politics.

Despite continuing violence and inequality, the Northern Ireland statelet has undoubtedly become more stable and more legitimate with the peace process and the GFA. When the Stormont Assembly is not suspended, it assumes a comical cross-community legitimacy with almost everyone in power – republican, nationalist, unionist and loyalist, Sinn Féin, SDLP, UUP and DUP. Bizarrely, the centrist and cross-community Alliance Party provides the only 'opposition'. Even when the executive is suspended – and Direct Rule returns 'pending re-establishment of the Assembly' – the statelet looks much less volatile than it did a decade ago. Suspended devolution is a 'temporary' arrangement with shades of permanence. The restoration of devolution to the Northern Ireland Assembly as Tuesday 8 May 2007 clearly marked a further bedding down of the 'peace process' – no doubt this has significant implications for the sociology of racism and sectarianism.

We find, however, that this new formation falls far short of what the GFA promised in terms of equality and human rights. As we have seen, racism and sectarianism are rampant in Northern Ireland and both continue to characterise the post-GFA state. In other words racism and sectarianism must be understood as defining elements of contemporary Northern Ireland rather than as unpleasant and vestigial legacies. They must both be situated and understood and resisted in terms of the post-GFA Northern Ireland state. The downplaying of racism and sectarianism does nothing to address their very real consequences in a place where racist and sectarian violence and discrimination remain routine.

Finally, it bears emphasis that suggesting that the post-GFA Northern Ireland state is 'more stable' and 'more legitimate' is not the same thing as suggesting that it is either stabilised or legitimised. A state formation that cannot support a sustainable, accountable government with a measure of democratic legitimacy remains vulnerable to collapse. Moreover, in the last ten years two events – the siege of the Garvaghy Road and the picket of Holy Cross School – have threatened to undermine the whole process of 'normalisation'. These episodes were obviously directly rooted in the continuing dynamics of sectarianism in Northern Ireland. In the meantime, this precarious, profoundly sectarianised state formation has also become identified as the 'race hate capital of Europe'. Both racism and sectarianism have a key part to play in the future development of this state and social forces within it. Whether the current accommodation collapses or not, we can be certain that both racism and sectarianism will remain definitive elements in the sociology of Northern Ireland.

Notes

Chapter 1 Population

1 The EU15 refers to the 15 countries in the European Union before the expansion on 1 May 2004.

2 Currently the State Retirement Pension is payable from either age 65 or 66 (this depends on whether or not you continue working).

3 This is a widely used measure that is arrived at by calculating the number of births a woman would have if over her reproductive lifespan she were to replicate the level of births found among all women in a particular year. Though expressed as births *per woman*, it is actually based on births *per year* and is a means of expressing annual birth rates in an easily understood way.

4 Technically, the replacement fertility rate is the number of births a woman of reproductive age would need to have in order to replace herself (i.e. that is to produce another woman of reproductive age). Human populations normally experience a slight gender imbalance in births in favour of males and this means that women on average need to have 2.06 births to have one female birth. In present mortality conditions, an additional 0.4 births per woman is needed to compensate for deaths of children and young adults prior to reaching average reproductive age, thus yielding a replacement fertility rate of 2.10. In populations with higher mortality among children and young adults, the replacement fertility rate would be correspondingly higher.

5 There are now many good websites from which demographic data and/or published compilations of data can be downloaded for free. Nearly all of the data presented in this chapter have been assembled in this way. For Ireland, see the excellent Central Statistics Office website at www.cso.ie. The EU equivalent is Eurostat's 'New Cronos' database at http://europe.eu.in/new chronos. The World Health Organisation in Europe makes available the European Health for All database at http://www.euro.who.int/hfadb. This is good not only on health but also on many other aspects of population. Another useful source is the demographic database of the United Nations Economic Commission for Europe (UNECE) at http://w3.unece. org/stat/pau.asp. The Council of Europe publishes an annual report entitled *Recent Demographic Developments in Europe* which includes an interactive CD-ROM that provides the data in tabular and graphic form (though the data are not available on the web).

Chapter 2 Immigration

1   The government has indicated that immigration and naturalisation will be dealt with by one body in the future, the Irish Naturalisation and Immigration Service.

2   Other major modes of entry include the Intra-Business transfer scheme (but this has temporarily been suspended), entry as a parent of Irish born children, arrival as a dependant.

3   Programme refugees are invited, usually in groups, by the government.

4   This estimate was made before the EU expanded to include 10 new states from Eastern Europe. The EEA included the 15 states in the EU, plus the members of the European Free Trade Association – Norway, Iceland and Liechtenstein.

Chapter 3 Irish mobilities

1   I acknowledge permission for the use of the POWSAR data set from the Central Statistics Office – Census Place of Work Microdata File © Government of Ireland.

2   Control over immigration is in fact an example of multi-level governance, since decisions involve the European Union and to a limited extent other inter-governmental and even non-governmental actors.

3   I acknowledge permission for the use of the COPSAR data set from the Central Statistics Office – Census of Population Sample of Anonymised Records © Government of Ireland.

Chapter 4 Individualisation and secularisation in Catholic Ireland

1   There were two phases to Irish modernisation. The first began after the Famine. The Church became central to attempts to modernise Irish farming and society. It was in and through the Church that many Irish people were able to bring rationalised order to family life, develop a decent standard of living, become emotionally self-disciplined and civilised like other Europeans and, at the same time, establish a separate identity to their colonial masters (Inglis 1998; Hynes 1978; Carroll 1999). This lasted until the 1960s when the state abandoned the Catholic vision of Irish society and ushered in a new phase of modernisation.

2   Bruce (2002a: 71–3) argues that Davie's notion of 'believing without belonging' is erroneous since, particularly in Britain, the decline in religious participation has been matched by a decline in belief. However, it is important to remember that while the general trend may hold, among some Protestant churches and sects both belief and practices remain high.

3   Bishop Jeremiah Newman was Bishop of Limerick 1974–95.

Chapter 6 Education

1   The differences are accounted for the higher incidence of short-cycle courses in Ireland and the smaller percentage of part-time higher education students, by comparison with those countries which report high levels of gross enrolment.

2   While there are some differences in management structure between comprehensive and community schools (Drudy and Lynch 1993) they both embody the same curriculum principles of combining academic and technical subjects.

3   Ireland ranked 7th, 16th, 20th and 21st out of 40 countries participating in the study of achievement in Reading, Science, Mathematics and cross-curricular problem solving, respectively (Cosgrove et al. 2005: xix).

4   It is likely that participation rates of about 90 per cent would constitute 'saturation' given ability and motivational thresholds.

5   Lynch distinguishes between the provision and consumption of a service such as education. The provision of an identical service to different groups in no way guarantees identical patterns of consumption; skills and resources are necessary to consume a service.

6   Gender issues are discussed in chapter 15 of this volume.

Chapter 9 A question of sport

1   It is worth noting that the term 'sport' generally tends to be widely used in a commonsense way to incorporate sport in schools (physical education), sport in the community (extra-curricular and club sports), elite sports, recreational and lifestyle activities, and leisure-based activities.

2   For example, functionalist explanations of sport focus on the purpose they serve (teleology) or on the organic analogy of sport as one interdependent part of the social system. Thus, sport functions to meet the needs of both the individual and the social system as a whole, and this argument is held to be true by virtue of its logic (tautology).

3   The research comprised a nationally representative survey of adults aged 16–75. Two thousand personal interviews were completed with a quota-controlled sample of the population. A 'seasonality monitor' was also conducted with a quota-controlled sample of 1,300 adults.

4   See Liston (2005c) for a more detailed discussion of aspects of the relationship between sport and gender in sports participation in Ireland.

5   The most strenuously active category of people is males in the 18–35 year age group.

6   The sociological concept of social capital is most closely associated with the work of Robert Putnam (1995, 2000), and Pierre Bourdieu (1986).

7   See *Irish Independent* (27 October 2006) for coverage of racist comments by Irish children towards non-nationals in children's sports.

8   The 2004 report on *Sports Participation and Health among Adults in Ireland* also identifies in passing that 'regular sports participants are more likely to drink higher numbers of units (of alcohol) per week compared to the general population, with higher levels of consumption being particularly common among female regular participants' (ESRI 2004: 49).

9   Sociologists of sport can raise critical questions about the paradox between the acceptance (if not the centrality) of alcohol within sporting cultures on the one hand, and the 'moral panic' that seems to exist about the negative consequences of alcohol overuse on the other. It seems implausible to encourage young people to participate in sports and physical activities for the essence of 'sports for sports sake' and the health benefits that arise from this when, at one and the same time, the concentrated intake of alcohol is approved (if not expected) in particular team sport cultures such as rugby, Gaelic games and soccer, some of which have identifiable post-match drinking rituals.

10 Research (see Waddington 2000) points to the benefits of moderate and regular physical exercise rather than over-exertion, over training (associated with some individual sports such as running), and physical contact (associated with competitive sports). Thus participation in individual and team sports often leads to injury and the pressure to play or compete, while injured rather than being 'good for health' in the physiological sense.

11 See Mennell (2006) for a summary of Elias and Dunning's threefold distinction between 'sports', 'games', and 'sport-games', written from a figurational sociological perspective.

12 For example, the Central Council of Physical Recreation argues that 'tackling social inclusion through sport can be a 'win-win' situation' (2002: 3); sport can be a 'key ingredient in tackling the causes of anti-social behaviour and street crime' (2002: 5); and 'the case for health improvement through physical activity and sport is proven' (2002: 6).

13 FIFA's report on the 1994 World Cup indicated that 12 per cent of all medical treatments for players were for chronic injuries predating the competition, while the costs of treatment to players with sporting injuries in Britain in 1991 was in the region of £420 m (Waddington 2000). To date, no comparable data exist for the Republic of Ireland.

Chapter 11 Power and powerlessness

1   For more on Jeremy Bentham's panopticon, see Foucault 1977, and Bentham 1995.

2   We are indebted to Una Crowley for drawing our attention to the Citizen Traveller campaign (Crowley 2005).

3   Travellers trace their ethnic origins back as far as the twelfth century (see McDonagh 2000).

Chapter 12 The environment and civil society

1 Focus groups are a recognised social research method used to examine in depth how selected groups talk about and discuss issues related to the research questions in hand.

Chapter 15 Gender and the workforce

1 Almost one in five (19.5 per cent) of cases taken in 2005 by the Equality Authority under the Employment Equality Acts related to gender grounds, second only to race (33.2 per cent) (Equality Authority 2006: 8).
2 The other grounds are marital status, sexual orientation, sexual orientation, disability, race or membership of the Traveller community.
3 Women are in the majority at the universities and have been since the early 1990s. In 2004 there were more girls than boys in the education system; the total participation rate for those aged 4–24 is 74.6 per cent for girls and 70.5 per cent for boys (Department of Education and Science 2005c: 7). Overall Irish women come to the labour market with better educational credentials than men. Only 39.2 per cent of Irish women between the ages of 35 and 64 have left school before the Leaving Certificate, compared to 44.2 per cent of men (CSO 2005b: 41).
4 As of 1 January 2007 there are 27 EU member states.

Chapter 16 Food and rural sustainable development

1 CORASON: A Cognitive Approach to Rural Sustainable Development, 2004–6, is a 12-country research project co-ordinated through Trinity College Dublin and funded under the EU Framework 6. My thanks to my Research Officer, Robert Mooney, and to students of Tipperary Institute, for collecting the data reported on here.

Chapter 17 Social class and inequality

1 The Gini coefficient is a measure of inequality ranging from zero (complete equality) to one (complete inequality).

Chapter 18 The changing working class in Northern Ireland

1 Even the term used in discussing the north east part of the island of Ireland is contentious (see Hillyard et al. 2005: 3–4). Here, I use Northern Ireland when referring to the administrative unit, and the North of Ireland otherwise.

2   The qualitative data come from a study of mothers, Protestant and Catholic, in areas of the North where there was more than 70 per cent child poverty in 2003. The study was commissioned by the Bogside and Brandywell Women's Group, funded by the Big Lottery Fund and carried out by the author in 2004–5. Seventy-two mothers were interviewed. All of the mothers were of working age; most were aged between 30 and 50 years. Half (51 per cent) of the mothers interviewed had either one or two children. A quarter had three or four children and a further quarter had five or more. They included women who had worked in traditional industrial and service sector jobs and some women who were part of families that had endured intergenerational unemployment and poverty. For more information on methodology and the final report, see www.bbwg.org.

3   The Gini coefficient is a measure of inequality ranging from zero (complete equality) to one (complete inequality).

4   The Noble Indices of Multiple Deprivation provide information about relative deprivation on an electoral ward level across a range of domains, including income; employment; health; education, skills and training; and crime and disorder.

5   Sen's 'capabilities framework' can sometimes seem difficult to understand. For a brief and accessible introduction, see Burchardt (2004).

6   See note 2 above.

Chapter 20   Identity, language and nationality

When I wrote this chapter I was a visiting scholar at the Institut für Soziologie in Albert-Ludwigs-Universität Freiburg and I am very grateful to Prof. Dr Hermann Schwengel for his invitation.

1   'That man is looking at us.'

2   In Irish mauve is bánchorcra, which is literally purple-white.

3   See for example the discussion and article 'Ulster Scots Language' on www.wikipedia.org.

4   In the 1851 Census 1,524,285 people were returned as Irish speakers, and 1,570,894 in the 2002 Census.

5   The Gaeltacht is an appellation employed to describe certain geographical areas containing a diverse group of communities that are predominantly Irish speaking. These communities are mainly in the West of Ireland, including areas in Counties Cork and Kerry (south-west), County Galway (west), Counties Mayo and Donegal (north-west), but also including a small community in County Meath (mid-east) and in County Waterford (south-east).

6   From 28 per cent in 1971 to 42 per cent in 2002. 'A new question on ability to speak the Irish language and frequency of speaking Irish was introduced in the 1996 Census of Population. The new version of the question marked a major departure from the version used in previous censuses. The version used in those years asked respondents to

write ' Irish only', ' Irish and English' , ' Read but cannot speak Irish' or to leave blank as appropriate. While the revised version used in 1996 is more direct, ' Can the person speak Irish?' , and also includes a question on frequency of speaking Irish, a major drawback is that it gives rise to a discontinuity with the results of previous censuses. The version introduced in 1996 was retained unchanged for 2002' (Census 2002 Report vol. II: 88). The increased percentage is quite dramatic not solely as a result of the change in the wording of the question.

7   P. Ó Ciardha, in a personal interview with the author on 19 February 1996.

8   Ironically, the Irish state was not able to sign the charter on behalf of the Irish language because it is defined as an official language of Ireland rather than a minority language.

Chapter 22 Protestants and Protestant habitus in Northern Ireland

1   The historic Province of Ulster includes six counties in Northern Ireland and three in the Republic of Ireland. The political Province refers only to the six counties which have remained in part of the United Kingdom. (See Northern Ireland Statistics website: www.nirsa.gov.uk)

2   Huguenots were refugees who fled France on the revocation of the Edict of Nantes in 1685.

3   Key texts which have seriously attempted to address the issue are relatively speaking, few in number. Important works include Gibbon 1975; Bew et al. 1979; Jenkins 1982; Jenkins 1983; Nelson 1984; Bell 1987; Bruce 1989; Bruce 1994; Miller 1978; Todd 1987; The more recent accounts presented by Whyte 1990; Boal et al. 1991; Beattie 1992; Moore and Sanders 1996; Shirlow and McGovern 1997; O'Dowd 1998; Ruane and Todd 1996; Miller 1998; Moore and Sanders 2002 and various journalistic accounts such as Bowyer Bell 1996 and McKay 2000 add to this.

4   Traditional Green (one nation) Marxists, the British and Irish Communist Party (two nation), regarded by some as Orange or revisionist Marxists, and Bew et al.'s (1979) (dialectical) third interpretation.

5   The Catholic Church no longer asks Protestants who marry Catholics to promise to raise the children as Catholics, but requires the Catholic partner to promise to ensure that this happens (Ruane and Todd 1996: 248).

6   There are at least 10,000 essays specific to the conflict in Northern Ireland, excluding works on conflict theory.

7   This included one of the biggest bank robberies in history which has largely been attributed to the IRA, and the revenge killing, for example of Denis Donaldson a close aid and adviser to senior Sinn Féin negotiators who was exposed as a British agent.

8   The literature ranges from the historical 'pre troubles' rural ethnography of Rosemary Harris to Jenkins community studies on the periphery of Belfast through to various sociological accounts by Bruce among others. Whyte (1990) presents a useful review of the literature.

9 'Friends' in the Northern Ireland context often refers to extended and distant kin.
10 For discussions on social capital see Putnam 1993b, 1995; Campbell et al. 1999; Kawachi and Kennedy 2002.

Chapter 23 Race and sectarianism in Northern Ireland

1 See *The Guardian,* 10 January 2004, for the origin of the 'race-hate capital of Europe' claim and *Der Spiegel,* 28 February 2005, for the origin of the 'world's most racist city' claim.

2 Hansard 1 Mar 2006: Col. 781w 'Racial hostility offences'.

3 It bears emphasis that these statistics require a strong health warning. The categories are the PSNI's own. The PSNI accepts that they may represent a marked under-recording. Nevertheless these are now the definitive statutory measure of hate crime. Moreover, the annual increase in 'racial' hate crime they have traced over recent years has informed much of the journalistic construction of the rise in racism in Northern Ireland. Finally, since these 1995–6 figures also represent the first ever official statistics on sectarian violence, their future annual appearance will no doubt provide key material for both journalists and academics tracing longitudinal changes in different forms of hate crime, especially racism and sectarianism.

4 See Lentin and McVeigh 'Situated racisms: A theoretical introduction' (2002: 1–48) for an overview of approaches to race and racism.

5 Recent publications have made significant contribution to historically grounding the subject (Brewer and Higgins 2002; Ford and McCafferty 2006) and building on analysis of the historic sectarianism of the Northern Ireland state (McVeigh 2006a).

6 Thus Connolly and Keenan (2000a: 19–20) were comparing their own work with that of Brewer and Dowds (1996) which had used a completely different sample method. The two studies were comparable but not statistically comparable. In any case, alarm bells should have been ringing about the reliability of their sample given that it suggested that only 10 per cent of the population were DUP voters and seven per cent Sinn Féin voters at a time when these were poised to become the majority unionist and nationalist parties (Connolly and Keenan 2000a: 28).

7   'Of most concern to the authors were the negative attitudes expressed towards members of the Traveller community. A majority of respondents (57 per cent) said they would not accept Travellers as residents in their local area, and two-thirds of those surveyed said they would not accept a member of the Traveller community as a work colleague' (University of Ulster Press Release, 14 April 2000).

8   INCORE is the Centre for International Conflict Research, a joint project of the United Nations University and the University of Ulster www.incore.ulst.ac.uk.

References

Adamson, I. 1986 *The Cruthin: The Ancient Kindred.* Belfast: Pretani Press.

Adler, F. 1983 *Nations Not Obsessed with Crime.* Littleton, CO: Rothman.

Agamben, G. 2005 *State of Exception.* Chicago: University of Chicago Press.

Agyeman, J., R. Bullard and B. Evans (eds) 2003 *Just Sustainabilities: Development in an Unequal World.* London: Earthscan.

Ahern, B. 1997 'Dáil speech to announce the creation of the Department of Tourism, Sport and Recreation' 26 June. www.taoiseach.gov.ie/index.asp Accessed 7 July 2000.

Ahn, N. and P. Mira, 2002 'A note on the changing relationship between fertility and female employment rates in developed countries', *Journal of Population Economics* 15: 667–82

Allen, C. and J. S. Nielsen 2002 *Summary Report on Islamophobia in the EU after 11 September 2001 on behalf of the EUMC.* Vienna: European Monitoring Centre on Racism and Xenophobia.

Allen, G. 1999 *The Garda Síochána: Policing Independent Ireland 1922–82.* Dublin: Gill & Macmillan.

Allen, K. 2000 *The Celtic Tiger: The Myth of Social Partnership in Ireland.* Manchester: Manchester University Press.

Allen, K. 2004 *Weber: A Critical Introduction.* London: Pluto.

Allison, L. 2000 'Sport and nationalism', pp. 344–55 in J. Coakley and E. Dunning (eds), *Handbook of Sports Studies.* London: Sage.

Andersen, M. L. 1998 *Thinking About Women: Sociological Perspectives on Sex and Gender.* London: Allyn & Bacon.

Anderson, B. 1983 *Imagined Communities: Reflections on the Origin and Spread of Nationalism.* London: Verso.

Anderson, R. 2004 'How to excel in S.C.' *Seattle Weekly,* 22 Sept.

An Gárda Siochána *Annual Reports* (various years) Dublin: Stationery Office.

Anthias, F. 1999 'Theorising identity, difference and social divisions', pp. 156–78 in M. O'Brien, S. Penna and C. Hay (eds), *Theorising modernity: reflexivity, environment and identity in Giddens's Social Theory.* London: Longman.

Ardoyne Commemoration Project 2002 *Ardoyne: The Untold Truth.* Belfast: Beyond the Pale.

Ardoyne Commemoration Project 2004 *Ardoyne: The Untold Truth (DVD),* Belfast: ACP.

Arendt, H. 1970 *On Violence.* London: Penguin.

Arensberg, C. and S. Kimball 1940 *Family and Community in Ireland.* Cambridge MA: Harvard University Press.

ARK Northern Ireland 2003 *Young Life and Times Survey.* www.ark.ac.uk/ylt

ARK Northern Ireland 2004 *Northern Ireland Life and Times Survey.* www.ark.ac.uk

Armstrong, J. A. 1982 *Nations Before Nationalism*. Chapel Hill: University of North Carolina Press.

Arnot, M., M. David, and G. Weiner 1999 *Closing the Gender Gap: Postwar Education and Social Change*. Cambridge: Polity.

Aspden, D. 2005 'Methodological improvements to UK foreign property statistics', *Economic Trends* 619 (June): 54–60. http://www.statistics.gov.uk/downloads/theme_economy/ET619.pdf Accessed 25 Sept. 2006.

Association of Garda Sergeants and Inspectors 1982 *A Discussion Paper Concerning Proposals for a Scheme of Community Policing*. Dublin: AGSI.

Athwal, H. and A. Kundnani 2006 'Sixty-eight racist murders since Stephen Lawrence', *IRR News*, 27 Apr.

Atkinson, J. and N. Meager 1986 *New Forms of Work Organisation*, Brighton: University of Sussex Institute of Manpower Studies.

Aughey, A. 2005 *The Politics of Northern Ireland: Beyond the Belfast Agreement*. London: Routledge.

Aughey, A. 2006 'The 1998 Agreement: three unionist anxieties', pp. 89–108 in M. Cox, A. Guilke and F. Stephen (eds), *A Farewell to Arms? Beyond the Good Friday Agreement*, Manchester: Manchester University Press.

Bacik, I., C. Costello and E. Drew 2003 *Gender Injustice: Feminising the Legal Professions?* Dublin: Trinity College Dublin Law School.

Bairner, A. 2002 'The dog that didn't bark? Football hooliganism in Ireland', pp. 118–30 in E. Dunning, P. Murphy, I. Waddington and A. E. Astrinakis (eds), *Fighting Fans: Football Hooliganism as a World Phenomenon*. Dublin: UCD Press.

Bairner, A. 2003 'Political unionism and sporting nationalism: an examination of the relationship between sport and national identity within the Ulster unionist tradition', *Identities: Global Studies in Culture and Power* 10 (4): 517–35.

Baker, J., K. Lynch, S. Cantillon and J. Walsh 2004 *Equality: From Theory to Action*. Basingstoke: Palgrave Macmillan.

Balanda, K. P. and J. Wilde 2001 *Inequalities in Mortality 1989–1998*. Dublin: Institute of Public Health in Ireland.

Bales, R. F. and P. E. Slater 1956 'Role differentiation in small groups', pp. 259–306 in T. Parsons and R. F. Bales (eds), *Family: Socialization and Interaction Processes*. London: Routledge & Kegan Paul.

Baran, P. 1957 *The Political Economy of Growth*. New York: Monthly Review Press.

Barnes, B. 1988 *The Nature of Power*. Cambridge: Polity.

Barr Tribunal 2006 *Report of The Tribunal of Inquiry into the Facts and Circumstances Surrounding the Fatal Shooting of John Carthy at Abbeylara, Co Longford on 20th April 2000*. Dublin: Stationery Office.

Barrell, R. and N. Pain 1997 'The growth of foreign investment in Europe', *National Institute Economic Review* 160: 63–75.

Barron, R. D. and G. M. Norris 1976 'Sexual division and the dual labour market', pp. 47–69 in D. Barker and S. Allen (eds), *Dependence and Exploitation in Work and Marriage*. London: Longman.

Barth, F. 1969 'Introduction', pp. 9–37 in F. Barth (ed.), *Ethnic Groups and Boundaries*, Oslo: Universiteforlaget.

Barton, J. 1992 *A History of Ulster*. Belfast: Blackstaff.

Basile, E. and C. Cecchi 2001 *La trasformazione post-industriele della campagna*. Turin: Rosenberg & Sellier.

Bathelt, H., A. Malmberg and P. Maskell 2004 'Clusters and knowledge: local buzz, global pipelines and the process of knowledge creation', *Progress in Human Geography* 28 (1): 31–56.

Bauer, P. T. 1984 'Remembrance of studies past', pp. 27–43 in G. Meier and D. Seers (eds), *Pioneers in Development*, Oxford: Oxford University Press.

Bauman, Z. 2001 *The Individualised Society*. Cambridge: Polity.

Bauman, Z. 2005 *Liquid Life*. Cambridge: Polity.

Bazen, S. and G. Benhayoun 1992 'Low pay and wage regulation in the European Community', *British Journal of Industrial Relations* 30 (4): 623–38.

Beardsworth, A. and T. Keil 1997 *Sociology on the Menu*. London: Routledge.

Beattie, J. 1992 *We are the People: Journeys through the Heart of Protestant Ulster*. London: Mandarin

Beck, U. 1992 *Risk Society: Towards a New Modernity*. London: Sage.

Beck, U. 1999 *World Risk Society*. Cambridge: Polity.

Beck, U. and E. Beck-Gernsheim 2002. *Individualization*. London: Sage

Beck-Gernsheim, E. 2002 *Reinventing the Family*. Cambridge: Polity.

Belfast Agreement 1998 http://www.nio.gov.uk/agreement.pdf Accessed 29 Mar. 2006.

Belfast City Council 2005 *Belfast City Council Policy and Resources Sub–Committee Report on Northern Ireland Multiple Deprivation Measure*. Belfast: BCC.

Bell, D. 1973 *The Coming of Postindustrial Society*. Boston: Free Press

Bell, D. 1987 *Acts of Union: Youth Culture and Sectarianism in Northern Ireland*. London. Macmillan.

Bell, K., N. Jarman and T. Lefebvre 2004 *Migrant Workers in Northern Ireland*. Belfast: Office of the First Minister and Deputy First Minister.

Bell, M. 1998 *An Introduction to Environmental Sociology*. London: Pine Forge Press.

Benner, C. 2002 *Work in the New Economy: Flexible Labor Markets in Silicon Valley*, Oxford: Blackwell.

Bentham, J. 1995 [1787] *Jeremy Bentham: The Panopticon Writings*, ed. Miran Boĺoviã (London and New York: Verso).

Benton, T. 2002 'Social theory and ecological politics: reflexive modernisation or green socialism?' pp. 252–73 in R. Dunlap, F. Buttle, P. Dickens and A. Gijswijt (eds), *Social Theory and the Environment*. Lanham, Maryland and Oxford: Rowman & Littlefield.

Berman, M. 1982 *All That Is Solid Melts Into Air: The Experience of Modernity*. London: Penguin.

Bernard, J. 1973 *The Future of Marriage*. London: Souvenir Press

Bernardes, Jon 1985 'Do we really know what the family is?' pp. 192–227 in P. Close and R. Collins (eds) *Family and Economy in Modern Society*. Basingstoke: Macmillan.

Bernstein, B. 1971 *Class, Codes and Control*, vol.1. London: Routledge & Kegan Paul.

Bew, P. 2006 'Myths of consociationalism: from Good Friday to political impasse', pp. 57–69 in M. Cox, A. Guelke and F. Stephen (eds), *A Farewell to Arms? Beyond the Good Friday Agreement*. Manchester: Manchester University Press.

Bew, P., P. Gibbon and H. Patterson 1979 *The State in Northern Ireland 1921–72.* Manchester: Manchester University Press.

Billig, M. 1995 *Banal Nationalism.* London: Sage.

Bissett, J. 1999 *Not Waiting for a Revolution: Negotiating Policing Through the Rialto Community Policing Forum.* Dublin: Rialto Community Policing Forum.

Blackwell, J. 1995 'The changing role of part-time work in Ireland and its implications', pp. 78–103 in F. Convery and A. McCashin (eds), *Reason and Reform: Studies in Social Policy.* Dublin: IPA.

Blomley, N. 2006 'Homelessness and the delusions of property', *Transactions of the Institute of British Geographers* 31 (1): 3–5.

Boal, F., J. Campbell and D. Livingstone 1991 'The Protestant mosaic: a majority of minorities', pp. 99–129 in P. Roche and B. Barton (eds), *The Northern Ireland Question: Myth and Reality.* Aldershot: Avebury.

Bohan, P. and D. Yorke 1987 'Law enforcement marketing: perceptions of a police force', *Irish Marketing Review* 2: 72–86.

Bond, P. 2005 *Elite Transition: From Apartheid to Neo–Liberalism in South Africa.* London: Pluto.

Borrel, C. 2006 'Enquêtes annuelles de recensement 2004 et 2005: Près de 5 millions d'immigrés à la mi-2004', *INSEE Première* no. 1098 (Aug.). http://www.insee.fr/fr/ffc/ipweb/ip1098/ip1098.htm accessed 25 Sept. 2006.

Boucher, G. W. 2004 'The land of conditional welcomes', pp. 185–95 in M. Peillon and M. Corcoran (eds), *Place and Non-Place.* Dublin: IPA.

Bourdieu, P. 1977 *Outline of a Theory of Practice.* Cambridge: Cambridge University Press.

Bourdieu, P. 1984 *Distinction – A Social Critique of the Judgement of Taste.* London: Routledge & Kegan Paul.

Bourdieu, P. 1986 'The forms of capital', pp. 241–58 in J. Richardson (ed.), *Handbook of Theory and Research for the Sociology of Education,* New York: Greenwood.

Bourdieu, P. 1990 *The Logic of Practice.* Cambridge: Polity.

Bourdieu, P. 1991 'Genesis and structure of the religious field', *Comparative Social Research* 13 (1): 1–44.

Bourdieu, P. 1998a *Practical Reason.* Cambridge: Polity.

Bourdieu, P. 1998b *On Television.* London: Pluto.

Bourdieu, P. and J. C. Passeron 1977 *Reproduction in Education, Society and Culture.* London: Sage.

Bourdieu, P. and L. Wacquant 1992 *An Invitation to Reflexive Sociology.* Cambridge: Cambridge University Press.

Bowden, M. and L. Higgins 2000 *The Impact and Effectiveness of the Garda Special Projects.* Dublin: Stationery Office.

Bowles, S. and H. Gintis 1976 *Schooling in Capitalist America.* London: Routledge & Kegan Paul.

Bowling, B. 1999 'The rise and fall of New York murder: zero tolerance or crack's decline?' *British Journal of Criminology* 39 (4): 531–54.

Bowyer Bell, J. 1996 *Back to the Future: The Protestants and a United Ireland.* Dublin: Poolbeg.

Boyle, M. 2002 'Cleaning up after the Celtic Tiger: the politics of waste management in the Irish Republic', *Transactions of the Institute of British Geographers* 27: 172–94.

Bradley, H. 1996 *Fractured Identities: Changing Patterns of Inequality*. Cambridge: Political Press.

Braverman, H. 1974 *Labor and Monopoly Capital*. New York: Monthly Review Press.

Breathnach, P. 2002 'Social polarisation in the post-Fordist informational economy: Ireland in an international context', *Irish Journal of Sociology* 11: 3–22.

Breathnach, P. 2004 'Occupational change and social polarisation in the post Fordist informational economy', Employment Research Centre: TCD.

Breen, M., A. Hynes and E. Devereux 2006 'Citizens, loopholes and maternity tourists', pp. 59–70 in M. Corcoran and M. Peillon (eds), *Uncertain Ireland*. Dublin: IPA.

Breen, R. and L. P. Cooke 2005 'The persistence of the gendered division of domestic labour', *European Sociological Review* 21: 43–57.

Breen, R. and Whelan, C. 1996 *Social Mobility and Social Class in Ireland*. Dublin: Gill & Macmillan.

Breuilly, J. 1982 *Nationalism and the State*. Manchester: Manchester University Press.

Brewer, J. 1992 'Sectarianism and racism, and their parallels and differences', *Ethnic and Racial Studies* 15 (3): 352–64.

Brewer, J. D. and L. Dowds 1996 'Race, ethnicity and prejudice in Northern Ireland' pp. 94–111 in R. Breen, P. Devine and L. Dowds (eds), *Social Attitudes in Northern Ireland: The Fifth Report 1995–6*. Belfast: Appletree.

Brewer, J. D. and G. I. Higgins 2002 *Anti-Catholicism in Northern Ireland, 1600–1998: The Mote and the Beam*. London: Macmillan.

Brewer, J., B. Lockhart and P. Rodgers 1997 *Crime in Ireland: 'Here be Dragons'*. Oxford: Clarendon.

Brody, H. 1973 *Inishkillane*. Suffolk: Penguin.

Brown, T. 1991 'British Ireland', pp. 72–84 in E. Longley (ed.) *Culture in Ireland: Division or Diversity*. Belfast: Institute of Irish Studies.

Brubaker, R. 2001 'Cognitive perspectives', *Ethnicities* 1 (1): 15–17.

Brubaker, R. 2002 'Ethnicity without groups', *Archives Européennes de Sociologies* XLII (2): 163–89.

Bruce, S. 1989 *God Save Ulster: The Religion and Politics of Paisleyism*. Oxford: Oxford University Press.

Bruce, S. 1994 The *Edge of the Union*, Oxford: Oxford University Press.

Bruce, S. 2002a *God is Dead: Secularization in the West*. Oxford: Blackwell.

Bruce, S. 2002b 'Praying alone? Church-going in Britain and the Putnam thesis', *Journal of Contemporary Religion* 17: 317–28.

Bruff, I. and J. Wickham 2005 'The implications of new forms of immigration for government socio-economic strategies and welfare state design: the case of Ireland', *Network for European Social Policy Analysis Conference*, Fribourg (Switzerland) 23 Sept.

Bryan, D. 1995 *Political Rituals: The Politics of Parading in Portadown*. Centre for the Study of Conflict, University of Ulster

Burawoy, M. 1985 *The Politics of Production*. London: Verso.

Burchardt, T. 2004 'Capabilities and disability: the capabilities framework and the social model of disability', *Disability and Society* 19 (7): 735–51.

Burgess, E. 1926 'The family as a unity of interacting personalities', *Family* 7: 3–9.

Burley, J. and F. Regan 2002 'Divorce in Ireland: the fear, the floodgates and the reality', *International Journal of Law, Policy and the Family* 16: 202–22.

Burton, F. 1978 *The Politics of Legitimacy: Struggles in a Belfast Community.* London: Routledge.

Cadwallader, A. 2004 *Holy Cross: The Untold Story.* Belfast: Brehon Press.

Cairns, D. 2000 'The object of sectarianism: The material reality of sectarianism in Ulster loyalism', *Journal of the Royal Anthropological Institute* 6 (3): 437–52.

Cairns, E., J. Van Til, and A. Williamson 2003 *Social Capital, Collectivism-Individualism and Community Background in Northern Ireland.* Belfast: OFMDFMNI/VCU.

Calhoun, C 1997 *Nationalism.* Basingstoke: Open University Press.

Calhoun, C. 1993 *Bourdieu: Critical Perspectives.* Cambridge: Polity.

Callinicos, A. 1983 *The Revolutionary Ideas of Karl Marx.* London: Bookmarks.

Campbell, C., R. Wood and M. Kelly 1999 *Social Capital and Health.* London: Health Education Authority.

Canny, N. P. 2001 *Making Ireland British 1580–1650.* Oxford: Oxford University Press.

Capek, S. 1993 'The "environmental justice" frame: a conceptual discussion and an application', *Social Problems* 40 (1): 5–24.

Carduso, F. H. 1972 'Dependency and development in Latin America', *New Left Review* 74: 83–95.

Carroll, M. 1999 *Irish Pilgrimage: Holy Wells and Popular Catholic Devotion.* Baltimore: Johns Hopkins University Press.

Castells, M. 1989 *The Informational City.* Oxford: Basil Blackwell.

Castells, M. 1996 *Rise of the Network Society.* Oxford: Basil Blackwell

Castles, S. and G. Kosack 1973 *Immigrant Workers and Class Structure in Western Europe.* London: Oxford University Press.

Castles, S. and M. Miller 1998 *The Age of Migration.* London: Macmillan.

Census 2002 http://www.cso.ie/census/Census2002Results.htm accessed 29 Mar. 2006.

Central Bank 2005 *Compendium of Irish Economic Statistics 2006.* Dublin: Central Bank.

Central Council of Physical Recreation 2002 *Everybody Wins.* London: CCPR.

Centre for Public Enquiry 2005 *The Great Corrib Gas Controversy.* Dublin: Centre for Public Enquiry.

Child Poverty Action Group 2002 *Poverty: The Facts.* London: Child Poverty Action Group.

Children Act 2001 no. 24 of 2001. Dublin: Stationery Office.

City Housing Initiative 1999 *Community Development Through Housing.* Dublin: Ringsend Action Project.

Civil Aviation Authority 1998 *Terminal Passengers 1987–1997.* London: Civil Aviation Authority.

Civil Aviation Authority 2005 *Annual UK Airport Statistics: 2004.* London: Civil Aviation Authority.

Clancy, P. 1982 *Participation in Higher Education: A National Survey.* Dublin: Higher Education Authority.

Clancy, P. 1989 'The evolution of policy in third-level education', pp. 99–132 in D. G. Mulcahy and D. O'Sullivan (eds), *Irish Educational Policy: Process and Substance.* Dublin: Institute of Public Education.

Clancy, P. 1996 'Investment in education: the equality perspective, progress and possibilities', *Administration* 44 (3): 28–41.

Clancy, P. 1999 'Barriers to entering higher education', pp. 113–35 in N. Ward and T. Dooney (eds), *Irish Education for the 21st Century.* Dublin: Oak Tree Press.

Clancy, P. 2001 *College Entry in Focus; A Fourth National Survey of Access to Higher Education.* Dublin: HEA.

Clancy, P. 2003 'The vocationalisation of higher education: the evolution of policy in the Republic of Ireland', *International Journal of Vocational Education and Training* 11 (1): 62–82.

Clancy, P. 2005 'Education policy' pp. 80–114 in S. Quin, P. Kennedy, A. Matthews and G. Kiely (eds), *Contemporary Irish Social Policy,* 2nd edn. Dublin: UCD Press.

Clancy, P. and T. Brannick 2004 *What the Papers Said: Analysis of Media Coverage of the Irish European Elections 2004.* Dublin: TASC.

Clayman, S. E. 2002 'Tribune of the people: maintaining the legitimacy of aggressive journalism', *Media, Culture and Society* 24 (2): 197–216.

Clayman, S. E. and J. Heritage 2002 'Questioning presidents: journalistic deference and adversarialness in the press conferences of U.S. Presidents Eisenhower and Reagan', *Journal of Communication* 52: 749–75.

Cleary, A. 2005 'Editor's introduction', *Irish Journal of Sociology* 14 (2): 5–10.

Coakley, J. 1999 'Society and political culture', pp. 36–71 in J. Coakley and M. Gallagher (eds), *Politics in the Republic of Ireland.* London: Routledge.

Coakley, J. 2001 *Sport in Society: Issues and Controversies,* 7th edn. New York: McGraw–Hill.

Coakley, J. and Dunning, E. (eds) 2000 *Handbook of Sports Studies.* London: Sage.

Coimisinéir Teanga 2006 *Annual Report 2005.*

Cole, C. 2000 'Body studies in the sociology of sport', pp. 439–60 in J. Coakley and E. Dunning (eds), *Handbook of Sports Studies.* London: Sage.

Cole, R. 1992 *Strategies for Learning: Small-Group Activities in American, Japanese, and Swedish Industry.* Berkeley: University of California Press.

Coleman, J. S., E. Q. Campbell, C. J. Hobson, J. McPartland, A. M. Mood, F. D. Weinfeld, and R. L. York 1966 *Equality of Educational Opportunity.* Washington DC.: US Government Printing Office.

Colley, L. 1992 *Britons: Forging the Nation 1707–1837.* London: Pimlico.

Collins, G. and J. Wickham 2004 'Inclusion or exploitation? Irish women enter the work force', *Gender Work and Organisation* 11 (1): 26–46.

Collins, M. 2004 'From bigotry to racism' *Searchlight,* Feb.

Collins, R. 1979 *The Credential Society.* New York: Academic Press.

Coltrane, S. 2000 'Research on household labour: modelling and measuring the social embeddedness of routine family work', *Journal of Marriage and the Family* 62: 1208–33.

Commins, P. 1996 'Agricultural production and the future of small-scale farming', pp. 87–125 in C. Curtin, T. Haase and H. Tovey (eds), *Poverty in Rural Ireland.* Dublin: Oak Tree Press.

Commission on the Family 1998 *Strengthening Families for Life: Final Report to the Minister for Social, Community and Family Affairs*. Dublin: Stationery Office.

Commission on Itinerancy 1963 *Report*. Dublin: Stationery Office.

Commission for Racial Equality 2005 *The Police Service in England and Wales: Full List of Recommendations of a Formal Investigation by the Commission for Racial Equality*. London: CRE.

Commission on the Status of People with Disabilities 1996 *A Strategy for Equality*. Dublin: Stationery Office.

Committee on the Administration of Justice 2006 *Equality in Northern Ireland: The Rhetoric and the Reality*. Belfast: CAJ.

Committee for a Worker's International 2003 'Stop racist attacks', socialistworld.net 23 July 2003.

Community Relations Commission 2003 'Anti-racism in the workplace week', *CRC Press Release*, 4 Nov.

Community Relations Commission 2004 *A Good Relations Framework: An Approach to the Development of Good Relations*. Belfast: CRC.

Community Workers Cooperative 2002 'Minister Martin Cullen reneges on his commitment to Traveller groups', news bulletin 2 July, Galway.

Connell, R. W. 1987 *Gender and Power: Society, the Person and Sexual Politics*. Stanford: Stanford University Press.

Connell, R. W. 2002 *Gender*. Cambridge: Polity.

Connolly, J. 1913 'North-East Ulster', in *Forward* transcribed for JCS and WW BBS by Workers' Web ASCII Pamphlet project.

Connolly, J. 2002 *Drugs, Crime and Community in Dublin*. Dublin: Dublin North Inner City Drugs Task Force.

Connolly, P. 2002 *'Race' and Racism in Northern Ireland: A Review of the Research Evidence*. Belfast: Office of the First Minister and Deputy First Minister.

Connolly, P. and M. Keenan 2000a *Racial Attitudes and Prejudice in Northern Ireland*. Belfast: Northern Ireland Statistics and Research Agency.

Connolly, P. and M. Keenan 2000b *Opportunities for All: Minority Ethnic People's Experiences of Education, Training and Employment in Northern Ireland*. Belfast: Northern Ireland Statistics and Research Agency.

Connolly, P. and M. Keenan 2001 *The Hidden Truth: Racist Harassment in Northern Ireland*. Belfast: Northern Ireland Statistics and Research Agency.

Connolly, P. and M. Keenan 2002 *Tackling Racial Inequalities in Northern Ireland: Structures and Strategies*. Belfast: Northern Ireland Statistics and Research Agency.

Connolly, P., A. Smith and B. Kelly 2002 *Too Young to Notice? The Cultural and Political Awareness of 3–6 Year Olds in Northern Ireland*. Belfast: Community Relations Council.

Connor, W. 1978 'A nation is a nation, is a state, is an ethnic group, is a . . . ', *Ethnic and Racial Studies* 1 (4): 379–88.

Conroy, P. and A. Brennan 2003 *Migrant Workers and Their Experiences*. Dublin: Equality Authority.

Conroy P. and M. Pierce, 2002 *Temporary Agency Work: National Reports, Ireland*. Dublin: European Foundation for the Improvements of Living and Working Conditions

Cooper, R. 2002 'The post-modern state', *The Observer Special Reports*, 7 Apr.

Corcoran, M. 2004 'The political preferences and value orientations of Irish journalists', *Irish Journal of Sociology* 13 (2): 23–42.

Corner, J. 2003 'Debate: the model in question: a response to Klaehn on Herman and Chomsky', *European Journal of Communication* 18 (3): 367–75.

Cosgrove, J., G. Shiel, S. Sofroniou, S. Zastrutzki, and F. Shortt 2005 *Education for Life: The Achievements of 15-Year-Olds in Ireland in the Second Cycle of PISA*. Dublin: Educational Research Centre.

Coulter, C. 1999 *Contemporary Northern Irish Society: An Introduction*. London: Pluto.

Coveney, E., J. Murphy-Lawless and S. Sheridan 1998 *Women, Work and Family Responsibilities*. Dublin: Larkin Unemployed Centre.

Cowan, R. 1998 'Parties agree on tax regime change', *Belfast Telegraph*, 20 June.

Cox, M., A. Guelke. and F. Stephen 2006 'Introduction: a farewell to arms? Beyond the Good Friday Agreement', pp. 1–5 in M. Cox, A. Guelke and F. Stephen (eds), *A Farewell to Arms? Beyond the Good Friday Agreement*. Manchester: Manchester University Press.

Craft, M. 1974 'Talent, family values and education in Ireland', pp. 47–67 in J. Eggleston (ed.), *Contemporary Research in the Sociology of Education*. London: Methuen.

Crawford, A. 2003 '"Contractual governance" of deviant behaviour', *Journal of Law and Society* 30 (4): 479–505.

Creaton, S. 2005 *Ryanair: How a Small Irish Airline Conquered Europe*. London: Aurum Press.

Croix, G. E. M. de Ste 1981 *The Class Struggle in the Ancient Greek World*. Duckworth: London.

Crompton, R. 1998 *Class and Stratification: An Introduction to Current Debates*. Cambridge: Polity.

Cronin, M. 2002 'Speed limits: Ireland, globalisation and the war against time' pp. 54–66 in P. Kirby, L. Gibbons and M. Cronin (eds), *Reinventing Ireland: Culture, Society and the Global Economy*. London: Pluto.

Crowley, U. 2005 'Paradoxical spaces of citizenship in contemporary Ireland', paper presented to the Political Studies Association of Ireland Annual Conference, Queen's University Belfast, 21–23 Oct.

Cruikshank, B. 1999 *The Will to Empower: Democratic Citizens and Other Subjects*. Ithaca and London: Cornell University Press.

CSO (Central Statistics Office) 2005a *Principal Statistics*. Dublin: CSO http://www.cso.ie/statistics/passengermovementbyair.htm accessed 8 Jan. 2007.

CSO (Central Statistics Office) 2005b *Women and Men in Ireland*. Dublin: Stationery Office.

CSO (Central Statistics Office) 2006a *Population and Migration Estimates*, April 2006. Dublin: Stationery Office.

CSO (Central Statistics Office) 2006b Quarterly National Household Survey: table 4 1997–2005 http://www.cso.ie/qnhs/main_result_qnhs.htm accessed 30 May 2006.

CSO (Central Statistics Office) 2006c *EU Survey on Income and Living Conditions*. Dublin: CSO.

Culliton Report, 1992 *A Time for Change: Industrial Policy in the 1990s.* Dublin: Stationery Office.

Cunningham, T., E. Isik and N. Moran 2005 '"Are you being served?": migrant workers multiculturalism and the state', pp. 201–20 in G. Boucher and G. Collins (eds), *The New World of Work: Labour Markets in Contemporary Ireland.* Dublin: Liffey Press.

Cunningham, W. 1998 'Conflict theory and conflict in northern Ireland', Unpublished Master of Literature in Political Studies thesis, University of Auckland,

D'Addio, A. C. and M. Mira d'Ercole 2005 *Trends and Determinants of Fertility Rates.* OECD Social, Employment and Migration Working Papers No. 27. Paris: OECD

Daly, M. 1985 *The Hidden Workers: The Work Lives of Part-Time Women Cleaners.* Dublin: Employment Equality Agency.

Daly, P. and I. Shuttleworth, 2000 'The pattern of performance at GCSE', in *The Effects of the Selective System of Secondary Education in Northern Ireland.* Belfast: Department of Education.

Darby, J. 1976 *Conflict in Northern Ireland: The Development of a Polarised Community.* Dublin: Gill & Macmillan.

Darby, J. 1986 *Intimidation and Control of Conflict in Northern Ireland.* Dublin: Gill & Macmillan.

Darby, J. 2006 'A truce rather than a treaty? The effects of violence on the Irish peace process', pp. 212–23 in M. Cox, A. Guelke and F. Stephen (eds), *A Farewell to Arms? Beyond the Good Friday Agreement.* Manchester: Manchester University Press.

Davie, G. 1994 *Religion in Britain Since 1945: Believing Without Belonging.* Oxford: Blackwell.

Davie, G. 2000 'Patterns of change in European religion', pp. 15–30 in T. Inglis, Z. Mach and R. Mazanek (eds), *Religion and Politics: East–West Contrasts from Contemporary Europe.* Dublin: UCD Press.

Davie, G. 2002 'Praying alone? Church-going in Britain and social capital: a reply to Steve Bruce' *Journal of Contemporary Religion* 17 (2): 329–34.

Davies, A. 2005 'Incinerator politics and the geographies of waste governance: a burning issue for Ireland?' *Environment and Planning C: Government and Policy* 23: 375–97.

Davies, A. 2006 'Environmental justice as subtext or omission: examining discourse of anti–incineration campaigning in Ireland?' *Geoforum*, forthcoming.

Davis, A. 2003 'Whither mass media and power? Evidence for a critical elite theory alternative', *Media, Culture and Society* 25 (5): 669–90.

Davis, K. and W. E. Moore 1966 'Some principles of stratification', pp. 47–52 in R. Bendix and S. Lipset (eds), *Class, Status and Power.* London: Routledge.

Davis, M. 1990 *City of Quartz.* London: Verso.

Davis, S. N. and T. N. Greenstein 2004 'Cross-national variations in the division of household labour', *Journal of Marriage and the Family* 66: 1260–71.

De Beauvoir, S. 1972 *The Second Sex.* Harmondsworth: Penguin.

Delaney, P. 2001 'Representations of the travellers in the 1880s and 1900s', *Irish Studies Review* 9 (1): 53–68.

Delaney, P. 2003 'A sense of place: Travellers, representation, and Irish culture', *The Republic* 3 (July): 79–89.

Delanty, G. 2003 *Community.* London: Routledge.

Delphy, C. and D. Leonard 1992 *Familiar Exploitation: A New Analysis of Marriage in Contemporary Western Societies.* Cambridge: Polity.

Department of Agriculture and Food 2005a *Annual Review and Outlook for Agriculture and Food 2004/5.* Dublin: Economics and Planning Division.

Department of Agriculture and Food 2005b *Fact Sheet on Irish Agriculture.* Dublin: Economics and Planning Division.

Department of Education 1992 *Education for a Changing World: Green Paper on Education.* Dublin: Stationery Office.

Department of Education 1997 *Targeting Sporting Change in Ireland: Sport in Ireland, 1997–2006 and Beyond.* Dublin: Stationery Office.

Department of Education 1998 *White Paper on Early Childhood Education.* Dublin: Stationery Office.

Department of Education and Science 1998 *Statistical Report 1996/7.* Dublin: Stationery Office.

Department of Education and Science 1999 *Ready to Learn: White Paper on Early Childhood Education.* Dublin: Stationery Office.

Department of Education and Science 2000 *Learning for Life: White Paper on Adult Education.* Dublin: Stationery Office

Department of Education and Science 2005a *Retention Rates of Pupils in Second Level Schools: The 1996 Cohort.* Dublin: Stationery Office.

Department of Education and Science 2005b *Delivering Equality of Opportunity in Schools.* Dublin: Stationery Office.

Department of Education and Science 2005c *Statistical Report 2003/4.* Dublin: Stationery Office.

Department of Education and the Health Promotion Unit 1996 *A National Survey of Involvement in Sport and Physical Activity.* Dublin: Stationery Office.

Department of Enterprise, Trade and Investment 2005 'Employment change by district council area 1995–2003', *Labour Market Bulletin* 19.

Department of the Environment 1997 *Sustainable Development: A Strategy for Ireland.* Dublin: Stationery Office.

Department of the Environment, Heritage and Local Government 2006 *Annual Housing Statistics Bulletin 2005.* Dublin: Stationery Office

Department of Health and Children and the Health Promotion Unit 1999 *Be Nifty and Fifty.* Dublin: Stationery Office.

Department of Health and Children and the Health Promotion Unit 2003 *The National Health and Lifestyles Survey.* Dublin: Stationery Office.

Department of Health, Social Services and Public Safety 2000 *Investing for Health.* Belfast: Department of Health, Social Services and Public Safety.

Department of Justice Equality and Law Reform 2004 *Developing Childcare in Ireland.* Dublin: Stationery Office.

Department of Justice, Equality and Law Reform 1999 *National Childcare Strategy: Report of the Partnership 2000 Expert Working Group on Childcare.* Dublin: Stationery Office.

Department of Justice, Equality and Law Reform 2002 *Value for Money and Management Audit of the Citizen Traveller Campaign and the Preparation of a Report on Financial Position, Final Report.* Dublin: Stationery Office.

Derrida, J. 2000 'Différance', pp. 87–93 in P. du Gay, J. Evans and P. Redman (eds), *Identity: A Reader.* London: Sage.

Devine, D., M. Nic Ghiolla Phádraig and J. Deegan 2004 'Time for children – time for change' in A. M. Jensen, A. Ben-Arieh, C. Conti, D. Kutsar, M. N. Phádraig, and H. M. Nielsen (eds), *Children's Welfare in Aging Europe*, vol. 1. Trondheim: Norwegian Centre for Child Research.

Devine, P. 2004 *Men and Family Life.* Men in Northern Ireland: Report 5, Belfast: Ark.

Dickson, B. 2006 'New beginnings? Policing and human rights after the conflict', pp. 170–86 in M. Cox, A. Guelke and F. Stephen (eds), *A Farewell to Arms? Beyond the Good Friday Agreement.* Manchester: Manchester University Press.

Dineen, D. 1992 'Atypical work patterns in Ireland: short-term adjustments or fundamental changes?' *Administration* 40 (3): 248–74.

Dixon, J. and C. Jamieson 2005 'The cross-Pacific chicken: tourism, migration and chicken consumption in the Cook Islands', pp. 81–93 in N. Fold and B. Pritchard (eds), *Cross-Continental Food Chains.* London: Routledge.

Dobbelaere, K. 1981 'Secularisation: a multi-dimensional concept', *Current Sociology* 29 (2): 1–215.

Doherty, P. and M. A. Poole 1995 *Ethnic Residential Segregation in Belfast.* Coleraine: University of Ulster.

Dolton, P. and M. Silles 2001 *Over-Education in the Graduate Labour Market.* Oxford: Centre for Economics of Education.

Donnelly, R., D. Grimshaw, J. Rubery and P. Urwin 2005 'Dynamics of national employment models: the UK national report', DYNAMO research project. http://iat-info.iatge.de/projekt/2005/dynamo_old/country-reports/dynamouk.pdf accessed 25 Sept. 2006.

Dooley, R. and M. Corbett 2002 'Child care, juvenile justice and the Children Act, 2001', *Irish Youthwork Scene: A Journal for Youth Workers* 36: June.

Downey, D. 1998 *New Realities in Irish Housing.* Dublin: CRUBE, DIT.

Downey, D. 2003 'Affordability and access to Irish housing: trends, policy and prospects', *Journal of Irish Urban Studies* 2 (1): 1–24.

Drew, E. 1991 *Who Needs Flexibility? Part-Time Working: The Irish Experience.* Dublin: Employment Equality Agency.

Drudy, P. J. and M. Punch 2001 'Housing and inequality in Ireland', pp 235–62 in S. Cantillon, C. Corrigan, P. Kirby and J. O'Flynn (eds), *Rich and Poor: Perspectives on Inequality in Ireland.* Dublin: Combat Poverty Agency and Oak Tree Press.

Drudy, P. J. and M. Punch 2002 'Housing models and inequality: perspectives on recent Irish experience', *Housing Studies* 17 (4): 657–72

Drudy, P. J. and M. Punch 2005 *Out of Reach: Inequalities in the Irish Housing System.* Dublin: TASC at New Island Books.

Drudy, S. and K. Lynch 1993 *Schools and Society in Ireland.* Dublin, Gill & Macmillan.

Dublin Transportation Office 2005 *Road User Monitoring Report 2005.* Dublin: DTO.

Dunn, S. (ed.) 1995 *Facets of the Conflict in Northern Ireland*. London: Macmillan.

Dunn, S. and V. Morgan 1994 *Protestant Alienation in Northern Ireland: A Preliminary Survey*. Coleraine: University of Ulster.

Dunning, E. 1999 *Sport Matters: Sociological Studies of Sport, Violence and Civilization*. London: Routledge.

Dunning, E. and Sheard, K. 2004 *Barbarians, Gentlemen and Players: A Sociological Study of the Development of Rugby Football*, 2nd edn. London: Routledge.

Dupuy, G. 1999 'From the "magic circle" to "automobile dependence": measurements and political implications', *Transport Policy* 6: 1–17.

Durkheim, E. 1984 *The Division of Labour in Society*. London: Palgrave Macmillan.

Economist, The 2004 'The luck of the Irish', 14 Oct.

ECRE (European Council on Refugees and Exiles) 2005 *Asylum Applications and Country of Origin Information in Europe 2004*, http://www.ecre.org/resources/statistics/695 Accessed 3 Jan. 2007.

Edgell, S. R. 1980 *Middle Class Couples*. London: Allen & Unwin.

Educational Disadvantage Committee 2003 *Moving Beyond Educational Disadvantage*. Dublin: Department of Education and Science.

Edwards, R. 1979 *Contested Terrain*. New York: Basic Books.

Eivers, E., G. Shiel, R. Perkins and J. Cosgrove 2005 *The 2004 National Assessment of English Reading*. Dublin: Educational Research Centre.

Elias, N. 1978a *What is Sociology?* London: Hutchinson.

Elias, N. 1978b *The Civilizing Process*. Oxford: Blackwell.

Elias, N. 2007 *Involvement and Detachment*, Collected Works vol. 8. Dublin: UCD Press.

Elias, N. and E. Dunning 1986 *Quest for Excitement: Sport and Leisure in the Civilisng Process*. Oxford: Blackwell.

Elias, N. and J. L. Scotson 1994 *The Established and the Outsiders: A Sociological Enquiry into Community Problems*. London: Sage.

Elliot, A. and C. Lemert 2006 *The New Individualism: The Emotional Costs of Globalization*. London: Routledge.

EPA (Environmental Protection Agency) 2006, *Environment in Focus 2006*. Dublin: EPA. http://www.epa.ie/OurEnvironment/EnvironmentalIndicators/ accessed 25 Sept. 2006.

Equality Authority 2006 *Annual Report 2005*. Dublin: Equality Authority.

Equality Commission for Northern Ireland 2003 *Corporate Plan 2003–2006*, Belfast: ECNI.

Esping-Andersen, G. 1999 *The Social Foundations of Postindustrial Economies*, Oxford: Oxford University Press.

Esping-Andersen, G. 2003 'Women in the new welfare equilibrium', *European Legacy* 8 (5): 599–610.

ESRI (Economic and Social Research Institute) 2004 *Sports Participation and Health Among Adults in Ireland*. Dublin: ESRI no. 178.

ESRI (Economic and Social Research Institute) 2005a *Social and Economic Value of Sport in Ireland*. Dublin: ESRI no. 180.

ESRI (Economic and Social Research Institute) 2005b *School Children and Sport in Ireland*. Dublin: ESRI No. 182.

Etzioni, A. 1993 *The Spirit of Community.* New York: Simon & Schuster.

European Commission, 2001 *Social Protection in Europe.* Luxembourg: EC.

European Commission 2005a *Green Paper, Confronting Demographic Change: A New Solidarity Between Generations.* Brussels COM 94 final.

European Commission 2005b *Employment in Europe.* Luxembourg: EC.

Eurostat 2004 *Structures of the Taxation Systems in the European Union.* Luxembourg: EC.

Eurostat 2005 *Europe in Figures: Eurostat Yearbook 2005.* Luxembourg: EC.

Evans, P. 1995 *Embedded Autonomy: States and Industrial Transformation.* Princeton, NJ: Princeton University Press.

Evans-Pritchard, E. 1940 *The Nuer.* Oxford: Clarendon Press.

Expert Group on Future Skills Needs 2005 *Skills Needs in the Irish Economy.* Dublin: Forfas.

Fahey, T. 1992 'Housework, the household economy, and economic development in Ireland since the 1920s', *Irish Journal of Sociology* 2: 42–69.

Fahey, T. 2001 'Trends in Irish fertility rates in comparative perspective', *Economic and Social Review* 32 (2): 153–80.

Fahey, T. 2003 'Is there a trade-off between pensions and home ownership? An exploration of the Irish case?' *Journal of European Social Policy* 13 (2): 159–73.

Fahey, T., B. Hayes and R. Sinnott 2005 *Consensus and Conflict: A Study of Values and Attitudes in the Republic of Ireland and Northern Ireland.* Dublin: IPA.

Fahey, T. and M. Lyons 1995 *Marital Breakdown and family law in Ireland.* Dublin: Oak Tree Press.

Fahey, T., B. Nolan and B. Maitre 2004 *Housing, Poverty and Wealth in Ireland.* Dublin: IPA and Combat Poverty Agency.

Fahey, T. and H. Russell 2001 *Family Formation in Ireland.* Dublin: ESRI.

Fahey, T., H. Russell and E. Smyth 2000 'Gender equality, fertility decline and labour market patterns among women in Ireland', pp. 244–67 in B. Nolan, P. O'Connell and C. T. Whelan (eds), *Bust to Boom? The Irish Experience of Growth and Inequality.* Dublin: IPA.

Fairclough, N. 2003 *Analysing Discourse: Textual Analysis for Social Research.* London: Routledge.

Falls, C. 1936 *The Birth of Ulster.* London: Methuen.

Fanning, B. 2002 *Racism and Social Change in the Republic of Ireland.* Manchester: Manchester University Press.

Fanning, B. and A. Veale 2001 *Beyond the Pale: Asylum Seeking Children and Social Exclusion in Ireland.* Dublin: Irish Refugee Council.

Farragher, M. A. 2001 'Degradation of the Dodder', *Irish Times,* letter, 14 Nov.

Fay, M. T., M. Morrissey, and M. Smyth 1998 *Mapping Troubles-Related Deaths and Deprivation in Northern Ireland.* Belfast: INCORE/CTS.

Fay, M., M. Morrissey, and M. Smyth 2000 *Northern Ireland's Troubles: The Human Costs.* London: Pluto.

Felstead, A., N. Jewson and S. Walters 2005 *Changing Places of Work.* London: Palgrave.

Ferguson, I., M. Lavalette and G. Mooney 2002 *Rethinking Welfare: A Critical Perspective.* London: Sage.

Ferguson, N. 2004 'Economics, religion and the decline of Europe', *Economic Affairs* 24 (4): 37–40.

Ferns Report, The 2005 Dublin: Stationery Office.

Ferriter, D. 2005 *The Transformation of Ireland 1900–2000*. London: Profile Books.

Fine Gael 2005 *Safe Streets*, www.safestreets.ie accessed 30 Nov. 2005.

Finnerty, J. 2002 'Homes for the working class? Irish public house-building cycles, 1945–2001', *Saothar: Journal of Irish Labour History* 27: 65–71.

Fischler, C. 1980 'Food habits, social change, and the nature-culture dilemma', *Social Science Information* 19: 937–53.

Fitzgerald, M. 2002 'BNP to contest seats in Ulster', *Belfast Telegraph*, 31 Oct.

Fletcher, R. 1966 *The Family and Marriage in Britain*. Harmondsworth: Penguin.

Florida, R. 2004 *The Rise of the Creative Class*. New York: Basic Books.

Fold, N. and B. Pritchard 2005 'Introduction', pp. 1–22 in N. Fold and B. Pritchard (eds), *Cross-Continental Food Chains*. London: Routledge.

Ford, A. and J. McCafferty (eds) 2005 *The Origins of Sectarianism in Early Modern Ireland*. Cambridge: Cambridge University Press.

Foucault, M. 1977 *Discipline and Punish*, trans. Alan Sheridan. London: Penguin.

Fox, R. 1967 'Kinship and land tenure on Tory Island', *Ulster Folklife* 12: 1–17.

Fox, R. 1978 *The Tory Islanders*. Cambridge: Cambridge University Press.

Frank, A. G. 1967 *Capitalism and Underdevelopment in Latin America*. New York: Monthly Review Press.

Freeman, R. B. and J. L. Medoff 1984 *What Do Unions Do?* New York: Basic Books.

Friedan, B. 1982 *The Feminine Mystique*. Harmondsworth: Penguin.

Friedman, A. 1977 *Industry and Labour*. London: Macmillan.

Friedman, T. 2005 'Follow the leapin' leprechaun', *New York Times*, 1 July.

Fuller, L. 2002 *Irish Catholicism Since 1950: The Undoing of Culture*. Dublin: Gill & Macmillan.

Fulton, G. 2005 'Northern Catholic fans of the Republic of Ireland soccer team', pp. 140–56 in A. Bairner (ed.), *Sport and the Irish*. Dublin: UCD Press.

Fynes, B., T. Morrissey, W. K. Roche, B. J. Whelan and J. Williams (eds) 1996 *Flexible Working Lives: The Changing Nature of Working Time Arrangements in Ireland*. Dublin: Oak Tree Press.

Gallagher, T and A. Smith, 2000 *The Effects of Selective Education in Northern Ireland*. Bangor: Department of Education.

Gallie, D. and C. Vogler 1993 'Unemployment and attitudes to work', pp. 1–46 in D. Gallie (ed.), *Social Change and the Experience of Unemployment*. Oxford University Press, Oxford.

Galligan, Y. 2000 *The Development of Mechanisms to Monitor Progress in Achieving Gender Equality in Ireland*. Dublin: Stationery Office.

Galway Travellers Support Group 1999 *Annual Report*. Galway: Galway Travellers Support Group.

Garda Síochána Complaints Board 2002 *Annual Report for 2002*. Dublin: Stationery Office.

Garda Síochána/Police Service of Northern Ireland 2004 *A Cross Border Organised Crime Assessment 2004*. Dublin/Belfast: Stationery Office/Northern Ireland Office.

Garfinkel, H. 1967 'Passing and the managed achievement of sex status in an intersexed person part 1', pp. 116–85 in *Studies in Ethnomethdology*. Englewood Cliffs NJ: Prentice Hall.

Garland, D. 2001 *The Culture of Control: Crime and Social Order in Contemporary Society*, Oxford: Oxford University Press.

Garvin, T. 2004 *Preventing the Future: Why was Ireland Poor for so Long*. Dublin: Gill & Macmillan.

Gash, V. and P. O'Connell. 2000 *The Irish Graduate Labour Market: A Six-Year Follow Up Survey of Third Level Graduates from 1992*. Dublin: ESRI.

Geary, J. 1999 'The new workplace: change at work in Ireland', *International Journal of Human Resource Management* 10 (5): 870–90.

Geertz, C. 1966 'Religion as a cultural system', pp. 1–46 in M. Banton (ed.), *Anthropological Approaches to the Study of Religion*. London: Tavistock.

Gelles, R. 1995 *Contemporary Families: a Sociological View*. Thousand Oaks, CA: Sage.

Gellner, E. 1964 *Thought and Change*. London: Weidenfeld & Nicolson.

Gellner, E. 1983 *Nations and Nationalism*. Oxford, Basil Blackwell.

Gellner, E. and A. D. Smith 1996 'The nation: real or imagined? The Warwick debates on nationalism', *Nations and Nationalism* 2 (3): 357–70.

Gendzier, I. 1985 *Managing Political Change: Social Scientist and the Third World*. Boulder CO: Westview.

General Consumer Council for Northern Ireland 2002 *In Poor Health (Northern Ireland: the Health Gap Between Rich and Poor)*. Belfast: General Consumer Council for Northern Ireland

Gerth, H. and C. W. Mills (eds) 1970 *From Max Weber*. London: Routledge.

Gibbon, P. 1973 'Arensberg and Kimball revisited', *Economy and Society* 2 (4): 479–98.

Gibbon, P. 1975 The *Origins of Ulster Unionism: The Formation of Popular Protestant Politics and Ideology in Nineteenth-century Ireland*, Manchester: Manchester University Press.

Gibbon, P. and C. Curtin 1978 'The stem family in Ireland', *Comparative Studies in Society and History* 20 (3): 429–53.

Gibson-Graham, J. K. 1996 *The End of Capitalism (As We Know It): A Feminist Critique of Political Economy*. Oxford: Blackwell.

Giddens, A. 1971 *Capitalism and Modern Social Theory: An Analysis of the Works of Marx, Durkheim and Max Weber*. Cambridge: Cambridge University Press.

Giddens A. 1991 *Modernity and Self-Identity: Self and Society in the Late Modern Age*. Cambridge: Polity.

Giddens, A. 1990 *The Consequences of Modernity*. Cambridge: Polity.

Giddens, A. 1998 'After the left's paralysis', *New Statesman*, 1 May.

Gilligan, C. and K. Lloyd 2006 'Racial prejudice in Northern Ireland', *Ark Research Update* no. 44.

Ging, D. 2005 'A "manual on masculinity?" The consumption and use of mediated images of masculinity among teenage boys in Ireland', *Irish Journal of Sociology* 14 (2): 29–52.

Gluckman, M. 1973 *Custom and Conflict in Africa*. Oxford: Basil Blackwell

Gmelch, S. B. 1987 'From poverty subculture to political lobby: the Traveller rights movement in Ireland', pp. 301–19 in C. Curtin and T. M. Wilson (eds), *Ireland from Below: Social Change and Local Community*. Galway: Galway University Press.

Goldberg, M. and J. Mercer 1992 *The Myth of the North American City*. Vancouver: UBC Press.

Goldblatt, D. 1996 *Social Theory and the Environment*. Cambridge: Polity.

Goldthorpe, J. H. 1982 'On the service class: its formation and future', pp. 162–88 in A. Giddens and G. Mackenzie (eds), *Social Class and the Division of Labour*. Cambridge: Cambridge University Press.

Goldthorpe, J. H. 2000 *On Sociology*. Oxford: Oxford University Press.

Goldthorpe, J. H., D. Lockwood, F. Bechofer, and J. Platt 1969 *The Affluent Worker in the Class Structure*. Cambridge: Cambridge University Press.

Goodbody Economic Consultants 2005 *Review of Area-Based Tax Incentive Schemes*. Dublin: Goodbody.

Goodman, D. 2003 'The "quality" turn and alternative food practices: reflections and agenda', *Journal of Rural Studies* 19 (1): 1–7.

Goodwin, J. 2002 'Irish men and work in North County Dublin', *Journal of Gender Studies* 11 (2): 151–66.

Grabowska, I. 2005 'Changes in the international mobility of labour: job migration of Polish nationals to Ireland', *Irish Journal of Sociology* 14 (1): 27–44.

Gradstein, M. and D. Nikitin 2004 *Education Expansion: Evidence and Interpretation*. Washington: World Bank Research Working Paper.

Granovetter, M. 1985 'Economic action and social structure: the problem of embeddedness', *American Journal of Sociology* 91: 481–510.

Greco, L. 2005 'Knowledge intensive organisations: women's promised land? The case of the Irish software companies', *Irish Journal of Sociology* 14 (1): 45–65.

Guelke, A., M. Cox and F. Stephen 2006 'Conclusion: peace beyond the GFA', pp. 443–53 in M. Cox, A. Guelke and F. Stephen (eds), *A Farewell to Arms? Beyond the Good Friday Agreement*. Manchester: Manchester University Press.

Guerin, P. 2002 'Racism and the media in Ireland', pp. 91–101 in R. Lentin and R. McVeigh (eds), *Racism and Anti–Racism in Ireland*. Belfast: Beyond the Pale.

Guinnane, T. W. 1997 *The Vanishing Irish: Marriage, Migration and the Rural Economy in Ireland, 1850–1914*. Princeton NJ: Princeton University Press.

Hainsworth, P. (ed.) 1998 *Divided Society: Ethnic Minorities and Racism in Northern Ireland*. London: Pluto.

Hajer, M. 1995 *The Politics of Environmental Discourse*. Oxford: Clarendon Press.

Hakim, C. 1995 'Five feminist myths about women's work', *British Journal of Sociology* 46: 429–55

Hakim, C. 2000 *Work–Lifestyle Choices in the 21st Century: Preference Theory*. Oxford: Oxford University Press.

Hall, S. 1996 'Introduction: who needs identity?', pp. 1–17 in S. Hall and P. du Gay (eds), *Questions of Cultural Identity*. London: Sage.

Hallin, D. 1987 'From Vietnam to El Salvador: hegemony and ideological change', pp. 3–25 in D. Paletz (ed.), *Political Communication Research*. Norwood: Ablex.

Halpin, B. and C. O'Donoghue 2004 'Cohabitation in Ireland: evidence from survey data'. University of Limerick Dept of Sociology Working Paper, no WP2004–01. http://www.ul.ie/sociology/pubs/

Halpin, B. and T. W. Chan 2003 'Educational homogamy in Britain and Ireland: trends and patterns', *British Journal of Sociology* 54 (4): 473–95

Hamilton, M. 1995 *The Sociology of Religion*. London: Routledge.

Hannan, D. and L. A. Katsiaounai 1977 *Traditional Families? From Culturally Prescribed to Negotiated Roles in Farm Families*. Paper no. 57. Dublin: ESRI.

Hannan, D. and S. Shortall 1991 *The Quality of Their Education*. Dublin: ESRI

Hannigan, J. 1995 *Environmental Sociology: A Social Constructionist Perspective*. London: Sage.

Hannum, E. and C. Buchmann 2003 *The Consequences of Global Educational Expansion: Social Science Perspectives*. Cambridge, MA: American Academy of Arts and Sciences.

Hanvey, E., I. McNicoll, R. Marsh, and F. Zuleeg 2005 *Report on Labour Market Dynamics. Phase Four: Equality of Opportunity Considerations*. Belfast: DTZ Pieda Consulting, OFMDFM.

Harney, M. 2000 'Remarks by Tánaiste, Mary Harney at a Meeting of the American Bar Association in the Law Society of Ireland', Blackhall Place, Dublin, 21 July http://www.entemp.ie/press/2000/210700.htm accessed 5 Jan. 2007.

Harris, C. (ed.) 2005 *The Report of the Democracy Commission: Engaging Citizens*. Dublin: TASC.

Harris, N. 1995 *The New Untouchables*. London: Penguin.

Harris, N. 2003 *The Return of Cosmopolitan Capital: Globalization, The State and War*. London: I. B. Taurus.

Harris, R. 1972 *Prejudice and Tolerance in Ulster: A Study of Neighbours and Strangers in a Border Community*. Manchester: Manchester University Press.

Hartmann, H. 1981 'The family as locus of gender, class and political struggle: the example of housework', *Signs: Journal of Women in Culture and Society* 6 (3): 366–94.

Hartmann, H. 1994 'The unhappy marriage of Marxism and feminism: towards a more progressive union', pp. 570–6 in D. B. Grusky (ed.), *Social Stratification: Class, Race, and Gender in Sociological Perspective*. Boulder, CO: Westview.

Harvey, D. 1982 *The Limits to Capital*. Oxford: Blackwell.

Harvey, D. 1985 *The Urbanization of Capital*. Oxford: Blackwell.

Harvey, D. 1989 The *Condition of Postmodernity*. Oxford: Blackwell.

Harvey, D. 2005 *A Brief History of Neoliberalism*. Oxford: Oxford University Press.

Hassan, D. 2005 'Sport, identity and Irish nationalism in Northern Ireland', pp. 123–39 in A. Bairner (ed.), *Sport and the Irish*. Dublin: UCD Press.

Haughey, N. 2002 'Travellers launch court challenge as trespass bill becomes law', *Irish Times*, 4 Nov.

Hayek, F. 1960 *The Constitution of Liberty*. London: Routledge.

Hayes, B. C. and I. McAllister 1999 'Ethnonationalism, public opinion and the Good Friday Agreement', pp. 30–48 in J. Ruane and J. Todd (eds), *After the Good Friday Agreement: Analysing Political Change in Northern Ireland*. Dublin: UCD Press.

Hayes, B. C. and I. McAllister 2005 'Public support for political violence and paramilitarism in Northern Ireland and the Republic of Ireland', *Terrorism and Political Violence* 17 (1): 1–19.

Helleiner, J. 2000 *Irish Travellers: Racism and the Politics of Culture*. Toronto, Buffalo and London: University of Toronto Press.

Hennessy, M. 2001a 'FG plan to move Travellers camping illegally', *Irish Times*, 6 Nov.

Hennessy, M. 2001b 'Travellers to oppose new laws on camps', *Irish Times*, 6 Nov.

Hepburn, A. C. 1996 *A Past Apart: Studies in the History of Catholic Belfast, 1850–1950*, Belfast: Ulster Historical Foundation.

Herman, E .1998 'The propaganda model revisited', pp. 191–205 in R. W. McChesney, E. M. Wood, and J. B. Foster (eds), *Capitalism and the Information Age: The Political Economy of the Global Communication Revolution*. New York: Monthly Review Press.

Herman, E. and N. Chomsky 2002 *Manufacturing Consent*. Boston: South End Press.

Hervieu-Léger, D. 2000 *Religion as a Chain of Memory*. Cambridge: Polity.

Hervieu-Léger, D. 2003 'Individualism, the validation of faith, and the social nature of religion in modernity' pp. 161–75 in R. Fenn (ed.), *The Blackwell Companion to Sociology of Religion*. Oxford: Blackwell.

Hicks, A. and L. Kenworthy 1998 'Cooperation and political economic performance in affluent democratic capitalism', *American Journal of Sociology* 103: 1631–72.

Hilliard, B. 2003 'The Catholic Church and married women's sexuality: habitus change in late 20th century Ireland', *Irish Journal of Sociology* 12 (2): 28–49.

Hilliard, B. 2006 'Changing gender roles in intimate relationships' pp. 33–42 in J. Garry, N. Hardiman and D. Payne (eds), *Irish Social and Political Attitudes*. Liverpool: University of Liverpool Press.

Hillyard, P., G. Kelly, E. McLaughlin, D. Patsios and M. Tomlinson 2003 *Bare Necessities: Poverty and Social Exclusion in Northern Ireland*. Belfast: Democratic Dialogue.

Hillyard, P., W. Rolston and M. Tomlinson 2005 *Poverty and Conflict: The International Evidence*. Dublin: CPA/IPA

Hobsbawm, E. 1990 *Nations and Nationalism since 1780*. Cambridge: Cambridge University Press.

Hobson, B. 1968 *Ireland, Yesterday, and Tomorrow*. Tralee: Anvil Books.

Hochschild, A. R. 1989 *The Second Shift: Working Parents and the Revolution at Home*. London: Piatkus.

Hochschild, A. R. 2000 'Global care chains and emotional surplus value', pp. 130–46 in W. Hutton and A. Giddens (eds), *On The Edge: Living With Global Capitalism*. London: Jonathan Cape.

Hoijer, B. 2004 'The discourse of global compassion: the audience and media reporting of human suffering', *Media, Culture and Society* 26 (4): 513–31.

Home Office 2002 *A Guide to Anti-Social Behaviour Orders and Acceptable Behaviour Contracts*. London: Home Office.

hooks, b. 1994 *Feminist Theory: From Margin to Centre*. Boston: South End Press.

Horgan, G. 2001 'Changing women's lives in Ireland', *International Socialism Journal* 91.

Horgan, J. 2001 *Irish Media: A Critical History*. London: Routledge

Hornsby-Smith, M. and C. T. Whelan 1994 'Religious and moral values', pp. 7–44 in C. T. Whelan (ed.), *Values and Social Change in Ireland*. Dublin: Gill & Macmillan.

House of Commons 2004 *Report of House of Commons Northern Ireland Affairs Committee on 'Hate Crime': the Draft Criminal Justice (Northern Ireland) Order 2004*. London: HMSO.

Howe, L. 1990 *Being Unemployed in Northern Ireland: An Ethnographic Study*. Cambridge: Cambridge University Press.

Hughes, G. and B. Nolan 1997 'Segmented labour markets and earnings in Ireland', *Economic and Social Review* 28 (1): 1–22.

Hughes, G. and B. Nolan 2000 'Competitive and segmented labour markets and exclusion from retirement income', pp. 123–44 in W. Salverda, C. Lucifora and B. Nolan (eds), *Policy Measures for Low-Wage Employment in Europe*. Cheltenham: Edward Elgar.

Humphreys, A. J. 1966 *New Dubliners: Urbanisation and the Irish Family*. London: Routledge & Kegan Paul.

Humphreys, P. C., S. Fleming and O. O'Donnell 2000 *Flexible and Innovative Working Arrangements in the Irish Public Service*. Dublin: IPA.

Huntington, P. 1968 *Political Order in Changing Societies*. Yale: Yale University Press.

Hutchinson, J. 1994 *Modern Nationalism*. London: Fontana.

Huws, U. 2003 *The Making of the Cybertariat: Virtual Work in a Real World*. New York: Monthly Review Press.

Hynes, E. 1978 'Irish Catholicism and the Great Famine', *Societas* VIII: 81–98.

Independent Commission on Policing for Northern Ireland 1999 *A New Beginning: Policing in Northern Ireland: The Report of the Independent Commission on Policing for Northern Ireland*. London: HMSO.

Inglis, T. 1980 'Dimensions of Irish students' religiosity', *Economic and Social Review* 11 (4): 237–56.

Inglis, T. 1985 'Separation of Church and state in Ireland', *Social Studies* 9 (1): 37–48.

Inglis, T. 1998 *Moral Monopoly: The Rise and Fall of the Catholic Church in Modern Ireland*, 2nd edn. Dublin: UCD Press.

Inglis, T. 2002 Searching for truth, revealing power, hoping for freedom', pp. 152–75 in E. Cassidy (ed.), *Measuring Ireland: Discerning Values and Beliefs*. Dublin: Veritas.

Inglis, T. 2003a 'Catholic Church, religious capital and symbolic domination' pp. 43–70 in M. Böss and E. Maher (eds), *Engaging Modernity: Readings of Irish Politics, Culture and Literature at the Turn of the Century*. Dublin: Veritas.

Inglis, T. 2003b *Truth, Power and Lies: Irish Society and the Case of the Kerry Babies*. Dublin: UCD Press.

Inglis, T. 2005 'Religion, identity, state and society', pp. 59–77 in J. Cleary and C. Connolly (eds), *The Cambridge Companion to Modern Irish Culture*. Cambridge: Cambridge University Press.

Inglis, T. 2006a 'From self-denial to self-fulfilment', *Irish Review* forthcoming.

Inglis, T. 2006b 'The religious field in contemporary Ireland: identity, being religious and symbolic domination', pp. 111–34 in L. Harte and Y. Whelan (eds), *Ireland Beyond Boundaries: Mapping Irish Studies in the Twentieth First Century.* London: Pluto.

Institute of Criminology 2001 *Crime in Ireland: Trends and Patterns, 1950–1998.* Dublin: National Crime Council.

Institute of Criminology 2003 *Public Order Offences in Ireland.* Dublin: National Crime Council.

Interdepartmental Group on Urban Crime and Disorder 1992 *Urban Crime and Disorder: Report of the Interdepartmental Group.* Dublin: Stationery Office.

International Organisation for Migration 2005 World *Migration Report 2005.* London: IOM.

Investment in Education 1965 *Report of the Survey Team Appointed by the Minister for Education.* Dublin: Stationery Office.

Irish Labour Party 2005 'Response to the draft race relations policy of the Northern Ireland Housing Executive, March 2005'.

Irish Prison Service 2004 *Annual Report for 2004.* Dublin: Stationery Office.

Irish Refugee Council 2006 *Irish Asylum Statistics,* www.irishregugeecouncil.ie/stats.htm Accessed 3 Jan. 2007.

Irish Traveller Movement 1999 'What is Citizen Traveller', www.paveepoint.ie/ accessed 6 Mar. 2006.

Irish Youth Justice Alliance 2005 *Anti Social Behaviour Orders ASBOs: A Briefing Paper prepared by the Irish Youth Justice Alliance,* 23 Feb., Irish Penal Reform website, www.iprt.ie/ accessed 20 Nov. 2005.

IRN 2006 'Critical issues in Irish industrial relations: an overview of a changing landscape', *IRN Industrial Relations News* 15, 13 Apr.

Irwin, A. 2001 *Sociology and the Environment: A Critical Introduction to Society, Nature and Knowledge.* Cambridge: Polity.

Irwing, P. and R. Lynn 2005 'Sex differences in means and variability on the progressive matrices in university students: a meta-analysis' *British Journal of Psychology* 96: 505–24.

Jackson, J. A. and T. Haase 1996 'Demography and the distribution of deprivation in rural Ireland', pp. 59–86 in C. Curtin, T. Haase and H. Tovey (eds), *Poverty in Rural Ireland.* Dublin: Oak Tree Press

Jacobs, M. 1999 'Sustainable development as a co.ntested concept', pp. 21–45 in A. Dobson (ed.), *Fairness and Futurity,.* Oxford: Oxford University Press.

Jagger, E. 1998 'Marketing the Self, buying an other; dating in a postmodern, consumer society', *Sociology* 32 (4): 795–814

Jarman, N. 2002a *Managing Disorder: Responding to Interface Violence in North Belfast.* Belfast: Office of the First Minister and Deputy First Minister.

Jarman, N. 2002b *Overview Analysis of Racist Incidents Recorded in Northern Ireland by the RUC 1996–1999.* Belfast: Community Development Centre.

Jarman, N. 2005 *No Longer a Problem? Sectarian Violence in Northern Ireland,* Belfast: Institute of Conflict Research.

Jarman, N. 2006 *Changing Patterns and Future Planning: Migration and Northern Ireland.* ICR Working Paper no. 1.

Jarman, N. and R. Monaghan 2003a *Analysis of Incidents of Racial Harassment Recorded by the Police in Northern Ireland.* Belfast: Institute for Conflict Research.

Jarman, N. and R. Monaghan 2003b *Racist Harassment in Northern Ireland.* Belfast: Institute for Conflict Research.

Jarvie, G. 2006 *Sport, Culture and Society: An Introduction.* London: Routledge.

Jencks, C., M. Smith, H. Acland, M. J. Bane, D. Cohen, H. Gintis, B. Heyns and S. Michelson 1972 *Inequality: A Reassessment of the Effects of Family and Schooling in America.* New York: Basic Books.

Jenkins, R. 1982 *Hightown Rules: Growing up in a Belfast Housing Estate.* Leicester: National Youth Bureau.

Jenkins, R. 1983 *Lads, Citizens and Ordinary Kids: Working-Class Youth Lifestyles in Belfast.* London: Routledge & Kegan Paul.

Jenkins, R. 2002 *Pierre Bourdieu.* London: Routledge.

Johnson, M. P. and K. J. Ferraro 2000 'Research on domestic violence in the 1990s: making distinctions', *Journal of Marriage and the Family* 62: 948–63.

Joint Committee on Justice, Equality, Defence and Women's Rights 2005 *Report on Community Policing.* Dublin: Stationery Office.

Jones, C. L., L. R. Marsden and L. J. Tepperman 1990 *Lives of Their Own: The Individualization of Women's Lives.* Oxford: Oxford University Press.

Jones, C. L. L. Tepperman and S. J. Wilson 1995 *The Futures of the Family.* Englewood Cliffs, NJ: Prentice Hall.

Jones, E. 1969 *A Social Geography of Belfast.* London: Oxford University Press.

Jones, H. and T. Sagar 2001 'Crime and Disorder Act 1998: Prostitution and the Anti-Social Behaviour Order', *Criminal Law Review* Nov.: 873–85.

Jordan, S. 2003 'Critical ethnography and the sociology of education', pp. 82–100 in C. A. Torres and A. Anikainen (eds), *The International Handbook on the Sociology of Education.* Lanham, MD: Rowman & Littlefield.

Kaczmarczyk, P. 2006. 'Labour migration from the new EU member states and its impact on sending and receiving countries', presentation to ERC/IIIS Workshop Employment in the Enlarging European Union, Dublin, 2 June.

Karnilowicz, W. 1982 'An analysis of the effects of ceremonial occasions on frequency of suicides in the United States, 1972–1978', unpublished Master's thesis, University of Illinois.

Katungi, D., E. Neale and A. Barbour 2006 *People in Low-Paid Informal Work: Need Not Greed.* Bristol: JRF/Policy Press.

Kaufmann, V. 2002 *Rethinking Mobility: Contemporary Sociology.* Aldershot: Ashgate.

Kawachi, I. 1997 'Long live community: social capital as public health', *The American Prospect*, Nov.–Dec.: 56–9.

Kawachi, I. and B. Kennedy 2002 *The Health of Nations: Why Inequality is Harmful to Your Health.* New York: New Press.

Kawachi, I., B. Kennedy and R. Glass 1998 'Social capital and self related health: a contextual analysis', *American Journal of Public Health* 89 (8): 1187–93.

Kay, P. and W. Kempton, 1984 'What is the Sapir-Whorf hypothesis?' *American Anthropologist* 86 (1): 65–79.

Kearns, A. 2003 'Mortgage arrears in the 1990s: lessons for today', *Central Bank Quarterly Bulletin* Autumn: 97–113.

Kelleher P. and Associates 2001 *Framing the Future: An Integrated Strategy to Support Women's Community and Voluntary Organisations*. Dublin: National Women's Council of Ireland.

Kelleher P. and Associates with M. O'Connor 1995 *Making the Links: Towards an Integrated Strategy for the Elimination of Violence in Intimate Relationships with Men*. Dublin: Women's Aid.

Kelly, A. 2002 *Compulsory Irish: Language and Education in Ireland 1870s–1970s*. Dublin: Irish Academic Press.

Kelly, M. 2007 *Environmental Debates and the Public in Ireland*. Dublin: IPA.

Kelly, M., F. Kennedy, P. Faughnan and H. Tovey 2003 *Cultural Sources of Support on which Environmental Attitudes and Behaviours Draw*. Dublin: Social Science Research Centre, UCD. www.ucd.ie/environ/home/htm.

Kelly, M., F. Kennedy, P. Faughnan and H. Tovey 2004 *Environmental Attitudes and Behaviours, Ireland in Comparative European Perspective*. Dublin: Social Science Research Centre, UCD. www.ucd.ie/environ/home/htm

Kelly, S. and A. MacLaran 2004 'The residential transformation of inner Dublin', pp. 36–59 in P. J. Drudy and A. MacLaran (eds), *Dublin: Economic and Social Trends Volume 4*. Dublin: Centre for Urban and Regional Studies.

Kelly, S. and I. Waddington 2007 'Abuse, intimidation and violence as aspects of managerial control in professional soccer', *International Review for the Sociology of Sport* (forthcoming).

Kemeny, J. 1992 *Housing and Social Theory*. London: Routledge.

Kemeny, J. 1995 *From Public Housing to the Social Market: Rental Policy Strategies in Comparative Perspective*. London: Routledge.

Kennedy, F. 2001 *Cottage to Crèche: Family Change in Ireland*. Dublin: IPA.

Kennedy, L. 1986 *Two Ulster's: A Case for Repartition*. Belfast: L. Kennedy.

Kennedy, R. E. 1973 *The Irish: Marriage, Migration and Fertility*, Berkeley CA: University of California Press.

Kennedy, S. 2003 'Irish Women and the Celtic Tiger economy', pp. 95–109 in C. Coulter and S. Coleman (eds), *The End of Irish History? Critical Reflections on the Celtic Tiger*. Manchester: Manchester University Press.

Kenny, M. 1997 *Goodbye to Catholic Ireland*. London: Sinclair-Stevenson.

Keogh, D. 1995 *Ireland and the Vatican: The Politics and Diplomacy of Church–State Relations 1922–1960*, Cork: Cork University Press.

Keohane, K. 1998 'Reflexive modernization and systematically distorted communications: an analysis of an Environmental Protection Agency hearing', *Irish Journal of Sociology* 8: 17–92.

Kilcommins, S., I. O'Donnell, E. O'Sullivan and B. Vaughan 2004 *Crime, Punishment and the Search for Order in Ireland*. Dublin: IPA.

Kimmel, M. and M. Messner (eds) 1995 *Men's Lives*, 3rd edn. London: Allyn & Bacon.

Kirby, P. 2002 *The Celtic Tiger in Distress: Growth with Inequality in Ireland*. London: Palgrave.

Klaehn, J. 2002 'A critical review and assessment of Herman and Chomsky's 'propaganda model', *European Journal of Communication* 17 (2): 147–82.

Kohn, H. 1944 *The Idea of Nationalism.* New York: Macmillan.

Kramer, L. 2000 *The Sociology of Gender: A Brief Introduction.* Los Angeles: Roxbury.

Kropiwiec, K. and R. King-O'Riain 2006 *Polish Migrant Workers in Ireland.* Dublin: National Consultative Committee on Racism and Interculturalism.

Kroska, A. 2004 'Divisions of domestic work: revising and expanding the theoretical explanations', *Journal of Family Issues* 25 (7): 900–32.

L'Estrange, S. 2005 'Catholicism and Capitalist Social Order in Ireland, 1907–1973 – An Historical Institutionalist Analysis.' Unpublished PhD. Queen's University, Belfast.

La Rossa, R. 1995 'Fatherhood and social change', pp. 448–60 in M. Kimmel and M. Messner (eds) *Men's Lives,* 3rd edn. London: Allyn & Bacon.

Labour Party 2005 *Taking Back the Neighbourhood: A Strategy For Tackling Anti-Social Behaviour,* Labour Party Discussion Paper, Apr., www.labour.ie/download/pdf/take_back_neighbour.pdf accessed 14 Dec. 2005.

Labov, W. 1973 'The logic of non-standard English', pp. 21–66 in N. Keddie (ed.), *Tinker Tailor . . . The Myth of Cultural Deprivation.* Harmondsworth: Penguin.

Lal, D. 1993 'The political economy of economic liberalization', pp. 97–126 in D. Lal (ed.), *The Repressed Economy.* Aldershot: Edward Elgar.

Lane, J. 2000 *Pierre Bourdieu: A Critical Introduction.* London: Pluto.

Larsen, S. 1982 'The two sides of the house: identity and social organisation', pp. 131–64 in P Cohen (ed.), *Belonging: Identity and Social Organisation in British Rural Culture.* Manchester: Manchester University Press.

Lash, S. 1994 'Reflexivity and its doubles: structure, aesthetics, community', pp. 110–73 in U. Beck (ed.), *Reflexive Modernization: Politics, Tradition and Aesthetics in the Modern Social Order.* Cambridge: Polity.

Lau, R. W.K. 2004 'Habitus and the practical logic of practice: an interpretation', *Sociology* 38 (2): 369–87.

Law, A. and G. Mooney 2006 "We've never had it so good': the 'problem' of the working class in the devolved Scotland', *Critical Social Policy* 26 (3): 523–42.

Law Reform Commission 2005 *Report on Public Inquiries, Including Tribunals of Inquiry.* Dublin: Law Reform Commission.

Layte, R. and C. T. Whelan 2000 'The rising tide and equality of opportunity: the changing class structure', pp. 90–108 in B. Nolan, P. J. O'Connell and C. T. Whelan (eds), *Boom to Bust? The Irish Experience of Growth and Inequality.* Dublin: IPA.

Leamer, E. and M. Storper 2001 'The economic geography of the internet age', *Journal of International Business Studies* 32 (4): 641–65.

Lee, E. 1969 'A theory of migration', pp. 282–97 in J. A. Jackson (ed.), *Migration.* Cambridge: Cambridge University Press.

Lee, G. and C. Bird 1998 *Breaking the Bank.* Dublin: Folens.

Lee, J. 1969 'Capital in the Irish economy', pp. 53–64 in L. M. Cullen (ed.), *The Formation of the Irish Economy.* Cork: Mercier.

Lennon, B. 2004 *Catholics in Northern Ireland: Ambivalence Rules? Northern Ireland Life and Times Survey Research Update No. 22.* Belfast: NILT.

Lentin, R. and R. McVeigh (eds) 2002 *Racism and Antiracism in Ireland.* Belfast: Beyond the Pale.

Lentin, R. and R. McVeigh 2006a *After Optimism? Ireland, Racism and Globalisation.* Dublin: MetroEireann.

Lentin, R. and R. McVeigh 2006b 'Irishness and racism: towards an e-reader', *Translocations: The Irish Migration, Race and Social Transformation Review* 1 (1): 22–40.

Leonard, M. 2004 'Teenage girls and housework in Irish society', *Irish Journal of Sociology* 13 (1): 73–87.

Leonard, M. 2006 'Sectarian childhoods in North Belfast', pp. 195–208 in M. P. Corcoran and M. Peillon (eds), *Uncertain Ireland: A Sociological Chronicle, 2003–2004.* Dublin: IPA.

Leroy, P. and J. van Tatenhove (2000) 'Political moderniztion theory and environmental politics', pp. 187–208 in G. Spaargaren, A. J. Mol and F. H. Buttel (eds), *Environment and Global Modernity.* London: Sage.

Lewis, H. 2004 'Community relations in Northern Ireland', PASSIA Training Program on Ireland and Palestine – Divided Countries United by History, 10–14 Oct.

Liston, K. 2005a 'Established–outsider relations between males and females in sports in Ireland', *Irish Journal of Sociology* 14 (1): 66–85.

Liston, K. 2005b 'Playing the "masculine/feminine" game: a sociological analysis of the fields of sport and gender in the Republic of Ireland', unpublished PhD thesis, UCD.

Liston, K. 2005c 'Some reflections on women's sports', pp. 206–23 in A. Bairner (ed.), *Sport and the Irish.* Dublin: UCD Press.

Liston, K. 2006a '"Women's soccer" in the Republic of Ireland: some preliminary sociological comments', *Soccer and Society* 7 (2–3): 364–84.

Liston, K. 2006b 'Sport and gender relations', *Sport in Society* 9 (4): 616–33.

Liston, K. and M. Rush 2006 'Social capital and health in Irish sports policy', *Administration* 53 (4): 73–88.

Loland, S., B. Skirstad and I. Waddington (eds) 2006 *Pain and Injury in Sport: Social and Ethical Analysis.* London: Routledge.

Lorenz, E. and A. Valeyre 2004 *Organisational Change in Europe: National Models or the Diffusion of A New 'One Best Way'?* Aalborg University: Danish Research Unit for Industrial Dynamics DRUID Working Paper number 4.

Love, S. 2002 'Travellers being pushed further to the edge of society', letter, *Irish Examiner*, 15 Apr.

Loy, J. and D. Booth 2000 'Functionalism, sport and society', pp. 8–27 in J. Coakley and E. Dunning (eds), *Handbook of Sports Studies.* London: Sage.

Loy, J., B. McPherson and G. Kenyon 1978 *Sport and Social Systems*, Reading, MA: Addison–Wesley.

LRC (Labour Relations Commission) 2005 *Annual Report.* Dublin: Labour Relations Commission.

Lundy, P. and M. McGovern 2005 *Community, Truth-telling and Conflict Resolution*, Belfast: Community Relations Council (NI).

Lundy, P. and M. McGovern 2006 'Participation, truth and partiality: participatory action research, community-based truth-telling and post-conflict transition', *Sociology* 40 (1): 71–88.

Lynch, K. 1989 *The Hidden Curriculum.* London: Falmer Press.

Lynch, K. 1992 'Education and the paid labour market', *Irish Educational Studies* 11: 13–33.

Lynch, K. 1995 'Solidarity labour: its nature and marginalisation', *Sociological Review* 37 (1): 1–14.

Lynch, K. and E. McLaughlin 1995 'Caring labour and love labour', pp. 250–94 in Clancy, P., S. Drudy, K. Lynch and L. O'Dowd (eds), *Irish Society: Sociological Perspectives*. Dublin: IPA.

Lyons, F. S. L. 1971 *Ireland Since the Famine*. Glasgow: Collins/Fontana

McAdam, D., J. McCarthy and M. Zald 1996 *Comparative Perspectives on Social Movements, Political Opportunities, Mobilizing Structures, and Cultural Framing*. Cambridge: Cambridge University Press.

McAleese, D. 2000 'The Celtic Tiger: origins and prospects', *Options Politiques* July–Aug.: 46–50.

McAuliffe, R. and T. Fahey 1999 'Responses to social order problems', pp. 173–90 in T. Fahey (ed.), *Social Housing in Ireland*. Dublin: Oak Tree Press.

McCabe, B. 2007 'Commitment to work in changing social and economic times: the case of Ireland', pp. 69–94 in B. Hilliard and M. Nic Ghiolla Phádraig (eds), *Changing Ireland in International Comparison*. Dublin: Liffey Press.

McCall, C. 2006 'From "long war" to the "war of the lilies": "post-conflict" territorial compromise and the return of cultural politics', pp. 302–16 in M. Cox, A. Guelke and F. Stephen (eds), *A Farewell to Arms? Beyond the Good Friday Agreement*, Manchester: Manchester University Press.

McCann, E. 1998 *War and Peace in Northern Ireland*. Dublin: Hot Press.

McCarthy, C. 2003 'Corruption in public office in Ireland: policy design as a countermeasure', *Quarterly Economic Commentary* (Autumn): 1–15.

McCullagh, C. 1996 *Crime in Ireland: A Sociological Introduction*. Cork: Cork University Press.

McCullagh, C. 1999 'Rural crime in the Republic of Ireland', pp. 29–44 in G. Dingwall and S. R. Moody (eds), *Crime and Conflict in the Countryside*. Cardiff: University of Wales Press.

McCullagh, C. 2002 *Media Power: A Sociological Introduction*. London: Palgrave.

McCullagh, C. 2003 'The disrespects and deceptions of informality', *Inside Cork*, 2 Dec.

McCullagh, C. 2005 'Giving Charlie the bird', *Inside Cork*, 10 Feb.

McCullough, M. 1986 'The social construction of unemployment', pp. 307–25 in P. Clancy, S. Drudy, K. Lynch and L. O'Dowd (eds), *Ireland: A Sociological Profile*. Dublin: IPA.

McDonagh, M. 2000 'Origins of the Travelling people', pp. 21–5 in E. Sheehan (ed.), *Travellers Citizens of Ireland*. Dublin: Parish of the Travelling People.

Mac Éinrí, P. 2003 *Labour Migration in Ireland*. Dublin: Immigrant Council of Ireland.

McElroy, G. 1991 *The Catholic Church and the Northern Ireland Crisis 1968–1986*. Dublin: Gill & Macmillan.

McFarlane, G. 1989 'Dimensions of Protestantism: the working of Protestant identity in a northern Irish village', pp. 23–45 in C. Curtin and T. Wilson (eds), *Ireland From Below: Social Change and Local Communities*, Galway: Galway University Press.

McGarry, P. 2004 'Mc Dowell says inequality an incentive in the economy', *Irish Times*, 28 May.

McGinty, F., H. Russell, J. Williams and S. Blackwell 2005 *Time-Use in Ireland 2005: Survey Report.* Dublin: ESRI.

McGovern, M. 2004 'The old days are over: Irish republicanism, the peace process and the discourse of equality', *Terrorism and Political Violence* 16 (3): 622–45.

Mac Gréil, M. 1996 *Prejudice and Tolerance in Ireland Revisited.* Maynooth: St Patrick's College.

McKay, S. 2000 *Northern Protestants: An Unsettled People.* Belfast: Blackstaff.

McKeown, K. and H. Ferguson 1998 *Changing Fathers? Fatherhood and Family Life in Ireland.* Cork: Collins Press.

McKeown, K. and M. Brosnan 2001 *Police and Community: An Evaluation of Neighbourhood and Community Alert in Ireland.* Dublin: Stationery Office.

McKittrick, D., S. Kelters, B. Feeney and C. Thornton 1999 *Lost Lives: The Stories of the Men, Women and Children Who Died as a Result of the Northern Ireland Troubles.* London: Mainstream Publishing.

McLaughlin, E. and M. Monteith 2006 *Child and Family Poverty in Northern Ireland.* Belfast: OFMDFM.

McLaughlin, E. and N. Faris 2004, *The Section 75 Equality Duty: An Operational Review.* Belfast: OFMDFM.

McNeil, W. 1979 'Historical patterns of migration', *Current Anthropology* 20 (1): 95–102.

McNiffe, L. 1997 *A History of the Garda Síochána.* Dublin: Wolfhound.

Macpherson, W. 1999 *The Stephen Lawrence Inquiry: Report of an Inquiry by Sir William Macpherson of Cluny.* London: HMSO.

McRae, S. 2003 'Constraints and choices in mothers' employment careers: a consideration of Hakim's preference theory'. *British Journal of Sociology* 54 (3): 317–38.

McVeigh, R. 1992 'Racism and Travelling people in Northern Ireland' *17th Report of the Standing Advisory Commission for Human Rights.* Belfast: HMSO.

McVeigh, R. 1995 'Cherishing the children of the nation unequally: sectarianism in Ireland', pp. 320–51 in Patrick Clancy S. Drudy, K. Lynch and L. O'Dowd (eds), *Irish Society: Sociological Perspectives.* Dublin: IPA.

McVeigh, R. 1997 'Irish Travellers and the logic of genocide', pp. 155–64 in M. Peillon and E. Slater (eds), *Encounters with Modern Ireland.* Dublin: IPA.

McVeigh, R. 1998 'Is sectarianism racism? theorising the sectarianism/racism interface', pp. 179–98 in D. Miller (ed.), *Rethinking Northern Ireland: Culture, Ideology and Colonialism.* London: Longman.

McVeigh, R. 2002 *A Place of Refuge? Asylum Seekers and Refugees in NI.* Belfast: Refugee Action Group.

McVeigh, R. 2006a '"Special powers": racism in a permanent state of exception', in A. Lentin and R. Lentin (eds), *Race and State.* Cambridge: Cambridge Scholars Press.

McVeigh, R. 2006b *The Next Stephen Lawrence? Racist Violence and Criminal Justice in Northern Ireland.* Belfast: NICEM.

McVeigh, R. 2006c. *Migrant Workers and their Families in Northern Ireland: A Trade Union Response.* Belfast: NICICTU.

McVeigh, R. and B. Rolston 2007 'From Good Friday to good relations: sectarianism, racism and the Northern Ireland state' *Race and Class* 48 (4): 1–23.

McVerry, P. 2003 *The Meaning is in the Shadows*. Dublin: Veritas.

Magee, J. 2005 'Football supporters, rivalry and Protestant fragmentation in Northern Ireland', pp. 172–90 in A. Bairner (ed.), *Sport and the Irish*. Dublin: UCD Press.

Maguire, J. 1999 *Global Sport: Identities, Societies, Civilizations*, Oxford: Polity.

Maguire, J. and J. Tuck 2005 'National identity, rugby union and notions of Ireland and the Irish', *Irish Journal of Sociology* 14 (1): 86–109.

Mann, M. 1986 *The Social Sources of Power: Vol. 1, A History of Power from the Beginning to A.D. 1760*, Cambridge: Cambridge University Press.

Marsden, T. 2003 *The Condition of Rural Sustainability*. Assen: Royal van Gorcum.

Marsden, T., A. Flynn and M. Harrison 2001 *Consuming Interests: The Social Provision of Foods*. London: UCL Press.

Marshall, G. 1997 *Against the Odds: Social Class and Social Justice in Contemporary Societies?* Oxford: Clarendon Press.

Marshall, G., R. Roberts, and C. Burgoyne 1996 'Social class and underclass in Britain and the United States', *British Journal of Sociology* 47 (1): 22–44

Marshall, T. H. 1992 [1950] *Citizenship and Social Class*. London: Pluto.

Marx, K. 1972 *Capital*, vol. III. London: Lawrence & Wishart.

Marx, K. 1975 [1844] 'Economic and philosophical manuscripts', pp. 322–400 in K. Marx, *Early Writings*. Harmondsworth: Penguin.

Marx, K. 1976 *Capital*, vol. 1. Harmondsworth: Penguin.

Marx, K. 1989 'Critique of the Gotha Programme', pp. 75–99 in K. Marx and F. Engels, *Collected Works*, XXIV. London: Lawrence & Wishart.

Marx, K. and F. Engels 1985 *The Communist Manifesto*. Harmondsworth: Penguin.

Massey, D. 2000 'Why does immigration occur? A theoretical synthesis', pp. 34–52 in C. Hirschman, P. Kasinitz and J. DeWind (eds), *The Handbook of International Migration: The American Experience*. New York: Russell Sage Foundation.

Massey, D., J. Arango, G. Hugo, A. Kouaouci, A. Pellegrino and E. Taylor 1994, 'An evaluation of international migration theory: the North American case', *Population and Development Review* 20: 699–751.

Massey, D., J. Arango, G. Hugo, A. Kouaouci, and E. Taylor 1993 'Theories of international migration: a review and appraisal', *Population and Development Review* 19: 431–65.

Massey, D., R. Alarcon, J. Durand and H. Gonzalez 1987 *Return from Aztlan: The Social Process of International Migration from Western Mexico*. Berkeley CA: University Of California Press.

Mbeki, T. 2005 'Letter from the President: was it a happy May Day after all?', *ANC Today* 5 (18): 6–12.

Mead, M. 1962 *Male and Female*. Harmondsworth: Penguin.

Melaugh, M. and F. McKenna 2002 'Northern Ireland: population and vital statistics', *Conflict Archive on the Internet (CAIN)* http://cain.ulst.ac.uk/ni/popul.htm, Accessed 15 Aug. 2006

Mennell, S. 2006 'The contribution of Eric Dunning to the sociology of sport: the foundations', *Sport in Society* 9 (4): 514–32.

Mercer 2003 'Wide variations in EU holiday entitlements – UK amongst lowest' www.mercerhr.com.pressrealease. 11 Aug.

Messenger, J. 1969 *Inis Beag: Isle of Ireland.* New York: Holt, Reinhart & Winston.

Miele, M. 2001 *Creating Sustainability: The Social Construction of the Market for Organic Produce.* Wageningen: University of Wageningen.

Migrant Rights Centre Ireland 2004 *A Public Concern: The Experience of Twenty Migrant Women Employed in the Private Home in Ireland.*

Miles, R. 1989 *Racism.* London: Routledge.

Millar, F. and G. Moriarty 2006 'DUP and Sinn Féin move closer to agreement', *Irish Times*, 14 Oct.

Miller, D. (ed.) 1998 *Rethinking Northern Ireland: Culture, Ideology and Colonialism.* London: Longman.

Miller, D. W. 1978 *Queen's Rebels: Ulster Loyalism in Historical Perspective.* Dublin: Gill & Macmillan.

Millward Brown 2004 *Research on Opinions and Attitudes to Minority Groups.* Dublin: Know Racism.

Millward, C. 1998 *Family Relationships and Intergenerational Exchange in Later Life,* Working paper no. 15. Melbourne: Australian Institute of Family Studies.

Mintz, S. 1980 *Sweetness and Power: The Place of Sugar in Modern History.* New York: Penguin.

Mitchell, C. 2003 'From victims to equals? Catholic responses to political change in Northern Ireland', *Irish Political Studies* 18: 51–71.

Moore, O. 2006 'Farmers' markets', pp. 129–40 in M. Corcoran and M. Peillon (eds), *Uncertain Ireland: A Sociological Chronicle 2003–4.* Dublin: IPA.

Moore, R. 2004 'Lambegs and Bódhrans: religion, identity and health in Northern Ireland', pp. 123–48 in D. Kelleher and G. Leave (eds), *Identity and Health.* London: Routledge.

Moore, R. and A. D. Sanders 1996 'The limits of an anthropology of conflict? Loyalist and republican paramilitary organisations in Northern Ireland', pp. 131–43 in A. Wolfe and H. Yang (eds), *Anthropological Contributions to Conflict Resolution,* Athens and London: University of Georgia Press.

Moore, R. and A. D. Sanders 2002 'Formations of culture: nationalism and conspiracy ideology in Ulster loyalism', *Anthropology Today* 18 (6): 9–15.

Moore, R., S. Harrison, C. Mason and J. Orr. 1996 *An assessment of health Inequalities in Two Northern Ireland Communities: An Ethnographic Approach.* Belfast: Queen's University of Belfast.

Morgan, D. H. J. 1975 *Social Theory and the Family.* London: Routledge & Kegan Paul.

MORI Ireland 2004 *Turning on and Tuning in to Irish Language Radio in the 21st Century,* A research report prepared by MORI Ireland on behalf of the Broadcasting Commission of Ireland and Foras na Gaeilge. Dublin: BCI.

Mortimore, P., P. Sammons, L. Stoll, D. Lewis and R. Ecob 1988 *School Matters: The Junior Years.* Salisbury: Open Books.

Motherway, B., M. Kelly, P. Faughnan and H. Tovey 2003 *Trends in Irish Environmental Attitudes between 1993 and 2002.* Dublin: Social Science Research Centre, UCD.

Mulcahy, A. 2005 'The "other" lessons from Ireland? Policing, political violence and policy transfer', *European Journal of Criminology* 2 (2): 185–209.

Mulcahy, A. 2006 *Policing Northern Ireland: Conflict, Legitimacy and Reform.* Cullompton, Devon: Willan.

Mulcahy, A. and E. O'Mahony 2005 *Policing and Social Marginalisation in Ireland.* Dublin: Combat Poverty Agency.

Munck, R. 2005 *Globalization and Social Exclusion: A Transformationalist Perspective.* Bloomfield CT: Kumarian Press.

Murdock, G. 1949 *Social Structure.* London: Collier-Macmillan.

Murphy, C. 2005 'Attack on Corporate Greed Censored', *Village*, 1 Dec.

Murphy, D. 1978 *A Place Apart.* London: Murray.

Murphy-Lawless, J. 2000 'Changing women's lives: child care policy in Ireland' *Feminist Economics* 6 (1): 89–94.

Murtagh, B. 1996 *A Study of Belfast's Peace Lines: Community and Conflict in Rural Ulster.* Coleraine: University of Ulster.

Murtagh, B. 2002 *Social Activity and Interaction in Northern Ireland,* Northern Ireland Life and Times Survey research update 10. Belfast: Ark.

Murtagh, L. 2003 'Retention and attrition of Irish as a second language', PhD thesis, University of Groningen, http://www.ite.ie/lmurtagh/RAISLeng.htm Accessed 29 Mar. 2006.

Nairn, T. 1977 *The Break-up of Britain: Crisis and Neo-Nationalism,* 2nd edn. London: New Left Books.

National Centre for Partnership and Performance 2003 *Survey of Irish Workplaces.* Dublin: National Centre for Partnership and Performance.

National Education Convention 1994 *Report.* Dublin: Convention Secretariat.

Nelson, S. 1984 *Ulster's Uncertain Defenders.* Belfast: Appletree.

NESC 2005 *The Developmental Welfare State.* Dublin: NESC.

Newman, P., J. Kenworthy and P. Zintila 1995 'Can we overcome automobile dependence? Physical planning in an age of urban cyncism', *Cities* 12 (1): 53–65.

Nic Ghiolla Phádraig, M. 1976 'Religion in Ireland: preliminary analysis', *Social Studies* 5 (3): 113–80.

Nic Ghiolla Phádraig, M. and J. Kilroe 2002 'Irish language results in the certificate examinations 1990–2001 a report prepared for Foras na Gaeilge'. Dublin: Foras na Gaeilge.

NISRA (Northern Ireland Statistics and Research Agency) 2001 *Labour Force Survey Religion Report.* Belfast: NISRA www.nisra.gov.uk Accessed 6 Jan. 2007.

NISRA (Northern Ireland Statistics and Research Agency) 2003 *Ireland: North and South.* Belfast: NISRA.

NISRA (Northern Ireland Statistics and Research Agency) 2005 *Registrar General Annual Report.* Belfast: NISRA.

Nixon II, H. L. 2000 'Sport and disability', pp. 422–38 in J. Coakley and E. Dunning (eds), *Handbook of Sports Studies.* London: Sage.

Noiriel, G. 2001 *État, nation et immigration.* Paris: Gallimard.

Nolan, A. J. 2005 'Special issue on the Moriarty Tribunal', *Communique: An Garda Síochána Management Journal* (Sept.).

Nolan, B. 1993 *Low Pay in Ireland.* Dublin: ESRI.

Nolan, B., D. O'Neill and J. Williams 2002 *The Impact of the Minimum Wage on Irish Firms.* Dublin: ESRI.

Northern Ireland Council of Voluntary Action 2003 'Comments on the race equality strategy: NICVA's response to the consultation on the race equality strategy', July.

Northern Ireland Office 2002 'Race crime and sectarian crime legislation in Northern Ireland: a summary paper', Northern Ireland Office, Nov.

Northern Ireland Tourist Board 2006, *Visitor Guide 2006,* available at www.discovernorthernireland.com accessed 28 July 2006.

Oakley, A. 1974 *The Sociology of Housework.* Oxford: Martin Robertson.

O'Brien, L. and B. Dillon 1982 *Private Rented: The Forgotten Sector.* Dublin: Threshold.

Ó Broin, A. 1995 *Beyond the Black Pig's Dyke: A Short History of Ulster.* Cork: Mercier.

O'Carroll, A. 2005 'In the Shadow of the Clock', unpublished PhD thesis, University of Dublin.

O'Connell, M. 2002 'The portrayal of crime in the media: does it matter?' pp. 245–68 in P. O'Mahony (ed.), *Criminal Justice in Ireland.* Dublin: IPA.

O'Connell, P. 1999 'Sick man or tigress? The labour market in the Republic of Ireland', pp. 215–49 in A. Heath, R. Breen and C. T. Whelan (eds), *Ireland North and South: Perspectives from Social Science.* Oxford: Oxford University Press.

O'Connell, P. 2000 'The dynamics of the Irish labour market in comparative perspective', pp. 58–89 in B. Nolan, P. O'Connell and C. T. Whelan (eds), *Bust to Boom? The Irish Experience of Growth and Inequality.* Dublin: IPA.

O'Connell, P., D. Clancy and S. McCoy 2006 *Who Went to College in 2004?* Dublin: HEA.

O'Connor, F. 1993 *In Search of a State: Catholics in Northern Ireland.* Belfast: Blackstaff.

O'Connor, J. S., A. S. Orloff and S. Shaver 1999 *States, Markets, Families: Gender, Liberalism and Social Policy in Australia, Canada, Great Britain and the United States.* Cambridge: Cambridge University Press.

O'Connor, P. 1998 *Emerging Voices: Women in Contemporary Irish Society.* Dublin: IPA.

O'Connor, P. 2000 'A man's world?' *Economic and Social Review* 31 (1): 81–102.

O'Connor, P. 2005 'Private troubles, public issues: the Irish sociological imagination', Keynote paper, SAI Annual Conference.

O'Donnell, I. 2005a 'Crime and justice in the Republic of Ireland', *European Journal of Criminology* 2 (1): 99–131.

O'Donnell, I. 2005b 'Lethal violence in Ireland, 1841–2003: famine, celibacy and parental pacification', *British Journal of Criminology* 45 (5): 671–95.

O'Donnell, I. and E. O'Sullivan 2001 *Crime Control in Ireland: The Politics of Intolerance.* Cork: Cork University Press.

O'Donnell, T. 2004 'Building public confidence through the deliberation of police strategy', *Communique*, Dec.: 17–29.

O'Dowd, L. 1983 'Beyond Industrial Society', pp. 198–220 in P. Clancy, S. Drudy, K. Lynch and L. O'Dowd (eds) *Ireland: A Sociological Profile.* Dublin: IPA.

O'Dowd, L. 1992 'State legitimacy and nationalism in Ireland', pp. 25–42 in P. Clancy, M. Kelly, J. Wiatr and R. Zoltaniecki (eds), *Ireland and Poland: Comparative Perspectives.* Dublin: Department of Sociology, UCD.

O'Dowd, L. 1998 'New Unionism' British nationalism and the prospects for a negotiated settlement in Northern Ireland', in D. Miller (ed.), *Rethinking Northern Ireland, Culture, Ideology and Colonialism.* London: Longman.

O'Dowd, L., B. Rolston and M. Tomlinson 1980 *Northern Ireland: Between. Civil Rights and Civil War.* London: CSE Books.

O'Dwyer, K., P. Kennedy, and W. Ryan 2005 *Garda Public Attitudes Survey 2005* (Research Report No. 1/05). Templemore: Garda Research Unit.

OECD 1990 *Employment Outlook Study.* Paris: OECD.

OECD 1991 *Review of National Policies for Education: Ireland.* Paris: OECD.

OECD 2004 *Review of National Policies for Education: Review of Higher Education in Ireland.* Paris: OECD.

OECD 2005 *Education at a Glance 2005.* Paris: OECD.

Office for National Statistics 2005 *Annual Survey of Hours and Earnings 2005.* London: ONS.

Office for National Statistics 2006 *Interim Life Tables 2003–5.* London: ONS.

Office of the First Minister and Deputy First Minister 2005a *A Race Equality Strategy for Northern Ireland: A Racial Equality Strategy for Northern Ireland.* Belfast: OFMDFM.

Office of the First Minister and Deputy First Minister 2005b *A Shared Future: Policy and Strategic Framework for Good Relations in Northern Ireland.* Belfast: OFMDFM.

O'Hearn, D. 1998 *Inside the Celtic Tiger: The Irish Economy and the Asian Model.* London: Pluto.

O'Hearn, D. 2001 *The Atlantic Economy: Britain, the US and Ireland.* Manchester: Manchester University Press.

Ohmae, K. 2003 'The end of the nation state', pp. 214–18 in F. Lechner and J. Boli (eds), *The Globalization Reader.* Oxford: Blackwell.

Oliver, Q. and P. McGill 2002 *A Wake Up Call on Race: Implications of the Macpherson Report for Institutional Racism in Northern Ireland.* Belfast: ECNI.

Olsthoorn, X. 2003 'Implications of globalization for CO_2 emissions from transport', *Transportation and Planning* 26 (1): 105–33.

O'Mahony, E., S. Loyal and A. Mulcahy 2000 *Racism in Ireland: The Views of Blacks and Ethnic Minorities.* Dublin: Amnesty.

O'Mahony, P. (ed.), 2002 *Criminal Justice in Ireland.* Dublin: IPA.

O'Rawe, M. 2008 'Policing change in Northern Ireland: To reform or not to transform?', in C. Coulter and M. Murray (eds), *Northern Ireland After the Troubles: A Society in Transition.* Manchester: Manchester University Press.

O'Reilly, D. and M. Stevenson 1998 'The two communities in Northern Ireland: deprivation and ill health', *Journal of Public Health Medicine* 20 (2): 161–8.

Ó Riagáin, P. 1988 'Introduction', *Language Planning in Ireland: International Journal of the Sociology of Language* 70: 5–9.

Ó Riagáin, P. and M. Ó Gliasáin 1994 *National Survey on Languages 1993: Preliminary Report.* Dublin: ITÉ.

Ó Riain, S. 2000 'Net-working for a living: Irish software designers in the global workplace', pp. 175–202 in M. Burawoy et al. (eds), *Global Ethnography: Forces, Connections and Imaginations in a Postmodern World.* Berkeley CA: University of California Press.

Ó Riain, S. 2002 'High-tech communities: better work or just more work?' *Contexts* 1 (4): 36–41.

Ó Riain, S. 2004 *The Politics of High Tech Growth: Developmental Network States in the Global Economy,* Cambridge: Cambridge University Press.

Ó Riain, S. 2006 'New deal or no deal? Knowledge workers in the information economy', pp. 63–77 in J. Amman, T. Carpenter and G. Neff (eds), *Surviving the New Economy.* Boulder, CO: Paradigm.

O'Riordan, T. 2006 'An award ceremony for successful criminals?' *Working Notes* 53: 17–22.

Osterman, P. 1999 *Securing Prosperity.* Princeton: Princeton University Press.

O'Sullivan, D. 1989 'The ideational base of Irish educational policy', pp. 219–69 in D. G. Mulcahy and D. O'Sullivan (eds), *Irish Educational Policy: Process and Substance.* Dublin: Institute of Public Education.

O'Toole, F. 2003 *After the Ball.* Dublin: TASC.

Padfield, N. 2004 'The Anti-Social Behaviour Act 2003: the ultimate nanny-state act?' *Criminal Law Review* Sept.: 712–27.

Pakulski, J and M. Waters 1996 *The Death of Class.* London: Sage.

Palmer, J. 2002 'Smoke and mirrors: is that the way it is: themes in political marketing', *Media, Culture and Society* 24 (3): 345–63.

Panayiotopoulos, P. and Capps,C. 2001 *World Development: An Introduction.* London: Pluto.

Parsons, T. 1943 'The kinship system of the contemporary United States', *American Anthropologist* 45: 22–38. (Repr. as ch. 9 in *Essays in Sociological Theory* 1949 New York: Free Press.)

Parsons, T. 1959 'The school class as a social system: some of its functions in American society', *Harvard Educational Review* 29 (4): 297–318.

Parsons, T. 1977 *Social Systems and the Evolution of Action Theory.* New York: Free Press.

Parsons, T. and R. F. Bales 1956 *Family: Socialization and Interaction Process.* London: Routledge & Kegan Paul.

Partnership 2000 for Inclusion, Employment and Competitiveness 1996 Dublin: Stationery Office.

Patten Commission 1999 *A New Beginning: Policing in Northern Ireland.* Belfast: Stationery Office.

Patterson, T. 1994 *Out of Order.* New York: Vintage Books.

Peace, A. 1993 'Environmental protest, bureaucratic closure: the politics of discourse in rural Ireland', pp. 189–204 in K. Middleton (ed.), *Environmentalism: The View from Anthropology.* London: Routledge.

Peillon, M. 1982 *Contemporary Irish Society: An Introduction.* Dublin: Gill & Macmillan.

Pensions Board 2005 *National Pensions Review.* Dublin: Pensions Board

Perlow. L. 1997 *Finding Time: How Corporations, Individuals and Families Can Benefit From New Work Patterns.* Ithaca, NY: Cornell University Press.

Piore, M. 1979 *Birds of Passage.* Cambridge: Cambridge University Press.

PIPS Project 2006 *Public Initiative for the Prevention of Suicide and Self–Harm.* http:// www.pipsproject.com accessed 1 Feb. 2006.

Polanyi, K. 1944 *The Great Transformation,* Boston: Beacon Press.

Political Vetting of Community Work Working Group 1990 *The Political Vetting of Community Work in Northern Ireland.* Belfast: Northern Ireland Council for Voluntary Action.

Pollak, A. 1997 'New disability to oversee policy and services', *Irish Times,* 19 Nov.

Potts, L. 1991 *The World Labour Market.* London: Zed Books.

Poulantzas, N. 1975 *Classes in Contemporary Capitalism.* London: Verso

Powell, B. 2003 'Economic freedom and growth: the case of the Celtic Tiger' *Cato Journal* 22 (3): 431–48

Pro Bono Publico 1931 'Tinkers' children', *Irish Times,* letter, 16 May.

Punch, M. 2005 'Uneven development and the private rental market', pp 119–43 in M. Norris and D. Redmond (eds), *Housing in Contemporary Ireland: Economy, Society, Space and Shelter.* Dublin: IPA.

Putnam, R. 1993a *Making Democracy Work: Civic Traditions in Modern Italy.* Princeton NJ: Princeton University Press.

Putnam, R. 1993b 'The prosperous community: social capital and public life', *American Prospect* 13: 35–42.

Putnam, R. 1995 'Bowling alone: America's declining social capital', *Journal of Democracy* 6 (1): 65–79.

Putnam, R. 2000 *Bowling Alone: The Collapse and Revival of American Community.* New York and London: Simon & Schuster.

Quinn, E and G. Hughes 2004 *The Impact of Migration on European Societies: Ireland.* Dublin: ESRI.

Radford, K., J. Betts and M. Ostermeyer 2006 *Policing, Accountability and the Black and Minority Ethnic Communities in Northern Ireland.* Belfast: Institute for Conflict Research.

Raftery, A. E. and M. Hout 1993 'Maximally maintained inequality: expansion, reform and opportunity in Irish education', *Sociology of Education* 66: 41–62.

Ramsay, P. 2004 'What is anti-social behaviour?', *Criminal Law Review* Nov.: 908–5.

Ravenstein, E. G. 1976 [1883] [1885] *The Laws of Migration.* New York: Arno.

Ray, C. 1998 'Culture, intellectual property and territorial rural development', *Sociologia Ruralis* 38 (1): 3–20.

Redmond, D. and Norris, M. 2005 'Setting the scene: transformations in Irish housing', pp 1–20 in M. Norris and D. Redmond (eds), *Housing in Contemporary Ireland: Economy, Society, Space and Shelter.* Dublin: IPA.

Reich, M., D. Gordon and R. Edwards 1973 'A theory of labour market segmentation', *American Economic Review* LXIII (2): 359–65.

Reich, R. 1991 *The Work of Nations.* New York: Vintage Books.

Reid, J. 2004 *The United States of Europe: The Superpower That Nobody Talks About, From the Euro to Eurovision.* London: Penguin.

Revenue Commissioners 1997 'Signature of New Tax Convention between Ireland and the US' Press Release 28 July.

Review Group on Health and Personal Social Services for People with Physical and Sensory Disabilities (1996) *Towards an Independent Future.* Dublin: Stationery Office.

RICS (Royal Institution of Chartered Surveyors) 2006, *European Housing Review 2006*, http://www.rics.org/Property/Residentialproperty/Residentialpropertymarket/ehr_2006.htm accessed 25 Sept. 2006.

Roche, E. 2005 'Riding the Celtic Tiger', *Harvard Business Review* 83 (11): 39–50.

Roche, W. K. 1998 'Between regime fragmentation and realignment: Irish industrial relations in the 1990s', *Industrial Relations Journal* 29 (2): 112–25.

Roche, W. K. and J. Geary 2000 '"Collaborative production" and the Irish boom: work organization, partnership and direct involvement in Irish workplaces', *Economic and Social Review* 31 (1): 1–36.

Rodrik, D. 2002 'After neoliberalism, what?' Paper presented to Alternatives to NeoLiberalism Conference, Washington.

Rolston, B. 2004 'Legacy of intolerance: racism and unionism in South Belfast', *IRR News* 10 Feb.

Rostow, W. W. 1960 *The Stages of Economic Growth: A Non-Communist Manifesto.* Cambridge: Cambridge University Press.

Roxborough, I. 1979 *Theories of Underdevelopment.* London: Macmillan.

Ruane, J. and J. Todd 1996 *The Dynamics of Conflict in Northern Ireland: Power, Conflict and Emancipation.* Cambridge: Cambridge University Press.

Ruane, J. and J. Todd 2003 'The roots of intense ethnic conflict may not in fact be ethnic: categories, communities and path dependant', Institute for the Study of Social Change Discussion Paper, UCD.

Ruhs, M. 2005 *Managing the Employment of Non-EU Nationals in Ireland.* Dublin: Trinity Policy Institute.

Runnymede Trust 1998 *Islamophobia: A Challenge To Us All.* London: Runnymede Trust.

Russell, H. and M. P. Corcoran 2000 *The Experience of Those Claiming the One-Parent Family Payment: A Qualitative Study.* Dublin: Department of Social, Community and Family Affairs.

Russell, H., E. Smyth and P. J O'Connell 2005 *Degrees of Equality: Gender Pay Differentials Among Recent Graduates.* Dublin: ESRI.

Russell, H., E. Smyth, M. Lyons and P. J. O'Connell 2002 *'Getting Out of the House': Women Returning to Employment, Education and Training.* Dublin: Liffey Press.

Rutter, M., B. Maughan, P. Mortimore, J. Ouston and A. Smith 1979 *Fifteen Thousand Hours: Secondary Schools and their Effects on Children.* London: Open Books.

Ryan, A. B. 2003 'Contemporary discourses of working, earning and spending: acceptance, critique and the bigger picture', pp. 155–74 in Colin Coulter and Steve Coleman (eds), *The End of Irish History? Critical Reflections on the Celtic Tiger.* Manchester: Manchester University Press.

Ryan, L. 1979 'Church and politics: the last twenty-five years', *The Furrow* 30 (1): 3–18.

Sabato, L.1991 *Feeding Frenzy.* New York: Free Press.

Sage, C. 2003 'Social embeddedness and relations of regard: alternative "good food" networks in South-West Ireland', *Journal of Rural Studies* 19 (1): 47–60.

Salt, J. 2001 'The business of international migration', pp. 86–108 in M. Siddque (ed.), *International Migration into the 21st Century*. Cheltenham: Edward Elgar.

Sassen, S. 1991 *The Global City*. Princeton NJ: Princeton University Press.

Saunders, P. 1990 *Social Class and Stratification*. London: Routledge.

Savage, M. 1992 *Property, Bureaucracy and Culture: Middle Class Formation in Contemporary Britain*. London: Routledge

Savage, M. 2000 *Class Analysis and Social Transformation*. Buckingham: Open University Press

Sayad, A. 2004 *The Suffering of the Immigrant*. Cambridge: Polity.

Scase, R. 1992 *Class*. Buckingham: Open University Press

Schnaiberg, A and K. Gould 1994 *Environment and Society, the Enduring Conflict*. New York: St Martins.

Schnapper, D. 2003 *La Communauté des citoyens*. Paris: Gallimard.

Schofer, E. and J. W. Meyer 2005 'The worldwide expansion of higher education in the twentieth century', *American Sociological Review* 70: 898–920.

Scott, J. 1997 'Changing households in Britain: do families still matter?', *Sociological Review* 45 (4): 591–620.

Scott, J. 2000 'Class and stratification', pp. 20–54 in G. Payne (ed.), *Social Divisions*. Cambridge: Cambridge University Press.

Scraton, S. and A. Flintoff (eds) 2002 *Gender and Sport: A Reader*. London: Routledge.

Sen, A. 1980 'Equality of what?' pp. 195–220 in S. McMurrin (ed.), *The Tanner Lectures on Human Values*. Cambridge: Cambridge University Press.

Sen, A. 1985 *Commodities and Capabilities*. Oxford: North-Holland.

Sennett, R. 1998 *The Corrosion of Character*. New York: WW Norton.

Sharone, O. 2004 'Engineering overwork: Bell-Curve management at a high-tech firm', pp. 191–218 in C. Epstein and A. Kalleberg (eds), *Fighting for Time*. New York: Russell Sage.

Shavit Y. and H. P. Blossfeld 1993 *Persistent Inequality: Changing Educational Attainment in Thirteen Countries*. Boulder CO: Westview.

Shaw, H. 2005 *The Irish Media Directory*. Dublin: Gill & Macmillan.

Sheller, M.and J. Urry 2006 'The new mobilities paradigm', *Environment and Planning A* 38: 207–26.

Shelton, B. A. and D. John 1996 'The division of household labor', *Annual Review of Sociology* 22: 299–322.

Shiel, G. and D. Kelly 2001 *The 1999 National Assessment of Mathematical Achievement*. Dublin: Educational Research Centre.

Shirlow, P. 1999 *Fear, Mobility and Living in the Ardoyne and Upper Ardoyne Communities*, School of Environmental Studies, University of Ulster, Coleraine.

Shirlow, P., B. Graham and K. McEvoy 2005 *Politically Motivated Former Prisoner Groups: Community Activism and Conflict Transformation*. Belfast: Community Relations Council.

Shirlow, P. and M. McGovern 1997 *Who are 'the People'?* London: Pluto.

Shirlow, P. and B. Murtagh 2006 *Belfast: Segregation, Violence and the City*. London: Pluto.

Shove, E. 1998 *Consuming Automobility*. Dublin: Employment Research Centre.

Shuttleworth, I. and C. Lloyd 2006 'Are Northern Ireland's two communities dividing? Evidence from the Census of Population 1971–2001', *Shared Spaces* 2: 5–14

Shuttleworth, I. and R. Osborne 2004 *Fair Employment in Northern Ireland: A Generation On.* Belfast: Blackstaff.

Sivanandan, A. 2004 'Racism in the age of globalisation' *IRR News*, 29 Oct.

Skillington, T. 1997 'Politics and the struggle to define: a discourse analysis of the framing strategies of competing actors in a "new" participatory forum', *British Journal of Sociology* 48 (3): 493–513.

Skillington, T. 1998 'The city as text: constructing Dublin's identity through discourse on transportation and urban re-development in the press', *British Journal of Sociology* 49 (3): 456–73.

Sleebos, J. E. 2003 *Low Fertility Rates in OECD Countries: Facts and Policy Responses*, OECD Social, Employment and Migration Working Papers No. 15. Paris: OECD.

Smart, B. 2003 *Economy, Culture and Society: A Sociological Critique of Neo-liberalism.* Buckingham: Open University Press.

Smith, A. and K. Green 2005 'The place of sport and physical activity in young people's lives and its implications for health: some sociological comments', *Journal of Youth Studies* 8: 24–53.

Smith, A. D. 1994 'Gastronomy or geology? The role of nationalism in the reconstruction of nations', *Nations and Nationalism* 1 (1): 3–23.

Smyth, E. and S. McCoy 2004 *At Work in School: Part-Time Employment among Second Level Students.* Dublin: Liffey Press.

Smyth, J. and A. Cebulla 2008 'The glacier moves? Economic change and class structure in Northern Ireland', in C. Coulter and M. Murray (eds), *Northern Ireland After the Troubles: A Society in Transition.* Manchester: Manchester University Press.

Spaargaren, G. 2000 'Ecological modernisation theory and the changing discourse on environment and modernity', pp. 41–71 in G. Spaargaren, A. Mol and F. H. Buttel (eds), *Environment and Global Modernity.* London: Sage.

Spaargaren, G., A. J. Mol and F. H. Buttel (eds) 2000 *Environment and Global Modernity.* London: Sage.

Spencer, G. 2004 'The impact of television news on the Northern Ireland peace process', *Media, Culture and Society* 26 (3): 603–23.

Squires, P. and D. E. Stephen 2005 'Rethinking ASBOs', *Critical Social Policy* 25 (4): 517–28.

Stark, R. and W. Bainbridge 1987 *A Theory of Religion.* New York: Peter Lang.

Stewart, A. T. Q. 1986 *The Narrow Ground: Patterns of Ulster History.* Belfast: Pretani Press.

Sullivan, M. 2004 'Data shows dramatic shift of profits to tax havens', *Tax Notes* 13 Sept.

Sullivan, O. 2000 'The division of household labour: twenty years of change?', *Sociology* 34 (3): 437–56.

Sutcliffe, B. 2004 'World inequality and globalisation', *Oxford Review of Economic Policy* 20 (1): 15–57.

Szatz, A. 1994 *Ecopopulism, Toxic Waste and the Movement for Environmental Justice.* Minneapolis: University of Minneapolis Press.

Szatz, A. 1997 'Environmental inequalities: literature review and proposals for new directions in research and theory', *Current Sociology* 44 (2): 99–120.

Task Force on the Travelling Community 1995 *Report*. Dublin: Stationery Office.

Taylor, G and B. Flynn 2003 'It's green, but is it of a light enough hue? Past performance, present success and the future of the Irish Greens', *Environmental Politics* 12 (1): 225–32.

Teichler, U. 2006 'Major findings of the survey of Former Erasmus students', Centre for Research on Higher Education and Work, University of Kassel.

Thomas, W. I. and F. Znaniecki 1918 *The Polish Peasant in Europe and America*. Boston: Richard Badger.

Thompson, C. A., L. L. Beauvais and K. S. Lyness 1999 'When work-family benefits are not enough: the influence of work-family culture on benefit utilization, organisational attachment and work-family conflict', *Journal of Vocational Behaviour* 54: 392–415.

Thompson, E. P. 1968 *The Making of the English Working Class*. Harmondsworth: Penguin.

Todd, J. 1987 'Two traditions in unionist political culture', *Irish Political Studies*, 2: 1–26.

Todd, J. 1999 'Nationalism, republicanism and the Good Friday Agreement', pp. 49–70 in J. Ruane and J. Todd (eds), *After the Good Friday Agreement: Analysing Political Change in Northern Ireland*. Dublin: UCD Press.

Tola, F. and Dragonetti, C. 2003 'Bhartrihari's philosophy of language (5th–6th centuries AD)', *Pensamiento* 59 (225): 377–92.

Tong, R. P. 1998 *Feminist Thought: A More Comprehensive Introduction*. Boulder CO: Westview.

Tonge, J. 2005 *The New Northern Irish Politics?* Houndmills: Palgrave Macmillan.

Tonge, J. 2006a *Northern Ireland*. Cambridge: Polity.

Tonge, J. 2006b 'Polarisation or new moderation? Party politics since the GFA', pp. 70–88 in M. Cox, A. Guelke and F. Stephen (eds), *A Farewell to Arms? Beyond the Good Friday Agreement*. Manchester: Manchester University Press.

Tormey, R. 1999 'Cutting at the wrong edge: gender, part-time work and the Irish retail sector', *Irish Journal of Sociology* 9: 77–96.

Tovey, H. 1997 'Food, environmentalism and rural sociology: on the organic farming movement in Ireland', *Sociologia Ruralis* 37(1): 21–37.

Tovey, H. 2000 'Milk and modernity: dairying in contemporary Ireland', pp. 47–74 in H. K. Schwarzweller and A. P. Davidson (eds), *Dairy Industry Restructuring, Research in Rural Sociology and Development*, vol. 8. New York: JAI Press

Tovey, H. 2002a 'Alternative agricultural movements and rural development cosmologies', *International Journal of Agriculture and Food* 10 (1): 1–17.

Tovey, H. 2002b 'Morality and the sociology of animals – reflections of the foot and mouth outbreak in Ireland', *Irish Journal of Sociology* 11 (1): 23–42.

Tovey, H. 2007 'New movements in old places? The alternative food movement in rural Ireland', pp. 168–89 in Linda Connolly (eds), *Social Movements in Ireland*. Manchester: Manchester University Press.

Tovey, H. 2008 *Environmentalism in Ireland: Movement and Activists*. Dublin: IPA.

Tovey, H and P. Share 2003 *A Sociology of Ireland*, 2nd edn. Dublin: Gill & Macmillan.

Transparency International 2005 *Transparency International Global Corruption Report – Ireland*. http://www.transparency.ie/about_cor/corireland.htm Accessed May 2006.

Troy, A. 2005 *Holy Cross: A Personal Experience*. Dublin: Currach Press.

TUC 2005 'TUC welcomes proposed EU Directive on agency workers', http://www.tuc.org.uk/work_life/tuc-4602-fo.cfm Accessed 4 Jan. 2007.

UNDP 2005 *Human Development Report 2005*. New York: United Nations.

UNESCO 2005 *Global Education Digest 2005*. Montreal: UNESCO Institute for Statistics.

Urry, J. 1990 *The Tourist Gaze: Leisure and Travel in Contemporary Societies*. London: Sage.

Urry, J. 2000 *Sociology Beyond Societies: Mobilities for the Twenty-First Century*. London: Routledge.

US Department of State 2005 'Ireland: 2005 Investment Climate Statement' http://www.state.gov/e/eb/ifd/2005/42063.htm Accessed 8 Oct. 2006

Voas, D. and A. Crockett 2005 'Religion in Britain: neither believing nor belonging' *Sociology* 39 (1): 11–28.

Von Tangen Page, M. 2006 'A "most difficult and unpalatable part": the release of politically motivated violent offenders', pp. 201–11 in M. Cox, A. Guelke and F. Stephen (eds), *A Farewell to Arms? Beyond the Good Friday Agreement*. Manchester: Manchester University Press.

Wacquant, L. 1997. 'For an analytic of racial domination', *Political Power and Social Theory* 11: 221–34.

Wacquant, L. 1999 'How penal common sense comes to Europeans: notes on the transatlantic diffusion of neoliberal doxa', *European Societies* 1 (3): 319–52.

Waddington, I. 2000 *Sport, Health and Drugs: A Critical Sociological Perspective*. London: E&FN Spon.

Walker, A., K. Kershaw, and S. Nicolas 2006 *Crime in England and Wales 2005/06* (Home Office Statistical Bulletin 12/06). London: HMSO.

Watson, D. 2000 *Victims of Recorded Crime in Ireland*. Dublin: Oak Tree Press.

Watson, I. 1996 'The Irish language and television', *British Journal of Sociology* 47 (2): 255–74.

Watson, I. 2003 *Broadcasting in Irish: Minority Language, Radio, Television and Identity*. Dublin: Four Courts.

Watts, M. and D. Goodman 1997 'Agrarian questions: global appetite, local metabolism: nature, culture and industry in *fin-de-siècle* agro-food systems', pp. 1–32 in D. Goodman and M. Watts (eds), *Globalising Food: Agrarian Questions and Global Restructuring*. London: Routledge.

Weber, E. 1979 *Peasants into Frenchmen: The Modernization of Rural France 1870–1914*. Stanford: Stanford UP.

Weber, M. 1978 *Economy and Society: An Outline of Interpretative Sociology*, ed. G. Roth and C. Wittich. Berkeley CA: University of California Press.

Weeks, J. 2005 'Fallen heroes? All about men', *Irish Journal of Sociology* 14 (2): 53–65.

Whannel, G. 2000 'Sport and the media', pp. 291–308 in J. Coakley and E. Dunning (eds), *Handbook of Sports Studies*. London: Sage.

Wheelock, J. and K. Jones 2002 'Grandparents are the next best thing: informal childcare for working parents in urban Britain', *Journal of Social Policy* 31 (3): 441–63.

Whelan, C. and Layte, R. 2004 'Economic change, social mobility and meritocracy: reflections on the Irish experience', *Quarterly Economic Commentary* (Autumn): 307–52.

Whelan, C. T. (ed.) (1994) *Values and Social Change in Ireland.* Dublin: Gill & Macmillan.

Whyte, J. 1990 *Interpreting Northern Ireland.* Oxford: Clarendon Press.

Whyte, J. H. 1980 *Church & State in Modern Ireland 1923–1979.* Dublin: Gill & Macmillan.

Whyte, J. H. 1981 *Catholics in Western Democracies.* Dublin: Gill & Macmillan.

Wichterich, C. 2000 *The Globalized Woman: Reports from a Future of Inequality.* London: Zed Books.

Wickham, J. 1997 'Part–time work in Ireland and Europe: who wants what where?' *Work, Employment and Society* 11 (1): 133–51.

Wickham, J. 2006 *Gridlock: Dublin's Transport Crisis and the Future of the City.* Dublin: TASC at New Island Books.

Wickham, J. and A. Vecchi 2006a 'Travelling and connecting, messaging and meeting: business travel, information technology and the virtual organisation', EGOS European Group of Organisation Studies Colloquium, Bergen, Norway, July.

Wickham, J. and A. Vecchi 2006b 'Clusters and pipelines, commuters and nomads: Business travel in the Irish software industry', Fifth Proximity Conference, Bordeaux, June.

Williams, B., P. Shiels, and B. Hughes 2003 'Access to housing: the role of housing supply and urban development policies in the Greater Dublin Area', *Journal of Irish Urban Studies* 2 (1): 25–52.

Williams, P. 2004 *Crimelords.* Dublin: Merlin.

Wilson, B. 2000 'Salvation, secularization and de-moralization', pp. 39–51 in R. Fenn (ed.), *The Blackwell Companion to the Sociology of Religion.* Oxford: Blackwell.

Wilson, J. Q. and G. Kelling 1982 'Broken windows', *Atlantic Monthly* (Mar.): 29–38.

Wilson, R. and R. Wilford 2003 *Northern Ireland: A Route to Stability?* http://www. devolution.ac.uk/Policy_Papers.htm Accessed 4 Jan. 2007.

Wimmer, A. and N. Glick Schiller 2002 'Methodological nationalism and beyond: nation state building, migration and the social sciences', *Global Networks* 2 (4): 301–34.

Winter, M. 2003 'Embeddedness, the new food economy and defensive localism', *Journal of Rural Studies* 19 (1): 23–32.

Wittgenstein, L. 1967 *Philosophical Investigations.* Oxford: Oxford University Press.

Wood, E. M. 1986 *The Retreat from Class.* London: Verso.

Woods, P. 1983 *Sociology and the School: An Interactionist Viewpoint.* London: Routledge & Kegan Paul.

World Bank 1995 *Priorities and Strategies for Education, A World Bank Sector Review.* ESP.

Wren, M. A. 2003 *Unhealthy State: Anatomy of a Sick Society.* Dublin: New Island.

Wright, E. O. 1985 *Classes.* London: Verso.

Wright, E. O. 1997 *Class Counts. Comparative Structure in Class Analysis*. Cambridge: Cambridge University Press.

Yago, G. 1984 *The Decline of Transit: Urban Transportation in German and US Cities 1900–1970*. Cambridge: Cambridge University Press.

Young, M. and P. Willmott 1957 *Family and Kinship in East London*. London: Routledge & Kegan Paul.

Young, M. and P. Willmott 1973 *The Symmetrical Family*. London: Routledge & Kegan Paul.

Zelditch, M. 1956 'Role differentiation in the nuclear family: a comparative study', pp. 307–52 in T. Parsons and R. F. Bales (eds), *Family: Socialization and Interaction processes*. London: Routledge & Kegan Paul.

Zolberg, A. 1989 'The next waves: migration theory for a changing world', *International Migration Review* 23: 403–30.

Zweig, F. 1961 *The Worker in an Affluent Society*. London: Heinemann.

Index